Doing Hard Time

The Addison-Wesley Object Technology Series

Grady Booch, Ivar Jacobson, and James Rumbaugh, Series Editors
For more information check out the series web site [http://www.awl.com /cseng/otseries/] as well as the pages
on each book [http://www.awl.com/cseng/I-S-B-N/] (I-S-B-N represents the actual ISBN, including dashes).

David Bellin and Susan Suchman Simone, *The CRC Card Book*, ISBN 0-201-89535-8

Robert V. Binder, *Testing Object-Oriented Systems: Models, Patterns, and Tools*, ISBN 0-201-80938-9

Bob Blakley, *CORBA Security: An Introduction to Safe Computing with Objects*, ISBN 0-201-32565-9

Grady Booch, *Object Solutions: Managing the Object-Oriented Project*, ISBN 0-8053-0594-7

Grady Booch, *Object-Oriented Analysis and Design with Applications, Second Edition*, ISBN 0-8053-5340-2

Grady Booch, James Rumbaugh, and Ivar Jacobson, *The Unified Modeling Language User Guide*, ISBN 0-201-57168-4

Don Box, *Essential COM*, ISBN 0-201-63446-5

Don Box, Keith Brown, Tim Ewald, and Chris Sells, *Effective COM: 50 Ways to Improve Your COM and MTS-based Applications*, ISBN 0-201-37968-6

Alistair Cockburn, *Surviving Object-Oriented Projects: A Manager's Guide*, ISBN 0-201-49834-0

Dave Collins, *Designing Object-Oriented User Interfaces*, ISBN 0-8053-5350-X

Jim Conallen, *Building Web Applications with UML*, ISBN 0-201-61577-0

Bruce Powel Douglass, *Doing Hard Time: Designing and Implementing Embedded Systems with UML*, ISBN 0-201-49837-5

Bruce Powel Douglass, *Real-Time UML, Second Edition: Developing Efficient Objects for Embedded Systems*, ISBN 0-201-65784-8

Desmond F. D'Souza and Alan Cameron Wills, *Objects, Components, and Frameworks with UML: The Catalysis Approach*, ISBN 0-201-31012-0

Martin Fowler, *Analysis Patterns: Reusable Object Models*, ISBN 0-201-89542-0

Martin Fowler, *Refactoring: Improving the Design of Existing Code,* ISBN 0-201-48567-2

Martin Fowler with Kendall Scott, *UML Distilled, Second Edition: Applying the Standard Object Modeling Language*, ISBN 0-201-65783-X

Peter Heinckiens, *Building Scalable Database Applications: Object-Oriented Design, Architectures, and Implementations*, ISBN 0-201-31013-9

Christine Hofmeister, Robert Nord, Soni Dilip, *Applied Software Architecture*, ISBN 0-201-32571-3

Ivar Jacobson, Grady Booch, and James Rumbaugh, *The Unified Software Development Process*, ISBN 0-201-57169-2

Ivar Jacobson, Magnus Christerson, Patrik Jonsson, and Gunnar Overgaard, *Object-Oriented Software Engineering: A Use Case Driven Approach*, ISBN 0-201-54435-0

Ivar Jacobson, Maria Ericsson, and Agneta Jacobson, *The Object Advantage: Business Process Reengineering with Object Technology,* ISBN 0-201-42289-1

Ivar Jacobson, Martin Griss, and Patrik Jonsson, *Software Reuse: Architecture, Process and Organization for Business Success,* ISBN 0-201-92476-5

David Jordan, *C++ Object Databases: Programming with the ODMG Standard*, ISBN 0-201-63488-0

Philippe Kruchten, *The Rational Unified Process: An Introduction,* ISBN 0-201-60459-0

Wilf LaLonde, *Discovering Smalltalk*, ISBN 0-8053-2720-7

Dean Leffingwell and Don Widrig, *Managing Software Requirements: A Unified Approach*, ISBN 0-201-61593-2

Chris Marshall, *Enterprise Modeling with UML: Designing Successful Software through Business Analysis*, ISBN 0-201-43313-3

Lockheed Martin Advanced Concepts Center and Rational Software Corporation, *Succeeding with the Booch and OMT Methods: A Practical Approach*, ISBN 0-8053-2279-5

Thomas Mowbray and William Ruh, *Inside CORBA: Distributed Object Standards and Applications*, ISBN 0-201-89540-4

Bernd Oestereich, *Developing Software with UML: Object-Oriented Analysis and Design in Practice*, ISBN 0-201-39826-5

Meiler Page-Jones, *Fundamentals of Object-Oriented Design in UML*, ISBN 0-201-69946-X

Ira Pohl, *Object-Oriented Programming Using C++, Second Edition,* ISBN 0-201-89550-1

Rob Pooley and Perdita Stevens, *Using UML: Software Engineering with Objects and Components*, ISBN 0-201-36067-5

Terry Quatrani, *Visual Modeling with Rational Rose 2000 and UML,* ISBN 0-201-69961-3

Brent E. Rector and Chris Sells, *ATL Internals*, ISBN 0-201-69589-8

Paul R. Reed, Jr., *Developing Applications with Visual Basic and UML*, ISBN 0-201-61579-7

Doug Rosenberg with Kendall Scott, *Use Case Driven Object Modeling with UML: A Practical Approach*, ISBN 0-201-43289-7

Walker Royce, *Software Project Management: A Unified Framework,* ISBN 0-201-30958-0

William Ruh, Thomas Herron, and Paul Klinker, *IIOP Complete: Middleware Interoperability and Distributed Object Standards,* ISBN 0-201-37925-2

James Rumbaugh, Ivar Jacobson, and Grady Booch, *The Unified Modeling Language Reference Manual*, ISBN 0-201-30998-X

Geri Schneider and Jason P. Winters, *Applying Use Cases: A Practical Guide*, ISBN 0-201-30981-5

Yen-Ping Shan and Ralph H. Earle, *Enterprise Computing with Objects: From Client/Server Environments to the Internet*, ISBN 0-201-32566-7

David N. Smith, *IBM Smalltalk: The Language*, ISBN 0-8053-0908-X

Daniel Tkach, Walter Fang, and Andrew So, *Visual Modeling Technique: Object Technology Using Visual Programming*, ISBN 0-8053-2574-3

Daniel Tkach and Richard Puttick, *Object Technology in Application Development, Second Edition*, ISBN 0-201-49833-2

Jos Warmer and Anneke Kleppe, *The Object Constraint Language: Precise Modeling with UML*, ISBN 0-201-37940-6

Doing Hard Time

Developing Real-Time Systems with UML, Objects, Frameworks, and Patterns

Bruce Powel Douglass

ADDISON–WESLEY
An Imprint of Addison Wesley Longman, Inc.
Reading, Massachusetts • Harlow, England • Menlo Park, California
Berkeley, California • Don Mills, Ontario • Sydney
Bonn • Amsterdam • Tokyo • Mexico City

Many of the designations used by manufacturers and sellers to distinguish their products are claimed as trademarks. Where those designations appear in this book and Addison Wesley Longman Inc., was aware of a trademark claim, the designations have been printed in initial capitals or in all capital letters.

The author and publisher have taken care in the preparation of this book, but make no expressed or implied warranty of any kind and assume no responsibility for errors or omissions. No liability is assumed for incidental or consequential damages in connection with or arising out of the use of the information or programs contained herein.

The publisher offers discounts on this book when ordered in quantity for special sales. For more information, please contact:

AWL Direct Sales
Addison Wesley Longman, Inc.
One Jacob Way
Reading, Massachusetts 01867
(781) 944-3700

Visit AWL on the Web: http://www.awl.com/cseng/

Library of Congress Cataloging-in-Publication Data

Doing hard time : developing real-time systems with UML, objects, frameworks, and patterns / Bruce Powel Douglass.
    p.   cm. — (The Addison-Wesley object technology series)
Includes bibliographical references and index.
ISBN 0-201-49837-5 (alk. paper)
   1. Embedded computer systems—Programming. 2. UML (Computer science) I. Title. II. Series.
QA76.6.D655   1999
005.1'17—dc21
                                       99–18093
                                            CIP

Executive Editor: J. Carter Shanklin
Project Editor: Krysia Bebick
Editorial Assistant: Rebecca Bence
Production Coordinator: Maureen A. Willard
Copy Editor: Arlene Richman
Proofreader: Pam Andrada
Composition: Stratford Publishing Services
Cover Design: Jennifer L. Collins

ISBN 0-201-49837-5
Text printed on recycled and acid-free paper.
2 3 4 5 6 7 8 9 10—CRW—0302010099
Second printing, September 1999

This book is dedicated to my lover, for her emotional support, caring, and encouragement. Thanks, Sweetie.

Contents

Figure List

About the Author

Bruce Powel Douglass was raised by wolves in the Oregon wilderness. He taught himself to read at age 3 and calculus before age 12. He dropped out of school when he was 14 and traveled around the United States for a few years before entering the University of Oregon as a mathematics major. Douglass eventually received his M.S. in exercise physiology from the University of Oregon and his Ph.D. in neurophysiology from the USD Medical School, where he developed a branch of mathematics called autocorrelative factor analysis for studying information processing in multicellular biological neural systems.

Bruce has worked as a software developer in real-time systems for almost 20 years and is a well-known speaker and author in the area of real-time, embedded systems. He is on the advisory board of the *Embedded Systems* and *UML World* conferences, at which he has taught courses in software estimation and scheduling, project management, object-oriented analysis and design, communications protocols, finite state machines, design patterns, and safety-critical systems design. He has developed and taught courses in real-time object-oriented analysis and design for many years, and has authored articles about the real-time domain for a number of journals and periodicals.

Bruce is currently the chief evangelist[1] for i-Logix, a leading producer of tools for real-time systems development. Bruce worked with Rational Software Corporation and other UML partners on the specification

---

[1] Being a chief evangelist is much like being a chief scientist, except for the burning bushes.

of the Unified Modeling Language. He is one of the co-chairs of the Object Management Group's Real-Time Analysis and Design Working Group, which is concerned with possible extensions to the UML to allow it to better meet the needs of real-time and embedded systems. He also consults, trains, and mentors a number of companies that build large-scale, real-time, safety-critical systems. He is the author of four books on software, including *Real-Time UML* (Addison-Wesley, 1998), as well as a short textbook on table tennis.

Bruce enjoys classical music and has played classical guitar professionally. He has competed in several sports, including table tennis, bicycle racing, running, and full-contact Tae Kwon Do, although he currently fights only inanimate objects that don't hit back. He and his two sons contemplate epistemology in the Frozen North. He can be reached at bpd@ilogix.com.

Foreword

In 1971, there were about 142,000 computers world-wide (and Bill Gates was just 16).[1] In 1999, there are now some 350 to 400 million personal computers alone[2] and at least an order of magnitude more embedded devices.[3] Although PCs are perhaps the most visible artifact of the microprocessor revolution, there are many more devices behind the scenes—such as elevators, pacemakers, cellular phones, industrial machine controllers, watches, automobile transmission and braking systems, home automation systems, and even appliances—which require software to carry out their functions. Software for embedded devices is particularly challenging to develop: it must interact with the real world (which is typically very noisy and unpredictable), it must do so under time and performance constraints (with responses measured from milliseconds to nanoseconds), and it must do so reliably and safely (especially in the case of human-critical systems). With the advent of technologies such as Sun's *Jini*, Microsoft's Universal Plug and Play, and IBM's T-Spaces, we will likely see a dramatic growth of ubiquitous distributed and embedded devices, all connected using the Internet. Someone has to write all that software.

In *Doing Hard Time*, Bruce makes the process of developing embedded systems approachable. I especially like his focus on abstraction and the use of the UML (although my opinion may be a little biased in that regard!). He covers all the essential issues: timeliness, rate monotonic scheduling, concurrency, safety, debugging, event-driven modeling, interaction with real time operating systems, architecture—this is indeed a very comprehensive work. His easy style of writing and his wit (he often quotes from the *Book of Douglass*) make a topic that could be a very dreary work, full of hairy mathematics, instead something that's a joy to read.

I've learned a lot from Bruce, and I'm sure you will as well.

Grady Booch
Rational Software Corporation

---

[1] John Gantz, International Data Corporation, as reported on www.idc.com/jgcdxdt.htm
<http://www.idc.com/jgcdxdt.htm>

[2] <http://www.intel.com/pressroom/archive/speeches/pg110298.htm>

[3] <http://www.eg3.com>

Preface

Goals

Today's world runs on embedded computers. Virtually every field of endeavor in our modern society depends on embedded computers from manufacturing to transportation to medicine. The typical household is a computing ecosystem that includes telephones, televisions, washing machines, ovens, and a host of other silicon-based fauna. Many, if not most, of these computing devices have timeliness requirements to their functionality, so that *late* action is often *wrong* action. Many embedded devices have the capability to do great harm if they malfunction or fail.

Not only are more things handled by embedded computing devices, but the scope, complexity, and criticality of the things handled is increasing geometrically. Technological advances are crucial in order to keep up with the increasing demands on the developer of such systems. Gone are the days when hardware complexity was the limiting factor in the development of electrical devices. Most companies involved in the manufacture of real-time and embedded systems have realized the truism of "the tail that wags the dog" and have begun seriously looking at ways to improve software productivity. These better ways to develop real-time and embedded systems are the source and soul of this book.

Doing Hard Time: Developing Real-Time Systems with UML, Objects, Frameworks, and Patterns focuses on model-based development of real-time and embedded systems using the Unified Modified Language (UML) and a risk-based iterative development lifecycle called ROPES.

UML is a third-generation modeling language that rigorously defines the semantics of the object metamodel and provides a notation for capturing and communicating object structure and behavior. The UML became a standard modeling language in the OMG in late 1996, and the author remains heavily involved in its ongoing effort. This book is based on the 1.3 revision of the UML standard.

Model-based development is crucial in today's high-complexity, short-development-cycle business environment. It is important to focus on the fundamental abstractions of the problem rather than on the low-level details of its implementation—to focus on, "Should the control rods be in the reactor core to avoid a meltdown?" rather than on, "Should I jump on non-zero or carry?" By increasing the level of abstraction, it is possible to build more-complex systems with fewer defects in less time—a winning combination for everyone concerned.

Because the UML is executable, it is possible to automatically generate executable systems from UML models. The importance of this goes well beyond simply saving the time and effort of hand-translating code from abstract models. It is an enabling technology, allowing the developer to move rapidly from the inception of a concept to the testing of that concept. This allows early risk reduction and encourages exploration of the solution space. Conceptual defects can be identified and fixed very early, before many dependencies on the flawed concepts are created, resulting in higher-quality systems in less calendar time.

This book is meant to be a fusion of several subject domains almost universally left disjoint—real-time concepts, such as timeliness and performance; object modeling; a rapid development process; and system safety. This unified approach allows the developer to follow simple and well-understood process steps, culminating with the delivery of correct and timely embedded solutions.

There are few books on using objects in real-time systems and even fewer that use the latest in object modeling languages—the UML. Virtually all object-oriented books focus primarily on business or database application domains and do not mention real-time aspects at all. On the other hand, texts on real-time systems have largely ignored object-oriented methods. For the most part, such books fall into two camps: those that bypass methodological considerations altogether and focus solely on "bare metal" programming, and those that are highly theoretical and have little advice for actually implementing workable systems. *Doing Hard Time* is meant to bridge the technologies, presenting the development of deployable real-time systems using the object semantics and notation of the UML. It does so in a tool-independent manner, even though it does use a particular tool to demonstrate examples.

Audience

The book is oriented toward the practicing professional software developer and the computer science major who is in the junior year or higher. The book could serve as an undergraduate or graduate level text, but the focus is on practical development rather than a theoretical introduction. A few equations are found in this book, but more-theoretical and mathematical approaches are referenced where appropriate. The book assumes a reasonable proficiency in at least one programming language and at least a cursory exposure to the fundamental concepts of object orientation and real-time systems.

Organization

This book is organized into five sections.

1. Basics

   This section introduces the object semantics and notation of the UML, real-time systems, safety criticality, and development processes.

2. Analysis

   This section deals with the various kinds of analysis, including the capture of requirements with use cases, scenarios, and state machines; the identification of the key abstractions in a problem; and modeling the fundamental behavior.

3. Design

   This section focuses on the addition of design-level information, such as the concurrency model, creation of run-time artifacts (libraries, executables, and so on), mapping to physical architectures, the application of design patterns to optimize collaborations of objects, and modeling of algorithms.

4. Advanced Real-Time Modeling

This section discusses topics of interest in difficult or complex real-time and embedded applications. The topics include the determination of the schedulability of object models through mathematical analysis, the reification of general state machine solutions to commonly occurring behavioral problems into behavioral design patterns, and the structure and function of real-time frameworks.

5. Appendices

The book provides three appendices.

- Summary of UML Notation—A short guide to the notations used in the UML and in the book
- Rhapsody: A Fully Constructive UML Visual Programming Tool—An introduction to the UML visual programming tool provided in the accompanying CD-ROM
- TimeWiz: An Integrated Tool for Timing Analysis—An introduction to the schedulability analysis tool provided in the accompanying CD-ROM

CD-ROM

The CD-ROM provided with this book contains three kinds of things:

- Examples presented in the pages of the book—These models are given as Rhapsody projects and can be copied to your local hard drive, where they can be opened and manipulated with Rhapsody.
- Rhapsody—The visual programming tool installation files.
- TimeWiz—The schedulability analysis tool installation files.

I believe (and hope) that the needs of the student, as well as the professional developer, will be addressed by this book, and it is in this spirit that I offer it.

Bruce Powel Douglass, Ph.D.
Deep Dark Winter, (early) 1999

Acknowledgments

I wish to express thanks to my reviewers who tried hard to keep me honest and on topic, and who, I think, more or less succeeded:

Eran Gery	i-Logix
Jim Collins	i-Logix
Larry McAlister	ENSCO, Inc.
Therese M. Douglass	Air Traffic Software Architecture, Inc.
Gary Cernosek	Rational Software Corp.

I would also like to thank Neeraj Chandra and Gene Robinson of i-Logix for their support in allowing me to spend so much effort on this book; Doug Jensen of Mitre for his input on schedulability; Therese Douglass for her expertise in air traffic control systems; and the editorial team at Addison-Wesley, including Carter Shanklin, Krysia Bebick, and Maureen Willard, to name a few.

Part I

The Basics

Part I serves as a precursor to the main body of the book. It introduces four distinct domains of knowledge: object-orientation, real-time systems, safety and reliability, and software development process management. Developers of real-time and embedded systems need knowledge and experience in all four domains to be effective in their jobs.

Chapter 1 introduces the basics of objects, using the current state-of-the-art object modeling language, the Unified Modeling Language (UML). The basics of objects, classes, and relations are presented. In addition, the reader will be familiarized with the more advanced UML concepts of use cases, packages, and deployment models. By the end of this chapter, the basics of UML should be well understood.

The next chapter explains the issues of real-time and embedded systems. Special attention is spent on the concepts of time, responsiveness, concurrency, predictability, and correctness. This chapter provides a set of concepts essential for the discussion in later chapters on schedulability and concurrency management.

Chapter 3 focuses on the concepts of safety as it applies to real-time and embedded systems. This is a confusing topic for many, and is not usually part of a standard computer science curriculum. However, as computer-controlled devices assume more safety-critical functions, this topic is crucial. No mere discussion of the concepts of fault tolerance, fault identification, and fail-safe states, this chapter also provides a number of commonly used safety architectural patterns, which can be specialized and extended in application-specific environments.

The last chapter in this part, Chapter 4, concerns itself with *how* projects are run, what the phases of the development process are, and when the concepts in the previous chapters can be effectively used. The process provided, called the rapid object-oriented process for embedded systems (ROPES), also identifies deliverable artifacts created in each of these phases. ROPES is based on an iterative development lifecycle that uses the executabilty of the UML models to aid in early risk reduction and rapid development.

The basic concepts identified in this part will be used heavily in the three parts that follow. Part II details the concepts required for the analysis of real-time systems. Part III discusses in depth the design of real-time systems using object technology. The last part focuses on some more-advanced concepts, such as the determination of the schedulability of real-time systems, advanced behavioral models, and real-time frameworks.

Chapter 1

Introduction to Objects and the Unified Modeling Language

Anything worth doing is worth overdoing.

—Book of Douglass, Law 1

Real-time applications vary in size and scope from wristwatches and microwave ovens to factory automation and nuclear power plant control systems. Applying a general development methodology to the development of real-time systems means that it must meet the tight performance and size constraints of small 4-bit and 8-bit controllers yet scale up to networked arrays of powerful processors that coordinate their activities to achieve a common purpose. Object models are scalable structures built upon a different fundamental unit—the object. Individually, objects are small models of fundamental problem-domain concepts. Using object models allows the construction of high-performance, robust systems that are resilient in the presence of change. The newest third-generation modeling language is the Unified Modeling Language, or UML. The UML provides a consistent landscape with simple notation and a rigorous semantic framework for developing systems with high performance and correctness requirements.

1.1 Advantages of Objects

Developing software is difficult. It is difficult primarily because the "ether" of software—the material of its existence—is complexity itself. While hardware and mechanical systems are limited by physical laws, no such limitations exist on software. It can become infinitely complex.[1] Hardware is very good at some things (particularly doing simple things very fast), but complexity evades a purely hardware solution. I would argue that even with *infinite resources*, you could never build a hardware-only version of Windows 95.[2] This doesn't mean that hardware isn't difficult—certainly, having immovable constraints makes it difficult to push the envelope of functionality and performance. But it does mean that not only is software difficult, it is its very nature to be so. Software engineers are in no danger of being replaced by some pimply-faced teenager saying, "Y'all want fries with that?"[3]

As Fred Brooks said, there is no "silver bullet" that will magically make software easier. But we can make incremental improvements in the way we think about systems and the way we develop them. One such tool was structured languages, introduced in the 1970s. Although their use also introduced some run-time overhead, structured lan-

---

1. Just *try* to modify the registry of your Windows 95 system!
2. Windows 95 consists of approximately 30 million lines of code. Each line of code exercises several million transistors.
3. Marketers maybe; but engineers, no.

guages were a powerful technology that enabled developers to build much larger systems, with many fewer defects, and in much less time.

In the last two decades, a new way of thinking about software has emerged that further enables developers to be bigger, better, and faster. This new technology is called object-oriented development.

The primary advantages of an object-oriented approach are

- Consistency of model views
- Improved problem-domain abstraction
- Improved stability in the presence of changes
- Improved model facilities for reuse
- Improved scaleability
- Better support for reliability and safety concerns
- Inherent support for concurrency

The perceived disadvantages of objects are

- Objects are an immature technology
- Objects are inefficient
- Lack of compiler and other tool support

As it happens, these perceived disadvantages are groundless. As for the maturity of the technology, object technology is rooted in the Simula language of the 1960s. It has been used heavily since the early to mid 1980s and is currently the preferred technology for personal desktop software development. Embedded-systems developers tend to be conservative in the adoption of new technology, and given the nature of their applications, that concern is appropriate. However, a great number of embedded and real-time systems have been successfully developed using object technology.

The second concern, efficiency, is based on reason. It *is* possible to write inefficient software using objects, and it may even be easier to do than with structured methods. The reasons have more to do with the use of well-established software engineering concepts, such as abstraction and encapsulation, than with anything specific to objects. However, even though objects make the use of these principles more enforceable, the developer need not adhere to them. Another possible reason for inefficiency of a software system based on object technology is the inexperience of the developer with the nuances of that technology.

Specifically, C++ is a complex language, far more so than C. If the developer has only a rudimentary understanding of the C++ language, inefficiencies are likely to occur. However, used properly, C++ is roughly as efficient as properly used C. Nevertheless, it is certainly possible to implement an object design in a structured language, such as C or even assembly language.

The last concern also has some basis in fact. There are few C++ compilers for 8- and 16-bit processors. If the real-time or embedded system is a 32-bit processor, then there are multiple choices available. However, an object design can be implemented in languages other than C++, as noted. These concerns are real. However, they can be avoided or mitigated through training, processor selection, and compiler or source code language selection, and the developer can still reap the very real benefits of using object technology.

The net result is that the object way is *better*. It's not dramatically better in the sense that software will suddenly become easy.[4] It's better because it enables us to build more-complex systems in less time, with fewer defects than is possible with structured development. Let's discuss each of these benefits in turn.

Consistency of model views

One problem with structured methods is difficulty in mapping analysis views to design views, and vice versa. Even though both representations are views of the same system, it is nontrivial to show the exact correspondence between the analysis views (data-flow and entity-relationship diagrams) and the design views (structure charts). The fact that an infinite set of designs can fulfill the same analysis model doesn't help either. Once you're down in the code, it is difficult to show which data flow or process it relates to. The concepts used in data-flow modeling and code writing are fundamentally disjoint. This makes it hard to show that the code in fact implements the analysis model.

In object-oriented systems, the same set of modeling views is used in all phases of development. Objects and classes identified in the analysis model have direct representations in the code, so it is almost trivial to show the relationship between the definition of the problem (analysis) and its solution (the code).

---

4. Don't worry—your job is secure.

Object-oriented systems are developed using one of two approaches. Either the analysis model is elaborated by adding design concepts (the "elaborative" development model) or a translator is built that embodies the design decisions directly (the "translative" development model). In either case, the analysis model maps directly to the implementation.

Improved problem-domain abstraction

Structured methods have some limited facilities for abstraction and encapsulation. However, they enforce an artificial separation of structure and behavior that greatly weakens their effectiveness. A "sensor" must be modeled on one hand as a set of data values and on the other as a set of operations, but the inherent link between them that exists in the real world is severed.

Object-oriented modeling maintains the strong cohesion among data items and the operations that manipulate them. Because this is how the real world exists, object-oriented abstractions are more intuitive and powerful. Even the vocabulary for naming the objects comes from the problem domain. Users and marketers can understand the implications of their requirements more clearly because the abstract model is constructed using their own concepts. The object perspective is at a higher level, closer to the problem domain and further from the computer science implementation domain. This results in a system that has loose coupling between the independent aspects of the system while maintaining good cohesion of aspects that are inherently tightly coupled.

Improved stability in the presence of changes

Every developer has experienced a small change in requirements that had a catastrophic effect on the software structure. This is because the foundation on which structured systems is based is *fundamentally unstable* and subject to radical changes. The structured development world is rather like a Dali painting in which a priori truths are subject to a posteriori modification. It works fine for art, but that's no way to live.

Because object-oriented system abstractions are based on the real world, they tend to be much more stable. The fundamental structure of the real universe doesn't undergo daily fluctuations.[5] Changing

---

5. To the consternation of marketers everywhere.

requirements tend to add or remove aspects of the model rather than totally restructure the system.

Improved model facilities for reuse

Structured systems have had "limited" success with reuse.[6] If the component does exactly what you need, great—you can reuse it (provided it links to the compiler on your operating system even though it was developed with an older revision of a now unavailable compiler). Reuse in structured systems is generally a matter of modifying the source code of the component to meet your new requirements or to integrate with your new environment. The net result has been a truly abysmal record of reuse.

Object-oriented modeling includes three tactical means for improving reuse—aggregation, generalization, and type parameterization. *Aggregation* is the process of constructing a new "whole" from possibly reusable "parts." This whole-part relationship permits the developer to construct higher-level abstractions from lower-level component pieces. In the same way that a computer system is constructed of hardware components reused in various ways to construct different systems, appropriately designed software component objects can build up different higher-level abstractions. For example, a control system might consist of a controller, a set of actuators, and a set of sensors. Each of these component parts might be reused within other control systems.

Generalization (a.k.a. "inheritance") supports reuse by deriving new components from existing ones. The developer may create new specialized and extended components without changing the existing components on which they are based. Specialization refers to redefining a behavior to be more appropriate for the newly specialized component. Extension is the process of adding behaviors or information to the new component. This is the powerful notion of "programming by difference" and allows the developer to code only the things that are different.

Type parameterization supports reuse by incompletely specifying the data elements (called formal parameters) of the component. Later, the

---

6. In the same sense that "the Russians have had limited success with capitalism."

developer completes the specification by supplying the missing elements (the actual parameters). Thus, parameterized types define a basic structure, which is reusable for different data elements. It is possible to write a sort routine once and bind it to different data types, such as integers, floats, accounts, EEG measurements, and target coordinates. The code that actually sorts the collection has to be written only one time, but it can be applied to many circumstances.[7]

Improved scaleability

The point of any kind of method for developing software is to manage complexity. Small systems are less complex than larger ones; if the system is small enough, no method is required at all. At the other end of the spectrum, we *really* need development methods when the systems are large and complicated. Structured methods work fine for small-to-medium-scale systems, but they fail when confronted with large-scale problems.

The lack of scaleability of structured systems is due to several weaknesses within the structured way of thinking and modeling. Structured systems have weaker abstraction and encapsulation facilities, meaning that these systems have some level of pathological coupling that becomes more severe as the scale of the problem grows. The use of different modeling notations and concepts in multiple phases means that "getting there from here" is harder and more error-prone. And last, too many system aspects aren't directly modeled, meaning that ad hoc approaches must be applied. As the system grows, these ad hoc approaches become less tenable.

Objects do it better. Improved abstraction and encapsulation maintains looser coupling among components, decreasing pathological coupling. The use of the same notation throughout the development process means that there is no "can't get there from here" syndrome when moving from analysis to design to code. The notation itself is obvious and simple and not full of ad hoc artifacts necessary to circumvent deficiencies in the method.

---

7. The reuse facilities in object-oriented methods are an enabling technology that permits reuse to occur. They do not automatically guarantee that reuse *will* occur—that is a sociological issue beyond the scope of this book.

Better support for reliability and safety concerns

Because of better abstraction and encapsulation, the interaction of object-oriented components can be limited to a few well-defined interfaces. This improves reliability because it is possible to control how the components interact. In addition, it is possible to more clearly and cleanly enforce pre- and post-conditions required to make your system run properly. For example, C standard arrays require the component's user to make sure that array bounds are not exceeded. Object language allows you to build the range checking into the array itself. Also, object systems offer exception handling for ensuring that exceptional and fault conditions are handled correctly. Finally, because of the improved support for reuse, previously tested components can be reused so that less of each new system must be developed from scratch.

Inherent support for concurrency

Concurrency is a fact of life—and a very important one for real-time, embedded-systems developers. Structured methods have no notion of concurrency, task management, or task synchronization. These important aspects of your system can't even be represented using standard structured methods.

Object-oriented systems are inherently concurrent, and the details of tasking and task synchronization can be explicitly represented using orthogonal components in statecharts, active objects, and object messaging. These are powerful tools in the struggle to build correct systems that meet tight performance requirements.

1.2 Terms and Concepts

An *object* is a unique real-world or conceptual entity. An object has identity, attributes (values), and behaviors (operations). Objects are instances of classes. A *class* is an abstraction of the things commonly shared by a set of objects. Classes relate to other classes by means of *relations*. Relations allow the construction of taxonomies of classes and allow objects to participate in collaborations that enable large-scale behaviors.

Objects and classes share an *instance-type* dichotomy that pervades virtually all of the object model. *Associations* (a type of relation) bind classes together to enable communication via messages. *Links* are instances of association between objects at a specific point in time.

Messages are an abstraction of object communication. Most commonly, messages are realized as direct calls to operations defined in the receiver object, but many other realizations are possible.

Use cases describes the primary and secondary functions of a system. A specific path through a use case is a *scenario,* which is composed of a sequence of operations in which several objects collaborate to achieve the purpose of the use case. Use cases provide an external black-box view of the system and its environment. Objects of interest outside the scope of the system are called *actors.* Actors associate with use cases and, ultimately, with system objects, sending messages and events back and forth.

1.3 Object Orientation with the UML

The Unified Modeling Language (UML) is a language for expressing the constructs and relationships of complex systems. It was begun as a response to the *Object Management Group's* (OMG) request for proposal for a standard object-oriented methodology. Spearheaded by Rational Software's Grady Booch, Jim Rumbaugh, and Ivar Jacobson, the OMG accepted the UML as the standard. It was jointly developed by some of the major software companies in the world, including I-Logix, Digital, HP, ICON Computing, Microsoft, MCI Systemhouse, Oracle, Texas Instruments, and Unysis. Contributions have been made by many top object modelers, including David Harel,[8] Peter Coad, and Jim Odell.

The UML is more complete than other methods in its support for modeling complex systems. It is particularly suited for modeling real-time, embedded systems. Major features include

- Object model
- Use cases and scenarios
- Behavioral modeling with statecharts

---

8. David Harel of I-Logix invented statecharts, the visual formalism used by the UML to model complex behavior.

- Packaging of various kinds of entities
- Representation of tasking and task synchronization
- Models of physical topology
- Models of source code organization
- Support for object-oriented patterns

Through the course of this book, these features will be described in more detail and their use shown by examples. For now, let's explore the fundamental aspects of the UML object model.

1.3.1 Objects

Objects have both data and behavior. They may represent real-world things, such as dogs, airfoil control surfaces, sensors, and engines. They may also represent purely conceptual entities, such as bank accounts, trademarks, marriages, and lists. Objects can be visual things, such as fonts, letters, ideographs, histograms, polygons, lines, and circles. All these things have various aspects, such as:

- Attributes (data)
- Behavior (operations or methods)
- State (memory)
- Identity
- Responsibilities

Let's take an example from each of the object categories just listed. A real-world thing might be a sensor that can detect and report both a linear value and its rate of change, as in Table 1-1.

The sensor object contains two attributes: the monitored sensor value and its computed rate of change (RoC). The behaviors support data acquisition and reporting. They also permit configuration of the sensor. The object state consists of the last acquired/computed values. The identity specifies exactly which object instance is under discussion. The responsibility of the sensor is defined to be how it contributes to overall system functionality. Its attributes and behaviors must collaborate to help the object achieve its responsibilities.

Table 1-1: *Aspects of a Sensor Object*

Attributes	Behavior	State	Identity	Responsibility
• Linear value • Rate of change (RoC)	• Acquire • Report • Reset • Zero • Enable • Disable	• Last value • Last RoC	• Instance for robot arm joint	• Provide information for the precise location of the end of the robot arm in absolute space coordinates

A message transaction is a conceptual entity, but it is an important object, as well. Its properties are listed in Table 1-2.

The message-transaction object also has enabling attributes and behaviors. The attributes include the current retry count, the maximum number of times to resend the message, and the period of time to wait between retries. The behaviors allow the object to send the message, accept the returning acknowledgement, and notify the sender if the message was not successfully sent.

Table 1-2: *Aspects of a Message-Transaction Object*

Attributes	Behavior	State	Identity	Responsibility
• Retry count • Max retries • Time to retry	• Send • Receive • Notify sender	• Idle • Sending • Waiting	• Transaction for msg 0x1199876	• Implements reliable transmission for the sender • Resends message after fixed period of time has elapsed until some max retry count is exceeded • Notifies the sender if unable to complete transaction

A font is a visual object. Its properties are shown in Table 1-3.

Table 1-3: *Aspects of a Font Object*

Attributes	Behavior	State	Identity	Responsibility
• Point size • Serif • Color	• Draw char • Erase char • Load • Unload • Set color	• Current character set	• Times New Roman 16 pt. normal sans serif (first load)	• Provides a visually attractive typeface in a particular size for the display of readable English text messages

Certain of these characteristics may be more important for some objects than for others. One could envision a sensor class that has no state—whenever you ask it for information, it samples the data and returns it rather than store it internally. An array of numbers is a container object that doesn't have any really interesting behaviors.

The key idea of objects is that they combine these properties into a single cohesive entity. The structured approach to software design deals with data and functions as totally separate entities. Data-flow diagrams show both data flow and data processes. Data can be decomposed, if necessary. Independently, structure charts show the static call tree to decompose functions (somewhat loosely related to the data processes). Objects fuse related data and functions together. The object is the fundamental unit of decomposition in object-oriented programming.

Abstraction is the process of identifying key aspects of the entity and ignoring the rest (see Figure 1-1). A chair is an abstraction defined as "a piece of furniture with at least one leg, a back, and a flat surface for sitting." That some chairs are made of wood while others may be plastic or metal is inessential to the abstraction of "chair." When we abstract objects, we select only those aspects that are important relative to our point of view. For example, as a runner, my abstraction of dogs is as "high-speed, teeth-delivery systems." The fact that they may have a pancreas or a tail is immaterial to my modeling domain, whereas top speed and territory boundaries are crucial.

The object metaphor is powerful for a couple of reasons. First and foremost, it aligns well with common daily experience. In the real

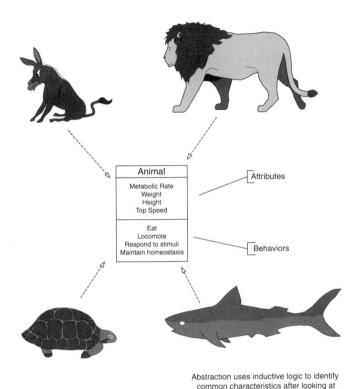

Figure 1-1: *Object Abstraction*

world, we deal with objects all the time, and each one has all the properties we've assigned to objects earlier. Okay, rocks may not have interesting behavior—but they do have attributes, such as color, weight, and size. They certainly have responsibilities, such as intimidating hungry pit bulls. Most objects have behavior as well. Engines turn on and off, deliver torque, guzzle gas, and require maintenance. Object-oriented decomposition allows us to use the hard-won intuition we've gained by simply living in the world and interacting with it. This is not true of functional decomposition.

ALGOL-based languages introduced the concept of an abstract data type (ADT). Rather than define only the underlying data bit patterns, ADTs include the operations that make sense in terms of their use and purpose. An enumerated type is an example of an ADT. Pascal provides three operators for enumerated types—ord(), pred(), and succ(), or ordinal value, predecessor, and successor, respectively. Ada provides the same operators as attributes, A'POS, A'PRED, and A'SUCC, in addition to a few more. C has much weaker abstraction facilities. It short circuits the abstraction by making visible the internal unsigned integer structure of enumerations. It is important to consider the ADTs and the operations defined on them together.

In their simplest expression, objects are nothing more than ADTs bound together with related operators. This is a low-level perspective and doesn't capture all the richness available in the object paradigm. Software developers use such ADTs and operators as low-level mechanisms all the time. Stacks, queues, trees, and all the other basic data structures are nothing more than objects with specific operations defined. Consider common ADTs in Table 1-4.

Table 1-4: *Abstract Data Types and Operations*

Data Structure	Operations
Stack	Push
	Pop
	Full
	Empty
Queue	Insert
	Remove
	Full
	Empty
Linked List	Insert
	Remove
	Next
	Previous
Tree	Insert
	Remove
	Next
	Previous

At a low level of abstraction, these are objects that provide the operations intrinsically rather than ADTs with separate functions to provide the services. In Pascal, to insert an item in a stack, you might have code that looks like this:

```pascal
type
    OKType = {NoCanDo, CanDo}
    stackFrame = array [1..100] of float;
    record stack
        st: stackFrame;    { holds stack values }
        top: integer;    { holds top of stack }
    end;

function insert(var s: stack; f: float) : OKType;
begin
    if s.top > 100 then
        insert := NoCanDo
    else
        begin
        s.st[s.top] := f;
        s.top:= s.top + 1;
        insert := CanDo;
        end;
end; { insert }

var
    s: stack;
    result: OKType;
begin
    s.top := 1; { start at the beginning }
    result:= insert(s, 3.14159265);
end.
```

There are some open issues. Who ensures that s.top is initially set to 1? Here it is decoupled from the declaration of the stack variables and appears after the main BEGIN. Does the insert() function apply to other stack-type objects that might store integers or strings instead of floats? These questions arise because, in Pascal, there is no way to bind the ADT to the operations defined for it. Compare the above code with a C++ implementation.

```cpp
class stack {
    int size;
    int top;
    float *st;
```

```
public:
    // constructor sets up top ok
    stack(int s=100) : size(s), top(1) { st = new
    float[size]; };
    void insert(float f) {
        if (top > size)
            throw StackOverflow;
        else
            st[++top] = f;
        };
    ~stack() { delete st[];};
};

void main() {
    stack s, t(400);
    s.insert(3.14159265);
    t.insert(2.7182818284);
};
```

Although in this case, it may not look like much of an improvement, the stack object binds the data and its associated operations together. Because the concept of a stack is meaningless without both the operations and the data, it makes most sense to bind these things tightly together—they are different aspects of a single concept. This is called *strong cohesion*—the appropriate binding together of inherently tightly coupled properties. The result of the cohesion is that we can easily create a different-size stack (the default gives us our 100-element stack). The stack object itself handles the details of creation and deletion of variables of type stack. The insert operation is also part of the stack object.

In a more general sense, objects may be thought of as autonomous machines. Our bodies are constructed of diverse sets of cells that have different attributes, roles, behavior, states, and responsibilities. They come together in higher-level collaborations, called organs, to achieve some higher-level systemic function, such as digestion, locomotion, and thermoregulation. The cells themselves are autonomous and take care of their internal details, just as software objects do.

Because objects are autonomous machines, it is easier to ensure that they are loosely coupled with the objects around them. In fact, the execution of behaviors is far more general under this notion than in the standard functional model. In the functional model, it is assumed that the caller calls a function and waits until it is complete and returns, whereupon the caller resumes. This is only one of several available models of inter-object communication. Objects may implement this synchronous (direct function) call, but they may also implement asynchronous calls, as well, as when the called object runs within a different thread of execution or even a different processor. Different mechanisms for handling guards and blocking are also available. The model of object-as-machine is a very general one.

Rather than depict one object calling a service of another, the general model is that one object sends a message to the other requesting a service or operation. Messages may be implemented in many ways to achieve different effects. At the modeling stage, message implementation is not an essential detail; as such, it should not be visible. Figure 1-2 shows how objects collaborate.

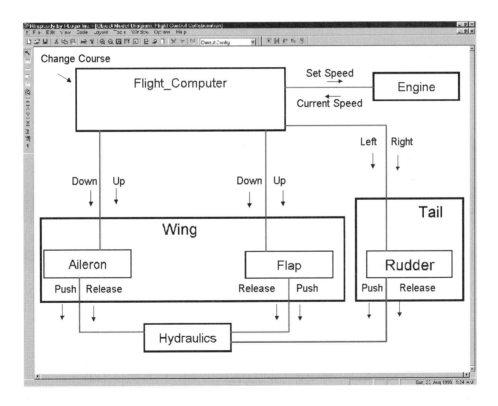

Figure 1-2: *Objects Collaborate to Achieve System Functionality*

1.3.2 Attributes

Attributes, in OO-speak, refer to the data encapsulated within an object. It might be the balance of a bank account, the current picture number in an electronic camera, the color of a font, or the owner of a trademark. Some objects may have one or a small number of simple attributes. Others may be quite rich. In some object-oriented languages, all instances of data types are objects, from the smallest integer type to the most complex aggregate. In an effort to minimize the difference between C and C++, variables of the elementary data types of C++, such as *int* and *float*, are not really objects. Programmers may treat them as if they were objects,[9] but C++ does not require it.

1.3.3 Behavior

Interesting objects do interesting things. Passive objects supply behaviors for other objects—that is, they provide services other objects may request. ADTs are typically passive objects. In the previous C++ example, the stack objects provide storage for simple data values, the means for inserting and removing them from storage, and some simple error checking to ensure their integrity. Active objects form the roots for threads and invoke the services (behaviors) of the passive objects.

In the UML, an *operation* is a named behavior of a class. A *method* is the implementation of an operation. Classes provide one or more interfaces to other classes. An *interface* is a named collection of operations. Additional hidden operations may be defined within a class to implement the behavior implied by the interface. All of a class's behaviors are ultimately realized by its set of operations, but they may be constrained by applying behavioral models to the class. These behavioral models limit the execution of operations into sets of well-defined sequences.

Logically, these constraining behavioral models can be thought of as one of three distinct types: simple, automaton, and continuous. All three are important, although the second has a particular importance in real-time systems.

The least complex kind of behavior is called simple. The object performs services on request and keeps no memory of previous services.

---

9. Well, almost anyway—but that's a programming, rather than a modeling, issue.

Each action is atomic and complete, at least from an external perspective. A simple object may maintain a collection of primitive data types and operations defined on them. A binary tree object, for instance, shows simple behavior. Another example is a cos(x) function; cos(π/2) always returns the same value, regardless of what value it was invoked with before. It retains no memory of previous invocations. This kind of object is also called *primitive.*

The second type of object behavior treats the object as a particular type of machine, called an automaton or finite state machine (FSM). This kind of object possesses a bounded (*finite*) set of conditions of existence (*states*). It must be in one and only one state at a time. An automaton exhibits modal behavior, each mode constituting a state. A state is a dichotomous condition of existence defined by the set of events it processes and the actions it performs. Because objects with state machines react to events in well-defined ways, they are also called *reactive objects.*

Incoming events can induce transitions between object states in a predefined manner. Some object-oriented methods claim that all objects exhibit state behavior. A sample-and-hold A/D converter, as in Figure 1-3, is such an object. It shows the following states:

- Enabled
- Sampling
- Holding
- Disabled

The third kind of object behavior is called continuous. An object with continuous behavior is one with an infinite, or at least unbounded, set of existence conditions. One example is an *algorithmic object.* This is an object that executes some algorithm on a possibly infinite data stream. For example, an object implementing a moving-average algorithm performs a smoothing function over an incoming data stream. Objects with continuous behavior are objects whose current behavior depends on past behavior and inputs, but the dependency is of a continuous, rather than discrete, nature. Fuzzy systems and PID control loops are examples of continuous systems, as are pseudo-random number generators and digital filters. Their current behavior depends on past history but in a quantitative, not qualitative, way.

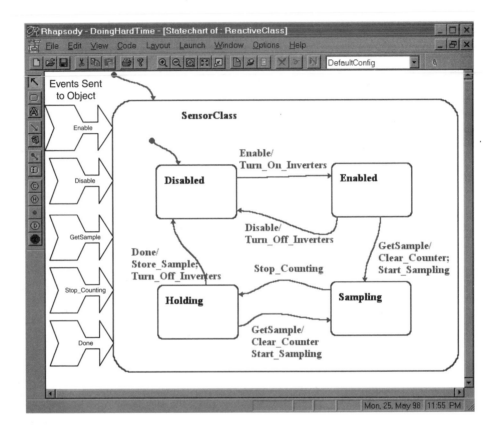

Figure 1-3: *State Machine for a Sample-and-Hold A/D Converter*

1.3.4 Messaging

The logical interface between objects is done with the passing of messages. A message is an abstraction of data and/or control information passed from one object to another. Different implementations are possible, for example:

- A function call
- Mail via a real-time operating system (RTOS)
- An event via an RTOS
- An interrupt
- A semaphore-protected shared resource

- An Ada rendezvous
- A remote procedure call (RPC) in a distributed system

Early analysis identifies the key messages. Later design elaborates an implementation strategy that defines the synchronization and timing requirements for each message. Internally, the object translates the messages into acceptor operations, state transitions, commands, or data to munch on, as appropriate. Messages occur only between objects that have an association (see Figure 1-4).

Use of message passing enables loose coupling. In analysis, one does not specify interface details, such as synchronicity, function call format, rendezvous, time outs, etc. These are design and implementation details that can be decided later, once the overall problem is better understood.

Figure 1-4: *Sending a Message to an Object*

An object's interface may be thought of as a contract it makes with the world and is defined by the set of protocols within which the object participates. An interface protocol consists of three things:

1. Pre-conditions
2. Signature
3. Post-conditions

Pre-conditions are the conditions guaranteed to be true before the message is sent or received. They are normally the responsibility of the object sending the message. Post-conditions are the things guaranteed to be true by the time the message is processed and are the responsibility of the receiver of the message. The message signature is the exact mechanism used for message transfer. This can be a function call with the parameters and return type or RTOS message post/pend pair, or it could be bus message protocol.

The interface should reflect the essential characteristics of the object that require visibility to other objects. Objects should hide inessential details. Objects enforce strong encapsulation. In C++, for example, common practice is to hide data members (in the private or protected sections of the class declaration), but to publish operations that manipulate the data (in the public section).

1.3.5 Responsibility

The responsibilities of an object are the roles it serves within the system. The interface and behaviors provide the means by which responsibilities are met, but they do not define them. Consider a front-end loader tractor as an object, as shown in Table 1-5.

The responsibilities are the roles the tractor will play for the road construction firm that uses it. The behaviors must be sufficiently rich to enable the responsibilities to be fulfilled, but they do not of themselves define those responsibilities. It is normal that several behaviors acting on potentially several attributes are required to realize a responsibility.

1.3.6 Concurrency

Unlike subroutines in structure charts, objects are inherently concurrent unless otherwise specified. It is theoretically possible for each

Table 1-5: *Object Properties*

Tractor Characteristics	
Attributes	• Carrying capacity • Wheel size • Maximum engine output • Clearance height • Weight
Behaviors	• Lift • Drop • Move • Set direction • Change gear
Responsibilities	• Move dirt from road bed to truck • Dig holes for bridge supports • Fill holes mistakenly dug

object to run on its own processor. It is the physical structure of modern computers that drives sequential threads. The concurrency model in the UML is based on the concept of an active object. Active objects are the roots of threads, so the process of identifying threads in the UML involves the creation of a set of active objects to own them.

A *thread* is a set of operations executed in sequence. Concurrent threads can run on separate processors, which means that the relative speeds with which they progress are uncoupled. On the same processor, we must rely on pseudo-concurrency provided by the underlying operating system or write our own executive. These concurrency mechanisms allow the threads to progress more or less independently.

1.3.7 Objects as Autonomous Machines

Taken together, the characteristics of objects, such as attributes, behaviors, interfaces, encapsulation, and concurrency, allow each object to act as a separate entity—an autonomous machine. This machine does not have to be very smart, but it must own its responsibilities and collaborate with other machines to achieve some higher-order goals. At a minimum, objects must ensure

- Data integrity
- Interface protocols are followed
- Their own behavior

This is true of small, simple objects, as well as more-complex, elaborate ones. Simple objects are akin to biological cells. Cells manage their own metabolism, absorb nutrients, maintain intracellular homeostasis, and fulfill whatever small function they provide to the system as a whole. Large groups of cells collaborate to form organs that excrete hormones, locomote, maintain systemic homeostasis, and play video games. Even larger collaborations form individual people, and collaborations of these (in pathological cases) form ANSI standards committees! Within the context of their responsibilities, these objects protect their own interests (especially in the standards committees).

This leads to a fundamental rule of object systems—*distributed intelligence.* Each object, however lowly and simple, has enough brains to manage its own resources and perform its own behaviors. This is different from functional decomposition in which it is common to have elaborately complex master subroutines know everything about everybody. The truth is that it is far easier to construct dozens of semi-smart objects than a single really smart object that knows everything.

1.4 Class Diagrams

In the object-oriented world, the term *class* is used in precisely the same way as in philosophy. A class is an abstraction of the common properties from a set containing many similar objects.

A class can be thought of as the *type* of an object.[10] The values 0, –3, and 7,879 are all instances (objects) of the class *integer*. Further, all

---

10. Strictly speaking, the type refers to the interface of the object—objects with the same interface are of the same type, regardless of their class. The class of an object defines its internal implementation. This is not normally a useful distinction unless you are using languages that make the difference visible, such as Java.

instances of a class have all the properties defined by the class. A mammal has fur, bears its young live, and is homeothermic. This is true of all members of the class *mammals*—cats, mice, bears, and even rock stars. This does not mean that instances of the class are all the same—cats are certainly different from rock stars—but they share at least some set of common properties.[11] The values of these properties may be different among instances, but all properties must be present. For example, an account class may define a balance attribute—that is, all accounts have balances. Some accounts may have positive values while other hover around zero or even dip into negative numbers.

Object-oriented designers uncover classes much the same way as philosophers—by observing a number of objects and abstracting the common properties. Table 1-6 presents some example classes.

Table 1-6: *Classes and Objects*

Class	Attributes	Behaviors	Example objects	Responsibilities
Ventilator Breath	Inspiration time Expiration time Tidal volume	Set insp time Get exp time Set tidal volume	Breath #1 Breath #98	Ventilate the patient to infuse O_2 and remove CO_2
Elevator	Capacity Current floor Current direction	Go to floor Stop Open door	Elevator 1 Blg 6 Elevator 3 Blg 1	Carry passengers to their desired floor
Airspeed Sensor	Airspeed magnitude Airspeed direction	Get airspeed Calibrate Set filter value	Primary AS sensor Secondary AS sensor	Determine current airspeed of the aircraft *(continued)*

11. Most notably: fur, indifference to the needs of others, and a universal inability to sing.

Table 1-6: (*cont.*)

Class	Attributes	Behaviors	Example objects	Responsibilities
Marriage	Wedding date Number of children Children	Wed Divorce Create children	Cindy's first marriage	Maintain stable social group
Airline Flight	Flight number Date Point of origin Destination Departure time	Take off Land Lose luggage	My flight to Jamaica Thursday at 11:45 AM	Safely carry passengers and luggage to destination
ECG Signal	Heart rate PVC count ST segment height Display rate Scale factor	Get heart rate Set alarm limits Display waveform	George's ECG signal	Monitor and report status of patient's cardiac function to the attending physician; alarm for possibly dangerous conditions

In each of these cases, it is possible to imagine specific object instances of these classes. Just as a *struct* in C defines data structure, a class defines the type of objects created in its likeness (see Figure 1-5).

A class defines the attributes and behaviors of the objects it instantiates,[12] but not their responsibilities. All attributes of objects of a class are the same in type, but not in value. That is, if a class has an attribute, such as color or charm, then instances of the class have the characteristic, although their particular value of the attribute may differ. Respon-

---

12. The term *instantiation* comes from the term *instance,* as in *making an instance* (that is, object) of a class.

Bruce (object)

Catherine (object)

Sam (object)

Figure 1-5: *Classes and Objects*

sibilities, however, are context-specific, and are determined by the use of the object within that context. A simple container object may hold checking accounts and be responsible for coordinating access to the accounts. A container object of the same class may hold inventory records and coordinate access for an inventory control system. The responsibilities are similar in type, but they differ in the specifics. An object's class defines the responsibilities of an object only when all such objects are used in the same context and in the same way.

UML classes are shown using rectangles with the name of the class inside the rectangle. A variation uses a three-segment box—the top segment holds the name of the class; the middle segment contains a list of attributes; the bottom segment contains a list of operations. Not all the attributes and operations need to be listed. Figure 1-6 shows a simple autopilot system that consists of an autopilot class and the various sensor and actuator classes it uses.

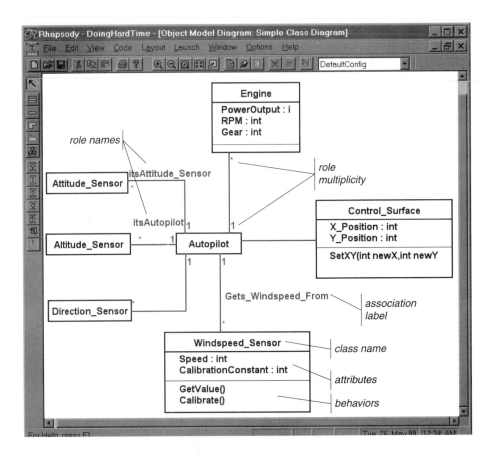

Figure 1-6: *A Simple Class Diagram*

1.4.1 Relations among Classes and Objects

For one object to send messages to another, they must associate with each other in some way. You can imagine that some association exists between the following pairs of objects.

Class	Association	Class
Engine	*has a*	Piston
Flight computer	*controls an*	Engine
Linear position sensor	*is a type of*	Sensor

Ship	*contains some*	Planks
Elevator	*is called by*	Call button
Bank customer	*stores money in a*	Bank account

In the UML, relationships exist among classes. Five common types of object relationships exist: association, aggregation, composition, generalization, and dependency.

Associations are relationships that typically manifest themselves at run-time to permit the exchange of messages among objects. Associations are shown using simple lines connecting two objects. Unless otherwise specified, UML associations are bi-directional and support messaging in either direction. When it is clear that messages go in only one direction, an open arrowhead points to the receiving object.

Many elements in the UML share the type-instance dichotomy, including associations. An association is a relation between classes. An instance of an association is called a link. Links exist between objects instantiated from the classes related by the association.

Aggregation associations are shown with diamonds at the owner (aggregate) end of the relationship. Aggregation is used when one object logically or physically contains another. *Composition* is a strong form of aggregation in which the owner is explicitly responsible for the creation and destruction of the part objects. Composition is shown either with filled-in aggregation diamonds or the physical containment of classes within the composite class.

Directed lines with closed arrowheads indicate a *generalization*, or *is-a-kind-of*, relationship. *Dependency* is shown with an open arrowhead and a dashed line. The UML defines several kinds of dependency, each represented as a stereotype of the relation.[13] One of the most important stereotypes of dependency is «bind». The «bind» dependency attaches a set of actual parameters to a partially specified template class.

The numbers at each end of the relationship line denote the number of objects that participate in the relationship at each end. This is called the *multiplicity* of the role. We see in Figure 1-7 that one Window object can have 0, 1, or 2 scroll bars. Because the window can have no scroll bars, this is an *optional* relationship. The scroll bar, for its side, works

---

13. A stereotype is a special kind of UML model element and is shown by embedding the stereotype name between guillemets, such as «bind» or «friend».

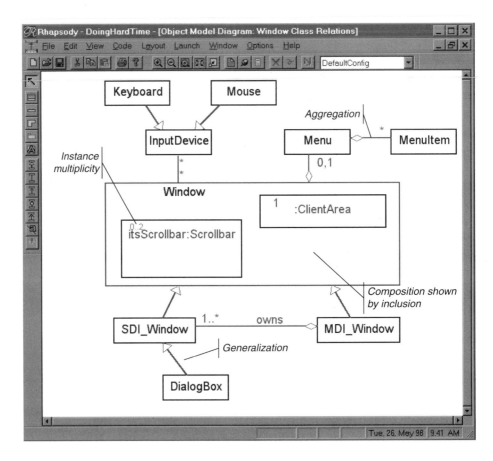

Figure 1-7: *Window Class Relationships*

only with a single window, so the number at the window side of the relationship is one. If multiple windows share a scroll bar, the multiplicity would be "*" (an indicator for "unspecified but greater than or equal to 0") or the fixed number, if known. Figure 1-8 shows a more real-time example, a sensor.

1.4.1.1 Association

When one object uses the services of another but does not own it, the objects have an association. Associations are appropriate when any of the following is true.

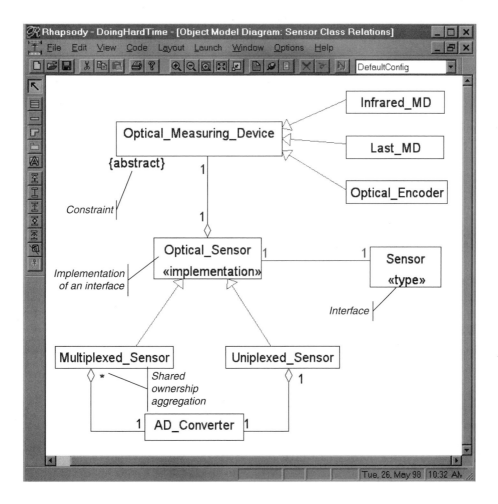

Figure 1-8: *Sensor Class Relationships*

- One object uses the services of another but is not an aggregate of it.
- The lifecycle of the used class is not the responsibility of the user class—that is, it is not responsible for the used object's creation and destruction.
- The association between objects is "looser" than one of aggregation.
- The association can be characterized as client-server.
- The used object is shared and used equally by many others.

The class diagrams show that a *Window* class *uses* (specifically, "gets user input from") various input devices. The two types shown are a mouse and a keyboard, but other devices are conceivable, including tablets, microphones, and even a modem for a remote session.

1.4.1.2 Aggregation

An aggregation relationship applies when one object physically or conceptually contains another. The aggregating class is referred to as the *owner,* or *whole,* and it contains the diamond end of the aggregation. The aggregated class is the *owned, part,* or *component* class. The owner is typically responsible for the creation and destruction of the owned class. The UML allows components of aggregates to be shared among owners. When an object has shared ownership, some ad hoc rule must specify who has the responsibility for its creation and destruction.

In Windows programming, a *window* is a kind of object that contains a *client area.* The client area cannot stand on its own, without being contained by a window. The client area comes into existence during the creation of the window and is destroyed when the window is destroyed.

1.4.1.3 Composition

Composition is a strong form of aggregation in which special constraints are levied on the participating objects. Components are usually shown by actual inclusion of the component class within the composite. Alternatively, an aggregation association can be used, but with a filled diamond. Components of composites cannot be shared (that is, they can have only one owner), and the composite is required to create and destroy its components. Composites are often more-abstract things that may be thought of as implemented in terms of more-primitive component parts. The composite receives messages and typically delegates them to one or more of these components. A common use of composites is as active objects—that is, objects that are the roots of threads. These active objects create the threads to operate in, and their components execute within this thread. The composite receives messages and events from the RTOS and other threads and dispatches them to the appropriate components within its own thread.

1.4.1.4 Generalization

When one class is a specialization of another, the relationship is called generalization, or inheritance. It means that the child or descendent class has all the characteristics defined by the parent, although it might specialize them. The child may also extend its parent class by adding additional attributes and behaviors. Fundamental to generalization is that it is an "is-a-kind-of" relationship among classes. A mammal is-a-kind-of animal and an infrared sensor is-a-kind-of sensor.

Type hierarchies are created from classes and their inheritance relationships. Such hierarchies form the basis of some kinds of frameworks, such as Microsoft Foundation Classes (MFC) and Borland's Object Windows Library (OWL).

In the *Window* class diagram above, the *Window* parent class has two direct descendants, *SDI* (single document interface) and *MDI* (multiple document interface) classes. The *SDI* class is further subtyped into a *Dialog Box* class. A dialog box is an *SDI* window that does not have a menu,[14] but has visual controls placed in its client area. Multiplicity makes no sense for inheritance relationships, and so is not depicted. Since the parent *Window* class *has* a client area, all its descendants do, as well.

Generalization is an extraordinarily powerful facility, despite its seeming simplicity. It allows objects to be *specified by difference* rather than from scratch each time. In standard structured methods, extending or specializing a function requires modification of the source code to produce a new routine that meets your needs. In object-oriented systems, you may subclass the parent to create a child class and merely add the additional attributes and behaviors needed. If a behavior needs to be implemented differently for a subclass, that's no problem either. You redefine the behavior in the subclass. The object-oriented paradigm ensures the correct version of the behavior will be called based on the object type you have.

Generalization is a mechanism to represent generalization-specialization. That is, the parent class is a generalized version of the child class. One of the important principles of generalization is the Liskov Substitution Principle (LSP), which states that a subclass must be freely substitutable for its superclass. This means that a subclass must continue to

---

14. Note that all subtypes of the class *Windows* can have a menu (the multiplicity of "0,1" makes it optional), but dialog boxes commonly do not.

act as though it were also an instance of its superclass. A dog may be a specialized, extended form of mammal, but an instance of dog is still a mammal and has all the properties of mammals. LSP requires that subclasses do not constrain superclass behavior, such as by "blocking" or "selectively inheriting" some properties.

Almost always, a single inheritance hierarchy is specialized along a single characteristic or a small set of closely related characteristics. Multiple inheritance usually makes sense only if the sets of inheritance hierarchies are specialized along orthogonal[15] characteristics. Otherwise, another solution will probably be more appropriate.

1.4.1.5 Dependency

The «bind» dependency relationship takes an incompletely specified entity and adds the previously unspecified aspects. The UML notational guide identifies other types of dependency, as well.

- Relation between one element that is derived from another («derive»)
- Relation between an element that provides another a special level of accessibility («friend»)
- Relation between a high-level construct at a coarse granularity and a lower-level construct at a finer granularity («refine»)
- Relation between a type and an instance («instantiate»)
- Relation between two use cases in which one extends the behavior of another («extends»)
- Relation between two use cases in which one includes the behavior of another («include»)

A very common use of dependency you'll see is taking a generic, but incomplete, class specification and creating from it an instantiable class. A parameterized class (*template* in C++-speak) is not, strictly speaking, a class. It is a template defined in terms of a set of formal parameters. The «bind» dependency applies actual parameters to the parameterized class, resulting in a class from which objects may be instantiated.

The «bind» dependency is similar to generalization in that it also creates more-specialized classes. At first glance, the distinction seems

---

15. *Orthogonal characteristics* here is defined as "properties with nothing in common."

subtle, indeed. In either case, you are specializing some entity to get a class. Inheritance is used when you want to specialize how some behavior is performed or how some class is constructed. Generic instantiation is used when you want the same behavior or structure applied on a novel component type.

Collection or container classes are a common application of the refinement relationship. A collection class is one that aggregates many component objects. These component objects are usually homogenous (of the same class) or at least from a single inheritance hierarchy. Exactly the same behavior applies, regardless of the class collected. Things you want to be able to do with a collection of classes might include

- Get the first object in the collection
- Get the next object in the collection
- Add an object to the collection
- Remove an object from the collection

These behaviors are exactly the same, regardless of whether you are dealing with a group of bank accounts, photodiode sensors, or automobiles. The behaviors of the objects themselves are vastly different, but the collection itself should behave in the same way, nevertheless.

This is difficult to implement using generalization. It is straightforward, however, using generic instantiation. Figure 1-9 shows how generics are represented. They use a dashed line with a closed arrowhead, similar to a generalization. The refining parameters are shown on the association with a «bind» stereotype[16] or shown with the parameters in the class box between angled brackets. The classes created as a result of the «bind» dependency look the same except that the base type is defined, and the base type appears inside a box with a solid line. This example declares a generic stack and then instantiates three stack classes: one for integers, one for strings, and one for transaction objects.

Note that in Figure 1-9, one of the bound classes has no dependency relationship shown with the generic. It is implied by the use of the generic's name and the inclusion of the replacing parameters enclosed by angled brackets.

---

16. A stereotype is the class of an entity in the UML metamodel. Stereotypes are discussed in more detail in the Section 1.8.4.

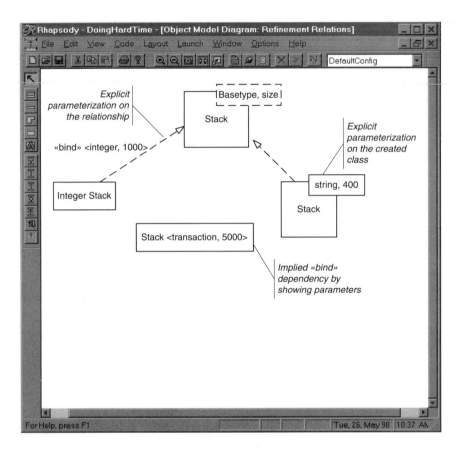

Figure 1-9: *«bind» Dependency Relationship*

1.5 Use Cases

A use case is a function that returns an observable value to an actor (object outside its context), without revealing the design structure of that function. A use case is roughly the same as a function point—a cohesive piece of functionality of the system that is visible from outside. Use cases are a form of functional, rather than object, decomposition.

Use cases are not classes. An attempt to map a use case to a specific class results in poor choices of use cases or (more likely) a bad object model. Use cases must ultimately be realized by collaborations of objects working together to achieve the use case functionality. These objects often participate in collaborations for many different use cases.

Use cases associate with actors. This means that the use case can receive messages from actors and send messages to them. Actors are objects that exist outside the scope of your system. They may be physical devices or users interacting with the system, depending on whether those devices forming the physical interface are subsumed by the system per se.

Use cases are shown as ovals with solid borders, while the icon for an actor is a stick figure. Associations are shown as lines, just as with class associations. (See Figure 1-10.) Use cases may have relations with

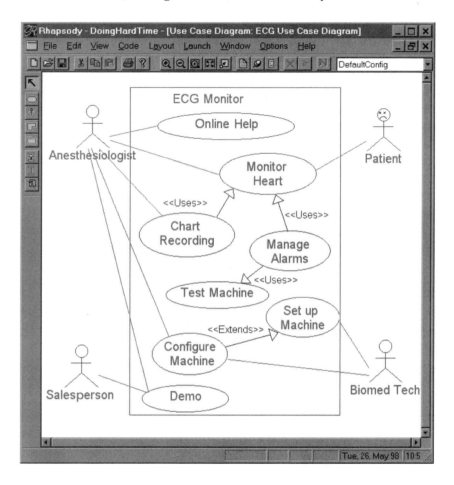

Figure 1-10: *ECG Use Case Diagram*

other use cases. The UML uses generalization for this, meaning that one use case is a more general form of another. Two stereotypes[17] of use cases are defined.

1. «extends» means that one use case is a more expanded version of another.

2. «uses» means that one use case uses the facilities provided by another.[18]

1.6 Sequence Diagrams

Similar to most concepts in object-oriented languages, use cases also have the type-instance dichotomy. A particular path through a use case is a scenario, a step-by-step sequence of message exchanges among the actors and the associated use case. Most often, sequence diagrams are used to capture the set of interesting scenarios. One such scenario, depicting the use of a patient ventilator, is shown in Figure 1-11.

Not all sequence diagrams map directly to use cases. Once the "cover is off the box" and objects inside the system are identified, the sequence diagram is useful for identifying how internal objects collaborate. Such a sequence diagram is shown in Figure 1-12.

The only difference between use case scenarios and object scenarios is the kind of instances that participate. The former will primarily consist of a single "system" object and the actors relevant to the scenario. The latter may contain actors, but it will primarily contain objects internal to the system.

Sequence diagrams are useful in two contexts. When used to realize a use case scenario, they are extraordinarily helpful in extracting and understanding requirements. The other context is the testing of object structures—for example, walking through a collaboration with several scenarios will identify whether the structure supports the responsibility of the collaboration.

---

17. See Section 1.8 for more information on stereotypes.
18. In the 1.4 revision of the UML, «uses» (a stereotype of generalization) is replaced by «includes» (a stereotype of dependency). For more details, see Chapter 5.

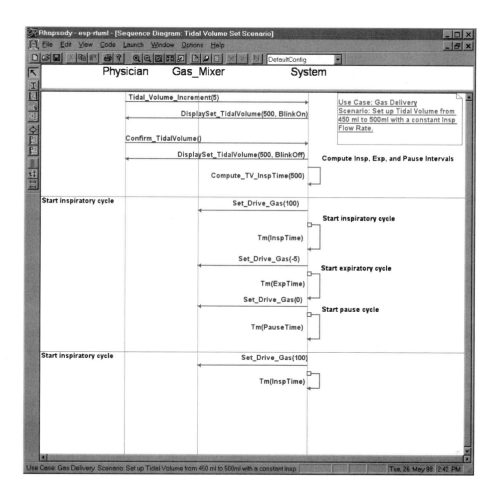

Figure 1-11: *Use Case Sequence Diagram*

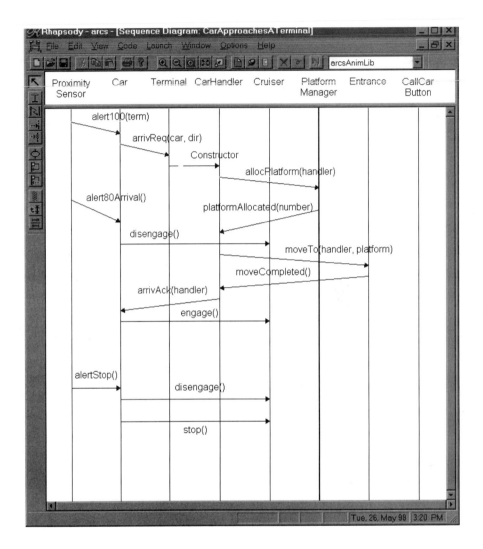

Figure 1-12: *Object Sequence Diagram*

1.7 Physical Representation

One thing that makes embedded systems "special" is that they must map to various hardware devices. Previous software modeling methods did not provide a way to specify or even clarify the relationship between the logical contents of the software and these physical things. The UML provides two primary diagram types, the deployment and the component diagram, to represent these kinds of physical things.

A *deployment diagram* is a simplified representation of the electronic architecture on which the software will execute. The primary entities on the deployment diagram are *nodes* (physical things) and *connections* among them. The UML defines some types of nodes via the UML's stereotype mechanism (see Section 1.8.4). The nodes that execute the software have the «processor» stereotype. Devices controlled or monitored by the software have the «device» stereotype. In the area of embedded real-time systems, several more stereotypes are appropriate (see Section 1.8.4).

Nodes are most often shown blank but may also contain deployable software units called *components*. The deployment diagram depicts the execution location of the various software components, as well as the physical devices of interest to the software.

The UML uses the component to represent a development artifact that exists at run-time. Components may be static organizations of software, such as files containing source code, unit tests, and software-design artifacts represented as configuration items in a configuration-management system. Components may also be dynamic, such as executable libraries and subsystems. This organization is independent of the logical structuring of the software into classes and objects. For example, a subsystem component may contain objects from communications, user interface, and device I/O domains. Components may nest other components within themselves. Some components may exist only on a single node (such as a user interface) or may exist on all nodes (such as communications). The difference between a package and a component is that a package is a generalized grouping mechanism, usually used to group logical elements into a logically cohesive structure. Components, on the other hand, are either a static-design artifact to facilitate project control (such as a file) or a dynamic executable artifact (such as a subsystem). Figure 1-13 shows some run-time components executing on a physical deployment architecture.

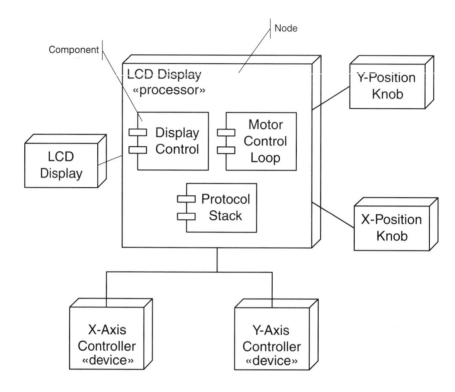

Figure 1-13: *Deployment and Component Diagram*

1.8 Things Common to Diagrams

A number of elements of the UML may be used in all or most diagrams. These include things such as notes, packages, constraints, and stereotypes. These are useful things to annotate, organize, or to more-fully describe the different elements provided by the UML.

1.8.1 Notes

A text note is a diagrammatic element with no semantic impact. They are common to all UML diagrams and are used to provide textual annotations to diagrams in order to improve understanding. Text notes are visually represented as a rectangle with the upper-right corner folded down. Free-standing text notes, without the box, are also permitted. Rhapsody (from I-Logix) also provides a *pushpin note,* which is intended to be used as a temporary note of something to be done, rather than as a long-term description or explanation.

1.8.2 Packages

A package is shown as a tabbed folder. It represents a logical grouping of elements. These elements may be virtually anything; most often, they are classes and objects. Formally, packages represent a namespace, but they do not imply any other semantics. As discussed later, a popular idiomatic usage of packages is to represent domains. A *domain* is an independent subject matter with its own vocabulary and object model, such as "user interface" or "device I/O." A feature of this kind of design is the relative isolation of areas of concern, which allows independent analysis of these concerns. It also facilitates replacement of the domain (such as "Windows 95") with an equivalent (such as "MacIntosh").[19] Figure 1-14 shows how packages can be used to organize a system along domain lines.

Packages may have interfaces, as can classes, and packages may be specialized. A package interface is usually defined as the set of services, classes, and objects visible from outside that package's namespace. A package may be specialized into subclasses. For example, the UserInterface package in the figure could be subclassed into Windows, Motif, and X-Windows packages. This is interpreted to mean that the interface to the package remains the same, but the implementation of the services, classes, and objects provided by the package is specialized.

1.8.3 Constraints

A constraint is some additional condition applied against a modeling element. Timing constraints can be shown on sequence diagrams,[20] specifying the time between messages, for example. Constraints are always shown inside curly brackets and may appear inside text notes.

---

19. Not everyone would consider Windows 95 as an equivalent replacement to a Mac, however.
20. Sequence diagrams are discussed in some detail in Chapters 5 and 7.

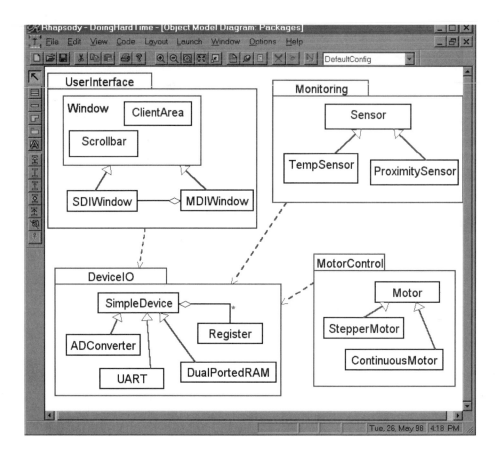

Figure 1-14: *Packages*

Figure 1-15 shows text notes and constraints used together. On the left, the class model for a double-linked list is shown as a single class with constrained associations. On the right, the associations between classes *Worker* and *Team Member* are constrained in that the *manager_of* association is a subset of the *member_of* association.

1.8.4 Stereotypes

A stereotype is a new kind of modeling element, derived (by specialization) from an existing metaclass in the UML metamodel. The UML

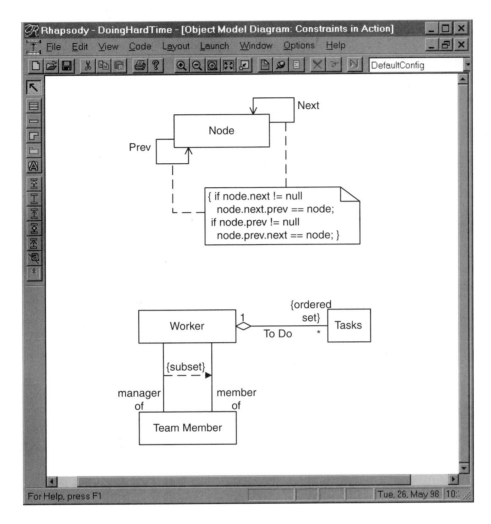

Figure 1-15: *Constraints in Action*

metamodel is the model of UML itself, expressed in UML. Stereotypes provide an important extension mechanism to the UML, allowing users to extend the modeling language to better address their needs. Each modeling element in the UML is represented as a metaclass. A stereotyped metaclass is ultimately derived from an existing UML metaclass. For example, it is possible to create a new (meta)class of the

UML class construct, which is just like the normal UML class but is extended, or specialized. A class that represents the type (interface) of a class is just such a stereotyped class.

The usual notation for stereotypes is to enclose the stereotype in guillemets[21] preceding the name of the entity, as in "«interface» stack," which is the name of a class providing a stack interface for another implementation. Special icons can be used instead of guillemets for common stereotypes. The UML defines a number of common stereotype icons, but you should feel free to add your own application-domain-specific icons.[22]

All modeling entities in the UML can be stereotyped. For example, messages can be stereotyped. Some stereotypes with iconic representations useful in the design of real-time systems are shown in Figure 1-16 and Figure 1-17. These include stereotypes that are either predefined within the UML itself or ones I have added to support real-time concerns.

Not all stereotypes have explicit iconic representations. All stereotypes may be shown using the icon of the stereotyped element and the stereotype enclosed within guillemets. The primary stereotypes used in this book are given in Table 1-7.

Table 1-7: *Some Important UML Stereotypes for Real-Time Systems*

Base UML Type	Stereotype name	Description
Class	«active»	(UML) Class is the root of an OS thread.
Message	«synchronous»	Association will be realized as a simple function or method call.
	«blocking-local»	Association will cross a thread boundary, but caller will block until receiver returns a value.

---

21. If guillemets are unavailable, then double angled brackets are acceptable. For example, <<interface>> may be substituted for «interface».
22. At the risk of introducing some non-portability, of course.

Table 1-7: (*cont.*)

Base UML Type	Stereotype name	Description
Message (*cont.*)	«asynchronous-local»	Association will cross a thread boundary by placing the message in the target thread's incoming message queue.
	«waiting-local»	Sender will wait for a fixed period of time or until receiver responds, whichever is first.
	«synchronous-remote»	Association will cross a processor boundary, and sender will block until explicit return from receiver.*
	«asynchronous-remote»	Association will cross a processor boundary, and sender will continue immediately, without waiting for a return value.
	«periodic»	Message is sent periodically.
	«episodic»	Message is sent based on some event of interest, such as a value change.
	«epiperiodic»	Message is sent *both* periodically and episodically.
Operation	«guarded»	Operation execution will be guarded by a mutual exclusion semaphore and is therefore "thread-reliable."
Node	«processor»	(UML) Node represents a device that executes software of interest.
	«device»	(UML) Node represents a device that does not execute software of interest but does have an interface.
	«sensor»	Device monitors the external world or another internal device's operation.
	«actuator»	Device affects the external world or another internal device's operation.
	«display»	Device displays information to a human user.
		(*continued*)

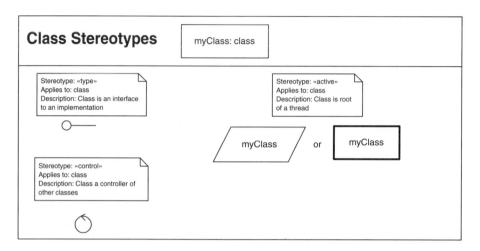

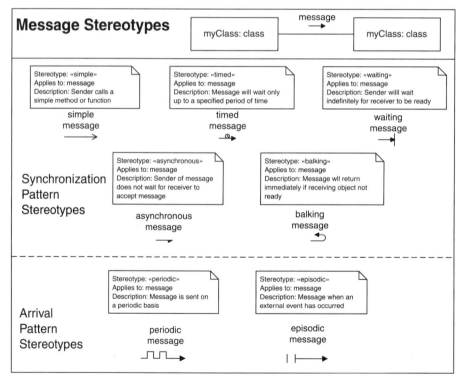

Figure 1-16: *Some UML Stereotypes for Real-Time Systems*

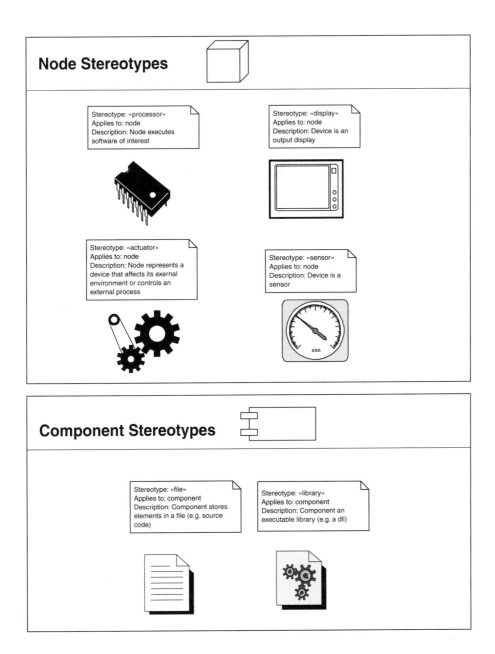

Figure 1-17: *More UML Stereotypes for Real-Time Systems*

Table 1-7: (*cont.*)

Base UML Type	Stereotype name	Description
	«knob»	User interface control knob.
	«button»	User interface control button.
	«switch»	User interface control switch.
	«watchdog»	A type of sensor that causes safety fail-safe behavior to occur when not stroked within proper time window.
*Usually, a message must be "marshalled" and demarshalled by any intervening communications protocol stack, respectively by each processor.		

It is important to note that the UML is adequate for the complete development of real-time embedded systems. The stereotypes presented here are added only because they help explain the purpose of a model element and occur commonly within the real-time and embedded domains. The ability of the UML to extend itself for notational convenience is a powerful one, but it can lead to nonportable and confusing diagrams if over-used.

1.9 Summary

In this chapter, we discussed why objects are better than structured methods. Structured methods work, but they have problems with scaleability, concurrency, and reuse. Structured designs tend to be fragile in the presence of new or changing requirements, and they don't model all the issues of concern to the software developer. Object methods may not be perfect, but they offer significant improvement in each of these areas.

An object is a thing with both property values and behavior. The property values are called attributes. The behaviors of the object typically are operations that act on those attributes or perform services utilizing those attributes. A class is the implementation structure of an object. This is distinct from its type, which refers only to the interface of the object. Thus, it is possible to have many classes (implementations) that have the same type (interface).

Objects are a relatively small unit of decomposition. To do anything interesting, objects must collaborate. They do this by having relations with other objects. The most important types of relations in the UML are generalization, association, aggregation, composition, and dependency. Generalization means that one object is a more specialized form of another, just as a primate is a more generalized form of a mammal. This allows developers to construct taxonomies in which classes inherit the more general constructs of their parents. Associations allow messages to be passed among objects when the system runs. Just as objects are instances of classes, links are instances of associations. Aggregation is a type of association in which one object is the owner and one or more objects are owned. Composition is a strong form of aggregation, which permits only one owner and explicitly assigns the responsibility for the creation and destruction of the owned objects. Dependencies allow constructs to be refined through the addition of information. The primary use of dependency is the creation of instantiable classes from templates or generic descriptions of classes, although the UML defines many kinds of dependency.

Use cases are not object oriented per se. But they are very commonly used in conjunction with the analysis of object-oriented systems. A use case is a broad area of functionality of a system. Use cases associate with actors (external objects outside the scope of the system under design). Use cases may also have relations with other use cases. The most important of these relations are the «extends» and «uses» («includes» in the current UML revision) relations. The former allows one use case to be a more specialized form of another. The latter allows one use case to use the facilities provided by another. Use cases do not lead one in any obvious or automatic way to a class or object structure, but they are useful in refining the requirements of a system.

Scenarios are instances of use cases. They are specific paths through the use of the system. Scenarios are also used to test object interactions to ensure that the static object model supports the necessary collaboration.

The UML uses deployment diagrams to represent the electronic hardware of a system and the mapping of software components onto that hardware. The basic elements found in deployment diagrams are nodes (devices) and connections. Nodes may also contain components, or deployable software structures built from the logical design. Components also may be used to represent software design artifacts, such as documents, source code files, and so on.

1.10 A Look Ahead

The next three chapters will introduce three broad areas of concern for the real-time software developer. Chapter 2 will discuss the fundamental concerns of real-time and embedded systems and some of the important concepts used to deal with these concerns, which include how to deal with time, concurrency management, sharing resources, and memory management. Chapter 3 introduces the basics of safety and reliability, a crucial concern for many real-time and embedded systems. The chapter also discusses the procedural means commonly employed to develop safety-critical systems, such as hazard analysis and architectural redundancy in its many forms. Chapter 4, the last chapter in this section, provides an overview of process, the procedures and tasks associated with taking a set of requirements and constructing an object-oriented system that adheres to it. The process presented is called real-time object-oriented process for embedded systems (ROPES). The ROPES process provides a context for the discussion of the use of the UML and its conceptual elements, which will constitute the remainder of this book.

1.11 Exercises

1. Name three benefits of object-orientation over structured analysis and design.
2. What is an object? Give five real-time examples of objects.
3. What are the primary properties, or characteristics, of objects?
4. What is a class?
5. What are the primary types of relations in the UML?
6. What is the difference between aggregation and composition?

7. What is the Liskov Substitution Principle?

8. What is the difference between a use case and a scenario?

9. What is the difference between a package and a component?

10. On what diagram type do nodes appear?

11. What is the advantage of the UML stereotype feature?

12. What elements can appear on most or all UML diagrams?

13. Give an example of a constraint on an association.

1.12 References

[1] Leveson, Nancy. *Safeware*, Reading, Mass.: Addison-Wesley, 1995.

[2] Neumann, Peter. *Computer Related Risks*, Reading, Mass.: Addison-Wesley, 1995.

[3] Jones, Richard, and Rafael Lins. *Garbage Collection: Algorithms for Automatic Dynamic Memory Management*, New York: John Wiley and Sons Publishers, 1996.

[4] Ellis, John. *Objectifying Real-Time Systems*, New York: SIGS Press, 1994.

[5] Rumbaugh, James, Michael Blaha, William Premerlani, Frederick Eddy, and William Lorenson. *Object-Oriented Modeling and Design*, Englewood Cliffs, NJ: Prentice-Hall, 1991.

[6] Douglass, Bruce Powel. *Real-Time UML: Developing Efficient Objects for Embedded Systems*, Reading, Mass.: Addison-Wesley, 1998.

Chapter 2

Basic Concepts of Real-Time Systems

Timeliness is next to godliness.

—Book of Douglass, Law 175

By definition, real-time and embedded systems control and monitor physical processes in a timely fashion. They must operate under more-severe constraints than "normal" software systems and yet perform reliably for long periods of time. Some of the constraints are inherent in their problem domain, such as schedulability, predictability, and robustness. Other constraints come from the need to reduce recurring system cost by cutting the amount of memory or capability of the processor. Most real-time and embedded systems must operate with a minimum memory footprint and with a minimum of support hardware. Taken together, these constraints greatly complicate the development of such systems.

2.1 What is *Real-Time*?

According to some people, building a real-time system means hacking assembler code on an 8-bit processor with 2K bytes of ROM and 256 bytes of RAM. Many real-time systems fall into this category, including some microwave ovens, cardiac pacemakers and defibrillators, and automobile-engine-control computers. At the other end of the spectrum are networks of dozens of processors collaborating to control entire factories, suites of critical-care instrumentation, flight-control systems for air- and spacecraft, and nuclear-power-plant control systems. These large systems are built using high-level languages, such as C++ and Ada; have megabytes of RAM; and may use mass-storage devices, such as hard disks and CD-ROM drives.

Real-time systems often do not provide a conventional computer display or keyboard, but may lie at the heart of some apparently non-computerized device. The user of these devices may never be aware that the embedded CPU makes decisions about how and when the system should act. The user is not intimately involved with the device as a computer per se, but rather relates to it as an electrical or mechanical device that provides services. These systems must often operate for days or even years without error in the most hostile environments. The services and controls provided must be autonomous and timely. Frequently, these devices have the potential to do great harm if they fail unsafely.

Real-time systems encompass all devices with performance constraints that, when violated, constitute a system failure of some kind.

2.2 Terms and Concepts

A *real-time system* is one that has performance deadlines on its computations and actions. Real-time systems are often *embedded*, meaning that the computational system exists inside a larger system, with the purpose of helping that system to achieve its overall responsibilities. A *reactive* or *event-driven system* is one whose behavior is primarily caused by specific reactions to external events rather than being self-generated. A *time-driven system* is one whose actions are driven primarily by either the passage of time or the arrival of time epochs. Time-driven systems are those primarily driven by periodic tasking rather than by the arrival of aperiodic events.

A *timely system* is one that meets its performance requirements. Performance requirements are most commonly specified in terms of deadlines.[1] A *deadline* is either a point in time (time-driven) or a delta-time interval (event-driven) by which a system action must occur. *Hard deadlines* are performance requirements that absolutely must be met each and every event or time mark. Timeliness is essential to correctness in such systems. A missed deadline constitutes an erroneous computation and a system failure. In these systems, *late* data is at best worthless data and at worst, *bad* data. Figure 2-1 shows a simple timing diagram illustrating these relationships. *Soft* real-time systems may be constrained simply by average execution time—examples include on-line databases and flight reservation systems—or by more-complex constraints. In these systems, *late* data may still be *good* data. Some systems have both soft- and hard-deadline performance constraints. These so-called *firm deadlines* arise when individual deadlines may be missed, as long as two things occur. First, a sufficient average performance maintained at all times. Second, each deadline must be met no later than a certain time. A *schedulable system* is one that can be guaranteed to meet all its performance requirements.

A *task* is an encapsulated sequence of operations that executes independently of other tasks.[2] In a multitasking system, tasks are scheduled to run via a scheduling policy. Most real-time systems use the *priority* of a task to control when it runs in relation to other tasks that are ready to run. The priority of a task depends on the *urgency* of the task completion and its *importance.* If multiple tasks are ready to run, then the task with the highest priority[3] will execute preferentially. The scheduling policy of tasks may be either event-driven (that is, the task depends on an awaited event) or time-driven (that is, the task waits for its next

---

1. A more general view of timeliness is provided in Chapter 11.
2. Some authors differentiate between a task (very encapsulated) and a thread (less well encapsulated). These may be different in the coding level because they invoke different RTOS services. But at the modeling level, they are indistinct. Therefore, in this book, we will treat them identically.
3. Some RTOSs treat the higher numerical value as the higher priority while others treat the lower numerical value as a higher priority.

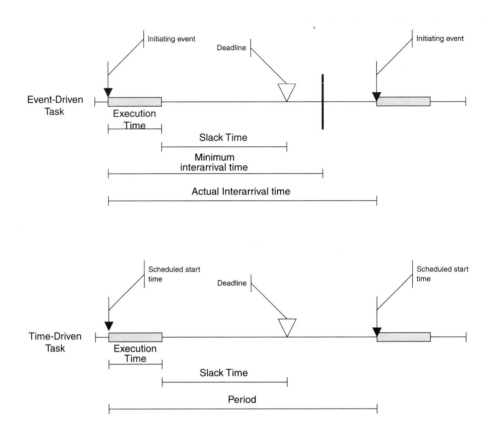

Figure 2-1: *Deadlines*

scheduled start time to arrive). As a practical matter, most event-driven systems respond to discrete events whose time is relatively unpredictable, while most time-driven systems deal with continuous control systems, such as PID control loops, which become unstable outside the computed timeliness requirements.

2.3 Timeliness

The timeliness of an action has to do with the action meeting time constraints, such as a deadline. Deadlines may be hard or soft. Missing a hard deadline constitutes a system failure of some kind, so great care must be taken to ensure that all such actions execute in a timely way. The important modeling concerns of timeliness are modeling execution time, deadlines, arrival patterns, synchronization patterns (see concurrency below), and time sources.

Timeliness requirements may be addressed by first determining the end-to-end performance requirement of an event-response action sequence. These are usually determined during use case or context analysis. For example, a deadline might exist from an external perspective.

> "When the actor VolumeControl sends an Increase command, the system shall respond within 10 ms +/− 2 ms."

Performance budgets are first computed from a black-box perspective and serve as a means of capturing external requirements, such as overall performance and response times. Later in analysis, these overall system reaction deadlines propagate into performance budgets on the individual operations and actions within the system design, as illustrated in Figure 2-2.

The basic concepts of timeliness in real-time systems are straightforward. Actions must be begun in response to event arrival or due-time arrival, and they must complete within a certain time after they begin. These actions may be simple digital actuations, such as turning on a light, or complex loops that control dozens of actuators simultaneously. Typically, many subroutines or tasks must execute between the causative event and the resulting system action. External requirements bound the overall performance of the control path. Each processing activity in the control path is assigned a portion of the overall time budget. The sum of the time budgets for any path must be less than or equal to the overall performance constraint.[4]

For example, consider a telebot. A telebot is a remotely controlled robot. Telebots are useful in hazardous environments because the operator can be yards (or even miles) away defusing a bomb or handling dangerous chemicals or radioactive material. To be useful, the telebot must respond to the hand movements of a data glove quickly enough to take advantage of the user's inherent motor-control system. If the

---

4. This includes initiation, preemption (postponement of execution by a higher-priority task, including interrupts) and blocking times (prevention of the execution of a high-priority action by a lower-priority action), if applicable.

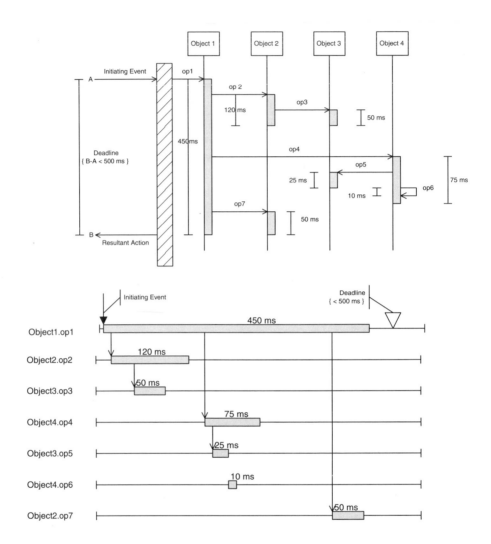

Figure 2-2: *Assignment of Time Budgets*

telebot responds too slowly, the user will overreact, creating an unstable control loop. Likewise, the control loop can become unstable if the telebot is slow to provide tactile or visual feedback. Figure 2-3 shows an architecture of such a telebot.

Let us say that the telebot should respond to finger movements, such as gripping and releasing, in a timely fashion. What is timely?

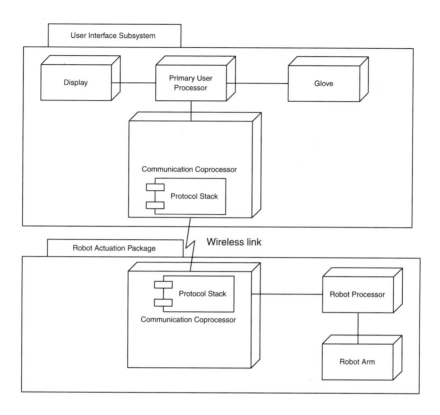

Figure 2-3: *Telebot Deployment Diagram*

Assume a maximum finger movement speed of 10 cm/sec (we *are* handling dangerous materials here, after all). The telebot must track a linear motion with no more than a 50 ms delay. The visual feedback is similarly bound. This puts a bound on the activities that sense the finger motion—the entire sensing and controlling path must be less than 50 ms, including transmission time.[5] A scenario of telebot usage is provided in Figure 2-4 using both sequence and timing diagrams.

---

5. Note that this also puts a limit on the distance between the telebot and the user. Such a device could be used to repair satellites with an earth-bound controller, as long as the satellite is above the controller. A 200-mile–distant satellite invokes a 1 ms time-of-flight delay for the message (assuming line-of-sight communications). At 10,000 miles, time-of-flight exceeds the performance bound.

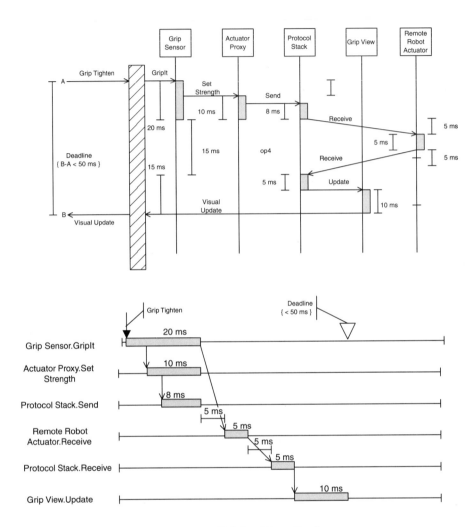

Figure 2-4: *Telebot Time Budgets*

2.4 Responsiveness

Virtually all real-time systems connect to either monitoring or controlling hardware, or both. Sensors provide information to the system about the state of the external environment. Medical monitoring devices, such as electrocardiography (ECG) machines, use sensors to monitor patient and machine status. Air speed, engine thrust, attitude, and altitude sensors provide aircraft information for proper execution of flight-control plans. Linear and angular position sensors sense a robot's arm position and adjust it via direct current or stepper motors.

Many real-time systems use actuators to control their external environment or to guide some external processes. Flight-control computers command engine thrust and wing and tail flap orientation to meet flight parameters. Chemical-process-control systems control when, what kind, and the amounts of different reagents added to mixing vats. Pacemakers make the heart beat at appropriate intervals by means of electrical leads attached to the inside walls of the heart.

Naturally, most systems containing actuators also contain sensors. Although there are many open-loop control systems, the majority of control systems use environmental feedback to ensure that the control loop is acting properly.

Standard computing systems respond primarily to the user.[6] Real-time systems, on the other hand, may interact with users, but they have more concern for interactions with their sensors and actuators.

One problem that arises with environmental interaction is that the universe has an annoying habit of disregarding our opinions of how and when it ought to behave.[7] External events are often not predictable. Nevertheless, the system must react to events when they occur rather than when it might be convenient. An ECG monitor must alarm quickly after the cessation of cardiac activity if it is to be of value. The system cannot delay alarm processing until later that evening, when the processor load is less.

Even worse, the real world is *not* linear, nor are its elements truly independent.[8] Linearity, in this context, means that a small perturbation on an input has a proportionally small effect on the output. There are many cases in which a small perturbation in the input results in a large change in the output. Consider the membrane potential of a biological neuron. If the electrical potential across the membrane reaches a

---

6. It is true that behind the scenes, even desktop computers must interface with printers, mice, keyboards, and networks. The point is they do this only to facilitate the user's whim.

7. It is similar to teenagers in this regard.

8. *At best*, on a good day, the world is *still* only piecewise-linear.

critical value, the neuron undergoes a patch-wise reversal of polarity followed by a slower repolarization. The electric field of this patch then affects the patches next to it, causing them to depolarize, as well. This propagation of depolarization generates a neural signal called an *action potential*, which is strongly nonlinear and has, in fact, been modeled by catastrophe theory. Our conceptual and computer models often make assumptions of linearity and independence, and things go awry when these assumptions are severely violated. This is true in PID control loops, fuzzy logic systems, neural networks, and most other control systems.

We often model reactive systems as finite state automata (FSA). Such machines make strong assumptions about their ontological conditions.

- An FSA can only be in one state at a time and must be in exactly one state at all times.
- States of one FSA are independent from the states of all other FSAs.
- Transitions between states are not interruptable and run to completion.
- Actions are atomic and take approximately zero time.
- Actions may be executed
    1. On entry to a state
    2. On exit from a state
    3. During the transition from one state to another

FSAs are firmly based on discrete mathematics—that is, states have crisp, distinct boundaries from other states. This can lead to difficulties in control systems. Consider an automotive cruise-control system. One might expect that in principle the force and frequency of application of the throttle should depend, at least in part, on current speed. So we can break up speed into states (0-5 mph, 5-20 mph, 20-50 mph, >50 mph) and use different actions, depending on the state. However, the discontinuity between the states at their boundaries can lead to no end of difficulty in stabilizing the system response.[9]

---

9. This is, in fact, how the cruise control in my old Plymouth station wagon worked. Acceleration was either OFF or we pulled about 3g, usually oscillating between the two at about 0.2 Hz.

2.5 Concurrency

Concurrency is the simultaneous execution of multiple sequential chains of actions. These action chains may execute on one processor (pseudoconcurrency) or multiple processors (true concurrency). Issues surrounding the execution of concurrent systems have to do with the scheduling characteristics of the concurrent threads, the arrival patterns of incoming events, the rendezvous patterns used when threads must synchronize, and the methods of controlling access to shared resources. These can be nontrivial issues to deal with, particularly when one must consider the performance, as well as the functional requirements, of the system.

2.5.1 Scheduling Concurrent Threads

Many strategies for concurrency control are possible. The most prevalent are

- FIFO run-to-completion event handling
- Nonpreemptive task switching
- Time-slicing round robin
- Cyclic executive
- Priority-based preemption

Some simple systems can use run-to-completion semantics to handle incoming events. These are usually executed on a first-in-first-out (FIFO) policy and may be implemented as an independent set of interrupt handlers, without the services of an RTOS. Unfortunately for large or complex systems, this simple approach quickly proves inadequate because it requires significant over-design of the computing platform.

Nonpreemptive task switching relies on the application threads to voluntarily release control to the OS. Once it receives control back, the OS can select the next task to run. It can do so on the basis of priority or of a fairness doctrine that attempts to ensure all tasks get equal time.

Time-slicing policies preempt tasks when they exceed their allotted time. Once a task suspends, the highest-priority waiting task then runs. This type of preemptive scheduler is not sensitive to changing demands.

A cyclic executive is based on run-to-completion semantics and has a set of statically ordered threads. It runs the first thread. When it completes, it runs the second, and so on, eventually returning to the first. The advantage of a cyclic executive is that it is brain-dead simple to write and test. The primary disadvantage is that it couples tightly to the timing and feature set of the applications being run. Every time the applications are modified, the cyclic executive requires modification, as well. Cyclic executives are not efficient in their overall usage of available CPU processing, and they do not provide optimal response time to external events. Because of their simplicity, they are used extensively in complex safety-critical systems, such as air flight-control systems. NASA frequently uses cyclic executives in space vehicle control systems, although there has been a recent shift to priority-based preemption [1].

A real-time operating system is often used because it provides control over task execution in a multitasking system. RTOSs typically provide separate services to create and execute tasks. The OS maintains information about a task in a task control block (TCB). The TCB contains the location and size of the task's stack frame, its executable code pointer, and its unique task ID. When the task is ready for execution, the scheduler places it in a Ready Queue. Priority-based preemptive schedulers suspend the currently executing task when a task of higher priority becomes ready to run. The currently executing task is first suspended by placing its TCB in the ready queue. The highest priority task in the Ready Queue then runs.

Life is more challenging when tasks share resources. A lower-priority task owning a required resource can block a higher-priority task from running. This is called *priority inversion* because a higher-priority task is ready to run but cannot. Blocked tasks are suspended until they can run. There they wait on an event, such as a signal, a time event (for periodically scheduled tasks), or the availability of a resource. The scheduler cannot remove tasks from the Waiting Queue and put them into the Ready Queue until the conditions on which they are waiting are satisfied. These problems will be discussed in more depth in Chapter 11.

2.5.2 Event Arrival Patterns

In reactive systems, most threads are scheduled in response to incoming events. One issue with these systems is the arrival patterns of the initiating events. Arrival patterns may be either periodic or aperiodic. A periodic arrival pattern means that the thread is reinitiated on a fixed period plus or minus a small variation (jitter). Such threads are commonly called *periodic tasks*. Aperiodic tasks don't occur with a regular period. As far as the system is concerned, they appear to occur randomly. For such systems to be schedulable, the frequency of occurrence of the initiating event must be bounded in time. The timing of aperiodic events may be

Irregular	A known, but varying, sequence of intervals between events
Bursty	A sequence in which events may occur arbitrarily close to each other, but the number of events within a burst cannot exceed a known bound
Bounded	A sequence of events with a known minimum interarrival interval, called the *bound*
Bounded average rate	A sequence of events in which individual event times are unpredictable, but they cluster around a mean
Unbounded	A sequence of events whose arrival intervals can only be predicted statistically. They are drawn from a probability density function as either a renewal or a nonrenewal process[10]

Analysis characterizes the timing characteristics of the events. This is crucial to the design of a reliable real-time system because it determines the mechanisms you employ to handle the events. For example, the characterization of the event arrival pattern, along with the timing characteristics of your system, can be used to determine reasonable buffer sizes to ensure events are not lost.

The process of analysis uncovers the period and jitter of periodic events. Frequently, bursty or bounded events need to be characterized

---

10. A renewal process is one in which intervals are drawn from the probability density function independent of each other.

only in terms of the minimum inter-arrival time. Unbounded event sequences are more problematic. Queuing theory is often employed to determine reasonable buffer sizes.

2.5.3 Thread Rendezvous Patterns

If concurrent threads were truly independent, life would be much less interesting.[11] Fortunately (or unfortunately, depending on your point of view), threads must communicate to synchronize control or share resources. Communication in object systems takes place via messages. Messaging is a logical abstraction that includes a variety of rendezvous patterns, such as synchronous function calls, asynchronous, waiting, timed, and balking. By far, the most common are synchronous function calls. Objects directly call the methods of other objects, effectively operating within the same thread of control. Asynchronous calls are supported by real-time operating systems by queuing a message from another thread and acting on it when it is convenient. Meanwhile, the caller continues, without waiting. A *waiting rendezvous* means that the calling task waits indefinitely for the called task to become ready; in a *timed rendezvous*, the caller waits for a specified length of time before aborting the synchronization attempt. A *balking rendezvous* means simply that if the called task is not immediately available, the caller aborts the attempt and takes other actions.

A rendezvous is specified within object methods by stereotyping messages and events with a rendezvous pattern. Some common message stereotypes are discussed in Chapters 8 and 11. It is important to characterize the rendezvous patterns of cross-thread messaging in order to ensure deadlines will always be met.

By their nature, tasks are fundamentally asynchronous. Processing within each thread is synchronous, but the whole point of having tasks is to separate the timing of their execution from other threads. As long as the tasks do not need to share data or control information, task synchronization is not required. However, real systems require tasks to frequently communicate with other tasks. RTOSs provide asynchronous mechanisms for task communication, such as mailboxes and events, which are computationally relatively heavyweight. Other task rendezvous supply faster, synchronous approaches but have additional

---

11. As in the ancient Chinese curse, "May you live in interesting times."

costs, such as the breaking of encapsulation, pathological coupling between threads, and so on.

2.5.4 Sharing Resources

Another common problem in concurrent systems is the robust sharing of resources. Most correct solutions involve the serialization of access through mutual exclusion semaphores, or queues. In object systems, such access control may be done through the Semaphore Pattern (see Chapter 11). This can be indicated using the pattern notation of the modeling language (if supported) or by adding a {guarded} constraint on the relevant operation.

Data corruption can occur whenever there is nonatomic access to a data structure within a concurrent architecture. Consider the simple example of a floating-point number shared among several tasks. In most processors, writing or reading such a value takes several processor instructions. A task switch can occur at any time, including between the write accesses of the individual bytes of the float. If the float is half-written when the OS swaps the task out, another task may come along and read it, not aware that the value is only partially updated. Thus, the second task reads an incorrect value. This is the *mutual exclusion problem*. The only real solution is to ensure that only one task at a time can access the value.

2.5.4.1 Asynchronous Access

The simplest way to control access is to serialize requests with an explicit queue. For example, most RTOSs supply a message queue for each executing task. If the only extra-thread access to the resource is via the message queue, then the system can be assured the mutual exclusion problem will not occur. The disadvantage of this approach is that it uses heavyweight abstractions (queues and task switching) to access the resource, and it is not possible in many circumstances.

2.5.4.2 Critical Sections

Another approach is to allow direct access to the resource but to make the accesses atomic—that is, prohibit task switching during variable access. The code that must execute without interruption to avoid deadlock and race conditions is called a *critical section*. Most real-time programmers make critical sections atomic by disabling interrupts and task switching, performing the critical section processing, and then reenabling interrupts and task switching.

This approach is simple, but has several drawbacks.

- The mechanism must be manually performed whenever the data is accessed. There is no protection from someone forgetting to turn interrupts off. Likewise, there is no protection from someone forgetting to reenable interrupts. More precisely, there is no way to guarantee the pre-conditional and post-conditional invariants of the resource access.[12]

- It may not always be possible to know the proper interrupt state of the machine prior to the critical section, so it may not be possible to restore it.

- Interrupts and events can be lost if they occur during a critical section with interrupts turned off.

- High-priority tasks are blocked when task switching is disabled. This causes priority inversion, which may lead to missed deadlines of the high-priority tasks.

- Some data structures have many frequent readers but only rarely have writers. It may be desirable to allow multiple access as long as the tasks are readers, but not when any task wants to write the value. This is difficult to accomplish using interrupt disabling alone to protect critical sections.

- Further, it usually does not solve the problem of mutual exclusion for tightly coupled processors sharing data, because disabling interrupts on one processor will not have any effect on the other.

A better way to enforce the critical section is to use mutual exclusion (mutex) semaphores of the underlying RTOS.

2.5.4.3 Semaphores

Edsger Dijkstra [2] created the *semaphore* as one solution to the protection of critical sections. A semaphore is essentially a "lock" that serial-

---

12. The use of objects can eliminate this drawback because these invariants can be built into the access functions themselves.

izes access to the resource it protects. Dijkstra used the p() and v() operations to allow tasks to grab the resource if the semaphore is free and to
relinquish ownership of it, respectively. The p() operation returns only
when the resource is available; otherwise, it waits. Once the resource is
available, the p() operation locks the resource and the call returns. The
v() operation releases the lock and relinquishes ownership. Semaphores
are simple, lightweight abstractions, which may not provide the behavioral richness required for more-complex resource sharing. Chapter 11
discusses semaphores in more detail, as well as how they can be effectively used in object-oriented systems.

2.6 Predictability

A key aspect of many real-time systems is their predictability. This is
crucial for many safety-critical and high-reliability systems, such as
nuclear power plants, avionics systems, and medical devices. The predictability of a system is the extent to which its response characteristics
can be known in advance. This can be determined, in some cases, by
static mathematical analysis, such as rate monotonic analysis (RMA).
In other cases, it can be ensured by disallowing preemption and using
simple control algorithms, such as cyclic executives. Using active objects to represent tasks and identifying the performance characteristics
of the tasks allows a variety of scheduling algorithms to be used.

2.6.1 Memory Management

The more common aspect of predictability is with respect to schedulability. We have discussed that aspect already in Section 2.5.1. Another
aspect of predictability is with respect to memory. There are two
orthogonal views of memory: *usage* and *persistence*. In terms of usage,
memory is typically thought of as divided into several categories:

- Execution memory, where the executable code resides
- Data memory
  1. Stack
  2. Heap
  3. Static

In terms of persistence, most real-time developers categorize memory into:

- Non-writable persistent
- Writable persistent
- Volatile

In addition, in multiprocessor systems, memory may be unique or shared and memory may be real or virtual.[13]

These categories are obviously not truly independent. Although *stack-writable persistent* memory and *heap-volatile* memory make perfect sense, *stack-nonwritable persistent* memory does not. During design, the tradeoffs of picking the correct mix can be evaluated.

In terms of predictability, the areas of concern are the stack and the heap. The stack is the simplest. The developer must ensure only that the amount of stack space is sufficient to hold the "automatic" variables and return addresses in all cases. This is relatively simple to do.

The heap is more challenging for a variety of reasons. Heaps usually work by requesting a block memory from the operating system (through the malloc, or new operators of the programming language). Most heap managers do not require a constant (or even bounded) time to allocate a block of memory. This is because most heap managers must traverse the free store to find a piece of memory that can fulfill the pending request. This means that deadlines may be missed.

A more insidious problem is *memory fragmentation*. Most heaps are nothing more than large blocks of memory out of which blocks of any size can be allocated on a first-come-first-served basis. Through the process of repeated allocation and deallocation, the free memory heap can become fragmented into many small isolated blocks. In such a case, should a request come in for a block that is bigger than any available free block, the request must be denied, which can lead to catastrophic consequences. The normal alternative, garbage collection, halts all computation at unpredictable intervals and performs heap management chores, such as compacting the heap and identifying blocks to which no valid pointer exists. This process is usually difficult to analyze. For this reason, few real-time systems can afford the luxury of

---

13. Few real-time systems can function in the nondeterministic world of virtual memory, so it will not be discussed in this text.

standard heaps. Java and Smalltalk provide built-in automatic garbage collection. C++, of course, avoids the issue altogether and expects the programmer to manage those aspects directly.

Some simple systems can surmount this problem by simply allocating all memory on boot-up. This totally avoids the heap fragmentation and nondeterminism, but it is not applicable to larger or more-complex systems.

A more-common solution is to use fixed-size block-allocation heaps. In this scheme, the heap is divided into several subheaps. Each subheap allocates memory of a fixed size. By tuning the amount of memory in each subheap and its respective block size, the developer can use memory optimally. This approach has the added advantage that it is directly supported by most RTOSs.

2.7 Correctness and Robustness

A system is *correct* when it does the right thing all the time. Such a system is *robust* when it does the right thing under novel (unplanned) circumstances, even in the presence of unplanned failures of portions of the system. Naturally, correctness and robustness are considered good things, but achieving them in a complex design is anything but trivial. One must be on guard for deadlock, race conditions, and other exceptional conditions.

2.7.1 Deadlock

A deadlock is a condition in which a task waits indefinitely for conditions that can never be satisfied. It is equivalent to a state with no exiting transitions or a state with exiting transitions based on events that can never occur. There are four conditions that must be true for deadlock to occur [3].

1. Tasks claim exclusive control over shared resources.
2. Tasks hold resources while waiting for other resources to be released.
3. Tasks cannot be forced to relinquish resources.
4. A circular waiting condition exists.

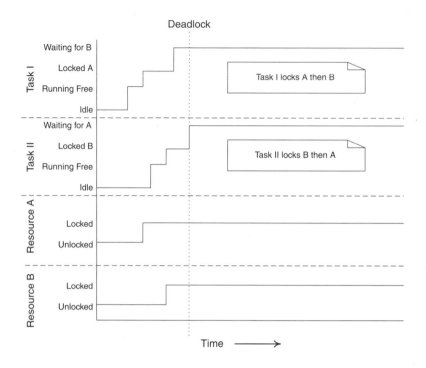

Figure 2-5: *Deadlock Situation*

The circular waiting condition exists when the preconditional invariant for task A is the completion of task B, while the precondition for task B is the completion of task A.

Note that in the circumstance shown in Figure 2-5, all four of these conditions are present.

Because all four conditions are required for deadlock to occur, it is enough to ensure that any one of them is false to totally avoid deadlock. Of the conditions listed, 2 and 4 are the easiest to negate. To negate condition 2, you must enforce a system policy that no shared resource may be locked while another shared resource is requested. This is usually, but not always, possible with careful design. The use of guarded critical sections is commonly employed to ensure that this cannot occur. To negate condition 4, it is necessary to block all other tasks from continuing every time a task claims a shared resource. The other tasks remain blocked until the task releases all shared resources. This is called a critical section, as described in Section 2.5.4.1.

Another way to negate condition 4 is to use a timed rendezvous. This is usually done using a timed mutex from an RTOS, or a timed entry call in Ada, such as the following:

```
-- Ada example
select
    accept ACKNOWLEDGE;
or
    delay 0.1*SECONDS;
    raise Safety_Shutdown;
end select;
```

or

```
// C++ Example with VxWorks RTOS calls
if (semTake(mySem, 1000)==OK) // wait 1000 ticks max
    {
        // do stuff
    }
else
    throw("Resource Unavailable");
```

This approach prevents deadlock because it breaks the circular waiting condition after waiting some fixed period of time.

2.7.2 Exceptional Conditions

A robust system is one that continues to do the right thing even in the presence of system faults. Such faults may be failures (that is, something that used to work no longer does) or errors (a designed-in mistake[14]). For example, a cardiac pacemaker might be subject to strong electromagnetic interference (EMI) that could modify the stored pacing rate, changing the rate from 66 paces/minute to 600 paces/minute.

A robust system must

- Identify the fault
- Take "evasive action," such as
  1. Correct the failure and continue processing
  2. Repeat the previous computation to restore the correct system state
  3. Enter a fail-safe condition

---

14. Some software companies commonly refer to these as "features."

The use of exception handling to improve system correctness requires active means to identify faults. This generally means that computational pre-conditional invariants must be explicitly verified during system execution. If these invariants are satisfied, then normal processing continues. If the invariant condition tests fail, then evasive action is taken. In a robust system, these invariants are checked whenever they are relied upon, *even if the software is formally proven correct*. This is vital because there are many paths to the violation of pre-conditional invariants.

- Software error
- Hardware error
- Hardware failure (transient)
- Hardware failure (persistent)

For example, a satellite system is subject to high levels of ionizing radiation that frequently modify the values of bits in memory. Just because a correct value was written to memory does not mean the value remains correct while waiting to be used. One could imagine a class that verifies its values with redundant 1s-complement storage:

```
class LaserPosition {
    long x, y, z;
    long notX, notY, notZ;
public:
    void set(a,b,c) {
        x = a;    notX = ~a;
        y = b;    notY = ~b;
        z = c;    notZ = ~c;
    };
    long getX(void) {
        if (x == ~notX)
            return x;
        else
            throw("Corrupted X");
    };
    // etc
};
```

This topic is dealt with in more detail in the next chapter.

2.7.3 Race Conditions

A race condition occurs when the state of a resource depends on timing factors that are not universally predictable. Race conditions typically occur when two or more threads access a shared resource with at least one modification to that resource, but the relative sequence of their actions to the resource is not predictable.

Consider the naïve implementation of a semaphore class:

```
class semaphore {
    int isLocked;
public:
    semaphore(void): isLocked(0) { };
    void semTake() {
        while (isLocked) {     // line "a"
            taskDelay(100);    // line "b"
            // (let other tasks run)
        isLocked = 1;          // line "c"
        };
    void semGive() {
        isLocked = 0;
        };
};
```

This implementation suffers from a race condition because it is possible for one task to enter line b, and another task, waiting for the same resource, can preempt the first and enter line b, locking the resource. Later, the first task gets a chance to run, and it continues, also locking the resource. Now two tasks think they have exclusive access to a resource, a condition that can wreak havoc with a system. This situation is shown in Figure 2-6.

This condition arises because the call to the naïve semaphore *semTake* operation is not atomic. If we can turn off task switching appropriately in the class methods, the race condition can be averted.

```
class semaphore {
    int isLocked;
public:
    semaphore(void): isLocked(0) { };
    void semTake() {
        enterCriticalSection();
        while (isLocked) {
            exitCriticalSection();
```

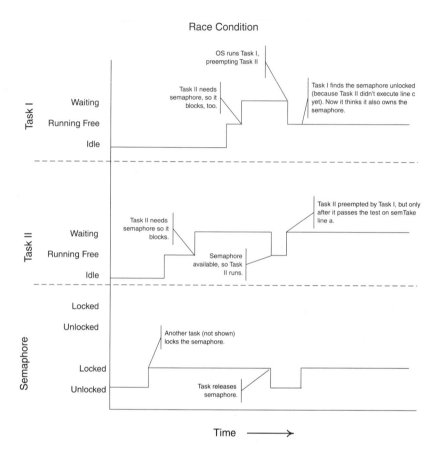

Race Condition

Figure 2-6: *Naïve Semaphore Race Condition*

```
        taskDelay(100);
        enterCriticalSection();
        // (let other tasks run)
    isLocked = 1;
    exitCriticalSection();
    };
void semGive() {
    enterCriticalSection();
    isLocked = 0;
    exitCriticalSection();
    };
};
```

The second version is better because the enterCriticalSection() operation prohibits other tasks from running (and preempting the current task) while the semaphore is being locked or unlocked.

In order to avoid race conditions with a concurrently accessed resource, the following methods must be employed.

1. No two tasks may be in their respective critical sections at the same time.

2. No assumptions are made about relative speeds of different tasks.

3. No task outside one of its critical sections should block another task from continuing.

4. No task should have an unbounded wait to enter its critical section.

The mutex semaphores provided by RTOSs provide the primary means used to avoid race conditions. Simply surround critical sections with calls to lock and release the semaphore associated with the resource.

2.8 Distributed Systems

Large real-time systems may be distributed across many processors and, indeed, across disparate physical locations. Larger-scale systems like these must concern themselves with additional aspects, such as coordination of tasks on different processors, managing boot-up processes, and the details of cross-processor communication. It is profitable to construct such systems using large-scale architectural abstractions, such as components and subsystems, as a means to decompose the system and control its apparent complexity.

2.9 Fault Tolerance and Safety

Many embedded systems have high availability requirements. In such systems, it is undesirable for the system to fail. Typical applications include fire control, avionics, nuclear power, and medical systems. Many of these systems must not only be reliable, but they must also be safe—that is, if they do fail, they do so without causing injury or loss of life.

There are many approaches to the development of reliable and safe systems, but they all involve architectural redundancy in some form [4]. The common approach to capturing and representing this redundancy is through the use of architectural design patterns (see Chapter 8). The next chapter will discuss reliability and safety systems in detail.

2.10 Dealing with Resource-Limited Target Environments

Embedded systems ship the hardware along with the software as part of a complete system package. As many products are extremely cost-sensitive, marketing and sales concerns push for smaller processors and less memory. Smaller CPUs with less memory lower the manufacturing cost. This per-shipped-item cost is called *recurring cost*; it recurs as each device is manufactured. Software has no significant recurring cost—all costs are bound up in development, maintenance, and support activities. Lowering the computing facilities available to the software may reduce recurring cost, but it is not free. It can greatly increase the cost and effort of all these activities. Adequate sales volume can sometimes compensate for the increased software cost.[15] However, the embedded-system developer is rarely, if ever, free from the push to reduce hardware component cost, physical size, heat production, and weight by reducing the number, size, and capability of the target computing platform.

Real-time developers most often use tools hosted on PCs and workstations but target their applications to smaller, less capable computer platforms. This means that they must use cross-compiler tools, which are often more temperamental than the more widely used desktop tools. In addition, the hardware facilities available on the target platform—such as timers, A/D converters, and sensors—cannot be easily simulated on a workstation. The discrepancy between the development and the target environments adds time and effort for the devel-

---

15. Unfortunately, many companies opt for decreasing hardware recurring costs without considering all the development-cost ramifications, but that's fodder for another book.

oper who wants to execute and test his or her code. The lack of sophisticated debugging tools on most small targets complicates testing, as well. Small, embedded targets often do not even have a display on which to view error and diagnostic messages.

Frequently, the real-time developer must design and write software for hardware that does not yet exist. This creates very real challenges because one cannot validate his or her understanding of how the hardware functions. Integration and validation testing become more difficult and lengthy. The use of executable models, discussed in Chapters 12 and 13, can mitigate some of these difficulties.

2.11 Low-Level Hardware Interfacing

One of the hallmarks of real-time and embedded systems is the low-level control of hardware. Hardware devices often require custom drivers because the hardware is novel, the RTOS vendor does not have drivers for that particular device, or the device drivers that do exist are inadequate in performance or size.

2.12 Real-Time Operating Systems

Most moderate-to-complex real-time systems use a real-time operating system, or RTOS. The functions of an RTOS are much the same as for a normal operating system.

- Managing the interface to the underlying computer hardware
- Scheduling and preempting tasks
- Managing memory
- Providing common services, including I/O, to standard devices, such as keyboards, video and LCD displays, pointing devices, and printers

They differ from normal operating systems in a variety of ways. The most important of these are

- Scaleability
- Scheduling policies
- Support for embedded, diskless target environments

2.12.1 Scaleability

First of all, RTOSs are usually *scaleable*, meaning that the RTOS is structured so that only the needed components are included in the RTOS image executing on the target. The innermost core, called the kernel, provides the most essential features of the RTOS. Other features are added as necessary. Scaleability makes an RTOS widely applicable to small, single-processor applications and to large, distributed ones. RTOS vendors call this a *microkernel architecture*, emphasizing the small size of the minimalist kernel.

2.12.2 Scheduling

Fairness doctrines determine task scheduling in many operating systems. This ensures that all tasks have equal access to the CPU. Nonpreemptive scheduling relies heavily on the proper execution of the application threads. Such schedulers cannot schedule other tasks until the currently executing thread explicitly releases control. One misbehaved task can starve all other threads by not releasing control to the OS in a timely fashion. RTOSs most commonly provide priority-based preemption[16] for control of scheduling. In this kind of scheduling, the higher-priority task always preempts lower-priority tasks when the former becomes ready to run. In real-time systems, average performance is a secondary concern. The primary concern is that the system meet all computational deadlines, even in the absolute worst case.

2.12.3 Typical RTOS Features

RTOSs are tailored for embedded systems. They typically provide the ability to boot from ROM—a real advantage in systems without disk

---

16. The *priority* of a task determines which task will run preferentially when more than one task is ready to run. Priority is different than urgency (how near a deadline is) and importance (value of the task completion to the overall system functionality).

storage. Many can even operate out of ROM. This decreases the time necessary for system boot-up and improves their reliability. Electromagnetic interference is less likely to corrupt ROM, so executing out of ROM increases the reliability of most systems.

An RTOS provides a number of services to the real-time developer. In particularly small or time-critical applications, the system may operate without an RTOS. An RTOS greatly simplifies the moderate or large-scale system designs by providing hardware independence, frameworks for execution and concurrency, resource management, and data resource protection. Not all operating systems will provide all these services—some may offer additional ones. In conjunction with the hardware design, you will probably want to evaluate a number of RTOSs to see which best meets your needs.

2.12.3.1 Hardware Independence

One of the primary advantages of an operating system is that it provides device drivers to talk to common hardware devices. Commonly supported hardware devices[17] are

- Printers
- Displays
- Keyboards
- Pointing devices (for example, mice)
- Memory management units (MMUs)
- Timers and real-time clocks
- Dual-ported RAM (DPR)
- Serial devices, such as RS-232 UARTs
- Networks
- Communication buses

Availability of third-party device drivers can be a great advantage because it means the developer need not write code to arbitrate an SCSI bus or to display characters and pixels on an LCD display. Instead, they can concentrate on the application-domain software. Device drivers

---

17. Remember, however, that many real-time systems won't have *any* of these devices to support.

integrate tightly with the operating system so that their functions appear as OS services to the application software.

The innermost microkernel is usually written in assembly language and optimized for the particular CPU on which it executes. Other services are written in a higher-level language, such as C. This means that it is a relatively simple matter to port the RTOS to other platforms, which is an advantage to developers working in a heterogeneous environment. Many companies ship products with a variety of processors, such as 8051s, 68HC16s, 80960s, 68000s, and so forth. Using a single OS means that the learning curve, once climbed, need not be climbed again if the next project uses a different processor family.

A major advantage of using an RTOS is that the embedded application is abstracted away from the implementation details of the underlying target platform. This is important for portability in two ways. First, it eases the transition of the embedded application to other devices should it become important to move to a different CPU or target environment. Second, it provides a common framework for application execution. This allows the developer to more-easily create multiple applications that run on the same platform.

2.12.3.2 Scaleable Architectures

As mentioned earlier, most RTOSs provide scaleable architectures, allowing the developer to link in as much or as little of the optional support services as needed. This broadens the range of applications that can take advantage of the OS. Figure 2-7 schematically shows a typical microkernel architecture layering of services.

Not only do optional library services require more target-system memory, but the RTOS vendor usually charges more for them, as well. Some vendors sell the entire source code for a one-time fee (per development platform), but most require a per-CPU royalty payment (per shipped target platform). Not purchasing parts of the RTOS means a lower development cost, but even more important, a lower per-(target) CPU recurring cost, as well. Depending on the application environment, this can be vitally important in cost-sensitive markets.

Typical optional libraries are shown in Table 2-1.[18]

18. The author once wrote a multitasking RTOS for a cardiac pacemaker that included, among other things, a file system for managing pacing application programs.

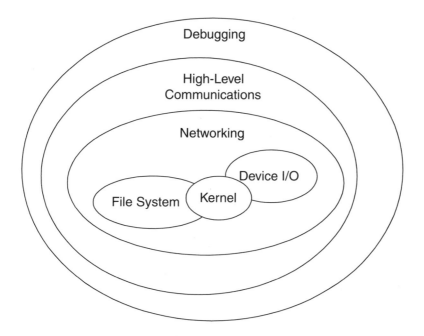

Figure 2-7: *Microkernel Architecture*

Table 2-1: *Typical RTOS Library Services*

Component	Typical Services Provided
Kernel	• Task scheduling • Memory management • Resource protection • Interrupt handling • Task-message passing • Task-event pend and post
File system	• File creation and deletion • File I/O • Directory structures and navigation (*continued*)

Table 2-1: (*cont.*)

Component	Typical Services Provided
Device I/O	• Device drivers for standard hardware devices
Networking	• Low-level protocol and device-driver support for network communications
High-level communications	• Hi-level communications protocols, such as TCP/IP, SMTP, and FTP
Debugging	• Monitor task execution • Start and stop tasks

Naturally, the particular set of services will depend on the specific RTOS.

2.12.3.3 Resource Management (Memory Allocation)

One of the most important jobs of an RTOS is to control access to memory. Most OSs provide the memory allocation and deallocation services that underlie dynamic memory mechanisms of high-level languages. The mechanisms used in desktop OSs are often not applicable to the real-time environment.

Application software must explicitly request that dynamic memory be allocated and released during run-time. The area used for dynamic allocation is the *heap*. Programming languages support memory requests through functions or operators such as *malloc* and *new*. The run-time system generated by the compiler translates these calls into OS calls for chunks of memory. The other side of the coin is the request to release memory, supported by programming-language functions, or operators, such as *free* and *delete*. The OS tracks currently allocated, as well as free, memory blocks. Application programs must select a general policy for allocation of run-time memory using the language facilities.

Few systems can determine all variable storage needs at compile time, so a policy is clearly needed. A number of policies are available for the run-time allocation of objects and data. The simplest and most expensive is to allocate them during the boot phase of the system. The system must allocate the maximum number of each kind of object or variable to operate under all conditions. This is extraordinarily wasteful of memory and is usually not possible in the minimalist environment of real-time systems.

The next simplest approach allocates memory blocks using the dynamic memory features of the programming language. This solves the problem of inefficient use of memory. When the system needs an object, it allocates memory. When the system no longer needs the object, it releases the memory. In real-time systems, however, this naïve implementation has a serious flaw—memory fragmentation.

Malloc and *new* operators request a contiguous block of memory large enough to store the required information (along with any additional information required for the OS to manage the memory block). These operators specify the amount of memory needed in the OS call. This allows different objects (or structs, arrays, and so forth) to be different sizes and to use correspondingly sized blocks of memory. Application tasks allocate and deallocate different-sized memory blocks at random, at least as far as the OS is concerned. Eventually, they heap fragments into randomly sized allocated blocks separated by randomly sized unallocated blocks. Figure 2-8 shows a simplified situation.

Aesthetics is not the problem. It is possible, because of fragmentation, to not have a block big enough to meet a request, even though the total amount of free memory is more than adequate. Remember that the OS allocates memory as a contiguous block. In Figure 2-8, suppose the application task needs a 2K block of memory. Clearly, more than 2K is available in the heap, yet the system cannot allocate a contiguous block to meet the request. In a real-time system that must run continuously for days or even years, this is a serious concern.

Dynamic allocation is generally an O(n) or O(log n) process, where n is the number of currently allocated blocks. It is usually not a constant-time process. The implication is that the more dynamic memory is used, the longer it may take to allocate it. This complicates timing analysis and weakens the developer's assurance that deadlines will always be met.

Another possible policy is to use a *garbage collection* scheme.[19] Garbage collection is the process of reclaiming memory that is no

---

19. Not all garbage collectors defragment memory. Some look only for lost memory blocks and reclaim them. This has a smaller effect on performance but doesn't address the fragmentation issue.

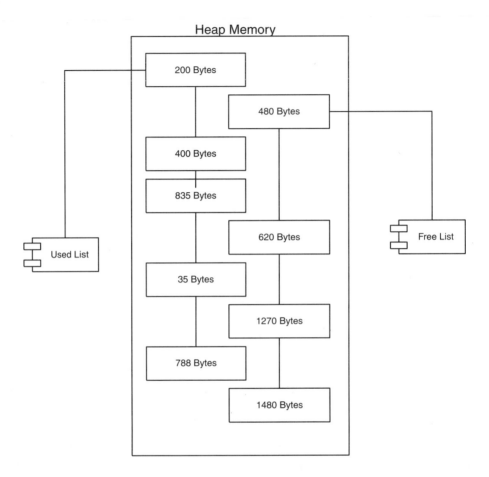

Figure 2-8: *Memory Fragmentation*

longer usable or referenced, and it may also be in charge of defragmenting or compacting memory. Garbage collection occurs either periodically or in response to some episodic event. Whenever garbage collection begins, the OS freezes the applications and moves all allocated blocks into a single contiguous block. For this to work, the applications must use a double-pointer scheme in which pointers to memory actually point to an OS table that, in turn, points to the actual memory. After compaction, the OS adjusts the pointers within its table to account for the new locations of allocated memory objects moved during compaction. Thus, moving the memory objects does not affect the application pointers.

Garbage collection is a powerful mechanism for memory-allocation control. It can totally avoid the fragmentation problem because a request can trigger memory compaction when necessary. It also solves the problem of memory leaks. A memory leak occurs when allocated memory is never released, even when it is no longer accessible. Some languages lack a means of memory release because the garbage collector reclaims inaccessible allocated memory. Such languages do not suffer from memory leaks. In other languages, such as C or C++, memory leaks are the result of software defects.[20] Combining a garbage collector with these languages solves the memory-leak problem.

Two problems exist with defragmenting garbage collection for real-time systems. The first and less important is the overhead for double pointers, which is required to reduce fragmentation. Every access to memory must go through an additional pointer dereference. In many real-time systems, the processor is barely powerful enough to do its primary job, without adding additional computational loads. The more-severe problem is that the garbage collector must freeze the application software for an indeterminate amount of time at unpredictable intervals. Incremental garbage collection (as opposed to stop-and-copy algorithms) addresses this problem somewhat, but not entirely.

Most RTOSs provide another mechanism to deal with memory fragmentation—*fixed-block-sized heaps.* In such a heap, there is no fragmentation because all blocks are exactly the same size. Each fragment is guaranteed to be big enough to meet the needs of its possible clients. Most RTOSs provide the ability to allocate a number of different heaps, each managing blocks of a specific size. By creatively using these heaps, the application developer can usually find an acceptable compromise that minimizes wasteful allocation of large blocks while avoiding memory fragmentation. Of course, this usually means that

---

20. One easy way to get a memory leak in C++ is by using raw pointers in the presence of exception handling. Memory allocated through raw pointers is not released because pointers have no destructors. The problem is that it looks like correct code—memory may be explicitly deallocated using delete, but the delete statements are not executed because an exception was thrown. Rule of thumb: Using raw pointers with exceptions in C++ is almost always an error!

the application developer will have to write his or her own memory-allocation constructs to use these extended OS features. In C++, this is done by overloading the *new* and *delete* operators. Some RTOSs provide support libraries for your language of choice, saving the developer the effort.

2.12.3.4 Concurrency Management

Concurrency is the simultaneous execution of multiple threads. A *thread* is a set of statements that execute in a synchronous, sequential fashion. Multiprocessor systems provide true concurrency, with separate tasks running at exactly the same instant on different processors. On a single CPU, only a single thread can actually be executing at one time. The RTOS interleaves the execution of the threads to give the appearance of concurrency. Task switching in this way actually increases the total compute time because of the overhead of the task-switching mechanism, but it facilitates the timely handling of events and execution of actions. Real-time software developers extensively use task switching to handle multiple tasks with independent events and actions. Many tasks wait for events to occur, such as timer events, user input, and sensor feedback. While one task waits, the RTOS schedules other tasks to run. Higher-priority tasks preempt those of lower priority, improving the system's ability to meet time-critical deadlines.

The RTOS provides services to create, schedule, execute, terminate, and destroy tasks. The RTOS autonomously schedules tasks according to its scheduling policy. Some RTOSs provide multiple policies, only one of which may be active at once. But most provide only a single choice. Concurrency management is discussed in more detail in Chapters 8 and 11.

2.12.3.5 Data-Access Control and Protection

Multiple threads execute asynchronously. In real-time systems, however, they may need to meet and synchronize at specific points to share data or to coordinate control. In Ada, this is called a *rendezvous*. When threads cooperate in this fashion, they share data or control information. RTOSs typically provide low-level mechanisms to support reliable data sharing through heavyweight and lightweight mechanisms. The heavyweight mechanisms provide asynchronous rendezvous through the use of task-message queues or pending/posting events to OS event queues. Lightweight mechanisms are usually based on mutual-exclusion semaphores that "lock" the resource and disallow access until the resource is released.

2.12.3.6 Time Management

Because real-time systems are preoccupied with time, it is only reasonable that an RTOS provide time services. Available services include *pend* for a time event (elapsed or absolute time), get the current time, measure elapsed time, and schedule future events.

These services allow efficient use of the CPU because tasks waiting for timed events needn't poll or execute idle loops. Timers are used with finite state automata to signal state changes in a lightweight way. (See Chapters 7 and 12.)

2.12.3.7 Networking

Many RTOSs provide built-in support for networking. The network support is frequently only for Ethernet networks, which use carrier sense multiple access/collision detect (CSMA/CD) algorithms, which may not be suitable for your application. Support may also be available for priority-based networks, such as ARCNET or CAN, but such support is vendor-specific. If you need networking support, it is far cheaper to buy it than to build it.

2.12.3.8 I/O Services and File Systems

Many embedded systems embed disk drives for booting, storing executable code, and providing persistent data storage. Removable media, such as CD-ROMs and floppy disks, are used for software upgrades, archival storage, and communication with desktop PCs. Such facilities require a file system to organize the data. There are real advantages to using a standard file system, such as the ubiquitous FAT-16 (DOS) file system, FAT-32 (Windows NT and 95/98), HPFS (OS/2), and UNIX file systems. With a standard file system, data is immediately available to third-party software for off-line processing.

File systems may even provide disk space for virtual-memory paging. Paging schemes swap tasks out to disk in low-memory situations, enabling other tasks to run. This allows many more tasks to run in the same amount of RAM. The large address space is not real memory, hence the term *virtual*. However, page swapping to disk can require many CPU cycles at unpredictable intervals. The OS may even swap out tasks running at high priorities, making them miss their deadlines because of the incurred overhead delays. This makes paging inappropriate for most real-time systems. Even though some OSs permit the locking of specific pages (running specific tasks) into memory, most real-time systems avoid virtual-memory paging altogether.

2.12.3.9 High-Level Language-Support Libraries

Many RTOSs provide C, C++, Ada, or Pascal libraries that can be linked in and executed on the target platform. This is a great aid to the developer because it limits the amount of effort he or she must spend writing code unrelated to the application domain. Generally available libraries must often be customized to be thread-reliable[21]—that is, to be robust in the presence of multiple threads with potential reentrancy. This often means using facilities peculiar to the specific RTOS. RTOS vendors ease the developer's life considerably when they supply these libraries, which typically include standard I/O, network services, math support, and memory management.

2.12.3.10 Graphics Toolkits

The use of graphical user interfaces (GUIs) has spread to embedded systems. No longer are textual menus and displays acceptable in many real-time applications. If your real-time system requires the use of a GUI, check with your RTOS vendor to see if graphics toolkits are available. A word of caution: Frequently, commercially available GUI toolkits are not reentrant or thread-reliable. In order to use them, the developer must serialize access to the GUI libraries, which may not meet with the performance requirements of the system.

---

21. The commonly used term is *thread-safe*. However, the literature inconsistently applies the term *safe* in this regard. We will use the terms *safe* and *reliable* more precisely in this book. Hence, thread-reliable. Safety is discussed in detail in Chapter 3.

2.13 Summary

For all the reasons already mentioned, developing real-time software is generally much more difficult than developing non-real-time software. The real-time development environments have fewer tools, and the ones that exist are often less capable than those for desktop environments or for big-iron mainframes. Additional concerns translate into more complexity for the developer. To put salt on the wound, in order to reduce recurring costs, these systems must frequently execute in much less memory, using much less raw compute power.

2.14 Looking Ahead

Many real-time embedded systems are mission- or life-critical. Unfortunately, very few universities provide any education on what constitutes safety and how it differs from reliability, how to analyze systems for safety, and appropriate design measures to ensure safety. Chapter 3 discusses the issues of safety and reliability in the context of real-time embedded systems.

In Chapter 4, we'll introduce a simple development process model called real-time object-oriented process for embedded systems (ROPES). Although the concepts and methods presented in this book can be applied in any reasonable development process, ROPES provides a context for our subsequent discussion of the development of real-time systems.

2.15 Exercises

1. Define the following terms:
   - Priority
   - Criticality
2. What is the difference between a cyclic executive, a round robin scheduling policy, and a priority-driven preemptive scheduler?

3. What is the primary problem with dynamic-memory allocation in real-time systems? What are some strategies to solve it?

4. What is the purpose of a semaphore? What is another means to achieve the same purpose?

5. Name five services that a typical RTOS provides to real-time applications.

6. What is memory fragmentation? Name three means to deal with or avoid it.

7. Define the following event-arrival patterns:
   - Periodic
   - Irregular
   - Bursty
   - Bounded
   - Unbounded

8. What are the four necessary conditions for deadlock? What are some strategies to avoid it?

9. What are the conditions necessary for a race condition? How can it be avoided?

2.16 References

[1] Stolper, Steven. "Embedded Systems on Mars," *Embedded Systems Conference West*, San Jose, Calif.: Miller Freeman Publishing, 1995.

[2] Dijkstra, E. W. *Cooperating Sequential Processes*, Eindhoven, Netherlands: Technology Report EWD-123, 1965.

[3] Hughes, Cameron, and Tracy Hughes. *Object-Oriented Multithreading Using C++*, New York: John Wiley and Sons, 1997.

[4] Storey, Neil. *Safety-Critical Computer Systems*, Reading, Mass.: Addison-Wesley, 1996.

Chapter 3

Basic Concepts of Safety-Critical Systems

"Safe enough" looks different at 35,000 feet.

—Book of Douglass, Law 198

Many real-time embedded systems have very high criticality. Failure of such systems can lead to loss of property, injury, and even loss of life. The frequency with which one comes across these systems is increasing at a rapid rate. Aircraft, nuclear power plants, industrial automation, and medical systems are the most obvious. However, other more-mundane devices, such as microwave ovens, automobiles, and other modes of transportation are increasingly software-controlled. This chapter introduces the fundamental concepts of high-reliability and safety-critical systems and the common means for ensuring safety.

3.1 Introduction to Safety

Software is being applied to increasingly diverse problems every day. It wasn't long ago that car engines were almost entirely mechanical devices, with just a few simple electronics. Nowadays, the car environment is "computer rich" and employs a local area network bus (for example, the controller area network, or CAN, bus) just to cope with it. As devices become "smarter," safety roles previously met solely by mechanical or electrical interlocks are being assumed by software. This is true in high-tech medical equipment, such as anesthesia-delivery machines, patient monitors, and implanted cardiac pacemakers. It is true of nonmedical devices, such as cars, airplanes, trains, and nuclear power plants. Failures in such systems can affect the lives of many people. As software plays an increasingly important role in safety-relevant systems, it becomes more important to understand the risks of software-controlled systems and how to address them.

3.1.1 The Therac-25 Story

The most published software-related safety failure occurred in a radiation-therapy device, the Therac-25. Released to the market by Atomic Energy of Canadian Limited in 1982, it used software to enhance its usability and lower the cost of production, providing real benefit to its users. However, through a compounding of process, design, and implementation failures, software defects caused massive radiation overdoses to six patients, killing three and contributing directly to the death of a fourth. Nancy Leveson details the history of the Therac-25 in her book, *Safeware* [1]. She concludes that merely fixing the identified defects in the code did not make the device safer.

3.1.2 Other Stories

Although the Therac-25 is the one of the best known software-related safety failures, other examples abound.[1]

---

1. Many of these examples are taken from [2].

- The Patriot missiles deployed in Saudi Arabia failed because of clock drift—their effectiveness in stopping missiles was downgraded from 95 percent to 13 percent. This failure was blamed for allowing a SCUD missile to hit an American barracks, killing 29 and injuring 97.

- Software flaws in the Aegis tracking system on the *USS Vincennes* contributed to the ship shooting down an Iranian Airline flight, at the cost of 290 lives.

- An 8080-based cement factory process-control system mistakenly stacked large boulders 80 feet above the ground until they fell, crushing cars and damaging the building.

- Stray electromagnetic interference is blamed for up to 19 robot-inflicted deaths per year in Japan.

- Low-energy radiation reprogrammed cardiac pacemakers, causing several deaths.

Software failures can have profound effects even in nonembedded systems. Because of an error in a medical-database computer, a German woman was incorrectly informed that she had incurable syphilis and had passed it on to her children. She strangled one to death and attempted to kill herself and the other.

The list of safety failures in software-controlled systems is long—and getting longer. As electrical, software, and systems engineers, it is crucial that we stand back and take a critical look at how the introduction of software into traditionally electro-mechanical devices affects safety. As Grady Booch points out, "The last announcement I want to hear from a pilot when I am flying is this: 'Is there a programmer on board?'"[3]

There is some confusion in the industry about the difference between safety and reliability. Although both are valuable, they are distinct concepts. They may at times even be conflicting concerns. The literature has muddied the picture by using these terms imprecisely, particularly the term *safety*. Because safety and reliability are so important to embedded systems, we will try hard to use the terms clearly and precisely.

3.2 Terms and Concepts

Reliability is a measure of the up-time, or availability, of a system—specifically, it is the probability that a computation will successfully complete before the system fails. It is usually estimated with mean time between failure, or MTBF. MTBF is a statistical estimate of the probability of failure and applies to stochastic failure modes. Electrical engineers are familiar with the "bathtub" curve, which shows the failure rates of electronic components over time. There is an initial high failure rate that rapidly drops to a low level and remains constant for a long time. Eventually, the failure rate rises rapidly back to initial or higher levels, giving the characteristic bathtub shape, as shown in Figure 3-1. This is why electrical components and systems undergo the burn-in process. The high temperature increases the probability of failure, thereby accelerating the bathtub curve. In other words, the components that are going to fail early do so even earlier (during the burn in). The

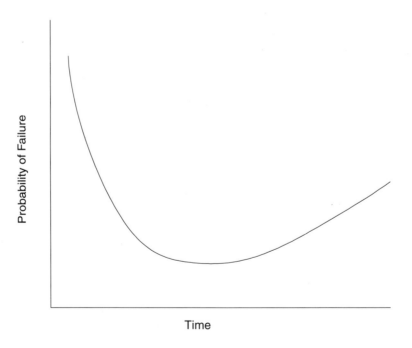

Figure 3-1: *Bathtub Curve for Electronic Component Failure*

remaining components or systems fall into the low failure basin of the bathtub curve and have a higher average life expectancy.

Reducing system down-time increases reliability by increasing the MTBF. Redundancy is one design approach that increases availability, because if one component fails, another takes its place. Of course, redundancy improves reliability only when the failures of the redundant components are independent.[2] The reliability of a component does not depend on what happens after the component fails. Whether or not the system fails safely, the reliability of the system remains the same. Clearly, the primary concern relative to the reliability of a system is the availability of its functions to the user.

Another term used loosely is *security*. Security deals with permitting or denying system access to appropriate individuals. A secure system is one that is relatively immune to attempts, intentional or not, to violate the security barriers set into place.

Safety is distinct from either reliability or security. A safe system is one that does not incur too much risk to persons or equipment. A *risk* is an event or condition that can occur but is undesirable. Risk is measured in terms of both severity and probability. The failure of a jet engine is unlikely, but the consequences can be very high. Thus, the risk of flying in a plane is tolerable; even though it is unlikely that you would survive a crash from 30,000 feet, it is an extremely rare occurrence. At the other end of the spectrum, there are events that are common but of lesser concern. There is a risk that you can get an electric shock from putting a 9-volt battery in a transistor radio. It could easily occur, but the consequences are small. Again, this is a tolerable risk.

A *risk* is the chance that something bad will happen. Nancy Leveson [1] defines risk to be "a combination of the likelihood of an accident and the severity of the potential consequences."

Some authors go so far as to define it exactly:[3]

Risk = Probability of Failure × Severity

The "something bad" is called a *mishap* or *accident* and is defined to be damage to property or harm to persons.

---

2. Strict independence isn't required to have a beneficial effect. Weakly correlated failure modes still offer improved tolerance to faults over tightly correlated failure modes.
3. See Chapter 5 in [4].

Leveson goes on to define a hazard as "a state or set of conditions of a system (or an object) that, together with other conditions in the environment of the system (or object), will inevitably lead to an accident (loss event)."

Hazards arise in five fundamental ways [1].

1. Release of energy

2. Release of toxins

3. Interference of life-support functions

4. Supplying misleading information to safety personnel or control systems

5. Failure to alarm when hazardous conditions arise

The unsafe release of energy is perhaps the most common threat. Energy occurs in many forms, including chemical, electrical, atomic, potential, and kinetic. Chemical energy can result in fires and explosions. Electrical energy can result in electrocutions. Atomic energy can lead to immediate death or agonizing radiation sickness. Airplane crashes release enormous kinetic energy. Any time a large amount of energy is controlled, protecting humans from its inadvertent sudden release is the primary safety concern.

The release of toxins is important in many environments today, particularly in the medical and chemical industries. Many of the worst catastrophes in recent times have been due to release of toxins. The Bhopal, India, chemical accident released a huge cloud of methyl isocyanate from a Union Carbide plant, killing at least 2,000 people in the surrounding area.

Incidents can also occur when the system interferes with a process necessary to sustain life. The most obvious examples are with medical products, such as patient ventilators and heart-lung machines. However, life-support systems also maintain human-compatible environments in airplanes, submarines, and spacecraft. Even the failure of a thermostat in a sufficiently harsh environment[4] could contribute to the loss of life.

Many safety-critical systems are continuously or periodically monitored by humans and include humans within the safety loop. A monitoring system that actively misleads a human contributes to a hazardous

---

4. Northern Minnesota comes to mind.

condition. Imagine an ECG monitor that displays a cardiac waveform, but, because of a software defect, it displays the same waveform over and over. The patient could enter cardiac arrest, but the trusted ECG system would display only old data. An attending physician might well conclude that the patient is fine because the supposedly real-time data shows a good patient condition. Off-line diagnostic systems can also contribute to an unsafe condition. Many deaths in hospitals occur because of mislabeling patient medications and laboratory results. These errors actively mislead the personnel responsible for safety-related decisions and contribute to the resulting incidents.

The previous examples deal with actively misleading the human-in-the-loop. Passive systems that fail to alarm can be just as deadly. Failure of pressure and temperature alarms in a nuclear power plant can lead to reactor leaks. Many people fail to recognize that the reverse is also true—too many "nuisance" alarms can hide important safety-related conditions. Exactly this kind of problem contributed to the Therac-25 incidents, in which the system falsely alarmed frequently and reported alarms with obscure error codes. The operators soon learned to ignore the nuisance alarms and silenced them immediately. In addition, the Therac-25 made no distinction between critical and routine alarms. Too many false alarms frequently lead to the operator disabling alarms altogether.

In some systems, the number of alarms can be so great that silencing the alarms takes all the operator's time, leaving none to deal with the underlying problems [1]. Alarms with cryptic messages can be worse than no indications at all; they do not suggest appropriate corrective action, yet distract the operator from monitoring tasks.

3.3 Safety-Related Faults

Hazards can occur because the system was designed to unsafe specifications or because of failures—that is, the nonperformance of a system to achieve its intended function within its specifications. *Failures* are events occurring at specific times. *Errors* are more static and are inherent characteristics of the system, as in *design errors*. A *fault* is an unsatisfactory system condition or state. Thus, failures and errors are different kinds of faults.

Faults can affect a system in a variety of ways.

- *Actions*—inappropriate system actions taken or appropriate actions not taken
- *Timing*—actions taken too soon or too late
- *Sequence*—skipping actions or doing them out of order
- *Amount*—inappropriate amount of energy or reagent used

3.3.1 Safety Is a System Issue

Many systems present hazards, which the system can identify and address or ignore. However, note that safety is a system issue. A system can remove an identified hazard or reduce its associated risk in many ways. For example, consider a radiation-therapy device. It has the hazard that it may over-radiate the patient. An electrical interlock activated when the beam is either too intense or lasts too long is one design approach to reduce risk. The interlock could involve a mechanical barrier or use an electric switch. Alternatively, the software could use redundant heterogeneous computational engines (verify the dosage using a different algorithm) to verify the setting before permitting the dose to be administered. The point is that the *system* is either safe or it isn't—not the software, not the electronics, not the mechanics. Of course, each of these affects the system safety, but it is ultimately the interaction of all these elements that determines system safety.

3.3.2 Random Faults vs. Systematic Faults

All types of components can contain design defects. These are errors in the component design that can lead to mishaps. However, not all can have failures. Notably, software does not fail. If it does the wrong thing, it will always do the wrong thing under identical circumstances. Contrast that with electrical components that reach end-of-life or mechanical switches that break. The designs of such components might have been fine, but they no longer meet their design characteristics. It makes sense, then, to divide faults into systematic and random faults. Errors are systematic faults—they are intrinsic in the design or implementation. Writing the FORTRAN statement

DO I=1.10

rather than

> DO I=1,10

is a transcription error—an inadvertent substitution of a period for a comma. A single inadvertent semicolon has been known to bring down entire mainframes![5]

The term *failure* implies that something that once functioned properly no longer does so. Failures are random faults that occur when a component breaks in the field.

Hardware faults may be systematic or random. Hardware may contain design flaws, or it may fail in the field. Random faults occur only in physical entities, such as mechanical or electronic components. End-of-life failures are common in long-lived systems, but the probability of random faults is well above zero even in brand new systems. The likelihood of failure is estimated from a probability distribution function, which is why they are called "random faults." Random faults cannot be designed away. It is possible to add redundancy for fault detection, but no one has ever made a CPU that cannot fail.

Software faults are always systematic because software neither breaks down nor wears out. Many engineers routinely remove run-time range checking from shipped programs because testing supposedly removes all faults. However, run-time checking can provide the only means within a system to identify a wide variety of systematic faults (as well as random hardware failures) that occur in rare circumstances.

3.3.3 Single-Point Failures

Devices ought to be safe when there are no faults and the device is used properly. Most experts consider a device safe, however, only when any single-point failure cannot lead to an incident. That is, the failure of any single component or the failure of multiple components due to any single failure event should not result in an unsafe condition.[6]

For example, consider total software control on a single CPU for a patient ventilator. What happens if the CPU locks up? What if EMI

---

5. Been there, done that.

6. Whether or not the system must consider multiple independent faults in its safety analysis depends on the risk. If the faults are sufficiently likely and the damage potential sufficiently high, then multiple-fault scenarios must be considered. Nuclear power plants fall into this category.

corrupts memory that contains the executable code or the commanded tidal volume and breathing rate? What if the ventilator loses power? What if the gas supply fails? What if a valve sticks open or closed?

Given that an untoward event can happen to a component, one must consider the effect of its failure on the safety of the system. If the only means of controlling hazards in the software-controlled ventilator is to raise an alarm on the ventilator itself, then the means of control may be inadequate. How can a stalled CPU also raise an alarm to call the user's attention to the hazard? This fault, a stalled CPU, affects both the primary action (ventilation) and the means of hazard control (alarming). This is a *common mode failure*—that is, a failure in multiple control paths due to a common or shared fault.

The German safety-assessment organization TUV uses a single fault assessment tree for determining the safety of devices in the presence of single-point failures [5,6].

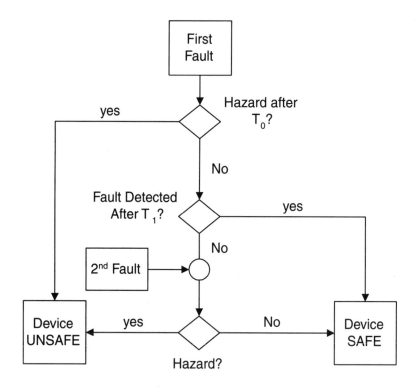

Figure 3-2: *TUV Fault Assessment*

In Figure 3-2, T_0 is the fault-tolerance time of the first failure (the time the fault can be tolerated without incident). T1 is the time after which a second fault is likely (which can be estimated by the MTBF).

If the purpose of run-time testing is to identify faults, then testing must be repeated periodically. The fault-tolerance time determines the maximal period of the test—as in:

$$T_{test} < T_0 < T_1$$

That is, the time between tests must be less than the fault-tolerance time. If the system cannot guarantee test completion within this time frame, then it must provide some other mechanism for fault identification and control.

A *hazard analysis* is a document that identifies faults, resulting hazards, and the hazard-control measures. The hazard analysis requires periodic review during the development process. The development process must also track identified hazard-control measures forward into design, implementation, and validation testing. Design decisions add additional failure modes to the hazard analysis.

For safety analysis, you cannot consider the probability of failure for the single fault. Regardless of how remote the chance of failure, a safe system continues to be safe in the event of *any* single-point failure. This has broad implications. Consider a watchdog circuit in a cardiac pacemaker. A watchdog is a circuit that requires periodic service or it forces the system to go into a fail-safe state. A watchdog must use a different time base from that used by the CPU running the software. If the same crystal drives both the CPU and the watchdog, the watchdog cannot detect a doubling or tripling of the pacing rate in the event of a crystal failure. Pacing the heart at 210 beats per minute is an unsafe condition for anyone. Crystals are typically reliable components, but they do fail. When they fail, the system must continue to be safe.

3.3.4 Common Mode Failures

The pacemaker example illustrates a *common mode failure,* a single failure that affects multiple parts. Safety measures must not have any common mode failures with the processes they seek to check. If a medical linear accelerator uses a CPU to control the radiation dose, then none of the safety mechanisms can reside on that CPU.

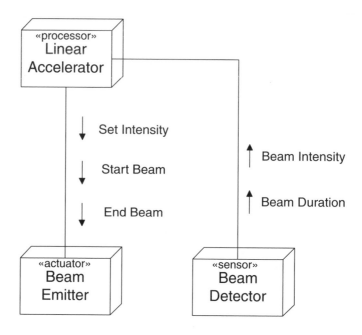

Figure 3-3: *Unsafe Linear Accelerator*

The unsafe linear accelerator in Figure 3-3 shows a CPU controlling a medical linear accelerator. The CPU first sets the accelerator intensity level. Then it turns on the beam. When the duration is adequate, it turns off the beam. A sensor provides feedback to the CPU. If the intensity is too high or the duration too long, then the CPU can turn off the beam.

However, there is a common mode failure that can disable the safety mechanism. What if the CPU fails after it has turned on the beam? Because the beam control uses the same CPU as the safety shutoff, the beam remains in an unsafe ON state. What if EMI corrupts the data inside the CPU, resulting in 100 times the proper dosage? If the safety mechanism simply compares the returned sensor value with the command-beam dose, the condition will pass, even though the condition is unsafe.

The safe linear accelerator in Figure 3-4 illustrates a safer design.

Several differences make this a safer design in the presence of faults. The main difference is the inclusion of a hardware interlock controlled by the separate CPU. This is basically a curtain that is opaque to radia-

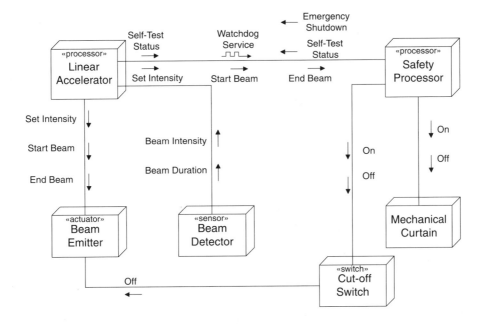

Figure 3-4: *Safe Linear Accelerator*

tion. The curtain is suspended and requires an active process to keep it up. The curtain will fall if not actively instructed otherwise, terminating the patient irradiation. This provides safety in the presence of a power loss. The system will fail with the curtain down, so when power is restored, the linear accelerator cannot release radiation. A mechanical switch connected to the curtain deenergizes the linear accelerator when it is down. Bidirectional communication of the separate CPU power-on self-tests (POSTs) provides an additional safety mechanism. Both CPUs must report passing their respective POSTs before the system begins therapy. The safety CPU tests the raising and lowering of the curtain, using an optical sensor as part of its self-test.

A radiation sensor feeds the safety CPU so that it can monitor the radiation dosage. Should the controlling CPU command an inappropriately high dose, the safety CPU closes the curtain and deenergizes the accelerator when the safety threshold is reached. To prevent the linear accelerator from being left on in the event of a primary CPU failure, the primary CPU sends the safety CPU a periodic message indicating proper functioning.

If the safety CPU fails, the system is safe because the primary CPU is unaffected by that failure. If the primary CPU fails, then the safety CPU prevents overdose. Note that the failures of the two CPUs are independent so that a single failure cannot make the device unsafe.

3.3.5 Latent Faults

An undetected failure is a *latent fault*. Because safety measures improve safety only when they function correctly, a measure can only be relied on if it is known to be valid. Put another way, if a system cannot routinely validate a safety measure, then the safety measure cannot be relied on. For example, if the linear-accelerator curtain was never tested, a failure of the curtain would be a latent fault. A failure in the primary CPU 10 years later could lead to an accident. Because the system tests the curtain periodically and at each power up, the curtain provides a safety measure against a single-point failure. If it does fail, the system would not start because the error would be reported to the primary CPU. Further, the curtain fails in a safe (down) state, meaning that the system fails into a safe condition.

3.3.6 Fail-Safe State

The concept of a fail-safe state is central to many safety-critical system designs. The fail-safe state is a condition a safety-critical system must achieve when faced with an unrecoverable fault. Nancy Leveson has identified several types of safe failure modes:

- Off state
    1. Emergency stop—immediately cuts power
    2. Production stop—shuts down as soon as the current task is completed
    3. Protection stop—shuts down immediately but not by removing power
- Partial shutdown—goes to a degraded level of functionality
- Hold—no functionality, but safety actions are taken automatically
- Manual, or external, control—system continues to function but only via external input
- Restart—system is rebooted or restarted

The problem-domain context usually disallows several of these choices. An engine in an airborne aircraft cannot merely be shut down in the event of a failure (OFF) unless there is another engine that can take over. In the case of unmanned space vehicles, the fail-safe state usually is to blow up the rocket (HOLD). Attended medical devices often shut down and alarm the user (emergency stop), although sometimes they enter a monitor-only condition (partial shutdown). When a person enters a hazardous area, a robot-control system may finish the current task before shutting down, to protect persons and equipment (production stop).

A safety-critical system may have several fail-safe states to handle failures in different control or data paths. A detailed analysis of the failure modes of the system determines the most appropriate fail-safe states.

3.3.7 Achieving Safety

The most fundamental safety design concept is the separation of safety channels from nonsafety channels. This is called the *firewall pattern*. A *channel* is a static path of data and control that takes some information and produces some output. Failure of any component of the channel constitutes a failure of the entire channel. A channel can be a control-only path with no feedback, or it can be a tightly coupled control loop, including sensors and actuators.

One application of the firewall concept involves isolation of all nonsafety-related software and hardware components from those with safety responsibility. Because developing safe subsystems is so difficult, this separation can usually be economically justified. The separation of safety-critical components simplifies their design and implementation, making them more tractable.

Another example of the firewall idea is the separation of control from its correlated safety measure, as in our safe linear accelerator example in Figure 3-4. This requires some kind of redundancy. The redundancy can be on a small scale, as in the protection of local data using 1's-complement multiple storage or cyclic redundancy checks (CRCs) on stored data. The redundancy can be large scale, as well, replicating an entire subsystem chain. The large-scale redundancy is commonly done in the context of a safety pattern or framework [9].

This redundancy can be *homogeneous* or *diverse* (also called *heterogeneous*). Homogeneous redundancy uses channel clones or exact replicas and protects only against random failures. Commercial airplanes use redundant engines and flight-control computers to protect against random component failures. Diverse redundancy uses different means to perform the same function. It is called diverse because the redundancy is not achieved by simply cloning the channel.

Redundant storage of data offers a simple example. Homogenous redundant storage might store the data three times and compare them before use. Diverse redundant storage might store a second copy of the data in 1's-complement format or stash a CRC with the data. An industrial process can be homogeneously redundant by replicating the control loops on identical computers. It can be diversely redundant by using a PID control loop on one computer and a fuzzy-logic or neural-network algorithm on another to solve the same problem.

Diverse redundancy is the stronger of the two because diverse redundancy protects against systematic, as well as random, faults. If a software flaw in the flight-control computer turns the plane upside down when you cross the equator, having three different computers contain the same code won't help on those flights to Rio de Janeiro.[7]

Software can be redundant with respect to either data or control, or both. Data redundancy can be as simple as storing multiple copies, or as complex as needed. Different types of redundancy provide varying degrees of protection against various kinds of faults. Many mechanisms identify data corruption, such as:

- Parity
- Hamming codes
- Checksums
- Cyclic redundancy checks (CRCs)
- Homogenous multiple storage
- Complement multiple storage

Simple 1-bit parity identifies single-bit errors, but not which bit is in error; nor does it protect against multiple-bit errors. Hamming codes contain multiple parity bits to identify n-bit errors and repair $(n-1)$-bit errors. Checksums simply add up the data within a block, using modulo arithmetic. CRCs provide good data integrity checks and are widely

---

7. Don't laugh. Such a software fault was uncovered in the F-16.

used in communication systems to identify data-stream corruption. CRCs have the advantage of fairly high reliability, with a small size and low computational overhead.

Data may be stored in multiple locations and compared prior to use. A stronger variant of multiple storage is to store the data in a 1's-complement form. The 1's-complement form is a simple bit-by-bit inversion of the original data. This form protects against certain hardware faults in RAM, such as stuck bits.

Redundant software control replicates controlling algorithms. The system compares the results from the replicates prior to control-signal use. Homogenous control redundancy is of no use in the detection of software faults. Diverse redundancy requires different algorithms computing the result, or the same algorithm written by different teams.[8] The redundant algorithm can be less complex than the primary one if it needs only to provide reasonableness checks.

Reasonableness checks may be simple and lightweight. If the primary system algorithm has a simple inverse operation, the reasonableness check may simply invert the result and compare the answer with the initial data. Algebraic computation usually, although not always, can be inverted.

In many cases, the inverse operation may not exist or may be too complex to compute. Instead of algorithmic inversion, a reasonableness check may perform an alternative forward calculation using a different algorithm, such as using a fuzzy-logic inference engine to check a PID control loop. In this kind of redundancy, it is not always necessary for the secondary system to have the same fidelity or accuracy as the primary system. It may be necessary to check only that the primary system is not grossly in error. In all but the highest-risk-category devices, a lightweight but less accurate reasonableness check may be sufficient.

Redundancy can implement either *feedback error detection* or *feedforward error correction*. Feedback error detection schemes identify faults but do not attempt to correct the action. Instead, they may attempt to redo the processing step that was in error, or they may terminate processing by signaling the system to go to a safe shutdown state.

---

8. Unfortunately, the faults found in redundant systems written by different teams are not entirely statistically independent [7]. This can be mitigated somewhat by purposefully selecting different algorithms when possible.

Some systems use feedback error detection to identify when it should enter a fail-safe state. Many systems do not have a safe shut-down state. For example, it may be unsafe for an error in a computational step of a flight-control computer to shut down the computer while flying at 35,000 feet. An unattended patient ventilator might not want to shut down when it detects an error.

Most systems do have a safe shutdown state. A nuclear reactor can safely shut down by inserting its control rods into the core. An attended ventilator can cease ventilation provided it alerts the attending physician. However, there may be nonsafety reasons for not forcing the fail-safe state. A high frequency of false negative alarms might lower the availability of the system to unacceptable levels. In this case, retrying the computation may be a better choice, depending on the risks associated with continuing and stopping.

Feedforward error correction schemes try to correct the error and keep processing. This is most appropriate when there is significant risk associated with shutting the system down, or when the fault's cause is unambiguous and correctable. A common implementation of feedforward error correction is the reconstruction of correct data from partially corrupted values.

3.4 Safety Architectures

Safety can be built into a system in small or large scale, but most commonly by using a combination of both. The large-scale mechanisms involve the construction of an architectural framework that provides both redundancy and separation. Such large-scale mechanisms are instances of architectural patterns.

3.4.1 Single-Channel Protected Design (SCPD)

In a SCPD architecture, a single channel exists for the control of some process. For example, consider an electronic train-braking system, illustrated in Figure 3-5.

In such a system, the Pedal Sensor detects when the engineer engages the brake lever. This relays the information to the train's Computer, which sends out commands along the Computer Bus—one to

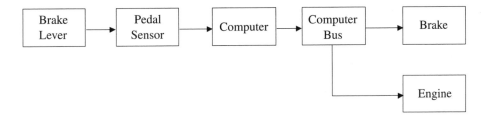

Figure 3-5: *Single-Channel Protected Architecture*

engage the brake and another to disengage the engine. This is a single channel of control, and any breakage in the chain could lead to an incident. However, this single channel can be made safe by applying sufficient hazard control within the channel. A periodic life tick ensures bus integrity—in the event of a failure, the brake engages itself and the engine disengages automatically. The computer watchdog activates the brake if it is not updated in the proper way and with the proper interval. This sequence of actions is shown in the sequence diagram in Figure 3-6.

SCPDs can be difficult or impossible to implement because of performance constraints. Suppose the fault-tolerance time for a corruption of the executable code is 10 seconds. That means that the periodic ROM CRC and RAM tests must detect any change in the executable code within that time. This is not possible in many computer designs. If the system is 50 percent loaded with execution of the embedded application

---

A Note About Patterns

A pattern is a general solution to a common problem. Patterns consist of three aspects: a problem context (which defines the problem the pattern addresses), a solution (the pattern itself), and consequences (implications of the use of the pattern). Although we haven't introduced the UML notation yet, we will use this notation to graphically depict the pattern. We will also provide a sequence diagram to show how the objects or components involved in the pattern might act in a dynamic context. Interested readers might want to skip ahead to Chapter 8 and learn about the notation.

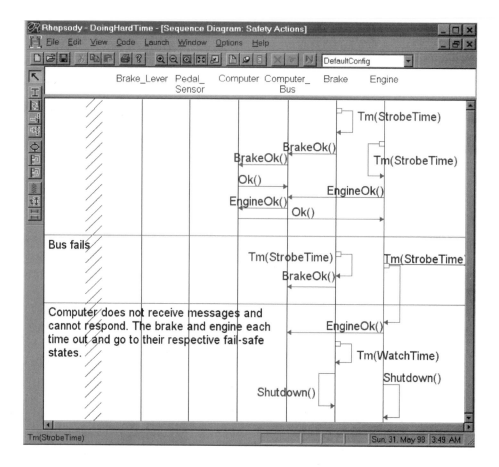

Figure 3-6: *Safety-Action Sequence*

and the RAM test itself takes five seconds, then the tests cannot be executed in a timely fashion. The feasibility of the single-channel approach depends on many features, such as:

- Fault-tolerance time
- Speed of the processor
- Amount of ROM and RAM
- Whether hardware assistance (such as CRC chips and redundant checked RAM) is available
- Sensitivity of the product to recurring cost versus development costs

Another problem with SCPD is that it is more difficult to provide fault independence of the primary and redundant processing. Remember, a system is usually considered safe only when it does not lead to an accident in the presence of any single-point failure. Single-channel systems are typically filled with opportunities for common mode failures that take out both primary and redundant processing. For such systems to be safe, mechanisms must ensure entrance to a fail-safe state should the entire channel stop functioning.

3.4.2 Multi-Channel Voting Pattern

One popular architecture for safety-critical systems uses an odd number of redundant channels that vote on the validity of incoming data or outgoing actuations. In case of disagreement, the majority rules. As mentioned earlier, these redundant systems may be homogeneous or diverse, depending on the costs, as well as the kind, of fault protection desired.

3.4.3 Homogeneous Redundancy Pattern

The *homogeneous redundancy pattern* uses identical channels[9] to increase reliability. All redundant channels are run in parallel, and the output of the channels is compared. If an odd number of channels is used, then a "majority wins" policy can be implemented that can detect and correct failures in the minority channels.

The advantage of this pattern is improved robustness in the presence of failures in the channels, without a large development overhead. Because all the channels are identical, they need only be "cloned" rather than redeveloped. Care should be taken that the channels are not only identical but also fully redundant so that single-point failures do not take out all channels simultaneously.[10]

A failure is an event that happens at a particular point in time. This is distinct from an error which is a systematic fault. An error is a flawed system condition—a system with an error has always had the error.

---

9. A *channel,* in this context, means a set of devices (including processors and software running on processors) that handle a related, cohesive set of data or control flows from incoming event to ultimate system response.

10. A Bell-Boeing V22 Osprey crashed because two roll-rate sensors were cross-wired, allowing the two faulty units to outvote the correct one. Similar faults were found in other flying V22 Ospreys [6].

The big disadvantage of homogeneous redundancy is that it detects only failures and not errors. Homogeneous redundancy cannot detect errors because, by definition, all channels are identical. If one channel contains an error, then all redundant channels contain the same error. This implies that homogenous redundancy protects only against hardware failures but not against software faults, because *software cannot fail.* Software can be wrong and full of errors, but it cannot suddenly break.

There are other disadvantages to redundancy. There is an increase in recurring cost because of the duplicated hardware devices. Redundant hardware also requires more space and power and generates more heat. In some real-time systems, this can be an important limitation. Figure 3-7 shows the pattern as an organization of subsystems.

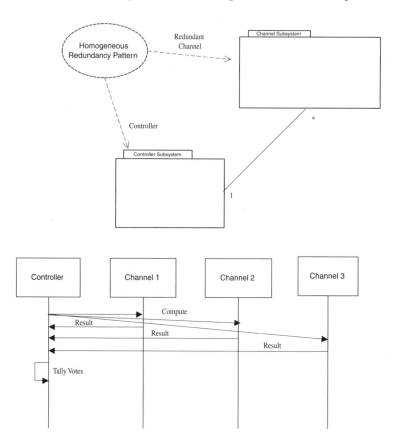

Figure 3-7: *Homogeneous Redundancy Pattern*

3.4.4 Diverse Redundancy Pattern

The *diverse redundancy pattern* mitigates the primary disadvantage of homogeneous redundancy by providing redundant channels that are implemented by using different means. This can be accomplished in several ways:

- Different but equal
- Lightweight redundancy
- Separation of monitoring and actuation

The first option is similar to the homogeneous redundancy pattern in that the channels are all approximately equal in terms of accuracy, throughput, and reliability. Each channel is implemented differently, using different software and hardware components, providing additional protection against errors, as well as failures. This is the most expensive of the three, but it does not only detect failures and errors but can also continue to execute correctly in the presence of such faults.

The second option is to use a lightweight secondary channel to ensure the correctness of the primary. This lightweight channel provides a reasonableness check on the results from the primary channel, but it does not have the same accuracy or range. It costs less to implement and manufacture but is better at fault detection than fault tolerance. The secondary channel can identify when the primary channel is broken, but it typically cannot take over all the primary's duties when this occurs. Other fault-tolerance means must be present if the system must remain operational in the presence of errors.

The separation of monitoring and actuation is discussed as a separate pattern in the next section.

Note in Figure 3-8 that the diverse channels share a common interface but have different implementations. It is not strictly required that the interfaces be identical, but it simplifies the software development. The requirement is that the channels do not have any common mode faults—that is, that they do not have the same systematic errors, nor can a single-point failure bring down multiple channels.

3.4.5 Monitor-Actuator Pattern

The *monitor-actuator pattern* is a special type of diverse redundancy. In this case, however, the channels are separated into monitoring and

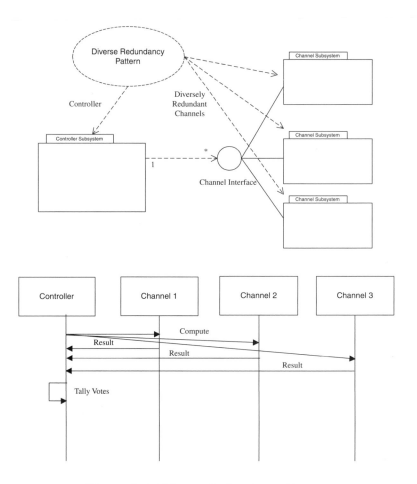

Figure 3-8: *Diverse Redundancy Pattern*

actuator channels. The actuator channel performs the actions, such as controlling the wing flaps, moving the control rods, and pacing the heart. The monitor channel keeps track of what the actuation is supposed to be doing and monitors the physical environment to ensure that the results of the actuator are appropriate. Note that the actuator itself cannot rely on this monitor—closed-loop actuators must use separate sensors that are independent of the sensor used in the monitoring channel.

The basic concept behind the monitor-actuator pattern is that the monitor channel identifies actuation-channel failures so that appropriate fault-handling mechanisms can be executed. Under the single-fault isolation assumption, if the monitor channel fails, it means that the actuator didn't fail, so it continues to be correct. As with all forms of redundancy, common mode failures must be eliminated to achieve the safety and fault-tolerance goals of the redundancy. The monitor and actuator channels exchange messages periodically to ensure both are operating properly, as well. The messages can also be sent to the controller, which decides the appropriate actuation.

The primary downside to this pattern is the (small) increased recurring cost caused by the additional monitoring channel. Nevertheless, in safety-critical or fault-sensitive situations, it can be a cost-effective

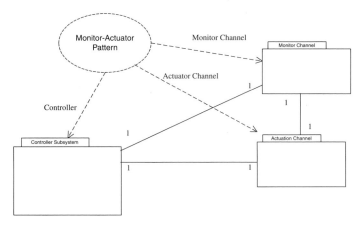

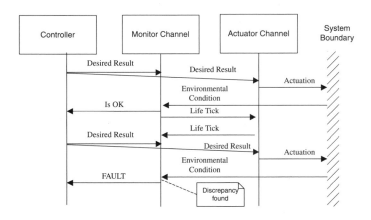

Figure 3-9: *Monitor-Actuator Pattern*

means for improving safety and reliability, compared with full homogeneous or diverse redundancy.

The scenario in Figure 3-9 shows how the desired result is sent to both the actuator and the monitor channels. The actuator uses this to decide the exact action it should take. The monitor uses this to check up on the result of the action to see if the goal was achieved. In the first case, the actuation was correct; in the second case, the monitor detected a large discrepancy between the commanded result and the actual environment. The controller can then take whatever corrective action seems appropriate.

Notice also the exchange of life-tick messages in the middle of the scenario. In this way, the actuator can detect when the monitor fails and vice versa.

3.4.6 Watchdog Pattern

A watchdog is a common concept in real-time embedded systems. A watchdog is a subsystem that receives messages from other subsystems on a periodic or sequence-keyed basis. If a service of the watchdog occurs too late or out of sequence, the watchdog initiates some corrective action, such as reset, shutdown, alarming to notify attending personnel, or signaling a more elaborate error-recovery mechanism. Watchdogs themselves tend to be simple and are often implemented in hardware to protect them from software faults. Although watchdogs are rather more mechanistic, they are usually used within a global scope of safety and redundancy, and so are included here.

Sometimes, software watchdogs are more active. Such watchdogs are woken up periodically and perform some built-in test (BIT) suite, such as performing CRC checks over the executable code, checking RAM, looking for evidence of stack overflow, and so forth. Although these are not watchdogs in the classic sense, they are simple to implement and are required in many safety-critical environments.

The advantage of watchdogs is that they are cheap and easy to implement. They don't require a lot of hardware or software support. However, many systems do not have a simple response to the detection of a system fault. Simply resetting an unattended ICU patient ventilator may not be the most appropriate action. This is the primary disadvantage of software watchdogs—they may be too simple to support complex error handling and fault recovery. Figure 3-10 shows the watchdog pattern.

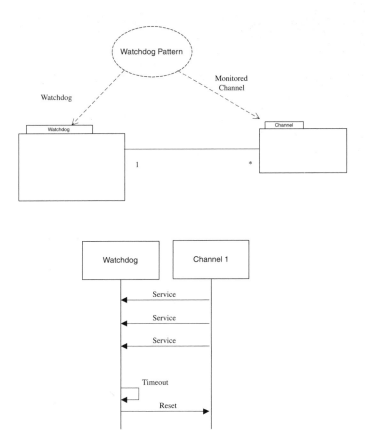

Figure 3-10: *Watchdog Pattern*

3.4.7 Safety Executive Pattern

The *safety executive pattern* uses a centralized coordinator for safety monitoring and control of system recovery from faults. It is also known as the safety kernel pattern. The safety executive acts like a really smart watchdog that tracks and coordinates all safety monitoring. Typically it captures the following inputs:

- Watchdogs timeouts
- Software error assertions
- Continuous or periodic BITs
- Faults identified by monitors in the monitor-actuation pattern

For larger and more-complex systems, a safety executive provides a consistent, centralized point for safety processing. This simplifies the application software, which might otherwise be riddled with extra checks and resulting actions that obscure the primary application purpose. Because the safety control is centralized, it becomes a simpler process to verify and validate the safety measures. Figure 3-11 shows the more elaborate structure of subsystems involved in the safety executive pattern.

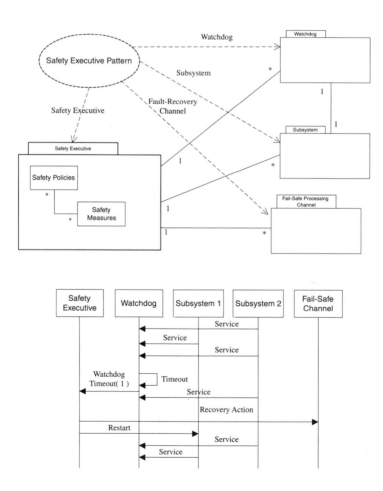

Figure 3-11: *Safety Executive Pattern*

3.5 Eight Steps to Safety

Building safe systems is not easy. Safety mechanisms can account for most of the complexity of a system. Nonetheless, building and deploying safe systems is the most important task of today's real-time systems developer. The process of constructing safe systems can be broken up into a multistep plan, called the eight steps to safety.

The eight steps to safety are

1. Identify the hazards
2. Determine the risks
3. Define the safety measures
4. Create safe requirements
5. Create safe designs
6. Implement safety
7. Assure the safety process
8. Test, test, test

The first three, Identify the hazards, Determine the risks, and Define the safety measures, all precede the finalization of the system requirements. The products of these activities—the hazards, risks, and measures—combine to form the hazard analysis, which contains all the identified hazards and specifies the risks and the measures to handle the hazards. This document then feeds into the system specification, which must identify the system-level architecture that provides the specified measures. The design and implementation steps then build the measures into the system. Testing creates the faults through a technique called *fault seeding,* to demonstrate the correct handling of the hazards.

The following sections discuss each issue in turn, but let us first consider the hazard analysis document itself.

3.5.1 Step 1: Identify the Hazards

The first step in developing safe systems is to determine the hazards of the system. Recall that a hazard is a condition that could allow a mishap to occur in the presence of other nonfault conditions. In a patient ventilator, one hazard is that the patient will not be ventilated, resulting in hypoxia and death. In an ECG monitor, electrocution is a hazard. A microwave oven can emit dangerous (microwave) radiation, cooking the tissues of the user. It is not uncommon for embedded systems to expose people to many potential hazards.

Naturally, a normally functioning system should provide no hazards. The identification of potential hazards is the first step; the compilation of the hazards forms the initial hazard analysis.

The hazard analysis is a report written at the same time, or even preceding, the system specification. This living document is continuously updated throughout the development process. It contains

- The identified hazards, including
  1. The hazard itself
  2. The level of risk
  3. The tolerance time—how long the hazardous condition can be tolerated before the condition results in an incident
- The means by which the hazards can arise:
  1. The fault leading to the hazard
  2. The likelihood of a fault
  3. The fault detection time
- The means by which the hazards are handled:
  1. The means
  2. The fault reaction (exposure) time

Such a table looks like Table 3-1.

Table 3-1 shows just a few entries for a hazard analysis of a patient ventilator.

Hypoventilation is a severe hazard, but one that can be tolerated for about five minutes. Several faults can lead to this hazard. The first is that the ventilator just quits working. We see that the system includes a secondary pressure alarm that detects the fault in 30 seconds. By 35 seconds, it raises an alarm to the user. This is an appropriate means for handling the hazard, because usual operation requires attendance by a qualified user. This would be an inappropriate means of control for an unattended ventilator.

Another fault that can occur is that the user fails to properly intubate the patient, and instead of inserting the endotracheal tube in the

Table 3-1: *Hazard Analysis*

Hazard	Level of risk	Tolerance Time T_t	Fault	Likelihood	Detection Time T_d	Reaction or Control Means	Exposure Time T_e
Hypo-ventilation	Severe	5 min	Vent fails	Rare	30 sec	Independent pressure alarm	35 sec
			Esophageal intubation	Medium	30 sec	CO_2 sensor alarm	40 sec
			User mis-attaches breathing circuit	Never	N/A	Different mechanical fasteners for intake vs. output	N/A
Over-pressur-ization	Severe	0.05 sec	Release valve failure	Rare	0.01 sec	Secondary valve opens	0.01 sec

trachea, he or she manages to put it in the esophagus. The secondary CO_2 monitor detects this hazard within 30 seconds. The breathing gas mixture delivered to the patient lacks significant CO_2, but CO_2 is present in high levels in normally expired gas. An insufficiently high level of CO_2 in the expiratory gas means the patient is not expiring. Thus, a secondary CO_2 monitor is an appropriate means for handling the hazard, again provided that an operator is in attendance.

The third fault identified is that the user attaches the breathing circuit hose to the wrong connectors of the ventilator. This can easily happen in an operating room, where there may be dozens of hoses lying around in the crowded area of the anesthesiologist. Designing different sizes of connectors eliminates this fault entirely.

The next hazard is that the patient's lungs are over-inflated, producing pulmonary barotrauma. This is a serious hazard that can also lead to death, particularly in neonates who lack a strong rib cage. Note that this fault cannot be tolerated for more than 50 ms, so alarming is an inappropriate measure for handling the condition. Here, a secondary mechanical over-pressure valve releases the pressure before it can rise to dangerous levels. The response time for the valve is 10 ms, well below the tolerance limit of 50 ms.

3.5.1.1 Determine the Faults Leading to Hazards

The hazard analysis identifies the hazards. Once hazards are identified, the faults causing the hazards must be determined. Fault-tree analysis, or FTA, is a common method for analyzing faults. An FTA graphically combines fault conditions using Boolean operators, OR, AND, and (less frequently) NOT. The typical use is to begin with an unsafe system state and work backward to identify the causal conditions that allowed it to happen. The analysis can be done from obvious fundamental faults and propagate forward as is done with failure modes and effect analysis (FMEA), discussed later.

The symbols identified in Figure 3-12 represent the Boolean equations for the combination and propagation of faults into hazards. The AND gate outputs a logical TRUE if and only if all its inputs are true—that is, the precursor events have occurred or conditions are present. The OR gate outputs a logical TRUE if any of its antecedents are true. The NOT gate outputs a TRUE only if its antecedent is false. The AND and OR gates may take any number of precursor events or inputs greater than one. The NOT gate takes a single input.

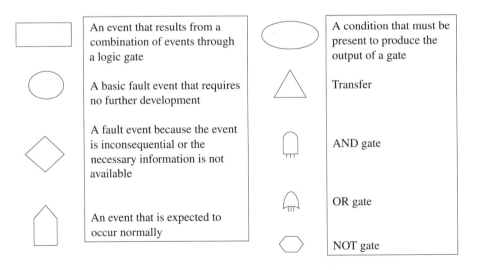

Figure 3-12: *Fault-Tree Analysis Notation*

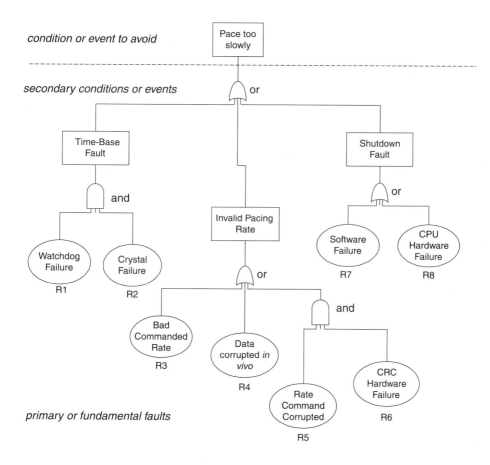

condition or event to avoid

secondary conditions or events

primary or fundamental faults

Figure 3-13: *Subset of Pacemaker Fault-Tree Analysis*

An example of a terminal (as in "highest level") fault condition is a pacemaker pacing too slowly, as shown in Figure 3-13.

Along the bottom of the figure appear the fundamental, or root, faults. Along the top is the unsafe resulting condition. This example limits itself to a single hazard—pacing too slowly. This can result from a number of fundamental faults. The time base that drives the pacing cycle could be incorrect, for example. This could be due to the CPU crystal drifting or failing. However, the independent watchdog circuit should detect such a fault, so it must also be in error for the hazard to arise in that fashion.

A fault condition might be that the stored pacing rate is incorrect. This could be due to any of a number of root causes. The physician could have incorrectly programmed the rate. EMI could corrupt a properly communicated rate after reception. The command telemetry itself could have been corrupted during transmission.

FTAs are nothing more than Boolean equations and can be written more compactly in that form. The example FTA can be written as

> Pacing Too Slowly = (Watchdog Failure ^ Crystal Failure) | (Bad Commanded Rate | Data Corrupted in vivo | (Rate Command Corrupted ^ CRC Hardware Failure)) | (Software Failure | CPU Hardware Failure)[11]

or more compactly yet:

$$T_1 = (R_1 \wedge R_2) \mid (R_3 \mid R_4 \mid (R_5 \wedge R_6)) \mid (R_7 \mid R_8)$$

However, such compact representations rarely assist in analyzing faults with problem-domain experts or regulatory-agency representatives.

FTA is a tool to assist in the identification of root faults leading to hazards. Remember that safe devices cannot lead to a hazard in the presence of a single fault. By this rule, it seems that the pacemaker is safe from time-base failure. This failure condition requires two undetected faults, one in the pacing time base and one in the watchdog. However, if the watchdog is not periodically checked, then its failure becomes a latent fault. In addition, it may be possible that a failure in the crystal also affects the watchdog. Specifically, if the CPU crystal provides the time base for the watchdog, as well, then the watchdog cannot detect an alteration in the time base.

The time-base failure can be discounted according to the single-point-failure rule only if both of the following conditions are met.

1. The watchdog is periodically checked.

2. There is no common mode failure between the pacing engine and the watchdog.

---

11. The "^" operator here stands for "and"; the " | " operator stands for "or."

FTA starts at hazards and tries to identify underlying precursor faults. FMEA starts with all components and their failure modes and looks forward to determine consequences. Many electrical engineers are familiar with FMEA from reliability assessment, so it is a well-known technique.

There are three main problems with FMEA in safety analysis. FMEA requires that all components be identified and characterized prior to analysis. However, these are usually not known until quite late in the design process. Because safety must be designed in, it is inappropriate to look *ex post facto* to see if your design is safe. The second problem is that it quickly becomes unwieldy in nontrivial designs. Components can typically fail in many ways, complicating a detailed analysis. Last, the failure modes for the components may not be well understood, limiting the usefulness of the analysis.

Other techniques have been applied to safety analysis, such as flowcharts, cause-effect graphs, and cause-consequent diagrams, but not as widely.

3.5.2 Step 2: Determine the Risks

The Food and Drug Administration (FDA) identifies three risk classes—minor, moderate, and major—with the definitions[12] shown in Table 3-2.

Table 3-2: *FDA Levels of Concern*

Level of Concern	Definition
Minor	Failures or latent design flaws would not be expected to result in injury or death.
Moderate	Failures or latent design flaws result in minor to moderate injury.
Major	Failures or latent design flaws result in death or serious injury.

---

12. The relevant standards for several standards organizations are discussed at the end of this chapter.

The German organization TUV has defined eight risk requirement categories that take into account the:

- Severity of the risk
- Duration of the period of exposure to the risk
- Prevention of the danger
- Probability of occurrence of the hazard

The TUV risk-level-determination chart in Figure 3-14 summarizes the process for risk determination.

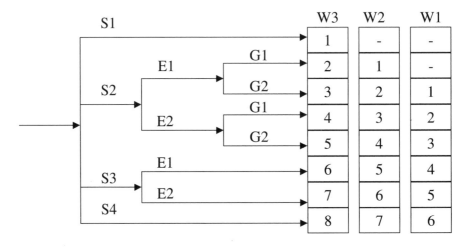

Risk Parameters
S: Extent of Damage
         S1: Slight injury
         S2: Severe irreversible injury to one or more persons or the death of a single person
         S3: Death of several persons
         S4: Catastrophic consequences, several deaths
E: Exposure Time
         E1: Seldom to relatively infrequent
         E2: Frequent to continuous
G: Hazard Prevention
         G1: Possible under certain conditions
         G2: Hardly possible
W: Occurrence Probability of Hazardous Event
         W1: Very Low
         W2: Low
         W3: Relatively High

Figure 3-14: *TUV Risk-Level-Determination Chart*

Table 3-3: *Risks of Various Devices*

Device	Hazard	Extent of Damage	Exposure Time	Hazard Prevention	Probability	TUV Risk Level
Micro-wave oven	Irradiation	S2	E2	G2	W3	5
Pace-maker	Pacing too slowly Pacing too fast	S2	E2	G2	W3	5
Power station burner control	Explosion	S3	E1	—	W3	6
Airliner	Crash	S4	E2	G2	W2	8

We can see that one of the parameters—Extent of Damage—closely correlates with the FDA risk classes.

TUV regulates the safety of many kinds of devices, including industrial robots; mass transit vehicles, such as airplanes and trains; and conventional and nuclear power plants. The FDA limits its concerns to medical devices[13] that expose one or a small number of people to risk at any one time. TUV deals with hazards to hundreds or thousands of people at a time.

To use the TUV risk-level-determination chart, consider how each parameter applies to your system. Some examples are shown in Table 3-3.

TUV requires risk determination for each hazard in your system. Table 3-3 shows the risk for only one hazard per device. TUV requires specific means of control for each risk category.

3.5.3 Step 3: Define the Safety Measures

A safety measure is a behavior added to a system to handle a hazard. There are many ways to handle a hazard.

---

13. They also regulate drugs, but that is beyond the scope of this book.

- *Obviation* The hazard can be made physically impossible.
- *Education* The hazard can be handled by educating the users so that they won't create hazardous conditions through equipment misuse.
- *Alarming* Announce the hazard to the user when it appears so that he or she can take appropriate action.
- *Interlocks* The hazard can be removed by using secondary devices or logic to intercede when a hazard presents itself.
- *Internal checking* The hazard can be handled by ensuring that a system can detect it is malfunctioning prior to an incident.
- *Safety equipment* Goggles, gloves, and so forth can be used.
- *Restriction of access* Access to potential hazards can be restricted so that only knowledgeable users have such access.
- *Labeling* The hazard can be handled by labeling—for example, *High Voltage, DO NOT TOUCH.*

Many considerations arise when applying a means of control to a hazard, such as:

- Tolerance time
- Risk level
- Supervision of the device—constant, occasional, unattended
- Skill level of the user—unskilled or expert users; trained or untrained
- Environment in which the system operates
- Likelihood of the fault that gives rise to the hazard
- Exposure time to the hazard because of the detection and response times of the means
- Scope of the fault's effects—can the condition that induced the fault also affect the means of control?

A control measure must factor in all these considerations to effectively handle a fault condition.

3.5.4 Step 4: Create Safe Requirements

A reliable system is one that continuously meets its availability requirements. A safe system is one that prevents mishaps and avoids hazardous conditions. Specifying a safe system often means specifying negations, such as: *The system shall not energize the laser when the safety interlock is active*, or: *The system shall not pass more than 10 mA through the ECG lead.*

Good specifications do not unnecessarily constrain the design. Safety requirements handle hazards that are intrinsic to the system and its environment. Design decisions introduce design hazards. Requirement specifications generally do not address design hazards. Design hazards must be added to the hazard analysis and tracked during the development process.

3.5.5 Step 5: Create Safe Designs

Creating safe designs is not an easy task. The design must take into account the complexity of the fundamental problem and add the complexity of the additional safety measures while identifying and handling possible common mode failures.

A general approach for safe designs is

- Work from safe requirements.
- Adopt a fundamentally safe architecture.
- Periodically, during design, revisit the hazard analysis to add hazards due to failures specific to the design.
- Select programming-in-the-small measures that provide the appropriate levels of detection and correction.
- Ensure that independent channels truly lack common mode failures.
- Adopt a consistent and appropriate set of strategies for handling faults once they are identified.
- Build in power-on and periodic run-time tests to identify latent faults.

This chapter has discussed most of these steps already. The last issue now bears discussion.

Almost all systems perform tests when they reset or power up. This is commonly called the power-on self-test, or POST. Embedded systems typically also include continuously executing or periodic tests, called built-in tests, or BITs. To ensure safety, the POST must test all system features used to detect faults. The BIT may also need to test for the same faults, depending on the fault-exposure time and the fault-tolerance time. For hazards with significant exposure—class E2 in the TUV risk-assessment chart—the BIT must test the fault-detection measure more frequently than the fault-tolerance time. BITs commonly contain tests for RAM and ROM to ensure data and code integrity, as well as tests for custom hardware. Some systems periodically activate the safety system as part of their BIT.

Consider a system monitoring a pressure sensor in a chemical tank designed to handle an over-pressure condition for 10 seconds. The system CPU monitors the tank and implements a control measure, such as venting the tank, when it detects the hazard. The BIT must test for all faults that can affect the safety function at least every 10 seconds—the fault-reaction time. This may mean testing 1 MB RAM with a "walking bit" test, performing a CPU test, executing a ROM CRC test, and so forth. Special hardware can be added to simulate excessive pressure, to periodically check the safety sensor. If the required BIT cannot execute within the fault-tolerance time, then the system must provide another safety control measure, such as an automatic secondary venting system.

BITs typically identify only hard failures—that is, persistent hardware failures. They usually cannot identify soft or systematic failures. Soft failures involve corruption of information or state, such as the flipping of a bit due to EMI, without permanent damage to the hardware. Systematic faults cannot, in principle, be identified by the BIT, or the system would never ship in the first place. Other means, such as data and control redundancy, can identify these faults. The underlying programming language often provides native mechanisms, such as runtime range checking and exception handling.

3.5.6 Step 6: Implementing Safety

Even with a safe design, implementation decisions affect system safety. Some of the issues are

- Language choice
  1. Compile-time checking (C vs. Ada)
  2. Run-time checking (C vs. Ada)
- Exceptions vs. error codes
- "Safe" language subsets (for example, avoiding void *)

3.5.6.1 Language Selection

It has been said: *"C treats you like a consenting adult. Pascal treats you like a naughty child. Ada treats you like a criminal."*

When considering a language for a safety-critical system, the language features that improve safety include

- Strong compile-time checking
- Strong run-time checking
- Support for encapsulation and abstraction
- Exception handling

Compilers for strongly typed languages perform compile-time checking so that the feature has no execution-time overhead. The compiler checks the grammar of the language to guarantee that no grammatical rules are broken. In Pascal, for example, the code

```
Program WontCompile1;
type
   MySubRange = 10 .. 20;
   Day = {Monday, Tuesday, Wednesday, Thursday,
      Friday,   Saturday, Sunday};
var
   MyVar: MySubRange
   MyDate: Day;
begin
   MyVar := 9; { will not compile — range error!}
   MyDate := 0;  { will not compile — wrong type! }
end.
```

won't compile because two rules are broken. The first assigns an out-of-range value to a subrange type. Because the compiler knows the constant value, it can check and reliably assert that the statement breaks the subrange-value-declaration rule. The second bad line attempts to assign an integer numeric value to an enumerated type—a violation of the strong typing rule.

·There are certainly cases in which the compiler cannot know ahead of time that the grammatical rules will be broken. Strongly typed languages usually execute run-time assertions when the software breaks grammatical rules during run-time.[14] Consider the Ada code segment

---

14. C++ bucks this trend to stay compatible with C, but C++ provides the means to safely extend the language to include run-time checking.

```
Procedure MyProc is
Var
   MyArray: array (1..10) of integer;
   j: integer;
   b: byte;
begin
   for j in 0 .. 10 loop
      MyArray(j) := j^6; -- raises an exception
            - on first time through
   end loop;
   b := MyArray(10); -- will fail run-time range check
end MyProc;
```

Ada is not the only language that will catch the errors in the code above. So will Pascal, Modula-2, and other ALGOL-derived languages. Pascal and Modula-2 will raise the error and terminate the program. This is usually unacceptable for embedded systems. Some languages, such as Ada and C++, extend the run-time checking to include run-time recovery by using user-defined exceptions and exception handlers.

The downside of run-time checking is, of course, that it takes place at run-time. Consider the Pascal statement

```
a[j] := b;
```

The compiler must generate additional code for this statement, which slightly increases the size of the executable code. Even worse, from most embedded developers' points of view, is that it must take the time to execute this additional code. A C program would just take the value from *b* and stick it into an address at offset *j* from the start of the array *a*. The Pascal run-time system would first verify that the index *j* is neither below the first valid index for the array nor above the last valid index. C performs no array index bound checking, but Pascal guarantees array assignments are only written within the confines of the array. Second, the Pascal run-time system must check that the current value of *b* is within the valid range for elements of array *a* prior to actually making the assignment. These kinds of run-time checks are *program-invariant assertions*. They verify invariant (that is, constantly valid) conditions during program execution. The good news is that Pascal totally insulates programmers from the most common C programming errors; the bad news is that the run-time system is larger and the program runs slower.

The fundamental rules of safe programming are

- *Make it right before you make it fast.*
- *Verify that it remains right during program execution.*
    1. *Explicitly check pre-conditional invariants.*
    2. *Explicitly check post-conditional invariants.*

Many real-time programmers avoid run-time checking because of the overhead involved, violating the second rule. *In a safety-critical system, it is unacceptable not to check for array index validity or subrange value bounding or other invariant assertions.*

Exceptions are a commonly available language feature that can improve safety. Pascal can detect some run-time failures, but the language provides no means for dealing with them. Ada was the first widely available commercial language to provide exception handling as a way to handle run-time errors. The C idiom of returning error codes as function values exemplifies the traditional approach to error handling. Returning a 0 means that the function was successful; nonzero, if it was not. The problem is that checking the return values is a manual process—the user of the function must remember to check the return value every time the function is used. In C, this is often not done. When was the last time you saw the result from a *printf* statement checked? It is all too easy to circumvent the error-handling system, so errors go unhandled even if detected!

The other problem is that the traditional approach thoroughly intermingles the error-handling code with the normal execution code, obscuring both. Consider the following code.

```
a = getfone(&b,&c);
if (a) {
   switch (a) {
      case 1: ...
      case 2: ...
   }
}
d = getftwo(b,c);
if (d) {
   switch (a) {
      case 1: ...
      case 2: ...
   }
}
```

In this code, the normal execution path is simply:

```
a = getfone(&b,&c);
d = getftwo(b,c);
```

and the rest is error-handling code. If the error-handling code is present, then it obscures the source code. If it is not, then errors are neither detected nor handled.

The exception-handling model addresses both concerns, guaranteeing that errors are not ignored and that the normal execution path is separate from the error-handling code. In Ada, exceptions are a scalar type that the user can extend. Built-in operations, such as mathematical operators, can raise exceptions, as can the programmer. What makes exceptions so powerful, though, is that the built-in exception type can be extended to add new problem-domain exceptions. An enqueue procedure may add the *overflow* and *underflow* exceptions:

```
procedure enqueue (q: in out queue; v: in FLOAT) is
begin
   if full(q) then
      raise overflow;
   end if;
   q.body(q.head + q.length) mod qSize := v;
   q.length := q.length + 1;
end enqueue;
```

The caller of the enqueue procedure then must handle the overflow condition, as in:

```
procedure testQ(q: in out queue) is
begin
   for j in 1..10 loop
      enqueue(q, random(1000));
   end loop;
   exception
      when overflow =>
         puts("Test failed due to queue overflow");
end testQ;
```

If the testQ procedure does not handle the exception, it terminates when the exception is raised and its caller's exception handler gets control.

C++ extends the exception-handling capabilities beyond that of Ada. C++ exceptions are extended by *type* rather than by *value*. This means it is possible to create hierarchies of exception classes and catch the exception by the thrown[15] subclass type. This allows the class to contain different types of information, depending on the kind of failure. A hardware failure might contain the information about the kind of device that failed and its physical address or port. A data-structure-integrity failure might contain the method used to detect it, such as CRC, range checking, and so forth. This allows the agent throwing the exception to return information relevant to the fault, which facilitates error recovery, debugging, and user-error reporting.

Booch suggests that exception classes should at least contain the name of the exception thrown, who threw it, and why the exception was thrown [8]. He suggests a textual representation for the exception information, implying that the information is to be displayed to a user. This may or may not be reasonable for an embedded system. The ANSI C++ committee has recently accepted a similar exception hierarchy for inclusion into the standard library for C++, as shown in Figure 3-15.

Strongly typed languages, such as C++, Pascal, and Ada, lessen the opportunities for design errors to creep into code. Run-time checking makes it even more likely that the software is actually performing correctly. C++ does not provide native run-time checking, but objects can easily add it. Overloading the [] operator with index range checking improves the robustness of arrays. Making classes of scalars and overloading the assignment operator allows additional range and value checking. Exception handling is a powerful tool for the separation of normal code from error-handling code, guaranteeing errors are handled.

Language selection is an emotionally charged issue with many developers and regulatory agencies alike. At least one TUV consultant has gone so far as to suggest that no safety-critical system should ever be written in C!

3.5.7 Step 7: Assure Safety Process

ISO 9000 is a quality standard and concerns itself solely with defining repeatable processes. The FDA defines a good manufacturing process (GMP) guideline that addresses the same issues. A quality process is one in which the quality of the product is stable and repeatable from product to product. Implementing some key process activities can improve product safety.

---

15. In Ada, exceptions are *raised*. In C++, they are *thrown*.

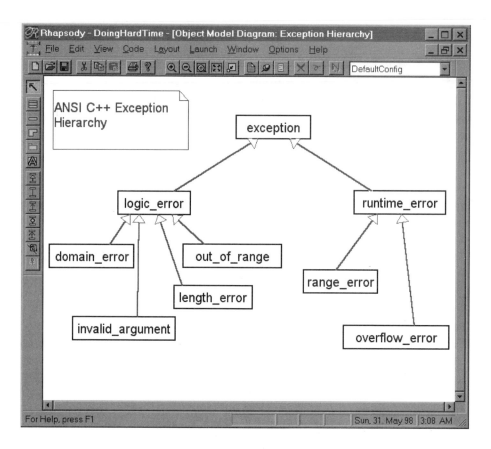

Figure 3-15: *ANSI C++ Exception Class Hierarchy*

- Continuously track against hazard analysis.
- Use peer reviews to assure quality.
- Verify design adherence.
- Verify coding standard adherence.
- Identify how each hazard is handled.

Most of these activities occur in any well-defined development process.[16] The draft safety standard IEC 65A/1508 defines a formidable safety process, the Overall Safety Lifecycle, as shown in Figure 3-16.

---

16. Which is to say, in far too few R&D departments.

IEC Overall Safety Lifecycle*

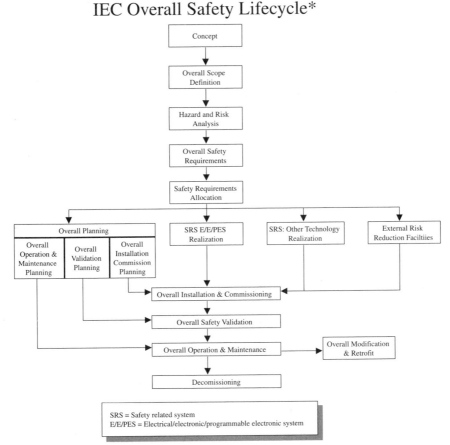

*Adapted from Draft IEC 65A/1508-1 Functional Safety:
Safety Related Systems, Part 1: General Requirements

Figure 3-16: *Overall Safety Lifecycle*

3.5.8 Step 8: Test, Test, Test

The final barrier to hazards that the developer can control is to test the bejeezus out of it. Many excellent texts exist on how to test systems; that information will not be repeated here. One concept to stress, however, is *fault seeding*. By the time code is available for testing, the hazard analysis should identify all faults that affect safety. Fault seeding is nothing more than inducing (or simulating) those faults to verify that the system acts in the safe, correct manner when the faults occur.

Unit testing is primarily white-box, meaning that the tests themselves must understand the detailed inner workings of the system. Unit tests check things like arithmetic statements, fence-post (boundary) conditions, and path execution. Fault seeding during unit testing means doing things like violating system invariants by passing in out-of-range values, or corrupting the data halfway through a procedure.

Integration testing is typically gray-box. In a distributed processor system, each processor is usually unit tested before it undergoes any level of integration. Integration testing adds the components together in a piece-wise fashion. The integration platform simulates missing or unavailable components as needed. Integration testing checks the interfaces among the interacting components, as well as checking some broad measure of the functionality. Fault seeding during integration might be done by:

- Breaking the communications bus
- Forcing or simulating a component failure
- Sending messages with the incorrect parity or CRC
- Abruptly removing power or inducing a current surge
- Flooding the bus with messages (valid or invalid)
- Exposing the system to strong EMI

Validation testing is usually totally black-box, meaning it tests the end-user requirements rather than internal design decisions. Fault seeding can uncover safety-related failure modes by inducing environmental conditions that can lead to failures, such as spilling coffee in the air vents, inducing a power surge, and so forth. To test large-scale structures, such as dual-channel architectures, safety compliance testing can use internal information for fault seeding.

All three kinds of testing are useful in uncovering safety-related failure modes. Each test phase requires a test plan that outlines each test, its purpose, use, and interpretation. The handling of each hazard in the hazard analysis must be verified by at least one test.

3.6 A Few Safety-Related Standards

There are many safety standards. The FDA has long applied its regulations to medical devices. The FDA's standard, however, addresses more a quality process than determination and assurance of safety. In this respect, the FDA standard is similar to the ISO 9000 series of standards. The FDA and ISO 9000 standards do not directly address safety but assume that a quality process enhances product safety. Although this is changing, the FDA has traditionally kept out of the internals of medical devices and has, instead, audited development processes.

Europeans have taken a different view. The German draft standards VDE 0801 and the similar TUV DIN 19250 have been around for a long time. The German organization TUV regulates the safety of a wide variety of products. German standards are much more concerned with identifying specific hazards and with verifying that proper safety measures are in place.

The draft UL standard takes a similar approach to VDE 0801 but is less detailed. The German standards identify distinct risk categories and levels of safety measures required for each. The UL standard identifies a number of measures but does not specify the conditions under which various measures are appropriate.

These standards are being supplanted by the new IEC 65A/1508 series of standards, which rigidly prescribe both process and safety measures. The process requirements are quite rigorous, as previously shown.

The risk category and required level of safety together determine the technical safety measures that must be applied. Table 3-4 shows the IEC 65A/1508 safety integrity levels, the corresponding VDE 0801 risk level, and the general requirement for the number of dangerous failures per year.

This chapter defines the important concepts of safety and safe systems. To be compliant with the standards requires detailed reading of the standards and very specific implementation of their requirements. The interested reader is referred to the standards themselves for the specific tasks required for standards adherence.

Table 3-4: *Equivalence of Safety Standards*

IEC Safety Integrity Level	VDE 0801 Risk Level	FDA Risk Classes	Demand Mode of Operation*	Continuous/High Demand Mode of Operation†
4	4-5	Major	$>= 10^{-5}$ to $< 10^{-4}$	$>= 10^{-5}$ to $< 10^{-4}$
3	3-4	Major	$>= 10^{-4}$ to $< 10^{-3}$	$>= 10^{-4}$ to $< 10^{-3}$
2	2-3	Moderate	$>= 10^{-3}$ to $< 10^{-2}$	$>= 10^{-3}$ to $< 10^{-2}$
1	1-2	Minor	$>= 10^{-2}$ to $< 10^{-1}$	$>= 10^{-2}$ to $< 10^{-1}$

*Probability of failure to perform its design function on demand.
†Probability of a dangerous failure per year.

Source: Table adapted from the IEC standard 65A/1508-1, quoted in the next section.

3.6.1 Some Important Safety Standards

IEC 65A/1508-1 Functional Safety: Safety-Related Systems, Part 1: General Requirements, June 1995 Draft.

IEC 65A/1508-2 Functional Safety: Safety-Related Systems, Part 2: Requirements for Electrical/Electronic/Programmable Electronic Systems, June 1995 Draft.

IEC 65A/1508-3 Functional Safety: Safety-Related Systems, Part 3: Software Requirements, June 1995 Draft.

IEC 65A/1508-4 Functional Safety: Safety-Related Systems, Part 4: Definitions and Abbreviations of Terms, June 1995 Draft.

IEC 65A/1508-5 Functional Safety: Safety-Related Systems, Part 5: Guidelines on the Application of Part 1, June 1995 Draft.

IEC 65A/1508-6 Functional Safety: Safety-Related Systems, Part 6: Guidelines of the Application of Parts 2 and 3, June 1995 Draft.

IEC 65A/1508-7 Functional Safety: Safety-Related Systems, Part 7: Bibliography of Techniques and Measures, June 1995 Draft.

DIN V 19250 Measurement and Control: Fundamental Safety Aspects for Measuring and Controlling Protective Equipment, January 1989 Draft.

DIN V VDE 0801: General Requirements for Safety in Computer-Controlled Electronic Devices, October 1991 Draft (English translation).

Standard for Safety-Related Software UL 1998 First Edition, Underwriter Laboratories, January 1994 Draft.

Reviewer Guidance for Computer-Controlled Medical Devices Undergoing 510(k) Review, FDA, 1991.

3.7 Summary

Software is becoming more pervasive in safety systems all the time. Software developers must become increasingly aware of the hazards to the users and bystanders from the systems they develop. The key document for the construction of safe systems is the hazard analysis. This living document is maintained throughout the project, evolving in the design, coding, and testing phases.

Hazards can be handled in many ways. Designing out hazards where possible is usually best, but it is not always possible or feasible. Safe designs use either protected single channels that can protect themselves within the fault-tolerance time from errors, or dual-channel systems that use different channels to watch each other to ensure safety.

Coding issues for safety are language selection and use of safe coding styles. Languages that provide strong compile-time and run-time checking are considered "safer" than those that do not. Exceptions provide a valuable tool for improving safety, without obscuring the intent of the normal execution code.

Finally, testing is vitally important for any safety-related system. Apart from other test methods, fault seeding is crucial to verify that the identified hazards are truly handled properly.

There are many standards relating to safety. Some standards focus exclusively on system quality through development and manufacturing process control. Others, such as the European safety standards, address specific architectures and measures to meet required levels of safety.

3.8 Looking Ahead

The first chapter discussed the basic concepts of objects ala the UML. The second chapter introduced basic concerns and issues of real-time systems. This chapter identified the issues surrounding the development of safe and highly reliable systems. The next chapter will conclude our introduction by discussing the software-development process in general, and the ROPES process in particular. This will round out the conceptual framework that we will use in the rest of this book.

3.9 Exercises

1. Define the difference among safety, reliability, and security.
2. How is reliability measured?
3. How is safety determined?
4. What is the difference between a hazard and a risk?
5. Do random faults occur in hardware? Software? What about systematic faults?
6. In what ways do hazards manifest themselves?
7. What is the fault-tolerance time?
8. State the most fundamental safety-architecture concept.
9. What are the two types of redundancy?
10. What must be defined for each hazard listed in a hazard analysis?
11. Consider a computer-controlled chemical-mixing system that consists of many elements—reagent vats, mixing vat, valves for each reagent flow to the mixing vat, mixture draining valve, pressure and temperature sensors, and a venting valve. Identify the faults that could lead to an explosion, using fault-tree analysis. What is the risk level using the TUV risk-determination chart?
12. Design a single-channel protected architecture that prevents an explosion if the temperature or pressure gets too high for the above chemical-mixing system.

13. Design a dual-channel architecture for the chemical-mixing system to meet the same objectives.

14. Name five means of controlling a hazard.

15. What is the fundamental rule of safe programming?

16. What is fault seeding, and why is it used?

17. Identify some possible common mode failures for a computer-controlled drive-by-wire automobile in which a single computer replaces all mechanical linkages (see Figure 3-17).

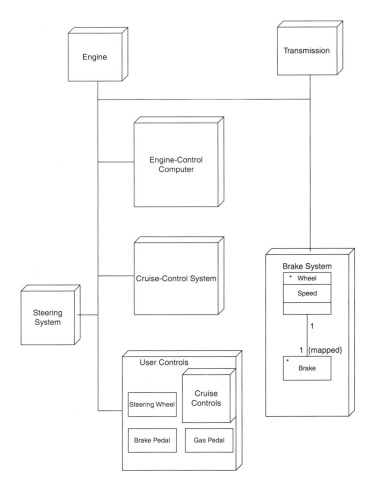

Figure 3-17: *Drive-by-Wire Automobile Architecture*

3.10 References

[1]   Leveson, Nancy. *Safeware*, Reading, Mass.: Addison-Wesley, 1995.

[2]   Neumann, Peter G. *Computer Related Risks*, Reading, Mass.: Addison-Wesley, 1995.

[3]   Booch, Grady. *Object Solutions: Managing the Object-Oriented Project*, Reading, Mass.: Addison-Wesley, 1996.

[4]   Friedman, Michael and Jeffrey Voas. *Software Assessment: Reliability, Safety, and Testability*, New York: John Wiley and Sons, 1995.

[5]   Weber, Marcus. "Functional and Software Safety—The German Approach," In *International Medical Device and Diagnostic Industry*, March/April 1991.

[6]   *VDE-0801 Principles for Computers in Safety-Related Systems*, German Electrotechnical Commission of the German Standards Institute, 1990.

[7]   Brilliant, Susan, John Knight, and Nancy Leveson. "Analysis of Faults in an *N*-Version Software Experiment," *IEEE Transactions on Software Engineering*, SE-16(2), 1990.

[8]   Booch, Grady. *Object-Oriented Analysis and Design with Applications*, Redwood City, Calif.: Benjamin Cummings Press, 1994.

[9]   Douglass, Bruce Powel. *Real-Time UML: Developing Efficient Objects for Embedded Systems*, Reading, Mass.: Addison-Wesley, 1998.

[10] Storey, Neil. *Safety-Critical Computer Systems*, Reading, Mass.: Addison-Wesley, 1996.

Chapter 4

Rapid Object-Oriented Process for Embedded Systems

Think horizontally, implement vertically.

—Book of Douglass, Law 69

The UML defines a generic semantic framework for capturing and expressing object models, including epistemological metamodel elements and a graphical notation for capturing models expressed using these elements. Real-time and safety concepts can be captured using these metamodel elements and can serve as building blocks for system models. So far, we haven't discussed how to use these metamodel elements in the sequence of development activities to profitably and efficiently construct systems. Although the UML and the more specific concepts of real-time and safety systems can be used in a variety of processes, this chapter will present one called ROPES. ROPES is a development process that emphasizes rapid turnaround, early proofs of correctness, and low risk. ROPES will serve as a context for the discussion of detailed activities of systems development to come later in this book.

4.1 Introduction

Creating software is not truly an engineering activity in which the application of known rules against a problem statement repeatedly results in a highly reliable, cost-effective solution. The creation of good software is notoriously difficult and depends in great measure on the skill of the individual developers. The current state of the art portrays developing software as a technological craft rather than as an engineering discipline. The creation of software is difficult primarily because software is essentially a model of a real or conceptual world. Any such world is filled with a complexity that exceeds the capabilities of any person to completely comprehend at one time.

The language and semantic models of software models are reasonably mature, although they are still evolving. Nevertheless, the systems they model defy complete and formal description. The more complete the model, the more accurate and representative the model becomes, but also the more difficult it is to create and prove correct.

The developer is left with a problem. On one hand, he or she has a real-world system that must be created. On the other hand, the developer has semantic models and notations to capture the essential characteristics of the system and its informational and control context. How can our developer use these modeling elements to represent the system in a complete and accurate way that is understandable, portable, modifiable, and correct? What steps are necessary in this quest and in what order should they be applied? The problem is little different from knowing a large number of French words but not knowing how to string them together into sentences. The problem to be solved, however, is not to make sentences; it is to create a book of poetry in which the various phrases, refrains, and poems come together into an integrated whole. *How* to accomplish this task is ultimately answered by the development process.

A question commonly asked by managers is, "Why bother with process?" Aside from keeping Scott Adams, author of the Dilbert comic strip, dutifully employed, process allows us to

- Produce systems of consistent quality
- Reliably produce systems with complex behavioral requirements
- Predict when systems will be complete
- Predict how much systems will cost to develop
- Identify milestones during development, enabling mid-course corrections when necessary
- Enable efficient team collaboration for moderate and large-scale systems

4.2 Terms and Concepts

A *methodology* consists of several parts: a semantic framework, a notational schema, a set of sequenced work activities, and a set of deliverable work artifacts. The semantic framework and its notational schema together comprise the *modeling language,* such as the UML. The *development process* describes the activities that govern the use of the language elements and the set of design artifacts resulting from the application of these in a defined sequence of activities.

4.2.1 Development Phases

This process is divided up into large-scale activities in an effort to simplify and clarify what needs to be done and when. These phases are called analysis, design, translation, and testing. *Analysis* consists of identification of the essential characteristics of all possible correct solutions. *Design* adds elements to the analysis that define one particular solution on the basis of the optimization of some criteria. *Translation* creates an executable, deployable realization of the design. *Testing* verifies that the translation is equivalent to the design and validates that the implementation meets all the criteria for correctness identified in the analysis.

All these phases work on the *model* of the system, which is an organized, internally consistent set of abstractions that collaborate to achieve system description at a desired level of detail and maturity. It is important to understand that the analysis model, design model, translation (source code) model, and testing model are not different models that are somehow linked. They are (or at least ought to be) different *views* of the same system model. If you understand the work artifacts of the various phases to capture different models, then you permit them to vary independently. All software engineers have had the experience that the more abstract models can deviate from the source code. This is always a bad thing. An essential ingredient to the ROPES process is that all the artifacts of the model under development must always be of the same underlying thing. They are allowed to focus on different aspects, just as architects use different views (floor plans, electrical conduit plans, and plumbing plans, for example) to focus on different aspects of the same building.

Analysis may be divided into several subphases: requirements analysis, systems analysis, and object analysis. *Requirements analysis* is the process of extracting the requirements from the customer and structuring them into a comprehensible form. *Systems analysis* builds more-rigorously defined models, and based on these requirements, partitions the system behavior into mechanical, electronic, and software components. Systems analysis is used in the development of complex systems such as those in the aircraft, automotive, and factory automation industries. Many real-time domains may skip the systems analysis step because the system architecture is sufficiently simple that it does not require it.

Both requirements and systems analysis are in their very essence functional descriptions of the system and rely heavily on behavioral and functional decomposition. The structural units of this decomposition are behaviors, functions, and activities. These structural elements are arranged into *system models*. The system model, along with the requirements model, form the *system specification*.

The third aspect of analysis is *object analysis*. This is a fundamentally different way to model the system under development. Object analysis consists of two subphases. *Structural object analysis* identifies the structural units of object decomposition as classes and objects, their organizational units (packages, nodes, and components), and the inherent relations among these elements. *Behavioral object analysis* defines essential dynamic behavioral models for the identified classes. Moving from systems analysis to object analysis requires a nontrivial translation step.

Design may likewise be divided into the subphases of architectural, mechanistic, and detailed designs. *Architectural design* identifies the large-scale organizational pieces of the deployable software system. Architectural design consists of different views of the underlying semantic model. The *deployment view* organizes the elements of the object analysis into executable components that execute on various processor nodes. The *development view* organizes the nonexecutable artifacts (such as source code) on which individuals work into pieces that enable team members to effectively manage their work and their collaboration with other team members. The *concurrency view* identifies the concurrency context of the objects. The structural elements defined during architectural design constitute strategic design decisions that have wide-reaching impact on the software structure. The decisions are largely driven by the application of architectural design patterns, as discussed in Chapter 8.

An object itself is a small unit of decomposition. Objects collaborate in clusters to achieve larger-scale purposes. A *collaboration* is a collection of objects collaborating to achieve a common purpose, such as the realization of a use case. A *mechanism* is the reification of a collaboration (such as a design pattern). The process of gluing these mechanisms together from their object parts constitutes *mechanistic design*. Similar to architectural design, much of mechanistic design proceeds by using mechanistic design patterns, adding "glue" objects to facilitate the collaboration.

Detailed design defines structures and organizes the internals of individual classes. This often includes translation patterns for how model structures will be coded, the visibility and data typing of attributes, and the realization of associations, aggregations, and compositions in the selected programming language.

Design can proceed using either of two strategies. The most common is *elaboration*. Using this approach, design proceeds by refining and elaborating the analysis models until the model is implementable. In this approach, the design information is added to the analysis model. The other approach, called *translation*, captures the design information in a translator, which is then applied against the analysis model to produce the executable system. The translation approach commonly uses a context-specific framework and rules for translating analysis concepts into programming language statements automatically. Rhapsody, from

I-Logix, is a UML-compliant design automation tool that works in exactly this way. The details of Rhapsody are discussed in Appendix B, and a demo copy of Rhapsody is provided on the CD-ROM that accompanies this book.

Elaboration does not require as much tool support, but generally takes longer. This is because once constructed, the translator can be applied against many analysis models and must be modified only when design decisions change. In addition, the use of a real-time framework greatly facilitates the construction of real-time systems, because most of the common mechanisms required for such systems are captured in the framework and used automatically by the translated analysis elements.

4.2.2 Ordering

Not only does a process consider the work activities and the products of that work, it must also define the order in which these activities are

---

Is Automatically Generated Code a Reality?

A question I often hear is whether the technology for generating code automatically from UML object models is mature enough to use in real systems. Certainly, the elaborative approach is more common. However, automatically generated code can and is being used today in a variety of hard real-time and embedded systems. Most systems are between 60 percent and 90 percent "housekeeping" and framework software. This software really varies little from system to system, but it must, nevertheless, be typically written from scratch for each system. Some design automation tools not only provide this framework, but also "glue" your object models into that framework. Microsoft MFC library provided such a framework for Windows programmers and greatly facilitated the development of Windows-based applications. Real-time frameworks do the same for embedded real-time systems today. Real-time frameworks provide a consistent way for dealing with event reception and handling, finite state machine operation, control of concurrency, operating system abstraction, and so on. For more detail, see Chapter 13.

performed. The entire set of work activities that are organized into a sequence is called a *lifecycle*. Different lifecycle models are in use, with varying degrees of success.

While the phases identify *what* must be done, the lifecycle model specifies *when* it must be done. This can take place at both the micro-cycle level and the macro-cycle level [1]. A micro cycle defines the ordering of activities within a portion of a macro cycle or within a single iteration of an iterative macro cycle.

4.2.3 Maturity

Deciding on these phases and the order of development-related activities is not enough. Each phase contains *activities* (things that developers do) and results in *artifacts* (deliverable work products). These artifacts have different levels of *maturity*. The maturity of an artifact refers to both its *completeness* and its *quality*. The completeness of an artifact refers to how much of the intended scope of the artifact has been considered and taken into account within the artifact. An artifact's quality is a comparison between the specific artifact and the optimal qualities of artifacts of its kind. This is often subjective, leading to the statement that, as with art, "I know bad software when I see it."[1]

4.3 Development-Task Sequencing

Before we discuss the methods, procedures, and artifacts of the ROPES process, let's consider lifecycles in more detail. There are two primary approaches to sequencing development phases. The *waterfall lifecycle* is the most common lifecycle and orders the phases in a linear fashion. The waterfall lifecycle has the advantage of simplicity and strong tool support. Other lifecycles are based on iterations of the phases. The advantage of these *iterative lifecycles* is that they allow early risk reduction and better mid-course control over development projects.

---

1. One indication that a design or source code is "bad" is when the reviewer suddenly drops the source code on the floor, clutches his eyes and yells "I'm blind! I'm blind!" while running from the room.

4.3.1 Waterfall Lifecycle

The waterfall lifecycle approach is based on the serialization of development phases into a strict order. The artifacts produced within the phase must all meet a certain level of maturity before the start of the next phase is permitted. The waterfall lifecycle has the advantage of easy scheduling. However, it is not without its problems. The primary difficulty is the incompleteness problem—artifacts of any phase cannot be complete until subsequent phases elaborate them and identify their problems. As a practical matter, experience has clearly shown that analysis cannot be complete until at least some design has been done; design cannot be complete until some coding has been done; coding cannot be complete until testing is done. In the waterfall lifecycle, each of these phases depends on the completeness and accuracy of artifacts from the previous phases, but *this never happens*. So our model of the development process is inadequate. This is another way of saying that we *plan* one way but *do* another. Although this facilitates planning, those plans are inaccurate and we cannot, in general, tell where we are with any certainty. For example, if you admit that some analysis must be redone, and your team has scheduled six weeks for analysis and "finishes" in five weeks, are you late or not? Figure 4-1 depicts the waterfall lifecycle.

4.3.2 Iterative Lifecycles

Iterative lifecycles deal with the incompleteness problem by using a more representative (that is, complex) model. The basic concept is that each waterfall lifecycle model is not planned to execute only once, but possibly many times.[2] Each "turn of the wheel" results in a *prototype*. The iterative lifecycle allows for early testing of analysis models even though they are not complete. This is a powerful notion because it takes cognizance of the fact that the phases won't be complete the first time through and allows us to plan our projects accordingly. Iterative lifecycles are more flexible and can be tailored easily to the size and complexity of the system being developed. In addition, by using reasonable criteria on the contents and ordering of the prototypes, we

---

2. Similar to the Hindu concept of reincarnation in which we come back in a higher form, but only if we've been good.

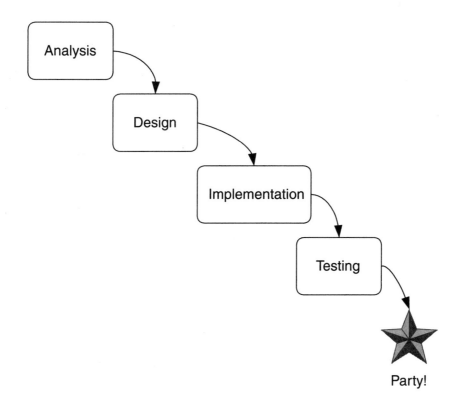

Figure 4-1: *Waterfall Lifecycle*

can assist project tracking with earlier feedback on high-risk project issues.

This more accurate representation comes at a cost—iterative lifecycle projects are more difficult to plan and control, and they are not directly supported by project management tools. With the increased flexibility and accuracy afforded by these models comes more complexity.

Barry Bohem published early work on iterative lifecycles [3], which he referred to as the *spiral lifecycle,* shown in Figure 4-2. Managers often have concerns about whether the spiral is convergent[3] and how to plan and manage projects along these lines. This topic will be dealt with later in the chapter.

---

3. Hence, its other name as the "software spiral of death."

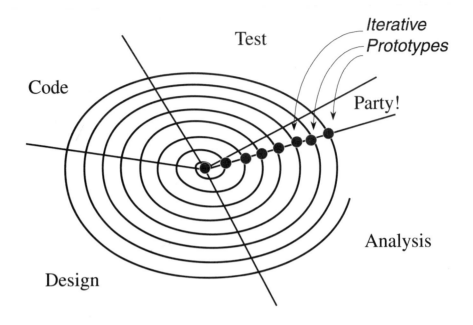

Figure 4-2: *Spiral Lifecycle*

4.3.3 Prototyping

A *prototype* is an instance of a system model. In the software context, prototypes are almost always executable in some sense. They may be either throw-away or iterative. A *throw-away prototype* is one that will not ultimately show up in the final product. For example, it is common to use GUI-building tools to construct mock-ups of user interfaces in order to provide early exposure of a planned interface to a set of users. This visual prototype, which might be done in Visual Basic, will not be shipped in the final product, but it helps the developers to understand their problem more completely and to communicate with nontechnical users.

Iterative prototypes are executable models of the system and will ultimately be shipped in the final product. This means that the quality of the elements (design and code) that make up the prototype must be of a higher quality than if the prototype was meant to be discarded. Iterative prototypes are constructed using elements of previous ones that have been modified to correct defects uncovered in them plus some additional elements. In this way, prototypes become increasingly elaborate over time in much the same way trees grow in spurts indicated by their growth rings. At some point, the prototype meets the system validation criteria, resulting in a shipable prototype. The prototype continues to be elaborated even after release, in the form of service packs, maintenance releases, and major upgrades.

Each prototype should have a *mission*. This mission is the primary purpose for which the prototype has been constructed. This mission might be to reduce some risk or set of risks, provide early integration of system architectural units, implement a use case, or provide an integrated set of functionality for alpha or beta testing. A common strategy is to implement use case prototypes in order of risk.

Many designs are organized into architectural layers based on the level of abstraction. The most concrete layers exist at the bottom and consist of abstractions related to the low-level manipulation of the underlying hardware. The more abstract layers exist above the more concrete layers and realize their behavior by invoking these lower-level services. At the very top are the abstractions that exist within the application domain. This is a marvelous way to decompose a set of abstractions; however, it is rarely a useful way to organize the content and delivery of prototypes. If the prototypes are organized around use cases, then the implementation policy is *vertical,* which means that the prototype typically contains elements from most or all of these layers of abstraction. This approach is also called *incremental development.*

Figure 4-3 illustrates vertical prototyping. The model is structured as a set of horizontal layers, but the prototypes implement relevant portions from most or all of these layers.

The technology that really enables the iterative prototyping process is *automatic translation of description models into executable models.* Executable models are crucial because the only things you can really validate are things you can execute. For example, an early prototype to realize a single use case might consist of a couple of dozen classes, five of which may be nontrivial state machines. To manually create an implementation of this simple use case would take, at a minimum, several days and might require up to several weeks to get it correct. The developer would have to answer many low-level questions like: What is the implementation of a state? An event? How do I implement timeouts? How should I handle events that are not yet handled? What about crossing thread boundaries? All these questions must be answered, but they are ancillary to the work at hand—judging whether

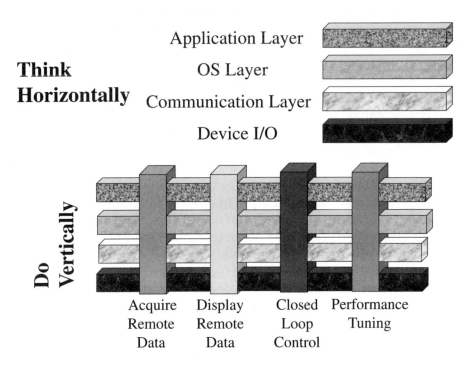

Figure 4-3: *Vertical Prototyping*

the collaboration of objects realizing the use case is, in fact, correct. With a translative approach, the code can be generated, compiled, and run within seconds.

4.4 Scheduling and Estimation

There is ample evidence in the software industry that we have not been tremendously successful in terms of predicting the resources, time, and budget required to develop products.[4] *PC Week* reported in 1994 that 52 percent of all software projects in the U.S. were at least 189 percent over budget, and 31 percent of all projects were cancelled before completion. Other studies give similarly depressing statistics.

---

4. This is no doubt the source of the phrase: There are lies, damn lies, statistics, fantasies, and software schedules.

There are a number of theories about why this is the case. A common theory is that software engineers are morons who couldn't schedule a trip to the bathroom. Understandably, software engineers take the opposing view that managers are clueless, pointy-haired individuals that wouldn't know an accurate estimate if it ran over them. And, of course, everyone gets to blame marketing.

My own view is that everybody gets to share the blame, if there is any, and this poor performance is due to both technical and sociological issues.

Sociological issues include

- The unwillingness of many managers to accept reasonable estimates
- Authoritative managerial style
- Accuracy in estimation is often actively discouraged[5]
- Nonstationary requirements
- Unwillingness on the part of management to believe that software is *inherently* difficult
- A lack of understanding of the true cost of replacing personnel
- Managers giving the "desired" answer[6]
- Engineers providing the "desired" answer even while knowing that it is inaccurate
- The use of schedules as a motivational tool in the belief that stress is a good motivator

Of these, the last is the least defensible, the most insulting to the engineering staff, and incurs the greatest long-term cost for the business.

Technical issues are

- Software involves invention, and estimation of invention is fundamentally difficult.
- Engineers are not trained in estimation techniques.
- Managers use waterfall rather than iterative lifecycles.

Of the two, the technical problems are by far the more solvable.

---

5. I once heard a manager respond to an estimate, "That's the wrong answer—do it again."

6. Another manager once told me, "You have six months to do this. How long will it take you?" Even *I* knew the answer to that one!

4.4.1 Advantages of Accurate Schedules

Despite their rarity, accurate schedules have a number of business advantages. Probably the main advantage is that they help the selection of appropriate projects to pursue. I believe one reason why the failure rate of software projects is so high is that many of these projects would not have been started had the true cost of the project been known at the start. A manager once told me in response to an estimate, "That might be correct, but I can't report that to upper management. They'd cancel the project!" He seemed unconcerned that this might actually be the best thing from a business standpoint. Projects that will not recoup their costs and return a profit generally should not be started in the first place. However, in the absence of accurate information about the cost of projects, making good decisions about which projects to do is difficult.

Another advantage of accurate schedules is that they facilitate the planning of ancillary activities, such as:

- Manufacturing
- Disk copying
- Manual and documentation reproduction
- Ad campaigns
- Hiring employees
- Gearing up for the next project

It is very expensive to gear up a manufacturing effort, which might include the purchase of expensive equipment and hiring manufacturing personnel, only to have manufacturing wait for a late project to complete.

Another benefit near to my own heart is the reduction of the very real "human cost" of software engineering. It is all too common for software engineers to work inhuman hours, often for months at a time, to achieve goals that were unrealistic in the first place. I once worked 120 hours per week for three weeks to make a schedule date. On another project, I worked 90 hours per week for six months. The whole notion of the software-engineer-as-hero becomes much less appealing when one actually has a life (and family).

Of course, many managers use "aggressive,"[7] schedules. As Tom

---

7. As in, "The probability of coming in at the scheduled time is less than the probability of all the molecules in the manager's head suddenly Brownian-motioning in the same direction causing his head to jump across the table."

DeMarco and Timothy Lister [4] point out, using schedules as a motivational tool means that they cannot be used to accurately predict the time and cost of the project. Despite the fact that the premise underlying this approach is particularly insulting to the engineers, even from the strictly business financial aspect, the approach fails miserably in practice. It tends to burn the engineering staff out, and they take their hard-won expertise and use it for the competition. The higher turnover resulting from a consistent application of this management practice is very expensive. It typically costs about $300,000 to replace a $70,000 engineer. The use of schedules as planning, rather than motivational, tools avoids this problem.

4.4.2 Difficulties of Accurate Scheduling

The advantages of accurate schedules are clear. However, we are nevertheless left with the problem of how do we get them. As stated earlier, the difficult problems are sociological in nature. I have consulted to a number of companies and greatly improved their estimation and scheduling accuracy through the consistent application of a few key principles.

Estimates are always applied against estimable work units (EWUs). EWUs are small, atomic tasks, typically no more than 80 hours in duration. The engineer estimating the work provides three estimates:

1. Mean (50 percent) estimate
2. Optimistic (20 percent) estimate
3. Pessimistic (80 percent) estimate

Of these, the most important is the 50 percent estimate. This estimate *is the one the engineer will beat half of the time.* The central limit theorem of statistics states that if all estimates are truly 50 percent estimates, then overall the project will come in on time. However, this estimate alone does not provide all the necessary information. You would also like a measure of the perceived risk associated with the estimate. This is provided by the 20 percent and 80 percent estimates. The former is the time the engineer will beat only 20 percent of the time; the latter will be beat 80 percent of the time. The difference between these two estimates is a measure of the confidence the engineer has in the estimate. The more the engineer knows, the smaller that difference will be.

These estimates are then combined to come up with the estimate actually used in the schedule.

$$\frac{\text{Low} + 4 \times \text{Mean} + \text{High}}{6} \times \text{EC}$$

Equation 4-1: *Computing Used Estimate for Scheduling*

The EC factor is the "estimator confidence" factor, which is based on the engineer's accuracy history. An ideal estimator would have an EC value of 1.00. Typically EC values range from 1.5 to 5.0.

In order to improve their accuracy, engineers must track their estimation success. This success is then fed back into the EC factor. A sample from an estimation notebook is shown in Table 4-1.

To construct a new EC value, use the following formula.

$$EC_{n+1} = \Sigma(\text{Deviations using } EC_n)/(\text{\# Estimates}) + 1.00$$

For example, to construct a new EC value from the previous table, you would compute:

$$EC_1 = (0.425 + 0.56 + 0.842 + 0.1)/4 + 1.00 = 1.48$$

In this example, the engineer went from an estimator confidence factor of 1.75 to 1.48 (a significant improvement). This EC value will be used to adjust the Unadjusted Used computed estimate for insertion in

Table 4-1: *Sample from Estimation Notebook*

Date	Task	Low	Mean	High	Unad-justed Used	EC	Used	Actual	Dev.	% Diff.
9/15/97	User interface	21	40	80	43.5	1.75	76.1	57	17	0.425
9/17/97	Database	15	75	200	85.8	1.75	150.2	117	42	0.56
9/18/97	Database conversion	30	38	42	37.3	1.75	65.3	60	32	0.842
9/20/97	User manual	15	20	22	19.5	1.75	34.1	22	2	0.1

the schedule. It is important to track estimation success in order to improve it.

A schedule is an ordered arrangement of EWUs. The EWUs are ordered to take into account inherent dependencies, level of risk, and the availability of personnel. The process of creating a schedule from a set of estimates is well covered in other texts and won't be discussed here.

4.5 The ROPES Macro Cycle

The ROPES process is based on an iterative lifecycle that uses the standard UML metamodel for its semantic framework and notation. It encourages, but does not require, automatic code generation within a real-time framework from these models to facilitate rapid generation of prototypes. Although the elaborative approach can be used, the translative approach creates deployable prototypes much faster and with much less effort. Figure 4-4 shows an overview of the ROPES process.

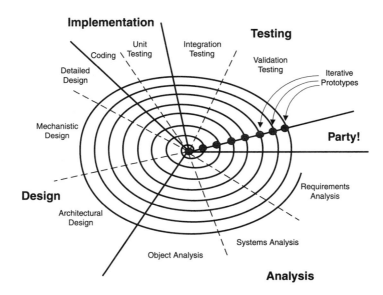

Figure 4-4: *ROPES Process*

The purpose of a process is to improve what we do. In particular, the primary purposes of any development process are to (1) increase the quality of the end product, (2) improve the repeatability and predictability of the development effort, and (3) decrease the effort required to develop the end product at the required level of quality. Other requirements may be levied on a development process, such as aid in accountability, visibility, and regulatory approach. If your development process does not provide these benefits, then it is a bad process and should be replaced or revised.

To achieve these purposes, a process consists of phases, activities, and artifacts. A phase is a set of activities that relate to a common development purpose usually done at a consistent level of abstraction. Each phase contains *activities* (things that developers do) and results in *artifacts* (deliverable work products). The primary artifacts of the ROPES process phases are shown in Figure 4-5.

Figure 4-5 shows the different phases of a single iteration; in practice, these phases iterate over time to produce the development prototypes. The primary artifacts are the different views of the system model. Different phases produce the models represented in these artifacts. A prototype really consists not only of the executable thing, but also of the artifacts used to generate it.

Each prototype in the ROPES process is organized around the use cases of the system. Once the set of use cases is identified and characterized, they are ordered to optimize the effort. The optimal ordering is determined by a combination of the use case:

- Priority
- Risk
- Commonality

For example, suppose you lead a team that builds an embedded communications protocol, which is modeled after the seven-layer ISO communications protocol standard. This protocol is to be implemented on several processors, using different RTOSs and compilers. The processor platforms include a heterogeneous set of 16-bit, 32-bit, and DSP processors. In addition, some subsystems are to be implemented in C while others are in C++. The team wants the same source code to compile and operate on all platforms, so this is identified as an early risk. You agree in this case to create an object model and implement the pro-

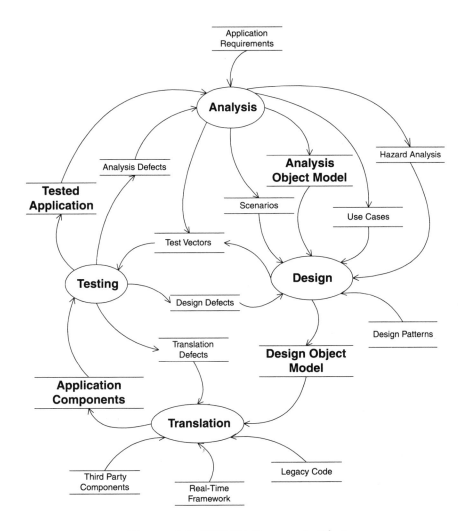

Figure 4-5: *ROPES Process Artifacts*

tocol using only the standard C that is also present in C++. The layered architecture looks like that shown in Figure 4-6.

You want to reduce risk while providing the subsystems with the ability to do at least some useful communication with others as early as possible. You then identify a series of prototypes that optimize both risk reduction and early availability, as shown in Figure 4-7.

- *Application Layer*: Application services
- *Presentation Layer*: Data encode/decode
- *Session Layer*: Organized extended dialogs
- *Transport Layer*: Connection-oriented and connectionless transportation
- *Network Layer*: Packet routing
- *Data Link Layer*: Error-free frame transmission, flow control
- *Physical Layer*: Encapsulate and abstract physical media characteristics

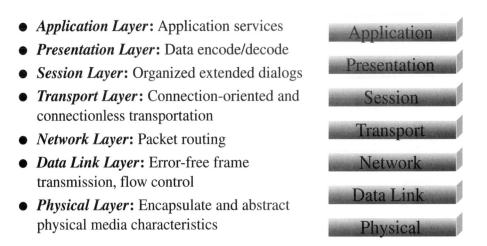

Figure 4-6: *Communication Protocol Architecture*

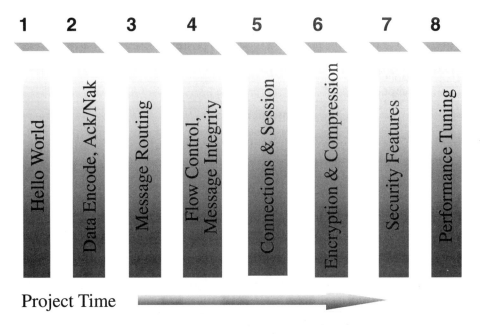

Figure 4-7: *Communication Protocol Prototypes*

In just such a development project I lead, the project was a great success. Interestingly, as a result of the Hello World prototype, which was compiled on every subsystem, we found that none of the ANSI C-compliant compilers were, in fact, ANSI C-compliant. By creating this prototype first, we were able to find the minimum set of language translation rules that worked on all subsystem compilers. At this point, only a small amount of code had to be rewritten. Had we waited until later, the rewrite would have been much more substantial and costly.

In the following sections, we will look at each phase of the ROPES process (the ROPES micro cycle) and identify the activities and deliverables. Each subphase is described in detail, including its activities (things you do during the subphase), the metamodel elements used (things you manipulate or define), and the artifacts (things produced). In some situations or business environments, some of the activities or artifacts of the sub-phases may be skipped. For example, if your system is not safety-critical, you won't spend the effort and time to produce a hazard analysis document. Pick the activities and artifacts that make the most sense for your system and work culture.

4.6 Analysis

As mentioned earlier, the analysis of a system identifies all characteristics of the system that are essential to correctness. That is, it should be devoid of design characteristics that are free to vary. Figure 4-8 shows the subphases and deliverables for the ROPES analysis activity, including the generated and delivered artifacts.

4.6.1 Requirements Analysis

Requirements analysis extracts requirements from the customer. The customer may be anyone who has responsibility for defining what the system does. This might be a user, a member of the marketing staff, or a contractor. There are several barriers to the extraction of a complete, unambiguous, and correct set of requirements.

First, most customers understand the field use of the system, but they don't think about it in a systematic manner. This results in requirements that are vague or incomplete. Even worse, they may specify

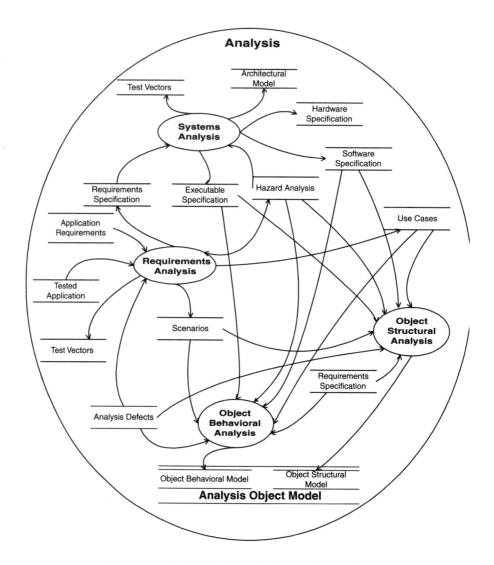

Figure 4-8: *ROPES Analysis Model Artifacts*

requirements that are mutually exclusive, impossible, or too expensive to implement. The customer may forget to specify requirements that seem too "obvious" and may specify requirements that are really implementations.

Second, customers will specify what they think they need. However, this is often not the best solution to their problem. If you deliver a system that is what the customer requested but does not meet his or her needs, you will nevertheless shoulder the blame. It behooves you to figure out what the real requirements are.

It is important to note that requirements analysis is almost exclusively a functional view. It does not identify objects or classes. It comes as a disappointment to many beginners that after spending significant effort identifying use cases and elaborating their behavior, not a single object is identified by the end of requirements analysis. That remains the task of object analysis, a later subphase.

4.6.1.1 Activities

The basic activities are

- Identify the use cases and associated actors.
- Decompose use cases with the generalization, uses (or includes), and extends relations.
- Identify and characterize external events that affect the system.
- Define behavioral scenarios that capture the system dynamic behavior.
- Identify required constraints, including required interfaces to other systems and performance constraints.

The first tool is the use case. As mentioned in Chapter 1, a use case is a cohesive end-to-end, externally visible behavior of the system, and can often be identified by talking with the customer. Most systems consist of three kinds of use cases. *Primary use cases* are the most obvious, and capture typical externally visible functionality. *Secondary use cases* are less common but still identify important pieces of functionality. Most of the time, safety and reliability issues are addressed within these types of use cases. However, sometimes it is possible to identify *safety-related use cases*. These use cases exist when, in addition to normal functionality, the system also acts as a safety monitor or safety means for another system. In a medium-sized system, you will expect to find from a few to a few dozen use cases.

Remember, however, that a use case is a function that returns a visible result to an actor, without revealing internal structure. This means that the identification of use cases and their relations *does not* indicate or imply an object structure. Use cases map to mechanisms and collaborations, not to objects. This is a stumbling block for many beginners who expect the set of use cases to automatically determine an object structure. There is no automatic way to bridge the gap from a functional black-box view of the system to an object-oriented white-box view.

Once use cases are identified, scenarios can be examined in more detail. Remember, scenarios are instances of use cases. They walk a particular path through a use case. Requirements scenarios are a primary means for requirement extraction.[8] You will start with the obvious set of scenarios but quickly identify branching points at which different decisions are made. Whenever a branching point appears in a scenario, it indicates the existence of another scenario (in which the other decision was made). If the latter scenario is "interestingly different," then it should be added to the scenario set of the use case.

The identification of events relevant to the system and their properties is also done during requirements analysis. This analysis includes the messages and events that actors send to the system, as well as the system response to those messages. The performance properties of those messages at this level include

- Associated actor
  1. Sender of message
  2. Receiver of response
- Arrival pattern (periodic or episodic)
- Arrival time for the message
  1. Period and jitter for periodic message
  2. Minimum inter-arrival interval or burst length for episodic message
- Message response properties
  1. Deadline for hard deadline message
  2. Average response time for soft deadline message

---

8. I like to visualize a scenario as a rather large syringe that I plunge into the brain of a marketer to suck out the hidden requirements. I find such visualization helpful in long meetings.

- State information
    1. Pre-conditional invariants for the message
    2. Protocol (acceptable message sequence)
    3. Message data
    4. Post-conditional invariants for the response

This information is typically captured on use case, object context, and sequence diagrams, statecharts, and perhaps in an external event list.

4.6.1.2 Metamodel Entities Used

Two kinds of modeling elements are used in requirements analysis: contextual elements and behavioral elements. It is important to remember that during this subphase, the system view is black-box and only elements that are visible from an external perspective are specified. The contextual elements define

- Actors (objects that exist outside the scope of your system)
- The "system object"
- Use cases
- Use case relations
- External messages (including events)
- Hazards

Use case relations may be between a use case and an actor or between use cases. Use cases capture typical and exceptional uses of the system that are visible to actors. Actors are objects outside use case context and may be human users of the system, devices with which the system must interact, or legacy software systems. Actors associate with use cases. The association between an actor and a use case means that the actor can send or receive messages that participate in the scenarios of that use case.

Hazard identification is crucial for safety- or mission-critical systems, or for any system for which the cost of system failure is high. At a minimum, you must define the hazards and their associated risks. Many times, the description will also include the safety measure if it is externally visible, although it is more common to define the safety measure later in design.

Behavioral elements include

- Constraints, such as performance requirements and fault-tolerance times
- Statecharts, including states and transitions
- Scenarios
- Message protocols in actor-system interactions

The behavioral elements define how the system behaves, but only from a black-box perspective. It is relatively common to use statecharts to define the behavior of message protocols of external interfaces and in the required behavior of use cases. Statecharts are *fully constructive*. This means that a single statechart can define the complete behavior of its associated contextual element. Scenarios are only *partially constructive*. It is impossible to fully define the complete behavior of a complex machine with a single scenario. Scenarios may be used to describe important paths through a state machine, or they may be applied when the behavior is not state-driven. It is common to define up to a few dozen scenarios per use case.

4.6.1.3 Artifacts

There are many artifacts produced during this subphase. The ones listed in Table 4-2 are the most common.

For some systems, it is appropriate to produce all these artifacts; for others, only some of these will be produced. The set of generally required artifacts are identified as "basic" in the middle column of Table 4-2. The structure and contents of these artifacts will be discussed in more detail in later chapters.

4.6.2 Systems Analysis

Systems analysis is an important phase in large, complex embedded systems, such as aerospace and automotive applications. Systems analysis usually elaborates key algorithms and partitions the requirements into electronic, mechanical, and software components. Often, behavioral

Table 4-2: *Requirements Analysis Artifacts*

Artifact	Representation	Basic	Description
Requirements document	Text	Yes	A textual description of the system contents, interface to external actors, and its externally visible behavior, including constraints and safety requirements.
Use cases	Use case diagrams	Yes	Identification of the major functional areas of the system and the interaction of actors with the use cases.
	Statecharts	No	Some set of use cases will be reactive—i.e., have state behavior. The full behavioral space of such use cases may be captured in statecharts.
	External event list	No	A spreadsheet describing the properties of events received by the system or issued from the system. This includes properties such as period and jitter (for periodic events), minimum inter-arrival time and burst length (for episodic events), deadlines, event data, etc.
	Context diagram	No	An idiomatic use of a UML object diagram. It contains the system "object" and actors that interact with the system. The messages and events passing between actors and the system are identified.
Use case scenarios	Sequence diagrams	Yes	Paths through individual use cases, these represent scenarios of uses of the system. They show specific paths through a use case, including messages sent between the use case and its associated actors.

(continued)

Table 4-2: (*cont.*)

Artifact	Representation	Basic	Description
Use case scenarios (*cont.*)	Timing diagrams	No	Another representation of scenarios, timing diagrams are also instances of use cases. Usually applied only to reactive use cases, they show state along the vertical axis and linear time along the horizontal axis.
Hazard analysis		No	Usually a spreadsheet format document that identifies the key hazards that the system must address and their properties, such as fault-tolerance time, severity and probability of the hazard, and its computed risk.
Test vectors	Textual	Yes	Specification of tests to validate the system against requirements.

modeling tools such as Statemate[9] and Simulink[10] are used to construct executable models and explore system dynamics. This is especially true when the system displays nontrivial state or continuous behavior.

It should be noted that, like requirements analysis, systems analysis is still fundamentally a functional, not an object, view. It does not imply, let alone identify, objects and classes. Systems analysis therefore will *not* generally result in a set of objects and classes. It is possible to perform system and, for that matter, hardware analysis using object model methods. However, systems analysts, as a group, seem reluctant to adopt this technology. Meanwhile, it is best that we software types accept that and plan to bridge the gap between their functional view and our object view.

---

9. Statemate is a systems analysis tool for building and testing executable models of complex, reactive systems. It is available from I-Logix. See *www.ilogix.com.*
10. Simulink is an interactive environment for modeling, analyzing, and simulating a wide variety of dynamic systems, including discrete, analog, and mixed signal systems. It is available from Mathworks. See *www.mathworks.com.*

4.6.2.1 Activities

The primary activities are

- Identify large-scale organizational units for complex systems
- Build and analyze complex behavioral specifications for the organizational units
- Partition system-level functionality into three engineering disciplines
  1. Software
  2. Electronics
  3. Mechanics
- Test the behavior with executable models

The large-scale organization is often time-specified in the systems analysis subphase. The result is a functionally decomposed architecture that contains black-box nodes that, in turn, contain behavioral elements called *components*. These components are then analyzed in detail, and hardware/software tradeoffs are made. The interfaces among the components must be defined, at least at a high level. This allows the engineers of different disciplines to go off and work on their respective pieces.

The analysis of the behavior components is done as finite state machines, continuous control systems, or a combination of the two. For reactive systems, it means constructing complex statecharts of the component behavior, which results in finite state machines with potentially hundreds or thousands of states. For continuous control systems, linear or nonlinear PID control loops are the most common way to capture the desired behavior.

In complex systems, it is crucial to execute the models to ensure that they are correct, unambiguous, and complete. Errors in specification during this phase are the most costly to correct later, because the errors are often discovered only after the system is completely implemented. Correcting errors in systems analysis requires substantial rewrites of major portions of the system under development. Early proofs of correctness, such as formal proofs and functional and performance testing, can greatly reduce this risk at minimal cost. It is important that any tests designed during systems analysis be constructed in such a way that they may also be applied later to the developed system. This not only saves work in producing tests, it helps ensure that the delivered system has the correct behavior.

4.6.2.2 Metamodel Entities Used

The metamodel elements used in systems analysis are both structural and behavioral. The structural components are used to decompose the system functionality into functional blocks (nodes on deployment diagrams). These are typically what is meant by the systems analysis term *subsystem.*[11] The UML component can be used to represent unelaborated boxes. When the hardware pieces are identified, they become UML «processor» nodes on which software-only components reside.

    The UML does not define a way to specify continuous mathematics. Continuous algorithms are best specified using equations or pseudocode. UML activity diagrams can be used as a type of concurrent flowchart to represent algorithms, as well. Performance constraints are generally elaborated at this subphase. The performance constraints are applied at the component level, meaning that the end-to-end performance of behaviors defined for the components must be specified.

4.6.2.3 Artifacts

Table 4-3 provides descriptions of systems analysis artifacts.

4.6.3 Object Analysis

Object analysis is the subphase in which the essential objects and classes are identified and their important properties captured. The previous subphases defined the required behavior of the system. These requirements must be met by the object structure identified in this phase. It is important to note that this is the first point at which objects and classes appear. It is also important that only the objects and classes

---

11. A subsystem, to a systems analyst, is a box that contains hardware and software and meets some cohesive functional purpose. This is somewhat different from, although related to, the UML use of the term. A UML subsystem is a subclass of two metamodel entities, Package and Classifier. Thus, a subsystem can group model elements (since it is a type of package) and may also have attributes, associations, and may itself be specialized.

Table 4-3: *Systems Analysis Artifacts*

Artifact	Representation	Description
Architectural model	Deployment diagrams	Identify hardware boxes that contain executable components.
	Component diagrams	Identify functional boxes potentially residing on nodes, which may be composed of a combination of hardware and software. Some components may be specialized to interact with «device» nodes (hardware that does not execute software of interest) or may be software-only components.
Executable specification	Statecharts	Finite state machines defined at the component level.
	Mathematical models	Mathematical descriptions of continuous functionality, such as PID control loops.
	Activity diagrams	UML diagrams that roughly correspond to concurrent flowcharts. These have some of the properties of Petri nets, as well, and can model complex algorithms.
	Sequence diagrams	Paths of interest (such as typical and exceptional) through the statecharts.
Software specification	Text	Detailed requirements of allocated responsibilities and behaviors required of the software.
Hardware specification	Text	Detailed requirements of allocated responsibilities and behaviors required of the hardware platform.
Test vectors	Sequence diagrams	Scenarios used to test that the implemented system, in fact, meets the systems analysis.
	System test plan	A plan for how the system will be tested to ensure that it correctly implements the system analysis requirements.

that are *essential to all possibly correct solutions* are captured.[12] That is why the analysis object model is often referred to as the "logical," or "essential," model.

Object analysis consists of two subphases: structural object analysis and behavioral object analysis. In practice, these subphases are most often done concurrently. For example, exploration of the important scenarios (behavior) leads to the identification of additional objects within a collaboration (structure) that realizes a use case.

4.6.3.1 Activities

The primary activities of object analysis are

* Apply object identification strategies to uncover essential objects of the system
* Abstract the objects to identify classes
* Uncover how the classes and objects relate to each other
* Construct mechanisms of object collaboration that meet the use case behavioral requirements
* Define the essential behavior of reactive objects
* Identify the essential operations and attributes of the objects
* Test the identified mechanisms with scenarios
* Decompose the end-to-end performance constraints to performance constraints on class operations

4.6.3.2 Metamodel Entities Used

The modeling elements used are the standard ones found in class and object diagrams: classes, objects, relations, and so on. In addition, mechanisms are instances of collaborations. Collaborations in the UML are namespaces that contain interactions of classifiers (such as classes).

It is common to divide up the classes into different areas of subject matter, called *domains*. A domain is an area of concern in which classes and objects are related. Typical domains include Device I/O, User

---

12. It is difficult to imagine, for example, an accounting system object model that does not include the class *Account*, or a fire-control system that does not include the classes *Target* and *Weapon*, at least in some form.

Interface, Alarm Management, and Persistence (long-term storage). A Device I/O domain might contain classes, such as A/D Converter, Hardware Register, Port, and so on. A User Interface domain might contain classes, such as *Window, Scrollbar, Button, Font, Bitmap,* and *Icon.* Each system will also have one or more specific application domains, such as spacecraft management, avionics, electrocardiography, or reactor management.

Generalization taxonomies are usually held within a single domain. Naturally, collaborations must span domain boundaries so that classes may associate across domains. Domains are commonly represented as packages on class diagrams. Part of the usefulness of domains comes from the fact that because they are well encapsulated and self-contained, analysis may proceed on domains independently.

In order to divide up the analysis work among team members, development components are usually identified. Development components are those representing nondeployable organizations of model elements (artifacts), such as documents and files. These differ from deployable components, such as data tables, pluggable components, libraries (for example, dlls), and executable programs. The identification of deployment components allows team members to divide up the work. This work is, of course, generally done on top of a configuration management layer to facilitate the efficient collaboration of team members.

Finite state machines continue to be used to capture reactive behavior, but during this subphase they are applied to classes only—that is, if you identify a statechart during object analysis, then there must be a class to which the statechart belongs.[13] This means that the statecharts identified in use cases and components from the earlier subphases of analysis must be partitioned among the classes identified during object analysis. This usually results in some reorthogonalization of the state behavior, and care must be taken to show that in all cases the resulting set of class state machines is isomorphic with the use case and component state machines.

Message sequence, collaboration, and timing diagrams are used to specify the dynamic collaboration of objects within mechanisms. Early in analysis, most people prefer to use sequence diagrams. But later, as the object structure stabilizes, some prefer to move to collaboration

---

13. Less common, a statechart may be added to a collaboration. Usually, however, such a statechart has already been defined for the use case realized by that component.

diagrams. When timing is important, timing diagrams can clearly represent operation or state behavior over time.

4.6.3.3 Artifacts

Table 4-4 shows the typical artifacts produced during object analysis.

Table 4-4: *Object Analysis Artifacts*

Artifact	Representation	Description
Object structural model	Class and object diagrams	Identify key abstractions and their logical organization in packages and mechanisms.
	Domain diagrams	An idiomatic usage of a class diagram, consisting primarily of packages organized around subject matters of interest and their dependency relations.
	Component diagrams	Identify development components, such as files and documents, to enable team members to collaborate by sharing work units.
Object behavioral model	Statecharts	Finite state machines defined at the class level.
	Activity diagrams	UML diagrams that roughly correspond to concurrent flowcharts. These have some of the properties of Petri nets, as well, and can model complex algorithms.
	Sequence diagrams	Paths of interest, such as typical and exceptional, through the collaborations of identified classes.
	Collaboration diagrams	Same as sequence diagrams, but visually organized similar to object diagrams.
	Timing diagrams	Specify the timing of operations and state transitions in collaborations of identified classes.

4.7 Design

While analysis identifies the logical or essential model of a system, design defines a single solution that is in some sense "optimal." For example, design will identify things such as:

- Which objects are active (concurrency model)
- Application task scheduling policies
- Organization of classes and objects within deployable components
- Inter-processor communication media and protocols
- Distribution of software components to nodes (especially if the systems analysis step was skipped)
- Relation implementation strategies (How should associations be implemented? Pointers? References? TCP/IP sockets?)
- Implementation patterns for state machines
- Management of multivalued roles (that is, 1-* associations)
- Error-handling policies
- Memory-management policies

Three subphases of design exist: architectural, mechanistic, and detailed. Architectural design defines the strategic design decisions that affect most or all of the software components, such as the concurrency model and the distribution of components across processor nodes. Mechanistic design elaborates individual collaborations by adding "glue" objects to bind the mechanism together and optimize its functionality. Such objects include containers, iterators, and smart pointers. Detailed design defines the internal structure and behavior of individual classes. This includes internal data structuring and algorithm details.

The work artifacts of the ROPES design process are shown in Figure 4-9. The primary deliverable artifact is the design model.

Much of design consists of the application of design patterns to the logical object model. These patterns may be large, medium, or small scale, mapping to architectural, mechanistic, or detailed design. Of course, to be correct, both the design model and the analysis model are different views of the same underlying system model, albeit at different levels of abstraction. It is obviously important that the design be consistent with the analysis. Moving from the more abstract analysis model

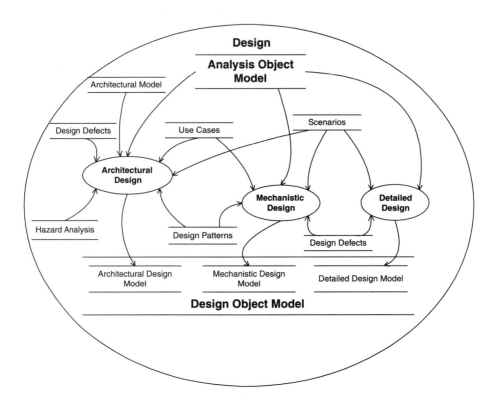

Figure 4-9: *ROPES Design Model Artifacts*

to the design model may be done in ROPES, using either the elaborative or translative approach.

The translative approach has much to recommend it. In a translative macro cycle, a translator is built, which embodies the design decisions and patterns to be used. This translator is then applied against the object model to produce an executable system. The advantage of a translator is that once built, turning around a prototype from an analysis model is a matter of seconds or minutes, rather than days or weeks. The translator usually has two parts: a real-time framework (see Chapter 13) and a code generator. The real-time framework works much like a GUI framework (such as MFC or Motif). Base classes provide attributes and behavior common to such elements in the domain. A real-time framework provides classes, such as timers, threads, semaphores, state machines, states, events, and a set of operating system abstractions.

The code generator generates code from your modeled classes, relations, and statecharts, which in turn use these framework classes (by subclassing or associating with them). The generated code is then compiled and executed.

Tools such as Rhapsody provide translators and frameworks out-of-the-box that embody a default set of design decisions. These decisions can be used without change, particularly for early prototypes but even in final deployable systems, as well. However, the user may modify the translator or the framework if desired. This may be done by

- Subclassing the classes provided by the framework, specializing the behavior as necessary
- Replacing parts of the framework
- Setting code generation configuration properties of the translator

In addition, because translating tools provide the generation of code and the real-time framework, they can insert animation instrumentation that allows them to monitor the execution of the generated program and graphically depict that behavior using analysis and design-level abstractions rather than source code. In the case of Rhapsody, this instrumentation communicates back to the tool as the generated application system runs, allowing it to graphically depict the execution of the model using UML constructs. Thus, statecharts animate, showing the acceptance of events and the transition within state machines; sequence diagrams animate, showing the messages sent among objects; the object browser animates, allowing you to view the current value of attributes and associations—all as the application executes. This provides a model-level debugger that can graphically show the execution of the system using the same diagram views used to create it, complete with breakpoints, event insertions, scripting, and so on. This debugging environment can be used while the generated system executes on the user's host machine or on remote embedded target hardware.

The more traditional method for designing object-oriented software uses a different approach. The analysis model is elaborated with design detail. This process still works by applying design patterns to the analysis model, but it is done by manually adding the classes to the analysis diagrams and by manually typing in code that implements the modeled semantic constructs.

A common question I am asked about the elaborative approach is whether the design model should be maintained as a distinct entity from the analysis model. There are two schools of thought here. The first school holds that the analysis model is a "higher-level," more-abstract view and should be maintained separately. The second school feels that it is important that the design and analysis models always coincide, and the best way to achieve that is to add the design elements to the analysis model. There are advantages to both approaches. However, my strong preference is the latter. I have seen far too many problems arise from the deviation of the analysis and design models to suggest any other approach. On the other hand, there are cases where the same analysis model will be used in multiple designs. If this is true, then it might be best to live with the potential for dual-maintenance of the analysis and design models. Care must be taken to ensure their continuing consistency.

4.7.1 Architectural Design

Architectural design is concerned with the large-scale strategic decisions that affect most or all of the software in the system.

4.7.1.1 Activities

The primary activities in architectural design are

- Identification and characterization of threads
- Definition of software components and their distribution
- Application of architectural design patterns for:
  1. Global error handling
  2. Safety processing
  3. Fault tolerance

Some (even most) of the architecture may be dictated by the systems analysis. Usually, however, there is still plenty of work left to define the concurrency and reliability/safety model even if systems analysis is performed (small engineering projects may skip the systems analysis step altogether).

4.7.1.2 Metamodel Entities Used

Since the design model is an elaboration of the analysis model, it consists of the same set of elements. The basic elements are collaborations, classes, objects, and their relations. Of particular concern in architectural design are the nodes, components, and active classes. Nodes and components capture the physical deployment architecture. Active objects are objects that are the roots of threads. They form the basis of the UML concurrency model. Finally, protocol classes are usually added to manage communications in a multiprocessor environment.

4.7.1.3 Artifacts

Table 4-5 shows the common artifacts produced during architectural design.

Table 4-5: *Architectural Design Artifacts*

Artifact	Representation	Description
Architectural design model	Class and object diagrams	Updated to include architectural design patterns.
	Component diagrams	Identify development components, such as files and documents, to enable team members to collaborate by sharing work units.
	Statecharts	Finite state machines defined at the class level.
	Activity diagrams	UML diagrams that roughly correspond to concurrent flowcharts. These have some of the properties of Petri nets, as well, and can model complex algorithms.
	Sequence diagrams	Paths of interest (such as typical and exceptional) through the collaborations of identified classes.
	Collaboration diagrams	Same as sequence diagrams, but visually organized similar to object diagrams.
	Timing diagrams	Specify the timing of operations and state transitions in collaborations of identified classes.

4.7.2 Mechanistic Design

Mechanistic design is the medium level of design. The scope of design elements in this subphase is generally from a few to a dozen objects. Similar to architectural design, most of the work in mechanistic design proceeds by the application of design patterns to the analysis models.

4.7.2.1 Activities

In mechanistic design, the details of collaborations of objects are refined by adding additional objects. For example, if a controller must manage many pending messages, the Container-Iterator pattern can be applied. This results in the insertion of a container (such as a FIFO queue to hold the messages) and iterators that allow the manipulation of that container. The container and iterator classes serve as "glue" to facilitate the execution of the collaboration.

4.7.2.2 Metamodel Entities Used

The metamodel elements used in mechanistic design are no different from those used in object analysis. Most of the emphasis is at the level of the class and object.

4.7.2.3 Artifacts

The artifacts commonly produced in mechanistic design are shown in Table 4-6.

Table 4-6: *Mechanistic Design Artifacts*

Artifact	Representation	Description
Mechanistic design model	Class and object diagrams	Updated to include mechanistic design patterns.
	Component diagrams	Identify development components, such as files and documents, to enable team members to collaborate by sharing work units. *(continued)*

Table 4-6: (*cont.*)

Artifact	Representation	Description
Mechanistic design model (*cont.*)	Sequence diagrams	Paths of interest (such as typical and exceptional) through the collaborations of identified classes.
	Collaboration diagrams	Same as sequence diagrams, but visually organized similar to object diagrams.
	Timing diagrams	Specify the timing of operations and state transitions in collaborations of identified classes.

4.7.3 Detailed Design

Detailed design is the lowest level of design. It is concerned with the definition of the internal structure and behavior of individual classes.

4.7.3.1 Activities

Most classes in a typical system are simple enough not to require much detailed design. However, even there, the implementation of associations, aggregations, and compositions must be defined. In addition, the pre- and post-conditional invariants of the operations, the exception-handling model of the class, and the precise types and valid ranges of attributes must be specified. For some small set of classes, complex algorithms must be clarified.

4.7.3.2 Metamodel Entities Used

4.7.3.3 Artifacts

Table 4-7 shows the artifacts commonly produced in detailed design.

Table 4-7: *Detailed Design Artifacts*

Artifact	Representation	Description
Detailed design model	Object model	Define the structure and valid values for attributes, as well as the decomposition of behaviors into a set of operations within the class.
	Statecharts	Finite state machines defined at the class level.
	Activity diagram	Definition of algorithmic behavior in terms of the operations invoked, their sequence, and their branching decisions.
	Pseudocode	Definition of algorithmic behavior.

4.8 Translation

The translation phase turns the UML model into source code and, via the compiler, into an executable system. See Figure 4-10 for a diagram of translation model artifacts.

4.8.1 Activities

In a translative development micro cycle, translation happens more or less automatically. In the elaborative approach, the developer must map the UML model elements to programming language elements. If an object-oriented language is used, this process is fairly rote, because all the important decisions have already been made during analysis and design. If a non-object-oriented language is used, then the programming effort is more "creative," in which case it is common to write a translation style guide. This guide defines the translation rules so that the programmer can implement the UML model in the target language, whether it is C, Pascal, or assembly language.

The ROPES process also includes unit testing in this phase. Unit testing is a set of white-box tests that ensure that the unit under test, in fact, is internally correct and meets the design. This generally consists

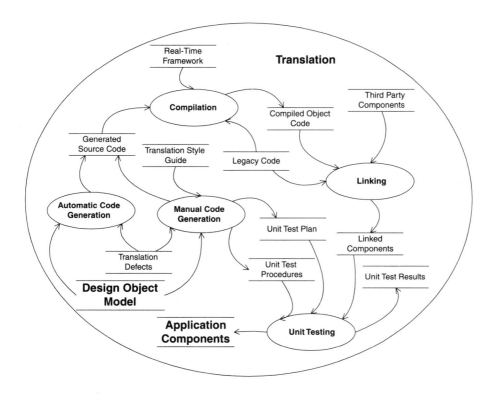

Figure 4-10: *ROPES Translation Model Artifacts*

of unit test plan and unit test procedures documents, and culminates in a unit test results document. The unit test plan is usually organized around the basic unit of the class. The document is written at the package or component level. Each class within the package is represented in a separate chapter. Within a class's chapter, the set of tests for each operation are identified.

The unit test procedures document is organized around identical lines but includes great detail of the actual execution of each test, including the operation of external equipment and test fixtures. In my teams, we don't even review source code until it passes its unit tests. Properly run, unit-level testing greatly increases quality and speeds the development process by identifying errors early and in a minimalist context.

4.8.2 Artifacts

Table 4-8 shows the artifacts produced during translation.

Table 4-8: *Translation Artifacts*

Artifact	Representation	Description
Generated source code	Textual source code	Programming language statements in the target language.
Translation style guide	Textual document	A set of rules for converting the UML models into source code statements.
Compiled object code	Compiler-dependent output format	Compiled executable code.
Legacy code	Source code Compiled object code	Existing source or compiled object code that provides services used by the application.
Real-time framework	Source code	Framework classes from which application classes are specialized (see Chapter 13).
Third-party components	Binary object code	Libraries and components to be used by the application, such as container and math libraries.
Unit test plan	Text organized by object and operation	Internal, white-box testing documentation for the classes, describing the breadth and depth of testing.
Unit test procedures	Text organized by object and operation	Detailed, step-by-step instructions for unit test execution, including pass/fail criteria.
Unit test results	Textual document	Test execution information, including tester, date, unit under test and its version, and pass or fail for each test.
Linked components	Executable components or applications	Components compiled and linked but not yet tested.
Application components	Executable components or applications	Components after they've been tested.

4.9 Testing

The testing phase in the ROPES process includes both integration and validation testing. Testing applies a set of test vectors to the application, which have observable results. The test vectors are based primarily upon the scenarios identified in the requirements and object analysis phase. The resulting artifacts are a tested application and defects, as shown in Figure 4-11.

4.9.1 Activities

All tests should be executed against a test plan and in strict accordance with a test procedures document. In integration testing, the system is constructed by adding a component at a time. At each point at which a new component is added, the interfaces created by adding that

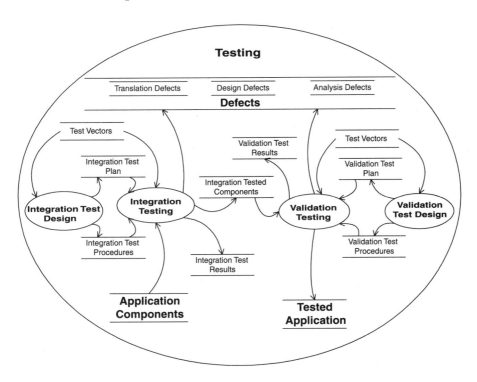

Figure 4-11: *ROPES Testing Model Artifacts*

component are tested. Validation tests are defined by a test team and represent the set of requirements and system analysis done early on. Validation tests are fundamentally black-box. The only exceptions are the tests of the safety aspects, which are white-box because it is usually necessary to go inside the system and break something to ensure that the safety action is correctly executed.

4.9.2 Artifacts

Table 4-9 provides descriptions of testing artifacts.

Table 4-9: *Testing Artifacts*

Artifact	Representation	Description
Integration test plan	Textual document	Identify and define the order of addition of the system components and what set of tests will be executed to test the introduced interactions among the components.
Integration test procedures	Textual document	Detailed description of how to execute each test, including clear and unambiguous pass/fail criteria.
Integration test results	Textual document	Results from the execution of the integration test plan, including the tester, name and revision of the components being integrated, date of test, and pass or fail for each test.
Integration-tested components	Executable component	Tested component.
Validation test plan	Textual document	Identify and define the set of tests required to show the system is correct. These tests are black-box and map to the requirements from the requirements and systems analysis.
Validation test procedures	Textual document	A detailed description of how to execute each test, including clear and unambiguous pass/fail criteria.

(continued)

Table 4-9: (*cont.*)

Artifact	Representation	Description
Validation test results	Textual document	The results from the execution of the validation test plan, including the tester, name and revision of the application being tested, date of test, and pass or fail for each test.
Tested application	Executable application	Validated executable application.

4.10 Summary

In this chapter, we have looked at a number of issues surrounding the process of software development. Early on, we looked at the process for the estimation of software work. As an industry, we are dismal failures at predicting how long software development will take and how much it will cost. There are both sociological and technical reasons for this. If the sociological issues can be addressed, the technical solutions provided in this section can greatly improve estimation accuracy. I've received many reports from companies to which I have consulted that their ability to accurately predict software projects has been enhanced significantly as a result of application of these techniques.

Most of this chapter was spent on the ROPES process model. This model breaks software development into four primary phases: analysis, design, translation, and testing. Analysis and design are both divided up into several subphases. Analysis is divided into requirements, systems, and object analysis phases. Design is broken up into architectural, mechanistic, and detailed designs. Each of these subphases has a set of deliverable artifacts, which constitute the work products for the subphase.

The phases identified in the ROPES model are organized into an iterative lifecycle. Each prototype typically implements one or more use cases organized by risk (greater risk first). This allows the early exploration of risks and minimizes the number of model aspects that must be modified because of those risks. In order to explore those risks, executable prototypes must be developed, as only executable things can be tested. Thus, the key enabling technology to making this process rapid and efficient is the automatic translation of models into executable code. This reduces the time necessary to do complete iterations from weeks or months to hours or days. ROPES supports both elaborative and translative development micro cycles, but it leans towards the latter.

4.11 Looking Ahead

This chapter concludes the introduction to real-time systems development. In the next section, we'll explore the analysis and design phases in more detail. We'll provide strategies for the elaboration of these subphases and work through some examples to illustrate how these strategies work.

The last section of the book discusses in more detail some of the issues relevant to the development of real-time systems, including issues surrounding scheduling, code generation, model debugging, and real-time frameworks.

4.12 Exercises

1. Define methodology, modeling language, and development process.
2. What is the difference between the waterfall and iterative lifecycles?
3. What is meant by "vertical prototyping"?
4. Name five sociological barriers to accurate scheduling. Name three technical barriers to accurate scheduling.
5. What are some advantages of accurate schedules? Why is it hard?
6. In Table 4-1, why is the value of the deviation column 17 and not −19.1?
7. What does ROPES stand for?
8. What are the primary phases of the ROPES process?
9. In what subphase are use cases used?

10. When in the ROPES process are classes and objects first identified?
11. What is a context diagram? How does it relate to a use case diagram?
12. What are the activities in systems analysis?
13. In what phase is unit testing performed?
14. What are the subphases of analysis? Design?

4.13 References

[1] Booch, Grady. *Object Solutions: Managing the Object-Oriented Project*, Reading, Mass.: Addison-Wesley, 1996.

[2] Kant, Immanuel, Guyer, Paul (translator), and Allen Wood, (translator). *Critique of Pure Reason*; Cambridge, Mass.: Cambridge University Press, 1998.

[3] Boheim, Barry. *Software Economics*, Englewood Cliffs, N.J.: Prentice Hall, 1981.

[4] DeMarco, Tom and Timothy Lister. *Peopleware: Productive Projects and Teams*, New York: Dorset House Publishing Company, 1987.

Part  II

Analysis

Part I of this book dealt with the basics. The first three chapters focused on elements of object-oriented systems, the basics of real-time and embedded systems, and safety and reliability concerns. That provides a common language for the discussion of how to develop object-oriented systems, the subject of Parts II and III. Chapter 4 provided a framework for the discussion of software project management and control via the ROPES process. It identified phases of development, work activities, and deliverable artifacts created during each of these phases. Now we have enough background to discuss in detail the actual process of object-oriented development targeted toward real-time and embedded systems. We will begin with analysis.

Analysis is the process of identifying the properties necessary for a solution to be both correct and proper. This can be decomposed into several steps, as identified in Chapter 4. The primary steps in analysis are the identification and analysis of the requirements per se, the identification of the structural object model, and the required behavioral models. Each of these topics is discussed in detail in the chapters to follow.[1]

---

1. Systems analysis is omitted because it is often not used except in very large-scale and complex systems. In most systems, the requirements analysis phase subsumes the systems analysis activities, as needed.

Chapter 5 incorporates use cases and scenarios in the specification of the requirements of the system. These requirements specify the externally visible behavior of the system, without revealing or implying any internal structure. The chapter provides a number of ways to specify the details of this behavior.

Use cases are realized in object models as collaborations. This is the topic of Chapter 6, which focuses on so-called structural object analysis—the identification of the elements and interactions of these collaborations. The chapter provides useful strategies for the identification and refinement of objects within the realizing collaborations.

Of course, the end user is primarily concerned with what the system does, not with how it is structured. The details of object behavioral models are provided in Chapter 7. This chapter identifies the three types of behavior and spends special effort on the use of finite state machines. Both types of UML state machines (statecharts and activity diagrams) are examined in terms of how they can be applied to the refinement of the object collaborations defined in the previous chapter.

Chapter 5

Requirements Analysis of Real-Time Systems

*Those arguing that something is impossible should
get out of the way of those actually doing it.*

—Book of Douglass, Law 72

Real-time systems interact with their external environment. The set of external objects of significance and their interactions with the system form the basis for the requirements analysis of the system. This is expressed in two forms—an external event context and the Use Case model. The external event context is expressed as an object model in which the system itself is treated as a single black-box composite object sending and receiving messages to external actor objects. The Use Case and scenario models decompose the primary functionality of the system and the protocols necessary to meet these functional requirements.

5.1 Introduction

Early analysis of systems can be thought of as discovering, in detail, the requirements of the final product. The UML provides an integrated set of modeling tools to capture and explore these requirements. From there, the developer can use the UML's other concepts and notations to drill down in more detail to elaborate the interior of the system.

One of the strengths of the UML's representation of requirements is that it is intuitive while still allowing the developer to select detailed representation to model the system in terms of user-selectable rigor and completeness.

The primary concerns during requirements analysis are

- Determine the large scale "clumps" of functionality that appear to be relatively independent and refine the behavior of these clumps in an understandable and unambiguous manner
- Identify the actors in the external environment that interact with the system in interesting ways
- Identify the semantics and characteristics of the individual messages (including those associated with signaling the occurrence of events) that pass between the system and its set of actors
- Refine the protocols of interactions that use the individual messages, including required sequences, pre-conditional, and post-conditional invariants

Tools the UML brings to bear on these concerns are the use case, statecharts, and sequence diagrams.

5.2 Terms and Concepts

5.2.1 Use Cases

Requirements are typically understood and specified by *domain experts*, who may be the ultimate system users, marketing staff, or academics working in the field. Most of these domain experts are not used to rigorous thinking along the same lines as system developers, and this disparity remains one of the key gaps that must be closed by the analyst. The problem is well known and accounts for requirements specifications that are ambiguous, contradictory, or just plain wrong. The analyst's job is to extract the requirements and capture them so that they can be analyzed and refined.

System requirements generally fall into two categories. *Functional requirements* are the expectations of system behavior as viewed from outside the system and will be such things as move air control surfaces to maintain a steady flight; display a waveform of cardiac electrical activity; and adjust the position of the reactor control rods to maintain a constant core temperature. These functional requirements are devoid of performance, reliability, or safety considerations.

The other kind of requirements are called *quality of service (QoS) requirements*. Such requirements specify the necessary performance, reliability, and safety of the functional requirements. QoS requirements never stand alone; they elaborate one or more functional requirements. For example, QoS requirements might be that the control surface must be fully stable with an airspeed of up to 800 knots; the waveform data is displayed with no more than 0.25s lag; and the control rod actuation control must be able to maintain core temperature within a 1.5 degree accuracy. For most embedded and real-time systems, QoS requirements are just as important as functional requirements, so their extraction and exploration must be a primary concern to the analyst.

In practical terms, the main tool that analysts bring to bear to capture requirements is the *use case*, which is a coherent piece of functionality of a system that is visible (in black-box form) from outside the system [1]. Use cases are strictly behavioral and neither define nor imply a set of objects or classes. In fact, moving from a strictly external behavioral-only view into the structural-and-behavioral view is not a task that can be automated with today's technology. The fact that a use case is externally visible implies that this system behavior interacts with objects in the system's external universe. These objects are called *actors*. Use cases associate with actors, enabling them to exchange messages.

Actors may be human users or externally visible subsystems and devices, such as sensors and actuators. It is a common mistake by neophyte modelers to assume that actors must be people. Whether the actor is a device used by a human or the human itself depends on the scope of the system. If the system development includes the development of devices that interact with a human, then the human is the actor. If the system must interact with existing (or separately supplied) devices that are, in turn, used by human users, then the interface devices are the actors because they are the first thing outside the system scope that actually interacts with the system.

Figure 5-1 shows a typical use case diagram. The (optional) rectangle represents the system boundary, the stick figures represent the actors, and the ovals represent the use cases. The lines between actors and use cases are associations, allowing the exchange of messages. Use cases may relate to other use cases, as shown by the generalization of one use case into another.

It is vital for the analyst to understand that *use cases don't define or even imply any specific internal structure*. Use cases are realized by collaborations of objects acting in concert. These collaborations are made up of societies of objects working together to achieve the functionality of the use case. To complicate things further, objects usually participate in multiple use cases. Thus, drilling down from requirements analysis to object analysis involves a many-to-many map of use cases and objects. This process is one of discovery and invention and remains a nontrivial step that defies automation. I've worked with a number of aerospace companies, helping to elaborate a process for moving from systems engineering to software engineering, and the solutions remain problematic at best.

5.2.2 Messages and Events

Capturing use cases and identifying participant actors is only one of the analysts' chores. They must also identify the messages passing between the actors and the system, their relevant properties, and their protocols of interaction.

As discussed in Chapter 1, a message is an abstraction of the exchange of information between a sender and a receiver. The implementation details of the exact mechanism of message exchange is ignored during use case analysis. However, messages have properties that are required in order to characterize the functionality and quality of service requirements of the system.

Logically, messages consist of several aspects. The first and most obvious is their *semantic content*. This is the meaning of the message,

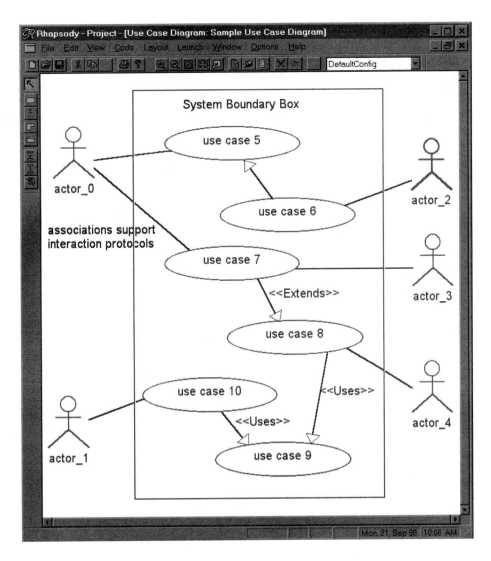

Figure 5-1: *Use Case Diagram*

such as "insert the control rod" or "the current temperature is 576 degrees." The structure of the message, called its *signature,* is generally limited in requirements analysis to a list of parameters, which aid the understanding at the black-box level of system abstraction. Pre- and post-conditional invariants are ontological states assumed to be true prior to the sending of a message and following its receipt, respectively. This is of particular concern in systems in which messages must occur in one of a set of predefined sequences or when the system's response to messages varies based on its state of existence.

Just as important are the QoS characteristics of the message. Most common for real-time and embedded systems, message arrival pattern and message synchronization pattern must be fully defined, as discussed in Chapter 2. Other QoS properties may be defined, as well, such as reliability.

Events can precipitate the sending of a message. As will be discussed in Chapter 7, an event is an occurrence in space and time, which has significance to the system. Events in the external environment can be manifested as messages to which the system responds. The UML defines four stereotypes of events: signal events, call events, change events, and time events.[1] Signals are associated with asynchronous SignalEvents. Signals are subtypes of a Request; Requests, in turn, are associated with MessageInstances in the UML metamodel. CallEvents are events that occur as the result of an operation call or service request. CallEvents are associated with OperationCalls; an OperationCall is also a subtype of a Request. Change events occur when a value of interest changes. Time events can occur either with the elapse of a specified period of time or the arrival of the system at a predetermined absolute time. All of these kinds of events are relevant to use case analysis, although by far the most common are Signals.

5.2.3 Scenarios, Protocols, and State Machines

A use case is a definition of a coherent chunk of system functionality. An instance of a use case is a particular path through the behavior. Such a path is called a scenario. A scenario consists of a set of objects (in this case, of the "system" and some set of actors) and an ordered list of messages exchanged among them. Scenarios have branching points at which there may be several responses or actions available to either the actor or the system. Every path with a unique set of branch points constitutes a separate scenario. By this definition, many scenarios are required to fully elaborate a use case—typically one dozen to several dozen.

---

1. In the UML metamodel, events are a submetaclass of the metaclass *Classifier*. Classifiers in general can have associated state machines, but events generally do not.

A scenario contains both important and incidental branching points. In general, at least one scenario of every important branch must be modeled. Scenarios that differ only in incidental branches are typically ignored. The remaining set of scenarios are "interesting."

For example, an air traffic control use case might be "identify aircraft track" in which the system identifies a track from primary (surface reflection) and/or secondary (transponder request) radars and assigns it to a previously identified aircraft in the airspace or it creates a new one. Interesting scenarios include

- Coincident primary and secondary tracks match the predicted position of a single previously identified aircraft
- Track is identified by primary radar only and it matches the predicted position of a single previously identified aircraft
- Track is identified by secondary radar only and matches the predicted position of a single previously identified aircraft
- Track is identified by primary radar only and fits the potential flight envelopes of two previously identified aircraft equally well, extrapolated from their last known positions and flight capabilities
- Coincident primary and secondary tracks but no previously identified aircraft matches position (new aircraft enters airspace)
- Primary and secondary tracks differ by a significant margin (is it two aircraft or one?)

The first scenario might look something like Figure 5-2.

The scenarios in our list are all interestingly different from each other because the system behavior in each is different. Not all scenarios differ in interesting ways. For example, the presence of additional aircraft in the airspace far removed from the new track does not change the system behavior with respect to the new track. Modeling all scenarios is impossible because the complete set of scenarios is either infinite or close enough to infinite that the difference doesn't matter. However, it is important that all the interesting scenarios, the ones during which the system behaves qualitatively differently, are modeled. The set of interesting scenarios is finite (although it may be large) and should be captured in its entirety.

Experience has shown that use cases and scenarios are understandable by virtually all domain experts. This is extremely valuable to the

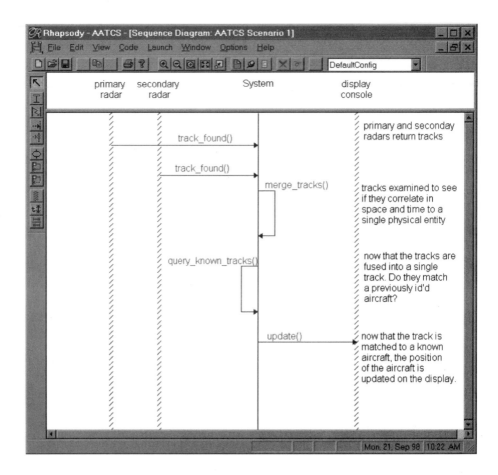

Figure 5-2: *Air Traffic Control Scenario 1*

analyst; it provides a common notation and semantic means to discuss system behavior. However, scenarios are at best only semi-constructive. Because any scenario, by definition, omits most of the behavior of the system, the totality of scenarios must be examined in detail to capture all the requirements correctly.

Another means by which use case behavior can be captured is via statecharts. These have the advantage of being more formal and rigorous. However, they are beyond the ken of many, if not most, domain experts. Statecharts also have the advantage that they are fully constructive—a single statechart represents the full scope of the use case behavior. Where statecharts are appropriate, it is common to use both statecharts and scenarios to model the use case behavior.

5.3 Use Cases

In early analysis, the use case diagram is similar to a traditional context diagram [3]. It shows the general cases of interaction among the system and the external objects. The use case diagram relies on the underlying event and message flows that would be shown on a context diagram.

The top-level use case diagram is a view of the system context. It provides an overview of the system—not of classes and objects, but of function points.[2] A function point is a broad scope area of functionality of the system and is isomorphic to a use case. Note that actors may participate in some use cases but not in others.

Use cases are generic transactions that potentially involve many actors and many messages. Use cases are important because they provide a valuable tool for capturing system requirements.

In the UML, a use case is a metasubtype of the metaclass *Classifier*. Classifiers can have attributes, operations, and statecharts. It is important to keep in mind that even though a use case may have such structural elements, the use case does not define object or implementation structure. Attributes, operations, and statecharts must be realized in some way by the object implementation, but usually not in a direct mapping.

Attributes of a use case are generally used to denote the (externally visible) state of the use case. This is important, especially when the use case participates in complex interactions with its associated actors. They may also be used to hold values in the behavioral description of the use case. Again, the presence of such use case attributes does not mean those attributes will appear in that form in the implementation.

A use case can have operations. Use case operations are pieces of functionality the use case uses to decompose the behavioral specification of the use case. They are not directly accessible outside the use case but serve as a means to partition and define the use case in more detail.

---

2. These function points and use cases can relate to vertical partitioning of the system. Internal organization of the system objects is discussed in the next chapter.

Behavior may be defined by a statechart, textual description, activity diagram, or formal language declaration. The behavioral description of the use case should include not only the main behavior, but common variants and exceptional (for example, error) conditions, as well.

Use cases are almost exclusively used to describe black-box system functionality. It does this via association with actors. An actor is a user of a classifier that is external to it. Because use cases are mostly applied to the entire system, virtually all actors are things in the system's environment. However, use cases can be used to describe internal pieces (also classifiers) at a lower level of abstraction. When this is done, the "system" to which the use case is applied may be any other classifier, such as a class. The peer classes that associate with the class to which the use case is being applied constitute the actors at that level of abstraction.

5.3.1 Use Case Relations

UML 1.1 (the first OMG-approved UML standard) provided two specialized stereotypes of the generalization relationship: «*uses*» and «*extends*». The generalization relation allowed one use case to be a more general version of another. The «uses» relation was employed primarily when one piece of the functionality was extracted out as a separate use case, analogous to a functional subroutine, except that the isolated functionality is included directly in the base use case. The «extends» relation meant that one use case was an extended version of another—it had the same behavior as the base use case, and something more.

This set of relations was somewhat controversial within the UML Revision Task Force (RTF), as well as with modelers in the object-oriented community. For example, many people (including myself) found it counter-intuitive for the «uses» relation to be a stereotype of generalization. As I write this, the RTF has pretty much settled on a somewhat different use case relation model, which I will describe here. It is possible that by the time the UML RTF is finished, the final use case relation model will differ from the following description.

In the new and improved use case relation model, there are still three types of use case relations: generalization, includes, and extends. The primary difference is that the «includes» is what «uses» used to be, and both «includes» and «extends» relations are stereotypes of the dependency relation rather than of generalization.

5.3.1.1 Use Case Generalization Relation

This relation declares that one use case (called the *base use case*) is a more general form of another (called the *derived use case*). Just as with class generalization, the more specialized use case inherits all the attributes and operations and the statechart (if any) of the base use case. The derived use case may both extend and specialize the base use case.

5.3.1.2 Use Case Extension Relation

The «extends» relation is a stereotype of the dependency relation between two use cases. The use case to be extended is called the *base use case;* the extended use case is called the *client use case*. The idea is that the base use case identifies a number of specific extension points in its behavioral description. These extension points are locations within the base use case at which the client use case may insert additional behavior. A base use case may have any number of extension points. The client use case defines the extension sequences for the extension points in the base. The dependency arrow points toward the base use case.

5.3.1.3 Use Case Includes Relation

The «includes» use case relation is also a stereotype of dependency. It defines a behavioral segment that will be included in the base use case. The use case that imports the behavior is called the *client use case;* the use case provided the included behavior is the *supplier use case*. This is especially useful when a unit of behavior is used by several other use cases. Rather than replicate the behavior in each, it can be extracted out into a supplier use case. The dependency arrow points toward the supplier use case. The use relations are shown in Figure 5-3.

5.3.2 Use Case Example: Air Traffic Control System

Let's put use cases to work on an example problem—an air traffic control system.

ACME Air Traffic Control System

The Acme Air Traffic Control System (AATCS) is meant to manage the information necessary for human controllers to control the local

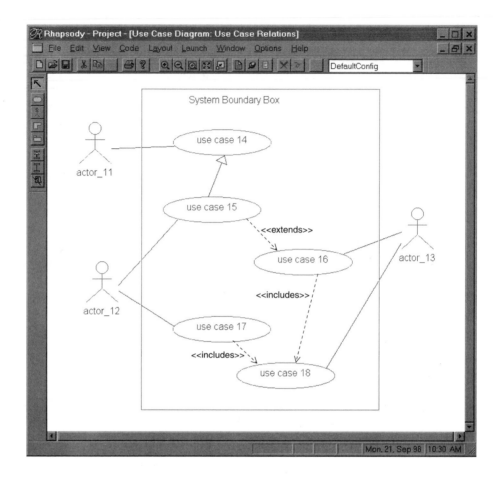

Figure 5-3: *Use Case Relations*

airspace and ground space for incoming and outgoing aircraft. Each aircraft preparing to leave or enter the control space must file a flight plan. This flight plan consists of a point and time of departure, a point and time of arrival, and an average ground speed, in addition to the information necessary to uniquely identify the aircraft. The aircraft identification includes a call sign, an owning company and flight number, and an aircraft type, which denotes its flight limitations (for example, altitude and air-speed range). AATCS maintains a list of all aircraft moving or preparing to move within the airspace and surface. The flight plan is approved by the controllers or returned with suggestions for change. When filing a flight plan prior to departure, this negotiation must be complete before the aircraft is cleared.

When an aircraft is cleared for taxiing, it taxis from its gate to the designated runway, where it awaits clearance to take off. Once final clearance is given (subject to current runway use and other flights awaiting final clearance), the plane is allowed to take off using the runway designated by the tower controller. At any time after a plane has left the gate but before it is given take-off clearance, it may be routed to a holding area. This may be due to environmental or scheduling conditions.

When an aircraft approaches for landing, it does so along its flight plan. As the aircraft approaches the airport, it must request clearance to land. The controller may grant clearance and provide a runway ID and directions, or he may give an alternate flight path, such as circling the airport at a designated altitude, distance, and air speed.

The system maintains the original flight plan, along with an actual flight plan, which is updated during the course of the flight. All aircraft in the local airspace are monitored using a primary radar, which uses a rotating emitter/receiver and aircraft skin reflection to identify targets in the airspace. The primary radar masks out ground-based obstructions (such as mountains and buildings). Processing associated with the primary radar signals identifies tracks based on computed position (requiring direction and time-of-flight of signal) and the known last position of all aircraft in the airspace. In addition to the primary radar, a secondary radar also provides information on aircraft. This radar sends out a transponder code request. Upon receiving the transponder identification request, the aircraft responds automatically, within a narrow and fixed time window. The return signal contains the aircraft beacon code and the aircraft's estimate of its altitude. Distance is computed via the signal time-of-flight. Aircraft may be monitored using only primary radar (for aircraft that have not filed a flight plan and do not have an active transponder—for example, smugglers) or secondary radar (for stealth aircraft), but normally both are used. A special icon is shown for planes that have been detected but not yet identified.

The airspace is displayed to the controller on one or more display screens. The aircraft are shown as plane icons pointing in the direction of flight, with relevant information textually tagged, including call sign, altitude, ground speed, and identification confidence level (how sure the system is that the radar image is that of the identified aircraft). Should the aircraft get within a specified distance of another (the distance varies with the types of aircraft involved, their trajectory vectors, and their proximity to the airport), the conflicting aircraft icon colors change from blue to yellow. There is also a smaller separation distance defined between aircraft, indicating a high level of warning in which the colors of the relevant aircraft change to red and the plane icons flash. These warning colors also apply to aircraft traveling too close to surface topology features.

The display may be shown in different levels of zoom, with radial rings indicating distance, under user control. Supported zoom levels show radial rings at 1, 5, 10, and 50 miles. Fixed surface topological features (buildings and mountains) are shown. Weather cells can also be shown to aid the controller in proper aircraft routing. When visible, weather is shown in false color—background indicating calm and clear gradually approaching bright red for severe weather. When a plane icon overlays a weather or surface feature, the portion of the icon overlaying the feature changes color to be highly visible against it. Menus for operator commands can pop up next to the aircraft icons by moving a cursor over the aircraft and hitting a menu button. One of the menu options shall be to display the planned flight plan (as a light blue line) for the aircraft, overlayed with the actual flight plan up to the current position (as a bright blue dashed line). However, none of the control, topological, or weather information is allowed to obscure the visibility of the aircraft icons at any time.

All actual monitored flight information must be stored for 30 days.

What are some use cases for this system? Some candidates are

- Allocate runways
- Guide planes though the take-off procedure

- Guide planes through the landing procedure
- Identify potential collision problems and manage such alarms
- Map radar sensor input to known aircraft, with confidence limits
- Update aircraft position on display
- Control zoom level
- Display airspace to the human air traffic controller
- Display weather and surface topology
- Acquire sensor data from primary and secondary radars

A little thought shows that these use cases are not merely simple data flows. Consider "Map radar sensor input to known aircraft, with confidence limits." The problem is

1. Take potentially unreliable data from multiple sources
2. Compare it to known aircraft populating or potentially populating the air space, along with their flight plans
3. Assign the sensor image as one of these aircraft, with computed confidence parameters (based on tracked actual flight plan and aircraft performance characteristics)
4. Discard redundant sensor indicators
5. Update the position and trajectory of the assigned aircraft or declare a new aircraft in the airspace

This lengthy and involved process can take multiple paths. Each sequence of messages is a different scenario. The totality of all such scenarios comprises the use case "Identify and update aircraft position."

Figure 5-4 shows the use case diagram for an air traffic control system. For simplicity, many normal functions of such a system are omitted. The scope of this system is the monitoring and control of nearby aircraft for the purpose of landing, take off, and runway management.

The figure identifies several actors. Some of these are sensors. The primary radar sweeps the local airspace vicinity by emitting radar and monitoring the returns created by skin reflection. The secondary radar works by asking the aircraft transponder to respond with its plane identification and its determination of its own position.

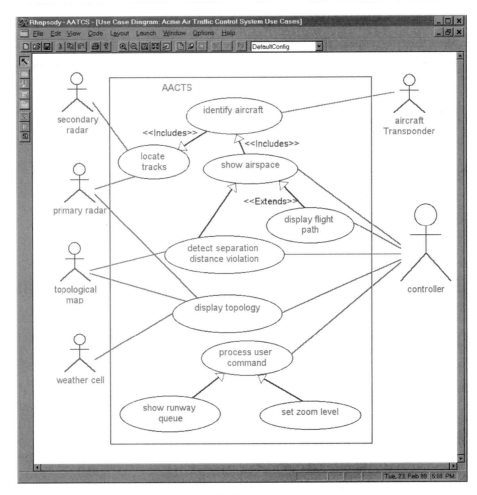

Figure 5-4: *AATCS Use Case Diagram*

5.4 External Events

The *system context* is a map of the world of interest to the system. We shall use the term *system* to include the conceptual whole, consisting of software, electrical hardware, and mechanical hardware under development. The use case diagram shows the system as a single entity surrounded by other objects in the real world and the important messages sent among them.

5.4.1 Context-Level Messages

The UML defines the *message* as the fundamental unit of object communication. Later in design, we'll decide whether this message is implemented in terms of a direction invocation of an object behavior, an RTOS message, or a message across a communications bus. At this point in the development process, it is more important to capture the essential properties of the messages that are exchanged among the system and the actors interacting with it. Subsequent design will define the implementation of each message.

5.4.1.1 Message Properties

An event is an occurrence that is important to the system. Events are like classes and can optionally contain data. Events are normally manifested to the system as messages[3] sent among objects or between an actor and the system. For example, a control knob can send an event when it is turned. One approach would send out an event for each click of the knob. Another approach is to band-limit the rate at which these events are sent and pass the number of clicks as a parameter of the event message. The event message then conveys not only the fact that the event occurred but also the number of clicks that occurred. Because events are generally manipulated as event messages (except within state machines, discussed in Chapter 7), we will use the terms *event* and *message* synonymously here.

The arrival pattern of the message describes the timing behavior of the set of message instances. The UML does not describe these directly, but the characterization of arrival patterns is crucial for analysis of schedulability and deadlines. This is important to define early because the feasibility of a cost-sensitive product is often determined by component and development costs. By understanding the message and event characteristics, it is possible to perform early performance analysis of different processor architecture choices and make good business

---

3. The actual parameters of the message are commonly used to represent the formal parameters of the event.

decisions about whether the product can be delivered within an acceptable cost window.

Message arrivals can be *episodic*[4] or *periodic*. An episodic arrival pattern is inherently less predictable than a periodic arrival pattern, but it may still be *bounded* in any number of ways. Clearly, nothing can be said about the schedulability of a system when the arrival times of messages to which it must respond are totally unknown. Characterizing the arrival times of episodic events is required for schedulability analysis. Episodic messages may be described by:

- Bounding times, such as a *minimum (or maximum) inter-arrival time*, which is a minimum (or maximum) time that must occur between message arrivals

- Central tendency and dispersion statistics, such as an *average arrival rate* with a *standard deviation* and *standard error*

- Autocorrelative dependencies among individual message arrivals

Bounding, or *sandboxing,* the inter-arrival times permits worst case analysis to be made even if the underlying probability density function is unknown. Often, an average arrival rate is known, along with associated dispersion statistics. When such information is available, more-detailed analysis is possible, particularly for soft real-time schedulability analysis (see Chapter 11).

Most simple analysis assumes that the arrivals of the events are independent. For example, the time between one pair of messages does not affect the time to the next message in the sequence. However, message arrival times may always be independent. It sometimes happens that messages may correlate in time. The presence of one message may make it more (or less) likely that another message will arrive soon after. These are called autocorrelative dependencies among the message arrival times. For example, some messages tend to arrive in clumps— such messages are referred to as *bursty*.

Periodic messages are characterized by a *period* with which the messages arrive and *jitter,* which is the variation around the period with which messages actually arrive. Jitter is normally modeled as a uniform random process but always totally within the specified interval.

---

4. Episodic event arrivals are also known as aperiodic. However, I find the term episodic more descriptive because the event arrivals correlate to an episode or event occurrence in the real world.

Synchronization patterns are explicitly, if somewhat weakly, supported by the UML standard. Synchronization defines characteristics of the rendezvous of two objects that occurs during the exchange of a message. The synchronization patterns explicitly defined by the UML are call, asynchronous, and waiting.

The call and waiting synchronization patterns are similar in that the sender is blocked from continuing until the target completes its message processing. The *call synchronization pattern* models the yielding of control during a function or method call that occurs within a single thread of control. The *waiting synchronization pattern* models the yielding of control to another thread until message processing is complete. Remote procedure calls (RPCs) are usually implemented with just this synchronization pattern. The *asynchronous synchronization pattern* is inherently multithreaded; it models a message being passed to another object, without yielding control.

Booch [4] also defines balking and timeout synchronization patterns, which are extensions to the core UML model. The *balking synchronization pattern* models the behavior of one object aborting the message transfer if the other is not immediately available. The *timeout pattern* models the balking pattern except that a fixed waiting time is defined for the receiver object to accept the message. The Ada programming language tasking constructs explicitly support balking and timeout synchronization.

5.5 Specifying External Messages

In real-time systems, external messages (including events) play an important role in constraining and defining the system behavior. For example, an air traffic control system must respond and deal with messages from a number of sensors, such as a radar "ping" indicating both azimuthal (radial) angle and distance, a transponder signal indicating aircraft identification and proposed position, and commands from the controller to manage the display (including set the zoom level, disable audible alarms, and so forth). An association between an actor and the system supports a potentially rich set of actual events that may be decomposed into an event hierarchy.

Events by themselves provide insufficient information for the development of a system. The expected system response to each event must be specified in terms of what the system should do and the timing requirements for this response. In addition, complex protocols that describe all possible legal sequences of event and message exchanges are often required. The characteristics of the individual events are often captured in the external event list. The protocols of event and message interactions are best described by sets of sequence diagrams and statecharts associated with the use cases.

5.5.1 External Event List

The external event list is a detailed list of the environmental events and messages that are of interest to the system. The list defines not only the events, but also the expected system response, their arrival patterns, and the event source. Table 5-1 shows an external event list for our air traffic control system.

As you can see, the external event list provides a number of attributes to capture the essential properties of events.

Table 5-1: *Acme Air Traffic Control System External Event List*

	Event	Description	Direction	Arrival Pattern	Response Performance
1	Primary radar ping	Periodic command to transmit a primary radar pulse	To primary radar	Periodic	20 ms period
2	Primary radar return	Surface reflection return from an aircraft or environmental feature	To system	Episodic	<10 ms response
3	Secondary radar ping	Periodic command to transmit a secondary radar pulse	To secondary radar	Periodic	20 ms period
4	Secondary radar return	Transponder response to a request	To system	Episodic	<10 ms response *(continued)*

Table 5-1: (*cont.*)

	Event	Description	Direction	Arrival Pattern	Response Performance
5	Radar control synch pulse	Pulse to system to confirm synchronization of radar transmitter position	To system	Periodic	2 sec period
6	User cursor movement	User moves cursor via pointing device	To system	Episodic	<5 ms response
7	User screen command	User selects a menu or menu item via a button push or click event	To display	Episodic	<100 ms response
8	Weather cell identification	External weather system updates weather cell map	To display	Periodic	<50 ms response
9	Separation distance violation detected	Violation must be visually tagged on the screen	To display	Episodic	<50 ms response
10	Log airspace activity	Periodically, airspace information for all aircraft and weather features must be logged	To log device	Periodic	100 ms period ± 10 ms

5.5.2 Response Time

In the realm of real-time systems, defining the external timing requirements is crucial to understanding the problem. An otherwise-correct result delivered past its deadline is a system failure in a hard, real-time environment. The key is to extend the external event table to include reactive timing.

A number of parameters are required to specify the timing requirements for real-time systems. Naturally, incoming messages must have their timing characterized. If they are periodic, then their periods and jitter must be identified. If they are episodic, then their stochastic properties must be defined. System response timing must be defined in terms of timeliness requirements (typically, deadlines). If the response has a hard deadline, then missing the deadline constitutes a system failure. In a soft deadline system, another timeliness measure, such as tolerable mean lateness, must be specified (see Chapter 11).

More-complex timing behavior requires more-complex modeling. In some cases, scalars (for example, deadlines) can adequately specify the timing of behavioral responses. However, this is a valid modeling technique only when traditional, hard deadline models of timeliness are used. In fact, in most systems, the use of hard deadlines is an unwarranted simplification; the use of utility functions are more appropriate.

Utility functions model the usefulness of an action (its "utility") as a function of time, from the occurrence of the event precipitating the action or from the start of the action itself. A hard deadline is a simple model in which the utility of the event response is 1 if it completes prior to the deadline and 0 otherwise (or - ∞ if the action is actively and severely counterproductive). That is, hard deadlines assume the utility of the event response is a binary function with a discontinuity at a certain point (the deadline). More-elaborate utility functions are possible, including

- Scaleable binary functions so that the relative utility of different event responses can be compared (for example, 4 versus 18)
- Smooth utility functions with no discontinuity at all, to model event responses that have a range in value but need not become valueless even if tardy
- Variant utility functions that permit the form of the utility function to vary over time ("progressive utility")

Many actions require relatively long periods of time to perform, and intermediate, even if partial, responses may be important. For example, an emergency shutdown of a nuclear reactor is implemented by insertion of control rods into the core. This may be initiated by an event such as a coolant leak or an explosive temperature and pressure build up. This takes some period of time. To avert an "incident," it is preferable to insert the rods 90 percent of the way as soon as possible even if the remaining 10 percent takes much longer. Control loops are another example. Quick, if incomplete, responses stabilize PID control loops, even if the system response asymptotically converges much later.

These issues are domain- and system-specific. For many situations, the only concerns are service time and latency. Modeling 50 percent or 80 percent response times may be important in some special applications. In other applications, several points from a stimulus-response curve may be required to adequately characterize the performance requirements. These topics are discussed in Chapter 11.

In most real-time systems, the time-response requirements are crucial because they define a performance budget for the system action. As objects and classes are defined, this performance budget propagates through the analysis and design phases. Ultimately, the performance requirement manifests itself as a performance (sub)budget for every operation and function call in the thread of execution responding to the event. The sum of the (sub)budgets must meet the overall system performance requirement specified here. For example, a message and the completion of its reaction may require 500 ms. The overall reaction may be implemented via a chain of six operations. Each of these operations must be allocated some portion of the overall performance budget.[5]

5.6 Detailing Use Case Behavior

Use cases are named pieces of coherent functionality. Good use case names are important because they aid in understanding the functional decomposition of externally visible behavior. Nevertheless, they are inadequate in defining the behavior implied by a use case in sufficient detail to build the correct system. Therefore, the UML allows more-detailed specification of behavior of use cases, even though it does not dictate the form. The most common ways are

- Informal textual description
- Formal textual description (for example, expressed in programming or constraint language)
- Scenarios
- Statecharts

---

5. The performance budget for each operation must include the worst case blocking as well, not only the time required to execute the individual actions of the method.

5.6.1 Informal Textual Description

Consider the use case "Detect airspace separation distance violation." A number of algorithms are possible. Let us suppose that the domain expert has given us one in the form of a textual description:

The system shall use an alpha-beta tracker:

$$\frac{\text{New}}{\text{position}} = \text{alpha} \times \frac{\text{predicted}}{\text{position}} + \text{beta} \times \frac{\text{measured}}{\text{position}}$$

Measured position comes from slant range (use the speed of light and two times the distance because we are reflecting, and use the time at which the signal came in—that is, there is a counter from the time the transmitted signal went out) and azimuth angle at which the target replied. We need to average the azimuths from the multiple replies to get the azimuth of the "return." Now we have slant range and az angle. To get to a range parallel to the flat earth, we need to know altitude. From the secondary radar, you know the altitude if you can correlate the track from the primary (which has no ID info) and the secondary. Generally, this correlation can be done because the aircraft tracks from the different sources are very close. So now you have range, az, and alt. The primary and secondary radars may be co-located, but this is not the general case. When they are not co-located, a geometric translation must be performed so that they reference objects using the same spatial origin.

Now you have measured position. So all you need is old, predicted position, which is obtained by extrapolation. In the beginning of the track, there is no old, predicted position to work with. So at first, position is measured position. Then on the second scan, you can measure velocity by subtraction (these are not Doppler radars). At first, you can't extrapolate with acceleration, but after a few measurements, you can use a finite difference as an estimate of the first derivative. That gives us position, velocity, and acceleration.

Separation is difference in position, and predicted separation is difference in predicted position.

In addition, when a flight plan is filed, the system looks at the set of known flight plans, to find predicted separation violations in the plans. This is done prior to accepting the flight plan. During this preflight plan approval stage, arrival times are scheduled so that there is no over-demand on the runway capacity (runways are the limiting item). One uses a standard arrival route (STAR) close in to the runway, so the distance can be measured along the path of the STAR based on the routine velocity in that portion (difference in arrival time is known, velocity is known, therefore spacing is known). Terrain maps, which include buildings, are provided by survey for separation calculations between them and aircraft positions and predicted positions. If there is low confidence in the position of a track, then a larger separation is required.

5.6.2 Scenarios

As mentioned previously, scenarios are specific instances of use cases. Scenarios model order-dependent message sequences among objects collaborating to produce system behavior. Scenarios within a given use case show permutations of object interactions. Even early in analysis, the advantage of scenarios is that domain experts and users can usually easily walk the analyst through dozens of typical system usage scenarios. The domain expert can explain why each step is taken, who initiates it, what the appropriate responses are, and what kinds of things can go awry. In going through this process, the analyst will uncover many important facets of the system behavior not mentioned within the problem statement. Scenarios provide an invaluable tool for validating the problem statement against the user's expectations, as well as for uncovering the less obvious requirements. Late in analysis, they can be used to test the object structure by ensuring the appropriate participation by each object in each scenario. Even at the end of development, they provide the core set of validation tests that ensure the delivered system meets its specifications.

Early in analysis, objects available for scenarios are the system and the external objects identified in the context and use case diagrams. Later analysis decomposes the system into objects, and the scenario process can be applied to them, as well. Ultimately, internal scenarios must map to the identified use cases. In fact, the objects identified decompose into multiple objects, and the messages are decomposed into protocols that consist of many messages. Just as iterative refinement of the object model identifies more classes, refinement of the scenarios adds more detail to the interactions.

It is important to stress that building and analyzing scenarios is a creative process of discovery. It is not simply a matter of starting with postulates and applying mathematical deduction to derive all possible behavior paths. Deep within the crevices of the domain experts' minds are hidden requirements that, if left to the experts' own devices, will never be explicitly identified. These cannot be deduced from the problem statement per se. The process of scenario modeling brings these hidden requirements to the surface, where they can be added to the system features.

Two primary scenario models exist within the UML: sequence diagrams and collaboration diagrams. However, collaboration diagrams are not often used in use case analysis and will not be discussed in this chapter.

5.6.3 Sequence Diagrams

Sequence diagrams show the sequence of messages between objects. The graphical syntax for sequence diagrams was shown in Figure 5-2. This figure shows all the elements used in most sequence diagrams. The vertical "instance lines" represent objects, with the name of the object written above or below the line. The horizontal or slanted directed lines are messages. Each message line starts at the *originator object* and ends at the *target object* and has a message name on the line. This name might, in later phases, specify an operation with a parameter list and a return value. Time flows from the top of the page downward so that "query_known_tracks" is sent before "update," and so on. The time axis shows only sequence; the scale is not linear, nor is a scale provided.

Note the textual annotation along the right side of the diagram. This descriptive text identifies initial conditions, actions, and activities not shown by the message sequence itself. Some of the messages are internal to the object—that is, they have the same originator and target object. This means that the message is sent internally from one method to another within the same object. It is not necessary to identify such messages, but it can be illuminating to do so.

Most sequence diagrams contain only the elements identified in Figure 5-2: objects, messages, (implicit) inactive periods, and scenario annotations. Sequence diagrams can contain a great deal more infor-

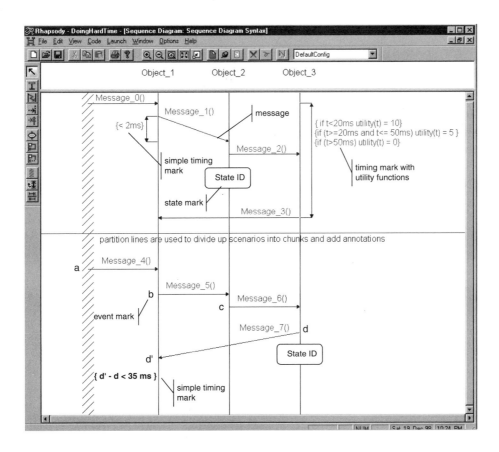

Figure 5-5: *Sequence Diagram Syntax*

mation when necessary, however. Figure 5-5 shows some additional features relevant to real-time system developers, including timing marks and states.

Each message in Figure 5-5 has an optional identifier off to the left or right of it; in this case, a letter from *A* to *D*. These are *event identifiers* and can be provided when it is necessary to reference the event that gives rise to the message. In addition, they can be included in timing-mark expressions to indicate relative time between events.

Timing marks are indicated in two fashions. The first is to use a marker bar with a time value between the two ends. This kind of time mark is shown between events *D* and *D'*. It defines the time between the two events as less than 35 ms in this example. Relational expressions can also indicate timing constraints. These are off to one side of the relevant messages and are delineated by curly braces. Event IDs are used in time expressions, as in

```
{ c - b <= 5 ms }
```

which means simply that the time between events *C* and *B* must be less than or equal to 5 ms.

Timing-mark expressions need not be for only adjacent events. Imagine two constraints:

1. The sum of the time among five events, *A* through *E*, must be less than 10 seconds.

2. The time between *C* and *D* must be less than or equal to 500 ms.

It is perfectly reasonable to write

```
{ e - a <   10 s
    d - c <= 500 ms        }
```

State marks bridge the gap between sequence and state diagrams. *State marks* are rounded rectangles[6] (the standard UML notation for a state on a state diagram) placed on the vertical object line. This allows the scenario to follow the state as it changes because of incoming events. More-specialized forms of sequence diagrams show detailed focus of control. These are discussed in later chapters.

In our AATCS example, we can see many opportunities for scenarios. Consider the use case "Locate tracks." A track is, according to my domain expert, a signal from an aircraft that has not yet been identified as an active aircraft and may be thought of as a state vector that contains 3-D position, 3-D velocity, and a time of validity. This use case needs to do several things:

1. Scan the airspace with the primary and secondary radars.

2. Create a new track upon either a primary or secondary radar hit.

3. Locate the track in three-space.

4. Resolve tracks from different sources into a smaller track set (determine co-hits).

---

6. SDL uses hexagons to mark states on sequence diagrams.

5.6.4 Statecharts for Defining Use Case Behavior

As discussed in Chapter 1, statecharts are a formal graphical language for specifying behavior. For this reason, they are especially applicable in the definition of use cases. Consider Figure 5-6. It shows a simple state machine for matching tracks from radar sources to known aircraft. Scenarios can be examined by following different paths through this statechart.

The detailed semantics and mechanisms of state machines are discussed in more detail in Chapter 7.

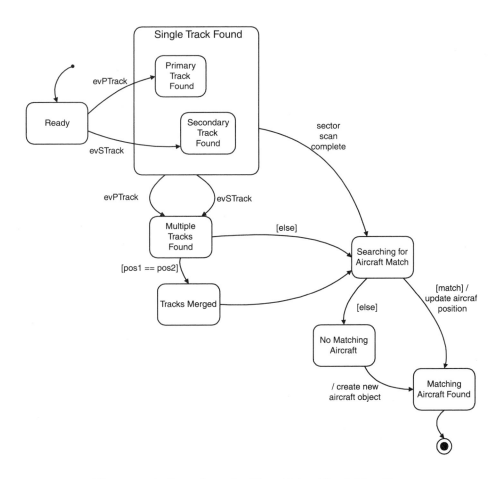

Figure 5-6: *Statechart for Identifying Track Use Case*

5.7 Identifying Use Cases

How does the analyst extract typical and nontypical uses of the system? Although some domain experts may think in abstract terms, the vast majority are more comfortable identifying specific scenarios rather than use cases. The analyst must identify the dozens (or hundreds) of scenarios that map the important system aspects and from these deduce the use cases. A number of approaches to identifying the scenarios are possible.

The analyst can sit with the customer and ask probing questions, such as:

- What are the primary functions of the system?
- What are the secondary functions of the system?
- With what physical devices or systems must the system interface?
- What are the different roles played by the human users of the system?
- Why is this system being built? What is it replacing and why?

The analyst must then identify for each use case:

- Roles the actors and system play in each scenario
- Interactions (flows) necessary to complete the scenario
- Sequences of events and data to realize the scenario
- Variations on the scenario that are possible (other related scenarios)

For example, the primary functions of the ECG monitor are to display waveforms for the physician, provide discrete patient numeric values (such as heart rate), and alarm when the patient is at risk. Secondary functions might be to provide a remote display for the surgeon, provide a permanent patient record, supply billing information to the hospital network, and so on. Why is the system being built? Perhaps it provides better arrhythmia detection, color displays for better differentiation of lead configurations, faster response times, or it interfaces to the hospital network and the operating room anesthesia machines.

Another approach works well with a small team. Each object in the context diagram is written on a 3" × 5" card,[7] including the system as one

---

7. These can evolve into class-responsibility-collaboration (CRC) cards for use later in the analysis phase.

of the objects. Each team member takes a card and assumes the identity of the object. The team members "role play" the scenario by passing written messages to each other. As each team member receives a message, the member must identify responses that he or she can reasonably make at this point. Each unique thread of responses is a scenario. The possible paths of these branch points define a decision tree. From this tree, a list of separate scenarios can be deduced.

The number of scenarios can quickly grow very large and require pruning. All scenarios that invoke identical system responses at each opportunity constitute a single interesting scenario. Primary scenarios elaborate the major ways the use case is realized in practice. Secondary scenarios are relatively minor variants of the primary scenarios to explore exception handling, safety issues, and other important (but at this stage, peripheral) issues. Booch suggests that a moderate project will have a few dozen use cases, an order of magnitude more primary scenarios, and an order of magnitude more secondary scenarios [5].

5.8 Using Use Cases

Use cases can provide a unifying strategy for the entire project development. They are an embodiment of what the customer wants and expects to see when the product ships. They also provide the base test suite for system validation. Use cases group together functionally related scenarios and provide valuable information into all phases, as illustrated in Table 5-2.

Table 5-2: *Use Cases in Different Development Stages*

Phase	Application of Use Cases
Analysis	• Suggest large-scale partitioning of the domain
	• Provide structuring of analysis objects
	• Clarify system and object responsibilities
	• Capture and clarify new features as they are added during development
	• Validate analysis model *(continued)*

Table 5-2: (*cont.*)

Phase	Application of Use Cases
Design	• Validate the elaboration of analysis models in the presence of design objects
Coding	• Clarify purpose and role of classes for coders
	• Focus coding efforts
Testing	• Provide primary and secondary test scenarios for system validation
Deployment	• Suggest iterative prototypes for spiral development

5.9 Heuristics for Good Requirements Analysis Diagrams

Good diagrams are like art—easy to identify but difficult to define the essential characteristics. Over the years, a number of attempts have been made to clarify what constitutes good diagrams in general. One of the most common is called the rule of 7 ± 2. However, this rule is overly simplistic and misinterprets the neurolinguistics research on which it was supposedly based. Neurolinguistics research found that most people can maintain seven concepts in their minds at once, within a common variance of about two concepts.

There are several problems with applying this research to the structuring of diagrams. First, the point of having a diagram is to present information. Because the road map is in front of you when you read a diagram, it isn't necessary to hold the information entirely in your mind, making the finding inapplicable at the outset. Second, in my experience, the normal application of this rule results in deeply nested sets of diagrams that are extremely difficult to navigate and comprehend. Third, the rule does not take into account the intrinsic complexity of the set of abstractions being represented. If a set of abstractions has a complex set of inter-relations, then it makes more sense to include enough context for the comprehension of the inter-relations rather than to artificially break up the intrinsically coupled abstractions. Last, the rule provides no guidance about how to break up a complex diagram into more understandable pieces. The slavish obedience to this rule has accounted for countless meaningless levels of decomposition that resulted in less-readable and less-understandable diagrams.

My basic rule for all diagrams is that each diagram should be *coherent*. That is, each diagram should have a mission and a level of abstraction. It should include everything relevant to its mission that is at that level of abstraction. If a class diagram's mission is to show a collaboration that realizes a use case, then the generalization hierarchies of those classes generally shouldn't be shown. Showing the details of the operations (such as their visibility, for example) doesn't aid in comprehension of the collaboration, so they should be omitted from this diagram. However, classes that participate in the collaboration should be shown, even if they number 20 or more.

Given that general rule, some heuristics for effectively constructing use case diagrams and use cases follow.

5.9.1 Use Case Diagram Heuristics

- Only in simple systems (<15 use cases, <12 actors) show all use cases on a single diagram.
- Show one use case generalization hierarchy per use case diagram.
- Show use of a common set of collaborating actors per use case diagram.
- Label each diagram with a note, including the system under development, the author, and initial date of creation, and the revision number for each diagram.
- Actors may be humans if the system scope includes user interface devices.
- Actors may be devices rather than humans if the system interfaces to devices outside its scope.

5.9.2 Use Case Heuristics

- Represent complex protocols of interactions via statecharts bound to the relevant use case.
- For rigorous use case definition, construct statecharts for the relevant use case.

- Minimize association-line crossing.
- Don't show associations among actors, only among actors and use cases.
- Mark extension points in whatever medium captures the details of the use case.
- If you have multiple domain experts, tag each use case with the relevant domain expert or reference documentation.

5.9.3 Use Case Sequence Diagram Heuristics

- Show only actors and the "system" as instances when the system is the scope.
- Build one sequence diagram per interesting scenario (system behavior differs at a branching point).
- Identify the pre-conditions for each scenario, as well as its purpose, using a text note.
- Identify the system under development, the use case, author and initial date of creation, and revision number for each diagram.
- Show timing marks to capture timing constraints where constrained in the problem domain.
- Multiple overlapping timing constraints should be analyzed for compatibility.
- Mark states of the use case on the sequence diagram where the use case is represented with statecharts.
- Label each message meaningfully, using problem-domain vocabulary.
- Use horizontal lines for normal messages.
- Use slanted lines for events.
- Show arrival and synchronization patterns for messages where dictated by the problem domain.
- Don't use branch points for focus on control for use case level sequence diagrams.
- Don't show explicit return from message unless the message is fundamentally asynchronous.

5.10 Summary

In this chapter, we explored the importance of capturing the system's environment to understand and characterize system behavior in a variety of circumstances. Use cases capture information about the system's environment in a different way. Use cases are a functional decomposition of the system's systemic behavior that does not reveal the system's internal structure. Use cases emphasize the behavior of the system rather than the incoming and outgoing events.

Use cases group together functionally related scenarios. Scenarios, in turn, group functionally related messages into a *protocol* as they pass among objects. The complete set of interesting scenarios defines the external behavior of the system. Scenarios are modeled using sequence and collaboration diagrams.

The information gathered during the construction of these diagrams is required before any object decomposition of the system can occur. The characterization of the external events and the integration of these events into the system use cases complete the external view of the system.

5.11 Looking Ahead

The next two chapters will "drill down" into the system and define objects, classes, and their relationships. Chapter 6 provides a number of strategies for the identification of objects and classes while Chapter 7 focuses on the specification of object behavior using state machines and operations.

5.12 Exercises

1. How does a use case differ from an object?
2. What is an actor and what does it contribute to the modeling of a system?

3. What are three kinds of relationships shown on a use case diagram? What kinds of things do each of these relationships relate?

4. What is the relation between a use case and a scenario?

5. What is the relation between a use case and a statechart?

6. What is the relation between a scenario and a statechart?

7. How does an analyst transition from a use case view to an object view?

8. What are the four kinds of events defined within the UML?

9. Define the use cases for a drive-by-wire automobile control computer, which monitors and controls braking, turning, acceleration control, and engine timing. What are the actors?

5.13 References

[1] Jacobson, Ivar, Magnus Christerson, Patrik Jonsson, and Gunnar Oevergaard. *Object-Oriented Software Engineering,* New York: ACM Press, 1992.

[2] Schneider, Geri and Jason Winters. *Applying Use Cases: A Practical Guide,* Reading, Mass.: Addison-Wesley, 1998.

[3] Ward, Paul and Steven Mellor. *Structured Development for Real-Time Systems,* Volumes 1-4, Englewood Cliffs, N.J.: Prentice Hall Press, 1985.

[4] Booch, Grady. *Object-Oriented Analysis and Design with Applications,* Redwood City, Calif.: Benjamin Cummings Press, 1994.

[5] Booch, Grady. *Object Solutions: Managing the Object-Oriented Project,* Reading, Mass.: Addison-Wesley, 1996.

Chapter 6

Structural Object Analysis

A good poem is worth a good proof—or a really great theorem!
—Book of Douglass, Law 17

Once the system's external environment is defined, the analyst must identify key objects and classes and their relationships within the system itself. This chapter presents several strategies that have proven effective in real-time systems development for the identification of the key objects and classes. These strategies may be used alone or in combination. Relationships and associations among classes and objects enable their collaborations to produce higher-level behaviors. This chapter goes on to identify some rules of thumb for uncovering and testing these relationships.

6.1 Introduction

The previous chapter discussed how the object-oriented analyst goes about identifying and capturing requirements. The UML provides use cases to represent externally visible pieces of system functionality that don't reveal the internal structure of the system. Once this process is more-or-less complete, the next logical step is to "open up the box" and examine the logical entities that make up the system and their inter-relations. However, this remains nontrivial. It is not possible today to perform this step automatically and end up with good-quality object models. The analyst must step in and manually intervene to make sure the core concepts of the problem domain are properly and appropriately reified as classes and that these classes have an appropriate set of relations with other concepts from the domain.

In this chapter, we'll discuss object and class identification and how to infer relationships and associations among them. The next chapter will deal with the definition and elaboration of object behavior and state. The topics covered in these two chapters form the basis of all object-oriented analysis and, ultimately, of all object-oriented development.

6.2 Terms and Concepts

The elementary concepts of object-oriented analysis and their notation were presented in Chapter 1. The metamodel elements of class and object, for example, were presented, along with the UML's semantics and notation. However, the information presented in Chapter 1 is an elementary introduction. Chapter 1 does not contain methods for effectively identifying and characterizing objects and classes during the course of system development, nor does it present criteria for discriminating between good object structures and poor ones. That is the purpose of this chapter—namely, to provide strategies and techniques for the identification of objects and classes and their structural relations to other classes and objects. Collectively, these activities form structural object analysis. This is one of three aspects of analysis in the ROPES process model discussed in Chapter 4.

Object analysis itself may be divided into a set of three primary activities:

1. Identifying and characterizing the things in the object model and how they relate to each other
2. Defining the behavior of the things in the object model
3. Validating the object model for consistency, completeness, and correctness

Each of these activities has subactivities, as well. Generally, the development process proceeds in the order of primary activities, as listed. However, within each of these primary activities, there is a great deal of variance regarding the specific order of the subactivities. Developers should feel free to order the subactivities in whatever manner they feel most appropriate.

Subactivities for structural object analysis include

- Identify essential objects that appear in the problem domain
- Propose candidate classes
- Identify essential attributes of these classes
- Identify essential operations and services of these classes
- Identify essential relations among the classes and objects
- Generalization taxonomies
- Associations (including multiplicities)
  1. Normal associations
  2. Aggregations
  3. Compositions
- Capture the structural object model in the tool repository
- Create diagrammatic views and reports of the structural object model

Remember that the information the analyst has at this point is either deep inside the domain expert's head or captured in terms of functional and quality-of-service requirements in use case, scenario, and state diagrams. Transitioning to a structural object model is an active process of discovery, with many pitfalls along the way. In practice, the object model must be iterated several times before it settles into a low entropy state.

Most structural information is captured using the graphical notation provided by the UML. Not all of it, however. It is important to remember that *the diagrams are not the model.* Diagrams are merely a *view* of the model. In keeping with this notion, do not fall into the trap of trying to represent too much in any one diagram.[1] As will be discussed later in the chapter, every diagram should have a purpose. The primary purposes for diagrams will be

- Show the classes and objects that participate in a single collaboration
- Show a generalization taxonomy
- Show the arrangement of logical partitions (that is, packages)

Along with not showing all classes on a single diagram, one should also not show all attributes and operations. The only reason for showing a class member on a class diagram is to illustrate some point. Therefore, it is virtually never a good idea to show all class members on one diagram. In fact, some attributes may never be shown on diagrams at all. Such members are usually more profitably viewed using reports or a model-browser tool.

6.3 Key Strategies for Object Identification

Unfortunately, objects don't always jump and dance and otherwise make themselves visible. The analyst must typically apply several strategies to identify the important objects in the system. The key strategy during structural object analysis is to identify only the essential objects and classes. Remember that the job of the analysis model is to identify the required aspects of the solution so that any delivered system lacking these aspects would be considered incorrect or incomplete. Therefore, the essential object model is the model that contains only

---

1. Sometimes, it may be useful to create a master class diagram which shows all classes and relations, but there is a limit to the number of boxes one can put on an *E*-size sheet of plotter paper and a limit to the size of readable fonts (4 pt can be read with help, depending on the thickness of the pen). In general, such diagrams are only useful to impress the "rubes" (that is, managers) and of little practical importance.

those objects without which *any* possible delivered system would be incorrect.

The essential model is useful because it separates out the lower-level design decisions from the important abstractions. This distinction is important for several reasons. First, by focusing on only the characteristics that are actually required, the model is simpler and easier to understand. A simpler model is more likely to be correct. Experience has shown that defects in analysis are orders of magnitude more expensive to correct than implementation defects, because the number of dependencies is highest on a model's fundamental constructs. Changing these fundamental concepts is likely to break a greater number of clients than changing a design detail, and it can result in significantly more rework. It really pays to get this part right.

Second, by separating out the analysis model, it may be reused in different contexts. This reuse is enabled by the omission of inessential detail. In addition, if the optimization criteria for a particular implementation should change (see below), the model can be simply modified to meet these criteria.

Finally, designs are always about optimization. The analysis model has a potentially infinite set of implementations. A design model has a single implementation. By allowing design decisions to float for as long as possible, more information is available for making optimal design decisions. Besides, analysis model characteristics, by their nature, are not permitted to vary. They represent the static foundation that the design model attempts to optimize. A great many optimization criteria are available, and the developer will usually be required to optimize along many or all of these simultaneously. By firmly cementing the analysis model first, a lower entropy state can be achieved in the design space through optimization.

Table 6-1 outlines what I have found to be the most effective of these object-identification strategies.

This chapter will discuss all these strategies, but note that the analyst need not use them all. These approaches are not orthogonal, and the objects they find will overlap to a significant degree. In fact, many subsets of the strategies will find exactly the same set of objects. Some methods will fit analysts' approaches better than others. As with all modeling strategies, use those that work well for you and discard the rest.

Table 6-1: *Object Discovery Strategies*

Strategy	Description
Underline the noun	Used to gain a first-cut object list, the analyst underlines each noun and noun phrase in the problem statement and evaluates it as a potential object.
Identify causal agents	Identify the sources of actions, events, and messages; includes the coordinators of actions.
Identify coherent services	Coherent services are sets of operations that seem to be intrinsically bound—for example, operations on a base data type, such as a complex number (add, subtract, multiply, etc.) and services provided by the same "thing," that share the same pre-conditional invariants, or that must execute in a specific order(s).
Identify real-world items	Real-world items are entities that exist in the real world, but are not necessarily electronic devices. Examples include objects such as respiratory gases, air pressures, forces, anatomical organs, chemicals, vats, etc.
Identify physical devices	Physical devices include the sensors and actuators provided by the system, as well as the electronic devices they monitor or control. In the internal architecture, they are processors or ancillary electronic "widgets."
Identify essential abstractions of domains	Essential abstractions may be modeled as objects. Bank accounts exist only conceptually but are important objects in a banking domain. Frequency bins for an online auto-correlator may also be objects.
Identify transactions	Transactions are finite instances of associations between objects. They persist for some significant period of time and are manifested as associative objects. Examples include bus messages and queued data.
Identify persistent information	Information that must persist for significant periods of time may be objects or attributes. This persistence may extend beyond the power cycling of the device.
Identify visual elements	User interface elements that display data are objects within the user interface domain, such as windows, buttons, scroll bars, menus, histograms, waveforms, icons, bitmaps, and fonts. *(continued)*

Table 6-1: (*cont.*)

Strategy	Description
Identify control elements	Control elements are objects that provide the interface for the user (or some external device) to control system behavior.
Execute scenarios on the object model	Walk through the scenarios, using the identified objects. Missing objects will become apparent when required actions cannot be achieved with existing objects.

6.3.1 Underline the Nouns

The first strategy works directly with the problem or mission statement from the concept phase. Underline each noun or noun phrase in the statement and treat it as a potential object. Objects identified in this way can be put into one of the following categories:

- Objects of interest
- Uninteresting objects
- Attributes of objects
- Synonyms of each of the above three things

The point of the exercise is to find objects within the first category—objects of interest. Uninteresting objects are objects that have no direct relevance to your system. Attributes also show up as nouns in the problem statement. Sometimes, an attribute is clearly just a property of an object. When in doubt, tentatively classify the noun as an object. If subsequent analysis shows the object is insufficiently interesting, it can be included as an attribute of some other object.

Consider the problem statement for an air traffic control system, which was used in the last chapter, as an illustration of use cases:

ACME Air Traffic Control System

The <u>Acme Air Traffic Control System</u> (AATCS) is meant to manage the <u>information</u> necessary for <u>human controllers</u> to control the local <u>airspace and surface</u> for incoming and outgoing <u>aircraft</u>. Each <u>aircraft</u> preparing to leave or enter the <u>control space</u> must file a <u>flight plan</u>. This <u>flight plan</u> consists of a <u>point</u> and <u>time of departure,</u> a point and time of arrival, and an average ground speed, in addition to the information necessary to uniquely identify the aircraft. The aircraft identification includes a call sign, an owning company and flight number, and an aircraft type, which denotes its flight limitations (for example, altitude and ground speed range). AATCS maintains a list of all aircraft moving or preparing to move within the airspace and surface. The flight plan is approved by the controllers or returned with suggestions for change. When filing a flight plan prior to departure, this negotiation must complete before the aircraft is cleared.

When an aircraft is cleared for taxiing, it taxis from its gate to the designated runway, where it awaits clearance to take off. Once final clearance is given (subject to current runway use and other flights awaiting final clearance), the plane is allowed to take off using the runway designated by the tower controller. At any time after a plane has left the gate but before it is given take-off clearance, it may be routed to a holding area. This may be due to environmental or scheduling conditions.

When an aircraft approaches for landing, it does so along its flight plan. As the aircraft approaches the airport, it must request clearance to land. The controller may grant clearance and provide a runway ID and directions, or he may give an alternate flight path, such as circling the airport at a designated altitude, distance, and air speed.

The system maintains the original flight plan, along with an actual flight plan, which is updated during the course of the flight. All aircraft in the local airspace are monitored using a primary radar, which uses a rotating emitter/receiver and aircraft skin reflection to identify targets in the airspace. The primary radar masks out ground-based obstructions (such as mountains and buildings). Processing associated with the primary radar identifies tracks based on computed position (requiring direction and time-of-flight of signal) and the last known position of all aircraft in the airspace. In addition to the primary radar, a secondary radar also provides information on aircraft. This radar sends out a transponder code request. Upon receiving the transponder identification request, the aircraft responds automatically, within a narrow and fixed time window. The return signal contains the aircraft beacon code and the aircraft's estimate of its altitude. Distance is computed via the signal time-of-flight. Aircraft may be monitored using only primary radar (for aircraft that have not filed a flight plan and do not have an active transponder—for example, smugglers) or secondary radar (for stealth aircraft), but normally both are used. A special icon is shown for planes that have been detected but not yet identified.

The airspace is displayed to the controller on one or more display screens. The aircraft are shown as plane icons pointing in the direction of flight, with relevant information textually tagged, including call sign, altitude, ground speed, and identification confidence level (how sure the system is that the radar image is that of the identified aircraft). Should the aircraft get within a specified distance of another (the distance varies with the types of aircraft involved, their trajectory vectors, and their proximity to the airport), the conflicting aircraft icon colors change from blue to yellow. There is also a smaller separation distance threshold defined between aircraft, indicating a high level of warning in which the colors of the relevant aircraft change to red and the plane icons flash. These warning colors also apply to aircraft traveling too close to surface topology features.

The display may be shown in different levels of zoom, with radial rings indicating distance, under user control. Supported zoom levels show radial rings at 1, 5, 10, and 50 miles. Fixed surface topological features (buildings and mountains) are shown. Weather cells can also be shown to aid the controller in proper aircraft routing. When visible, weather is shown in false color—background color indicating calm and clear gradually approaching bright red for severe weather. When a plane icon overlays a weather or surface feature, the portion of the icon overlaying the feature changes color to be highly visible against it. Menus for operator commands can pop up next to the aircraft icons by moving a cursor over the aircraft and hitting a menu button. One of the menu options shall be to display the planned flight plan (as a light blue line) for the aircraft, overlayed with the actual flight plan up to the current position (as a bright blue dashed line). However, none of the control, topological, or weather information is allowed to obscure the visibility of the aircraft icons at any time.

All actual monitored flight information must be stored for 30 days.

The nouns in this problem have been underlined, and a quick glance allows us to classify most of them.

A number of likely objects of interest were identified. These include aircraft, flight plan, primary and secondary radar, transponder, call sign, ground speed and average ground speed, runway, display, plane icon, menu, signal, transponder code, and so on.

Several of the potential underlined objects are most likely synonyms for others. For example, aircraft is also referred to as "plane" and "flight," controller is also called "human controller" and "tower controller," and direction is also called "direction of flight." It may be that they are not actually synonyms, but the domain expert can resolve these issues. For example, it may turn out that there are several kinds of air traffic controllers—some for enroute airspace, some for local airspace, and others for the surface space.

Other underlined elements seem to be simple things more-properly modeled as attributes of objects. For example, as a first guess, the nouns and noun phrases found in Table 6-2 are made attributes of other objects:

Several identified elements are outside the scope of the system. Some are obvious. The air traffic controller will not be designed as an internal part of the system. Clearly, air traffic controllers are actors in some sense. Other uninteresting objects may not be so obvious. For

Table 6-2: *Objects and Attributes*

Object	Attribute
Aircraft	Position Ground speed Altitude
Flight plan	Point of departure Time of departure Point of arrival Time of arrival Average ground speed
Transponder code	Call sign Owning company

example, let us suppose that the problem statement is meant to describe a software-only solution that executes on the air traffic control computers. This means that it will use existing interfaces, such as the primary and secondary radars for gathering information, and the displays, cursor controls, and buttons for display management. In that case, these items are actors in the system environment to which the system must interface, not controllers themselves.

The simple problem statement provided earlier is insufficient to properly set the actual system boundary. To determine this, more analysis and discussion with the domain experts is required.

It may happen, as we explore the model in more detail, that some things we've temporarily classified as attributes will turn out to be nonprimitive and should become objects. It may also happen that some of the potential objects we've uncovered turn out to be simple, primitive things that are really attributes of yet another object. It is true that the strategy has not uncovered all the objects within the system. Even if the problem statement declared all the analysis objects (which it clearly does not), more objects will be introduced during design to facilitate the object collaborations. Nevertheless, this strategy has given us a starting point so we can begin thinking about the objects and their structural and taxonomic relations.

6.3.2 Identify Causal Agents

Once the potential objects are identified, look for the most fundamental ones. These are objects that:

- Produce or control actions
- Produce or analyze data
- Accept events or action requests from people or external devices

Causal agents may be thought of as objects that initiate or control actions or events. During architectural design, such objects are often (but not always) realized as *active objects*. Active objects in the UML are the roots of threads of control in multitasking systems and are generally implemented as the root composite object of a thread. Their components execute within the context of the thread of the owner composite. However, the selection of threads is always a design optimization concern and is never part of analysis per se.[2] Therefore, we will refer to them as causal agents rather than active objects in this chapter, although at some point they may become active objects in our design model.

Clearly, several AATCS causal agents exist. If we are interfacing to existing sensor subsystems (for example, primary and secondary radar), the objects that reify the interface to these actors are causal agents. Similarly, the display and control devices used by the controllers also introduce (cause) events into the system. Others may be implied. The problem statement clearly states that the system must identify aircraft separation violations so that this information can be communicated to the controller. Perhaps there will be a separation distance monitor object that scans identified aircraft for such violations, raising events when they are detected.

6.3.3 Identify Coherent Services

Passive service provider objects are usually less obvious than causal agents. They may provide passive control, data storage, and perform calculations. Display output devices, such as CRTs, LEDs, and LCDs, perform output services upon command. Objects that perform CRC calculations or digital filtering may also be passive service providers. These passive objects are also known as servers, because they provide services to client objects.

Some AATCS server objects might be the controller display, menu, and menu item.

6.3.4 Identify Real-World Items

Object-oriented systems often need to model the information or behavior of real-world objects even though they are not part of the system per

---

2. This is obvious from a couple of perspectives. First, it is possible (on a sufficiently powerful computer) to implement each object in a separate OS thread and use asynchronous messaging among all objects. It is also possible to implement any system using a single thread. Therefore, the thread model cannot, in principle, be part of the fundamental correctness of the model. In fact, the set of threads selected is always meant to optimize some aspect of system performance. We will discuss strategies to select an optimal thread set of an object model in Chapter 8 when we discuss architectural design.

se. The object representing a real-world thing generally represents the interface to that thing and translates operations in the executing object system into real-world causes and effects, such as enabling sensors, reading values, setting actuator positions, and so on. Another use of this strategy is to represent a real-world resource that must be managed, such as a runway or a standard flight path, or to represent a constraint on the system, such as a mountain to avoid. A less common use of an object that represents a real-world thing is to simulate its behavior. Such objects obviously occur within simulation systems, but they also may be used inside adaptive control algorithms.

The AATCS, like most embedded systems, provides many concrete, real-world things that must be modeled in the system, such as primary radar, secondary radar, display, aircraft, runway, flight path, air space, surface topology feature, weather cell, and transponder.

6.3.5 Identify Physical Devices

This object identification strategy is a subset of the previous one, but it is very prevalent with embedded systems developers. Embedded systems interact with their environment using sensors and actuators. These devices in turn must communicate through device interfaces. The system controls and monitors physical devices inside and outside the system. Devices providing information used by the system are typically modeled as objects. Devices themselves must be configured, calibrated, enabled, and controlled so that they can provide services to the system. For example, deep within the inner workings of the system, processors typically perform initial power-on self-tests (POSTs) and periodic (or continuous) built-in tests (BITs). Devices frequently have nontrivial state machines and must provide status information on command. When device information and state must be maintained, the devices may be modeled as objects to hold the information about their operational status.

Example AATCS objects using this strategy are primary and secondary radars, transponder, display, button, mouse, and the AATCS itself. This is important, because the AATCS is a real-time, safety-critical application and so must somehow be able to run POSTs and BITs to identify faults, and may contain multiple channels introduced during design to continue to provide its safety function in the presence of those faults.

6.3.6 Identify Essential Abstractions of Domains

A *domain* is an independent coherent subject matter that may be modeled as a set of objects with various relations among them.[3] For example, User Interface is a rich domain with such objects as *window, scroll bar, cursor, icon, bitmap, text, font, color,* and so on. Communications is another domain with its own set of essential concepts, such as *communication message, packet, frame, message transaction, data format, socket, session,* and *message quality of service.* For constructing complex systems, domains provide a means of decomposing a potentially unmanageable object space into smaller, more-manageable chunks. A large portion of object analysis can be then disseminated to multiple developers. Each developer or small team can perform independent structural and behavioral object analysis on the identified domains. Some of the analysis will bridge domains, but domains still provide a useful decomposition mechanism.[4]

Each domain has its own set of essential concepts, or abstractions. These concepts are important abstractions within the domain and have interesting attributes and behaviors. These abstractions often do not have physical realizations but must nevertheless be modeled by the system. Within the User Interface (UI) domain, *window* is an essential abstraction. In the banking domain, *account* is an important abstraction. In an autonomous manufacturing robot, *task plan* is the set of steps required to implement the desired manufacturing process. In the design of a C compiler, *functions, data types,* and *pointers* are essential concepts. Each of these objects has no physical manifestation. They exist only as abstractions modeled as objects within the appropriate domains.

The AACTS contains a number of domains. In our model, we identify several, as shown in Figure 6-1: Aircraft Management, Aircraft Monitoring, Display, and Topology. Some essential concepts for the aircraft management domain are aircraft, position, equipage of an aircraft, and flight plan. If the mission of the topology domain is to model physical space and relatively stationary objects within it, then some essen-

---

3. Generalization taxonomies usually fall entirely within a single domain. Domains have associations that are contained completely within the domain, but in addition, at least some associations within collaborations must, in principle, span multiple domains.
4. Domains can be realized as a stereotype of a package in the UML.

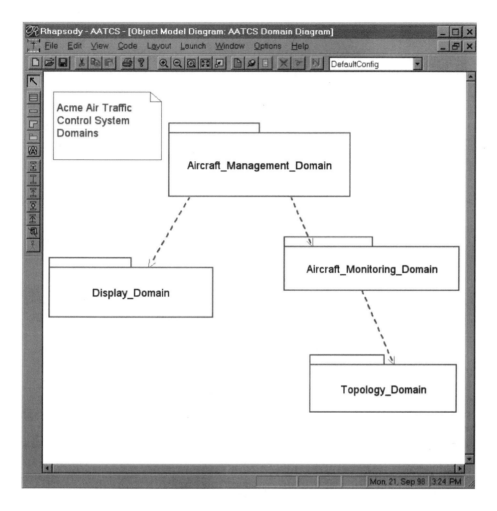

Figure 6-1: *AATCS Domain Diagram*

tial concepts are surface feature, weather cell, and standard approach route (STAR).

As we elaborate our analysis model into design, further domains will be identified. For example, an object-distribution domain may be required to deal with issues of object naming and to service requests across multiple processors. Such a domain will no doubt depend on a communication domain to provide an infrastructure for sending messages along wires to remote subsystems.

6.3.7 Identify Transactions

Transactions are objects that arise from interactions of other objects that have a temporarily persistent existence. Some example transaction objects are outlined in Table 6-3.

Separation distance is an example of such a transaction object within AATCS, as are a (radar) signal and a separation distance alarm. In discussions with domain experts, they will identify the notion of a

Table 6-3: *Example Transaction Objects*

Object 1	Object 2	Association	Transaction Object
Woman	Man	Marriage	Marriage object: • Wedding date • Wedding location • Prenuptial agreement • Witnesses
			Divorce object: • Filing date • Decree date • Maintenance schedule • Amount paid to lawyers
Controller	Actuator	Controls	Control message over bus
Customer	Account	Owns	Deposit Withdrawal Open account Close account
Customer	Store	Buys things at	Order Return
Display system	Sensor	Displays values for	Alarm Error
Elevator request button	Elevator	Issues request to	Request for elevator
Floor request button	Elevator	Issues request to	Request for floor
Task plan	Robot arm	Controls	Command

track, which is a yet-unidentified sensory datum with both position and time, which will be mapped to an aircraft, a topological feature, or a UFO.[5]

6.3.8 Identify Persistent Information

Persistent information is typically held within passive objects, such as stacks, queues, trees, and databases. Volatile memory (RAM or SRAM) or long-term storage (FLASH, EPROM, EEPROM, or disk) may store persistent data.

A robot must store and recall task plans. Subsequent analysis of the system may reveal other persistent data. For example, Table 6-4 reveals some persistent information.

Table 6-4: *Possible Persistent Information Objects*

Information	Storage Period	Description
Task plans	Unlimited	"Programs" for the robotic system must be constructed, stored, recalled for editing, and recalled for execution.
Errors	Between service calls	Error log holding the error identifier, severity, location, and time/date of occurrence. This will facilitate maintenance of the system.
Alarms	Until next service call	Alarms indicate conditions that must be brought to the attention of the user even though they may not be errors. Tracking them between service calls allows analysis of the reliability of the system.
Hours of operation	Between service calls	Hours of operation aid in tracking costs and scheduling service calls.
Security access	Unlimited	Stores valid users, their identifiers, and passwords to permit different levels of access.
Service information	Unlimited	Tracks service calls and updates that are performed: when, what, and by whom.

---

5. The truth is out there!

The AATCS must maintain actual monitored flight plans (including associated aircraft identification and time-stamped way points). It is likely that the POST and BIT must also log errors and alarms because of the safety criticality of the application.

6.3.9 Identify Visual Elements

Many real-time systems interact directly or indirectly with human users. Real-time system displays may be as simple as a single blinking LED to indicate power status, or as elaborate as a full Windows-like GUI with buttons, windows, scroll bars, icons, and text. Visual elements used to convey information to the user are objects within the User Interface domain.

In many environments, user interface designers specialize in the construction of visual interaction models or prototypes that developers will ultimately implement.

For example, assume the AATCS display is arranged much like Figure 6-2.

Such a display contains a number of common visual elements:

- Surface feature
- Radial distance line
- Weather feature
- Cursor
- Menu
- Menu item
- Text
- Plane icon

These are shown in a class diagram for the AATCS display domain, shown in Figure 6-3.

6.3.10 Identify Control Elements

Control elements are entities that control other objects and are specific types of causal agents. Some objects, called *composites*, often orchestrate the behaviors of their tightly aggregated component objects. These may be simple objects or elaborate control systems, such as:

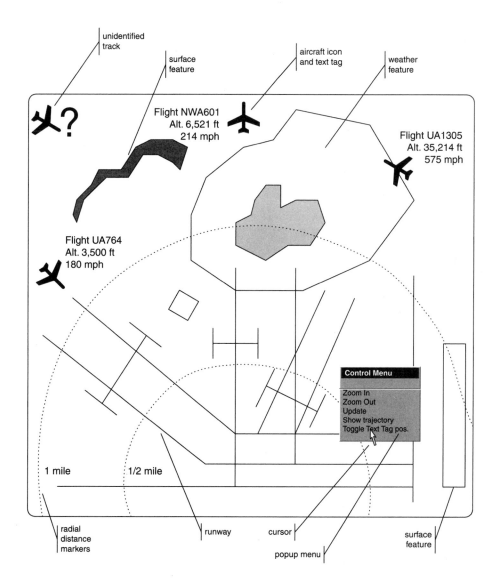

Figure 6-2: *AATCS Display Layout*

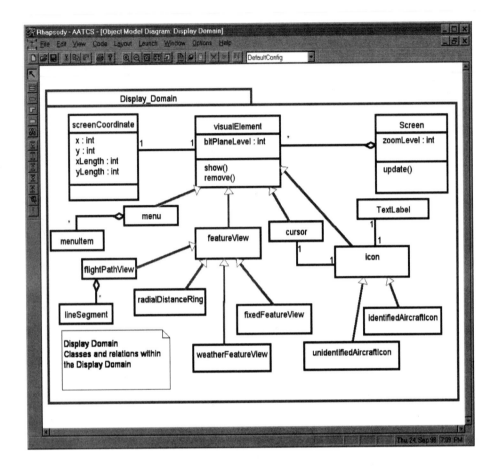

Figure 6-3: *AATCS Display Domain Diagram*

- PID control loops
- Fuzzy logic inference engines
- Expert system inference engines
- Artificial neural network computational engines

The AATCS has only a few that are explicitly mentioned, but one can see that others might be implied by the requirement to manage resources.

- Button (select things on the screen)
- Mouse

- Separation distance manager
- Runway manager

6.3.11 Execute Scenarios on the Object Model

The execution of use case scenarios is another strategy to identify missing objects. Using only known objects, step through the messages to implement the scenario. When "you can't get there from here" occurs, one or more missing objects may be identified.

This execution of the object model is most commonly done using manual means. It can be done by a single person walking through a scenario or by a group of people play-acting the roles of the collaborating objects. However, such a scenario is more effectively done by animating the execution of the object model. Some tools, such as Rhapsody, create executable code directly from the object model, even if the model is incomplete in places. If the collaborating objects are sufficiently well-specified in the object model, then this model can generate source code and can be compiled. Then, as the model executes, the developer can set breakpoints, insert events, and so on while he watches sequence diagrams being drawn, which reflect the scenario execution. The developer can as easily watch the state machines execute and examine the state of object attributes, if desired. When the animated sequence diagram shows an unexpected sequence of steps, the object model can then be examined to identify missing or incorrectly specified objects (see Chapter 13).

Consider the scenario involving the resolution of an active airspace track to a previously identified aircraft. Several objects participate in this process. The set of objects forms the collaboration shown in Figure 6-4.

This appears to be an adequate set of collaborating objects. The proper things seem to be represented. The radars are there to create the track, and the aircraft is there to be associated to the track. The aircraft position is there, so we know where the aircraft was last. Also, once it is associated with the track, the aircraft's position can be updated. The flight plan is there to provide information about what the aircraft is doing over time. Finally the aircraft equipage is there so that questionable links can be accepted or dismissed on the basis of possible maneuvering properties of the aircraft (turn radius, maximum climb rate, maximum air speed, and so forth).

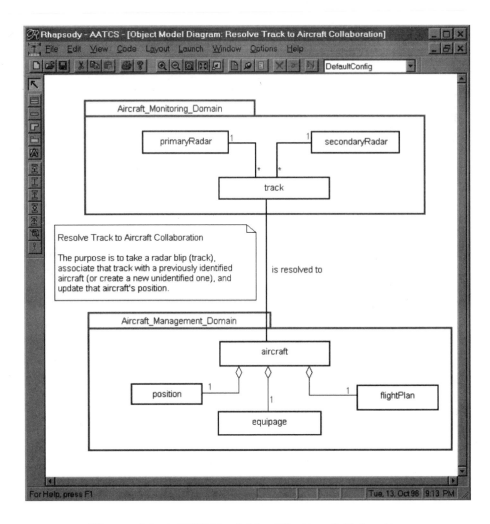

Figure 6-4: *AATCS Track Identification Collaboration*

Now consider the following scenario: Both radars detect the track of a previously identified aircraft, and the job of the collaboration should be to merge these two signals to a single track and then match it to an aircraft. This scenario is shown in Figure 6-5. We can see that the collaboration proceeds in a smooth fashion except for one thing. How does the track actually get matched with the aircraft? Who does the matching? The radar?

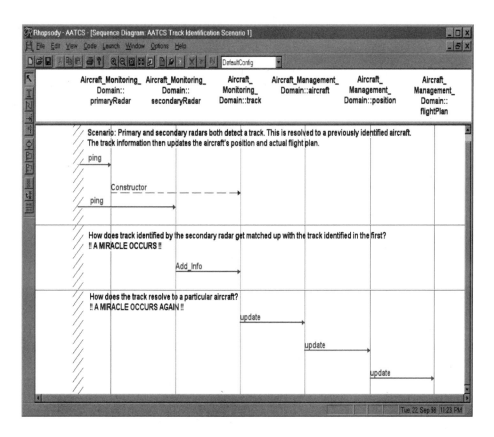

Figure 6-5: *AATCS Track Identification Scenario*

There are problems with each radar having an association with every aircraft. First, because aircraft come and go, some means must be provided to efficiently add and remove aircraft from this 1-* association dynamically. Even when this is done, however, it still must be done twice (once for each radar). Then there is the issue of which radar should search its list of aircraft. It would be inefficient to have both do it, but either radar may fail to detect the track, either because the device itself failed, a surface topology feature obstructed one radar but not the other, or the aircraft is stealth (primary radar will miss) or a smuggler (secondary radar will miss).

An additional concern is that resolving the tracks doesn't really seem to belong to the responsibility of a radar object. The natural expectation of a radar object is that it identifies things in the airspace, and that's all. This is especially important when you consider that the radars will typically scan continuously and identify multiple tracks per scan. Then there is the issue of resolving sensor echoes caused by radar reflection from surface features, such as buildings.

One solution is to use a track manager object to manage the known tracks and merge multiple senses of the same physical entity into a single track. That still leaves the issue of resolving which (if any) of the identified aircraft is the best fit for the track. The track manager could assume that responsibility, as well. However, looking ahead to other scenarios, there may be valid reasons for iterating over the known aircraft other than to merely resolve tracks to aircraft and update positions. For this reason, we'll add a known aircraft manager to the model. The known aircraft manager will have the responsibility of assigning a track to a particular aircraft.

The updated class model is shown in Figure 6-6. It is clear how the sequence diagram works, with these two new classes added.

6.4 Reification of Objects into Classes

Although we've talked about identifying objects, we've actually been identifying the types of those objects. For example, in the air traffic control domain, a track object represents a particular sensor bounce that indicates a physical element in 4-D space (x,y,x,t). We have not distinguished between different tracks, because we've already mentally classified all such track instances and created a mental track "type" in our minds. Because classification is endemic to the human cognitive process, we do this without much thought or consideration. However, the UML (and other object methods, as well) makes the distinction between things (objects) and types (classes). This is called the *type-instance dichotomy*.

Life is actually more complex than that. Even when we think about objects, we normally think about object roles, not objects themselves. An object role is the role an instance of a class plays in a particular context—a "prototypical object." Thus, we think of instance lines in a sequence diagram as representing objects, but they are really roles, or placeholders for objects.

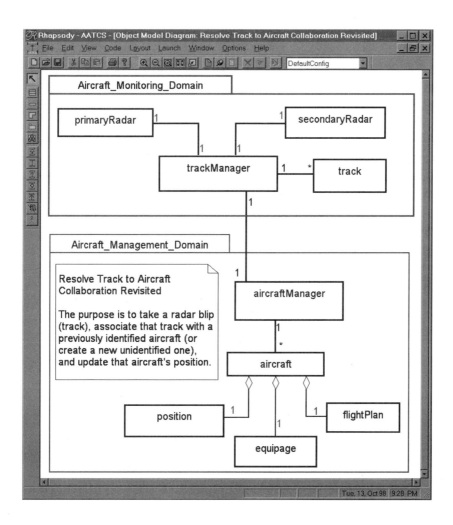

Figure 6-6: *Track Identification Collaboration Revisited*

One way to mentally envelope the distinctions is to think about a class as a template or recipe for an object. Think about a role as a prototypical object that, at a particular absolute time in the universe, will correspond to exactly one object. Think about object instances as a particular thing at a particular space-time coordinate. An aircraft, as we've used it so far, is really a class. It defines the characteristics of a large set of particular aircraft. An aircraft role, as it might appear in a sequence diagram, defines the interaction of an object, but it doesn't specify the place or time. An aircraft object occupies a particular memory address in the computer (for example, 0xf7760009) at a particular time (Oct 13, 1985, at 03:00.00 AM). The same scenario might repeat multiple times with different instances (for example, flight DAL335 may occur every day), so it clearly cannot contain objects (the scenario is the same whether the memory address is 0x7760009 or 0x10009999).

Once you've identified object instances, or roles, reify them into classes. Remember that all instances of any class have all the things declared by their class—attributes, operations, associations, and so forth. Once you have defined the classes for the identified objects, you can place them on class diagrams, create taxonomic classification schemes, and link them together at run-time.

6.5 Identify Object Associations

Objects are a small unit of decomposition. Societies of collaborating objects do interesting system-level things. The association relation is the glue that allows objects to send messages to one another and collaborate. One primary task in structural object analysis is to identify and clarify the important associations in the model. Just as object identification strategies provide some standard ways to find objects, there are strategies to identify object associations, as shown in Table 6-5.

Table 6-5: *Object Association Strategies*

Strategy	Description
Identify messages	Each message implies an association between the source and target objects.
Identify message sources	The sensors that detect information or events and the creators of information or events are all *message sources*. They pass information on to other objects for handling and storage.
Identify message storage depots	Message storage depots store information for archival purposes or provide a central repository of information for other objects. The depots have associations with the message sources, as well as with the users of that information.

(continued)

Table 6-5: (*cont.*)

Strategy	Description
Identify message handlers	Some objects centralize message dispatching and handling. They form connections to either or both message sources and message storage depots.
Execute scenarios on the object model	Walk through the scenarios, using the identified objects. When, in order to achieve the purpose of the collaboration, one object must send a message to another, it means an association exists between them.

As we might guess, the AATCS contains many associations, as shown in Table 6-6.

Table 6-6: *Some AATCS Associations*

Domain	Class	Associates with
Aircraft management	Feature Aircraft manager	Separation distance Aircraft
Aircraft monitoring	Radar Track manager	Track manager Track
Display	Visual element Icon Cursor	Coordinate Text label Icon
Aircraft management— Aircraft monitoring	Track manager	Aircraft manager

We purposely did not capture the aggregations and compositions here, even though they are specialized types of associations. They will be discussed later.

Class and object diagrams visually depict these associations. A line drawn between two objects represents a link (instance of an association) between those objects, supporting the transmission of a message from one to the other.

Associations are logically bidirectional unless explicitly constrained by the addition of a navigation adornment. In the UML, this adornment is an open arrowhead pointing toward the class to which navigation is defined. Navigation defines the direction of message flow. Note that this is not necessarily the same as information flow, because messages can both send and return information.

The object-oriented abstraction of communication is to send a message, using the association as a conduit. This conduit may be implemented in any number of ways: OS handles, RTOS message posts, RPCs, and transmission of bus and network messages. However, associations are most often implemented as simple pointers or references to objects. A unidirectional association means that only one object participating in the association has a logical reference (such as implemented by a pointer). For example, consider two classes, *dog* and *tail*, connected by an association that may be navigated only from *dog* to *tail*:

```
class dog {
    Tail* pT; // low level implementation of
    association
public:
    // these operations send a message to the tail
        object
    void BeHappy(void) { pT->Wag(20); );
    void BeSad(void) { pT->Wag(2); };
    void BeExcited(void) { pT->Wag(50); };
    void BeMelancholy(void) { pT->Wag(5); };
};
```

It may not be possible, given just a tail, to identify which dog is emoting. It is a question of navigability.

By far, associations are usually navigable only in one direction. Such cases are commonly called *client-server* associations. The *client* is the object with the reference; the *server* is the object with the data or operation invoked by the client. Servers are mostly passive or reactive objects, responding to requests from the client. Clients must know about the servers to be able to invoke services from them. Servers should not know about their clients, because this induces pathological coupling and makes the addition of new clients more difficult.

Commonly, bidirectionally navigable associations are called *peer-to-peer* associations. Although less common than client-server, collaborations sometimes require recursion of operations between the two classes. For example, this can happen in the callback design pattern.[6] In this pattern, one (server) object must have an association to another

---

6. The callback pattern is a simplified form of the observer pattern. See [1] and [2] for more details on the observer pattern.

(client) in order to register itself with the client. Once registered, the client object can invoke methods on the server object. This pattern is useful when the collaboration needs the ability to dynamically change the server at run-time. For example, a class may need different watch-dog monitoring with varying degrees of computational overhead and fidelity of coverage. Although the callback pattern is really a special-ized form of client-server, the dynamic nature of the link requires a bidirectional association. Figure 6-7 shows an example of this pattern.

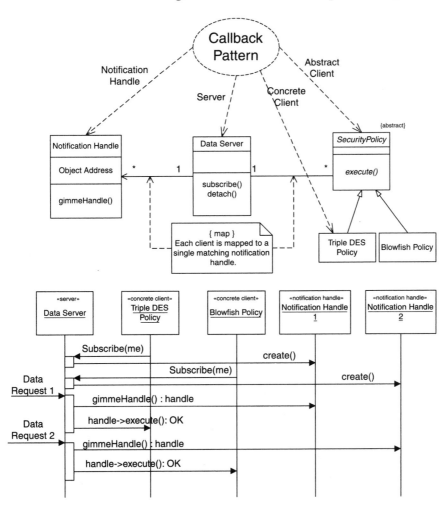

Figure 6-7: *Example of Callback Pattern*

Each end of the association is called an *association role*. Role ends may be named on the diagram by placing a textual label by the association end. The association role name identifies the role an instance of the class will play in collaborations that use that association. Generally, each navigable role of an association needs to be named unless it is a simple conjugate of the other end.

6.5.1 Multiplicity

Not only must the association and its navigability be defined, it is critically important to define the multiplicity of the association role. As discussed in Chapter 1, the multiplicity defines the number of objects that will participate in the role of an association at run-time. The UML defines a simple syntax for defining multiplicity, given in Table 6-7.

The normal use of an optional (1-[0,1]) association is that the link comes and goes during the execution of the object model. However, sometimes a pair of classes are connected by an optional association. This association is *always* present for certain instances of the class and *never* for others. This pattern of interaction suggests that the unary role class should be subclassed so that it does not have the association, but

Table 6-7: *Association Multiplicity*

Multiplicity Symbol	Description
n	Exactly *n* objects participate in the role (*n* is an integer constant). The most common value for *n* is 1.
m,n	Either *m* or *n* objects may participate in the role (*m* and *n* are both integer constants). The most common values for *m* and *n* are 0 and 1, meaning that it is an optional association.
m..n	Anywhere from *m* to *n*, inclusive, objects may participate in the role.
*	Zero or more objects may participate in the role.
1..*	One or more objects may participate in the role.

its subclass does (although the association changes from optional to mandatory).

6.5.2 Associations and Links

Note that the type-instance dichotomy also applies to associations. An association is a relation between classes that specifies that at run-time, an object of one class may send an object of the other class a message. At run-time, objects have links (instances of associations). This distinction is important because classes have associations that declare an intention for run-time. At run-time, however, programmatic mechanisms must realize that intention. For example, if class A has a 1-(0,1) association with class B, then at run-time, object A1:A (that is, instance A1, which is of class A) may or may not have a link with object B1:B. At some point, the link may exist (and be used as a logical conduit for sending messages); at another point, it may not. Fixed associations, such as 1,1, imply that the link always exists when A and B exist.

6.6 Aggregation and Composition

An *aggregation* is a special type of association that implies logical or physical containment. In the UML, aggregation is weak, comparable to Booch's aggregation by reference [3]. Nothing is implied about the responsibility of construction and destruction of the part, the relative lifecycles of the part vs. the whole, nor the number of possible owners. Aggregation in the UML is not significantly different from an association other than the weakly defined concept of logical or physical containment.

Composition is a strong form of aggregation, similar to Booch's *aggregation by value* [3]. Composition means that part objects (called *components*) are solely the responsibility of the composite class. Composites must create and destroy their components. For component objects with a fixed multiplicity (such as 1 or 4), the implication is that when the composite object is created, exactly this many components must exist bound to that association and that the composite has the responsibility to create them.

Components cannot be shared among composites.[7] This means that the multiplicity at the "owner" end must be exactly 1. Composition is shown by graphical inclusions of the components within the composite or with a filled-in aggregation diamond. When inclusion is used, the multiplicity of the component ("instance multiplicity") is provided at its upper-left corner.

6.7 Object Attributes

The UML defines an attribute as "a named property of a type." But in the UML, they are also expected to be simple primitive things that have behavior no more interesting than get_ and set_ operations. Attributes are "smaller" than objects. In some abstract sense, attributes are equivalent to unary, unidirectional aggregations, because you can navigate from the object to its properties. Practically speaking, attributes are the data portion of an object. A sensor object might include attributes such as a calibration constant and a measured value. If you find attributes to be nonprimitive, then they should generally be modeled as component objects owned by the original object. For example, if a sensor has a table of calibration constants rather than a simple scalar, the calibration table should be modeled as an object aggregated unidirectionally by the sensor object, as you can see in Figure 6-8.

Sometimes, the primary attributes of an object are obvious, but not always. Developers can ask themselves some key questions to identify the most important attributes of objects:

- What information defines the object?
- What information do the object's operations act upon?
- From the object's viewpoint, what do I know?
- Are the identified attributes rich in either structure or behavior? If so, are they objects rather than attributes?

---

7. Although they may collaborate directly with other noncomponent objects, components may themselves have only a single composite "owner." Composites are often treated as higher-level abstractions that are later decomposed into smaller parts. To maintain such levels of abstraction, the internal parts should not be made visible to objects outside the boundary of their owning composite class.

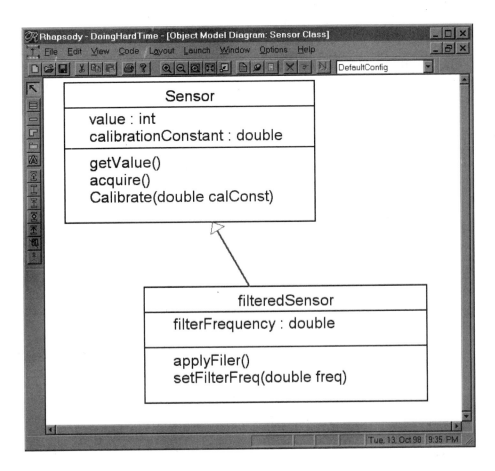

Figure 6-8: *Sensor Attributes*

- What are the responsibilities of the object? What information is necessary to fulfill these responsibilities?

The *aircraft* class within the context of an air traffic control system provides a good example of a real-time class with attributes. Let's ask these questions about the class:

- What information defines the object?
  The *aircraft* is a physical thing that traverses the airspace. AATCS models the aspects of the aircraft that allow it to know where it is, where it is going (flight plan), its capabilities (equipage), who it is (call signal), and its current direction.

- What information do the object's operations act upon?
  The aircraft must maintain its planned flight plan and create its actual flight plan during the course of a flight.

- From the object's viewpoint, what do I know?
  I know who I am, where I am, where I am going, and what I am doing right now.

- Are the identified attributes rich in either structure or behavior? If so, are they objects rather than attributes?
  Flight Plan, position (x, y, z, t, confidence), equipage.

- What are the responsibilities of the object? What information is necessary to fulfill these responsibilities?
  The *aircraft* class's primary responsibility is to represent the location and direction of a physical aircraft through the airspace to facilitate and support the controller's decisions about a flight path; runway selection; granting taxi, take-off and landing clearances; and to identify for the controller potential airspace and runway conflicts.

6.8 Generalization Relationships

Generalization is a taxonomic relationship between classes. The class higher in the taxonomic hierarchy can be called the *parent, generalized, base,* or *super* class. The class that inherits properties from the base class can be called the *child, specialized, derived,* or *subclass.*

Generalization in UML implies two things. The first is the substitutability of child classes for their parents. This property is called the Liskov Substitution Principle (LSP) [4]. Substitutability means that if A1:A (object A1, which is of class A) has an association to class B, the actual instance A1 links to at run-time may be of any subclass of B, without breaking the semantics of the model. This is another way of saying that *the subclass is a (more specialized) type of its superclass.*

The second implication of generalization in the UML is that subclasses inherit aspects of their superclass. Virtually *anything* that is true of the superclass must also be true of the subclass. Associations, attributes, and behaviors of the superclass are inherited by the subclass.

Anything less would break the related Substitution Principle.[8] Where, then, is the advantage of the generalization relationship?

Subclasses have all the properties of their parents, but may differ in two ways from their parent classes: Subclasses may either *extend* or *specialize* them (or both). Extension means that new properties are added to the subclass that are not present in the superclass. These are typically associations, attributes, and behaviors. A filteredSensor may have the structure of a *Sensor* class, including the attribute value and setPoint, and the behaviors of acquire(), getValue(), and setSetPoint(). It may also add a filterFrequency attribute, for example, and a filter() operation.

Specialization means that the operations defined by a superclass may be implemented differently, in a manner more appropriate to the subclass. In our *Sensor* example, the getValue operation may merely return the acquired value directly. However, in the *filteredSensor,* the getValue may call the filter() operation to filter the data to remove noise in the raw signal. None of these changes affect the fact that *filteredSensor* is a type of *sensor,* and everything that is true of *sensor* is also true of *filteredSensor.*

Figure 6-8 shows the relationship between the *Sensor* class and the *filteredSensor* class. Note that the *filteredSensor* class observes the LSP. It both extends and specializes its parent *Sensor* class.

Subclassing is most often done along one dimension, creating a set of subclasses that span the useful variants of that dimension. This dimension may be implementation (which may optimize some aspect of performance differently in various subclasses), behavior (more elaborate, for example), or some aspect of the class's responsibility. For example, the button subclasses in Figure 6-9 are specialized along the lines of behavior. Simple buttons issue an event message when pressed, but they have no state memory. Toggle buttons jump back and forth between two states on sequential depressions. Multistate buttons run through a (possibly elaborate) state machine on each depression. Group buttons deselect all other buttons within the group when depressed.

---

8. The only class property for which this is not true is the actual implementation of superclass operations. These are allowed to change in the subclasses. However, the signature of those operations is inherited.

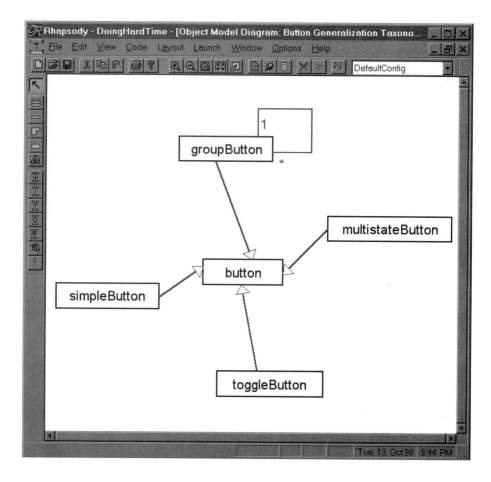

Figure 6-9: *Button Subclasses*

Superclasses may be used to define a "placeholder" without itself being instantiable. Such superclasses are called *abstract*. They provide a common interface to a set of (child) instantiable classes and, internally, a common structure for those base classes. Programmatically, C++ classes are made abstract by the inclusion of a *pure virtual function*. A C++ virtual function is a class method that is denoted by the keyword *virtual*. It need be so indicated in only one class in the inheritance tree, and it will be virtual for all derived classes. A virtual function is made *pure virtual* with the peculiar syntax of assigning the function declaration the value zero. For example,

```
class widget { // abstract class
public:
   virtual void doSomething() = 0; // pure virtual
   function
};
```

From a logical perspective, *all operations ought to be virtual* in all classes that may ever be overridden in a subclass. This helps ensure compliance with LSP. If a class has an association with a superclass, then at run-time any operation provided by the superclass may be called, even if the actual instance to which the class is linked is a subclass. Any operation that may be overridden in the subclass should be virtual. If it is not, the client class calling the operation will call the operation defined in the superclass and not the one redefined in the subclass. C++ compilers typically do not check this.

```
class B {
public:
   void doItForMe() {
      cout << "called B.doItForMe()" << endl;
   };
};

class sonOfB: public B {
   void doItForMe() {
      cout << "called sonOfB.doItForMe()" << endl;
   };
};

class A {
   public:
   B* myB;
   void doIt(void) {
      myB->doItForMe();
   };
};

void main(void) {
   A theA;
   sonOfB theB;
   theA.myB = &theB;
   theA->doIt(); // calls B.doItForMe not
sonOfB.doItForMe
};
```

The preceding code illustrates this point. The call to doIt() is statically bound by the compiler to b.doItForMe, but what is desired is probably sonOfB.doItForMe.

A corollary to the rule-of-thumb that all operations that may ever be overridden should be made virtual is that destructors should always be virtual, as well. Subclasses are free to create new attributes and associations that allocate memory or control devices, and the destructors in such specialized classes must generally deallocate the memory or decommission the devices.[9]

Another common generalization error found in object-oriented programs is a misunderstanding of the difference between generalization and instantiation. For example, an elevator system has a large number of buttons: up buttons to request an elevator to go up, down buttons to request an elevator to go down, and floor buttons to request that an elevator go to a particular floor. In such an environment, a class hierarchy such as that shown in Figure 6-10 is common. However, are the button subclasses shown in this figure really subclasses? Do they differ in their interface or the type and number of their attributes? Do they differ in how the behaviors are implemented? Or do they differ only in which target objects receive messages that indicate that a button was pushed? I strongly suggest that the latter case is true and that the different uses of buttons in the elevator system are not, in fact, different *kinds* of buttons. Thus, these different button objects are different instantiations of the very same button class and not of button subclasses.

It is not uncommon to show all the relations we've discussed on a single diagram when it helps to illustrate a collaboration or shows the interactions and abstractions within a domain. The simple model in Figure 6-11 shows all the primary ones: association, aggregation, composition, and generalization.

---

9. Note that in C++, constructors and destructors cannot be made pure virtual. C++ does not allow virtual constructors.

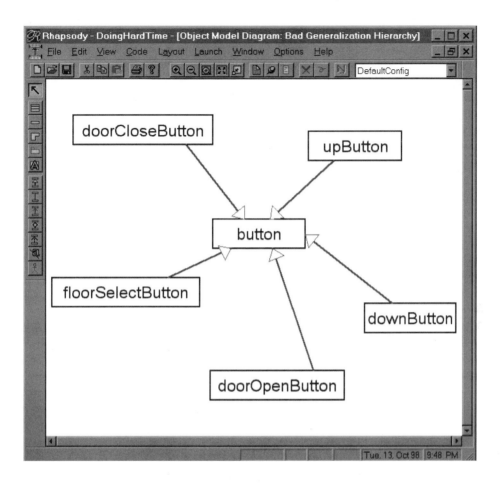

Figure 6-10: *Bad Generalization Hierarchy*

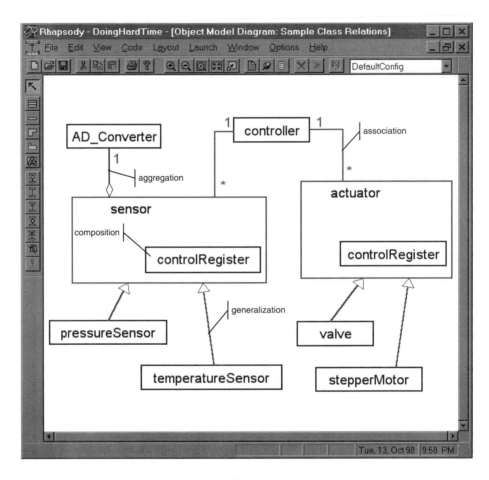

Figure 6-11: *Class Relationships*

6.9 AATCS Example: Class Diagrams

Figure 6-12 through Figure 6-17 show several important diagrams for the AATCS. Note that they are organized along multiple lines. Some class diagrams capture the classes and relations within a domain; others capture the class collaborations that cross domain boundaries. Rules for constructing useful class diagrams are discussed in the next section.

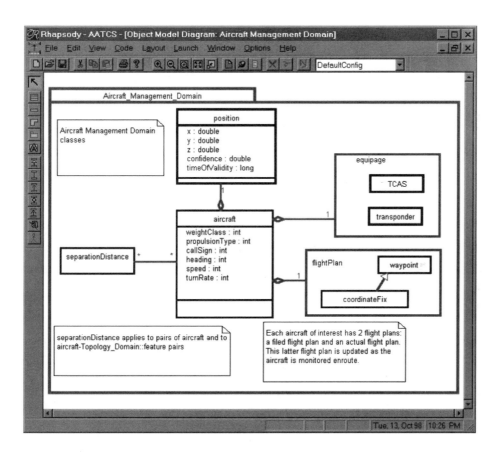

Figure 6-12: *AATCS Aircraft Management Domain Diagram*

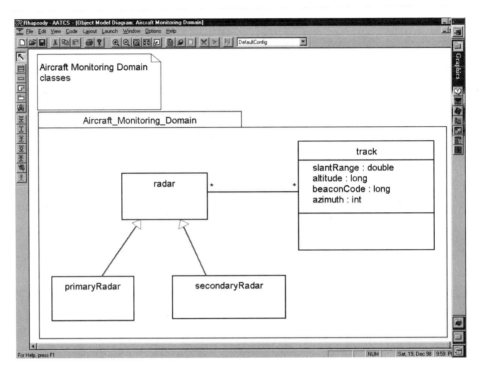

Figure 6-13: *AATCS Aircraft Monitoring Domain Diagram*

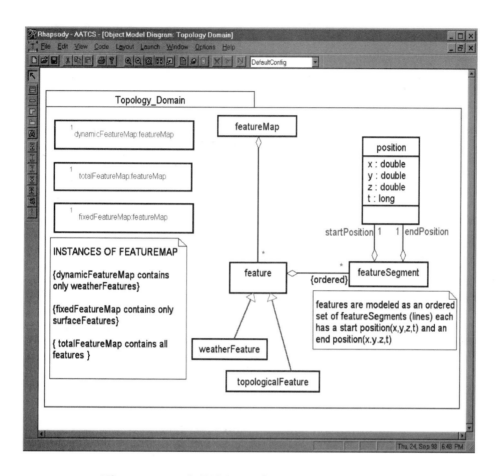

Figure 6-14: *AATCS Topology Domain Diagram*

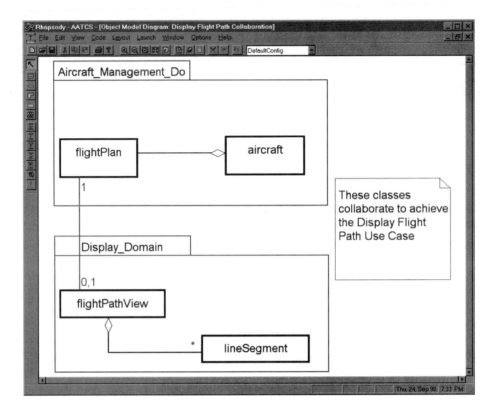

Figure 6-15: *Display Flight Path Collaboration*

Figure 6-15 and Figure 6-16 show the set of classes that collaborate to achieve a particular use case. Often a collaboration diagram is used instead of a class diagram. A collaboration diagram differs from a class diagram in two ways. First, object roles, rather than classes, are shown (indicated with object name:class name syntax). Second, explicit messages are shown. Collaboration diagrams show particular scenarios by prefacing the message names with sequence numbers. However, class diagrams may also be used, as in these figures, to represent all scenarios. Figure 6-17 shows how these objects collaborate to find a separation distance violation between the aircraft and a surface feature (mountain).

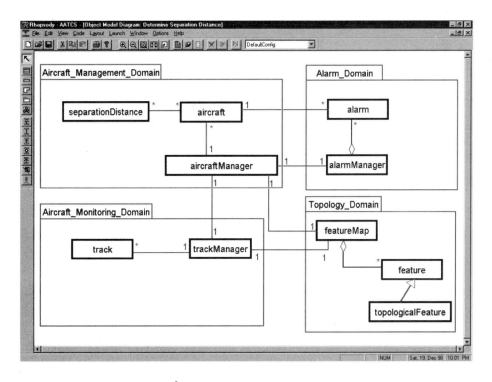

Figure 6-16: *Determine Separation Distance Violation Collaboration*

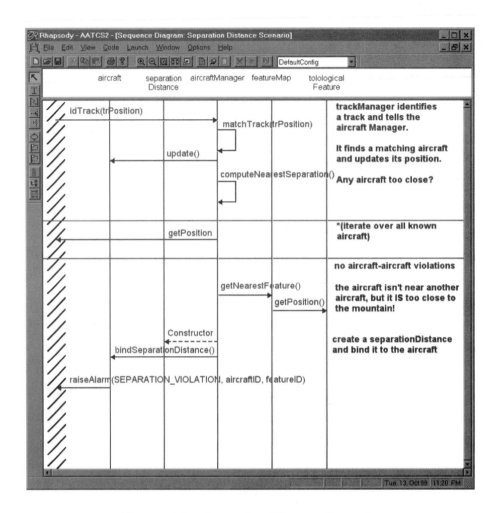

Figure 6-17: *Separation Distance Scenario*

6.10 Heuristics for Good Class Diagrams

One of the mistakes I see beginner object modelers make is the confusion between the diagrams of a model and the model itself. The whole point of modeling is to capture important abstractions within a system and define the semantics of these abstractions. This includes, of course, the attributes and operations defined on those abstractions, which are usually depicted on class diagrams. However, it also includes the roles the abstractions play in a variety of collaborations (generally captured in interaction diagrams, such as sequence and collaboration diagrams) and the state space of the abstractions (shown in statecharts). There may be any number of additional constraints and details that are important, including the responsibilities of the abstraction, the requirements met by the abstraction, and (manually or automatically) generated source code. All of these are parts of the model. Thus, the diagrams offer a view of the underlying semantic model of the user application, but they are not the model itself. Practically speaking, this means that one cannot understand a system with only the diagrams in hand. A report of the captured semantic model (yet another view of the model), in conjunction with the diagrams, is required for a full-detailed understanding of the object model.

This implies that the use of a drawing tool to construct pictures is inadequate, because you can create and maintain only a small set of the views. The diagrammatic view is the most common way to capture semantics, but the underlying model is the logical conjunction of the semantic information captured in all views.

That being said, diagrams provide a very important medium for capturing semantics. The class diagram is the primary view for capturing the structural object model, which includes the classes, their various relations to other classes, and (possibly) some set of the attributes and operations. The purpose of the class diagram view is to provide a medium in which one can capture and explore ("tinker with") the structural object model and, just as important, communicate this structural object model to peers.

The importance of class diagrams increases with the complexity of the underlying system model. As systems scale up, there quickly comes a time when the object structure is too rich to convey in a single diagram. What is needed is a set of ideas for how to decompose a complex model into separate structural pieces that maximize the purpose of the class diagrams. These are given in the sections that follow. These rules are not mutually exclusive but are provided as guidelines that may apply to some set of the diagrams you want to create.

6.10.1 Rules for Good Class Diagrams

- Each diagram should have a mission in life.

  One problem with many class diagrams is that they try to accomplish too many purposes and end up doing a rather poor job for all. If each class diagram has a single focus (to show a collaboration, a domain, or a generalization hierarchy), that purpose will be communicated more effectively.

- Build one diagram per collaboration (that is, use case).

  Collaborations of objects realize individual use cases. These objects may participate in other collaborations and act as helper classes in internal, domain-specific collaborations. Classes may also participate in generalization taxonomies. One approach to decomposing the object space is to capture each important collaboration in a separate diagram.

- Create one diagram per domain, including generalization hierarchies within that domain (domain diagram as high-level road map).

  Large object systems are always decomposed into packages. The semantics of package usage are not dictated by the UML. I find it particularly useful to divide up the system into a set of internally cohesive subject matters, called *domains*. Domains can often be well represented on one or a small set of class diagrams. Note that because collaborations must, in principle, span domains, domain class diagrams will not show all associations within a system.

- Create a single task diagram if there is significant multitasking.

  When multitasking is present, it is useful to represent the set of tasks on a single diagram. Such an idiomatic class diagram is called a *task diagram*. The UML models tasks as emanating from certain classes called *active classes*. A task diagram is a class diagram that shows only active classes.

- For rich hierarchies, create one diagram per generalization hierarchy.

  For the most part, generalization hierarchies fall entirely within a single domain. However, some domains may be too rich to show in a single diagram. One approach to decompose the domain into a reasonable set of diagrams is to show one generalization taxonomy per diagram.

- Don't mix generalization and collaboration unless it makes sense.

  Generally speaking, generalizations don't aid in the understanding of how collaborations work, and collaborations don't directly aid in the understanding of generalizations. Keeping these separate will clarify both.

- Create a master road map diagram of all classes only for very small systems (<50 classes) unless you have an E-size plotter and lots of wall space.

  Such roadmap diagrams are good for rubes (managers and their cohorts) but have little practical application.

- Don't show attributes and operations on class diagrams.

  Sometimes, it makes sense to show attributes and operations, but in the vast majority of cases, this level of detail only clutters the diagrams and discourages understanding. Show public members only when it adds understanding to the particular mission of the diagram.

- Don't replicate the repository on the diagrams.

  Show attributes and operations only on class diagrams on which they will directly aid understandability. It is virtually always a bad idea to show all attributes and operations of a class on a diagram. Similarly, it is rarely a good idea to show visibility (public, protected, private) on a class diagram. Such detail is better relegated to a textual model report.

- Don't cross lines.

  This is obvious, but it should be stated.

- Show multiplicities for all shown associations.

  The "groking"[10] of an association requires information about the numbers of objects that will participate in it at run-time.

- Show role names rather than association labels.

  Role names identify the purpose that an object serves within a collaboration. This is usually more useful than simply naming the association.

---

10. Heinleinian for "comprehending."

- Show only one role name for unidirectional navigation associations. Show both role names for bidirectional associations.

  In unidirectional associations, the role names are conjugates of the other (for example, "owner" and "owned"). This is not necessarily true of bidirectional associations. In the cases in which the roles are not conjugates, show both role names.

- Use containment composition notation (use containment to show creation/destruction responsibility).

  The containment way (nesting class boxes) to show composition is clearer and more distinct than using the filled aggregation diamond.

- Use composition to represent layers of abstraction within the class model.

  To maintain the abstraction layers, do not allow the component objects within the composite to associate with objects outside the scope of the composite. Instead, associate these external objects with the composite and have the composite delegate the appropriate messages to the component object.

- Show constraints in note boxes where appropriate. Don't forget the curly braces '{}' to denote the constraint.

  Constraints are limitations applied to metaelements. These constraints can be structural ("{node.prev.next == node.next.prev == node }") or behavioral ("{ execute time < 2 ms}"). They often aid in the understanding of the collaborations or generalization to which they apply.

- Show stereotypes where they add value—for instance, active, abstract, controller.

  Stereotypes have a sharp double edge. On one hand, they allow the developer to extend the UML's expressiveness to meet the particular characteristics of his or her application domain, company environment, or specific application. On the other hand, they are nonportable and can easily obscure intended meaning. Use stereotypes sparingly.

- Don't use color to convey information if you will share black and white hardcopies. It is better to use line styles (for example, rectilinear for associations, straight for generalizations, spline for event transition).

Color is useful only to distinguish things when the color is retained in all uses. I often see diagrams that look great on the computer screen languish on the printed page.

- Use a note box to label each diagram. Include the project, author and date of initial creation, and purpose.

   Remember that the diagram may be read out of context. It is always nice to know how old a diagram is, to what project it belongs, and its author. This can save considerable time and effort.

6.11 Summary

This chapter discussed the first half of analysis—identification of objects, classes, and relationships. Many strategies can be used to identify objects and classes—underlining the nouns, identifying the physical devices, looking for persistent data, and so on. Objects have attributes and behaviors that allow them to fulfill their responsibilities. Classes are abstractions of objects, so all objects instantiated from a particular class are structurally identical.

To support collaboration of objects, classes have relationships to each other. These may be associations among class instances, such as association and aggregation, or they may be relationships between classes, such as generalization. Objects use these associations to communicate by sending messages to each other.

6.12 Looking Ahead

The other half of analysis is concerned with defining the behavior of the classes. As we shall see in the next chapter, class behaviors may be classified in three ways—simple, state, and continuous. The dynamic properties of these classes allow them to use their structure to meet system responsibilities in real time.

6.13 Exercises

1. Name 10 elements commonly shown on a class diagram.

2. What is the purpose of structural object analysis?

3. What are the primary activities performed by the developer during structural object analysis?

4. Name and describe four strategies for the identification of objects and classes.

5. What is the value of early execution of an object model in structural object analysis?

6. Create a class diagram for the Acme Air Traffic Control System that identifies the structure of the collaboration of objects to realize the use case "Allocate runways to aircraft in airspace."

7. What are three uses of class diagrams?

8. What is the difference between m,n and $m..n$ multiplicities?

9. Describe the difference between aggregation and composition.

10. What is the Liskov Substitution Principle? How does it differ from the open-closed principle?

6.14 References

[1] Douglass, Bruce Powel. *Real-Time UML: Developing Efficient Objects for Embedded Systems*, Reading, Mass.: Addison-Wesley, 1998.

[2] Gamma, Erich, Richard Helm, Ralph Johnson, and John Vlissides. *Design Patterns: Elements of Reusable Software*, Reading, Mass.: Addison-Wesley, 1996.

[3] Booch, Grady. *Object-Oriented Analysis and Design with Applications*, Second Edition, Redwood City, Calif.: Benjamin Cummings Press, 1994.

[4] Liskov, Barbara. *Data Abstraction and Hierarchy*, SIGPLAN Notices, Vol. 23, Number 5, May 1988.

[5] Martin, Robert. *The Open-Closed Principle*, C++ Report, Vol. 8, Number 1, 1996.

Chapter 7

Behavioral Object Analysis

On its best-behaved day, the world is still *only piece-wise linear.*
— Book of Douglass, Law 75

The previous chapter showed how to define the system object structure by identifying the fundamental objects and classes and their relationships. In this chapter, we define and refine operations and behaviors of the objects. There are a number of ways to specify overall object behavior, the most important of these is to model the object as a finite state machine. Scenario modeling helps you test your behavioral models to ensure that the objects can collaborate to achieve the system responsibilities. The state and scenario models lead to the definitions of class operations required to process the incoming messages and events.

7.1 Introduction

Objects have both structure and behavior. Object behavior may be viewed solely within the context of individual objects, or behavior may be viewed in the larger context of object collaborations. In this chapter, we will explore both views, as well as the underlying semantics of behavior as defined by the UML.

One of the difficulties of behavioral models applied to functionally decomposed systems is the definition of the portion of the system to which the behavioral model applies. That part of the system must have both attributes (values that potentially persist) and operations (to accept events and perform actions). This difficulty arises because functionally decomposed systems artificially separate intrinsically tightly coupled things. Specifically, they separate the actions that the part of the system can perform from the data upon which those actions operate.

This difficulty does not arise in the definition of object-oriented systems because objects are things that naturally maintain this intrinsic coupling while they allow the designer to enforce an independence between things that are inherently loosely coupled. Thus, in object-oriented analysis and design, the subject to which a behavioral model applies is always clear. In the UML, it is always a *classifier*—most commonly a class, but it can also be other kinds of classifier, such as a use case.

7.2 Terms and Concepts

Behavior refers to the ways in which things change. An object's behavior is defined by the set of class operations and the constraints on their application. The functional aspect of behavior refers to *what* the object does. For example, the object may turn on a switch, retrieve a value, display a waveform, or modulate an RF wave.

Constraints on behavior may be specified in various ways. Functional constraints limit the use of operations into well-defined sequences in which pre- and post-conditional invariants are met. Functional constraints are often modeled using finite state machines. Other nonfunctional constraints frequently apply, as well. Such constraints are referred to as quality-of-service (QoS) constraints, and qualify how that behavior is accomplished. For example, how long should an action take? Performance requirements levied against behaviors are an example of such QoS requirements. Another example is the required accuracy or fidelity of a computation. Is two-digit accuracy enough? In real-time systems, both functional and QoS aspects must be taken into account when specifying an object's behavior. QoS constraints are generally modeled using a constraint language. The UML does not require particular constraint language, although it does provide one that it uses in its own definition (Object Constraint Language, or OCL). Developers should feel free to use a constraint language that meets their needs. Common constraint languages are structured English, mathematics (for example, differential equations), OCL, and temporal logic.

In this volume, we will discuss behavior as one of three types: simple, state, or continuous. These types of behavior are distinguished on the basis of how they treat the object's time history. Simple behavior does not depend on the history of the object whatsoever. Reactive objects divide up the behavioral space of the object into nonoverlapping chunks, called states. Continuous behavior depends on the object's time history, but it does so in ways that cannot be easily divided up into disjoint states.

7.2.1 Simple Behavior

An object with simple behavior performs services on request and keeps no memory of previous services. A simple behavior always responds to an input in exactly the same way, regardless of its history. Some examples of simple behaviors are

- Simple mathematical functions, such as cosine or square root
- A knob that returns the number of clicks for a given user action
- Return a value measured by a sensor at this instant
- Return the current value of an object attribute
- Send a point-event pulse down a wire

7.2.2 State Behavior

The second type of object behavior is called *state, state-driven,* or *reactive.* A *state* is an ontological condition that persists for a significant period of time, which is both distinguishable from other such conditions and disjoint with them. A distinguishable state means that it observably differs from other states in the events it accepts, the transitions it takes as a result of accepting those events, and the actions it performs. A transition is a response to an event that causes a change in state.[1]

Modeling an object as a *finite state machine* (FSM) attempts to reduce the behavioral complexity by making some simplifying assumption. Specifically, it assumes

- The object being modeled can assume only a finite number of existence conditions, called *states.*
- The object's behavior within a given state is essentially identical and is defined by:
  1. The messages and events accepted
  2. The actions associated with each incoming event
  3. The state's reachability graph
  4. The complete set of event-transition-target state triads (that is, the ongoing activities within the state and the actions done entering or leaving the state)
- The object spends all of its time in states. The object resides in individual states for significant periods of time.
- The system may change these conditions only in a finite number of well-defined ways, called *transitions.*
- Transitions are enabled by occurrences of interest, called *events.*
- Transitions take (approximately) zero time.

In the UML, a state machine defines the behavior of a classifier. (For the rest of this discussion, we will assume that we are discussing how it applies to classes and objects, but the reader should be aware that it applies equally well to other types of classifier.) It does this by constraining the object's overall behavioral space as defined by its operations. It is a way of explicitly codifying pre- and post-conditional invariants—that is, things that must be true prior to the execution of an action and things that must be true following its execution. In this

---

1. This is a somewhat more intuitive definition than the one provided by more-formal texts [1], but it is equivalent with them.

case, a state machine constrains the execution of the operations provided by an object into specific sequences that occur when specific preconditional predicates are satisfied.

The UML represents states in two ways: statecharts and activity diagrams. *Statecharts* are the primary representation of state machines. They are a visual formalism that depicts an object's state space. This visual formalism has several features that have been added to ensure that it successfully scales up to complex behavioral models [2]. Statecharts are particularly adept at representing reactive systems—that is, systems that wait for and react to asynchronous events.

The other type of state machine explicitly represented in the UML is an *activity diagram*—a type of state machine in which most or all the transitions between states occur not because of asynchronous events but, rather, following the completion of the activities performed while residing in the activity state itself. Thus, activity diagrams are adept at showing primarily synchronous behavior. Activity diagrams are discussed in more detail later in this chapter. For now, let's limit our discussion to the more common, primarily asynchronous state machine.

To explore the state machine just a bit, let's build a state machine to parse a string of parentheses to see if they are balanced—that is, the number and order of left and right parentheses is correct and equal (see Table 7-1).

This turns out to be hard to model as an FSM.[2] By our definition of states, each of the following is a different state of the expression.

Table 7-1: *Sample Parenthetical Expressions*

Expression	Description
( ) ( )	Balanced
((( ) ( )))	Balanced
(( ) ( )	Unbalanced: +1
( ) ( ))	Unbalanced: −1
) (	Unbalanced due to order
( ))(( ) ( )	Unbalanced due to order

---

2. Hard, as in *impossible*.

```
(
( (
( ( (
)
( )
) (
```

Because it is possible to be infinitely unbalanced to the left or right, a finite set of states, in principle, cannot model a parser of this grammar. If we limit the string length to a finite value, then it becomes possible, in principle, to capture the behavioral space using a finite set of states. For the purpose of illustration, let's limit the string length to four characters and the characters in the grammar to '(' and ').' Such a state machine looks like Figure 7-1.

The figure shows the state space for an expression parser for this simple grammar.[3] The valid balanced states are shown using heavy lines. The transitions are not named, to simplify the diagram.

Only 4 of the 31 states shown represent valid balanced expressions. Many of the expressions are simply unbalanced, such as ")))(." Others have an incorrect sequence, such as ")(." The resulting statechart is unsatisfying, because it seems like it *ought* to be simple, and that a more parsimonious graph, than a complete enumeration of all possible expressions, *ought* to be possible. Further, it makes intuitive sense that the string ought to be in one of two high-level states: balanced or unbalanced. Intuition, however, is misleading in this case. The implication is that while FSMs are theoretically helpful, in many applications their state spaces grow unmanageably large and complex for even simple problems.

A modified approach, however, can simplify the problem. You may note that three conditions are met by all valid expression states:

1. The number of characters is even (0, 2, or 4).

2. The number of left parentheses equals the number of right parentheses.

3. The next token received when the state corresponds to a balanced expression must be a left parenthesis.

---

3. Error transitions for illegal tokens (for example, 'w') are not shown; these would complicate the diagram further.

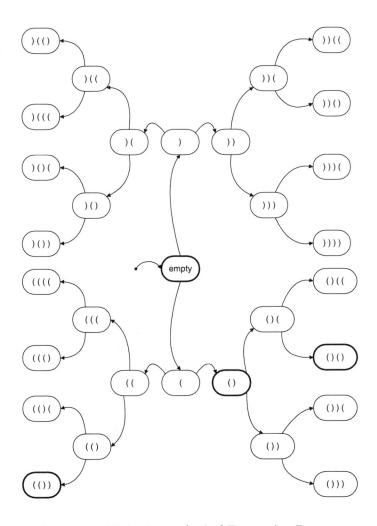

Figure 7-1: *Finite Parenthetical Expression Parser*

Figure 7-2 shows a greatly simplified FSM that does the same thing as the FSM in Figure 7-1. The exact syntax for statecharts is defined in a later section, but briefly, this FSM consists of three states and eight transitions. Transitions are labeled within the incoming token, optionally followed by a '/' character and an action expression, such as "++balance." This action expression is executed when the transition is taken. The © is a *conditional connector*, which allows different transitions to be taken when an event occurs based on a Boolean expression called a *guard* (shown in square brackets), such as the guard [balance <= 1].[4]

The FSM in Figure 7-2 is simplified greatly because we use memory (the attribute *balance*) to track the balance state for the expression. This is a great asset in this case, because all the left-unbalanced states can be represented with a single state (with memory), all the balanced states with another, and all the invalid expressions (incorrect sequence and right-unbalanced) with a third. Pure FSMs have no memory and must represent the automaton using only states. However, we can cheat and combine FSMs with memory to create the counting machine shown in Figure 7-2, which can represent our behavioral space more simply. Mixing state machines with other kinds of memory[5] permits the construction of more-powerful machines than pure FSMs. When we refer to an FSM throughout the remainder of this book, we mean one augmented with memory as necessary. State machines are a major focus of this chapter and will be discussed in more detail.

7.2.3 Continuous Behavior

The third kind of object behavior is continuous. Many objects show continuous behavior, including digital filters and PID control loops. All that is required is that the current output depends on the previous history in a way that does not lend itself to discretization. In the simplest of such cases, the behavior depends on history in a smooth way, but smoothness is not necessarily required. If there are discontinuities in the behavior itself, then the behavior should probably be modeled as a quasi-state machine with piece-wise continuous behavior.[6] If the difference is in the first or higher derivatives, then even quasi-statehood probably doesn't apply. However, we will be sloppy and use the term *continuous* to mean "nondiscrete."

An object with continuous behavior is one with an infinite, or at least unbounded, set of existence conditions. Mathematical control systems, fuzzy sets, and neural networks all display continuous behavior.

---

4. In UML, guards are evaluated prior to the execution of actions. Therefore, this guard "[balance <= 1]" is executed before the execution of the action "—balance." This means that the guard should check for '1' as the boundary, not '0', as shown in the figure.
5. Such as push-down stacks, queues, and more-elaborate data structures.
6. That is, the behavior is smooth within a given state, and state boundaries are defined by the discontinuities.

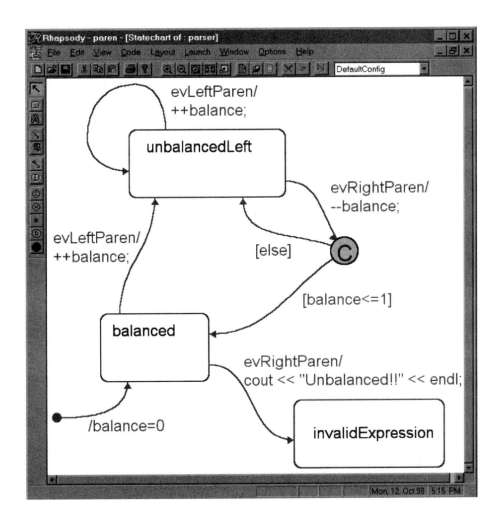

Figure 7-2: *Simplified Finite Parenthetical Expression Parser*

Most of this chapter will deal with state behavior. However, I hear questions about how to model continuous systems often enough that I would like to address it briefly in this section.

7.2.3.1 Fuzzy Systems

State machines fundamentally rely on Aristotelian logic and indirectly on the law of the excluded middle (LEM). The LEM states that existence conditions can be divided into two mutually exclusive groups. If the first is called *A*, then the second can be called *not A* or *~A*. Classical set theory, on which finite state analysis is based, is firmly rooted in the basic notion that states have hard, crisp boundaries and that an object must be either in the set *A* or in the set *~A*. It cannot be in both, but it must be in one. States in a normal finite state machine are essentially nothing more than disjoint sets of the object's behavior space, whereas *all* states of a fuzzy state machine are concurrently active. The degree to which the state holds varies, however.

Objects with continuous behaviors do not follow the LEM because the concept of states doesn't apply or because states are not disjoint. If a value is a real number between 0 and 1, it cannot be modeled by an FSM because it can assume any of an infinite set of values. Even when continuous systems have states, these states are not disjoint—this is the very basis for fuzzy set and control theory. Before we get into FSMs in more detail, let's examine a system with continuous behavior—in this case, a fuzzy logic system.

A fuzzy automobile braking-control system is a relatively simple example. Such a system would have the responsibility of slowing down the car smoothly as it approaches its destination. The amount of braking to be applied depends on two independent variables: automobile speed and distance from destination. When the car is moving fast and is close, the brakes must be applied more vigorously than when the car is either {moving fast and is far away} or {moving slowly and is close}.

The fuzzy car-braking system can be codified by defining the membership functions (inputs) and the rules applied to set members (outputs to the brake). A diagrammatic representation of the fuzzy sets used in the definition of an automobile-braking system are given in Figure 7-3.

In conventional terms, the speed of the automobile constitutes one state (set) variable and the distance another. Because these concerns are fundamentally orthogonal, it makes sense to consider each separately in its own state machine.[7] The state values for speed are *stopped, slow, sauntering,* and *galloping*. The state values for distance are *at, close, near, removed,* and *far*. In a fuzzy state machine, the object is in all these states simultaneously, but in varying degrees.

---

7. More specifically, they are orthogonal components of a single fuzzy state machine. Orthogonal components are discussed later in this chapter.

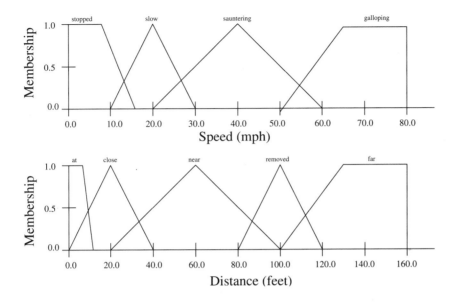

Figure 7-3: *Fuzzy Automobile Brakes*

The output of the control system is the braking pressure. It has four states: *none, light, medium,* and *hard.* Brakes should not be applied when trying to accelerate or maintain speed, but only when trying to slow down. The other states are of various strengths, related to the desired amount of instantaneous deceleration.

The rule set is defined in Table 7-2.

Table 7-2: *Fuzzy Automobile Braking Rules*

Speed State	Distance State	Output Rule (Braking Pressure Applied)
Stopped	Any	None
Slow	At	Medium
Slow	Close	Light
Slow	Near	Light
Slow	Removed	None *(continued)*

Table 7-2: (*cont.*)

Speed State	Distance State	Output Rule (Braking Pressure Applied)
Slow	Far	None
Sauntering	At	Hard
Sauntering	Close	Medium
Sauntering	Near	Medium
Sauntering	Removed	Light
Sauntering	Far	None
Galloping	At	Hard
Galloping	Close	Hard
Galloping	Near	Medium
Galloping	Removed	Light
Galloping	Far	None

In a fuzzy state machine, the system is in all states simultaneously, so *all* rules are applied *all* the time. The degree to which they are applied depends directly on the degree of membership within the particular state. For example, if the current speed is 25 miles per hour, then *slow* is half true (0.5) and *sauntering* is also partially true (0.25). If the distance is 85 feet, then *near* is true (0.4) and *removed* is true (0.2). Therefore, the following rules have nonzero outputs:

- Slow and Near—> Light
- Slow and Removed—> None
- Sauntering and Near—> Medium
- Sauntering and Removed—> Light

You can also see that the logical statement *"slow and near"* is more true than the statement *"sauntering and removed."* The resulting outputs are combined (using what is called a *defuzzifier*) to produce an output that is a weighted sum of the inputs, called the *centroid*.

Fuzzy systems can be used to model behavior that is not readily discretized into nonoverlapping sets or states. It does this by relaxing the

LEM and using weighted set membership functions to compute centroids. Fuzzy systems can be modeled in the UML in a straightforward way. Remember, that the "thing" that has the fuzzy behavior is still a class. This means that the structural object formalisms (for example, class diagrams) apply equally well to fuzzy systems as to object systems. What is lacking is a visual formalism within the UML for the representation of the fuzzy sets. One approach is to use the State Pattern (see Chapter 9 and [3]), which is an implementation pattern in which states are implemented by (design-level) objects to which the main class (called the *context*) associates. This pattern can be used equally well with fuzzy states. The main difference lies in the fact that rather than associate to a single state at a time (because states are nonoverlapping), in the Fuzzy-State Pattern the context associates to all fuzzy states at once, each with varying degrees of truth. For more detail on the Fuzzy-State Pattern, see Chapter 9.

Fuzzy systems are appropriate when the object's behavioral model can be divided up into possibly overlapping conditions of existence (fuzzy states) and the rules that affect the degree of membership in those fuzzy states are known. There are many circumstances when this is true, and fuzzy systems have been applied successfully to a wide variety of real-time systems problems, from anesthesia alarm systems [4] to control of trains [5] and avionics [6]. Fuzzy systems typically perform well with respect to timeliness.

One advantage is the availability of a number of fuzzy logic toolsets that can automatically generate control logic in languages such as C and C++. However, fuzzy logic is no more or less expressive than the other methods presented here. With properly constructed fuzzy sets, any nonlinear function can be captured. The difficulty in creating good fuzzy control systems is tuning the membership functions and rule sets, a task analogous to tuning PID control loop parameters. Still, fuzzy systems have been created that solve some problems that defy conventional mathematical approaches, such as balancing a three-segment inverted pendulum and backing up three-segment trucks.

7.2.3.2 Artificial Neural Network (ANN) Systems

Sometimes the rules (including the underlying mathematics) of a behavior or process are either unknown or intractable. Such problems routinely occur in pattern recognition. One solution to these problems is the construction of artificial neural networks (ANNs). A neural network is an organized collection of small autonomous machines of limited functionality that collaborate to achieve a larger behavior. There are a great many ways to wire these simple machines together [7,8], but we will limit this discussion to its most common computation form, the back-propagation network. It turns out that ANNs are adept at identifying key factors underlying variation in input-output response and the rules governing those factors even when these factors are not obvious upon inspection [9]. In fact, several neural network systems have been constructed to perform tasks such as tumor identification in images and in the diagnosis of early heart failure that have outperformed experts.[8]

Figure 7-4 shows the basic structure of the back-propagation network. The key object in the network is obviously the neuron. As mentioned earlier, individual neurons are simple things, although artificial neurons are simpler than their biological counterparts [10].

A back-propagation neural network consists of three or more layers. One layer, called the *input layer,* receives the raw information upon which it is supposed to work its magic. Another layer, the *output layer,* produces the desired output. In the middle are one or more intermediate layers that link a predecessor layer with a subsequent layer. During execution, information flows from the input layer toward the output layer. When a neuron in one layer fires (produces an output), its computed output flows (suitably scaled) toward all the neurons in the subsequent layer.

Biological neurons may be thought of as machines that perform integration both temporally and spatially—but that also leak. Mechanistically, this is because they perform integration by summing the electrical potential of membrane patches maintained by differences in ion concentrations across that membrane. Maintaining the ion concentration requires energy, and for a variety of biochemical reasons, the ions leak in the direction of the concentration gradient. It is exactly these properties that allow the neurons in the retina to perform 2-D

---

8. This is likely because the expert's theory is either inaccurate or he or she has incorrectly assessed the magnitude of an input's contribution. Neural networks care nothing for theory; but they can identify input-output patterns in the data itself.

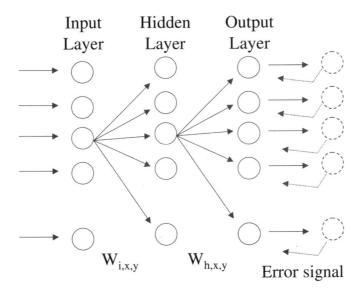

Figure 7-4: *Back-Propagation Neural Network*

Gaussian convolution of their inputs, which is crucial for the identification of edges in image analysis.[9] But I digress . . .

Each neuron N_i in any given layer L receives inputs from each neuron in the previous (L-1) layer. Each separate unidirectional link from Neuron$_{j,L-1}$ to Neuron$_{k,L}$ is called a synapse and has a unique weighting factor $w_{j,k,L-1}$. The input to Neuron$_{k,L}$ from Neuron$_{j,L-1}$ is computed by multiplying the output value of the neuron by its synaptic weight.

Each artificial neuron computes by adding up its input values to determine its output (see Figure 7-5). To prevent nonlinear explosion, this sum is typically bounded by a sigmoidal so-called "squashing function" such as $\tan(x)$. This value is then used as the neuron's output for the next layer's input (for that neuron). In some networks, the neural output is itself constrained to be 0 or 1, depending on whether the sum exceeds the threshold. This output is then scaled by the various synaptic weights.

---

9. The retinal neural system does not use a back-propagation network. Rather, it uses an arrangement called *reciprocal inhibition* in which inputs in the center of a field are sharpened by inhibition of the neurons surrounding the primary input.

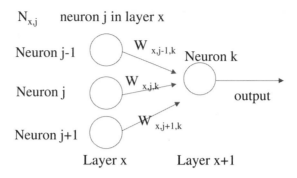

$$n_{x+1,k} = Squash(\mathbf{S} n_{x,j} w_{x,j,k})$$

Figure 7-5: *The Computational Neuron*

A neural network learns its proper input-output response (such as mapping an input set of pixels forming a character "A" to the output—the ASCII representation of the letter *A*) by adjusting the weighting factors to minimize the error of the computation. This is done in a recursive fashion by applying a training pair that consists of an input with a known output. The weights are then modified, layer by layer, to a value that minimizes the error between the known correct output and the computed output. This process is repeated for every input-output pair in the training set. Each run through the training set is called an "epoch" in the neural network biz. Initially, the weights are set to small random values (usually, less then 0.1 or so) and the training set is applied until the error in the training set reaches an acceptable minimum or until it is clear that the network will not converge. This typically takes several thousand epochs to achieve. If the network does not converge, the common approach is to reinitialize the network and try again. Once a neural network is trained to produce the proper output for the known inputs, the learning mode is disabled. In operation, a back-propagation network works in a feed-forward-only fashion, generating the output that the system computes to best match the input.

There are a number of ways to represent neural networks using UML models. All these models will have a neuron class. Whether or not the model also contains a layer class depends on the type of neural model being considered. Hebbian models do not require layers while other neural models, such as adaptive resonance theory (ART) networks, have a number of different layers. In this case, let us limit our focus to simple back-propagation networks and include the layers, not as constraints on associations (a perfectly valid approach), but as structural features (classes).

Figure 7-6 shows a simple way to represent a back-propagation neural network in the UML. Note that the layers are shown as container classes that aggregate their constituent neurons. In this example, we have assumed a three-layer network with a single hidden layer.

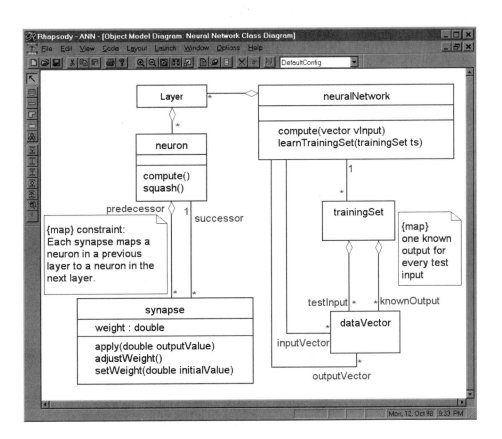

Figure 7-6: *Neural Network Model in UML*

7.2.3.3 General Mathematics with Recursion

The more traditional approach, particularly with control engineers, is to directly implement equations dictated by their understanding of the physical system under control. A small set of these equations have closed-form analytic solutions but, by far, most do not. In fact, in typical graduate courses on partial differential equations, virtually all the effort is focused on the conditions under which solutions exist, not on analytic methods for deriving those solutions. Thus, the control engineer is usually stuck with linear approximations of the behavior, or with performing numerical computations to estimate the solutions to the nonlinear formulations.

There are many ways to solve problems numerically. In order to use a numerical solution, a detailed analysis of error and error propagation (which can lead to the accumulation of increasing levels of error in subsequent calculations) is required. When problems are fully understood at an initial starting point (generally, including the value and first and second derivatives), it is said to be an *initial value problem*. When instead, the function values (but not the derivatives) are known at different points and a differential equation describes the system, it is called a *boundary value problem*. Boundary value problems are generally more difficult to solve than initial value problems, because the former can usually be solved by more-direct numerical methods. Consider a simple second-order differential equation:

$$\frac{dx^2}{d^2t} = f(t, x, \frac{dx}{dt})$$

and x(a) = A and x(b) = B. One approach to solving this boundary value problem is the shooting method in which one guesses at x'(a) and then the system is solved iteratively as an initial value problem. The error is computed between the computed estimate of x(b) and the actual known B; this feeds back into a correction of the estimate of x'(t); this solution is tried, and so on.

In terms of modeling such systems, if a set of differential equations applies to a single class, then the class can contain the difference equations (a discrete formulation of a differential equation). The context class (containing the problem) can then associate to a class containing the computational machinery to solve the problem. Computational classes can implement methods such as Runge-Kutta, Adams-Moulton, or other suitable computational approaches [11]. This is an example of the Policy Pattern, discussed in Chapter 9. These policies can even change during run-time if necessary.

The most common way to implement a set of equations is to iterate periodically. At the end of each period, the output of the equation set is used as the input for the subsequent iteration. This can be (and often is) driven by a simple state machine, such as shown in Figure 7-7. The application of the equations in the control loop is performed as an entry action (or an activity) in the *Iterate_Control_Eqs* state every so often, as defined by the timeout transition *tm(iterPeriod)*.

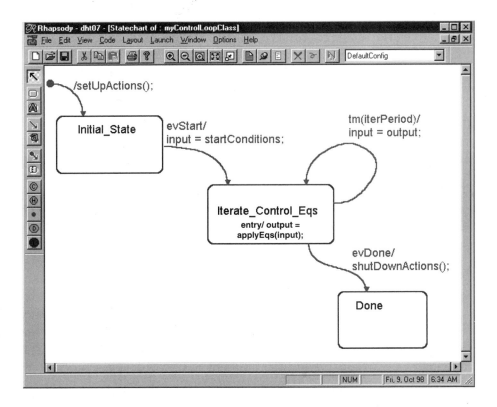

Figure 7-7: *Driving a Control Loop*

7.3 UML Statecharts

A primary feature of the UML is its support for finite state machines. Harel statecharts [2] form the basis of UML state diagrams, and we shall use the terms *statechart* and *state diagram* interchangeably. Statecharts overcome the limitations of traditional FSMs while they retain the benefits of finite state modeling. Statecharts include the notions of nested hierarchical states and orthogonal regions, while extending the notion of actions.

7.3.1 Basic State Semantics

An object whose behavior may be captured on a statechart is said to be *reactive.* Such an object's behavioral space is divided up into disjoint and nonoverlapping conditions of existence, called states. And as we've already defined state: A *state* is an ontological condition that persists for a significant period of time, which is both distinguishable from other such conditions and disjoint with them. A distinguishable state means that it observably differs from other states in the events it accepts, the transitions it takes as a result of accepting those events, and the actions it performs. A transition is a response to an event that causes a change in state.

Perhaps more simply put, a state is a condition of an object during which a set of events is accepted and some actions and activities are executed, and the object can reach some set of states based on the events it accepts. It differs from other states in any of the following ways:

- Input events accepted
- Output transitions taken as a result of the input events and the reachability graph of subsequent states achieved when the transitions are taken
- Actions executed on state entry
- Actions executed on state exit
- Activities performed

Basically, if two states differ in any way, they are different states of existence.

Extending this notion is the idea that a state may be decomposed into substates. For example, the state space of a sensor may be thought of at a high level as the set:

sensor state is one of {off, on}

The *on* state might be further decomposed into nonoverlapping substates:

on is one of {booting, active, broken}

Similarly,

active is one of {idle, calibrating, measuring, has valid measurement }

Using such recursion, arbitrarily complex state spaces may be decomposed.[10] Note also that such hierarchical state space decomposition is no more mathematically expressive than flat Mealy-Moore state models. However, it is, as we shall see, vastly more parsimonious for many complex state spaces.

The decomposition, or nesting (as it is commonly called), of states does not address one practical problem of constructing complex state spaces—islands of independent behavior within objects. For example, an object may have a memory requirement (small, medium, and large), an operating condition (self-testing, automatic, externally controlled, error), and a fidelity (coarse, medium, fine). The state space of such an object is the set defined by the cross products of these orthogonal regions of behavior. It will have states such as *small-automatic-medium* and *small-error-fine*. This requires the 2-D state diagram to explicitly represent $3 \times 4 \times 3 = 36$ independent states. The problem grows combinatorially worse as the number and size of the orthogonal regions grow.

The statechart solution is to represent the orthogonal regions as separate areas in which the semantics define the independence of the regions. Thus, statecharts define two kinds of superstates. One kind (called an *or-state*) declares that the object must be in exactly one substate of the superstate whenever the object can be said to be in the superstate at any given time. The other kind (called an *and-state* or

---

10. It should be noted that some methodologists, such as Steve Mellor, argue that such decomposition is always an indication that the object space has not been properly decomposed. However, the general opinion of methodologists actively involved in the UML, including the author, is that, much of the time, decomposition of state spaces into multiple levels of abstraction greatly aids understandability and, in a very practical way, the scaleability of the state machine formalism itself.

orthogonal region) declares that the object must be in all substates at the same time when the enclosing superstate is active.

Usually, or-states and and-states are combined, so in a superstate containing and-states, each and-state is further decomposed into or-states. This allows the following amendment to the earlier definition of state: *A state context is an enclosing state (called a superstate), which is further decomposed. An object "residing in" a substate is also "residing in" its superstate. An object must be in exactly one of all possible or-states at any given level of decomposition within a state context when that state context is active. An object must be in all and-states at any given level within a state context when that state context is active.*

7.3.2 Transitions and Events

An act of changing state is called a *transition*. Transitions are initiated by events. The UML defines four kinds of events:

1. *SignalEvent*—an occurrence of interest arising asynchronously from outside the scope of the state machine
2. *CallEvent*—an explicit synchronous notification of an object by another
3. *ChangeEvent*—an event based on the changing of an attribute value
4. *TimeEvent*—either the elapse of a specific duration or the arrival of an absolute time

It should be remembered, though, that an event is just that—something that occurs at particular space-time coordinates. Events have neither duration nor persistence (except where noted below). When an object cannot act on an event, either because the event does not result in an explicit transition or because a guarding condition evaluates FALSE, the event is discarded. This is why the state machine segment in Figure 7-8 is such a bad idea. A *completion event* (a.k.a. an *anonymous event*) transition is triggered immediately upon entry to the state and the completion of any defined activities. If the guard evaluates to FALSE at that time, the object is stuck in that state. That completion event will never occur again unless the state is exited and reentered.

The UML does provide syntax for deferring the handling of an event until a subsequent state is entered. An event handled in this way is said to be *deferred*. The event will persist until a state is entered in

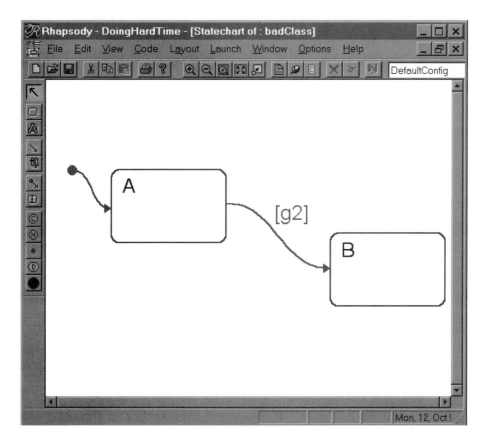

Figure 7-8: *Dangerous Event Pattern*

which that event is not deferred. At that point, the event will either be acted upon (if explicitly mentioned) or discarded (if not).

Signals associated with *SignalEvents* are modeled as *signal classes* (also known, somewhat misleadingly, as *event classes*). This means that signal hierarchies may be constructed in which some signals are more specialized versions of others, such as shown in Figure 7-9. Signal hierarchies are useful not only because they provide a means to structure and classify the taxonomy of signals and their associated events in a system but also because they allow polymorphic handling of events. This means that various objects can accept events at different levels (possibly simultaneously) in the hierarchy. They are also useful because

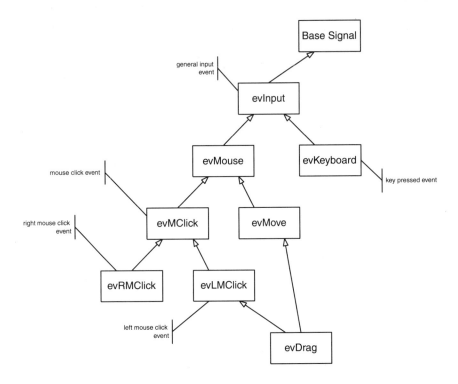

Figure 7-9: *Event Hierarchy*

a class may need to perform different actions based on both the general type of a signal, as well as the more specific type.

For example, consider the state machine in Figure 7-10. When an evRMClick occurs, it affects both the handleMouseInput region and the handleAllInput region. This is because a right mouse click (evRMClick) is a type of input event signal (evInput). Without a signal hierarchy, the logEvent() action would have to be proliferated throughout the state machine.

7.3.3 Actions and Activities

Actions are noninterruptible behaviors executed at particular points in state machines. An action may also be a sequence of actions that is also noninterruptible. Actions are considered to take essentially zero time.

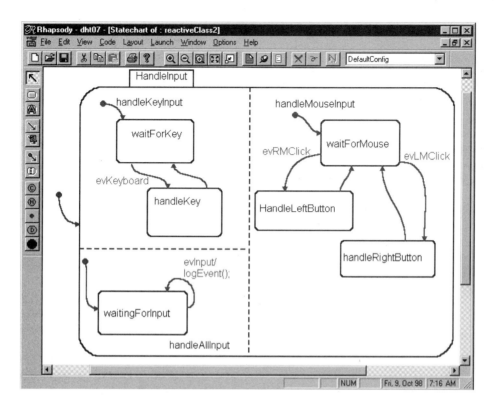

Figure 7-10: *Using an Event Hierarchy*

Activities are behaviors that can take significant time, so they must generally be interruptible. If it turns out that an action can take a significant time, then it should be made into an activity within some state. Actions may be done on entry to a state, exit from a state, or when a transition is taken. Activities may be done only within states.

State action properties are specified by an action-type keyword, a slash ('/'), and an action list. Action properties for states are

entry / [action-list]

exit / [action-list]

reaction/ [action-list]

do / [activity-list]

deferred / [event-list]

If an event in the current state's deferred event list occurs, the event will persist (although it does not block handling of nondeferred events) until a state is entered that does not list the action in its deferred event list.

Actions may be executed at any of the following times:

- When a state is entered
- When a state is exited
- When a transition is taken

Actions may be action sequences, consisting of an arbitrary-length list of actions. Actions themselves may be calls of operations defined within the class, or statements in a formal language. Some example actions are

- f(x,y,z) + g(b)
- ++a;
- b += c/a;

Actions are executed in the following order: First, the exit actions of the exit state(s) are executed, followed by the transition actions, followed by the entry actions of the entered state(s). The situation with nested states follows the same basic rule, but is slightly more complex. Entry actions are executed in the same order as the nesting, when entering a nested substate from outside its enclosing superstate. When transition t1 is taken in Figure 7-11, the sequence of actions is w then x,y then z. When transition t2 is taken, the reverse order applies (innermost -> out), so the sequence of exit actions is p then n then m. When transitioning between states, as with the transition t3, the exit actions of the source state are taken, followed by the transition actions, followed by the destination state's entry actions. In the case of transition t3, the sequence is p then n, then g then s. States may be nested arbitrarily deeply, and these rules apply recursively.

Internal transitions, also called *reactions*, are action responses taken when an event occurs while the state is true, without changing state. If a state has a reaction react1( ) to event e, then if the object receives event e while in that state, it will execute the action react1( ). This is different from a transition in which the source and target states are the same (called a "transition-to-self"), because the states entry and exit actions are not executed for a reaction but are executed for a transition-to-self.

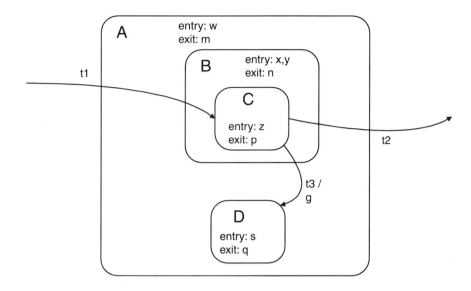

Figure 7-11: *Actions and Nested States*

As mentioned earlier, deferred events are events that persist until a subsequent state is entered. If this next state also defers the event, it will continue to be deferred until such time that a state is entered in which it is no longer deferred. At that point, it will be either handled or discarded.

Although actions and action lists are fundamentally noninterruptible, activities are. Activities are defined as behaviors performed by the object as long as it resides within the specified state. For example, the activity of a *calculating trajectory* state might be the application of an iterative numeric solution to a set of differential equations so that the accuracy of the solution increases over time. It is feasible that an external event could interrupt that process and the object would transition to a state *adjusting course* in which it would use the trajectory calculation with its current accuracy level. Behaviors that are executed periodically, such as polling a device to see if it has data of interest, are most likely better implemented using a separate orthogonal region with a timeout that initiates the polling action.

There is also some discussion within the UML Revision Task Force, the team within the OMG tasked with revising and solidifying the UML specification, whether to make event propagation just another action.

Currently, a transition can create an event sent to the same orthogonal state region within an object, peer orthogonal regions, or other objects. The existing syntax within the UML uses a carat ("^") for this, as in

e1 ^e2

This says that when the transition is triggered by the occurrence of e1, an event e2 will then be created. It is clear within the RTF that the generation of propagated events is a kind of action. One group within the RTF (and the author agrees with them) holds that such event propagation does not require a separate syntax. For example, Rhapsody uses the gen() operator defined for reactive classes within its framework for event propagation.[11]

Transitions may have parameters and guards, as well as actions (see Table 7-3). The complete syntax for transitions is

event-name(parameters) [guard] / action list ^ event list

All of these fields are optional. Even the name may be omitted in the case of an anonymous transition to be taken when a state completes its activities.

Table 7-3: *Transition Parameters*

Field	Description
Event-name	The name of the event triggering the transition.
Parameters	A comma-separated list containing the names of data parameters passed with the event signal.
Guard	A Boolean expression that must evaluate to TRUE for the transition to be taken, often used in conjunction with the conditional connector.
Action list	A comma-separated list of actions executed as a result of the transition being taken. These operations may be of this or another object.
Event list	A comma-separated list of events generated as a result of the transition being taken. This allows events to be propagated to other (concurrent) state machines.

---

11. Although, a sugaring macro, GEN(), is more commonly used.

A common transition in real-time systems is the timeout transition. It is denoted by the event name *tm(interval)*. This avoids the necessity of building explicit timer objects with propagate transitions to the other objects that use them. In addition, a common guard condition is whether another object (or orthogonal region) is in a given state. This is tested by the IS_IN( ) operation, which returns TRUE when the specified object is in the given state—for example,

> e1 [myPeer->IS_IN(waiting)]

In this case, the object has a pointer called myPeer off to another object. The guard tests whether this other object is in the state of *waiting* and returns TRUE if it is.

By far, most transitions have a single source state and a single target state. Also common are transitions with conditional connector pseudostates in which there is one source state but multiple potential target states from which, at most, one is selected, based on guards. Complex transitions occur when there are multiple concurrently active source or target states, or both. This can occur only in the presence of orthogonal regions in the state space. The semantics of such a transition are that if a) the preconditional states of the transition are all active, b) the named event on each of the independent transition segments occurs, and c) all relevant guards evaluate to TRUE, then each target state (one per orthogonal region) becomes active. This can occur only with peer orthogonal regions, not with orthogonal regions at different levels in the nesting hierarchy.

7.3.4 Pseudostates

The UML defines several things for state machines that are almost, but not quite, states. Collectively, these things are called *pseudostates*. The following are pseudostates:

- Initial state
- Terminal state
- History
- Conditional connector
- Diagram connector
- Synchronization pseudostate

The initial state pseudostate indicates the initial default state within a state context. This context can be the entire state space of the object or a nested state. If a transition enters the context without explicitly specifying a target substate, the initial state is entered.

The terminal state pseudostate indicates a termination of a local state. When this state is at the outermost level of context within a state machine, it indicates the destruction of the object.

The history pseudostate is used when the initial state within a state context is not fixed, but depends instead upon the substate within that context that was occupied last. The history pseudostate indicates the initial default (before a history exists). Subsequently, the initial state will be the last visited substate within the context. History comes in two flavors: shallow and deep. Shallow history applies only to the immediate context, not to substates or submachines. Deep history applies to the immediate context and all nested contexts. If only one is available, shallow history is preferable, because in using it, you must explicitly state your intentions at each level of decomposition. Also, if the context decomposition includes a submachine, there are no mnemonics indicating the presence of deep history. Systems that provide history usually also provide a cancelHistory action, which may be executed when history should be forgotten.

The conditional connector is a pseudostate with a single incoming transition and multiple outgoing guarded anonymous transitions. This is equivalent to multiple outgoing transitions from the source state that are triggered by the same event but with different guards. The conditional connector is used for selection (branching) based on guards—the state machine equivalent to if-then-else.

A diagram connector is a syntatic sugaring that takes into account the difficulty of drawing transitions clearly on complex diagrams. A diagram connector is a named pseudostate that appears twice in a diagram. At one point, it is entered within an incoming transition, and at another, it is exited and terminates upon a real state.

At the Helsinki OMG meeting in mid-1998, the UML RTF provisionally adopted a synchronization pseudostate ("synch state") to provide a clear syntax for solving a particular synchronization problem that arises in many state machines with orthogonal components. The problem is: How can I synchronize two or more orthogonal regions in general? The IS_IN( ) operator works reasonably well when the synchronization semantics demand that the other region must currently reside in that named state. But, what about the condition in which a required state has been visited in a region's past history but the region is not currently residing in the required state? How can that be modeled?

Well, one solution is to have another orthogonal region, which acts like a latch, set by the entrance of the target region into the required state (see the Latch-State Pattern in Chapter 12). However, even this doesn't directly solve the problem when you need to track the number of times the required state has been visited (the classic producer-consumer model). Thus, the UML RTF adopted a proposal to include a synchronization pseudostate. The pseudostate is indicated by a small circle circumscribing a number. This number indicates the capacity of the state (in Petri net terms, the number of tokens it can hold). The capacity is usually one, but allowing a nonunary capacity permits the states to loop and iterate independently in the different orthogonal regions and still synchronize not only that the state has been visited, but also the number of times through the loop.

7.3.5 Orthogonal Regions and Synchronization

Orthogonal regions are only *mostly* orthogonal, because statecharts do provide a number of ways for orthogonal regions (and separate objects) to communicate and synchronize. However, in the absence of these explicit synchronization mechanisms, the orthogonal regions remain independent.

The explicit synchronization among orthogonal regions in statecharts may be done via

- Guards on transitions
  - Conditions based on state conditions within the synchronizing region (using the IS_IN( ) operator).
  - Conditions based on object attributes (visible to both orthogonal regions).
- Propagated events
  - A transition in one region can create and send an event to another region to indicate its change of state.
- Broadcast events
  - One event sent to the object is sent to all currently active orthogonal regions.

- Multicast events
    - The event-sending mechanism can explicitly list the target objects to receive a specific event (multicast events).
- Complex transitions
    - A complex transition can serve as a synchronization point allowing multiple orthogonal regions to coordinate (similar to a thread boundary—see Chapter 12).
- Synch pseudostates
    - A pseudostate that explicitly shows the synchronization among substates in different orthogonal regions.

It should be noted that orthogonal regions imply independence of execution and, therefore, in some conceptual sense, concurrency. However, it is not necessary that they are implemented in terms of concurrent threads on a target machine. If an event e applies to multiple orthogonal regions, then the semantics of statecharts explicitly state that you cannot know or rely upon any particular order of execution among those regions. To do so invites race conditions that can lead to system failure. For example, in Figure 7-10, an *evRMClick* affects two regions (because evRMClick is a subclass of evInput). Whether the logEvent( ) operation executes before or after the state handleRightButton is achieved cannot be known.

7.3.6 Basic Statecharts Syntax

All the semantics so far discussed may be represented using the syntax of statecharts. In fact, statecharts may be thought of as a visual formalism for capturing those state semantics in a clear and obvious way. The important basic features of statecharts are illustrated in Figure 7-12.

The figure shows much of the basic statechart syntax directly. It is clear that the state space of the class is divided into four major states S0, S1, S2, and S3. Except for S1, all of them have nested substates. In this example, the substates are all visible. However, they can be shown on another diagram, in which case the substate references a *submachine* defined by the other diagram. Note that all levels of decomposition in the states have either an initial or a history pseudostate. This is crucial because all well-formed models must have all possible transition paths result in a known state.

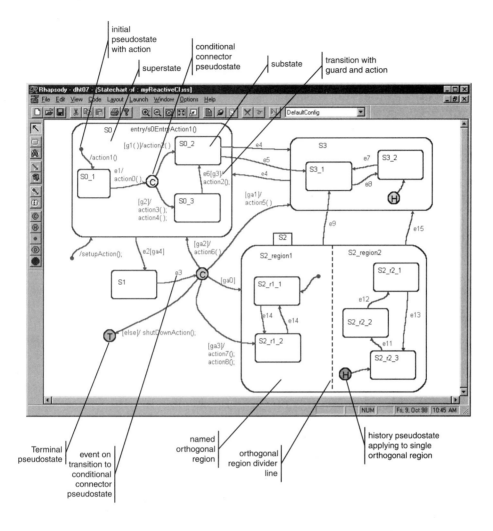

Figure 7-12: *Basic Statechart*

As mentioned previously, the high-level states, S0, S1, S2, and S3, are called or-states because the object may be in any of them, but only in one of them at a time. Similarly, states S0_1, S0_2, and S0_3 are or-states within the context of the S0 superstate. It is common that all state names within a statechart are unique, regardless of nesting. However, if you need to reference a nested state within its superstate context, the common syntax is to use dot notation, such as S0.S0_1. This syntax may be applied recursively to any level of nesting.

When the object resides in S0, it must also reside in exactly one of these substates. Put another way, if IS_IN(S0) is TRUE, then exactly one of the following must also be TRUE: IS_IN(S0_1), IS_IN(S0_2), or IS_IN(S0_3). Of these peer or-states, S0_1 is the initial state, as indicated by the presence of an initial transition terminating upon it. If a transition, such as the e4 transition coming from the S3 state, terminates on the superstate, then S0_1 will be the entered substate. However, transitions terminating directly on a substate, such as the e5 transition from S0_2 to S3_1, bypass the initial state within that context and go to the specified target state.

State S2 has two orthogonal regions, S2_region1 and S2_region2. Each region has multiple substates. These two regions are and-states. When IS_IN(S2) is true, *both* IS_IN(S2_region1) and IS_IN(S2_region2) return TRUE. As long as state S2 is active, exactly one substate from each peer orthogonal region must be active, such as S2_r1_2 and S2_r2_3.

When the object is created, which is its initial state? The statechart shows that S0 will be entered. Inside S0, the statechart specifies that S0_1 will be entered, as well. Note that in this instance, both of these initial pseudostates are anonymous[12] and have actions associated with them. The action is separated from the event name (in this case, blank) by a slash ('/'). Therefore, the sequence of actions taken when the object is created is setupAction( ), followed by action1( ), and finally s0EntryAction1( ). The statechart shows the actions are method calls, but the actions can be any behavioral statement, such as incrementing an attribute ("++x") or lists of actions.

Guards are Boolean expressions following the event name, such as that on event e2. If e2 occurs and the condition ga4 is TRUE, then the transition will be taken. If ga4 evaluates to FALSE, then the event is discarded. For example, one can imagine that if a microwave oven emitter is in its *off* state and it receives a *cookButtonPush* event, it might want to check that the door is not open before starting to emit microwaves. Such a transition might look like

cookButtonPush[myDoor->IS_IN(closed)]

---

12. As they should be!

Guards are also used in conjunction with conditional pseudostates (shown as a circumscribed 'c' as in the figure or as a small diamond). For example, if the object in the statechart given by Figure 7-12 resides in state S1 and an e3 event occurs, one of the following things will happen:

- Enter S2 if ga0 is TRUE
- Execute action5() and enter S3 if ga1is TRUE
- Execute action6( ) and enter S0 if ga2 is TRUE
- Execute action7( ) and action8( ) and enter S2 if ga3 is TRUE
- Otherwise, terminate (destroy the object)

The [else] clause applied to the transition named e3 allows a simple way to capture "all other conditions." If the else clause is not used and no guard evaluates to TRUE, then the event will be discarded. It is important that the guarding conditions are nonoverlapping. If ga0 and ga1 are both TRUE, for example, one of those branches will be taken, but you cannot in principle predict which one it is.

Figure 7-12 also shows the use of the history pseudostate. State S3 uses it to indicate two facts. First, it indicates the default initial state (S3_2) by pointing an explicit transition to it. This is the initial substate prior to the visitation of that state. The other thing the presence of the history pseudostate indicates is that on subsequent visitations, the initial state will be the last active substate of S3. S2 illustrates how history can apply to one orthogonal region but not the other, if desired.

The presence of orthogonal regions permits opportunities for leaving two and-states and entering an or-state (join), and leaving an or-state to enter multiple and-states (fork). This is shown in Figure 7-13.[13] In the UML, all initiating branches of a multi-segment transition must respond to the same event. Because events are point-occurrences in time, the chance that they occur at exactly the same time is extremely remote, so using two events allows for racing conditions to arise.

Also shown in this figure are the junction connector, which divides the transition into segments, and the diagram connector, a special type of junction connector. The diagram connector is used when the topology

---

13. This screen shot is taken from the Rhapsody tool. In standard UML, a short, thick horizontal or vertical line is shown at the joining or forking. If you see this visual symbol, it merely indicates a complex transition.

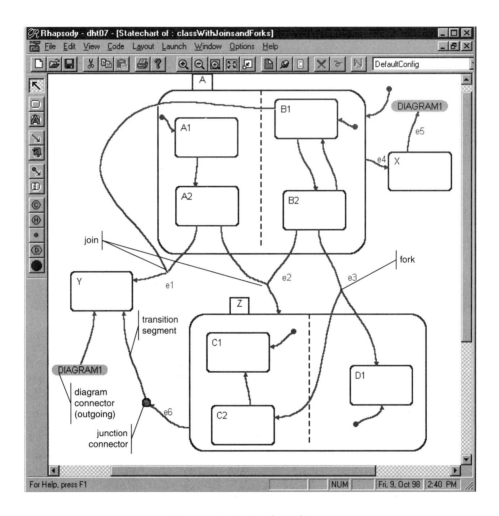

Figure 7-13: *Fork and Join*

of the diagram is such that it is difficult to draw a transition cleanly from the source state to the target state.

Like much of what is really useful about statecharts, the synchronization pseudostate (synch state) adds nothing new to the standard state machine in the formal sense, but it does make it far easier and simpler to express recurring behavioral patterns. Specifically, the synch state allows for a general kind of synchronization—"Allow this transition to fire only if another orthogonal region has visited one of its sub-

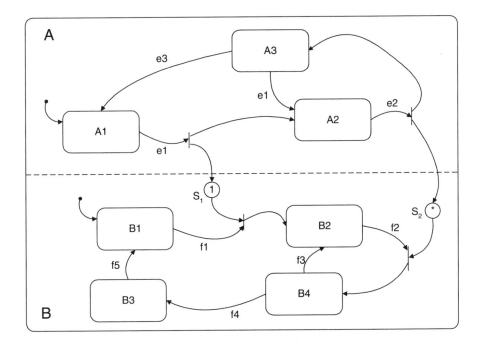

Figure 7-14: *Synch States*

states." Of course, it is simple to synchronize if another region is currently residing in a particular state—just use the IS_IN(requiredState) operator. It is less obvious how to synchronize if that orthogonal region previously visited that substate.

Figure 7-14 has two orthogonal regions, A and B, synchronized with two synch states, S_1 and S_2. S_1 allows the transition triggered by event f1 to occur (in region B) if and only if the transition triggered by event e1 has previously triggered. S_1 "remembers" that its triggering event has occurred until its accepting complex transition has occurred (in this case, that the transition triggered by f1 has occurred). Once the synchronization has occurred (f1 is accepted), S_1 "forgets" that the event occurred.

The way to think about the S_1 synch state is via the production and consumption of tokens. When the transition from state A1 to A2 occurs, it produces a token, which is held in S_1. If S_1 contains a token when region B is in state B1 and event f1 occurs, then two things occur:

Region B transitions to state B2, and the token in S1 is consumed—that is, it no longer holds a token. If S_1 does not contain a token when B is in state B1 and event f1 occurs, then the event f1 is discarded and no transition occurs.

S_1 can hold either zero or one token, denoted by the explicit 1 inside the synch state. This means that it has a *capacity* to hold at most one token. This number could be any positive number, such as 20, or '*' (an arbitrary number). If region A loops around and produces another token when S_1 still holds a token, the additional token is discarded because S_1 is "full."

Synch state S2 has an infinite capacity. This is shown by the '*' capacity within the synch state. This means that if region A loops 1,000 times faster than B, tokens will continue to accumulate in S2.

This simple formalism allows a very general kind of synchronization to be captured, which is difficult to show in regular state machine visual formalisms (see the State Synchronization Pattern in Chapter 12).

7.3.7 Inherited State Models

Two approaches are generally taken to support inheritance of class state behavioral models. The simplest is to just ignore the parent class's state model and reconstruct the child's state model from scratch. While this has the advantage of flexibility, it hardly seems in the spirit of object-orientation, in general, and reuse, in particular. The second approach is to inherit the parent's state model but specialize and extend it where necessary.

In order to help ensure compliance with the Liskov Substitution Principle, some rules must govern the modifications that can be made to an inherited state model.

- New states and transitions may be freely added in the child class, including substates of new or inherited states.
- States and transitions defined by the parent cannot be deleted (the subclass must accept all events and messages that can be accepted by the parent).
- Action and activity lists may be changed (actions and activities may be added or removed) for each transition and state.
- Actions and activities may be specialized in the subclass (that is, the actions may be polymorphic operations overridden in the subclass).

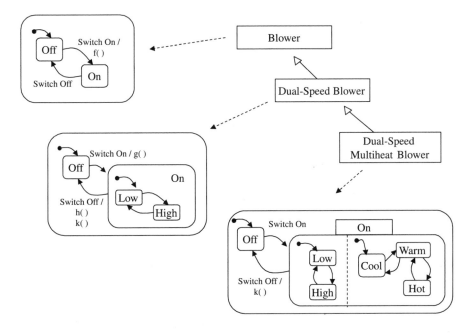

Figure 7-15: *Inherited State Models*

- Substates may not alter their enclosing superstate, including adding a new superstate ("reparenting").
- Transitions may be retargeted to different states.
- Orthogonal components may be added to inherited states.

A simple example of inherited state models is provided in Figure 7-15. The class model is shown at the right of the figure. The class *Blower* has a simple on-off state model. The *Switch On* transition has a single action in its action list, the function f( ). The *Dual-Speed Blower* class extends the *Blower* class by adding *Low* and *High* speed substates to the *On* state. Note that the action for the *Switch On* transition is now changed to the execution of the function g( ) and that two actions are now added to the *Switch Off* transition. The *Dual-Speed Multiheat Blower* class continues the specialization by adding three heat settings as an orthogonal component to the *Low* and *High* states added by the previous subclass. Also note that the g() action for the *Switch On* transition and the h() action for the *Switch Off* transitions have been removed.

7.3.8 Ill-Formed State Models

The purpose of any language is to capture and communicate meaning. Languages are always a compromise between ease of use, rigor, and correctness. All usable languages provide means to say things that are ridiculous, even formal languages. Such statements are said to be *ill-formed*. An ill-formed statement is not one that just happens to be false, it is a statement that inherently violates its own pre-conditions, or is meaningless. Therefore, one's construction of a finite state machine, a Petri net, or a statement in Z or temporal logic does not necessarily imply the statement is true, let alone that the statement has meaning. Consider the Russell Paradox: *A town's barber shaves all men who don't shave themselves. The barber is a man.*

The relevant question is: Who shaves the barber? A more insidious example is asserted by the analytic-synthetic dichotomy of Kant (paraphrased): *That which is real cannot be known. That which is known cannot be real.*

In this case, one wonders: How did he *know* that?[14]

Of course, languages do provide syntax to assist in understanding the stated semantics and to identify obviously ill-formed statements. Some syntactic rules are more helpful than others. For example, "All verbs have subjects (even if implied)," helps one parse statements and determine who is the actor, what is the action, and what the actor acts upon. Other rules are less obviously helpful for this purpose, such as the rule that one should not end a sentence with a preposition.[15]

Formal languages, such as statecharts, are not fundamentally different. Statecharts provide a well-defined syntax for capturing the state space semantics. Obvious syntax violations can be caught by model-checking tools, without exhaustively searching the state space. For example, states with no incoming transitions cannot be reached and indicate an ill-formed state machine. Transitions must have both a source and target state. Guards apply to transitions and not states. Other errors are possible, even with formal languages, that are not easily identified or verified. In fact, I would assert that any language in which it is not possible to make an ill-formed statement would be incredibly unusable.

---

14. And we haven't even discussed Schrödinger's damned cat!
15. Which led Winston Churchill to remark, having been corrected on that very point, "That is pedantry up with which I will not put!"

So, if we wish to consider only languages that are usable, we must live with the possibility that some of our less-talented colleagues[16] may make ill-formed statements from time to time, which we must be able to identify and correct. Some of the common mistakes are

- No initial state within a context
  All possible paths through a statechart must be specified. Therefore, if there is a transition to an enclosing superstate that does not explicitly specify the resulting substate, an initial pseudostate is required.

- Conflicting transitions
  The obvious case occurs when the same event triggers multiple transitions from one source state. However, less-obvious examples can occur, such as an event triggering an internal transition between substates, as well as leaving the superstate. This is even harder to find when these events on the conflicting transitions are not the same event but are related by a generalization relation.

- Overlapping guards
  This is a special cause of conflicting transitions. If a single event triggers multiple transitions with different guards, or if the transition enters a conditional pseudostate with multiple output transition segments that have different guards, then this can occur. It is up to the designer to ensure that, at most, one of a set of evaluated guards triggered by the same event evaluates to TRUE.

- Guards on completion-event transitions
  A completion-event transition is triggered only once. If it has a guard that evaluates to FALSE, the object may be stuck in deadlock in that state. This can be obviated if there are other transitions that can occur, but the guard will only be evaluated once. If the other event causes a transition to self, then the completion event will occur again, and the guard will be reevaluated. However, this is a controversial topic among state modelers, so it is probably best to avoid using guards in this way, anyway.[17]

---

16. Not that *we* would ever do such a thing!
17. To avoid the problem of getting stuck in a state, Rhapsody reevaluates the guards on completion events whenever the object receives *any* event.

- Guards on initial transitions
  Guards should never be used on initial transitions either. What should the object do if the guard evaluates to FALSE?

- Using action side effects within a guard in the same transition
  This is a common error. For example, in state A, the attribute x has the value 0. Now suppose e1 triggers an event with the action "++x" and this transition leads into a conditional pseudostate with three output transition segments. One segment has the guard [x<0], one has the guard [x==0], and the last has the guard [x>0]. Many beginner state modelers are surprised to discover that the middle transition segment is taken when e1 occurs. This is because the action is taken only if a guard condition evaluates to TRUE, and this necessarily implies that the actions must be executed only *after* the guards are evaluated.

- Synch pseudostate within a single orthogonal region
  Synch pseudostates must cross into an orthogonal region.

- Breaking substitutability in subclasses
  The normal rules for statechart inheritance (provided earlier) are good enough for most uses and, therefore, serve as a generally useful guide for how to avoid "breaking" LSP in child classes. However, even if you observe these rules, it is possible to violate LSP, particularly if you try.

7.3.9 Example: AATCS Alarm System

Consider, for our example, a portion of an air traffic control system that manages alarms.[18] Alarms are conditions that are serious enough to require the controller's attention. One source of alarms is the equipment itself—perhaps the primary radar has failed, a memory variable has been corrupted, or a periodic built-in-test (BIT) has failed. Alarming conditions might arise from the system's physical environment, such as an attempted hacker break-in,[19] the sudden appearance of a tor-

---

18. This example is fictitious and does not reflect the design of any system of which the author is aware. Nevertheless, it is relatively simple and illustrates various points about statecharts.
19. It was proposed to the FAA, at one point, to put ancillary systems related to air traffic control on the Internet. Some pointed out that this provided an indirect link to the actual air traffic control systems in the airports and the enroute centers; others felt the

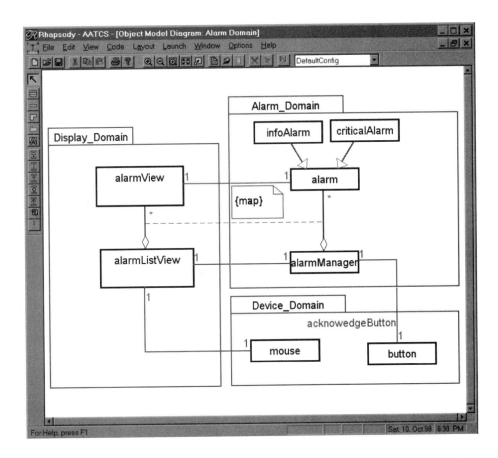

Figure 7-16: *Alarm Domain Class Diagram*

nado, or the arrival of an aircraft known to be in crisis. Alarms can also arrive from computations, such as the computation of separation distance violations of aircraft in the airspace. Figure 7-16 shows the class diagram for such an alarm domain.

Alarms on the AATCS are classified into three groups: *informational* (low criticality), *caution* (hazard will result eventually if no corrective action is taken), and *critical* (immediate impending accident if no cor-

---

system was safe enough, until FAA experiments demonstrated that high school students were able to easily hack into a lab prototype of the system. Physical isolation continued to be deemed necessary.

rective action is taken). Each of these alarms has a slightly different behavior.

Informational alarms are displayed for a brief period—no more than two minutes (less if they are replaced by higher-priority alarms). Informational alarms are displayed in green. Typical *informationalAlarms* might be that the controller shift-change time is approaching, or that a redundant system component has failed and a backup component is in use.

Caution alarms are displayed until acknowledged by the user (by pressing the alarm silence button). Caution alarms are displayed in yellow. A caution alarm might be that a moderate weather cell has appeared, or that a first-stage separation distance violation between a pair of aircraft or between an aircraft and a topological surface feature has occurred.

Critical alarms are displayed in red. If a critical alarm condition disappears before being acknowledged, then active annunciation via the speaker ceases and the alarm message is grayed out. If the alarm condition reappears before being acknowledged, it maintains its current position within the alarm window, becomes "ungrayed," and is reannunciated. If the alarm condition does not reappear before being acknowledged, then the alarm disappears when acknowledged. *criticalAlarms* are annunciated until acknowledged, but they reannunciate every 10 seconds until the condition clears. *criticalAlarms* include secondary separation distance violation, severe weather, and an aircraft-declared emergency.

The statecharts of the *alarmManager* and *alarm* class (and its subclasses) are interesting enough to show.

The *alarmManager* statechart in Figure 7-17 uses the same pattern as was suggested for continuous control systems previously. It chunks through its list of alarm rules every two seconds, updates the *alarmList*, and informs it to update the display.

The *alarm* class is used to handle caution alarms that must be explicitly acknowledged. The state machine for this class is shown in Figure 7-18. The *Active* state has two substates: *Waiting_For_Ack* and *Acknowledged*. The former state has two substates: *NotViewed* and *Viewed*. When the associated *alarmView* has been displayed by the *AlarmListView*, an *evWasSeen* event is sent by the *alarmView* back to the *alarm*. In the figure, we are trying to make sure that an unviewed alarm is not quietly

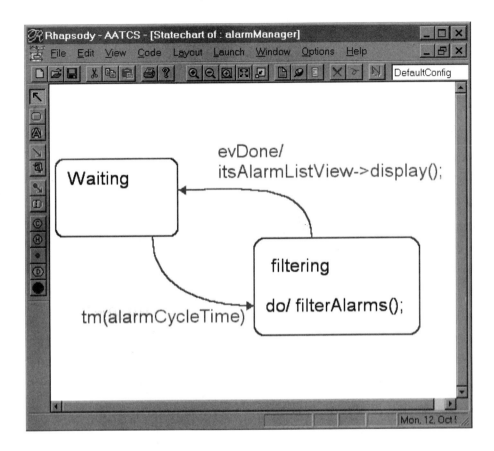

Figure 7-17: alarmManager *Statechart*

removed without the user having an opportunity to see it. Thus, explicit acknowledgement should affect an alarm only if it has been viewed.

The *alarm* class has two subclasses. The first is the *infoAlarm* class. This is a subclass because it has all the behavior of the *alarm* class plus more—it also has an automatic timeout, as shown in Figure 7-19. This is an example of *state inheritance*. Because the superclass (*alarm*) is reactive and its subclass is-a-kind-of its parent, it follows that the subclass must also be reactive. Further, it should include all the states and event transitions of its parent class.

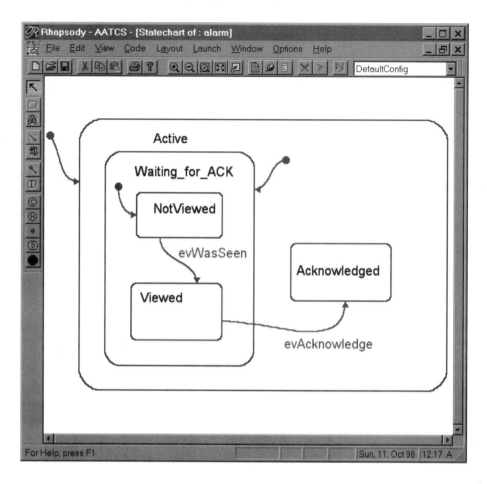

Figure 7-18: alarm *Statechart*

The second subclass is the *criticalAlarm* subclass. Its behavior is slightly more elaborate, as shown in Figure 7-20. In this case, if the alarm condition ceases, it must be "remembered" so that if it reappears before a certain time, the alarm will retain its position in the alarm list. If it does not reappear within that time, the alarm is removed.

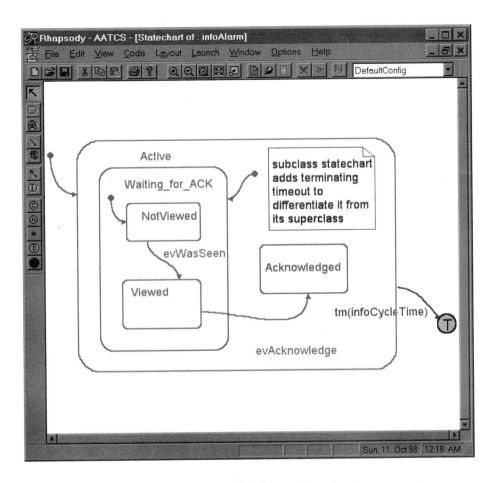

Figure 7-19: infoAlarm *Statechart*

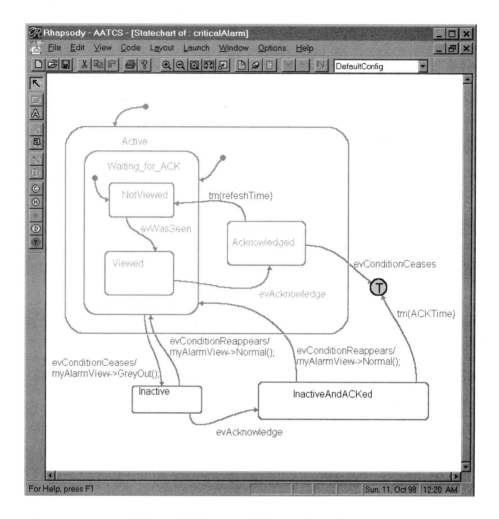

Figure 7-20: criticalAlarm *Statechart*

7.4 The Role of Scenarios in the Definition of Behavior

A state diagram provides a static view of the entire state space of a system. Because the complete behavior of a state-driven object can be represented by a sufficiently detailed state model, state models are said to be *fully constructive.* This means that they can be used to fully generate executable code for the object.

What state diagrams do not show are typical paths through the state space as the system is used. These typical paths are called *scenarios.* Scenarios may not visit all states in the system nor activate all transitions, but they provide an order-dependent view of how the system is expected to behave when actually used. Because a scenario does not have enough information to fully define the complete behavioral model of an object, scenarios are said to be *semi-constructive.*

Two methods for showing scenarios are particularly useful in real-time systems. The first is the timing diagram, which is best used when strict timing must be shown. The other is the sequence diagram, which normally shows order but not strict timing. Timing diagrams may show a particular time-stamped view of the behavior of an object, but, as we will see, they can also show the collaboration of multiple objects. Sequence diagrams almost always show the combined behavior of a collaboration of objects working to achieve a common purpose, such as the realization of a use case.

7.4.1 Timing Diagrams

Electrical engineers have used timing diagrams[20] for a long time in the design of electronic state machines. A timing diagram is a simple representation, with time along the horizontal axis and object state along the vertical axis. In most cases, electrical engineers concern themselves with only two states: ON and OFF. Software engineers can use timing diagrams just as easily on more-elaborate state machines to show the changes of state over time.

Timing diagrams depict state as a horizontal band across the diagram. When the system is in that state, a line is drawn in that band for the duration of time the system is in the state. The time axis is linear, although special notations are sometimes used to indicate long uninteresting periods of time. The simple form of a timing diagram is shown in Figure 7-21.

---

20. Timing diagrams are not explicitly supported by the UML. If the reader wishes to limit himself or herself to only explicitly defined UML features, this section may be omitted.

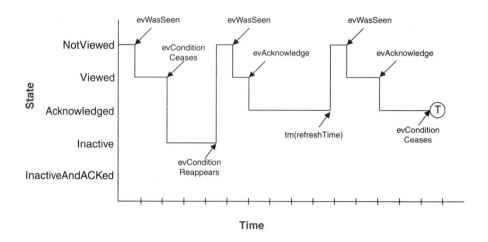

Figure 7-21: *Simple Timing Diagram*

This timing diagram shows a particular path through the alarm state machine. This *alarm* instance begins life in the *NotViewed* state.[21] The object receives an *evWasSeen* event (presumably from its associated *alarmView* object) and transitions to the *Viewed* state. While in that state, the alarm condition ceases (perhaps the aircraft put more distance between themselves, for example). However, while in the *Inactive* state, the alarm condition reappears. As specified in the problem statement, the *alarm* returns to its original *NotViewed* state. Again, the alarm receives an *evWasSeen* message and transitions to the *Viewed* state. This time, however, the user acknowledges the message, as shown by the alarm receiving the *evAcknowledge* event (presumably originating in the *alarmManager* and forwarded on to all alarms in the *Viewed* state). The *alarm* remains in this state until it times out and returns to the *NotViewed* state to remind the user that this condition is still in progress. The cycle repeats. But this time, instead of the timeout occurring, the acknowledged condition ceases and the alarm object is destroyed.

In this simple form, only a single object (or system) is represented. It is possible to show multiple objects on the same diagram. By separat-

---

21. Because the names are unique in this example, I will use only the name of the inner-most state rather than the fully qualified name, Active.Waiting_for_ACK.NotViewed.

Table 7-4: *Common Elements of Timing Diagrams*

Elements	Description
Period	The time between initiations for the same state.
Deadline	The time by which the state must be exited and a new state entered.
Initiation time	The time required to completely enter the state (that is, execute state entry actions).
Execute time	The time required to execute the entry and exit actions and the activities of the state.
Dwell time	The time the object remains in the state after the execute time and before the state is exited. Includes time for exit actions.
Slack time	The time between the end of actions and activities and the deadline.
Rise and fall time	The time required for the transition between states to complete. This includes the time necessary to execute the transition actions.
Jitter	Variations in the start time for a periodic transition or event.

ing these with dashed lines, the different (and possibly concurrent) objects can be clearly delineated. Propagated transitions can be clearly marked with directed lines showing event dependency.

Timing diagrams are very good at showing precise timing behavior and are often used to closely analyze the timing of periodic and aperiodic tasks. Table 7-4 shows some common elements.

When there are many tasks to be shown on a single diagram, task state can be shown by using pattern shading, as in Figure 7-22 and Figure 7-23. Although timing diagrams show no information beyond that available in annotated sequence diagrams, the absolute timing of events and state changes and the relative timing among objects is clearer and more obvious than on sequence diagrams, even when explicit timing constraints are added.

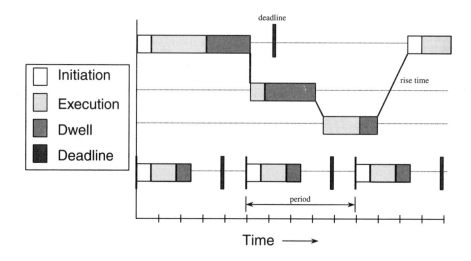

Figure 7-22: *Task Timing Diagram with Shading*

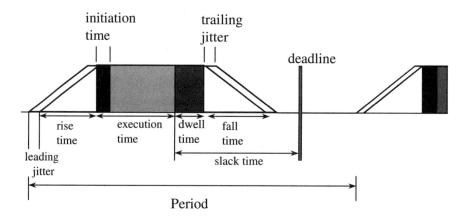

Figure 7-23: *Complex Timing Diagram*

7.4.2 Sequence Diagrams

Sequence diagrams are a more common way to show scenarios, as discussed earlier in this book. Sequence diagrams use vertical lines to represent the objects participating in the scenario and horizontal directed lines to represent the messages sent from one object to another. Time

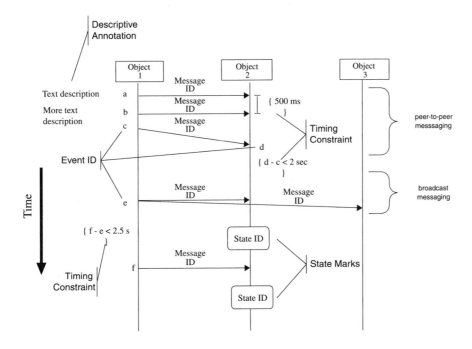

Figure 7-24: *Sequence Diagram*

flows from top to bottom—that is, messages shown lower on the page take place later than ones above it.

Sequence diagrams can be related more closely with associated state models when state marks are added to the instance lines, as shown in Figure 7-24. The state marks indicate the state of the object instance at that point in the scenario and serve to integrate the state model with the scenario model.

Sequence diagrams are discussed in more detail in Chapters 1 and 5.

7.4.3 Activity Diagrams

The primary reason for the introduction of activity diagrams[22] into the UML was to capture complex business activity models, in which some

---

22. At the time of this writing, there is no design automation tool in widespread use that supports activity diagrams. However a number of companies are developing such tools. At least some should be available by the time you read this.

of the activities might be people doing work, while others are inventory flow, and still others are processes performed by computers. Although that is a perfectly valid use of activity models, that is not the use we will explore here. In this section, we will explore the use of activity diagrams to capture algorithmic flow, a task for which it is well suited.

An activity diagram consists of activities, shown by rounded rectangles,[23] and transitions, shown by arrows. In fact, the UML considers activity diagrams to be a kind of state machine in which most or all the transitions are taken when the activity completes rather than wait for an external asynchronous event. Activity diagrams excel at showing procedural flow and, in fact, show concurrency in a more natural and obvious way than statecharts.

The activity-diagram-as-state-machine is one useful perspective. There are at least two more. The first is activity-diagram-as-Petri-net, for those readers familiar with Petri net formalism. Activity diagrams are essentially Petri nets with the constraint that each activity state has a maximal capacity of a single token. Another view is activity-diagram-as-flowchart; this will strike a familiar chord with more readers. However, activity diagrams are more powerful than flowcharts, because they apply as well to multitasking behaviors as they do to strictly sequential behaviors. Activity diagrams can even show data flow.

Figure 7-25 illustrates activity diagrams with a simple example. In this case, the activity diagram is bound to the addNode operation of an AVL binary tree class. Each activity state shows a single operation in the sequence that is necessary to add the node and maintain a balanced tree. The initial activity state connector shows where, on the diagram, to begin. The terminal activity states represent the end of the overall behavior (for example, a "return" in C++). The arrows represent the sequencing of the suboperations—that is, a transition from one activity state to the next. The diamonds are used for branching. As many branches as necessary may be used. The branches are discriminated upon by the guarding conditions, which are shown, as in statecharts, inside square brackets ("[ ]"). However, unlike statecharts, at least one branch must be taken, or the system will be in deadlock.

---

23. Close inspection will show that activity states are more rounded than normal states.

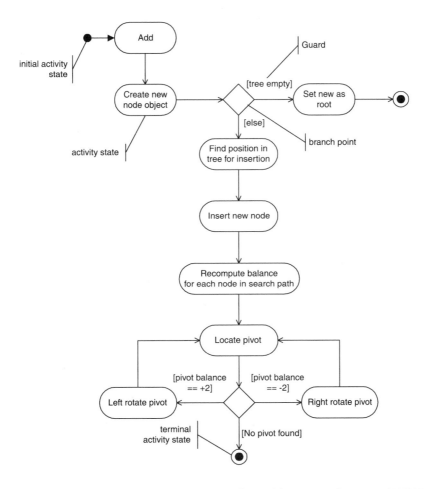

Figure 7-25: *Simple Activity Diagram for Adding a Node to an AVL Tree*

Figure 7-26 shows a more complete list of the symbols used in activity diagrams, in the context of an operation of a robot that grasps an object. In addition to the symbols used in the previous figure, several more are added. First, there are two oddly shaped boxes. Wait for Proximity Signal is a special kind of activity state in which the system waits for the receipt of an explicit signal. Annunciate Alarm sends an explicit signal to the alarm system.

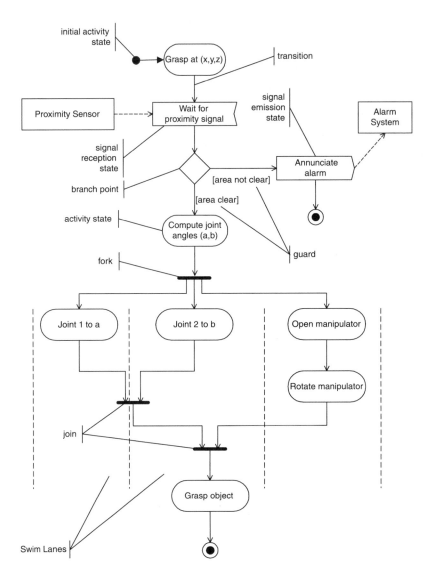

Figure 7-26: *Activity Diagram Notation*

Multitasking is an integral part of activity diagrams. The activity state Compute Joint Angles transitions to a *fork*, which branches out into three separate threads—one for each of two joints and one for the manipulator. The threads are separated by *swim lanes* to aid readability.

Swim lanes have no actual semantics but are used to visually partition the diagram into related activities. Most commonly, they are used to isolate the threads.

Multiple transitions can come together at a *join*, such as that leading into the Grasp Object activity state. In general, any number of incoming and output threads can be synchronized in this fashion.

Activity diagrams can be used to model high-level activity sequences or as individual program statements. Such elementary programming concepts as sequence, branching, and looping may be directly shown on activity diagrams, as shown in Figure 7-27.

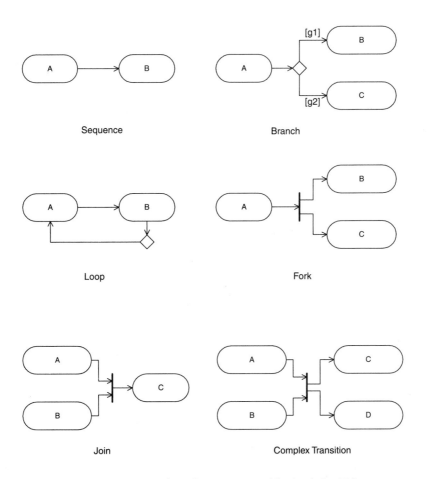

Figure 7-27: *Programming Constructs with Activity Diagrams*

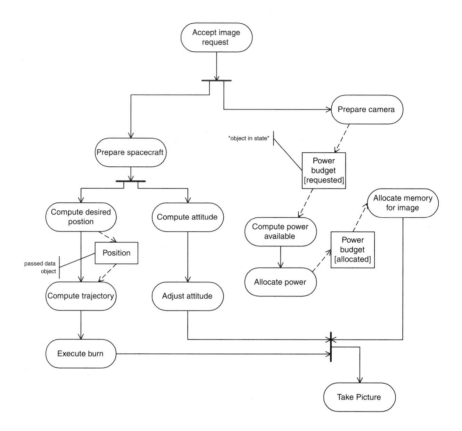

Figure 7-28: *Data Passing in Activity Diagrams*

If desired, data passing between objects can be shown on activity diagrams. Figure 7-28 represents the processing of a request to take an image. In the process of preparing the spacecraft, a position is computed. The position is represented as (what else?) an object and is explicitly passed to the Compute Trajectory activity state. Similarly, the Prepare Camera activity state computes a power budget and creates a power budget object. The power system then computes how much power it can spare and allocates that much power. The object is then passed to the Allocate Memory for Image activity state. The state of the object being passed is shown in square brackets in the object box.

7.5 Defining Operations

All class operations either handle messages or assist in their handling. This means that once a class's state machine is defined and important scenarios are elucidated, the messages and events shown on those diagrams become class operations.

An *operation* is the fundamental quantum of object behavior (the implementation of an operation within a class is called a *method*). The overall behavior of the object is decomposed into a set of operations, some of which are within the interface of the class and some of which are internal and hidden. Naturally, all objects of the same class provide the same set of operations to their clients. An object's operations must directly support its behavior and ultimately its responsibilities. In the simplest case, a 1-1 mapping exists between a class's behaviors and its operations, but this is not true in general. Often, behaviors are decomposed into multiple primitive operations to produce the overall class behavior. This is similar to the functional decomposition in structured system design.

Operations have a protocol for correct usage that consists of the following:

- Preconditional invariants—that is, assumptions about the environment that must be satisfied before the operation is invoked
- A signature containing an ordered list of formal parameters and their types and the return type of the operation
- Post-conditional invariants that are guaranteed to be satisfied when the operations complete
- Rules for thread-reliable interaction, including synchronization behavior

The responsibility for ensuring that pre-conditional invariants are met falls primarily in the client's realm. That is, the user of the operation is required to guarantee that the pre-conditional invariants are satisfied. However, the server operation should check as many of these as possible. Interfaces are hotbeds for common errors, and the inclusion of pre-conditional invariant checking in acceptor operations makes objects more robust and reliable.

In strongly typed languages, the compiler itself will check the number and types of parameters for synchronous operation calls. However, some language type checking is stronger than others. For example, enumerated values are freely and automatically converted to integer types in C++. A caller can pass an out-of-range integer value when an enumerated type is expected, and the compiler typing system will not detect it. Ada's stronger type checking flags this as an error and will not allow it unless an explicit *unchecked_conversion* type cast is performed. Even in Ada, however, not all range violations can be caught at compile time. In such cases, the operation itself must check for violations of its pre-conditional invariants.

For example, consider an array class. Because C++ is backwardly compatible with C, array indices are not checked. Thus, it is possible (even *likely*) that an array will be accessed with an out-of-range index, returning garbage or overwriting some unknown portion of memory. In C++, however, it is possible to construct a reliable array class:

```
#include <iostream.h>

template<class T, int size>
class ReliableArray {
T arr[size];
public:
    ReliableArray(void) { };
    T &operator[](int j) {
        if (j<0 || j <=size)
            throw "Index range Error";
            return arr[ j];
    };
    const T *operator&() { return arr; };
    T operator*() { return arr[0]; };
};

int main(void) {
    ReliableArray<int, 10> iArray;
    iArray[1] = 16;
    cout << iArray[ 1] << endl;
    iArray[ 19] = 0; // INDEX OUT OF RANGE!
    return 0;
};
```

Classes instantiated from the ReliableArray template overload the bracket ("[]") operator and prevent inappropriate access to the array.

This kind of assertion of the pre-conditional invariant ("Don't access beyond the array boundaries") should be checked by the client[24] but, nevertheless, is guaranteed by the server (array class).

7.5.1 Types of Operations

Operations are the manifestations of behavior. This behavior is generally specified on state diagrams (for state-driven classes) and/or scenario diagrams. These operations may be divided into several types. Booch [12] identifies five types of operations.

1. Constructor
2. Destructor
3. Modifier
4. Selector
5. Iterator

Constructors and *destructors* create and destroy objects of a class, respectively. Well-written constructors ensure the consistent creation of valid objects. This usually means that an object begins in the correct initial state; its variables are initialized to known, reasonable values; and required links to other objects are properly initialized. Object creation involves the allocation of memory, either implicitly, on the stack, or dynamically, on the heap. The constructor must allocate memory for any internal objects or values that use heap storage. The constructor must guarantee its post-conditional invariants—specifically, a client using the object once it is created must be assured that the object is properly created and in a valid state.

Sometimes, the construction of an object is done in a two-step process. The constructor does the initial job of building the object infrastructure, while a subsequent call to an initialization operation completes the process. This is done when concerns for creation and

---

24. If known. Clearly, a negative index into an array is probably nonsensical, but the client may not know the upper bounds of the array. If you always put range checking in the server array class, you can be assured that even if the client forgets, the array integrity will be maintained.

initialization of the object are clearly distinct and not all information is known at creation time to fully initialize the object.

Destructors reverse the construction process. They must deallocate memory when appropriate and perform other cleanup activities. In real-time systems, this often means commanding hardware components to known, reasonable states. Valves may be closed, hard disks parked, lasers deenergized, and so forth.

Modifiers change values within the object; *selectors* read values or request services from an object, without modifying them. *Iterators* provide orderly access to the components of an object. Iterators are most common with objects that maintain collections of other objects. Such objects are called *collections* or *containers*. It is important that these three types of operations hide the internal object structure and reveal, instead, the externally visible semantics. Consider a simple collection class:

```
class Bunch_O_Objects {
    node* p;
    node* current_node;
public:
    void insert(node n);
    node* go_left(void);
    node* go_right(void);
};
```

The interface forces clients of this class to be aware of its internal structure (a binary tree). The current position in the tree is maintained by the current_node pointer. The implementation structure is made visible by the iterator methods go_left() and go_right(). What if the design changes to an *n*-way tree? A linked list? A hash table? The externally visible interface ensures that any such internal change to the class will force a change to the interface and therefore changes to all the clients of the class. Clearly, a better approach would be to provide the fundamental semantics (the concept of a next and a previous node), as in:

```
class Bunch_O_Objects {
    node* p;
    node* current_node;
public:
    void insert(node n);
    node* next(void);
    node* previous(void);
};
```

However, even this approach has problems. This interface works fine, provided that marching through the objects in the collection is always in a sequential manner and only a single reader is active.

The first problem can be resolved by adding some additional operations to meet the needs of the clients. Perhaps some clients must be able to restart the search or easily retrieve the last object. Perhaps having the ability to quickly locate a specific object in the list is important. Considering the client needs produces a more elaborate interface:

```
class Bunch_O_Objects {
    node* p;
    node* current_node;
public:
    void insert(node n);
    node* next(void);
    node* previous(void);
    node* first(void);
    node* last(void);
    node* find(node &n);
};
```

This interface isn't primitive or orthogonal, but it does provide common-usage access methods to the clients.

Providing support for multiple readers is slightly more problematic. If two readers march through the list using next() at the same time, neither will get the entire list; some items will go to the first reader while others will go to the second. The most common solution is to create separate iterator objects, one for each of the various readers. Each iterator maintains its own current_node pointer to track its position within the collection:

```
class Bunch_O_Objects {
    node* p;
public:
    void insert(node n);
    node *next(node *p);
    node *previous(node *p);
    friend class BOO_Iterator;
};

class BOO_Iterator {
    node* current_node;
    Bunch_O_Objects& BOO;
```

```
public:
    BOO_Iterator(Bunch_O_Objects& B) : BOO(B) {
        current_node = BOO.p; };
    node* next(void);
    node* previous(void);
    node* first(void);
    node* last(void);
    node* find(node &n);
};
```

7.5.2 Strategies for Defining Operations

Defining a good set of operations for a class interface can be difficult. There are a number of rules that can help decide on the operations:

• Provide a set of orthogonal primitive interface operations.

• Hide the internal class structure with interface operations that show only essential class semantics.

• Provide a set of nonprimitive operations to enforce protocol rules and capture frequently used combinations of operations.

• Operations within a class and class hierarchy should use a consistent set of parameter types where possible.

• A common parent class should provide operations shared by sibling classes.

• Each responsibility to be met by a class or object must be represented by some combination of the operations, attributes, and associations.

• All messages directed toward an object must be accepted and result in a defined action.

    1. Events handled by a class's state model must have corresponding acceptor operations.

    2. Messages shown in scenarios must have corresponding acceptor operations.

    3. Get and set operations provide access to object attributes when appropriate.

• Actions and activities identified on statecharts must result in operations defined on the classes providing those actions.

• Operations should check their pre-conditional invariants.

Just as with strategies for identifying objects, classes, and relationships, these strategies may be mixed freely to meet the requirements of a system.

By providing the complete elemental operations on the class, clients can combine these to provide all nonprimitive complex behaviors of which the class is capable. Consider a *set* class, which provides set operations. The class below maintains a set of integers. In actual implementation, a template would most likely be used, but the use of the template syntax obscures the purpose of the class so it won't be used here.

```
class Set {
    int size;
    SetElement *bag;

    class SetElement {
    public:
        int Element;
        SetElement *NextPtr;
        SetElement(): NextPtr(NULL); {};
        SetElement(int initial): Element(initial),
            NextPtr(NULL) { };
    };
public:
    Set(): size(0), bag(NULL) { };
    Set union(set a);
    Set intersection(set a);
    void clear(void);
    void operator +(int x); // insert into set
    void operator -(int x); // remove from set
    int numElements(void);
    bool operator ==(set a);
    bool operator !=(set a);
    bool inSet(int x); // test for membership
    bool inSet(Set a); // test for subsethood
};
```

This simple class provides a set type and all the common set operations. Elements can be inserted or removed. Sets can be compared for equality, inequality, and whether they are subsets of other sets. Set unions and intersections can be computed.

Often, a series of operations must be performed in a specific order to get the correct result. Such a required sequence is part of the protocol for the correct use of that object. Whenever possible, operations should be structured to reduce the amount of information the clients of an object must have in order to use the object properly. These protocol-enforcing operations are not primitive, but they help ensure the correct use of an object.

A sensor that must first be zeroed before being used is a simple example. The *sensor* class can simply provide the primitive operations doZero() and get(), or it can provide an acquire() operation that combines them:

```
class sensor {
    void doZero();
    int get();
public:
    int acquire(void) {
        doZero();
        return get();
    };
};
```

The acquire() operation enforces the protocol of zeroing the sensor before reading the value. Not only does this enforce the pre-conditions of the get() operation, but it also simplifies the use of the class. Since the doZero() and get() operations are always invoked in succession, combining them into an operation provides a common-use nonprimitive.

Polymorphic operations are operations of the same name that perform different actions. Depending on the implementation language, polymorphism may be static, dynamic, or both. Static polymorphism is resolved at compile time and requires that the compiler has enough context to unambiguously determine which operation is intended. Dynamic polymorphism occurs when the binding of the executable code to the operator invocation is done as the program executes. Both static and dynamic polymorphism are resolved on the basis of the type and number of parameters passed to the operation.[25] Ada 83 operator overloading is purely static. C++ polymorphism may be either static or dynamic. Smalltalk polymorphism is always dynamic.

---

25. C++ class operations have an invisible *this* pointer in their parameter lists. Thus, even an operation with an otherwise identical parameter list can be polymorphic if a subclass redefines the operation, because the *this* pointer is a pointer to a different type.

7.6 Statechart Heuristics

Statecharts are like other diagrams in that there are good ones and bad ones. Although this is rather like art, some basic rules for avoiding bad statecharts are

- Use states to hold behaviors that take significant time (activities). Activities may take a long time to execute and so are, in principle, interruptible. Because they take a long time, they should not be attached to transitions, state entry, or state exit.
- Use actions on entry or exit if the action is always taken when a state is entered or exited, respectively.
- Use actions on transitions if the actions are executed only on some paths into a state.
- Use nested or-states when some transitions exit a number of peer or-states. Nested states provide great diagrammatic simplification when a set of events applies to several substates. Nested states also allow the capture of entry actions common to multiple substates in one place (the superstate).
- Use and-states (orthogonal regions) when multiple sets of states are independent and may be assumed independently. Many objects have relatively independent partitions that have state behavior. This is the best use of orthogonal regions and why they were originally added to statecharts.
- When inheriting state behavior, do not
  1. Remove transitions
  2. Reparent states (add a new superstate to an inherited state)
  3. Delete states

  You don't want to break LSP. Remember a subclass "is-a-kind-of," so everything that is true of a superclass must also be true of the subclass.
- When inheriting state behavior, you may
  1. Add transitions
  2. Change action lists on transitions or states

3. Change activities within states

4. Use polymorphic operations (redefined in the substate)

Such changes constitute either specialization or extension (see Chapter 6), so they are not likely to change substitutability.

- Obey the obvious well-formedness rules
  1. Always identify the initial state
  2. Use named transitions
- Don't use guards on anonymous or initial transitions
- Don't use side effects of actions in guards
- Don't use guards that have side effects
- Make sure guards have nonoverlapping true conditions

7.7 Timing-Diagram Heuristics

Timing diagrams excel at showing absolute timing, but they are not a panacea.

- Use timing diagrams when the absolute timing is the most essential aspects of a behavior to capture.
  Timing diagrams do this well.
- Use timing diagrams to capture paths through a state machine.
  Timing diagrams always capture a scenario. Many timing diagrams are necessary to get full coverage of a state machine.
- Use timing diagrams to capture timed paths through a set of collaborating state machines.
  The use of the dashed object partition lines separate the state spaces of collaborating objects on a timing diagram. This aids in understanding complex timing behavior of tightly coupled objects.
- Timing diagrams may be applied to both normal states and activity states.
  Timing diagrams are primarily concerned with time, so the distinction between a normal state and an activity state is irrelevant with respect to time.

7.8 Activity-Diagram Heuristics

Activity diagrams capture state spaces, particularly ones decomposed into a sequence of activities, one after another.

- Use activity diagrams when most or all transitions occur synchronously because of the completion of the preceding activity. This is what activity diagrams are good at.

- Use statecharts when most or all transitions occur asynchronously. This is what statecharts are good at.

- Use swim lanes to group related activities
  1. Activities within a single thread
  2. Activities performed by a single object

  Complex activity diagrams can be difficult to read if they don't contain a roadmap.

7.9 Summary

We have now seen both parts of analysis. The previous chapter covered means to identify the object structure of a system, find the classes of those objects, and link them together with relationships and associations. This chapter covered the dynamic aspects of objects—the definition of behavior, with special attention given to state-driven objects, and the operations necessary to implement those behaviors.

Two kinds of state machines were discussed in this chapter: statecharts and activity diagrams. Statecharts provide strong support for asynchronous, event-accepting state behavior. In statecharts, a state is generally active until it receives an explicit event causing a change of state. Activity diagrams only rarely receive external events; almost all their processing proceeds immediately after the completion of activities. Both support independent, orthogonal regions. This is done in statecharts with and-states. The representation of orthogonal actions is usually clearer in activity states, with the explicit representation of joins and forks. Orthogonal regions in both may be implemented as concurrent threads, but it is more common in the case of activity diagrams to do so.

Scenarios show paths through behavior and apply to nonreactive, as well as reactive, behavior. Sequence diagrams, discussed in previous chapters, are the most common representation of scenarios. Timing diagrams work well when explicit timing, rather than merely the sequence of behaviors, is the focus.

Operations are the smallest nuggets of behavior modeled in the UML. Operations are implemented by methods in the classes. Sequences of operations shown in scenarios are quite often implemented as direct method calls, but that needn't be the case. Operations in other objects, which may be in different threads, different processors, or for that matter on different continents, may use more-elaborate means for message passing.

7.10 Looking Ahead

The task of analysis is to find the object structure required of all acceptable solutions to the problem. Put another way, analysis finds the essential objects, classes, and relationships inherent in the system under study. Analysis defines the "what" of the system. The next process step, design, will add the "how." We have deferred many questions about implementation strategies and structures, such as the number of tasks running, how messages will be implemented, and the internal design of the objects themselves. Let's continue with the large-scale architectural design in the next chapter.

7.11 Exercises

1. What are the three kinds of behavior that objects exhibit?

2. What is the definition of a state? A transition? An action? An activity?

3. The following questions refer to Figure 7-12
   - When the object to which this statechart applies is created at run-time, what is the initial state?

- What action(s) do(es) the object perform prior to achieving that state?
- If we are currently in state S1 and an event e2 occurs, what is the resulting state if the guards {g1(), ga0, ga4} are TRUE and {g2, g3, ga1, ga2, ga3} are FALSE?
- If we are currently in state S1 and event e3 occurs, what is the resulting state if the guards {g1(), ga0, ga4} are TRUE and {g2, g3, ga1, ga2, ga3} are FALSE?
- If we are currently in state S1 and event e3 occurs, what is the resulting state if the guards {g1(), g2, ga4} are TRUE and {g3, ga0, ga1, ga2, ga3} are FALSE?
- Assume we start in state S0.S0_1 and apply the following events: e1 → e6 → e2 → e3 with the following Boolean statements evaluated TRUE {g2, ga2, g3, ga4} and the following Boolean statements evaluated FALSE {g1( ), g3, ga0, ga1, ga3}, then what is the resulting state?
- In the situation described above, give a complete list of actions performed as a result of accepting the event sequence.
- Starting in state S1, given that the following conditions are TRUE { } and the following conditions are FALSE { }, apply the event sequence: e4 → e1 → e3 → e14 → e1 → e12 → e4 → e11. What is the current state of the object?
- Continue from the resulting state of the previous event sequence and apply the event list e6 → e4 → e15 → e14 → e5 → e4 → e1 → e4. What is the resulting state?

4. Define substitutability (LSP) as it applies to reactive classes.

5. Name five heuristics for inherited state machines designed to help ensure substitutability.

6. Construct a state machine that is inherited from the superclass's state machine such that it violates LSP.

7. Why are scenarios said to be only partially constructive?

8. When would you use a timing diagram over a sequence diagram? How about the reverse?

9. What is the primary difference between normal states and activity states?

10. When would you use an activity diagram over a statechart? How about the reverse?

11. What is the difference between an operation and a method?

12. Name the five kinds of operations typically defined for classes.

13. Define a polymorphic operation. How is it indicated in C++?

7.12 References

[1] Brookshear, J. Glenn. *Theory of Computation: Formal Languages, Automata, and Complexity,* Redwood City, Calif.: Benjamin Cummings Publishing, 1989.

[2] Harel, David. "Statecharts: A Visual Formalism for Complex Systems," *Science of Computer Programming,* 1987; 8: 231–274.

[3] Douglass, Bruce Powel. *Real-Time UML: Developing Efficient Objects for Embedded Systems,* Reading, Mass.: Addison-Wesley, 1998.

[4] Douglass, Bruce. *Applications of Fuzzy Logic to Anesthesia Alarm Systems,* San Diego: International Conference on Fuzzy Systems, 1992.

[5] Terano, Toshiro, Kiyoji Asai, and Michio Sugeno. *Applied Fuzzy Systems,* Cambridge, Mass.: AP Professional, 1994.

[6] Jamshidi, Mohammad, Nader Vadiee, and Timothy Ross. *Fuzzy Logic and Control,* Englewood Cliffs, N.J.: PTR Prentice-Hall, 1993.

[7] Wasserman, Philip. *Neural Computing, Theory and Practice,* New York: Van Nostrand Reinhold, 1989.

[8] Wasserman, Philip. *Advanced Methods in Neural Computing,* New York: Van Nostrand Reinhold, 1993.

[9] Douglass, Bruce Powel. *Statistical Analysis of Simulated Multinerve Networks: Use of Factor Analytical Methods* (Ph.D. dissertation), Vermillion, S.D.: University of South Dakota School of Medicine, 1984.

[10] Durbin, Richard, Christopher Miall, and Graeme Mitchison, ed. *The Computing Neuron,* Reading, Mass.: Addison-Wesley, 1989.

[11] Douglass, Bruce Powel. *Numerical Basic,* Indianapolis, Indiana: Howard Sams and Co., 1983.

[12] Booch, Grady. *Object-Oriented Analysis and Design with Applications,* Redwood City, Calif.: Benjamin Cummings Press, 1994.

Part III

Design

By now, you should have a good grasp of the process and products of analysis. Analysis identifies the criteria of acceptance of any solution. The first part of analysis studies system-environment interaction and explores and captures this interaction with context and use case diagrams. The second part of analysis "drills down" inside the system to identify the fundamental concepts within the system that must be represented in terms of both structure and dynamics. These concepts are captured as classes and objects.

Design is the process of specifying a solution that is consistent with the analysis model. It is useful to divide design into three primary categories based on the scope and breadth of decisions within each category (see Figure III-1). They are architectural, mechanistic, and detailed design (see Table III-1). Architectural design details the largest-scale software structures, such as subsystems, packages, and tasks. The middle layer of design is called mechanistic because it includes the design of mechanisms composed of classes working together to achieve common goals. Detailed design specifies the internal primitive data structures and algorithms within individual classes.

For simple systems, most of the design effort may be spent in the mechanistic and detailed levels. For larger systems, including avionics and other distributed real-time systems, the architectural level is crucial to project success. This chapter will focus on the process of architectural design.

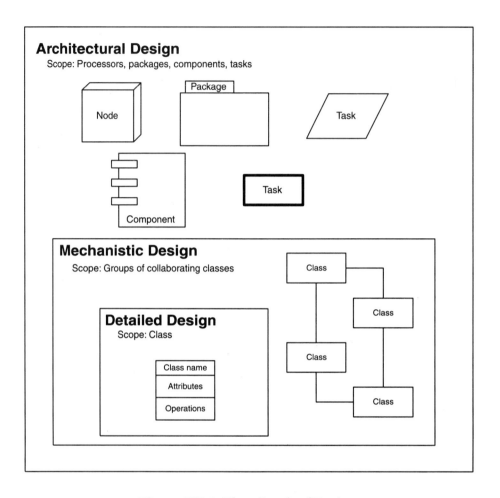

Figure III-1: *Three Levels of Design*

Table III-1: *Phases of Design*

Design Phase	Scope	What Is Specified
Architectural	System-wide Processor-wide	• Number and type of processors • Packages of objects running on each processor • Inter-processor communication media and protocols • Concurrency model and inter-thread communication strategies • Software layering and vertical slices • Global error-handling policies
Mechanistic	Inter-object	• Instances of design patterns of multiple collaborating objects • Containers and design-level classes and objects • Medium-level error-handling policies
Detailed	Intra-object	• Algorithmic detail within an object • Details of data members (types, ranges) • Details of function members (arguments, internal structure)

The design process can be either translative or elaborative. Translative design takes the analysis model and, using a translator, produces an executable system more or less autonomously. Great care must be put into the design of the translator, which is often highly customized for a particular problem domain and business environment. The other approach elaborates the analysis model by adding increasing amounts of design detail until the system is fully specified. The UML is process-independent and applies equally to both design approaches. Because the elaborative approach is more common and generally applicable, we will continue in an elaborative spirit in this book.

Chapter 8

Architectural Design

Embrace uncertainty.
> —Book of Douglass, Law 99 (I think).

Of the three phases of design, architectural design paints with the broadest brush. It is concerned with the strategic decisions that affect most or all of the system, such as the set of tasks and their interactions (the concurrency model), the set of artifacts that will exist at run-time and their interfaces (the component model), the mapping of these components to the physical hardware (the deployment model), and the creation of large-scale redundant structures to provide safety in the presence of faults (the safety model). The definition is crucial because it provides an infrastructure necessary for the lower-level design constructs to collaborate effectively.

8.1 Introduction

The last three chapters have dealt with analysis of the system. Chapter 5 looked at ways of capturing requirements using the context diagram and use cases. Chapters 6 and 7 presented approaches for identifying and characterizing classes and objects inherent in the problem. Analysis identifies key implementation-independent abstractions and structures in the system.

Now we're ready for design. Design specifies a solution that is based on the analysis model. Design can be broken into three parts, according to the scope of the decisions made in each: architectural, mechanistic, and detailed. This chapter discusses the first and broadest in scope—architectural design.

Architectural design selects the key strategies for the large-scale organization of the system. These strategies include mapping software packages to processors, interprocessor communication via bus and protocol selection, and the concurrency model and task-thread identification. The UML provides notation and semantics for the specification of large-scale architecture. This chapter presents methods for the specification of architectural design, the UML language features used to capture it, and how they can be applied to real-time systems.

Large-scale design strategies can be based on architectural patterns that are useful in a variety of similar systems. A number of patterns presented in this chapter exemplify how pattern-based architectures can simplify architectural design.

8.2 Terms and Concepts

The analysis model identifies objects, classes, and relationships, but it does not specify how they are organized into large-scale, run-time structures. Architectural design is concerned with large-scale design decisions that involve collaborations of components, tasks, and processors.

There are models and then there are Models. The Model of the system includes many perspectives. It is common to refer to the set of views from a single perspective as a model. For example, the set of views related to concurrency within a Model is commonly called the

Table 8-1: *Strategic Models in Architectural Design*

Model	Description
Tasking model	Packaging of objects into independent threads of execution and the strategies necessary to effectively manage and synchronize those threads
Component model	Packaging of the generated object artifacts that exist at run-time into libraries, executables, databases, and so on
Deployment model	Strategies for the distribution of run-time components onto processors and devices, and management of collaboration among the distributed objects (inter-thread and inter-processor communication)
Safety/Reliability model	Arrangement or addition of components within the deployment and component models to meet system safety and reliability requirements

concurrency model, or the *tasking model*. The set of run-time artifacts and their views is called the *component model*. We will continue with that verbiage here, but keep in mind that the entire system is contained within the Model, which consists of the sum of all perspectives of the system in the same way that a building Model includes floor plans, layouts for electrical conduits, water pipes and air flow, structure models for load-bearing members, and so on. All these (sub)models must be consistent within the larger context of the system Model.

Table 8-1 describes some major strategic models for architectural design.

8.3 Tasking Model

Real-time systems typically have multiple threads of control that execute simultaneously. A *thread* can be defined as a set of *actions* that execute sequentially. Actions are statements that execute at the same priority in a particular sequence or that perform some coherent function. These statements can belong to many objects. The entirety of a thread is also known as a *task*. Multiple objects typically participate within a single task. Often, a distinction is made between *heavyweight* and *lightweight* threads. Heavyweight threads use different data spaces and must resort to expensive messaging to communicate data among themselves. Such threads have relatively strong encapsulation and protection from other threads. Lightweight threads coexist within an enclosing data space and provide faster inter-task communication via this shared "global" space, but they offer weaker encapsulation. Some authors use the terms *thread* to refer to lightweight threads and *task* or *process* to refer to heavyweight threads. The UML itself includes stereotypes of active classes «process» and «thread» to make this distinction visible when necessary. We shall use these distinctions when it is necessary to do so, but for the majority of our discussion, they may be treated identically.

The packaging of objects appropriately into nodes and threads is vital for system performance. The relationships among the tasks are fundamental architectural decisions that have great impact on the performance and hardware requirements of the system. Besides identifying the tasks and their relationships to other tasks, the characteristics of the messages must themselves be defined. These characteristics include

- Message arrival patterns and frequencies
- Event response deadlines
- Synchronization protocols for inter-task communication
- Quality-of-service (for example, timeliness) requirements placed on the thread

Answering these questions is at the very heart of the system's concurrency model.

8.3.1 Representing Tasks

The UML can show concurrency models in a couple of ways. Class and object diagrams can show the tasks (represented as *active classes*, and their instances, *active objects*) directly. In the UML, an active object is the root of a thread. Typically, the constructor for an active object allocates a thread from the underlying OS in which to execute, and it specifies the scheduling policy and priority, as appropriate. Active objects are frequently composites, tightly aggregating component objects. Composites, as you will remember from Chapter 1, are responsible for both the creation and destruction of the component objects. Active objects usually have the responsibility for checking their OS message queue for messages sent asynchronously from other tasks and for delegating the response to those messages to component objects.

Class and object diagrams can use the stereotype «active» or the active object stereotype icon to represent tasks. By representing only classes and objects with this stereotype, the task structure can be clearly shown. A task diagram is nothing more than a class diagram that shows only active objects and their associations.

Another approach to capturing concurrency is to show it on statecharts using the orthogonal regions. Most of the time, orthogonal regions indicate only behavioral independence, not multithreading. It is not only possible, but usual, that the orthogonal regions of a superstate are kept entirely within a single thread. However, it is also possible for an object to dynamically create and destroy threads as orthogonal regions become active and inactive, respectively.

Statecharts show the state space for classes and objects. Because active objects are just a special kind of object, their behavior can be captured on state diagrams, as well. Using the complex transition notation (for example, join and fork), it is possible to show multiple threads rooted within a single active object. Broadcast and propagated events show the event communication between active objects. Activity diagrams may also be used to show the multithreaded state space of active objects, and in many ways is much clearer than the way it is shown in statecharts. In both cases, the complete set of thread interactions is shown. These different state machines and their representations were dealt with in some detail in the previous chapter.

Another type of metaclass in the concurrency model is the «interrupt» stereotype. This kind of active class has a special purpose—to accept and respond to hardware and software interrupts. Such classes are not generally part of the main concurrency model, but they must nevertheless be represented in the concurrency model. This class stereotype, although not one of the standard UML stereotypes, is common in embedded systems. It is common to subclass from an abstract «interrupt» class that provides methods to install and deinstall itself in the interrupt vector table, chain to previous interrupt handlers, restore the previous interrupt handler during deinstallation, and pass the information gathered during the interrupt to other parts of the system.

This latter functionality is achieved through the standard synchroniza-tion mechanisms discussed later in this chapter, with the exception that interrupts are almost never allowed to block, so they cannot participate in either blocking or timed rendezvous.

Class diagrams depict static structural relations in the system object model. Statecharts take a single class and show its complete behavioral state space. Scenarios depict paths through the behavioral space of sev-eral objects during a collaboration. Scenarios can be multithreaded, as well, but special care must be taken to show the threads and their syn-chronization points clearly. This may be done with all scenario views—sequence, collaboration, and timing diagrams. Neither sequence nor collaboration diagrams provide an intrinsically clear way of represent-ing multithreading, so the enumerated messages are prefaced with a thread name. Multiple threads are clearly shown in timing diagrams by physical separation of the objects.

8.3.1.1 Task Diagrams

Class and object models are intrinsically concurrent. Objects are them-selves inherently concurrent, and it is conceivable that each object could execute in its own thread. During the course of architectural design, the objects must be aligned into a smaller set of concurrent threads solely for efficiency reasons, so the partitioning of a system into threads is always a design decision.

In the UML, tasks are rooted in a single active object. The active object is a composite that aggregates the objects participating within the thread. Its general responsibility is to coordinate internal execution by dispatching messages to its constituent parts and providing infor-mation to the underlying operating system so that the latter can sched-ule the task. A task diagram can be easily created by constructing a class diagram that shows only the active classes. In most cases, a single diagram depicting all active objects (representing thread instances) is a key roadmap to the design of the run-time structure. The set of quality-of-service constraints that apply at the thread level can be easily cap-tured on this diagram, such as the scheduling policy, task priority,[1] task period, deadlines, and so forth. Sometimes, an active object receives

---

1. Task priority is generally represented as a tagged value rather than as a constraint. But in either case, the task diagram remains an ideal spot for it to be shown.

more than one initiating event and performs several action lists, depending on the message received. In such cases, each action list generally has its own independent timeliness properties (for example, period and deadline). Formal analysis of schedulability, discussed in Chapter 11, is certainly simpler when tasks are limited to a single action sequence, but this is not always an optimal design. Later in this chapter, we will discuss various strategies for identifying threads in real-time and embedded systems.

The official UML notation for an active class is a standard class box, with heavy border lines. Previously [1], I used the notation of a parallelogram to indicate active classes on class diagrams because I found that using heavy borders was insufficiently distinctive. Feel free to use whichever representation your tool may support and that you find useful.

Consider the Acme Air Traffic Control problem that was discussed in the last few chapters. Without thinking too hard about an optimal thread set, one might decide on individual threads to handle

- Primary radar data
- Secondary radar data
- Track merging and aircraft identification
- Updating feature map[2]
- Updating feature and aircraft positions on screen
- User command processing
- Alarm management

Associations between active classes represent conduits for message flow. These messages are most likely to be asynchronous messages sent via the OS message queue or via the OS pend and post operations. However, they can be synchronous calls made directly to component objects that execute within the composites. Mutual exclusion can be ensured by inserting semaphores in front of the operations called across the thread boundary. Such operations are *guarded*.

Another way to share information across a thread boundary, as well as synchronize the threads, as necessary, is to use *rendezvous objects*. A rendezvous object is one that does not reside in one thread or another,

---

2. Mountains may not move quickly, but weather features can!

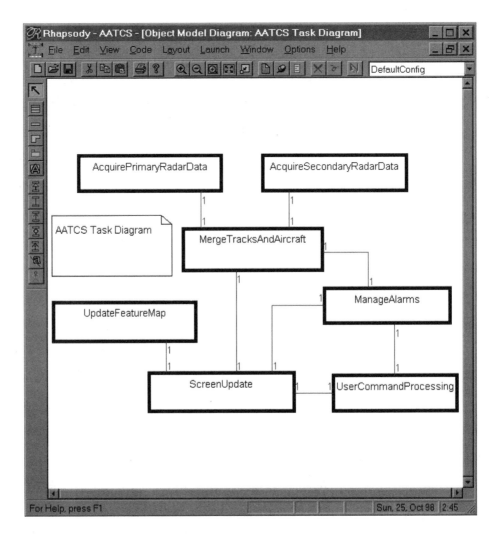

Figure 8-1: *AATCS Task Diagram*

but straddles several threads, executing its operations in the thread space of the caller. The feature maps shown in Figure 8-1 are exactly these kinds of objects. They passively hold topological feature information, are updated by the feature-update thread on one side, and are read for display by the display-update thread on the other.

8.3.1.2 Concurrent State Diagrams

Rumbaugh, *et. al.* [2] have suggested a means by which concurrent tasks can be diagrammed using statecharts. He notes that concurrency with objects generally arises by aggregation—that is, a composite object is composed of component objects, some of which may execute in separate threads. In this case, a single state of the composite object may be composed of multiple states of these components.

Active objects respond to events and dispatch them to their aggregate parts. This process can be modeled as a finite state machine. The other orthogonal component is due to the task thread itself having a number of states. Because the active object represents the task characteristics to the system, it is natural to make this an orthogonal component of the active object.

Figure 8-2 shows orthogonal components of a robot-arm object statechart. The initial (*Idle*) state is not multithreaded, but as it transitions into its positioning state (as a result of the *evMove* event), it gains active orthogonal regions. The object may spawn threads to perform these motions. Finally, when the motion is complete, the orthogonal regions become inactive, at which point the temporary threads can be destroyed. It should be noted that orthogonal regions do not necessarily imply multithreading, and, in fact, most commonly orthogonal regions actually execute within the same thread. The most common solution to this example would be to create active joint and manipulator objects, each with its own or-state model in its own thread. The robot arm would then associate to these objects, execute in their own threads, and pend upon an event from the robot-arm object to begin motion. However, the concurrent and-state approach shown in Figure 8-2 is equally valid.

Concurrent statecharts are most applicable when the object shows TRUE states (which wait for asynchronous signal events) and when orthogonal regions come and go. But for some reason, it is inconvenient to create objects to hold those threads.

8.3.1.3 Concurrent Activity Diagrams

Activity diagrams show orthogonality at least as conveniently as do statecharts. They are most applicable when the object states transition

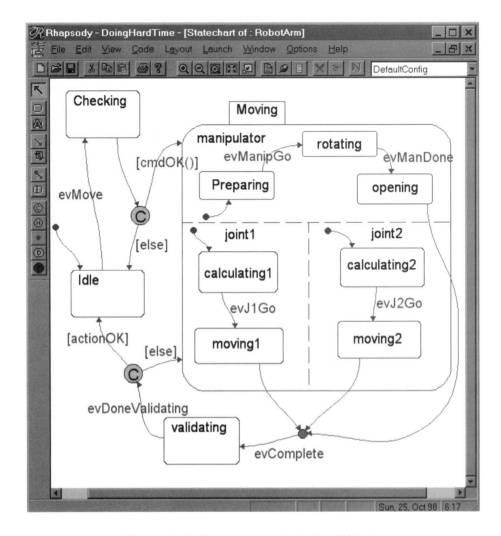

Figure 8-2: *Concurrency in Active Objects*

to subsequent states primarily because of the completion of the activities in the predecessor states (hence the name *activity states*) and when threads fork and merge during execution.

Figure 8-3 shows an example of a system that has sets of independent sequential actions, without any forks and joins.

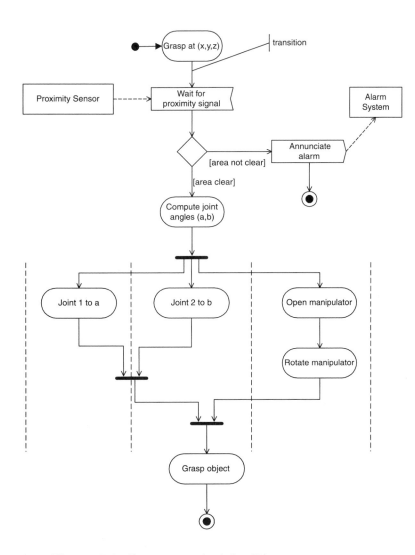

Figure 8-3: *Concurrent Activity Diagram*

8.3.1.4 Concurrent Sequence Diagrams

Sequence diagrams do a good job of showing sequence, but they do not provide a clear representation of threads without some help. Two approaches have been used, with varying degrees of success. The first is to color code the messages within the different threads—red for one thread, blue for the second thread, yellow for the third, and so on. This approach provides a usable on-screen view of a scenario that involves multiple threads. It fails when the sequence diagram is printed on a non-color printer, however. A related approach is to use different line styles, such as solid, dashed, dotted, dash-dot, and so forth. Although nonstandard, this approach can also be effective, as you can see in Figure 8-4.

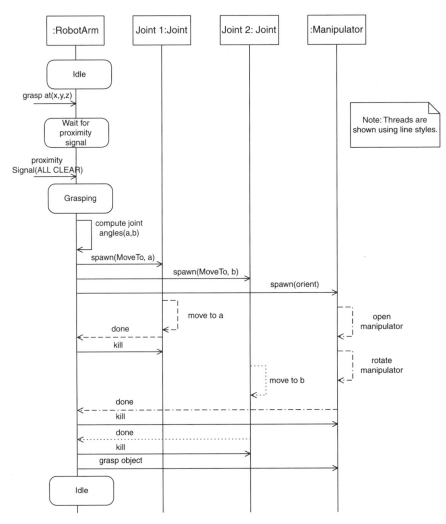

Figure 8-4: *Concurrent Sequence Diagram*

The standard UML approach is to preface the message names with a thread identifier, as shown in the collaboration diagram in Figure 8-5. Although not as visually distinctive as color or line-style coding, thread identifiers are supported by more tools. However, many people solve the problem by not using sequence diagrams to represent multi-threaded scenarios. Collaboration diagrams are more frequently used in this context, even though they are no more expressive of concurrency than sequence diagrams.

8.3.1.5 Concurrent Collaboration Diagrams

A collaboration diagram faces the same difficulty as a sequence diagram with respect to showing concurrency, and the same solution applies. Figure 8-5 shows the same scenario as the previous figure, but in the form of a collaboration diagram. Notice that the structure of the mechanism is clearer in Figure 8-5, but that sequence is harder to follow because the reader must visually hunt for the next message in the

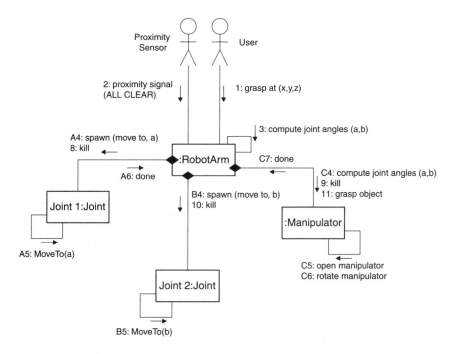

Figure 8-5: *Concurrent Collaboration Diagram*

sequence. The collaboration diagram uses thread identifiers (A, B, and C) for the temporary spawned threads. Messages executing within the primary (originating) thread are shown without a thread identifier.

8.3.1.6 Concurrent Timing Diagrams

Timing diagrams are a more natural representation of concurrent scenarios than either sequence or collaboration diagrams. That is because objects execute all their methods in the same thread of control most of the time and because timing diagrams separate the state spaces of objects. Again, timing diagrams are not a standard UML diagram, but they are very expressive in the context of absolute time and state behavior. Objects are shown in horizontal bands across the diagram, separated by dashed lines. States within the objects are shown as horizontal lines; messages and events are shown as directed lines. Note the use of diagram connectors in Figure 8-6 to aid readability of the messages passing between objects.

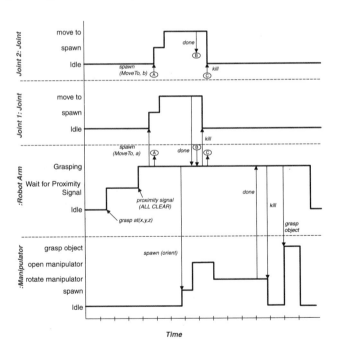

Figure 8-6: *Concurrent Timing Diagram*

8.3.2 Defining Task Threads

During analysis, classes and objects were identified and characterized and their associations are defined. In a multitasking system, the objects must be placed into task threads for actual execution. This process of task-thread definition is twofold.

1. Identify the task threads.
2. Populate the task threads with classes and objects from the analysis and design process.

Several strategies can help you define the threads based on external events and the system context. Their general approach is to group events in the system so that a thread handles one or more events and every event is handled by some thread.

There are conditions under which an event may be handled by more than one thread. One event may generate other *propagated events* to be handled by other threads. For example, the appearance of wave-form data may itself generate an event to signal another thread to scale the incoming data asynchronously. Occasionally, events may be broadcast or multicast to more than one thread. This may happen when a number of threads are waiting on a shared resource or waiting for a common event that permits them all to move forward independently.

8.3.2.1 Task-Definition Strategies

Tasks perform a set of actions in response to any of a set of related events. The key to identifying an optimal task set is to find an optimal grouping of the events. Events can be grouped together into threads in a variety of ways. Some common event grouping strategies are provided here. Note that, similar to the strategies presented in Chapter 6 for object identification, there is significant overlap in many of them.

- Single event groups
  In a simple system, it may be possible to create a separate task for each external and internal event. This is usually not feasible in complex systems that have dozens or even hundreds of possible events or when task switch time is significant relative to the event response timing.

- Sequential processing
  When it is clear that a series of steps must be performed in a sequential fashion, the set of actions may be grouped within a single thread to enforce this requirement.

- Event source
  This strategy groups together events from a common source. For example, group all the events related to ECG numerics into one thread (such as HR Available, ECG Alarms, and so forth), all the NIBP (noninvasive blood pressure) data in another, the ventilator data in another, the anesthetic agent in another, and the gas mixing data in yet another. In an automobile, sources of events might be the ignition, braking, and engine-control systems. In systems with clearly defined subsystems that produce events within roughly the same period, this may be the simplest approach.

- Interface device (a.k.a. *port*)
  This grouping strategy encapsulates control of a specific interface within a single thread. For example, the (periodic) SDLC data can be handled in one thread, the (episodic) RS232 data to the external models in another, and the (episodic) user buttons and knobs in another. This strategy is a specialization of the event source grouping strategy.

- Related information
  Consider grouping all waveforms within a single task and all measured numeric parameters within another task. Or perhaps, all information related to airfoil control surfaces in each wing and tail section might be manipulated by separate threads. This grouping may be appropriate when related data is used together in the user problem domain. Another name used for this grouping is *functional cohesion*. This strategy is especially effective when the data are manipulated together.

- Unrelated information
  This strategy is the conjunct of the previous one. When two actions or sets of actions seem unrelated, it is natural to want to make them independent. This simplifies processing each.

- Timing characteristics
  If data arrive at a given rate, a single periodic task thread could handle the reception of all relevant data and dispatch it to various objects, as necessary. Aperiodic events might be handled by a single

interrupt handler and similarly dispatch control to appropriate objects. Generally, this grouping may be most useful with internal events, such as timer interrupts, or when the periods of events naturally cluster around a small set of periods.

- Target object/Computationally intensive processing
One purpose of rendezvous objects is to encapsulate and provide access to data. As such, they are targets for events, such as to insert, remove, or filter data. A waveform queue object server might have its own thread for background scaling and manipulation while, at the same time, it participates in threads that deposit data within the queue object and remove data for display.

- Purpose
Alarms serve one purpose. They notify the system user of anomalies so that he can take corrective action or vacate the premises, whichever seems more appropriate. This might form one event group. Grouping safety checks within a watchdog task, such as checking for stack overflow or code corruption, might form another. Getting and dispatching user commands might be a third.

- Safety concerns
The system hazard analysis may suggest threads. One common rule of thumb in safety-critical systems is to separate safety monitoring from actuation. In terms of task identification, this means that a task that controls a safety-relevant process should be checked by an independent task. From a safety perspective, it is preferable to run safety checks on a separate processor so that common-mode hardware and software faults do not simultaneously affect the primary and the safety processing.

During concurrency design, you must add events to groups in which they appear appropriate so that each event is represented in at least one group. Each event that remains after the initial grouping can be considered independently. Create a task diagram in which the processing of each group is represented by a separate thread. Most events will occur only within a single task, but sometimes events must be dispatched to multiple tasks.

Frequently, one or more of these groupings will emerge as the primary decomposition strategy of the event space, but it is very common to mix grouping strategies. When the grouping seems complete and stable, you have identified an initial set of tasks that handle all events in your system. As product development evolves, events may be added to or removed from groups, new groups may suggest themselves, and alternative grouping strategies may present themselves. This will lead the astute designer to alternative designs that are worth consideration.

Let's think about applying some of these strategies to the AATCS. Picking some strategies more or less at random:

- What actions seem unrelated? This strategy might suggest the following task groupings:
    1. Screen updates
    2. User input processing
    3. Alarm management
    4. Dealing with radar images (acquiring and merging tracks, mapping tracks to aircraft, determining separation distance)
    5. Update weather features
- What are some unique event sources?
    1. Primary radar
    2. Secondary radar
    3. User input
    4. Weather updates
- What events are likely to have independent timing characteristics?
    1. Radar acquisition (periodic)
    2. Alarm updates (likely periodic)
    3. User input processing (episodic)
    4. Screen updates (episodic, depending on radar and weather input)
- What about safety and reliability?
    1. Built-in-test (BIT) (periodic or low-priority background task)
    2. Watchdog task (periodic, unless serviced)
    3. Separation distance sanity check (periodic)

Naturally, it is rather rare to use one strategy exclusively. In most real systems, a combination of strategies is applied, resulting in a task diagram that looks something like Figure 8-1.

8.3.3 Assigning Objects to Tasks

Once a good set of tasks is identified, you may start populating your groups with objects. Note that the previous sentence referred to "objects" and not "classes." Objects are specific instances of classes, which may appear in different tasks or as an interface between tasks. There are classes that create only a single instance in an application ("singletons"); other classes instantiate multiple objects, each of which may appear in a separate thread. For example, there may be queues of tasks, queues of waveform data, queues of numeric data, queues of network messages, command queues, error queues, alarm queues, and so forth. These might appear in a great many tasks, even though they are instances of the same class (queue). There will even be individual objects that participate in multiple threads, requiring some protection against mutual exclusion problems.

Most commonly, active classes are composites that, after creating the thread in which they will execute, create their component parts. The simplest kind of task rendezvous requires the active class at the root of the thread to receive messages (via its OS message queue) and then dispatch them to the appropriate component objects. This can be done by having the active object pend on the message queue or an OS event, or by having the active object run an "event loop" in which it repetitively checks for messages in its OS message queue. In either case, once it finds a waiting message, it dequeues and processes the message, usually by dispatching it to one or more of its component objects.

For example, examine Figure 8-7, which constructs a composite active class called *Process_Track*. This composite is shown to be active in two ways. First, it is drawn with a heavy border. Second, the «active» stereotype is attached to the composite. This active object strongly aggregates its component objects. Note that classes from multiple packages (Aircraft_Monitoring_Domain and Aircraft_Management_Domain) execute within that single thread.

It is also common for tasks to run every so often. In this case, the active object pends on an OS timer. When the timer goes off, the task awakens and performs its periodic function. An even more-general solution for periodic tasks is to create a state machine for the active object with an internal tm( ) (timeout) event transition similar to that shown in Figure 8-8. In the figure, you can see that the task periodically

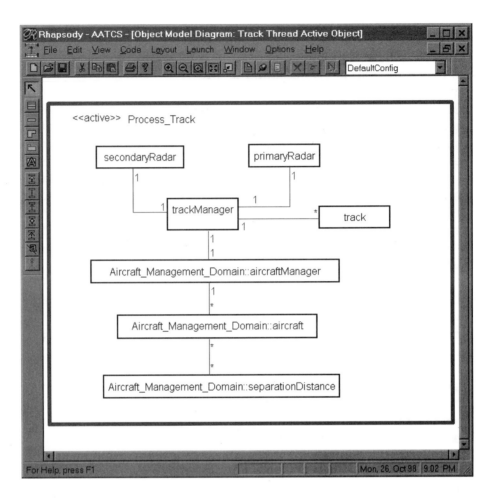

Figure 8-7: *AATCS Track Active Object*

wakes up, checks for messages, handles any pending ones, and does its periodic activities in the TaskProcessing state.

8.3.4 Defining Task Rendezvous

So far in this chapter, we have looked at what a task is, strategies to select a set of tasks, and how to populate tasks with objects. What remains is to define how the tasks communicate with each other.

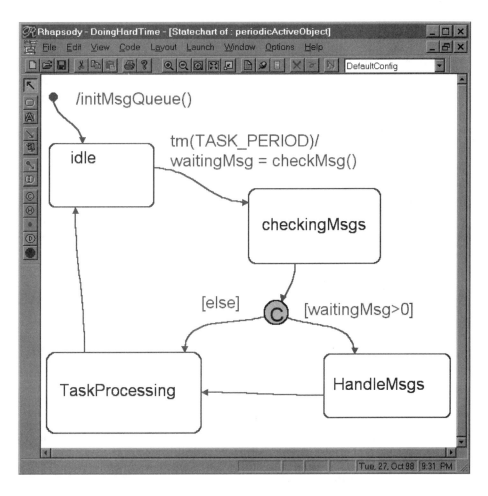

Figure 8-8: *Periodic Active Object Statechart*

There are several strategies for inter-task communication. The simplest by far is to use the OS to send messages from one task to another, as mentioned in the previous section. Although this approach maintains encapsulation and limits coupling among threads, it can be computationally expensive and may not provide prompt handling of certain high-bandwidth events. In many real-time systems, at least some inter-task communication must be done in a lightweight, expeditious fashion in order for the tasks to meet their performance requirements. In this section, we will consider some methods for inter-task communication that are both lightweight and robust, at the expense of some increase in complexity.

The two primary reasons for communication among tasks are to share information and to synchronize control. The acquisition, manipulation, and display of information may all occur in different task threads with different periods and may not even take place on the same processor, necessitating some means to share the information among these tasks. Synchronization of control is also a very common requirement in real-time systems. In asynchronous tasks that control physical processes, one task's completion (such as emptying a chemical vat) may form a pre-condition for another process (such as adding a volatile chemical to the vat). The task synchronization strategy must ensure that such pre-conditions are satisfied prior to the execution of actions that depend on them.

When tasks communicate, the rendezvous itself may have attributes and behavior which make it reasonable to model it as a class. The important questions to ask about task synchronization are

- What are the pre-conditions for the tasks' communication? A pre-condition is generally something like a data value that must be set, or particular states that objects must be in. If a pre-condition for task synchronization exists, it should be checked by a guarding condition before the rendezvous is allowed to continue.

- What should happen if the pre-conditions are not met, such as when the collaborating task is not available? The rendezvous can
  1. Wait indefinitely until the other task is ready (a *waiting rendezvous*)
  2. Wait until the required task is ready or a specified period has elapsed (*timed rendezvous*)
  3. Return immediately (*balking rendezvous*) and ignore the attempt at task communication
  4. Raise an exception and handle the task communication failure as an error (*protected rendezvous*).

- If data is to be shared via the rendezvous class, what is the relationship of the rendezvous object with the object containing the required information? Options include

1. The rendezvous object contains the information directly

2. The rendezvous object holds a reference to the object that contains the information or a reference to an object that serves as an interface for the information

3. The rendezvous object can temporarily hold the information until it is passed to the target thread

Remember that objects must ensure the integrity of their internal data. If there is a possibility that shared data can be simultaneously *write* or *write-read* accessed by more than a single task, then it must be protected by some mechanism, such as a mutual-exclusion semaphore. In general, synchronization objects must handle

- Preconditions

- Access control

- Data access

One approach is typified by the Rendezvous Pattern [1], which works by abstracting out the responsibility of synchronization into a separate rendezvous object. The rendezvous object associates with multiple active objects and awaits synchronous call events from each that signify that it is ready for synchronization. This results in the calling active object to be blocked by a lock object. The rendezvous object creates one lock object for each active object expected to send such a signal. Once all are locked, the rendezvous object releases them all, and the active objects are free to continue asynchronously according to their normal scheduling policy. This pattern is shown in Figure 8-9.

Let's consider an example in which threads must synchronize, as in Figure 8-1. A vitally important part of alarm management is the application of filtering rules on the active alarm set to reduce the number of nuisance alarms. This involves making sure that 1) the same condition is only annunciated once, and 2) only the root cause of an alarm (as opposed to a secondary effect of a primary cause) is annunciated. A simple example of this is a separation distance alarm between two aircraft. It would be annoying to the controllers to have such an alarm annunciated twice (once for each aircraft participating in the close encounter). If two alarms come in from the same encounter, only a single alarm should be annunciated. In addition, rules may apply that result in the removal of alarms that, under other circumstances, should

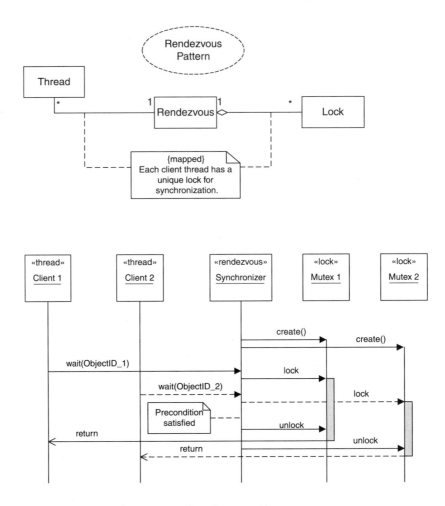

Figure 8-9: *Rendezvous Pattern*

be annunciated. A weather system might bring in several areas of both severe and moderate conditions. It would be inappropriate to alarm on all of them—a single severe weather alarm would suffice. Remember, the purpose of an alarm management system is to bring potentially hazardous conditions to the attention of the controller, with only enough information to allow the controller to make expeditious and correct decisions. Too much information can be just as bad as too little.

Given the foregoing discussion, an alarm management thread must wait until enough context is available to perform the alarm filtering prior to the annunciation of alarms. One way to accomplish this is to check for, filter, and annunciate the alarms periodically, once the radars have completed a sweep of the airspace. This requires synchronization between the two threads. Also, if separate threads are used by the primary and secondary radars, small timing differences could accumulate and get them out of synch. If these three tasks synchronize at the end of the sweeps for both radars, all these goals can be accomplished.

The class diagram shown in Figure 8-10 shows how the rendezvous pattern can be applied to this particular problem. At the end of its

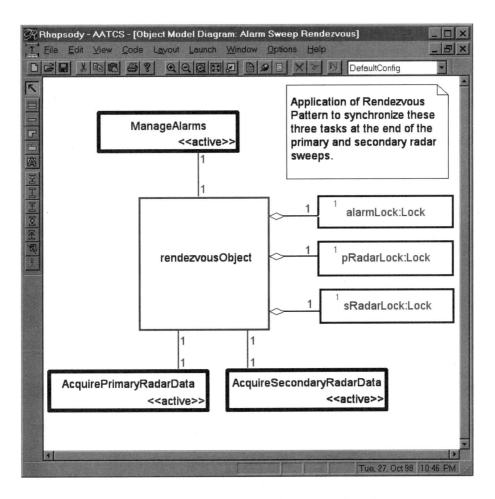

Figure 8-10: *Rendezvous of AATCS Threads*

sweep, each radar acquisition thread tries to synchronize with the alarm management thread. Each client thread blocks until all three have blocked, and then all are released to run.

Task synchronization is discussed in more depth in Chapter 11, along with problems of assigning priority and sharing resources.

8.4 Component Model

A *component* in UML is a software artifact that exists at run-time. Components are often things of concern to software developers, especially in real-time and embedded systems. The most common artifacts are executable programs and libraries, but there are many possibly interesting components, as shown in Table 8-2.

Like classes, components have interfaces. One component calling another must *conform* to that interface. A component implementing an interface is said to *realize* that interface. Large-scale interfaces are often called *application program interfaces* (APIs). A component that realizes an interface generally implements many objects that participate in potentially many collaborations within the component. The UML notation for components is shown in Figure 8-11.

Also like classes, components may have instances. The component

Table 8-2: *Components*

Component	Description
Executables	Stand-alone programs
Libraries	Collections of objects and functions that provide services to executables; such libraries may be dynamically or statically linked
Tables	Large-scale data structures, such as databases, device configuration tables, ROM-based calibration data, and so forth
Files	Organizations of data within a file system
Documents	Nonexecutable data describing other components, such as components of an online help system

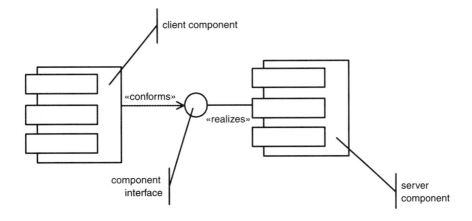

Figure 8-11: *Component Notation*

is in this sense a *type,* and instances are the things that exist at particular memory addresses on particular processors. It is not uncommon to have the same component replicated on multiple processors. For example, a communications component providing TCP/IP communications services may exist on all processors within a system.

Components are binary-replaceable things, and this distinction, more than anything else, sets them apart from classes. This means that as a revision of a component is created, it can replace a previous revision of the same component, without recompiling other components. In general, as long as a component meets the same interface, it can replace another component without requiring any change to its clients.

Components are important in any system in which updating, maintenance, distribution, and reuse are issues. If these issues are unimportant in your system, then a single, monolithic component will suffice. However, most real systems must concern themselves with each of these issues, and components provide a powerful means to address each, as shown in Table 8-3.

The component-based architecture metamodel is "drop and glue." That is, much of an application resides in already constructed components so that a great deal of application development can be reduced to dropping in the desired components and writing only enough code to glue the components together and drive them. This approach is exemplified by Visual Basic. While VB is not without its problems (most

Table 8-3: *Advantages of Components*

Issue	Description
Updating	In the absence of components, updating a system requires at least recompilation of the entire system. In a component-based architecture, it is usually a matter of introducing a replacement component while the system executes or while the system is temporarily shut down for updates, or, in the worst case, relinking the statically linked components.
Maintenance	Similar to updating a system, defects tend to be well-encapsulated in a component-based architecture. This means that defect removal is easier than in most other architectural patterns. Only the portion needing maintenance need be recompiled. Often, a system can be updated with a repaired component, without even shutting down the running system.
Distribution	Strong encapsulation is required to effectively control the distribution of software onto different processors within a multi-processor system. Components are a natural way to organize these run-time artifacts to enable effective distribution.
Reuse	Through generalization and parameterization, classes provide the reuse of logical conceptual elements. Although this is a powerful form of reuse, classes don't provide a means for the reuse of existing run-time artifacts, such as libraries or data and algorithmic servers. Components do.

notably scaleability to large projects[3]), in my experience there is no simpler way to put together a small Windows-based application. By dropping in provided, or third-party, components and gluing them together with small code snippets, applications can literally be constructed in minutes, even though they have TCP/IP sockets, bitmap manipulation, dialog boxes, list boxes, databases, or complete spreadsheet engines. Each of these run-time things is available as a component.

---

3. The largest VB application I worked on had about 50K lines of code plus a few dozen components. By this point, the weaknesses of using Basic as an application language had become clear. However, it was obviously a weakness of the Basic language rather than of the component architecture. Delphi and C++ Builder, both from Inprise, use the same approach with more-powerful languages to great effect (although not in the real-time domain).

During maintenance of a VB application, a component can be replaced with an updated version that corrects known defects[4] or adds new capabilities. Very little source-code-level changes are necessary to perform this maintenance. The result is extremely rapid development and greatly enhanced maintainability.

There are certainly fewer ready-made components suitable for the real-time and embedded systems than for the desktop market. Still, the existence of commercially available components still provides a compelling argument for their use. Certainly, some components exist—communication, math, device I/O components are available. Even an RTOS can be considered a component in this sense. For the most part, however, real-time and embedded-system developers must construct their own components to meet their particular needs because of novel (or at least relatively uncommon) hardware devices and severe performance constraints. However components come into being, the question of their large-scale organization remains. What is a reasonable way to arrange these components?

The UML package concept provides the ability to group components together, so the means exist to organize the set of components within a system. A common approach is to construct components as participants in layers of abstraction—the most abstract (closest to the application domain) at the "top," and the most concrete (closest to the hardware) at the "bottom." For example, an application might be structured into the following five independent layers:

1. Application
2. User interface
3. Communication
4. OS
5. Hardware abstraction

Layering packages and subsystems in this way is an example of the Microkernel Architecture Pattern [1]. In this pattern, packages represent layers of abstraction. Each package contains one or more components. The interface of the layer is the combined interfaces from all contained components. Alternatively, each component interface may be brought forward independently. Figure 8-12 shows the pattern.

---

4. And, of course, adds new ones.

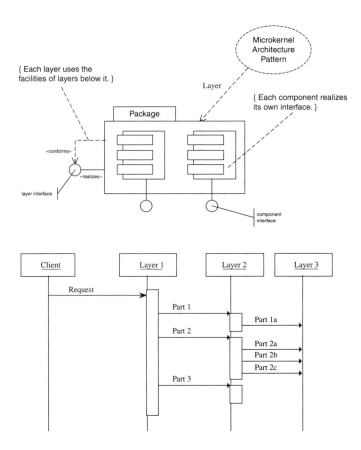

Figure 8-12: *Microkernel Architecture Pattern*

Note that the layer (represented by the package) both presents an interface (to the layers above it) and conforms to the interface (for the layers below it). The Microkernel Architecture Pattern is fundamentally a set of client-server relationships among the layers. The more abstract layers are the clients that invoke the services of the more concrete layers. This one-way dependency makes it possible to use the same lower-level server layers in different contexts, because they know nothing of their clients. Similarly, since the lower layers offer a well-defined set of interfaces, they can be replaced with different lower layers, making the entire subsystem easily portable to other physical environments.

Because the components and packages are logically layered in terms of abstraction does not in any way imply that the system should be developed a layer at a time. In fact, the opposite is true. It is most efficacious to design a layered architecture but actually implement the system as a series of vertical slices of functionality that cut through all layers.

For example, the OSI's seven-layer reference model is a common layered architecture for communications protocols, as shown in Figure 8-13. (The physical layer is not shown in the figures because it does not

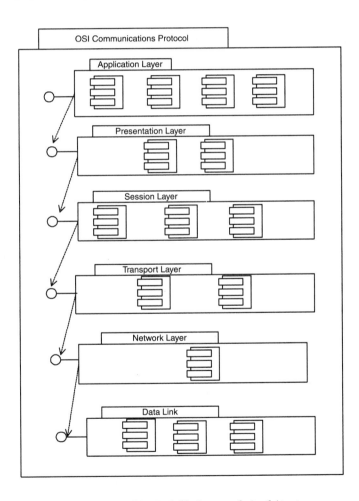

Figure 8-13: *OSI Model's Layered Architecture*

usually involve software.) The lollipop at the left of each package represents its *interface*, a set of classes and objects that may be externally accessed (service access points (SAPs), in OSI's nomenclature). The dashed arrow is the dependency relationship and indicates that each package depends on the packages below it.

A layered implementation strategy would build each layer independently and link them as they are completed. However, this approach has been proven to be risky and expensive in practice, because fundamental flaws that affect the overall subsystem functionality are not caught until integration. A better implementation strategy is to implement vertical slices.

Each vertical slice implements only the portion of each layer relevant to the purpose of the slice. This approach to implementation is called *iterative prototyping*, and each slice is called a *prototype*. The prototypes are implemented so that each prototype builds upon the features implemented in its predecessors. The sequence of prototypes is decided by which features logically come first, as well as which represent the highest risk. By doing "risk-based development," higher-risk items are explored and resolved as early as possible. This typically results in less rework and a more integrated, reliable system. As the components within the prototypes evolve, their version numbers can be shown with a constraint, such as "{Version 2.1.3 build 096}," which changes as updated components are introduced into the prototype.

A typical set of prototypes for such a protocol can be seen in Table 8-4.

Note how each prototype includes one or more components from each of the layers, and that the later prototypes build upon the services implemented in their predecessors. This is the essence of the iterative prototyping development philosophy—gradually add capability until the entire system is complete. Naturally, iterative prototyping applies to more than just communication protocol design. Any sufficiently complex piece of software can be broken down into a set of hierarchical layers, arranged in a client-server topology.

The layered interfaces are transparent from above but opaque from below. The components defined in the layer interface are visible only to components in layers at or above the package in the hierarchy. A *closed-layered architecture* is one in which each layer knows about only the layer immediately below it in the hierarchy. In an *open-layered architecture*, a layer can request services of any layer lower in the hierarchy.

Table 8-4: *Communication System Iterative Prototypes*

No.	Prototype Name	Description
1	Hello World	Implement enough of each layer (and stub the remainder) to send a message from one node to another.
2	Data format	Mostly presentation layer—implement data encode, decode, and network-data format conversions. Also include timed ACK/NAK transport layer protocol.
3	Routing	Mostly network and data-link layers to control routing of messages.
4	Flow control	Data-link Xon/Xoff flow control and message CRCs to implement data integrity checks with automatic retry on message failure.
5	Connections	Connections and sessions (transport, data-link, session layers).
6	Performance	Performance tuning of all layers to optimize high-bandwidth throughput.

Closed-layered architectures tend to sacrifice some performance for increased encapsulation and reusability.

There is much to recommend layered designs as they provide good portability at both the top and bottom layers. The bottom layers can be reused with different upper layers, because the latter are more concrete and more primitive. For example, a device I/O layer can be used in a wide set of applications on the same hardware platform. The upper layers can be reused on different hardware platforms by replacing only the device-specific lower layers. This is a great aid in porting a system to new physical architectures.

A potential disadvantage of the microkernel architecture is a loss of performance. A layered strategy often means that an execution path must pass through several layers in order to invoke the required service, when it would be more efficient to call the service directly. Also, because the lower layers know nothing of the higher layers, they must be general and not apply any optimization that would require knowledge of their clients. This inefficiency can be mitigated by identifying the high bandwidth among the objects and optimizing the propagation of the data along those paths.

8.5 Deployment Model

Components are the run-time things that execute or provide information. The deployment model is concerned with where these components execute and how they interact between processors. This is where the rubber (software) meets the road (electronics). The electronic design decisions that are particularly relevant to the software architecture are the number and type of devices in the system (particularly the processors) and the physical communications media linking them together.

It is crucial to the success of the system that the electrical and software engineers collaborate on these decisions. If the electrical engineers don't understand the software needs, they are unable to adequately accommodate them. Similarly, if the software engineers don't have a sufficient understanding of the electronic design, their architectural decisions are, at best, suboptimal, at worst, workable. For this reason, both disciplines must be involved in device selection, particularly processors, memory maps, and communication buses. It is an unfortunate truth that many systems do not meet their functional or performance requirements when this collaboration is missing in the development process.

The software concerns for each processor are

- Envisioned purpose and scope of the software executing on the processor
- Computational horsepower of the processor
- Availability of development tools, such as compilers for the selected language, debuggers, in-circuit emulators
- Availability of third-party components, including operating systems, container libraries, communication protocols, and user interfaces
- Previous experience and developer expertise with the processor

How the processors are linked is another far-reaching set of electronic design decisions. Should the communication media be arranged in a bus or star topology? Should it be bus-mastered or master-slave? Should it arbitrate on the basis of priority or fairness? Point-to-point or multidrop? How fast must the transmission rate be? These are the requirements of just the physical communications media. The software must layer appropriate communications protocols on top of that to ensure timely and reliable message exchange.

Naturally, these electronic design decisions can have a tremendous impact on the software architecture. Smaller processors can be used if there are more of them and they are linked appropriately, or a smaller number of larger processors can do the same work. If the bus mastering is not arbitrated in hardware, more software support is required to implement a peer-to-peer communications protocol required for distributed processing. Only by working together can the electronic and software engineers find an optimal solution within all the system constraints. The optimal solution is specific to both the application domain and the business goals and approaches.

8.5.1 Representing Physical Architecture in the UML

The UML represents physical architectures with deployment diagrams. There are two primary diagrammatic elements, as shown in Figure 8-14. The icon of primary importance on deployment diagrams is the *node*. Nodes represent processors, sensors, actuators, routers, displays, input devices, memory, custom PLAs, or any physical object of importance to the software. Typically, nodes are stereotyped to indicate the type of node. Connections represent physical inter-connections among nodes. They are most commonly electronic but can as easily be optical or telemetric. Stereotyping is more-common with nodes than with any other UML metaelement. It is common to use bitmaps resembling the stereotype for things like sensors, buttons, knobs, actuators, ports, and so on.

Processor nodes are occasionally shown to contain classes or objects, but usually processor nodes contain packages that may be broken down into subpackages and tasks. Components may be placed directly within the nodes, within packages within the nodes, or the dependency notation shown in Figure 8-14.

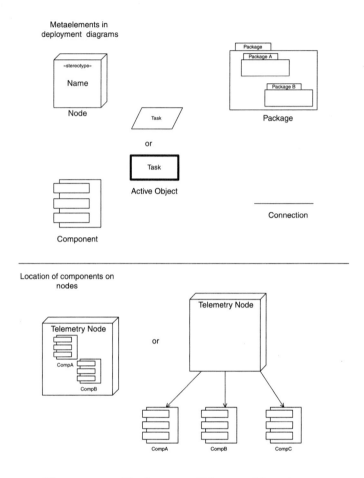

Figure 8-14: *Deployment Diagram Notation*

Figure 8-15 shows a simple example for a telescope position control system. The user interface consists of an LCD display and two rotary encoder knobs, which are tied to the same processor. The positioning subsystem consists of two independent subsystems, each containing a stepper motor and an independent sensor. The processors are linked across an Ethernet network, and both use Ethernet controller boards to access the network.

This figure shows two methods for specifying the software running on the processors. The first is shown in the *UI Processor* node. The

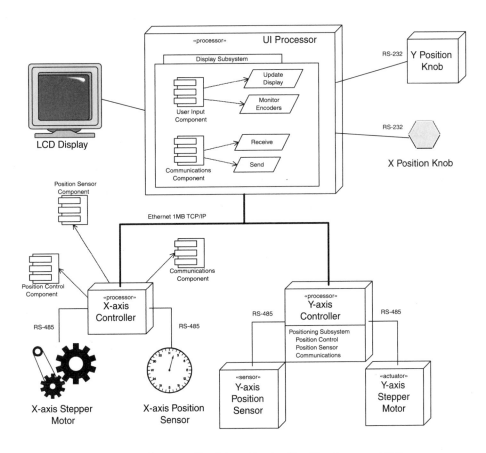

Figure 8-15: *Telescope Position Controller Deployment Diagram*

software components are shown as nested packages. The other notation method is to list the packages in a textual annotation, as is done for the position controllers. Note also that both forms of listing components are shown, as well as the use of the stereotype label and the use of stereotype icons. Naturally, in a real application design, more care would be taken to use a consistent presentation style.

The description for the user interface processor in the figure shows that it contains four threads (two per component, as it turns out). This is shown using the dependency relation. The positioning subsystem has two other components—one for controlling the stepper motor and one for monitoring the position of the telescope, but the number of threads are not indicated. Both processors have additional task threads for communicating across the network. Because this is a large-scale view, it does not typically include individual classes and objects.

The reader should also note that the same package can reside on multiple processors. The *User Interface* package may only reside on a single processor, but packages such as *Communications, Device I/O,* and *Containers* may very well reside on every processor node in the system.

8.5.2 Multiprocessor Systems

One of the most important things shown in a deployment diagram is the location of components in the system. There are three primary strategies for component location used in real-time and embedded systems. The most common strategy is static, compile-time location of components, called *asymmetric multiprocessing.* One reason this is so prevalent in embedded systems is that much of the embedded software is tightly bound to hardware devices and interfaces, making dynamic location difficult. Still, although asymmetric multiprocessing is easy to implement and conceptualize, maintenance of such a system can be difficult. For example, suppose that another processor is to be added to an asymmetric system in order to improve its performance. The software must be modified at the source-code level in order to execute on the new processor and achieve the performance gains.

Symmetric multiprocessing takes a different approach. When a task or component becomes ready to run, the OS analyzes available computational power on all the processors and selects one to execute the task or component. That is, the strategy takes advantage of dynamic load balancing. This has the advantage that increasing the available computational power improves performance with no software changes. In addition, for highly dynamic systems, a single static load balance that is efficient enough for all run-time scenarios may not exist.

Semi-symmetric multiprocessing takes a middle view. The system works like a symmetric system in that it examines the available computational power and determines where components and tasks will execute, but it does so only once, at boot-up. Thereafter, it acts like a static system, using the load balance settings determined when the system first started up.

8.5.2.1 Component Location and Access

All three of these deployment strategies support distributed object-oriented systems, but they differ in how objects communicate among themselves. In an asymmetric system, the location of objects is determined at compile time. If a target object is local, it can use a local mechanism, such as a direct method call or an OS message put operation. If the target object is remote, then it must marshal resources to construct a bus message and send it via the communications services to the hosting processor. Even in such a system, it is preferable to hide the location details from the programmer. Because the linkage is static, macros can be used to invoke various services, depending on the location of the source and target.

Another solution is to use a proxy pattern to handle the location control. A proxy class is a class that pretends to be the real data server but is really just a local stand-in. In this way, all clients of the server request information and services from the proxy. The proxy, on the other hand, encapsulates the information necessary to get the data and services from the actual server, whether or not it is in another address space.

Figure 8-16 shows the proxy pattern and an example. In the scenario shown in the figure, the server contains the heart rate as measured from its ECG leads. The client displays the current heart rate. The client is insulated from knowledge of the location of the actual data server via the proxy object, which holds a local copy of the heart rate. The client registers for automatic updates with the proxy class. In our scenario, a periodic policy updates the client from the proxy, but an independent episodic policy updates the proxy with the most recent value as it changes in the actual data server.

Naturally, the benefit gained from this is minimal with only a single client. However, this proxy can have many clients, such as an alarm manager (to check for arrhythmia), a trending client, and several display clients. The proxy subscribes to the server (which might have several proxy clients distributed throughout the system), and every so often the server sends an update to its proxies. The proxy insulates the clients from knowing anything about the location of the server and how to marshal bus messages to get the data. Further, the proxy is more efficient with distributed clients, because bus bandwidth is usually at a premium, and this way only the proxy must communicate with the server directly.

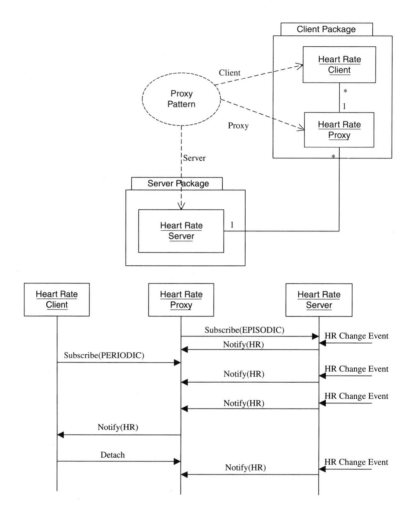

Figure 8-16: *Proxy Pattern*

The primary disadvantage of the Proxy Pattern is a possible loss of performance when only a single client resides on the processor. Another weakness is the coupling between the proxy object and the server. The proxy must know how to find the server, so it must know not only the operational syntax for requesting the data, it must also know the location of the server and how to marshal requests using the communication protocol. The proxy pattern can be elaborated to decouple the proxy from the server using the Broker Pattern, described next.

The problem is more difficult for symmetric and semi-symmetric systems, because it isn't known at compile time where the target object will be located. The Broker Pattern solves this problem by including an object repository, called a broker.

The Broker Pattern is an elaborated Proxy Pattern, which goes another step toward decoupling the clients from the servers. An object broker is an object that knows the location of other objects. The broker can have the knowledge a priori (at compile time) or can gather the information dynamically as objects register themselves, or a combination of both. The primary advantage of the Broker Pattern is that it is possible to construct a Proxy Pattern when the location of the server isn't known at compile time. This makes it particularly useful for systems that use symmetric or semi-symmetric multiprocessing.

The architectural components of the Broker Pattern are the Object Broker, Client, and Server Subsystems. It is rare to have a Broker with an isolated client and server. When it is used, the Broker Pattern is generally a key strategic design decision. Although many real-time systems may be able to use commercial object brokers,[5] it is not uncommon to implement a custom broker to optimize system resource usage.

The broker can be used to coordinate the boot of a multiprocessor system. Many such systems must boot in a particular sequence in order to make all the proper distributed linkages. As components or objects become available during the boot process, they register with the broker and request the address of their servers. If their servers are available, a valid address is returned. If not, the clients can either block on the availability of the servers or periodically retry until they become available.

During normal execution of the system, objects use the server addresses retrieved from the object broker. Should that object be unexpectedly destroyed (such as when the processor on which it executes fails), the usual procedure is to requery the broker (to see if the object has reregistered with a different address). If the broker cannot find the requested object, the client can then block, periodically retry, or execute some corrective action. In a fault-tolerant or safety-critical system, this might involve invoking a redundant channel, resetting the system, or shutting down.

---

5. The Object Management Group (OMG) is hard at work on both real-time and embedded CORBA (Common Object Request Broker Architecture) broker specifications.

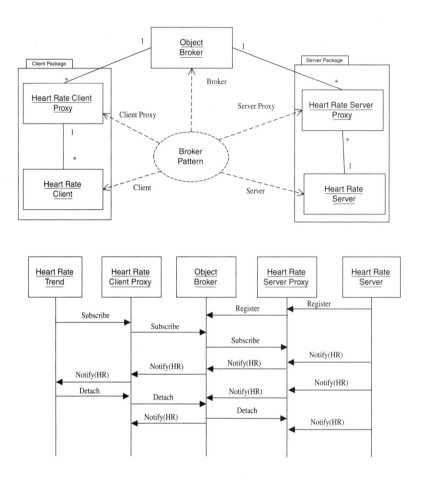

Figure 8-17: *Broker Pattern*

The scenario in Figure 8-17 shows how the participant objects collaborate with two levels of indirection. The first level is provided by the proxies, insulating the clients and servers from each other. The second level is provided by the object broker, which insulates the proxies from a priori knowledge of the server location. Note that the server object first registers with the broker so that it can handle incoming requests for the server. When the client subscribes to its local proxy, the proxy in turn subscribes to the server proxy. The object broker handles this request because only it knows the location of the server.

8.6 Safety/Reliability Model

By *safe*, we mean that the system does not create accidents leading to injury, the loss of life, or damage to property. By *reliable*, we mean a system that continues to function for long periods of time. It is possible to have reliable but unsafe systems, as well as safe but unreliable systems. A safe system can fail, as long as it does so without creating an accident. For example, an accounting program can fail and require a system reboot, but this can occur without the loss of life. Such an unreliable accounting system continues to be safe. On the other hand, a reliable system can function correctly but still lead to accidents. A handgun is a very reliable piece of equipment, but it is not particularly safe!

In many real-time systems, safe and reliable go hand-in-hand. This is especially true when there is no predetermined fail-safe condition. When flying at 35,000 feet, what is the fail-safe condition in the event of an engine malfunction? It may not be to shut down the engine! In such systems, safety is enhanced when the reliability is increased. But this is not always the case. Many systems are fault-tolerant by having redundancy, but if a redundant channel fails, the system may no longer be safe.

In safety-critical environments, applications must not only do the right thing when everything is okay, they must continue to do the right thing in the presence of single-point failures.[6] It is possible to improve both safety and reliability through an appropriate architecture, although not always at the same time. This section will explore some architectural patterns relevant to safety and reliability. The basic issues of safety criticality are discussed in Chapter 3.

8.6.1.1 Homogeneous Redundancy Pattern

The Homogeneous Redundancy Pattern uses identical channels[7] to increase reliability. All redundant channels are run in parallel, and the outputs of the channels are compared. If an odd number of channels is

6. In extremely safety-critical systems in which the lives of thousands or millions may be put at risk (such as nuclear power plants), double-point failure safety may be required.
7. A *channel*, in this context, means a set of devices (including processors and software components executing on processors) that handle a related, cohesive set of data or control flows from incoming event to ultimate system response.

used, then a "majority wins" policy can be implemented, which can detect and correct failures in the minority channels.

The advantages of this pattern are improved robustness in the presence of failures in the channels, without a large development overhead. Because all the channels are identical, they need only be "cloned" rather than redeveloped. Care should be taken that the channels are not only identical but also fully redundant so that single-point failures do not take out all channels simultaneously.[8]

A *failure* is an event that happens at a particular point in time. This is distinct from an *error,* which is a systematic fault. An error is a persistent defect due to a design or implementation mistake—a system with an error has always had the error. The big disadvantage of homogeneous redundancy is that it detects only failures, not errors. Homogeneous redundancy cannot detect errors because, by definition, all channels are identical. If one channel contains an error, then all redundant channels contain the same error. This implies that homogenous redundancy protects only against hardware failures but does not protect against software faults, because *software cannot fail.* Software can be wrong and full of errors, but it cannot suddenly break.

There are other disadvantages of redundancy. There is an increase in recurring cost caused by duplicated hardware devices. The redundant hardware also requires more space and power and generates more heat. In some real-time systems, this can be an important limitation (see Figure 8-18).

8.6.1.2 Diverse Redundancy Pattern

The Diverse Redundancy Pattern mitigates the primary disadvantage of homogeneous redundancy by providing redundant channels that are implemented by different means. This can be accomplished in several ways:

- Different but equal
- Lightweight redundancy
- Separation of monitoring and actuation

---

8. A Bell-Boeing V22 Osprey crashed because two roll-rate sensors were cross-wired, allowing the two faulty units to outvote the correct one. Similar faults were found in other flying V22 Ospreys [2].

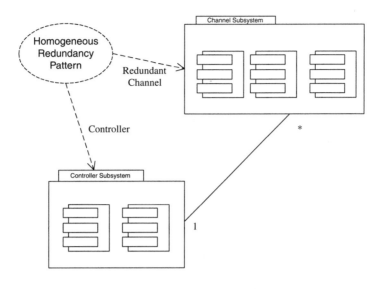

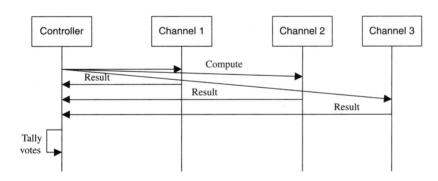

Figure 8-18: *Homogeneous Redundancy Pattern*

The first option is similar to the Homogeneous Redundancy Pattern in that the channels are all approximately equal in terms of accuracy, throughput, and reliability. Each channel is implemented differently, using different software and hardware components, so each will provide additional protection against errors, as well as failures. This is the most expensive of the three, but it can detect not only failures and errors, it can also continue to execute correctly in the presence of such faults.

The second option is to use a lightweight, secondary channel to ensure the correctness of the primary. This lightweight channel provides a reasonableness check on the results from the primary channel, but it does not have the same accuracy and/or range. It entails a lower cost to implement and manufacture but is better at fault detection than fault tolerance. The secondary channel can identify when the primary channel is broken but typically cannot take over all its duties when this occurs. Other fault tolerance means must be available if the system must remain operational in the presence of errors.

The last of these, the separation of monitoring and actuation is discussed as a separate pattern, in the next section.

You will note in Figure 8-19 that the diverse channels share a common interface but have different implementations. It is not strictly required that the interfaces be identical, but it simplifies the software development. The requirement is that the channels do not have any common mode faults—that is, that they do not have the same systematic errors, nor can a single-point failure bring down multiple channels.

8.6.1.3 Monitor-Actuator Pattern

The Monitor-Actuator Pattern is a special type of diverse redundancy. In this case, however, the channels are separated into monitoring and actuator channels. The actuator channel performs the actions, such as controlling the wing flaps, moving the control rods, and pacing the heart. The monitor channel keeps track of what the actuation is supposed to be doing and monitors the physical environment to ensure that the results of the actuator are appropriate. Note that the actuator itself cannot rely on this monitor—closed-loop actuators must use separate sensors that are independent of the sensor used in the monitoring channel.

The basic concept behind the Monitor-Actuator Pattern is that the monitor channel identifies actuation channel failures so that appropriate fault-handling mechanisms can be executed. If the monitor channel fails, it means that the actuator didn't fail (remember the assumption of single-point failure safety), so it continues to be correct. As with all forms of redundancy, common mode failures must be eliminated to achieve the safety and fault-tolerance goals of the redundancy. The monitor and actuator channels exchange messages periodically to ensure both are operating properly, as well. The messages can also be sent to the controller, which decides the appropriate actuation.

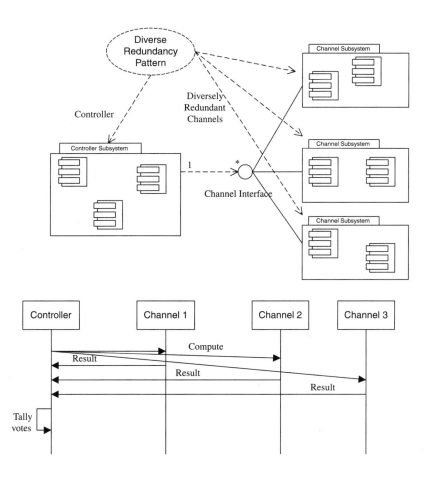

Figure 8-19: *Diverse Redundancy Pattern*

The primary downside to this pattern is the (small) increased recurring cost due to the additional monitoring channel. Nevertheless, in safety-critical or fault-sensitive situations, it can be a cost-effective means for improving safety and reliability when compared with full homogeneous or diverse redundancy.

The scenario in Figure 8-20 shows how the desired result is sent to both the actuator and the monitor channels. The actuator uses this to decide the exact action it should take. The monitor uses this to check up on the result of the action to see if the goal is achieved. In the first case, the actuation was correct, but in the second case, the monitor detected a

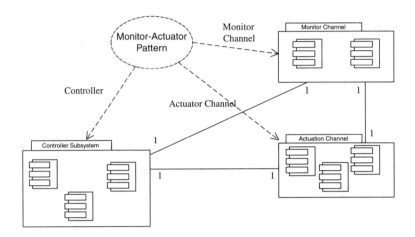

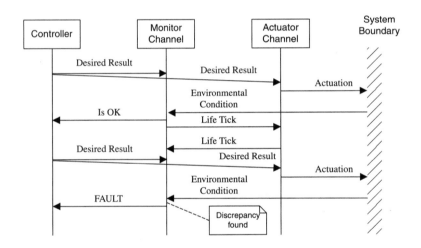

Figure 8-20: *Monitor-Actuator Pattern*

large discrepancy between the commanded result and the actual environment. The controller can then take whatever corrective action seems appropriate.

Notice also the exchange of life-tick messages in the middle of the scenario. In this way, the actuator can quickly detect when the monitor fails, and vice versa.

8.6.1.4 Watchdog Pattern

A watchdog is a common concept in real-time, embedded systems. A watchdog is a component that receives messages from other components on a periodic or sequence-keyed basis. If a service of the watchdog occurs too early, too late, or out of sequence, the watchdog initiates some corrective action, such as reset, shutdown, alarming to notify attending personnel, or signaling a more elaborate error-recovery mechanism. Watchdogs themselves tend to be very simple and are often implemented with hardware support to protect them from software faults. Although watchdogs are rather mechanistic, they are usually used within a global scope of safety and redundancy and so are included here (see Figure 8-21).

Sometimes, software watchdogs are more active. Such watchdogs are woken up periodically and perform some built-in test suite, such as performing CRC checks over the executable code, checking RAM, looking for evidence of stack overflow, and so forth. Although these are not watchdogs in the classic sense, they are simple to implement and are required in many safety-critical environments.

The advantage of using watchdogs is that they are cheap and easy to implement. They don't require a lot of hardware or software support. However, many systems do not have a simple response to the detection of a system fault. Simply resetting an unattended ICU patient ventilator may not be the most appropriate action. This is their primary disadvantage—they may be too simple to support complex error handling and fault recovery.

8.6.1.5 Safety Executive Pattern

The Safety Executive Pattern uses a centralized coordinator for safety monitoring and control of system recovery from faults. It is also known as the Safety Kernel Pattern. The safety executive acts like a very intelligent watchdog that tracks and coordinates all safety monitoring and action. Typically it captures the following inputs:

- Watchdogs timeouts
- Software error assertions
- Continuous or periodic BITs
- Faults identified by monitors in the Monitor-Actuation Pattern

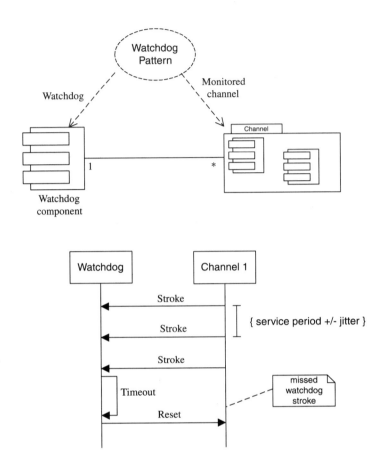

Figure 8-21: *Watchdog Pattern*

For larger and more-complex systems, a safety executive provides a consistent, centralized point for safety processing. This simplifies the application software, which might otherwise be riddled with extra checks and resulting actions that obscure the primary application purpose. Because the safety control is centralized, it becomes a simpler process to verify and validate the safety measures. The pattern is shown in Figure 8-22.

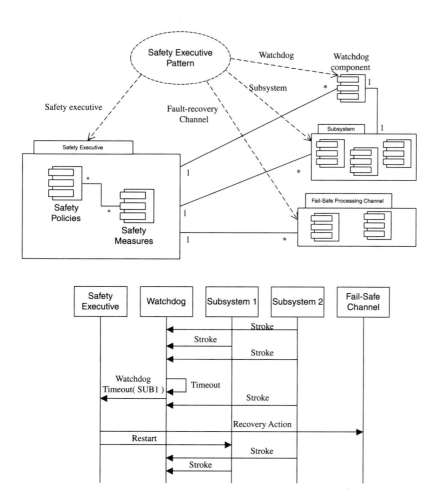

Figure 8-22: *Safety Executive Pattern*

8.7 Summary

Architectural design includes strategic design decisions that affect most or all software in the system. These decisions include the concurrency model, component model, deployment model, and the safety/reliability model.

The specification of the concurrency model is important to performance in real-time systems. This concurrency model identifies a relatively small number of threads and populates these threads with the objects identified in the analysis model. Inter-task communication allows tasks to share information and to synchronize control. This is often accomplished using a Rendezvous Pattern to ensure robust exchange of information.

Components are run-time artifacts consisting of collaborations of objects, such as executables, libraries, tables, files, and documents. Components are similar to classes in that they have interfaces and instances. Multiple instances of the same component may appear in the same system, usually on different processor nodes. The component model reifies the things that will be built, occupy memory, and execute. Components are binary-replaceable things that realize a set of interfaces. Properly designed, components provide a powerful means for updating, maintaining, and reusing systems and their parts.

A node is a physical device. Most nodes of interest to the software developer contain processors that execute components from the component model. Other nodes indicate devices that are controlled by or provide information to components executing on processor nodes. Deployment diagrams depict the nodes linked together with connections, which represent the physical inter-processor links, such as buses, serial lines, and networks. Components may be shown optionally on deployment diagrams to provide a map of the system as it exists at run-time.

The safety-reliability model is included in architectural design because the decisions that determine how safety and reliability will be ensured affect most or all the components in a system. The safety-reliability model is often implemented as instances of patterns of large-scale components or packages of components. Some common patterns discussed in this chapter include the Homogeneous Redundancy, Diverse Redundancy, Monitor-Actuator, Watchdog, and Safety Executive Patterns.

8.8 Looking Ahead

The next step is to specify the middle layer of design, known as mechanistic design. This level focuses on the collaboration of small groups of classes and objects. In the process of mechanistic design, we add classes to improve information flow and to specify details that have been so far ignored.

8.9 Exercises

1. What are the major strategic models of architectural design?

2. What is the semantic representation of tasks in the UML? What notation is used to indicate these?

3. Name four kinds of diagrams that can represent concurrency in the UML. Which is most common?

4. Name five task-identification strategies.

5. How can tasks share information in a robust fashion? Provide at least three mechanisms.

6. Describe the Microkernel Architecture Pattern.

7. What is the difference between a component, a class, and a node?

8. What is the purpose of the Proxy Pattern? What are its pros and cons?

9. Under what circumstances would the Broker Pattern be preferred to the Proxy Pattern?

10. What is the difference between the Homogeneous and Diverse Redundancy Patterns? Under what circumstances would each be a preferable architectural choice?

11. Construct component and deployment diagrams for the Acme Air Traffic Control System.

8.10 References

[1] Douglass, Bruce Powel. *Real-Time UML: Developing Efficient Objects for Embedded Systems,* Reading, Mass.: Addison-Wesley, 1988.

[2] Rumbaugh, James, Michael Blaha, William Premerlani, Frederick Eddy, and William Lorensen. *Object-Oriented Modeling and Design,* Englewood Cliffs, N.J.: Prentice Hall, 1991.

Chapter 9

Mechanistic Design

Pointers don't kill programs—people kill programs.
—Book of Douglass, Law 150

The middle level of design, called mechanistic design, deals with how small sets of classes and objects collaborate to achieve common goals. Mechanistic design is primarily organized around the discovery and use of patterns of object collaboration. These design patterns are reified solutions to structurally similar problems. Some architectural patterns are given in the previous chapter, but this chapter will identify several smaller-scale patterns useful in real-time, embedded systems.

9.1 Introduction

It all starts with use cases. As you no doubt recall, use cases reify externally visible system functions, without implying any specific implementation. Later, in structural object analysis, collaborations are identified that consist of key system domain abstractions that interact to *realize* the use case. This analysis model should, at least, contain only the abstractions without which the use case cannot be realized. It should not contain design or implementation details that are free to vary in equally correct design solutions.

This analysis-level object model has a minimal set of associations, attributes, and operations necessary to support the required collaborations. However, a naïve implementation of such analysis models, even when possible, is usually far from optimal. That's where design comes in.

Design is all about optimizing an analysis model according to some set of criteria. Typical criteria are

- Performance, such as a) average case performance, b) worst case performance
- Predictability
- Optimal use of some set of resources
- Memory usage
- Safety
- Reliability
- Maintainability
- Portability
- Development effort or cost (nonrecurring cost)
- Manufacturing effort or cost (recurring cost)

In the previous chapter, we saw how large-scale architectural structures are used to meet some of these criteria. Architectural design is concerned with broad-stroke strategic decisions that affect how all or most objects in a system work together. These decisions go well beyond the implementation of a single collaboration of objects.

The next tier down in design is called *mechanistic design* and is concerned with design optimization against a set of criteria that make sense in the smaller context of a set of collaborating objects. These design decisions take into account the strategic architectural design decisions and refine those decisions into more detail. The scope of mechanistic design is individual collaboration, although the same criteria (and hence the same design solutions) is often applied to a number of collaborations within a system.

Let's begin with a simple example. Figure 9-1 shows a collaboration of objects from a spacecraft object model. The particular use case being

Table 9-1: *Trajectory Planner Classes*

Classes	Roles
Trajectory planner	Plans the full trajectory, including positional and attitudinal changes
Trajectory	The plan itself created by the trajectory planner
Trajectory segment	A piece of a plan, consisting of a short sequence of precisely timed rocket burns to adjust attitude and position, starting position and attitude
Attitude sensor	A sensor that determines orientation (attitude) (*)
Attitude rocket	A small rocket used to change attitude (*)
Thrust rocket	A rocket used to change position (*)
Position sensor	A sensor that determines position relative to a coordinate fix (*)
Position	A coordinate position in space relative to a fixed coordinate origin (x,y,z,t)
Attitude	Amount of rotation in three axes that determine orientation
Attitude burn	A timed burn for an attitude rocket
Position burn	A timed burn for a positional rocket

realized is "Get the spacecraft from here to there." Table 9-1 spells out the classes involved in the collaboration and their roles.

One can see how this collaboration might work: The trajectory planner creates a complete trajectory, consisting of multiple segments. Each segment consists of a starting position and a short sequence of precisely timed burns from various positional and attitudinal rockets.

We can elaborate the model shown in Figure 9-1 by introducing threads and components, as shown in Figure 9-2, using the techniques and notations discussed in the previous chapter. This allows the construction of scenarios that follow the operations as the threads execute across the different components.

Nevertheless, some questions remain. Associations among classes permit messages to be sent to request information and services, enabling the required collaboration. How are these associations to be

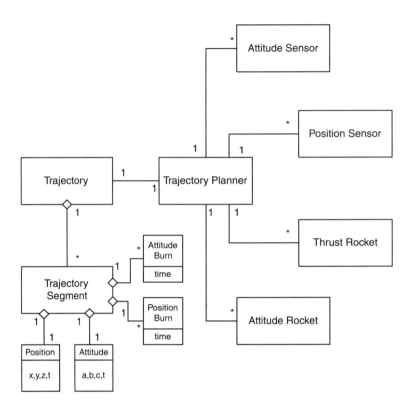

Figure 9-1: *Trajectory Control Object Analysis Model*

implemented? Common design solutions would be pointers or references (if they are within the same thread), posting to an OS message queue, guarded operations (that is, operations protected by a semaphore), and interprocess call (IPC) or remote procedure call (RPC) mechanisms. All these solutions are appropriate, depending on a variety of other design solutions and constraints. The simplest solution, using pointers to facilitate direct method invocation, is appropriate only when the objects are within the same address space and in the absence of potential mutual exclusion problems.

Even with that simple solution, problems remain. For example, how should multivalued roles[1] be handled? One solution is to have the

---

1. A *multi-valued role* of an association is one with a nonunity multiplicity, such as 0,1, or *.

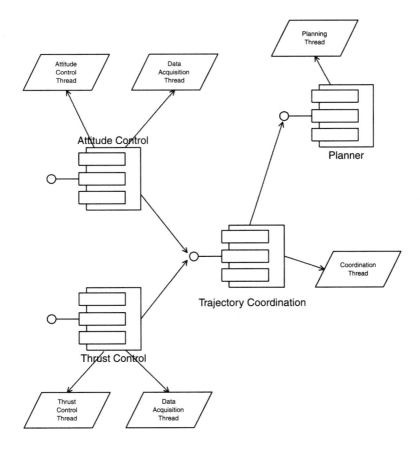

Figure 9-2: *Trajectory Component Architecture*

unary role end include the knowledge of how to manage the other, multivalued end. Perhaps the collection of objects at the multivalued role end can be managed with an array of pointers, a linked list, or a binary tree.

Another problem is controlling the rockets to achieve the desired effect. Burns of rockets can be executed open-loop, without feedback, or they can be closed-loop. If the trajectory segments can incorporate closed-loop feedback, then the trajectory planning is simpler, because it needs far less accuracy in terms of the current mass of the spacecraft (which diminishes due to burns and leaks) and its weight distribution. If we decide that closed-loop control is appropriate, how do we manage that? Should the trajectory planner do that? It seems beyond the intended scope of that object.

Figure 9-3 shows a design solution for these issues (dotted lines highlight the added design-level classes). The containment of multiple objects implied by the multivalued roles is managed by container classes. In the figure, list classes were used, indicating our choice. But other container classes could be used, as well, implementing any of a large variety of data structures. The implementation strategies for associations are shown as constraints that are in alignment with their function—standard pointer implementation for invoking operations within

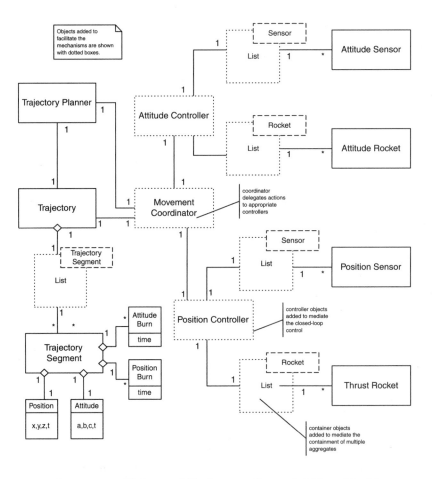

Figure 9-3: *Elaborated Trajectory Control Object Model*

the same thread, and for posting messages to OS message queues for the associations between threads. The responsibility for dispatching such operation invocations are made by the active object owning the thread. Even the problem of closed-loop control was addressed by introducing controller objects, which implement control logic (probably using difference equations to incorporate position or attitude information). True, we haven't solved the problem of what those equations look like exactly, but now at least we have a placeholder for them.

This is a very common way of proceeding with design—elaborate at successive levels of detail until the design solution is fully implementable.

So it is with all of mechanistic design. Classes are added to facilitate the implementation of the analysis model. This is the classic elaborative or iterative development method—repeated refinement of the model via reorganization and addition.

In the following section, we'll present a number of design patterns that can be applied profitably in the design of real-time systems. These patterns simplify the system's design and allow reuse on a grander scale than the reuse of individual objects and classes.

9.2 Terms and Concepts

Remember that use cases represent a named behavior within a specific context. Use cases associate with objects called actors that exist outside the boundary of that context. Use cases can be defined with an arbitrary level of detail, with respect to their functionality, but they never imply an implementation. Most use cases are identified at the system level of context; actors that associate with these system-level use cases reside outside the scope of the system. However, use cases can be defined at any level of decomposition. Use cases may be identified at the subsystem level or lower, but their semantics remains the same.

A *collaboration* is a set of class roles[2] that exchange messages in the pursuit of an overall, coordinated behavior. Collaborations are said to realize use cases—that is, they provide an implementable design that

---

2. A *class role* is the behavior of a class within the context of a specific collaboration. The same class may serve different roles in various collaborations.

provides the specified behavior. Coordination of the participant class operation is most commonly shown with a set of scenarios, ranging in number from a few to several dozen. However, as discussed previously, other means for specifying use case behavior abound, including statecharts, activity diagrams, formal languages, control logic, and so on.

However it is defined, the collaboration realizing a use case must be consistent with the defined behavior. In the case of scenario modeling, consistency is relatively easy to verify: Execute the scenario on the collaborating objects and see if the required results are produced. Demonstrating executional equivalence of other behavioral representations is somewhat more problematic. For example, if a use case is defined by a state machine, the states of all the reactive objects within the collaboration must map to that use case statechart. This is not always easy to show. Consider the state machine, shown in Figure 9-4, for the space-

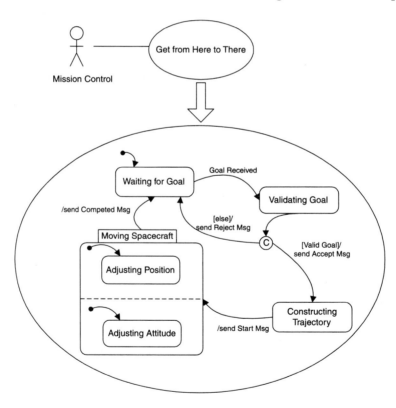

Figure 9-4: *Use Case Statechart*

craft use case "Get the spacecraft from here to there." Each state in Figure 9-4 actually maps to a state vector (at the next level down in abstraction), consisting of one or more states for each object within the realizing collaboration. Put another way, each state in a use case statechart is realized by a submachine with *n* orthogonal components, one for each reactive object within the collaboration.

To demonstrate, let us assume that the following objects from Figure 9-3 are reactive: trajectory planner, trajectory controller, position controller, attitude controller (position controller and attitude controller are descendants from class *Controller*), thrust rocket, and attitude rocket (rocket controller classes are of class *Rocket*). Let's assume the sensors, position, burns, and other classes are all stateless ("simple," in the terms of Chapter 7). The statecharts for these reactive classes are shown in Figure 9-5.

To simplify matters, let's assume that the statecharts for all controllers are identical, even though they may have polymorphic operations that allow them to achieve different effects. Similarly, the statecharts for rockets will be identical.

Planner

In this system, planning may occur when the system is at rest or when it is actively implementing a trajectory. It does this by running in its own thread (see Figure 9-2). In this way, the next trajectory can be calculated while the current one is being executed. When the Planner receives an *evGoal* event, it enters the *Building* state. In this state, it validates that the goal is valid and achievable, and if so, it constructs a set of subgoals for the various components. When a trajectory is completely constructed, the Planner enters its *Trajectory Ready* state. From here, a new trajectory can be calculated, or the just-calculated one can be implemented in response to a mission control command event *evApplyGoal*.

Movement Coordinator

The Movement Coordinator applies a trajectory received from the Planner in response to the propagated event *evApplyTrajectory*. This event is accepted in both the *Idle* (not doing anything) and *Coordinating* (currently executing a different trajectory plan) states. In the *Coordinating* superstate, two concurrent things are taking place: The position and the attitude are being independently adjusted. The Movement Coordinator steps through one trajectory segment at a time until, at last, all subgoals are achieved.

Controller

The system contains two controllers. The Position Controller works primarily with thrust rockets that move the spacecraft in a single direction. However, for fine positioning (such as required by docking maneuvers), small retrorockets may be used as antagonists. The Attitude Controller works similarly, except that the protagonist and antagonist rockets are more equally sized and tend to work in concert all the time. In both cases, the control is closed loop and uses sensors to ensure that it is working as planned.

Sensor

Sensor objects are used to ensure the spacecraft is moving correctly within the six-degree-of-freedom frame of reference. This means that sensors provide either linear position information in one of three orthogonal axes, or rotational information (roll, pitch, and yaw) in one of the other three orthogonal axes. In all cases, the basic state machine is the same. This is probably an abstract superclass which will be subclassed into two basic types—translational and rotational.

Rocket

Rocket objects provide thrust in a single direction relative to the spacecraft center of mass. Although one might use rockets that have controllable nozzles, for this spacecraft, the trajectory planner computes the trajectory such that the attitude of the spacecraft determines the vector of thrust. The primary thrust rockets are large, but a number of small rockets exist, such as thrust retrorockets and attitude rockets. The state machine for all rockets is the same.

Figure 9-6 shows a scenario for the collaboration of some of the objects in Figure 9-3. In this scenario, the Movement Coordinator gets a GoTo(x,y,z,t,a,b,c) command. It sends part of that command off to the positional control system (not shown in the scenario) and controls the attitude of the spacecraft via the Attitude Controller (shown). The states of the participating objects are shown on the instance lines, along with

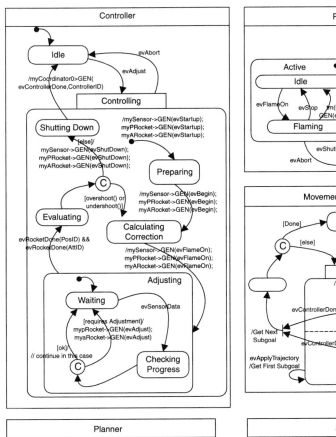
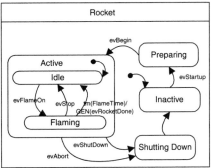
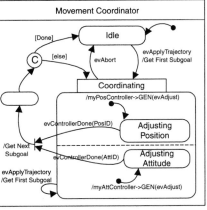
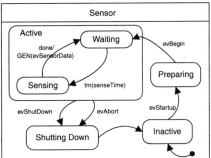
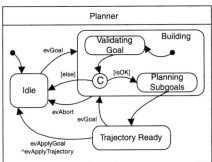

Figure 9-5: *Collaborating Reactive Object Statecharts*

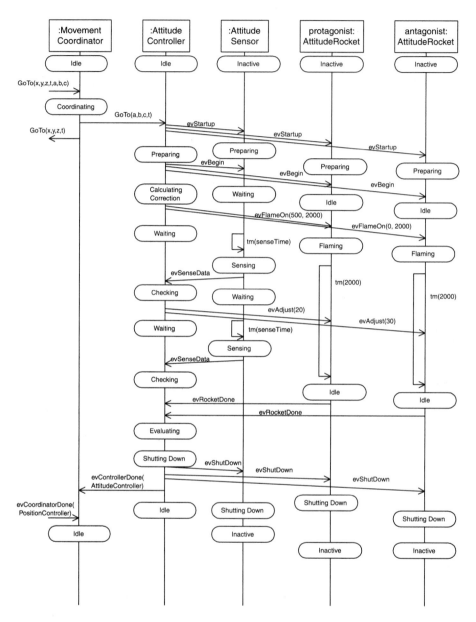

Figure 9-6: *Collaborating Reactive Object Scenario*

the scenario. Although this scenario is fairly simple (albeit with a large number of small steps), it shows how the objects communicate via messages and how their state machines change in a coordinated fashion over time.

That's all well and good, but we have a use case specification and state machine that describes the proper behavior from a black-box viewpoint. How do the states from Figure 9-4 map to the states of the reactive objects of Figure 9-5?

The collaboration must achieve the behavior identified within the use case statechart, shown in Figure 9-4. In an ideal world, mapping use case states to collaborating object states would be so straightforward as to be trivial. However, just looking at the state machines associated with the participating objects in Figure 9-5, it is less than obvious. Table 9-2 provides a mapping from the use case states to the states of the collaborating objects.

Table 9-2: *Mapping Use Case States to Object States*

Getting from Here to There **Use Case States**				
	Waiting for goal	Validating goal	Constructing trajectory	Moving spacecraft
Trajectory planner	Idle	Validating goal	Planning subgoals	Trajectory ready
Movement coordinator state(s)	(Don't care)	(Don't care)	(Don't care)	Coordinating, Adjusting position, Coordinating, Adjusting attitude
Attitude controller state(s)	(Don't care)	(Don't care)	(Don't care)	Preparing, Calculating correction, Adjusting, Evaluating, Shutting down
				(continued)

Table 9-2: (*cont.*)

Getting from Here to There **Use Case States**				
Attitude sensor state(s)	(Don't care)	(Don't care)	(Don't care)	Waiting, Sensing
protagonist: Attitude rocket state(s)	(Don't care)	(Don't care)	(Don't care)	Preparing, Active, Shutting down
antagonist: Attitude rocket state(s)	(Don't care)	(Don't care)	(Don't care)	Preparing, Active, Shutting down
Thrust rocket state(s)	(Don't care)	(Don't care)	(Don't care)	Preparing, Active, Shutting down

We can see in this table that the mapping may not be obvious, but it is at least straightforward. Because the planning of one trajectory can be done while the spacecraft is actually performing another, the states of objects other than the Trajectory Planner are irrelevant. If the spacecraft is not actively maneuvering, then they will all be in their *Idle* or *Inactive* states. Once the trajectory plan is complete, however, the other objects kick into action, controlled at the low level by the two controllers and ultimately coordinated by the Movement Coordinator object.

Traceability from the use case functional description to the object behavioral description is obviously important in any system that has to meet complex behavioral requirements. It is crucial when the costs of system failure are high.

9.2.1 Design-Pattern Basics

As discussed earlier, a collaboration is a set of classes that work together to realize a use case. A *mechanism* is "a design pattern that applies to a society of classes [7]." A collaboration is, in an important sense, an instance of one or more mechanisms in that it consists of a set of collaborating objects realizing that design pattern.[3] An instance of a collaboration consists of a particular set of object instances that occupy real memory addresses at some particular point in time. It is possible for a collaboration to be replicated—that is, have multiple instances— or to have no instances at some particular time.

A *design pattern* (or more succinctly, "pattern") is an abstraction of a collaboration—that is, a pattern in some sense is the type of a collaboration, and a collaboration is, in the conjugate sense, an instance of a pattern. Design patterns actually apply to concepts other than collaborations and so are more general that this. Nevertheless, most of the work that has been done in the identification of patterns has dealt exclusively with collaborations.

Figure 9-7 ties together the concepts of use cases, mechanisms, and collaborations. The use cases are taken from Chapter 5 for the Acme Air Traffic Control System. Two of these use cases, *detect separation distance violation* and *display flight path* are realized first as mechanisms. Mechanisms have some missing design-level detail, so they are *refined* into a collaboration that consists of instantiable classes. The collaborations may then be instantiated by creating the collaborating objects and linking them together.

Design patterns are parameterized mechanisms—that is, design patterns typically contain parameterized elements with formal parameter lists. During the creation of an instantiable collaboration, the pattern is refined by supplying the actual parameters to be used. For example, a design pattern may require a container of some kind, which implements containment of multiple objects, but it doesn't much care which kind of container is used. During refinement, the kind of container is selected, although with some other missing design-level detail.

Design patterns can be thought of as general solutions to commonly occurring design problems. They consist of three parts.

1. A common problem, including common problem context

2. A generalization approach to a solution

3. Consequences of the pattern

---

3. This definition is slightly different from the one given in [5], but it is consistent with [7] and so is used here to avoid confusion.

Figure 9-7: *Use Cases, Mechanisms, and Collaborations*

The problem statement describes the general characteristics of the problem at hand. This description may include context and preconditions. For example,

Problem: When exception handling is used, raw pointers can lead to memory leaks when exceptions are thrown. The use of temporary pointers within normal C++ functions or class member functions may not be properly cleaned up if an exception is thrown, because the inline delete operator may be bypassed. This does not apply to objects, because when objects go out of scope, their destructors are called. Raw pointers do not have destructors.

This problem statement identifies a problem common to designs within many domains. The context is broad—programs using C++ with exception handling. Because a generally applicable solution to this problem is available, it can be reified into a design pattern:

Solution: Rather than use a raw pointer, a *smart pointer* object can be used when a temporary pointer is called for. The smart pointer is responsible for identifying the time at which it must deallocate memory when the pointer is destroyed. This requires an internal mechanism, such as reference counting, to determine whether other smart pointers are referring to the same object in memory.

Naturally, design patterns have pros and cons. These are the consequences of the design pattern:

Consequences: The smart pointer makes the design more robust in the presence of thrown exceptions, but it increases the code complexity and requires an additional level of indirection for each pointer reference. Although this can be made syntactically invisible to the user, it involves a small run-time overhead. Enforcement of the smart pointer policy cannot be automated; it must be ensured by consensus and review. Further, if smart and raw pointers are both applied against the same object, reference counting should be disabled.

Mechanistic design patterns are medium-scale, involving as few as two or as many as a couple of dozen classes. Several patterns are provided in this chapter, but this is a rich area of active research. The interested reader is referred to references [1] through [5] for more patterns.[4]

A great deal of mechanistic design can be reduced to identifying and applying patterns that optimize collaboration along the system design criteria. There are usually some elements of mechanistic design that are not general enough to be reified as patterns, but the design optimization

---

4. Another good source of patterns is the Patterns home page at *http://st-www.cs.uiuc. edu/users/patterns/patterns.html*.

of almost all collaborations can be achieved through the application of appropriately selected patterns. To this end, let us consider a few design patterns appropriate for real-time and embedded systems.

9.3 Mechanistic Design Patterns

Collaborations define the overall interaction necessary to achieve a use case behavior. Patterns exist to provide common ways of wiring together collaborations that optimize some criteria of importance. Because functional issues are addressed by the collaboration itself, design patterns optimize some quality-of-service (QoS) criteria, such as those identified in the first section of this chapter. Rather than exhaustively catalog all potentially useful patterns, let us concern ourselves with some patterns that address problems faced by real-time and embedded-system developers—namely, correctness and execution (see

Table 9-3: *Real-Time Mechanistic Design Patterns*

Category	Pattern Name	Purpose
Correctness patterns	Smart pointer	Avoid problems associated with dumb pointers
	Second guess	Monitor collaboration results for reasonableness
	Exception monitor	Track and ensure pre- and post-conditions are met
Execution control patterns	Policy pattern	Abstract away a replaceable algorithm into a policy class
	State	Provide an optimal state machine implementation when some state changes are infrequent
	State table	Provide an efficient means to maintain and execute large complex state machines
	State walker	Use a controller to walk a state space graph *(continued)*

Table 9-3: (*cont.*)

Category	Pattern Name	Purpose
Execution Control Patterns (*cont.*)	Control loop	Execute closed-loop control mathematics
	Reactive control loop	Different control loops or a single control loop with different parameters used under different conditions
	Fuzzy state	Apply the state pattern to fuzzy logic control systems
	Neural network	Apply neural networks to control systems

Table 9-3). Other patterns useful for real-time systems are dealt with in more detail elsewhere [5, 6], and the interested reader is referred there for a more complete set of real-time design patterns.

9.3.1 Correctness Patterns

Some patterns for correctness have already been discussed at some length in the previous chapter. For example, the Homogeneous and Diverse Redundancy patterns provide safety through redundancy, a large-scale strategic decision. The patterns discussed here are applicable to an individual collaboration. They tend to be lightweight and local in scope.

9.3.1.1 Smart Pointer Pattern

Problems with pointers are well-known to C and C++ programmers. They fall into several categories:

- Pointers may be used before they are initialized.
- Pointers may be used after the memory they point to has been released (dangling pointer).
- Memory may not be released (memory leak).
- Pointer arithmetic may result in erroneous addresses.
- Target objects may be in different memory addresses.

Every experienced C and C++ programmer has not only seen these problems, they have also committed offenses against Truth, Justice, and the Object Way. These languages make it so easy to misuse pointers and so hard to find the errors. Even programs that appear to be robust can lead to subtle pointer problems. Just to prove how easy it is, consider some simple examples of memory leaks.

The first example is a procedure that accepts and uses a pointer.

```
void test(int* p) {
    int* a = p;   // line 1
    *p = 17;      // line 2
    delete a;     // line 3
    *p = 99;      // line 4
};
```

What if the parameter *p* is not initialized? Then lines 2 and 4 will wreak havoc. This is a common problem in C and C++ programs. What about when line 3 is executed? Then line 4 is in error, because *p* now points to memory that is released. Further, does the caller of *test* know that the memory *p* points to has been released? Are there other pointers to this memory left in the program?

Many pointer problems are more subtle. For example, can you identify the problem in the code below?

```
class myClass {
    int a;
public:
    int get(void) { return a; }
    void put(int temp) { a = temp; }
};

class usesMC {
public:
    void test(void) {
        myClass *pMC = new myClass;
        pMC->put(75);
        //
        myTestFunction(); // function defined outside
        class
        //
        delete pMC;
    };
};
```

The problem is that if myTestFunction() throws an exception, the myClass object pointed to by pMC will not be deleted, even though it is no longer accessible. Using raw pointers in C++ for local function objects is always an error when the compiler puts in exception-handling code. By default, all ANSI-compliant C++ compilers must put in exception-handling code because 1) they're required to, and 2) standard C++ libraries throw exceptions. Thus, this ostensibly correct code can lead to memory leaks.

The smart pointer is a common pattern meant to eliminate, or at least mitigate, the myriad problems that stem from the manual use of raw pointers:

- Although raw pointers have no constructor to leave them in a valid initial state, smart pointers can use their constructors to initialize them to NULL or force the pre-condition that they are constructed pointing to a valid target object.

- Although raw pointers have no destructor and so may not deallocate memory if they suddenly go out of scope, smart pointers determine whether it is appropriate to deallocate memory when they go out of scope and call the delete operator.

- Although a raw pointer to a deleted object still holds the address of the memory at which the object used to be (and hence can be used to reference that memory illegally), smart pointers can automatically detect that condition and refuse access.

The simplicity of the Smart Pointer Pattern shown in Figure 9-8 belies its usefulness. Although the mechanism is simple, significant functionality is hidden within the detailed design of the smart pointer class. In order to determine when it is safe to delete the memory, the smart pointer associates with a reference count. As smart pointers are added, the reference count is incremented by the smart pointer constructor; as smart pointers are deleted, the reference count is diminished in the smart pointer destructor. When the reference count is decremented to zero, the last smart pointer releases the memory being pointed to by calling the delete() operator on the referenced object.

9.3.1.2 Second-Guess Pattern

In a discussion of the theory of problem solving with Scott, my now-11-year old, I asked him to solve the following problem.

> Space Patrolman Jones and the evil alien approach each other in their respective spacecraft, each going 9,000 miles per hour. Space Patrolman Jones sends forth an atomic-powered robot that flies

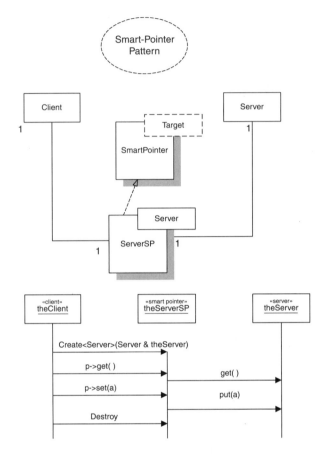

Figure 9-8: *Smart Pointer Pattern*

back and forth between the two spacecraft at 12,000 miles per hour until the two spacecraft collide in a fiery crash. How far does the robot travel if it begins when the spacecraft are 300,000 miles apart and finishes when they collide?

The obvious way to solve this problem is to sum the infinite series and thus compute the asymptote, which he dutifully did. "Now," I said, "how can you tell me, in 30 seconds or less, whether your answer is at least approximately correct?"[5] This led to a discussion of computation by rules of thumb and reasonableness checks.

---

5. Exercise left to the reader.

Whenever one does lengthy computations, there is an opportunity for error. Not only can the computations be erroneous (that is, erroneously programmed), but they may also suffer from accumulation of round-off error, violation of pre-conditional invariants, device failure, and other maladies. What's a computer to do?

The Second Guess Pattern (see Figure 9-9) is similar to the Policy Pattern that will be discussed later in the chapter. In effect, there are two algorithms represented, the primary one and another (often much

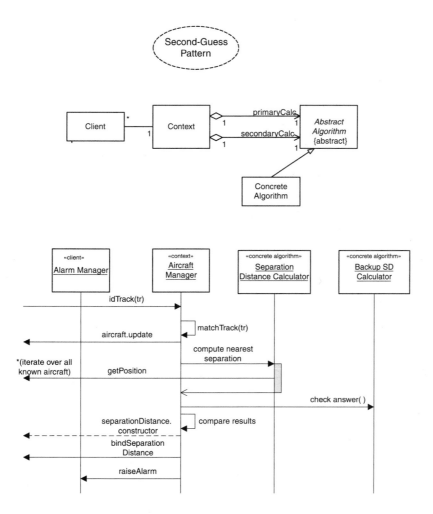

Figure 9-9: *Second Guess Pattern*

lighter, in terms of computation required). The context object computes the primary, high-fidelity answer, and then passes this off to the reasonableness check, which returns a Boolean value (TRUE, meaning that the answer is within a reasonable range).

9.3.1.3 Exception-Monitor Pattern

Building reliable and safe systems is on the order of three times more difficult than building systems that don't concern themselves explicitly with reliability and safety. This is true largely because there are more ways to fail than to succeed. There is also the additional difficulty of deciding what should be done in each failure mode. Sometimes, objects themselves have enough context to know what to do in the case of a failure; sometimes, it must be handled at the system level by transitioning to a system fail-safe state. However, frequently it is best to handle exceptions within the scope of the collaboration it affects. The Exception-Monitor Pattern is one mechanism for dealing with exceptions within the scope of an individual collaboration.

This pattern, shown in Figure 9-10, adds exception handling at the mechanistic level by adding a number of classes in the collaboration.

- Exception Safe Class
  The *Exception Safe Class* is an abstract class that associates to the various other members of the pattern. *Collaborating Objects,* implementing the primary functionality of the collaboration, subclass from *Exception Safe Class* in order to link into this pattern.

- Exception
  The *Exception* class reifies the exception object explicitly, allowing it to be passed in a standard way to the *Exception Monitor.* The *Exception* class includes a severity parameter, which is normally an enumerated type, such as *{warning, mild, caution, catastrophic},* or something similar. It also associates to a specific handler that is called by the *Exception Monitor* when the latter handles the former. *Exception* associates with *Exception Handler* rather than handle the rescue action directly. This permits multiple exceptions to use the same handler, and even change handlers at run-time.

- Exception Handler
  Exception Handler is known to *Exception* at creation time (allowing *Exception* to invoke its handle() operation). *Exception Handler* has an

optional association to *Client* so that it may invoke operations defined in those classes if and when necessary (such as shutting down equipment, retrying operations, and so forth).

- Exception Monitor
  Exception Monitor mediates the exception handling by accepting the exceptions, logging them with the *Exception Log,* and passing them off to the *Global Exception Handler* if they are not successfully handled. *Exception Handlers* that cannot handle the exception may still perform some clean-up activities, but they return unsuccessful to notify the *Exception Monitor* to call the *Global Exception Handler.*

- Exception Log
  Exception Log manages the persistent storage of exceptions, a requirement in many reliable systems.

- Global Exception Handler
  The *Global Exception Handler* handles exceptions that cannot be handled within the local collaboration in such a way that they can continue or retry the operation.

This pattern handles one of the issues with language-based, exception-handling mechanisms, particularly in C++ and Ada—that exception handling can take an unpredictable amount of time to execute. This is because the standard language mechanisms walk the call stack backward, looking for a handler that deals with the identified exception. By reifying the exception as a class and calling an explicit handler directly, this unpredictability can be removed.

9.3.2 Execution Control Patterns

The patterns in this section use encapsulation and abstraction to improve reuse of classes. They may also provide other advantages, as well. Their primary purpose, however, is to separate and encapsulate areas of concern within an object into separate objects.

9.3.2.1 Policy Pattern

Many times, classes realize the same interface but differ in terms of how they operate internally. For example, it is possible that a class looks the same but makes different time/space/complexity/safety/

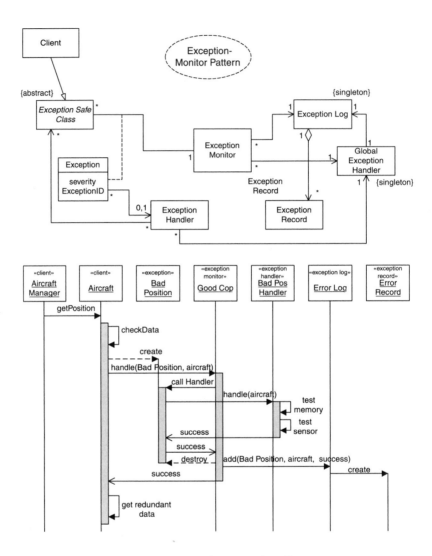

Figure 9-10: *Exception Monitor Pattern*

reliability optimization choices. The algorithm used to implement the black-box behavior is called a *policy*. Policies can be abstracted away from the main class to simplify the interface, improve reuse, and even allow dynamic choices of policies based on operating condition or state.

The objects participating in the Policy Pattern are

Client—Uses the services and operations of the *Context* object.

Context—Provides services to the *Client* and a context for the *Policy* object. It will invoke the services of the *Policy* object necessary to implement the policy within its context.

Abstract policy—Provides a virtual interface to the *Concrete Policy* object for the *Context object.*

Concrete policy—Implements the algorithm and services for the selected policy.

The scenario in Figure 9-11 shows a typical use of a Policy Pattern in safety-critical applications. A *Client* associates with the *Heart Rate Server* to get patient information. If this information is corrupted (and EMI in an operating room can be extremely high), then patient safety may be compromised. To improve safety, the *Heart Rate Server* uses a safety policy to detect corruption. Such a policy may use feedback error-detection schemes, such as checksums; cyclic redundancy checks; and 1's-complement storage, or feed-forward error correction, such as triple redundancy or Hamming codes. A CRC error-detection policy is used in the scenario in Figure 9-11.

This particular scenario shows a *Heart Rate Source* object that updates the *Heart Rate Proxy.* When new data is received from the *Heart Rate Source*, the *Heart Rate Proxy* requests that the *CRC Policy* object compute a CRC on the data. *theClient* object gets the heart rate from the *Heart Rate Proxy* via its get() operation. The *Heart Rate Proxy*'s get() operation checks the data against the CRC stored in the *CRC Policy* object via the latter's check() member function. If it returns OK, then the heart rate is returned to the client. If it returns BAD, then the *Heart Rate Proxy* requests a new value from the *Heart Rate Source,* recomputes the CRC, and then checks the CRC. If this now works, then the heart rate is returned. If it still fails (not shown in the scenario), the *Heart Rate Proxy* could retry or throw an exception to the *Client.*

9.3.2.2 State Pattern

Many systems spend most of their time in only a few states. For such systems, it is more efficient to have a heavyweight process for transitioning to the less-used state if it can make the more-used state transitions

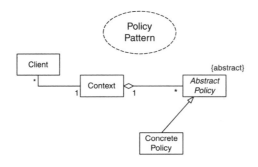

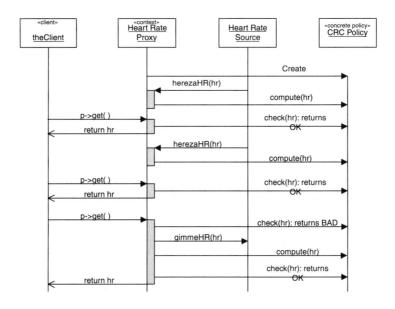

Figure 9-11: *Policy Pattern*

lighter weight. The state model shown in Figure 9-12 illustrates this problem.

A cardiac pacemaker is "programmed" by the physician into a pacing mode after it is implanted in the patient's chest. In a VVI pacing mode, the ventricle is paced (the first *V*), the ventricle is sensed (the second *V*) and when an intrinsic beat is sensed, pacing is inhibited (the *I*).

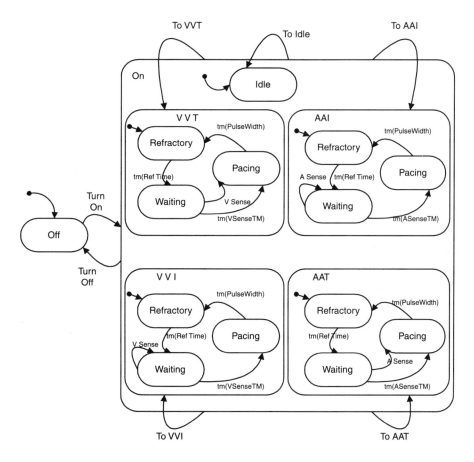

Figure 9-12: *Pacemaker State Machine Example*

The patient leaves the office with a pacemaker in this mode and may return on a yearly or bi-yearly basis. Because only the doctor can reprogram the pacemaker, the transitions between available pacing modes are very infrequent. However, it is important that within a pacing mode, the state transitions must be very lightweight to reduce battery drain.

The participants in the State Pattern shown in Figure 9-13 are

- Context
  The *Context* is a composite object that manages the state behavior. It accepts the transitions and either processes the transition directly

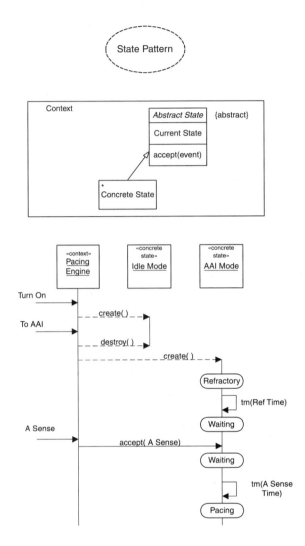

Figure 9-13: *State Pattern*

(for heavyweight transitions) or dispatches it to the currently active *State* object.

- Abstract State
  The *Abstract State* class defines the structure for a *State* class, which includes the events accepted and the actions executed. Being abstract, this class is never directly instantiated.

- Concrete State

  Concrete State objects implement a state—each corresponds to a single heavyweight state. Frequently, *Concrete States* themselves have substates, so they directly and clearly map to the nested hierarchical states found in statecharts; *Concrete States* implement superstates while the substates within the *Concrete States* are implemented using a lighter-weight mechanism, such as nested switch-case statements or state tables (see the State-Table Pattern, below).

The scenario in Figure 9-13 shows how the *Context* handles events in two distinct fashions. Some events cause the currently active *Concrete State* to change. If the event is not one of those, then it is dispatched to the *Concrete State* for processing. If the event is handled by the *Concrete State*, then it may be quietly discarded or cause an exception to be thrown, whichever is semantically appropriate in the system. Self-caused events, such as the timeouts shown in the scenario, are usually handled directly by the active state object.

9.3.2.3 State-Table Pattern

The State-Table Pattern (see Figure 9-14) provides a simple mechanism for managing large state machines with an efficiency of $O(c)$, where c is a constant. This makes it a preferred mechanism for very large state spaces, because the time to handle a transition is a constant (not including the time to execute actions associated with state entry, exit, and the transition itself). Another advantage is that this pattern maps directly to tabular state specifications, commonly used to specify many safety-critical systems.

The State-Table Pattern hinges upon the state table. This structure is typically implemented as an $n \times m$ array, where n is the number of states and m is the number of transitions. Each cell contains a single pointer to a *Transition* object, which "handles" the event with an *accept* operation. The operation returns the resulting state. Both events and states are represented as an enumerated type. Enumerated types are used as indices into the table to optimize performance. Because this pattern is designed to execute fast, it has a relatively high initialization cost, but execution cost is low.

This pattern is relatively complex,[6] although it contains only the following elements:

---

6. In this case, due to the tight coupling of the classes involved.

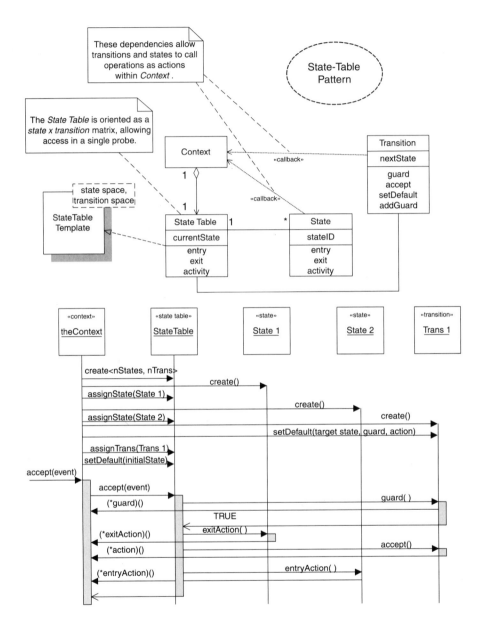

Figure 9-14: *State-Table Pattern*

- Context
  This is the class for which the state table manages the state machine. It also contains all the actions to be executed, including the transition actions and the state entry, exit, and activity actions. *Context* creates the state and transition objects and then passes responsibility for their management over to the *State Table.*

- State Table Template
  This is a template, or generic, that is refined based on the number of states and transitions.

- State Table
  The *State Table* is basically a *nState x nTransition* matrix of pointers to state transitions, and a vector of *nStates,* with some supporting methods, such as:

  1. accept, which accepts an incoming event and processes it based on the current state by indexing into the array. If the matrix cell is empty, the event is discarded; otherwise, the guard (if any) is evaluated. If the guard evaluates to TRUE, then the current state's exit action is executed, followed by the transition's action and the new state's entry action.

  2. setDefault, which sets the default initial state.

  3. assignState, which accepts state objects created by the *Context.*

  4. assignTrans, which accepts transition objects created by the *Context.*

  5. destructor, which destroys state and transition objects originally created by the *Context.*

- State
  State objects contain a state ID so that it can be queried, if necessary, and action statements. These action statements are all implemented using function pointers that point back to operations defined within the *Context.* This is done because, almost always, actions to be executed must be defined within the *Context* and manipulate its member variables. The following behaviors are defined for *State* objects:

  1. idState identifies the state, using an integer or enumeration value.

  2. entryAction is an action to be executed when the state is entered.

  3. exitAction is an action to be executed when the state is executed.

4. doActivity is an action to be executed as long as the state is active.

- Transition
  In the simplest case, a transition has a single guard (implemented as a function pointer to an operation defined within the *Context* that returns a Boolean), a single action (similar to *State* object actions), and a single target state to be entered when the transition is taken. However, to handle conditional connectors, transitions must handle multiple guards, each with a separate associated action and target state. Thus, this class contains the following elements:

  1. nGuards, an attribute that identifies the number of conditions to be handled. If this is 0, then there are no branching conditions.

  2. lastTrueGuard, an attribute that, for efficiency reasons, identifies the index of the last guard that evaluated to TRUE. It is generally maintained to a testable sentinel value indicating NOT TESTED.

  3. setDefault, an operation that, when there are no branches, sets the guard and action operations to point to the specified operations defined within the *Context.*

  4. addGuard, an operation that, when there are conditional branches, sets a {guard, action, target state} triad so that its corresponding action will be executed and its corresponding target state will be entered if the guard evaluates to TRUE.

  5. guard executes the guards in order until one evaluates to TRUE or until it runs out of guards. The attribute lastTrueGuard is set to the first guard evaluating to TRUE.

  6. accept, an operation that assumes the guard has been passed. It uses the lastTrueGuard attribute to identify the guard that evaluated to TRUE and then executes its associated action. It returns the new target state and resets lastTrueGuard back to its sentinel value.

This pattern is very efficient during execution, but it can take longer to initialize than other design strategies. Also, the pattern handles nesting by flattening the statechart (removing all nesting). That is not difficult to achieve in state machines that don't use orthogonal components; to achieve it for state machines with orthogonal components is more difficult. The way to flatten a set of and-states is to produce a set of states that correspond to the cross-product of orthogonal region substates.

9.3.2.4 State-Walker Pattern

A graph-theoretic definition of a state machine is that it is a set of nodes, called states, connected by directed lines, called transitions. This definition can be implemented directly by constructing a generalized state graph and by using a State Walker to execute transitions over the graph.

The pattern shown in Figure 9-15 is similar to the State-Table Pattern, except that it is structured as a graph rather than as a table. This has the effect of not requiring the entire state space graph to be in main memory at one time. When the State Walker transitions to a new state, it can load the state information off disk storage, or it can scan one transition ahead and load all possible successor states.

9.3.2.5 Control-Loop Pattern

People frequently ask how to implement continuous behavior using discrete modeling languages, such as the UML. The Control-Loop Pattern is one straightforward means to accomplish this, although the pattern is a simple, special case of the Policy Pattern.

Most control loops are discretized implementations of continuous mathematical expressions, and we will limit our discussion to that type of controller. The *Context* class typically runs periodically. This can be explicitly modeled as a finite state machine with a tm() transition-to-self, or it can be done via other means, such as with periodic RTOS scheduling.

The control loop itself is frequently captured with control diagrams (rather than with UML diagrams) on which various mathematical operators, such as addition, subtraction, multiplication, division, integration, and differentiation, are used. The control loop is captured as a set of differential equations and ultimately implemented as a set of difference equations. These difference equations can be written as operations

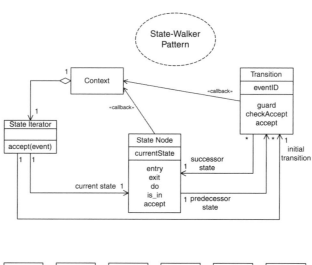

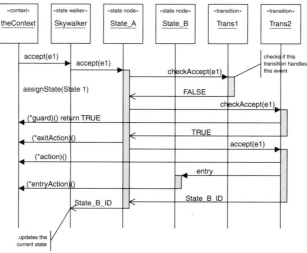

Figure 9-15: *State-Walker Pattern*

defined in the *Control Loop* class of Figure 9-16. This pattern consists of the following classes:

- Context
  This class owns the *Control Loop* and acts as a repository for the continuous variables manipulated within the *Control Loop*.

- Control Loop
  The *Control Loop* class is where the "magic" happens. It provides an interface consisting of initialize(), step(), and shutdown() operations. The key is the step() function, which executes the complete set of difference equations before returning. The step function usually calls private members that implement those difference equations. The *Control Loop* is a friend of the *Context* class, allowing it to access the latter's internal data members used to store the continuous variables required for the control loop.

- Abstract Sensor
  To simplify the construction of the control loop, the *Abstract Sensor* class defines a common interface to the *Concrete Sensor* classes. Most control loops perform closed-loop control of actuation, so the *Concrete Sensor* classes are vital.

- Abstract Actuator
  Similar in purpose to the *Abstract Sensor* class, this class provides a common interface and structure for the actual actuators used. Although many control loops control only a single actuator, generalizing their interface allows a system to be easily constructed from common parts.

- Concrete Sensor
  The *Concrete Sensor* represents the actual sensors used. These subclasses provide multiple implementations so that different types of sensors can be represented.

- Concrete Actuator
  This class represents different kinds of actuators. Many control loops use only a single actuator.

A simple control loop is shown in Figure 9-17. It basically takes a single input (x), scales it, combines it with a previous computation, and outputs the result. The top part of the figure shows the control loop. The middle part shows the corresponding object collaboration. The bottom part shows the algorithm that uses the activity diagram notation of the UML, discussed in Chapter 7. In this simple example, the step() operation probably executes the activity states in-line, manipulating the data members X_n, Y_n, Y_{n-1}, W_n, and Z_n residing within the *Context* class. In a more complicated example, each activity state might be implemented in a different operation in the *Control Loop* class.

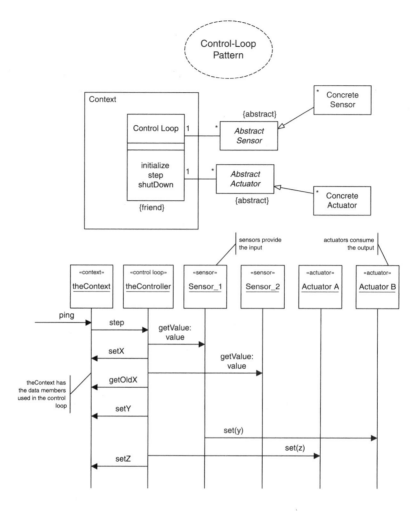

Figure 9-16: *Control-Loop Pattern*

9.3.2.6 Reactive Control-Loop Pattern

The Control-Loop Pattern works well for continuous behavior that spans the dynamic range of the inputs. Sometimes, however, different sets of equations must be used for the dynamic subranges of the input variables. This situation is handled best by treating the object behavior as piecewise continuous, requiring a combined approach of both statecharts and continuous mathematics. This Reactive Control-Loop Pattern shown in

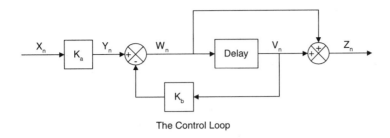

The Control Loop

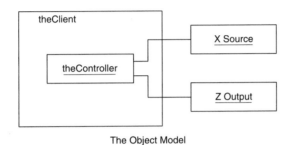

The Object Model

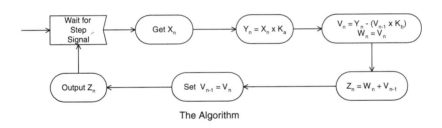

The Algorithm

Figure 9-17: *Control-Loop Example*

Figure 9-18 demonstrates a mechanism that achieves this combined behavior.

The pattern in Figure 9-18 combines the State and Control-Loop Patterns. The {map} constraint on the association between the *Abstract State* and *Abstract Control Loop* classes means that there is a one-to-one relation between the *Concrete State* and the *Concrete Control Loop* objects at run-time. The do() operation of the *Concrete State* class periodically calls the step() function of its corresponding *Concrete Control Loop* class.

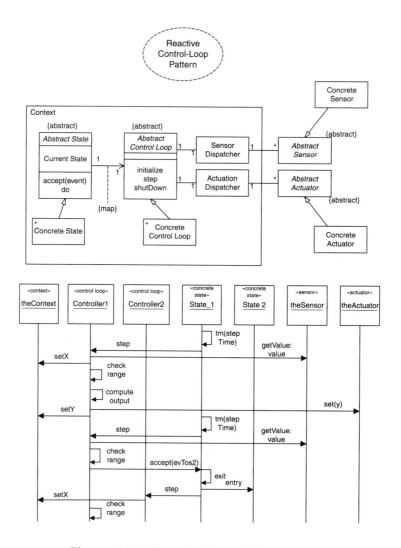

Figure 9-18: *Reactive Control-Loop Pattern*

This periodic invocation is generally modeled using an orthogonal region in the *Abstract State* class that contains a single *Waiting* state and a timeout transition-to-self. When this timer fires, it calls the step() function of the associated *Concrete Control Loop* class. All concrete subclasses of the *Abstract State* class inherit this high-level state machine and its periodic control function. This uses the Polling Behavior Pattern described in Chapter 12.

State transitions may be triggered by an external object, but the *Context* is usually assumed to automatically select the appropriate control function based on the inputs. This can be done in a couple of ways. One way is to check the range when the variable is read from the sensor and generate a propagated event to the currently active *Concrete State*. Another way is to provide a transition based on a change event on the input variables, suitably guarded to select the appropriate subsequent state. Still another way is to use a null-triggered transition with appropriate guards. Such an approach has a time complexity of $O(n)$, where n is the number of separately modeled input range states.

9.3.2.7 Fuzzy-State Pattern

Fuzzy sets have been used in a variety of closed-loop control problems with good success. They can be applied to any continuous control problem, and have successfully solved some problems that have not yet been solved by traditional closed-loop methods, such as balancing a multisegment inverted pendulum by controlling the x and y positions of its base.

Fuzzy systems are based on the premise of *fuzzy sets*—that is, sets that permit partial membership. Whenever traditional (called "crisp") sets are used, membership is an all-or-none proposition—the room is either *hot* or *not hot*. Statements like "The room is a little warm," or "The room is very cold," don't carry meaning in crisp logic, but they do in fuzzy logic. Membership in a fuzzy set is a continuous value from 0.0 ("completely false") to 1.0 ("completely true"), with all intermediate values possible. If two fuzzy states of room temperature are HOT and COLD, respectively, then "just right" might have a membership value of 0.5 in both sets at the same time.

The key to modeling fuzzy states is to remember that an object can be in every possible state at the same time, with possibly different degrees of truth. This means that the State Pattern, discussed earlier, is almost applicable. But rather than have a single state be the current state, all states are concurrently active, with different levels of membership. The controller then applies a set of mapping rules that map the input state memberships (depending on the value of the input variables) to the output states. The centroid is then computed on the fuzzy-state space of the output sets to arrive at a single output value for the controlled variable, in a process called *defuzzification*. The mapping rules themselves are represented in tabular format called *fuzzy associative memory*, or FAM. They represent IF (in input set) THEN (in output set) rules, which are then applied proportionally, depending on the degree that the predicate is true.

The Fuzzy-State Pattern is shown in Figure 9-19. The *Fuzzy Controller* steps the control process, much like the *Control Loop* does in the

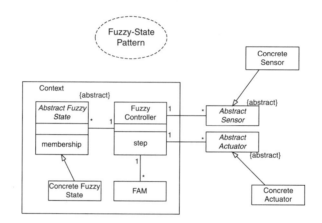

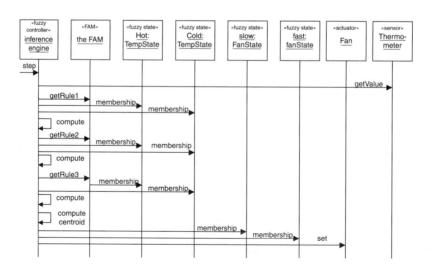

Figure 9-19: *Fuzzy-State Pattern*

Control-Loop Pattern. However, it gets the input values and, for each mapping rule in the FAM, it visits the *Fuzzy State* in the rule to determine the degree of membership based on the input values. It then applies the rule (which provides an output fuzzy-state membership) and scales it in according to that degree of membership. When all rules have been applied, the centroid of the output set memberships is computed, resulting in a single output control value. This completes the action of the step.

The closed-loop steam turbine controller in Figure 9-20 was adapted from [9]. The input data include the temperature from the *Temp Sensor* and the pressure from the *Pressure Sensor.*

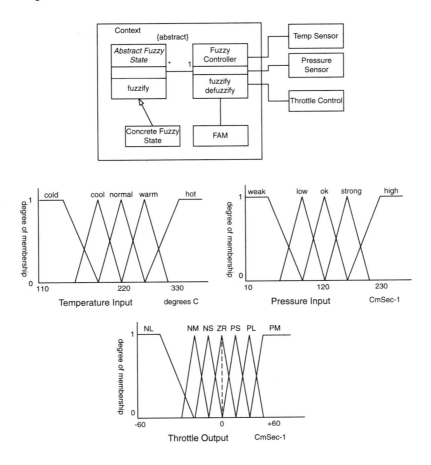

Figure 9-20: *Fuzzy Steam Turbine Controller*

Figure 9-20 provides both the object model for the collaboration and the set of membership functions. In this case, the steam turbine throttle is controlled by two inputs: temperature and pressure. Each of these inputs is divided into a set of fuzzy states, whose degree of membership, shown as a function of numeric value of the input, is shown graphically in the figure. Note that the membership functions are mostly triangular in shape (a common fuzzy idiom) and that the sets overlap. Note, for example, that a temperature of 200 degrees is about 0.72 in the *cool* state, about 0.45 in the *normal* state, and 0.0 in all other states. The membership functions for the two input variables, temperature and pressure, are given, along with that of the output control variable, throttle.

The fuzzy rule set, FAM, presented in Table 9-4, maps the state of the input variables to the state of the output variable. The way to think about this is that each cell is a separate equation mapping the input values to the commanded output. For example:

> IF (temperature is normal) AND (pressure is strong), THEN set turbine to NS.

The odd thing about fuzzy systems is that *all* these rules are applied all the time, scaled by the relative truth of the statement (the degree of membership). Because all the rules always apply, fine-grained control is possible. The mathematical result of simultaneous scaled application of all the rules computes the mathematical centroid of the output memberships. The computational process for arriving at a single output to the controlled variable, or *defuzzification*, is a topic too broad and deep to be considered here in any detail (the interested reader is referred to [9] and [10]).

Table 9-4: *Fuzzy Rule Set for Steam Turbine Controller*

	Weak	Low	OK	Strong	High
Cold	PL	PM	PS	NS	NM
Cool	PL	PM	ZR	NM	NM
Normal	PM	PS	ZR	NS	NM
Warm	PM	PS	NS	NM	NL
Hot	PS	PS	NM	NL	NL

9.3.2.8 Neural Network Pattern

Fuzzy states are appropriate when you know the mapping functions from the inputs to the output. However, this doesn't help when the mapping functions are unknown, hidden, or extremely complex. Neural networks[7] are a way of performing continuous control under such circumstances, because the neural network actually learns the mapping functions inherent in the data itself, by self-adaptation. It does this in a learning phase, in which training pairs, consisting of an input with a known output, are applied to the network. The synaptic strength of the inter-neuron connections is adjusted to minimize the error. This process is then applied to the next training pair, and so forth, until all training pairs in the training set have been applied. Then the entire process is repeated (typically, thousands of times) until the synapse weights have converged to values that generate a sufficiently low error on the training pairs or until the system gives up. Once trained, network learning is disabled, so application of the neural network is a simple and computationally efficient process.

Figure 9-21 shows a typical pattern for the implementation of a neural network. The behavior of neural networks was discussed in Chapter 7, and the reader is referred there for its operational semantics.

9.4 Summary

Mechanistic design is concerned with specifying the details of inter-object collaboration. Groups of objects acting together to achieve a common goal are referred to as *collaborations*. Collaborations can be generalized into design pattern *mechanisms* and applied in different situations that face similar problems. Mechanistic design takes the collaborative groups of objects identified in analysis and adds design-level objects to facilitate and direct their implementation. For example, containers and iterators are added to manage associations that consist of

---

7. There are zillions of different kinds of networks, but by far the most common in practice is the back-propagation neural network. The interested reader is referred to the references in Chapter 7 for more information in regard to other ways of wiring neural structures together. This pattern deals solely with back-propagation networks.

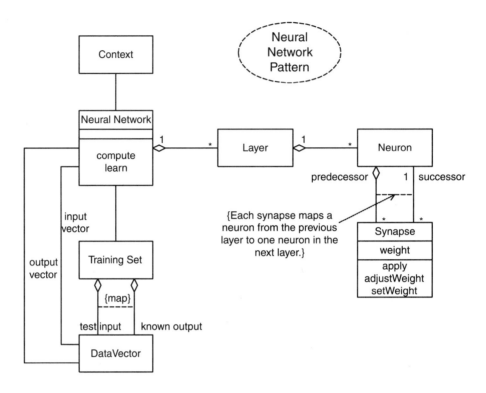

Figure 9-21: *Neural Network Pattern*

multiple objects. Smart pointer objects glue associations together in such a way as to eliminate memory leaks and inappropriate pointer dereferencing. Policy objects abstract away strategies and algorithms from their context so that they can be easily modified or replaced, even while the system executes.

Many of the objects added during mechanistic design reappear in designs because they solve common problems. These collaborations are reified into mechanistic design patterns. These patterns are templates of object interaction, consisting of a problem, a context, and a structural solution. The reification of the patterns allows them to be cataloged and studied systematically so that they can be reused in future projects. This chapter presented a number of patterns useful in mechanistic design. The interested reader is invited to explore the references for more patterns.

9.5 Looking Ahead

The final chapter in this section will discuss the detailed design of object-oriented systems in a real-time context. Detailed design is concerned with the implementation of data structures and algorithms within the scope of a single class. Space and time complexity tradeoffs are made during detailed design in order to achieve the performance requirements specified for your system.

9.6 Exercises

1. Compare and contrast use case, collaboration, and mechanism.
2. What are the three primary parts of a design pattern?
3. What are the common problems addressed by the Smart-Pointer Pattern?
4. When would you use the different patterns of State, State Table, and State Walker?
5. What pattern is appropriate to model collaborative behavior that is piece-wise continuous?
6. What is the different between a fuzzy state and a crisp state?

9.7 References

[1] Gamma, Erich, Richard Helm, Ralph Johnson, and John Vlissides. *Design Patterns*, Reading, Mass.: Addison-Wesley, 1995.
[2] Buschmann, Frank, Regine Meunier, Hans Rohnert, Peter Sommerlad, and Michael Stal. *A System of Patterns: Pattern-Oriented Software Architecture*, New York: John Wiley & Sons, Ltd., 1996.
[3] Coplien, James and Douglas Schmidt, ed. *Pattern Languages of Program Design*, Reading, Mass.: Addison-Wesley, 1995.
[4] Vlissides, John, James Coplien, and Norman Kerth, ed. *Pattern Languages of Program Design 2*, Reading, Mass.: Addison-Wesley, 1996.

[5] Douglass, Bruce Powel. *Real-Time UML: Developing Efficient Objects for Embedded Systems,* Reading, Mass.: Addison-Wesley, 1998.

[6] Douglass, Bruce. *Real-Time Design Patterns.* Forthcoming.

[7] Booch, Grady, James Rumbaugh, and Ivar Jacobson. *The Unified Modeling Language User Guide,* Reading, Mass.: Addison-Wesley, 1998.

[8] Meyer, Bertand. *Object-Oriented Software Construction, Second Edition,* Upper Saddle River, N.J.: Prentice Hall PTR, 1997.

[9] Cox, Earl. *The Fuzzy Systems Handbook,* Cambridge, Mass.: Academic Press, 1994.

[10] Jamshidi, Vadiee, and Ross. *Fuzzy Logic and Control,* Englewood Cliffs, N.J.: PTR Prentice Hall, 1993.

[11] Rumbaugh, James, Ivar Jacobson, and Grady Booch. *The Unified Modeling Language Reference Manual,* Reading, Mass.: Addison-Wesley, 1999.

Chapter 10

Detailed Design

You give power to that which you grant attention.

—Book of Douglass, Law 151

Of the three levels of design—architectural, mechanistic, and detailed—detailed design is the smallest in scope and the most concrete. Detailed design specifies details such as the storage format and range used for attributes, association-implementation strategy, the set of operations the object provides, how pre- and post-conditions will be ensured, the selection of internal algorithms, and the specification of exception handling, all within individual objects. In object-oriented systems, only a small percentage of objects typically require any special attention in detailed design, but those that do often play a crucial role in the overall performance of the system.

10.1 Introduction to Detailed Design

As one peruses the object-oriented literature, one is struck by how much the descriptions of behavior are dealt with by collaborations of objects. True, we discussed in some detail in Chapter 7 the construction of finite state machines, but for the most part, complex behavior has been delegated to societies of classes working together to achieve system-level behaviors. Indeed, these collaborations realize use cases, those named black-box functions. That's all well and good. This approach allows the development of systems that can produce arbitrarily elaborate behavior to deal with the most obtuse set of behavioral requirements. Nevertheless, there have been times when we have waved our hands and said, "Ignore the man behind the curtain." Certain objects do encapsulate rich, complicated data structures or complex algorithms. It is probably a mistake to implement a tightly coupled coherent function and spread it across too many objects, without a compelling reason. For example, a fast Fourier transform is probably best implemented by a single object. True, we can encapsulate some of the primitive matrix arithmetic within a matrix class, but linking together the matrix arithmetic into the Fast Fourier Transform (FFT) may be most efficaciously performed within a single object.

Remember that collaborations realize use cases. Collaborations are composed of objects of varying degrees of internal complexity. Any algorithms we design inside these objects must fit within the mission parameters of the collaboration. This means that whatever the optimization criteria is for the collaboration—minimal memory footprint, best average performance, best worst-case performance, and so forth—must also be applied to the individual objects within the collaboration. That process involves tradeoffs between the structuring of attributes and the set of operations that act on them. That's also a part of detailed design.

The focus of this chapter is to design in detail the "interesting objects" that appear from time to time in our collaborations.

10.2 Terms and Concepts

The scope of detailed design is limited to individual objects. Even though they may participate in complex collaborations at the mechanistic level, or complex strategic organizations at the architectural level, by far, most objects are structurally and algorithmically simple things. Nevertheless, in virtually all systems, some small set of objects is sufficiently rich and complicated to require special attention. The special concerns dealt with in detailed design are

- Data structuring of nonprimitive attributes or attribute collections
- Implementation of associations
- Detailed definition of the object interface
- Finalization of the operations defined for a class
- Algorithms implemented by those operations
- Exceptions handled and thrown

Data structuring is concerned with mapping complex data structures or, more commonly, effectively arranging multiples of structurally simple attributes. The UML perspective is that attributes ought to be structurally primitive things, and when they are not, they should be abstracted away into a separate class. This approach works well, in general, even when highly efficient access to the attribute is required. This doesn't mean, however, that it is always best to show that class on the class diagram, particularly in complex object spaces. The other issue of concern to data structuring is the selection and management of object collections. In mechanistic design, multivalued roles are reified into container objects, and these containers must be designed (or at least selected) to optimize the collaboration.

Associations are the glue that holds collaborations together. They are the conduits that allow the object messages to flow within the collaboration. Now that the concurrency model is complete and the mechanisms are elaborated, the implementation of the association must be selected. There are a number of possibilities: pointers, references, named handles, messages sent via the OS message queue, bus messages, RPCs, IPCs, and so on.

An interface in the UML is a cohesive, named collection of operations. An object can realize multiple interfaces just as one interface can be realized by different objects. The details of the object interfaces, if not yet fully defined, need to be completed in detailed design. These details include not only the set of operations and their signatures (parameter lists and return types), but also their protocols of interaction, pre-conditional invariants, post-conditional invariants, how and when these invariants will be validated at run-time, and what will be done if their assumptions are violated.

Algorithmic design is an area mostly ignored by books on object-oriented methods. However, it is vitally important in many, if not most, applications. Most applications have some localized pockets of algorithmic complexity that must be flushed out in detailed design.

The safety and reliability model is addressed at all three levels of design. The architectural design includes the definition of the safety and reliability channels. Mechanistic design deals with error and exception handling at the level of the collaboration. Now, at the level of individual objects, the objects' responsibilities for raising and handling exceptions and errors must be fully defined.

Let us now consider each of these concerns in more detail, with special attention paid to algorithmic design.

10.3 Data Structure

Data structuring has three primary concerns: the primitive representational types used to hold the attributes, the useful subranges of those primitive types (and the enforcement of those subranges), and the means by which we collect multiples of these attributes into encapsulated containers.

10.3.1 Primitive Representational Types

The UML doctrine calls for attributes to be structurally simple—things like ints and floats. Even strings are considered to be stretching the limit. However, it is not always efficient to treat a string as a separate object to which one must associate when such a data type already exists within the execution framework or implementation language. Rather than draw an association to a string class, sometimes it is just easier to say

OMString s;

within the object itself.

Likewise, when we manipulate a massive set of data, such as a queue of 20,000 waveform samples, the organizational principles must be aligned with the use of that information. Let us suppose that we have very tight timing constraints for the timely display of such waveform data, and that this data must be scaled in place in both time and amplitude. The organization we use for the entire set of data must facilitate the way in which this information will be manipulated. A linked list of samples implemented with pointers would be inefficient for such a purpose. Most likely, we would encapsulate this data in an array of some kind so that simple pointer increments could access the data in an efficient fashion. This doesn't mean that the samples themselves can't be individual objects of a waveform sample class, such as:

```
const WAVEFORM_SIZE = 20000;

class waveformSample {
protected:
    char sample; // signed values -128 to 127
public:
    char getSample(void) { return sample; }
    void setSample(char s) { sample = s; }
    // the char() operator does an explicit conversion
       when
    // the sample is used as a number.
    operator char() { return getSample(); }
}

class waveform {
protected:
    waveformSample data[WAVEFORM_SIZE];
public:
    waveformSample& operator[](unsigned int j) {
        if (j >= WAVEFORM_SIZE)
            throw range_error(j);
        return data[j];
    };
};

class STL_waveform {
protected:
    vector<waveformSample> data;  // STL vector
```

```
      vector_iterator<waveformSample> iter;   // STL
      vector iterator
   public:
      waveformSample& operator[] (unsigned int j) {
         if (j >= WAVEFORM_SIZE)
            throw range_error(j);
         return data[j];
      }; //
   };
```

The foregoing code shows how the waveformSample instances are collected together. The *waveform* class does so via a protected array member, while the *STL_waveform* class does it via the standard C++ STL vector container. These means of collecting the data need not be any less efficient than coding the operations directly in the *waveform* class, because the operations defined in the class body for *waveform* will be compiled as inline functions.

All attributes within an application must be implemented in terms of the primitive types provided by the implementation language. In detailed design, we must examine early choices of these primitive types and convince ourselves that they are most appropriate.

Naturally, a necessary condition for the attribute implementation type is that it can hold all the reasonable values that can be held by the attribute, and this ought to be true for all potential target platforms. Unfortunately, this is nontrivial to achieve. The size of int, for example, is permitted to vary within the C++ standard. This makes good sense because of the desire to make int-based arithmetic operations optimally efficient in the deployed application. However, this makes the selection of a base type more difficult, because the range an int can assume will differ between an 8-bit computing platform and a 32-bit platform. On the other hand, erring on the large size can use up more memory, which may be a constraining factor on the application. The common approach is to use the smallest-sized int type that can represent all valid values of the attribute in all cases.

Assuming that one can pick an appropriate, primitive data type for an attribute based on the range alone, however, is incorrect. One also must be concerned about issues such as round-off error and error accumulation, availability of math libraries of suitable precision for the selected primitive data type, and so on.

Consider a simple, complex number class. Most of the applications using complex numbers require fractional values, so that using ints for the real and imaginary parts wouldn't meet the need. What about using floats, as in:

```
class complex_1 {
public:
    float iPart, rPart;
    // operations omitted
};
```

That looks like a reasonable start. Is the range sufficient? Most floating-point implementations have a range of 10^{-40} to 10^{+40} or more, so that is probably okay. What about round-off error? Because the infinite continuous set of possible values is stored and manipulated as a finite set of machine numbers, just representing a continuous value that uses floating-point format incurs some error. Numerical analysis identifies two forms of numerical error—absolute error and relative error [1]. For example, consider adding two numbers, 123456 and 4.567891, using six-digit-precision, floating-point arithmetic:

$$123456.000000$$
$$+000004.567891$$
$$\overline{123460.567891} = 0.123460567891 \times 10^6$$

Because this must be stored in six-digit precision, the value will be stored as 0.123460×10^6, which is an absolute error of 0.567891. Relative error is computed as:

$$\frac{(A\text{-}B) - [m(A) - m(B)]}{A - B}$$

where $m(x)$ is the machine number representation of the value x. This gives us a relative error of 4.59977×10^{-8} for this calculation. Although this error is tiny, errors can propagate and build during repeated calculation, to the point of making your computations meaningless.

Subtraction of two values is a common source of significant error. For example,

$$-0.991012312$$
$$-0.991009987$$
$$\overline{-0.00002325} = 0.2325 \times 10^{-5}$$

But truncating these numbers to six digits of precision yields

$$-0.991012$$
$$-0.991010$$
$$\overline{-0.000002} = 0.20 \times 10^{-5}$$

which is an absolute error of 0.325×10^{-6} and a relative error of 14 percent. This means that we may have to change our format to include more significant digits, change our format entirely to use infinite-precision arithmetic,[1] or change our algorithms to equivalent forms when a loss of precision is likely—for example, when computing 1-cos(x) when the angle close to zero can result in the loss of precision. You can use the trigonometric relation

$$1 - \cos(\phi) = 2\sin\frac{\phi}{2}$$

to avoid round-off error.[2]

10.3.2 Subrange Constraints

Frequently, although a primitive data type is used, its entire range may not be needed. For example, an array index may be stored as an int, but negative values would be erroneous. If the valid set of attribute values is a subset of the range of the representational primitive type, then the set of valid attribute values is called the *subrange* of the primitive type. For cardinal types, such as int and long, it is common to have subranges. For example, consider the following *patient* class.

```
class patient {
protected:
    int weight_in_lbs;
    int height_in_inches;
    OMString name;
    int sex; // MALE==0 or FEMALE==1
    int age;
    long socialSecurityNumber;
};
```

---

1. Infinite-precision arithmetic is available in some LISP-based symbolic mathematics systems, such as Derive and MacSyma.
2. Widely different computational results of algebraically equivalent formulations can lead to hazardous situations. See [5].

Clearly, none of the numeric attributes of the class *patient* should be negative. If nothing else, we can at least use the unsigned types. However, even then, there are values that can be represented in the attribute that are clearly erroneous. What if weight_in_lbs should have the value 32,000? That is unlikely to be a reasonable value. Many programmers say that this just "can't happen" and ignore it. However, not only do programs have defects that can cause the value to be erroneously set, EMI and device malfunctions can lead to corrupted data even in otherwise perfect programs.

And, what are the consequences of this, should it happen? Suppose this attribute is used to compute a dosage for a syringe pump. A failure here could have catastrophic consequences to the patient.

For any kind of "hi-rel" (high-reliability) application, at minimum, values should not exceed the valid subrange of the attribute. In addition, the value itself should be validated with enough redundancy to detect corruption.

The common data ranges for numeric types in 32-bit C++ compilers are shown in Table 10-1, along with their size in bits. The value ranges are different for 8- and 16-bit computers, because compilers base the sizes of their numeric types on the bit sizes of the registers of the supported processors. Of course, confusing this is the issue of value alignment. On some processors, having attributes aligned on word boundaries makes their access more efficient. In a highly compute-bound process, it may be better to sacrifice the memory space in order to force word-boundary alignment of the attributes.

In terms of space efficiency and for the purpose of excluding obviously erroneous values, the *patient* class can be adapted as follows:

```
enum maleOrFemale {MALE, FEMALE};
class patient {
protected:
    unsigned int weight_in_lbs;
    unsigned char height_in_inches;
    OMString name;
    maleOrFemale sex; // MALE or FEMALE
    unsigned char age;
    unsigned long socialSecurityNumber;
};
```

However, even this isn't good enough. True, age can not be –10, but 255 is an unreasonably large value to permit. How can we suitably limit these attributes to reasonable values?

Table 10-1: *Common Type Ranges for 32-bit C++ Compilers*

Type	Low	High	Size in Bits
unsigned char	0	255	8
char	-128	127	8
short int	-32,768	32,767	16
unsigned int	0	4,294,967,295	32
int	-2,147,483,648	2,147,483,647	32
unsigned long	0	4,294,967,295	32
long	-2,147,483,648	2,147,483,647	32
float	3.4×10^{-38}	1.7×10^{38}	32
double	1.7×10^{-308}	3.4×10^{308}	64
long double	3.4×10^{-4932}	1.1×10^{4932}	80

There are two problems here. First, we must be able to capture the valid subranges. Second, we want to be able to enforce this representational and range invariant. In Pascal and Ada, you simply define a subrange type. However, C++ does not inherently support subranges. Nevertheless, the same approach works in C++, as well. What we want to do is create a subrange metatype in C++ where one does not exist now. The simplest way to do this is to use a C++ parameterized class, such as *subrange:*

```
enum maleOrFemale {MALE, FEMALE};

template <class tPrimitive, long tLow, long tHigh>
class subrange {
protected:
   tPrimitive value, copyOfValue;
   tPrimitive low;
   tPrimitive high;
public:
   subrange(tPrimitive initial=tLow):
      value(initial), copyOfValue(~initial) { };

   //
   // check that the value is in range. If not
```

```
       // throw an exception. Otherwise, store it
       // and its one's complement.
       //
       void setValue(tPrimitive sv) {
          if (sv >= tLow)
             if (sv <= tHigh) {
                value = sv;
                copyOfValue = ~sv;
                }
             else
                throw "Overshoot";
          else
             throw "Undershoot";
       }; // end setValue

       //
       // check that the stored value is a
       // ones complement of the copy. If
       // so, return the value, otherwise throw an
       // exception.
       //
       tPrimitive getValue(void) const {
          if (value == ~copyOfValue)
             return value;
          else
             throw "corrupt data";
          return tLow;
       }; // end getValue
       // assignment operator =
       subrange& operator=(const subrange& v) {
          if (this != &v) // not same instance
             setValue(v.getValue());
          return (*this);
       };

       // type conversion to the primitive type
       operator tPrimitive() { // cast to primitive type
          return getValue();
       };
}; // end template subrange

//
// define the relevant subrange types for the
// patient class
//
typedef subrange<int, 0, 10> tWeight;
```

```
typedef subrange<unsigned char, 0, 100> tHeight;
typedef subrange<unsigned char, 0, 150> tAge;
typedef subrange<unsigned long, 0, 999999999> tSSN;

class patient {
public:
   tWeight weight_in_lbs;
   tHeight height_in_inches;
   maleOrFemale sex;  // MALE or FEMALE
   tAge age;
   tSSN socialSecurityNumber;
};
```

The preceding code solves a number of issues with the original *patient* class. For example, the use of a parameterized class (template), along with the typedef type declarator, allows us to enforce the appropriate subranges for each of the subranged attributes: weight_in_lbs, for example, is no longer a simple int—now it is an instance of class *tWeight*. *tWeight* is, in turn, an instantiated class of the template *subrange.* The simple operation setValue checks to see that the value is in range before allowing its attribute to be updated. It solves another problem, as well—in memory, corruption of the attribute value. Because the value is stored twice (once in a 1's complement form), getValue can check it for corruption on every access. Should the data become corrupted, getValue can detect it and throw an exception for its client to handle.[3]

The really nice thing about this approach is that the details of subrange control are encapsulated away from the application class (*patient*). By abstracting the detail, it not only makes class *patient* easier to manipulate, it also allows the abstractions (represented by the typedefs) to be reused in other application-level classes. Should the subrange type need modification, there is now a central point (either the subrange template or the typedef) at which the change can be made to correct a defect for all the clients of this abstraction.

Subclasses may constrain their data ranges in different ways than their superclasses. Many designers feel that data constraints should monotonically decrease with subclass depth—that is, that a subclass may constrain a data range further than its superclass. Although systems

---

3. Because of the 1's-complement, the full primitive storage size was used in order to store the 1's-complement value, rather than the restricted subranges used previously.

can be built this way, this violates the Liskov Substitution Principle: An instance of a subclass must be freely substitutable for an instance of its superclass.

If a superclass declares a color attribute with a range of {white, yellow, blue, green, red, black}, and a subclass restricts it to {white, black}, then what happens if the client has a superclass pointer and sets the color to red?

```
enum color {white, yellow, blue, green, red, black};
class super {
protected:
    color c;
public:
    virtual void setColor(color temp); // all colors
    valid
};

class sub: public super {
public:
    virtual void setColor(color temp); // only white
    and black now valid
};
```

Increasing constraints down the superclass hierarchy is a dangerous policy if the subclass will be used in a polymorphic fashion.

At any rate, it is important that operations enforce their range constraints, including the range of indices used in array access.

10.3.3 Derived Attributes

Aside from normal attributes identified in the analysis model, detailed design may add *derived attributes*, as well. Derived attributes are values that can, in principle, be reconstructed from other attributes within the class but are added to optimize performance. They can be indicated on class diagrams with a «derived» stereotype, and by defining the derivation formula within an associated constraint, such as "{age = currentDate – startDate}".

For example, a sensor class may provide a 10-sample history, with a get(index) accessor method. If the clients often want to know the average measurement value, they can compute this from the history, but it is more convenient to add an average( ) operation.

```
class sensor {
    float value[10];
    int nMeasurements, currentMeasurment;
public:
    sensor(void): nMeasurements(0),
    currentMeasurement(0) {
        for (int j = 0; j<10; j++) value[j] = 0;
    };

        void accept(float tValue) {
            value[currentMeasurement] = tValue;
            currentMeasurement = (++currentMeasurement)
                \ 10;
            if (nMeasurements < 10) ++nMeasurements;
            };

        float get(int index=0) {
            int cIndex;
            if (nMeasurements > index) {
                cIndex = currentMeasurement-index-1;
            // last valid one
                if (cIndex < 0) cIndex += 10;
                return value[cIndex];
            else
                throw "No valid measurement at that index";
            };

        float average(void) {
            float sum = 0.0;
            if (nMeasurements > 0) {
                for (int j=0; j < nMeasurements-1; j++)
                    sum += value[j];
                return sum / nMeasurements;
                }
            else
                throw "No measurements to average";
            };
    };
```

The average() operation exists only to optimize the computational path (the client class could do it, as well, for example). If the average value was needed more frequently than the data was monitored, the average could be computed as the data is read:

```
class sensor {
   float value[10];
   float averageValue;
   int nMeasurements, currentMeasurement;
public:
   sensor(void): averageValue(0), nMeasurements(0),
         currentMeasurement(0) {
      for (int j = 0; j<10; j++) value[j] = 0;
   };

   void accept(float tValue) {
      value[currentMeasurement] = tValue;
      currentMeasurement = (++currentMeasurement) \ 10;
      if (nMeasurements < 10) ++nMeasurements;
         // compute average
      averageValue = 0;
      for (int j=0; j < nMeasurements-1; j++)
         averageValue += value[j];
         averageValue /= nMeasurements;
      };
   float get(int index=0) {
      int cIndex;
      if (nMeasurements > index) {
         cIndex = currentMeasurement-index-1;
         // last valid one
         if (cIndex < 0) cIndex += 10;
         return value[cIndex];
      else
         throw "No valid measurement at that index";
      };

   float average(void) {
      if (nMeasurements > 0)
         return averageValue;
      else
         throw "No measurements to average";
   };
};
```

In this case, the derived attribute averageValue is added to minimize the required computation when the average value is needed frequently.

10.3.4 Data-Collection Structure

Collections of primitive data attributes may be structured in myriad ways, including stacks, queues, lists, vectors, and a forest of trees. The layout of data collections is the subject of hundreds of volumes of research and practical applications. The UML provides a role constraint notation to indicate different kinds of collections that may be inherent in the analysis model. Common role-constraints for multivalued roles include

{ordered}   Collection is maintained in a sorted manner.

{bag}   Collection may have multiple copies of a single item.

{set}   Collection may have, at most, a single copy of a given item.

{hashed}   Collection is referenced via a keyed hash.

Some constraints may be combined, such as {ordered set}. Another common design scheme is to use a key value to retrieve an item from a collection. This is called a *qualified association,* and the key value is called a *qualifier.*

Figure 10-1 shows examples of constraints and qualified associations. An association qualifier is shown as a named box on one end of an association, such as the *Personnel ID* box at the *Roster* end of the association, between the classes *Roster* and *Person.* This means that *Personnel ID* is an attribute of class *Person,* which is used as a qualifier (an index or key into the *Roster* class). Similarly, *Log In ID* is a qualifier for *Person* into the *Launch Control* class, and *Missile ID* is a qualifier used to identify the appropriate *Missile* to launch.

There are also a number of constraints in Figure 10-1. Constraints are additional rules added to the normal predefined UML semantics to account for special limitations within the problem context. Most of the constraints in the figure apply to association roles. For example, the multivalued roles of the *Person* role in the *Roster* ←→ *Person* association, is constrained to be an ordered list, while the Missile role in the *Launch Control* ←→ *Missile* association is an ordered set. Also note that there is a subset that maps constraint between the *Person* and *Missile Operator* objects. This means that all *Missile Operators* are map 1-to-1 to *Persons,* but not vice versa.

The constraints in Figure 10-1 are design decisions that reflect essential characteristics of the organization of the collection of the mul-

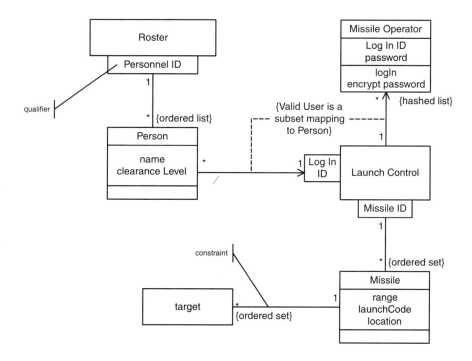

Figure 10-1: *Role Constraints and Qualified Associations*

tivalued role end. The selection of a collection structure depends on which characteristics should be optimized. Balanced trees, for example, are fast to search (O(log n)), but inserting new elements is complex and costly because of the need to rotate the tree to maintain balance. Linked lists are simple to maintain, but searching takes relatively long (O(n)). Balanced trees are most appropriate when the data structure is searched more frequently than it is updated. Linked lists are most appropriate when lists are updated more often.

10.4 Associations

Associations among objects allow client objects to invoke the operations provided by server objects. There are many ways to implement associations, depending on the nature and locality of the objects and their association. Implementations appropriate for objects within the same thread fail when used across thread or processor boundaries. Accessing objects with multivalued roles must be done differently than with a 1-to-1 association. Some implementation strategies that work for composition don't work for client-server associations. One purpose of detailed design is to resolve the management of associations between the objects.

The simplest cases are the 1-to-1 and 1-to-(0,1) associations between objects within the same thread. In this case, the 1-to-(0,1) is best done with a pointer to the server object, because there are times when the role multiplicity will be zero (that is, the pointer will be NULL). A 1-to-1 association may also be implemented with a reference (in the C++ sense) because the association link is always valid.[4] A 1-to-1 composition association may also use an inline class declaration, which would be inappropriate for the more loosely coupled client-server association. Normal aggregation is implemented in exactly the same way as an association. The following class shows these simple approaches.

```
class testAssoc {
    T myT;      // appropriate only for 1-to-1 composition
    T* myT2;    // ok for 1-to-1 or 1-to-(0,1) association
    // or composition
    T& myT3;    // ok for 1-1 association or composition
};
```

As discussed earlier, multivalued roles are most often resolved by using the Container Pattern. This involves inserting a container class between the two classes with the multivalued roles, and possibly iterators, as well, as shown in Figure 10-2. The basic idea of the Container Pattern is that whenever there is a multivalued role end in a collaboration, a class whose responsibility is the management of the containment of the multiple objects is inserted between the context and the contained objects. Iterators are used to provide multiple-client-safe iteration over the container. A simple example of this insertion is shown in Figure 10-2. In this case, the linked list class knows how to perform containment operations (insertion, deletion, and access), while the iterator knows how to reference individual contained objects within the collection. The container pattern is discussed in more detail in [4].

---

4. C++ requires that references always be valid—that is, a null reference is semantically illegal.

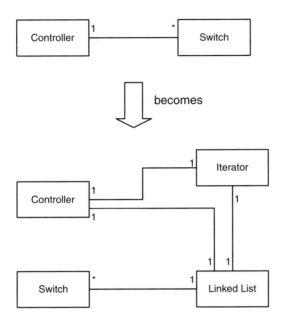

Figure 10-2: *Container Pattern Applied to Multivalued Role*

Crossing thread boundaries complicates the resolution of associations. Simply calling an operation across a thread boundary is not generally a good idea because of mutual exclusion and reentrancy problems. It can be done if sufficient care is taken. The target operation can be protected using mutual exclusion guards, and both sides must agree on the appropriate behavior if access cannot be immediately granted. Should the caller be blocked? Should the caller return immediately with an indication of failure? Should the caller be blocked, but only for a maximum period of time? All of these rendezvous are possible and appropriate in different circumstances.

Although directly calling an operation across a thread boundary is lightweight and efficient, it is not always the best way. If the underlying operating system or hardware enforces segmented address spaces for threads, it may not even be possible. Operating systems provide additional means for inter-task communication, such as OS message queues and OS pipes.

An OS message queue is the most popular approach for requesting services across a thread boundary. The receiver thread's active object reads the message queue and dispatches the message to an appropriate component object. This approach has a fairly heavy run-time cost, but it maintains the inherent asychronicity of the threads.

OS pipes are an alternative to message queues. They are opened by both client and server objects and are a slightly more direct approach for the client to invoke the services of the server.

When the service request must cross processor boundaries, the objects must be more decoupled. Common operating services to meet intra-processor communications include sockets and remote procedure calls (RPCs). Sockets usually implement a specified TCP/IP protocol across a network. The common protocols are the Transmission Control Protocol (TCP) and User Datagram Protocol (UDP). The TCP/IP protocol suite does not make any guarantees about timing, but it can be placed on top of a data link layer that does. TCP supports reliable transmission by using acknowledged transmission, and it also supports stream sockets. UDP is simpler and makes no guarantees about reliable transmission.

Finally, some systems use RPCs. Generally, RPCs are implemented using a blocking protocol so that the client is blocked until the remote procedure completes. This maintains the function call-like semantics of the RPC, but it may be inappropriate in some cases.

Any of the approaches that cross the thread boundary (with the exception of the direct guarded call) requires a different implementation in the client class. The client must now know the thread ID and a logical object ID to invoke the services. So rather than a C++ pointer or reference, ad hoc operating system-dependent means must be used. For example, a thread ID might be used to send a message to an active object (or one of its component parts) that is the root of a RTOS thread, or an object handle might be used in an application distributed across multiple processors.

In addition, several patterns can be used to streamline message passing along an association (see [4]). When there are multiple clients for a single server, the Observer Pattern facilitates timely updates of the clients. The clients register with the server and provide an address (typically, of a callback function). When the data in the server changes, the server then walks down the list of registered clients and notifies each of them. The Proxy and Broker Patterns (discussed in Chapter 8) are specialized forms of the Observer Pattern and are useful for situations in which clients are not in the same address space as the server and when it isn't known where the server and clients will reside at run-time.

Note that this discussion has been independent of the underlying physical medium of inter-processor communication. It can be implemented using shared memory, Ethernet networks, or various kinds of buses, as appropriate. Reusable protocols built using the Layered Architecture Pattern can replace one data link layer with another that is more suitable for a different physical medium, with a minimum of fuss.

10.5 The Object Interface

An interface is a named set of operations. An interface in the UML is an abstract notion that cannot be instantiated. Instead, interfaces are *realized* by either logical elements (classes and packages) or run-time artifacts (components). Interfaces may define an operation and its signature but not its implementation. Neither may interfaces have attributes. A client class may *depend on* (use) an interface. Interfaces decouple the declaration of a set of services from the entities that provide them. Some languages provide interfaces as a native construct (notably Java); in other languages, interfaces remain either an abstract notion or may be reified as classes that do nothing other than implement their operations by calling methods defined by other (implementation) classes.

Figure 10-3 shows two examples of interfaces that use the UML notation. In the upper part of the figure, the most common notational form is shown—the so-called *lollipop icon*. Note that the interface has a name (*iSensor*) and associates to the class *Optical Detector* to realize the interface. The client of the interface, in this case the *Alarm Manager,* depends on that interface, as shown by the dependency arrow.

This notation doesn't show the operations provided by the interface. When desired, the interface may be shown as a class box with the «interface» stereotype, as shown in the lower half of the figure. In this notation, the operations are shown, as well as several classes that can realize that interface. More information than this can be shown, as well. It is common to link constraints to the operations, such as pre-conditional and post-conditional invariants. Interfaces may also have associated statecharts that define acceptable sequences of operation invocations.

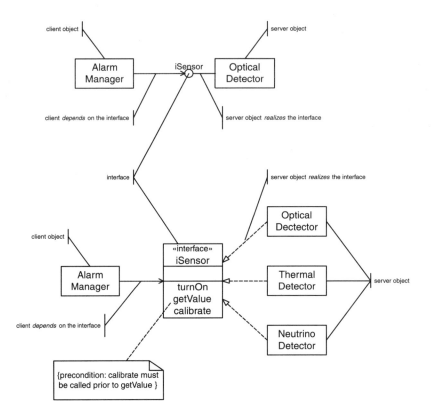

Figure 10-3: *Object Interfaces*

Interfaces may be realized by different classes. This provides a great deal of flexibility. For example, interfaces are generalizable elements, so interface and realizing classes may participate in independent generalization taxonomies. Interfaces are realized by different classes for a variety of reasons. A common reason is that a set of classes may implement the same set of operations but may be optimized for different purposes. One may be optimized for bounded worst-case behavior while another provides best average case, another predictability, another accuracy, and still another minimizes dynamic memory utilization. Another reason for the separation of class and interface is that the implementation of the various realizing classes may differ because of underlying technology. In Figure 10-3, the different classes that realize the *iSensor* interface do so on the basis of implementation hardware

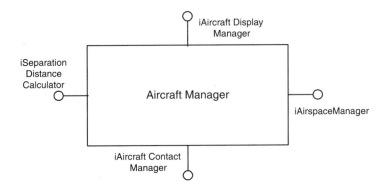

Figure 10-4: *Multiple Interfaces for a Single Class*

technology. The separation of the interface allows the developer to construct a system in which it is easy to link different parts to create customized applications.

Not only can a single interface be realized by a number of classes, the reverse is also true—a single class may realize different interfaces. Interfaces map closely to object roles—that is, the roles that objects play in collaborations. Roles are indicated on class diagrams with (optional) role names. A role is a purpose or responsibility of an object within the context of the collaboration. In a logical sense, every role played by a class defines an interface that must be realized by that class. For example, in our Acme Air Traffic Control System, the *Aircraft Manager* plays multiple roles. It is used to compute separation distance violations, get the aircraft information to display on the screen, and generally manage the airspace. Figure 10-4 shows several interfaces for the *Aircraft Manager* class, taken from various collaborations in which it participates.

10.6 Definition of Operations

The operations defined by a class specify how the data may be manipulated. Generally, a complete set of primitive operations maximizes reusability. A *set* class template typically provides operators, such as add item or set, remove item or subset, and test for item or subset membership. Even if the current application doesn't use all these operations, adding the complete list of primitives makes it more likely to meet the needs of the next system.

Analysis models class operations as the recipients of object messages (on class, object, sequence, and collaboration diagrams), state event acceptors (on statecharts), and as actions and activities (also on statecharts). The great majority of the time, these messages are directly implemented as operations in the server class, using the implementation strategy for the association supporting the message passing (see Section 10.4).

Analysis and early design models specify only the public operations. Detailed design often adds operations that are used only internally. These operations are due to the functional decomposition of the public operations or actions and activities on statecharts. For example, a queue might provide the following set of public operations:

```
template <class T, int size>
class queue {
protected:
    T q[size];
    int head, tail;
public:
    queue(void): head(0), tail(0);
    virtual void put(T  myT);
    virtual T get(void);
};
```

A cached queue caches data locally but stores most of it on a more remote, but larger, data store, such as a hard disk. Operations can be added to implement the caching so that it is invisible to the client, maintaining LSP:

```
template <class T, int size>
class cachedQueue : public queue<T, size> {
protected:
    void writeToDisk(void);
    void readFromDisk(void);
public:
    cachedQueue(void): head(0), tail(0);
    virtual void put(T  myT);        // new version uses
                                            writeToDisk
        // when cache fills
    virtual T get(void);                // new version uses
                                            readFromDisk
        // when data is not cached
};
```

These operations are added to support the additional functionality of the *cachedQueue* subclass.

10.7 Detailed Algorithmic Design

An algorithm is a step-by-step procedure for computing a desired result. The complexity of algorithms may be defined in many ways, but the most common is *time complexity,* the amount of execution time required to compute the result. Algorithmic complexity is expressed using the "order of" notation. Common algorithmic complexities are

$O(c)$

$O(\log_2 n)$

$O(n)$

$O(n \log_2 n)$

$O(n^2)$

$O(n^3)$

where c is a constant and n is the number of elements participating in the algorithmic computation.

All algorithms with the same complexity differ from each other only by a multiplicative and additive constant. Thus, it is possible for one $O(n)$ algorithm to perform 100 times faster than another $O(n)$ algorithm and be considered of equal time complexity. It is even possible for an $O(n^2)$ algorithm to outperform an $O(c)$ algorithm for sufficiently small n. The algorithmic complexity is most useful when the number of entities manipulated is large (as in "asymptotically approaching infinity") because then these constants become insignificant and the complexity order dictates performance. For small n, they can only be given rules of thumb.

Objects may be designed to optimize

- Run-time performance—for example, average performance, worst-case performance, predictability
- Run-time memory requirements
- Simplicity and correctness

- Development time and effort
- Reusability
- Extensibility
- Reliability
- Safety

Of course, to some degree, these are conflicting goals. For example, some objects must maintain their elements in sorted order. A Bubble sort is very simple, so it requires a minimum of development time. Although it has a worst case run-time performance of $O(n^2)$, it can actually have better performance than more-efficient algorithms if n is small. Quicksort is generally much faster ($O(\log_2 n)$) but is more complicated to implement. It is not always best to use a Quicksort and it is not always worst to use a Bubble sort, even if the Quicksort is demonstrably faster for the data set. Most systems spend most of their time executing a small portion of the code. If the sorting effort is tiny compared with other system functions, the additional time necessary to correctly implement the Quicksort might be more profitably spent elsewhere.

Some algorithms have good average performance, but their worst-case performance may be unacceptable. In real-time systems, raw performance is usually not the most important criterion—deterministic performance may be more crucial. Often, embedded systems must run in a minimum of memory, so efficient use of existing resources may be crucial. The job of the designer is to make the set of design choices that result in the best overall system.

Classes with rich behavior must not only perform correctly, they must also help meet the system level quality of service requirements, such as performance. Most often, average execution speed is the criterion used for algorithm selection, but as we saw earlier, many other criteria may be used. Once the appropriate algorithm is selected, the operations and attributes of the class must be designed to implement the algorithm. This will often result in new attributes and operations that assist in the execution of the algorithm.

10.7.1 Representing Algorithms in the UML

Single- and multi-threaded algorithms can be captured in the UML in several ways. Statecharts, dealt with in Chapter 7, are a common way of describing event-driven algorithms. It is not the best representation for algorithms that are driven by the completion of activities. For this kind of algorithm, the UML provides *activity diagrams,* also introduced in Chapter 7.

Activity diagrams may be categorized in many ways, depending on one's perspective. They are a kind of concurrent flowchart and can easily depict programmatic constructs of sequence, branch, loop, fork and join, as shown in Figure 7-27.

Sequence diagrams, shown in detail elsewhere in this book, can also be used to show algorithms within individual objects. Sequence diagrams usually show multiple objects collaborating by sending messages. These messages can be explicit function calls to show detailed algorithms. Sequence diagrams are weaker than activity diagrams in the sense that they don't show concurrency well.

Algorithms prescribe the activities that constitute a desired process [3]. That is, algorithms are in their very essence the decomposition of a function into well-defined sequences of smaller functions. This does not obviate the power of the object-oriented approach, it enhances it.

10.7.2 Algorithmic Example: Run-Time Data Interpolation

Let us consider a sample problem. Figure 10-5 shows the class model for a closed-loop control system. The *Controller* class has responsibility for monitoring the *Sensor* and outputting an appropriate value to the *Actuator.* In this example, the response is computed from a stimulus-response curve represented by a fixed number of *Data Samples.* Each *Data Sample* consists of a stimulus (x) value and a corresponding response (y) value. The data samples are not necessarily equally spaced in the stimulus space.

Because the stimulus is a real number, the value from the *Sensor* may not correspond to a value in our *Data Table.* Therefore, the *Response Calculator* may need to interpolate the data if the stimulus value doesn't exactly match the data stored in the *Data Table.* It is known that the stimulus-response curve is smooth but has great variation and fluctuation. Simple linear interpolation does not provide enough accuracy. In addition, this application requires exactly correct values for the stimuli directly captured in the set of samples. This means that nonlinear regression is out, as well, because regression finds the parameters of a curve that minimize the sum of the square of the error but always produce

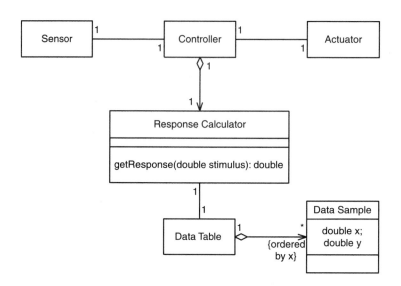

Figure 10-5: *Class Model for Algorithm Example*

some error. A Newton interpolating polynomial meets these criteria, but this technique results in a wildly fluctuating curve (even though it passes through all the represented data points) when the number of points is large. After some analysis, it has been determined that a cubic spline approximation will meet the needs of the interpolation accuracy.

A spline function works by dividing up a complex curve into a set of piece-wise curves, one curve for each interval between adjacent (x,y) data points. These smaller curves are then fitted together at the adjoining points with smoothness criteria. Because the curves meet at the represented points, the curves go through those points exactly (as required in our problem statement). If the stimulus is between two represented points, then the algorithm must select the appropriate piece-wise curve and use it to compute the response value. The process is computationally efficient and accurate—perfect for our own application needs.

In this application, we want to be able to upload new sets of data points as it runs, so the application must be able to construct the spline functions *in vivo*, as well as use them to calculate a response to an incoming stimulus.

Figure 10-6 shows how a spline function works. The figure shows 11 sets of stimulus-response points and 10 curves (S_1 through S_{10}) between

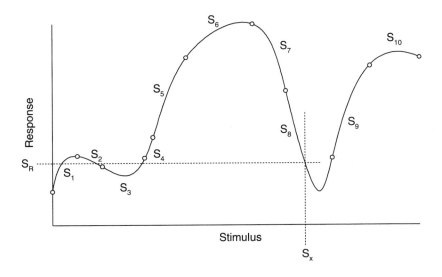

Figure 10-6: *Typical Spline Function*

them.[5] To compute a value for S_x, the *Response Calculator* would select the piece-wise curve S_8 and compute the resulting value S_R.

10.7.2.1 The Math

Cubic splines are one of several kinds of spline functions. Cubic splines are piece-wise cubic functions of the form

$$s_j(x) = a_j x^3 + b_j x^2 + c_j x + d_j$$

that go through two points (x_1, y_1) and (x_2, y_2). Adjacent spline functions meet at the represented data points—that is,

$$S_{j-1}(a) = S_j(a)$$

where a is the high endpoint of S_{j-1} and the low endpoint of S_j.

Additional smoothness criteria are added to uniquely define the parameters of the equation. One criterion is that the first and second

---

5. In general, for *n* points, *n*-1 spline curves are produced.

derivatives of adjoining splines at the point of intersection are equal. That is, if two spline functions S_{j-1} and S_j meet at point a, then

$$\lim_{x \to a^+} S_{j-1}^{(k)}(x) = \lim_{x \to a^-} S_j^{(k)}(x)$$

That is, the derivative at a is the same whether it is approached positively from S_{j-1} or negatively from S_j for all k derivatives of S_{j-1} and S_j. In cubic splines, the only derivatives of concern are the first and second derivatives (k=1 and k=2, respectively).

Two more conditions must be placed on the set of equations to use all available degrees of freedom and define a unique solution. A common restriction is to force the second derivative of the endpoints of the data points to be zero—that is,

$$S_1''(x_1) = S_n''(x_{n-1}) = 0$$

The constraint in the second equation makes the set of equations a *natural spline*.

Let use define the cubic function S_j over the region $[x_j, x_{j+1}]$, where x_j and x_{j+1} are values for which we know the value of the function a priori. The second derivative of S_j is a linear function that takes on the value a_j at x_j and a_{j+1} at x_{j+1}. This defines the function $S_j''(x)$:

$$S_j''(x) = \frac{a_{j+1}(x - x_j) + a_j(x_{j+1} - x)}{x_{j+1} - x_j}$$

Note that $S''(x_j) = a_j$ and $S''(x_{j+1}) = a_{j+1}$ (the specified derivatives of $S_j(x)$ at the endpoints), as required.

Integrating twice to get $S_j(x)$, we get

$$S_j(x) = \frac{a_{j+1}}{6(x_{j+1} - x_j)}(x - x_j)^3 + \frac{a_j}{6(x_{j+1} - x_j)}(x_{j+1} - x)^3 + b(x - x_j) + c(x_{j+1} - x)$$

where b and c are constants generated by the integration. These can be solved for because we know from our data table that $S_j(x_j) = y_j$ and $S_j(x_{j+1}) = y_{j+1}$.

If we define hj to be the size of the j-th interval (that is, $x_{j+1}-x_j$) and we combine the constraint so that the first derivatives at the endpoints between adjacent spline functions must be equal (that is, $S_j''(x_{j+1}) = S_{j+1}''(x_{j+1})$), then we can write

$$h_{j-1}a_{j-1} + 2(h_{j-1} + h_j)a_j + h_j a_{j+1} = 6\left[\frac{(y_{j+1} - y_j)}{h_j} - \frac{(y_j - y_{j-1})}{h_{j-1}}\right]$$

If n is the number of data (x,y) pairs, then the system to be solved is a set of n-2 equations in which everything is known from the data table except the a_j parameters. Furthermore, we know a priori that $a_0 = a_n = 0$ because we decided to use a natural spline.

It is possible to write this entire set of equations as a tridiagonal matrix equation and solve it by using techniques such as Gaussian elimination. It is possible to write the algorithm to compute the parameters as follows:

1. For j=0 to n-1, define $h_j = x_{j+1} - x_j$
2. Define the elements of a tridiagonal matrix **Ta = b** from the preceding equation, where
   - **a** is the vector of unknown a_j elements
   - **b** is the vector of values on the right side of the preceding equation,
   - **T** is the tridiagonal matrix in which

     Rows 2 through n-2 are the individual terms on the left side of the equation

     The first elements of the first row are $2(h_0+h_1)$ and h_1, respectively

     The last elements of the last row are h_{n-2} and $(2h_{n-2} + 3* (h_{n-1})/2$, respectively
3. Solve the matrix equation to find the elements of **a**. These are the parameters necessary to apply the spline functions to compute an interpolated output.

This algorithm needs to be executed only once on a given data set, such as when a data table is received by the *Response Calculator*. To compute a response to an input stimulus, use the second algorithm:

1. Find the segment, such as x resides in $[x_j <= x <= x_{j+1}]$.
2. Interpolate the value using the following equation.

$$y = \frac{a_j}{6}\left[\frac{(x_{j+1}-x)^3}{h_j} - h_j(x_{j+1}-x)\right] + \frac{a_{j+1}}{6}\left[\frac{(x-x_j)^3}{h_j} - h_j(x-x_j)\right] + y_j\left(\frac{x_{j+1}-x}{h_j}\right) + y_{j+1}\left(\frac{x-x_j}{h_j}\right)$$

10.7.2.2 Binding the Object Model with the Algorithm

Clearly, the algorithms defined in the previous section are implemented within the *Response Calculator* class. We can refine the class model in Figure 10-5 to add the pieces we need: an object that knows how to perform Gaussian elimination (an example of abstracting away a computational policy using the Policy Pattern (see [4])), the values that define the tridiagonal matrix **T** (which can be represented as the three vectors, because we know all other elements of the matrix are zero), and the **a** and **d** vectors. For interpolation, the *Response Calculator* must be able to efficiently search the data points to find the correct range and then apply the interpolation computation equation. The elaborated object model is shown in Figure 10-7.

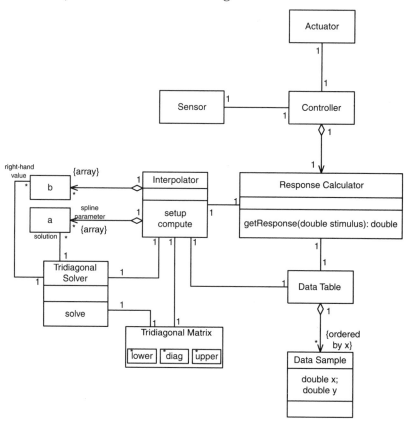

Figure 10-7: *Class Model Elaborated to Add Algorithm Details*

The policy class, called *Tridiagonal Solver,* uses an optimized form of Gaussian elimination. Other algorithms are possible, but let's use our third algorithm:

1. Define a tridiagonal system $\mathbf{Tx=d}$. $\mathbf{T}$ is represented as three vectors (**lower, diag, upper**)
2. Perform upper triangulation for j=2 to n
   - ratio $= \text{lower}_j / \text{diag}_{j-1}$
   - $\text{diag}_j = \text{diag}_j - \text{ratio} * \text{upper}_{j-1}$
   - if $\text{diag}_j == 0$ throw "Singular Matrix – No Solution," exit
   - $d_j = d_j - \text{ratio} * d_{j-1}$
3. Perform backward substitution
   - $x_n = d_n / \text{diag}_n$
   - for j=n-1 to 1 step –1
     $$x_j = (d_j - \text{upper}_j * x_{j+1}) / \text{diag}_j$$
4. Solution is in $\mathbf{x}$.

Now that we know where the algorithm will be added, how can we represent the algorithm itself? Let's use an activity diagram bound to the operations exposed in the interface in the *Response Calculator* and *Tridiagonal Solver* classes.

The activity diagram for the *setup()* operation of the *interpolator* class in Figure 10-8 is written at a high level. First we store the data set, then we compute the interval ranges (as a run-time optimization—they can also be computed when needed), and then we construct the various vectors needed for subsequent computation. The tridiagonal matrix $\mathbf{T}$ is constructed by making vectors **lower, diag,** and **upper**. This is all that is required to represent a tridiagonal matrix (a matrix in which all elements are zero except the main diagonal and the diagonals immediately above and below it). Then the vector $\mathbf{b}$ is constructed from the equations. Finally, the *Tridiagonal Solver::solve()* operation is called to construct the $\mathbf{a}$ vector. The $\mathbf{a}$ vector contains the parameters used in the set of spline functions shown in our interpolation computation equation. That completes the setup process. Now the *Response Calculator* (via the *interpolator::compute()* function) is ready to return a stimulus value for an input response.

interpolator::setup(x)

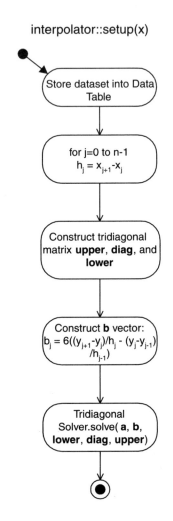

Figure 10-8: *Activity Diagram for* interpolator::setup() *Operation*

Figure 10-9 shows the activity diagram for the *interpolator::compute()* operation. This is shown in more detail. Most of the diagram is concerned with the efficient identification of the correct interval and spline function. The algorithm shown uses a binary search, which has O(log n) time complexity.

Finally, Figure 10-10 shows the algorithm for the optimized form of Gaussian elimination used for the triangular matrix decomposition.

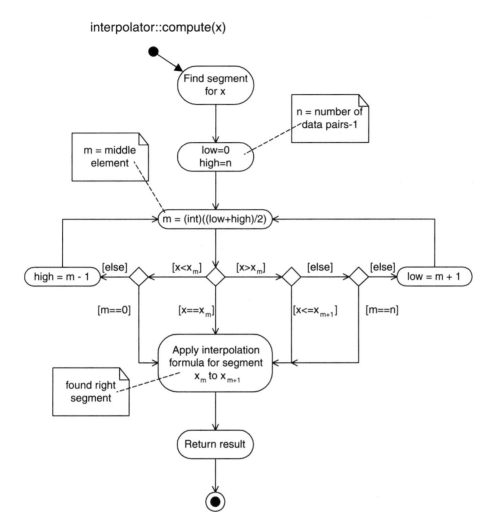

Figure 10-9: *Activity Diagram for* interpolator::compute() *Operation*

Activity diagrams are a great way to show algorithmic detail. Not only can they function as simple flowcharts, as we learned in Chapter 7, they also support concurrency modeling and the asynchronous communication of signals.

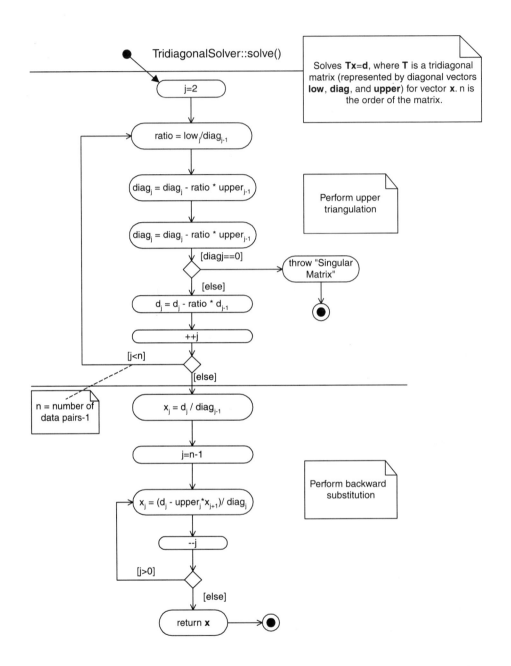

Figure 10-10: *Activity Diagram for* TridiagonalSolver::solve() *Operation*

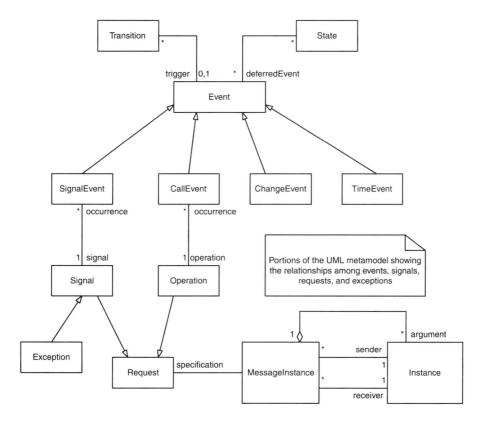

Figure 10-11: *UML Exceptions*

10.8 Exceptions

In the UML, a *Signal* is a metaclass defined as a "specification of an asynchronous stimulus communicated between instances" [4]. An *Exception* is a specialized kind of *Signal,* used when the stimulus is a fault of some kind, such as the violation of a pre-conditional or range invariant. An *Event* is a "specification of a significant occurrence that has a location in time and space" [4]. As we can see in Figure 10-11, *SignalEvent* is one of four kinds of *Event* (specifically, the type that associates with *Signal*). Furthermore, *Signal* and *Operation* are the two kinds of *Request,* which are specifications of *MessageInstances,* sent from one *Instance* to another during the execution of the application.

Fortunately, a detailed understanding of the subtleties of these metaclass relations isn't required to effectively model exceptions in applications. The thing to remember is that *Exception* is a specialized kind of *Signal* and a *Signal* associates with a specialized kind of *Event*. This allows us to create instances of *Exceptions* and deal with them in our applications. The common approach to explicitly model a *Signal* and its specialized child, *Exception*, is to represent both of them as class stereotypes. Once this is done, the taxonomies of *Signal* that are important to your application environment can be modeled and manipulated.

Class operations are the things that raise (or *throw*, in C++-speak) exceptions. In the UML, there is a special kind of dependency called «send», which represents the passing of a *MessageInstance* to an object. As you can see in Figure 10-11, a *MessageInstance* associates with a *Request*, one type of which is the *Signal*. This means that we can create class diagrams on which exceptions are drawn as stereotyped classes on which other class operations depend, as shown in Figure 10-12.

In the figure, the application domain classes *controller, deviceInterface, sensor,* and *actuator* collaborate to achieve a closed-loop control system. Several operations send signals and exceptions, when appropriate. The taxonomies for the *appSignals* and the *appExceptions* are shown in the figure, along with the operations that can send them. This class diagram documents the exceptions that can be thrown from the operations. Another approach is to add additional compartments, named «Signal» and «Exception», which explicitly list the signals and exceptions sent by the class. This approach is viable but doesn't show which operations can send the signals.

Class models provide a static structural view of the object model. It is frequently useful to show the sending of signals and exceptions in a scenario. This can be done by stereotyping the message instances sent among the object instances on a sequence diagram. For example, Figure 10-13 shows the interaction of the application domain classes from the previous figure. Certain of these messages are marked with stereotypes to indicate their special nature. Of course, based on the UML metamodel shown in Figure 10-11, the stereotype really applies to the request associated with the message instance and not the message instance itself, but it is clear enough to represent the passing of signals and exceptions during the execution of the collaboration.

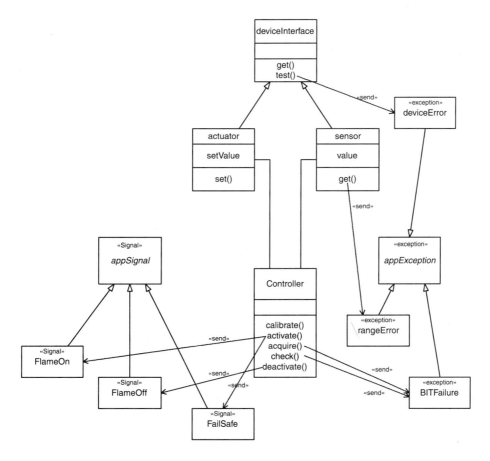

Figure 10-12: *Modeling Exceptions in the UML*

10.8.1 Source Language-Based Exception Handling

Exception handling is a powerful addition to programming languages. Language-based exception handling provides two primary benefits. The first is that exceptions cannot be ignored. The C idiom for exception handling is to pass back a return value from a function, but this is generally ignored by the clients of the service. When was the last time you saw the return value for printf checked?

The correct usage for the C fopen function is something like this:

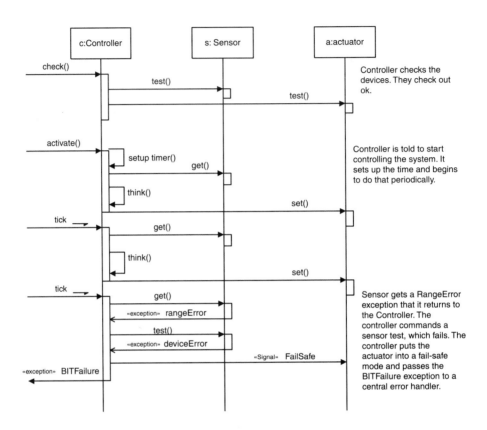

Figure 10-13: *Dynamic Exception Modeling*

```
FILE *fp;
if ( (fp = fopen("filename", "w")) == NULL) {
    /* do some corrective action */
    exit(1); /* pass error indicator up a level */
    };
```

Many programmers, to their credit, do just that. However, no law
states that the errors must be identified or handled. It is up to the good
graces of the programmer and the code peer review process to ensure
this is done. With exceptions, the error condition cannot be ignored.
Unhandled exceptions are passed to each preceding caller until they
are handled—a process called "unwinding the stack." The terminate-
on-exception approach has been successfully applied to programs in
Ada and C++ for many years.

The other benefit of exception handling is that it separates the exception handling itself from the usual execution path. This simplifies the normal processing code and the exception-handling code. For example, consider the following standard C code segment:

```c
if ( (fp = ftest1(x,y,z))) == NULL) {
   /* do some corrective action */
   printf("Failure on ftest1");
   exit(1); /* pass error indicator up a level */
   };

if (!ftest2()) {
   /* do some corrective action */
   printf("failure on ftest2");
   exit(1);
   };

if (ftest3() == 0) {
   /* do some corrective action */
   printf("failure on ftest3");
   exit(1);
   };
```

This is arguably more difficult to understand than the following code:

```cpp
// main code is simplified
try {
   ftest1(x,y,z);
   ftest2();
   ftest3();
}

// exception handling code is simplified
catch (test1Failure& t1) {
   cout << "Failure on test1";
   throw; // rethrow same exception as in code above
}
catch (test2Failure& t2) {
   cout << "Failure on test2";
   throw;
};
catch (test3Failure& t3) {
   cout << Failure on test3";
   throw;
};
```

The second code segment separates the usual code processing from the exception processing, making both clearer.

Each operation should define the exceptions it throws, as well as the exceptions it handles. There are reasons to avoid using formal C++ exceptions specifications [2], but the information should be captured nonetheless. Exceptions should never be used as an alternate way to terminate a function, in much the same way that a crowbar should not be used as an alternative key for your front door. Exceptions indicate that a serious fault requiring explicit handling has occurred.

Throwing exceptions is computationally expensive, because the stack must be unwound and local objects on the stack must be destroyed. The presence of exception handling in your code adds a small overhead to your executing code (usually around 3 percent) even when exceptions are not thrown. Most compiler vendors offer nonstandard library versions that don't throw exceptions, so this overhead can be avoided if exceptions are not used. Most operations can throw exceptions when they detect a fault.[6] However, destructors should *never* throw exceptions or call operations that might throw exceptions, nor should the constructors of exception classes throw exceptions.[7]

Each operation must answer two questions:

1. What exceptions should I catch?

2. What exceptions should I throw?

The general answer to the first question is that an operation should catch all exceptions it has enough context to handle or that will make no sense to the current operation's caller.

The answer to the second is "all others." If an object does not have enough context to decide how to handle an exception, then its caller might. Perhaps the caller can retry a set of operations or execute an alternative algorithm.

---

6. You should *not*, however, just use exception handling as a secondary means of control flow transfer.

7. In C++, if an exception is thrown while an unhandled exception is active, the program calls the internal function terminate() to exit the program. As the stack is unwound during exception handling, local objects are destroyed by calling their destructors. Thus, destructors are called as part of the exception-handling process. If a destructor is called because its object is being destroyed due to an exception, any exception it throws will terminate the program immediately.

At some point, exception handling runs out of stack to unwind, so at some global level, an exception policy must be implemented. Actions at this level depend on the severity of the exception, its impact on system safety, and the context of the system. In some cases, a severe error with safety ramifications should result in a system shutdown into a system fail-safe state. Drill presses or robotic assembly systems generally deenergize in the presence of faults, because that is their fail-safe state. Other systems, such as medical monitoring systems, may continue to provide diminished functionality or they may reset and retry, because that is their safest course of action. Of course, some systems have no fail-safe state—shutting down a jet engine at 35,000 feet might *not* constitute "transitioning to a fail-safe state." For such systems, architectural means must be provided as an alternative to in-line fault correction.

10.8.2 State-Based Exception Handling

In reactive classes, exception handling is straightforward—exceptions (a type of *Signal*) can associate with the triggering events specified in the class statechart, resulting in certain transitions and actions. This intuitively makes sense because the states of an object represent its possible condition of existence, *including* fault conditions.

Handling exception signals in a statechart is generally a language-independent way to manage exceptions, although it can be mixed with language-based exception handling. For example, if an operation does not have enough context to know how to handle an exception, it can throw it. If it is caught by an operation of a reactive class, that operation can handle it by generating an event associated with the exception signal, which can, in turn, cause a state transition and the execution of error-recovery actions. For example, Figure 10-14 depicts a state machine that works in exactly that way. The *evErrorCondition* event is associated with another object that is throwing an exception caught by an operation in this class. That operation generates an *evErrorCondition*, which, in turn, is handled by the state machine.

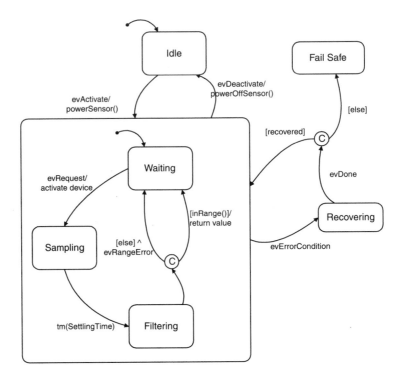

Figure 10-14: *State-Based Exception Handling*

10.9 Summary

One definition of an object is "a set of tightly coupled attributes and the operations that act on them." Detailed design uses this microscopic view to fully specify the characteristics of objects that have been hitherto abstracted away and ignored. These characteristics include the structuring of attributes and the identification of their representational invariants, resolution of abstract message-passing into object operations, and the selection and definition of algorithms, including the handling of exceptional conditions.

Attributes are the data values subsumed within the objects. They must be represented in some fashion and supported by the implementation language, but that is not enough. Most often, the underlying representation is larger than the valid ranges of the attribute, so the valid set of values of the attributes must be defined. Operations can then include checking the representational invariants to ensure that the object remains in a valid state.

Analysis models use the concept of message-passing to represent the myriad ways that objects can communicate. Detailed design must decide on the exact implementation of each message. Most often, messages are isomorphic with operations, but that is true only when the message source is always in the same thread of execution. When this is not true, other means, such as OS message queues, must be employed to provide inter-object communication.

Many objects are themselves algorithmically trivial and do not require detailed specification of the interaction of operations and attributes. However, in every system, a significant proportion of objects have "rich" behavior. Although this requires additional work, it also provides the designer with an opportunity to optimize the system performance along some set of criteria. Algorithms include the handling of exceptions, which is usually at least as complex as the primary algorithm itself. Algorithms can be expressed using state charts or activity diagrams. Other representations, such as mathematical equations, pseudocode, and text can be used as well.

10.10 Looking Ahead

This chapter finishes the section on design. The next several chapters provide some detail about a number of issues relevant to the design of real-time and embedded systems: schedulability and timeliness concerns, dynamic modeling, and real-time frameworks. Schedulability deals with the issues surrounding analysis of timeliness models so that statements can be made about the performance of a system against its timeliness requirements. The chapter on dynamic models focuses on what constitutes "good" state machines and the presentation of a variety of behavioral design patterns—generalized ways to construct state machines to solve a variety of common modeling problems. Last, but not least, Chapter 13 discusses what a framework is and what characteristics of a framework make it appropriate for real-time and embedded systems.

10.11 Exercises

1. What are the three levels of design?
2. What is the scope for detailed design?
3. Name four primary issues dealt with in detailed design.
4. What is round-off error? What mathematical operations lend themselves to its introduction in calculations?
5. What is the benefit of subranges?
6. What should be done with structurally rich class attributes?
7. Is it better to constrain values more in a subclass or less? Why?
8. Name four means of implementing associations. Under what circumstances would each be most appropriate?
9. What is an interface in the UML? How are they represented?
10. Name four optimization criteria typically applied in detailed design to algorithms.
11. What is the difference between a statechart and an activity diagram? When is each most appropriate?
12. What is the relation between the UML metaclasses *Event*, *Signal*, *Exception*, and *Request?*
13. How can exceptions be modeled on class diagrams? Statecharts? Sequence diagrams?

10.12 References

[1] Douglass, Bruce Powel. *Numerical Basic*, Indianapolis, Ind.: Howard Sams Press, 1983.
[2] Meyers, Scott. *More Effective C++*, Reading, Mass.: Addison-Wesley, 1996.
[3] Harel, David. *Algorithmics*, Reading, Mass.: Addison-Wesley, 1993.
[4] Douglass, Bruce Powel. *Real-Time UML: Developing Efficient Objects for Embedded Systems*, Reading, Mass.: Addison-Wesley, 1998.
[4] *UML Semantics Version 1.2*, Object Management Group, 1998.
[5] Neumann, Peter. *Computer Related Risks*, Reading, Mass.: Addison-Wesley, 1995.

Part  IV

Advanced Real-Time Object Modeling

Part IV is concerned with a number of advanced topics of interest to the real-time and embedded development community.

Chapter 11 discusses the notion of schedulability in real-time systems. Most work done in the computing literature on this topic has focused on the determination of schedulability of hard real-time systems—that is, systems in which missed deadlines are considered fault conditions. This chapter discusses deadlines as a special case of the more general concept of action utility, as well as mutual-exclusion primitives for resource management. It also provides methods for the analysis of schedulability for hard and soft real-time systems.

Patterns, introduced earlier in this book, are reifications of general solutions to commonly occurring problems. In the computing literature, these patterns are limited to generalized ways of organizing structural elements, such as classes, objects, components, and packages. Chapter 12 takes the concept another step and introduces the notion of a behavioral pattern—that is, a way of linking states of existence to solve common behavioral design problems. Behavioral patterns are provided that solve many commonly occurring difficulties in modeling complex state behavior. Finally, the chapter focuses on the difficulties of determining the correctness of a state model and offers some solutions based on model executability.

The last chapter of the book is about real-time frameworks. A framework is a partially written application that is specialized. Frameworks provide the essential application structure and non-application-specific code. They serve as an infrastructure for the rapid creation of new applications. The chapter discusses the role of frameworks in development, as well as sets of features commonly provided by them. Finally, we consider an example of a real-time framework, the OXF.

Chapter 11

Threads and Schedulability

The more you learn, the less you know.

—Book of Douglass, Law 15

By definition, real-time and embedded systems control and monitor physical processes in a timely fashion. They must operate under more-severe constraints than "normal" software systems and yet perform reliably for long periods of time. Some constraints are inherent in their problem domain: schedulability, predictability, and robustness. Other constraints are due to the need to cut recurring system cost by reducing the amount of memory or capability of the processor. Most real-time and embedded systems must operate with a minimum memory footprint and with a minimum of support hardware. Together, these constraints greatly complicate the development of such systems.

11.1 Introduction

Chapter 2 discussed the basics of real-time systems and introduced the notions of threads and their scheduling. Chapter 8 went on to discuss strategies for the identification of threads based on the characteristics of the object structure of the system. This chapter will discuss in more detail the issues surrounding how those threads may be effectively scheduled so that they meet their deadlines and provide adequate system performance. The chapter also provides some mathematical methods for analyzing a thread model to see if the set of threads can be guaranteed to be schedulable.

11.2 Terms and Concepts

One characteristic of real-time systems is that they typically have multiple threads of control. A *thread* is a set of executable actions that execute sequentially. *Actions* are sequentially executing statements that execute at the same priority or perform some cohesive function. These statements can belong to many subprograms or classes. The entirety of a thread is also known as a *task* or an *event sequence*. Multiple objects typically participate within a single task. In some systems, a distinction is made between *heavyweight threads* (a.k.a. *processes*) and *lightweight threads*. Heavyweight threads use different data address spaces and must resort to some sort of messaging to communicate data among themselves. Such threads have relatively strong encapsulation and protection from other threads. Lightweight threads coexist within an enclosing data space. They provide faster inter-task communication via this shared "global" space, but they offer weaker encapsulation. Some authors use the term *thread* to refer to lightweight threads and *task* to refer to heavyweight threads. We shall use *thread* and *task* synonymously in this book.

11.2.1 Time-Based Systems

Time-based systems are systems whose behavior is primarily controlled by time—either the arrival of an absolute time or the elapse of a time interval. Time is usually modeled as a monotonically increasing value. Logically, there are different kinds of time: absolute time, mission time, "friendly" time, simulation time, intervals, and durations.

Absolute time is real-world time that marches on pretty much independent of what we do.[1] *Mission time* is used in many aerospace systems. It is just like absolute time, except that it starts when the system starts, ends when the system shuts down, and may "hold" or stop at different points in the mission. *Friendly time* refers to user-readable time, which is expressed in terms of time of day relative to a specific date. *Simulation time* is important in many systems, particularly during analysis. The special thing about simulation time is that it is not monotonically nondecreasing—sometimes, you want to march time backward during simulation runs.

Intervals and durations are distinct. An *interval* is not a length of time. Rather, it has particular start and end points. To be identical, intervals must have both started and stopped at the same times. A periodic event is one that repeats with a constant duration once it is begun. A *duration* is a relative time measure. It is a scalar value that is independent of the start time. Thus, it is possible for two nonequal intervals to have the same duration if they started at different times.

11.2.2 Reactive Systems

Reactive systems are primarily composed of tasks whose execution is initiated in response to either internal or external *events.* During requirements analysis (see Chapter 5), the external events are identified and characterized. For example, a system may have to

- Respond to a user turning a knob within 20 msec
- Respond to a heart beat to invoke a ventricular pacemaker pulse within 10 μsec
- Periodically clamp and release brakes while the wheels of a car are in a skid
- Adjust the ailerons for a banked turn in response to flight control computer commands sent every 50 μsec

---

1. Well, OK, the world is somewhat more complex if you must account for relativistic velocities and time dilation, but we'll ignore that here.

11.2.3 Time Concepts

During design, additional threads may appear because of implementation concerns. These are due to internal events.

Tasks that occur with a regular, repeating duration between invocations are called *periodic*. The duration between task invocations is called the *period*. The length of time a task executes is called the task's *execution time*. Variation in the actual occurrence of a periodic event that invokes a task is called *jitter*. Most commonly, jitter is represented by a bound probability density function (PDF). More-elaborate analysis is possible if the statistical properties of the jitter distribution (for example, mean and variance) are known. In many, but certainly not all, systems, jitter can be safely ignored.

A common way to represent change in state over time is via a timing diagram. A simplified version of timing diagrams was introduced in Chapter 2. This kind of diagram shows only binary task states (running or not running). In this chapter, we'll use a more elaborate form of timing diagram, which permits an arbitrary number of states along the vertical axis. Such a diagram shows the current state along the vertical axis and linear time along the horizontal axis, as shown in Figure 11-1.

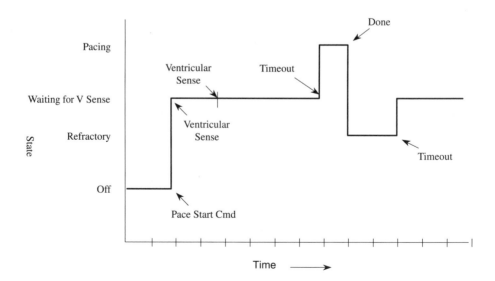

Figure 11-1: *Simple Timing Diagram*

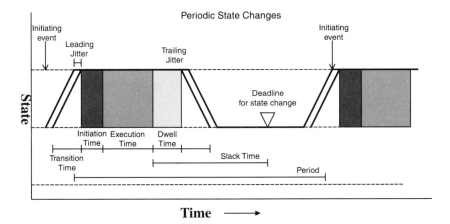

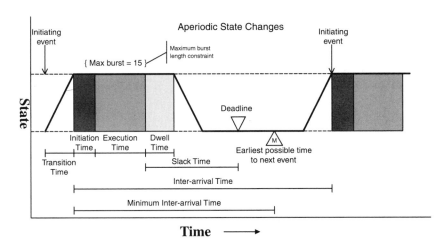

Figure 11-2: *Timing Diagram with Annotations*

Graphical annotations are used to indicate events (which occur at some instant of time), periods, intervals, durations, and so on. Figure 11-2 shows some of these annotations. Slanted lines indicate that the transition from one state to another takes a significant period of time relative to the time scale of the view. Although it is sometimes necessary to model transition times, it is more common to assume they are zero, because they are relatively small compared with the time spent actually in the state.

Those tasks whose invocation vary in time are called *aperiodic*. The duration between task invocations is called the *inter-arrival time*.[2] When analyzing tasks to see if they can be scheduled, it is necessary to know the lower bound on this time, the *minimum inter-arrival time*. Other constraints, such as the maximum burst length (the maximum number of events that can occur within a period of time), can be added using the standard UML constraint syntax.

Two independent properties of actions are of significance to real-time systems. *Urgency* is the timeliness constraint of an action; *importance* is the value of the computational action to the system. Scheduling systems do not commonly contain these abstractions; instead, they provide a lower-level abstraction called *priority* to schedule action execution.

The *priority* of a task is used to resolve disputes over which tasks execute when more than one task is waiting and ready to execute. Tasks of a higher priority[3] execute preferentially to those of a lower priority. Many people become confused over the concepts of *priority* and *importance* as it applies to tasks. The importance of the task is the value of the completion of the action relative to the overall system goals; the task's priority has to do with which task "wins" when more than one is available to run. For example, the American Academy of Monitoring Instrumentation (AAMI) standard dictates that an asystole alarm in an ECG monitor must be reported to the user within 10 seconds of the occurrence of the alarming condition. Alarm handling is crucial to the safe use of an ECG monitor, but the user wouldn't even notice a one-half second delay in alarm annunciation—it is critical, but has broad timeliness requirements, with a hard deadline. Waveform displays with delays of 100 ms are noticeably jerky and would be unacceptable to users—it is not critical, but it has tight timeliness requirements, with a soft deadline. Thus, system alarm handling should have a low priority to ensure that the high bandwidth waveform data usually "wins" and its display is smooth.

A real-time system is one in which correctness implies timeliness. A system operating in real-time executes actions in a timely fashion to

---

2. Many systems must respond to aperiodic events that can occur, at most, once, so they have no useful inter-arrival time.

3. Whether higher priority is represented with a numerically higher or lower value is OS-dependent.

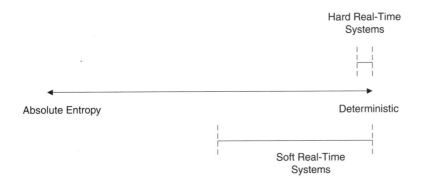

Figure 11-3: *Predictability Scale*

maintain an appropriate measure of correctness. This can be done by brute force approaches (overspecification of the processor capability) or by careful design. Most real-time systems carefully manage resources with respect to meeting predictability-of-timeliness constraints of operations. Such resources are often externally visible devices, interfaces, and processes.

Predictability refers to the accuracy with which one can declare in advance when and how an action will occur. It can be applied to the occurrence of a pre-conditional event that starts an action (usually, the period of the event) and the execution time required for the action. Predictability ranges from no information (absolute entropy) to deterministic (zero entropy), as shown in Figure 11-3. Predictability constraints take a variety of forms, the most common being "hard" and "soft" predictability. (Note that *real-time* does not mean *real-fast*, because the latter term does not concern itself with determinism or predictability, only with execution speed.)

A task that must finish by a specified time is said to be *hard*, or to have a *hard deadline*. In this case, a missed deadline is considered either a partial or a total system failure. A computation computed after its deadline is considered invalid or erroneous. A system is said to be hard real-time if it has one or more tasks with hard deadlines. Such systems may have nonhard real-time processes and activities, but the hard deadlines are the primary focus of system timeliness concerns.

Any other timeliness requirement of an action other than hard is, by definition, *soft*. Soft deadlines might require meeting a deadline on average. Some tasks have average response time requirements, as well as a hard deadline; these tasks are called *firm*. A deadline is usually specified in terms of time from the occurrence of the triggering event to the completion of the task's execution. In general, a task that can be determined to always meet its timeliness constraints is said to be *schedulable*. As a special case, a task that can be guaranteed to meet all its deadlines is said to be *deterministically schedulable*. This occurs when the event's worst-case response time is less than or equal to the task's deadline. Schedulability of all tasks is used to specify the overall system schedulability.

Of the two types, hard deadlines have received most of the attention in the literature. This is because the concepts around hard deadlines are more straightforward than for soft deadlines—in the same way that linearizing control systems makes the analysis of control systems tractable and solvable. Considering all deadlines to be hard is an approximation that makes scheduling analysis more straightforward. It can, however, be overly strict. By making strong worst-case assumptions of execution time, for example, analysis can derive conclusions about whether the system can be guaranteed to meet its deadlines. However, soft real-time systems can often be constructed that meet all their mission performance requirements but, nevertheless, fail all measures of hard deadline schedulability.

Soft deadlines may be considered on a number of levels of increasing mathematical and conceptual complexity. Soft real-time computing may be soft in either or both of two ways. The first is the relaxation of the constraint that missing a deadline constitutes a mission failure. A soft real-time system context may tolerate missing specific deadlines as long as some other measure of timeliness is maintained—for instance, average throughput. Second, a soft real-time context may evaluate the correctness of a computation with respect to its timeliness as nonbinary ("Good" or "Bad")—for example, as a multivalued or continuous function.

It is possible to think of an action's time constraint (as in Table 11-1) in terms of Aristotelian,[4] or fuzzy, logic. One can therefore think of hard deadlines as an important idealized subset of soft real-time timeliness, just as crisp logic is an idealized subset of fuzzy logic.

---

4. The hallmark of Aristotle's logic is the Law of the Excluded Middle, which prohibits partial membership in a set.

Soft real-time systems may then be optimized against a number of criteria, such as:

- Convergence toward a mean throughput or response time
- Minimization of deviation of response time
- Minimization of the number of missed deadlines
- Minimization of the average lateness
- Maximization of the number of events handled or computations performed
- Minimization of the worst-case response time

Different analytical and scheduling means must be applied to achieve each of these criteria. The relatively simple case of hard deadlines can be computed analytically, but soft real-time analysis must often be done via simulation rather than via rigorous mathematical proof.

To complicate matters more, soft real-time action execution time may be deterministic or stochastic. As more large-scale distributed systems are constructed, using hundreds or thousands of distributed

Table 11-1: *Timeliness Constraints*

Property	Non-Real-Time	Soft Real-Time	Hard Real-Time
Deterministic	No	Possibly	Yes
Predictable	No	Possibly	Yes
Consequences of late computation	No effect	Degraded performance	Mission failure
Mission-critical reliability	No	Yes	Yes
Response dictated by external events	No	Yes	Yes
Timing analysis possible	No	Analytic (sometimes), stochastic simulation	Analytic, stochastic simulation

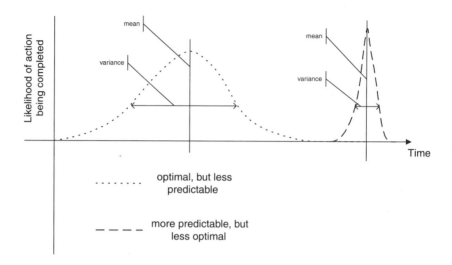

Figure 11-4: *Predictability versus Optimality*

resources, the execution times of system-level actions may be impossible to predict accurately with a useful degree of certainty. These actions may involve local concurrency scheduling issues, communications delays, and external asynchronous events, resulting in a lower-level action sequence that may have well-defined stochastic properties that stop short of determinism.

Real-time systems have attributes of optimality and predictability (see Figure 11-4). It is sometimes possible to trade one of these properties against another. For example, it is possible to create systems that minimize mean tardiness but are highly unpredictable, or the opposite. In other cases, it may be possible to make the system highly predictable but require an excessive amount of computation to ensure that predictability.

11.2.3.1 Utility Functions

Let us think abstractly about timeliness as it applies to actions performed by a system in response to an initiating event. In hard real-time systems, such an action has a value or utility (1 if valuable, 0 or $-\infty$ if not, depending on whether the late completion of the action is not helpful or actually counterproductive) as long as it is performed before the

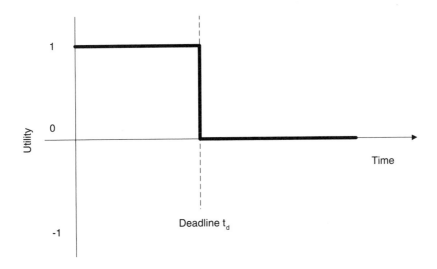

Figure 11-5: *Utility Function for an Action with a Hard Deadline*

expiration of a deadline. If we model this utility over time, the function looks like that shown in Figure 11-5. This function has value 1.0 when the action completes prior to the deadline, meaning it has its full value. The value of the function is 0.0 thereafter, meaning the value of the action completion is 0 after the deadline.

The usefulness of a computation may change with time and may not be binary. This is the concept of an action's *utility* [2], expressed as u(t). The utility of an action is the usefulness of that action (when it completes) as a function of time. An action with a hard deadline has a binary utility function—1 if the action occurs prior to the deadline; 0 thereafter. Actions with soft deadlines may have continuous utility functions that degrade over time. For example, a radar track of an air-craft for an air traffic controller may not be useless if it is two seconds late. If the flight plan for the aircraft, along with its last position and the time of measurement of that position, are known, correlative methods may be used to incorporate late data to estimate the aircraft's current position. This is not as good as having *current* data, but it is vastly supe-rior to having *no* data.

Figure 11-6 shows a number of utility functions. Figure 11-6a is the standard hard deadline. The value of the utility is 1.0 when the action is completed prior to the deadline and 0 thereafter. Figure 11-6b is a

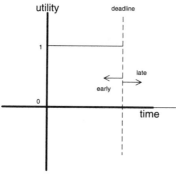

Figure 11-6a: Utility Function for a Hard
Deadline (late is useless)

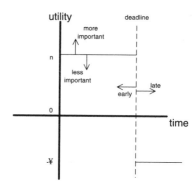

Figure 11-6b: Scaleable Utility Function for
Hard Deadline (late is counter-productive)

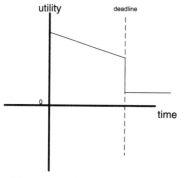

Figure 11-6c: More General Utility Function
with a Deadline

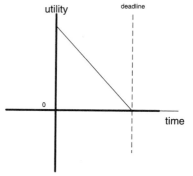

Figure 11-6d: Simple Decreasing Utility
Function with a Deadline

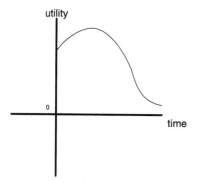

Figure 11-6e: General Utility Function
(no deadline)

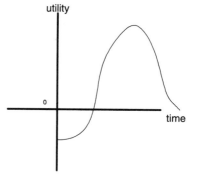

Figure 11-6f: Another General Utility Function
(no deadline)

Figure 11-6: *Utility Functions*

slightly more elaborate hard deadline utility function. In this case, the utility is a single value if completed prior to the deadline and $-\infty$ thereafter. However, the utility of the individual actions can be different and contribute different amounts of utility to the overall system functionality. These differences may be represented in the action's priority for priority-based preemption scheduling.

The next two figures, Figure 11-6c and Figure 11-6d, show a utility function that decreases linearly with time but still has a deadline. A deadline, in this context, may be defined as the first discontinuity (after 0) in the utility function or its first or second derivatives. In the case of the utility function shown in Figure 11-6c, the action continues to have usefulness after the deadline, although it is greatly diminished. In Figure 11-6d, the utility decreases linearly with time until the deadline and is 0 thereafter.

Utility functions can take on any general shape, as shown by the next two figures, Figure 11-6e and Figure 11-6f. In the former, the usefulness of the action's completion first increases, then peaks, followed by a curvilinear decrease. In the latter, early completion of the action is counterproductive, as indicated by the initial negative value of the utility function.

This notion of action utility refers to the usefulness of the completion of an action as a function of time. An extension to this notion is *progressive utility*, which refers to the progressive achievement of an external purpose, such as the insertion of control rods into a nuclear reactor core. The action may be to insert the control rods to shut down the nuclear process, and the progressive utility of this action may be thought of as the effectiveness of the activity as it nears completion. Thus, it may be very important to have the control rods inserted 75 percent of the way by a certain time, but the actual completion of the action may be deferred until later. We can see that progressive utility is different from completion utility. Progressive utility in our nuclear plant example refers to the utility of partial action completion over time, while the completion utility refers to the utility of the entire action as a function of time.

Progressive utility, $u_p(t,w)$ is clearly a function of two variables. The first of these is *time*, because the utility of the action varies with time, typically diminishing after some point. The other variable, w, is the percentage completion of the work performed by the action. In the standard utility function, the utility of the action is assumed to be 0 until the action completes. Many actions increase in value as work progresses. For example, the iterative solution of a set of trajectory differential equations for a space delivery vehicle or of (for a noncomputer example) your child brushing his or her teeth increase in value as they converge on an optimal solution. These actions still have value even if not performed to completion, although maximum utility is achieved at the completion of the action.

Progressive utility functions may be shown as surfaces in three-space. Figure 11-7 shows some different utility functions. Figure 11-7a shows the surface (a simple plane) for a normal utility function. Figure

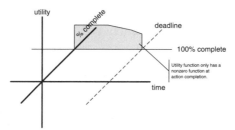

Figure 11-7a: Normal Utility Function

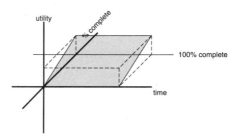

Figure 11-7b: Simple Progressive Utility Function

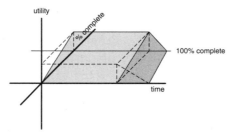

Figure 11-7c: More General Progressive Utility Function

Figure 11-7: *Progressive Utility Functions*

Table 11-2: *Types of Utility Functions*

Utility Function	Description
Unary	$U(t) = 1$ when action completes, if it completes <= deadline
	$U(t) = 0$ elsewhere
Scaled constant	$U(t) = c$ (a constant) when the action completes if it completes <= deadline, where c is the (constant) relative importance of the action $U(t) = 0$ elsewhere
Utility	$U(t) = x$ (a variable) when the action completes at time t
Progressive utility	$U_p(t,w) = x$ (a variable) when the action is w% complete at time t.

11-7b shows a linear progressive utility function in which the utility falls to 0 at the action's deadline. Figure 11-7c is a more general surface in which the utility begins to drop at a deadline but does not immediately go to 0. Of course, other surfaces are possible, as well.

In summary, utility functions may be thought of in terms of successive generalization, as shown in Table 11-2.

11.3 Scheduling Threads

Chapter 8 discussed different strategies for the allocation of application domain objects to threads. This section will concern itself with what comes after thread identification and allocation of objects to threads—the determination of the policies that decide which tasks execute when multiple tasks are ready to execute. This process is called *scheduling*. Scheduling is always a design concern, because it fundamentally involves decisions that optimize the overall system performance according to some criteria. In the case of hard deadlines, the overriding system concern is that the tasks (and their time-critical actions) meet every deadline. In soft real-time systems, many more criteria are possible, such as minimizing mean tardiness, minimizing missed deadlines, maximizing utility, and so on.

There are many methods for scheduling the execution of tasks. In some cases, the operating system will perform task switching on a cyclic or periodic basis, and it will swap out a task of lower priority when a higher-priority task becomes ready to run. Windows NT is such a *preemptive* system. In others, the task must voluntarily relinquish control. Windows 3.1 is such a *nonpreemptive* system. In many embedded systems, hardware interrupts drive at least some tasks. Even in Windows 3.1, serial communication is handled in this way. As the system designer, you usually can choose how tasks are scheduled to run.

Schedulers in real-time systems assign each task a priority. The priority of the task establishes the precedence of the task when multiple tasks are ready to run. Most commonly, schedulers use a run-to-completion policy or a preemptive policy to control task execution. A run-to-completion scheduling policy waits until the task explicitly relinquishes control before starting another task. Two implementations of run-to-completion schedulers are round-robin and cyclic executive schedulers.

The most common scheduling policy in real-time systems is preemptive scheduling. This policy preempts a lower-priority task as soon as a higher-priority task becomes ready to run. For example, if task A is running with a priority of 10, and tasks B and C are ready to run, with respective priorities of 8 and 6 (assuming the smallest value represents the highest priority), task A will be suspended and task C will execute. If no higher-priority task comes along, then task C will run to completion. When that occurs, the RTOS will execute task B, which has the highest priority of tasks ready to run. When task B completes, task A will finally be allowed to complete its execution.

Two keys to good real-time design are repeatability and predictability. They are essential in any system with hard temporal constraints. Modern fighter aircraft are so unstable that humans cannot directly manage the flight-control surfaces. Only by frequent *and timely* updates to the airfoil position and thrust application are these planes able to fly at all. A change that comes too late is no better than one that does not come at all. This is what system designers call a *BAD THING*. In pacemaker design, after the heart has beat, there is a period of time called the suprathreshold period. A pacemaker pulse to the heart during this period can induce fibrillation in the heart muscle. This is also a *BAD THING.* In order to make sure that task execution is timely, a real-time system uses one or more scheduling algorithms that control when a task begins execution, and whether or not a task may be suspended during execution and prior to its completion.

The key to determining predictability is to define the timing characteristics of the tasks and to properly schedule them using a predictable scheduling algorithm. Windows 3.1 uses a nonpreemptive scheduling executive that requires tasks to explicitly relinquish control to Windows for another task to run. Clearly, a single misbehaved task in such a system can lead to missed deadlines.

However, it is not trivial to determine whether deadlines can be missed. Even in a priority-based scheduling schema, high-priority tasks that are schedulable in isolation may be blocked from execution by lower-priority tasks. A task is said to be *blocked* when it is ready to run but cannot because a lower-priority task owns a required resource. Consider two tasks, A and B, that share a resource X, where A has the higher priority. If B is running and has locked resource X and A becomes ready to run, A can run only up to the point at which it requires resource X. At this point, A must suspend itself and allow B to run so that it can finish using and release resource X. Task A is blocked while it waits for B to release the resource. As soon as B releases X, A can immediately preempt B.

Blocking is unavoidable in preemptive scheduling in which resources are shared among tasks. However, it is vital that the blocking be bounded so that worst-case blocking can be computed. A system in which higher-priority tasks may be blocked from execution by an indefinite set of other tasks is said to suffer from *unbounded priority inversion*. A simple example should illustrate this.

Consider the system in the task diagram in Figure 11-8. The tasks are represented by heavy lines for the class box (the normal UML iconic stereotype for an active object). The thin-lined boxes are normal classes. The *Data Class* is a resource shared among the tasks. The *Data Class* uses a semaphore to protect and serialize access to the resource.

In this example, Task A has the highest priority (lowest number is the highest priority in this example), Task B the next, and Task C the lowest. The numbers by the lines connecting the tasks to the resource is the length of time the tasks use the resource.

Note that Task A is, in isolation, schedulable. It has a period of 100ms, a deadline of 80ms, and an execution time of 10ms. It is also the highest priority task in the system, so of course, it will meet its deadlines. Even if C locks the resource, A will meet its deadlines, because C

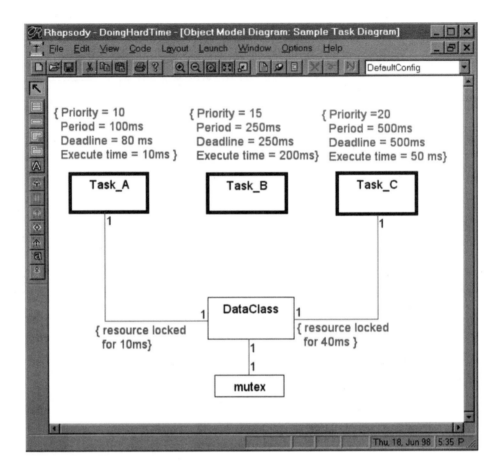

Figure 11-8: *Simple Task Diagram*

uses the resource for only 40ms, and that, plus A's execution time of 10ms is 50ms, is still less than A's deadline of 80 ms. So we can be assured that A will always meet its deadlines. Or can we? Consider the timing diagram in Figure 11-9.

1. Task C becomes ready to run and starts executing (time = 0). It locks the resource at this time.

2. Task A becomes ready to run but cannot run because it is waiting for the resource to be released. That is, Task A is *blocked* (time = 5ms).

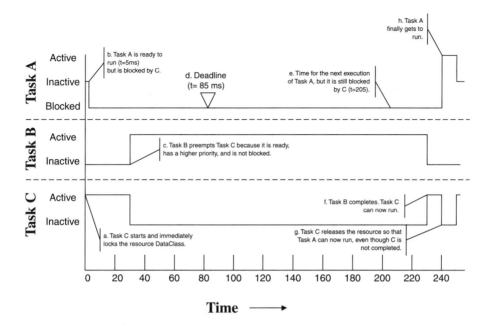

Figure 11-9: *Timing Diagram for Simple Task Model*

3. Task B becomes ready to run. Because it has a higher priority than Task C and it is not blocked (that is, does not need the resource), Task C is suspended and Task B begins (time = 30ms).

4. Task A's deadline passes (time = 85ms).

5. Task A must run a second time, but it is blocked because its required resource is still locked by Task C (time = 200ms).

6. Task B completes, allowing Task C to continue (time = 230ms).

7. Task C releases the resource, Task A now preempts Task C and runs (time = 250ms).

The deadline for Task A has long since elapsed. Unfortunately, far too many real-time systems suffer from unbounded priority inversions, as well as other sources of scheduling unpredictability. Their implementers probably get reports from the field that speak of intermittent failures but have no idea why, because the conditions that lead to the unbounded priority inversion occur only rarely.

In this section, we will briefly consider several scheduling algorithms. Detailed discussions of these algorithms are beyond the scope of this book, and the interested reader should check the references quoted at the end of the chapter. The algorithms we will mention here are:

- Rate monotonic (RM)
- Earliest deadline (ED)
- Least laxity dynamic (LL)
- Maximum urgency first (MU)

11.3.1 Rate Monotonic Scheduling

Rate monotonic scheduling (RMS) was initially developed in 1973 by Lui and Leyand [3], and it has been updated to handle a much broader set of conditions [4]. In the basic RMS schema, a task's priority depends on its period—the shorter the period, the higher the priority of the task. In RMS, priorities are determined at design time and remain fixed during system execution. Such a system is said to use a *static*, or *fixed*, scheduling policy. RMS systems can be analyzed in phases by applying increasingly precise calculations using a family of analytical techniques collectively called rate monotonic analysis, or RMA.

The way to compute schedulability is to use a single *utilization bound* for the entire set of tasks:

$$\sum_{j=1}^{n} \left(\frac{C_k}{T_k} \right) \le n \, (2^{\frac{1}{n}} - 1)$$

where C_j and T_j are the execution time and the period of task j, respectively, and n is the number of tasks.[5] The method assumes the deadline for each task is equal to its period and all tasks are preemptible at any time.

The term on the right of the inequality is called the *utilization bound*. It forms a severe condition for proof of task schedulability. If the condition is not met, then a more detailed analysis must be performed to

---

5. There is a special case in which the periods are all multiples of a single factor. In this case, the utilization bound is always 100 percent.

prove schedulability. The right-hand term converges to 69 percent as n approaches infinity. As a practical matter, however, the set of tasks is probably schedulable if the computed bound is less than about 88 percent.

This simple RMS algorithm makes it easy to analyze systems, because the scheduling is static—that is, it is determined at design time. The worst case can be shown to occur when all tasks are started simultaneously. The RMS *Critical Zone Theorem* states that if the computed utilization is less than the utilization bound, then the system is guaranteed to meet all task deadlines in all task phasings.

This algorithm can be extended to include simple blocking:

$$\sum_n \left(\frac{C_j}{T_j}\right) + \max \left(\frac{B_1}{T_1}, \ldots, \frac{B_n}{T_n}\right) \leq n \, (2^{\frac{1}{n}} - 1)$$

B_j is the maximum amount of time that task j can be blocked from execution by a lower-priority task.

RMS is *optimal* in that if the tasks can be scheduled by other static algorithms, then they can also be scheduled by RMS. That is, no other static algorithm can schedule better than RMS. RMS is also *stable* in the sense that when additional lower-priority tasks are added, the higher-priority tasks still meet their deadlines, even if the lower-priority tasks fail to do so (in the absence of blocking).

More-elaborate RMA methods are shown later in this chapter, including handling of aperiodic tasks, as well as more-detailed algorithms to apply when this pessimistic test fails.

11.3.2 Earliest-Deadline-First Scheduling

In this scheduling algorithm, tasks are selected for execution based on which has the closest deadline [9]. This algorithm is said to be *dynamic* because task scheduling cannot be determined at design time, only when the system runs. In this algorithm, a set of tasks is schedulable (in the hard real-time sense) if the sum of the task loading is less than 100 percent. The algorithm is optimal in the sense that if it is schedulable by other algorithms, then it is also schedulable by ED. However, ED is not stable; if the total task load rises above 100 percent, then at least one task misses its deadline, and it is not possible in general to predict which task will fail. This algorithm requires additional run-time overhead, because the scheduler must determine and store the next task to run on the basis of its deadline, whenever a task switch, task creation, or task deletion occurs. In addition, analytical methods are more complex than those for the simpler, fixed-priority case.

11.3.3 Least Laxity Dynamic Scheduling

Laxity for a task is defined as the time to deadline minus the task execution time remaining. Clearly, a task with a negative laxity will fail to meet its deadline. The algorithm schedules tasks in ascending order of their laxity. The difficulty is that during run-time, the system must know the expected execution time and also track the total time a task has been executing in order to compute its laxity. While this is not conceptually difficult, it means that designers and implementers must identify the deadlines and execution times for the tasks and update the information for the scheduler every time they modify the system. In a system with hard and soft deadlines, the LL algorithm must be merged with another so that hard deadlines can be met at the expense of tasks that must meet average response time requirements (see maximum urgency first, in the next section). LL has the same disadvantages as the ED algorithm. It is not stable and adds run-time overhead over what is required for static scheduling. In addition, this algorithm tends to devote cycles to tasks that are clearly going to be late, even though this means that a greater number of deadlines will be missed.

11.3.4 Maximum-Urgency-First Scheduling

This algorithm is a hybrid of RMS and LL. Tasks are initially ordered by period, as in RMS. An additional binary task parameter, *criticality*, is added. The first n tasks of high criticality that load under 100 percent become the *critical task set*. It is this set to which the least laxity scheduling is applied. Only if no critical tasks are waiting to run are tasks from the noncritical task set scheduled. Because MU has a critical set based on RMS, it can be structured so that no critical tasks fail to meet their deadlines.

The advantages of RMS are that it is simple, has relatively low run-time overhead, and formal methods may be applied to prove the set of tasks can all meet their deadlines. It lacks flexibility, however. For example, RMS assumes that tasks are "infinitely preemptable." Small deviations (short periods of atomic behavior) are generally tolerated well, but greater deviations may render the formal analysis meaningless. It is most appropriate when the set of tasks is characterized and blocking characteristics are easy to determine. ED and LL provide dynamic scheduling, so if a task is "slipping," they may be able to compensate by elevating its priority. These algorithms are more robust in the presence of assumption violations, but they are more complex, add run-time overhead, and are more difficult to guarantee that all tasks will meet their deadlines. MU is a hybrid that is most applicable when tasks vary in their ability to tolerate missing their deadlines. It can be thought of as primarily RMS, with some run-time checking to ensure that deadlines are met.

11.3.5 Weighted-Shortest-Processing-Time-First (WSPTF) Scheduling

Outside of the standard hard real-time computing literature, there exists an extensive body of scheduling theory that has to do with optimal shop scheduling [8]. This literature is concerned with optimal scheduling strategies for the use of machines in manufacturing and other industrial applications. These strategies are often different from those used in hard real-time computing, because the individual deadline is considered less important than total schedulability. In such circumstances, the WSPTF policy is optimal. Given the overall processing time

$$w_j C_j$$

where

C_j is the completion time for action j

w_j is the weight (relative importance) of action j

p_j is the processing time for action j

The WSPTF policy schedules tasks in decreasing order of the ratio w_j/p_j. This policy is optimal in the sense that any rearrangement of actions can do no better in terms of the optimizing sum of the preceding equation.

Although this scheduling policy is stated in deterministic terms, it also applies to the stochastic case, in which the processing time for actions is not constant. In that case, replace p_j with the mean p_j.

11.3.6 Minimizing Maximum Lateness Scheduling

Sometimes, a set of actions have start-finish precedence relations (that is, one task cannot start until another completes). In addition, the completion of each action j is associated with a cost function h_j (alternatively, it may be associated with a benefit function). An optimal schedule that minimizes cost can be constructed using the following iterative algorithm (adapted from [8]):

Definitions:

J   Ordered set of actions already scheduled.

J^c Set of actions still to be scheduled (J^c is the complement of J).

J' Set of actions that can be scheduled immediately before set J (that is, the set of all jobs all of whose successors are in J). This is the set of schedulable actions (J' is a subset of J^c).

Algorithm

1. Set J empty. Set J^c to the set of all actions to be scheduled. Set J' to the set of all jobs with no successors.
2. Select the action j* from set J^c that has the minimum cost function h_{j*} over J^c that has no predecessors in J^c.
3. Add j* to set J and remove from set J^c.
4. Adjust J' to represent the new set of schedulable actions.
5. If J^c is empty, stop. Otherwise, go to step 2.

This is clearly an off-line static scheduling algorithm.

This set of scheduling algorithms barely scratches the surface, and the literature is full of innovative work that is being done. One promising, but early, approach to scheduling is based on fuzzy reasoning in nondeterministic scheduling problems for air-traffic control [10]. Time will tell how applicable such methods will be for scheduling real-time computing resources.

11.4 Thread Synchronization and Resource Sharing

When threads are actually independent, life is good. However, one characteristic of real systems is that threads must share discrete resources, and for correct system execution, these resources must be shared in a thread-robust manner. Sharing resources is a case of the more general problem of thread synchronization. It is common for threads to share *synchronization points*. A synchronization point is a system state in which the transition to the continuation of the dependent tasks has a conjunctive pre-conditional invariant—namely, that each task is in a state of waiting to be released by the synchronization point. This is demonstrated by the activity diagram in Figure 11-10.

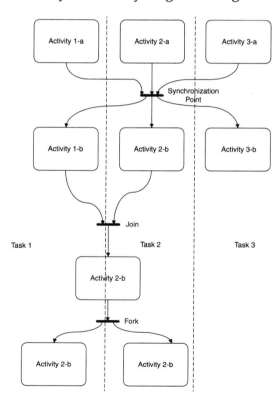

Figure 11-10: *Thread Control Synchronization*

Activity diagrams are basically constrained Petri nets. The most important of these constraints is that a place can contain, at most, one token.[6] Although the primary use of activity diagrams in the UML is to model business process, they are adept at showing multiple threads of control and their synchronization points, as well. Figure 11-10 shows three threads (for illustrative purposes, each thread is shown in its own swim lane). The heavy horizontal bars represent synchronization points. Because an activity can contain, at most, one token, each thread must be in the predecessor activity before the transition to the subsequent activities can occur. The figure shows three kinds of synchronization points—a generalized one with multiple inputs and outputs, a fork (single input, multiple outputs), and a join (multiple inputs, single output).

There are different ways in which tasks can synchronize control. The most common rendezvous strategies are

- Balking
- Waiting
- Timed waiting
- Asynchronous
- Synchronous

The *waiting rendezvous* acts just as expected—the task waits indefinitely until the resource (or other task) is available. *Timed waiting rendezvous* waits until the resource is available or until some timeout period has elapsed. An *asynchronous rendezvous* means only that the task sends a message to the resource (or other task) and goes on its merry way, not caring exactly when the message is acted on. The *synchronous rendezvous* is one in which resource access does not involve a task switch; it is called synchronously, just as is a normal function call in C.

---

6. A Petri net is a generalized graph that represents a Turing machine. A Petri net contains *places* (states) connected by directional *transitions*. Places may contain *tokens*, meaning that the place is active. For a transition to fire, all predecessor places must contain at least one token. When a transition fires, a single token is removed from each predecessor place and one token is put in each subsequent place. The number of predecessor and subsequent places need not be the same. The transition models generalized synchronization semantics. For those of you unfamiliar with Petri nets, see [7] or related texts.

There are several means for achieving thread synchronization. The ones we'll discuss include mutual exclusion (mutex) semaphores, counting semaphores, conditional variables, and rendezvous objects.

11.4.1 Mutual-Exclusion Semaphores

Dijkstra [6] suggested the semaphore as a means of resource protection. In the procedural world, a semaphore is a special variable that acts as a lock on a resource, such as a variable or a block of memory. Two primitive operations are defined on the semaphore: P() (from *proberen*, "test") and V() (from *verhogen*, "increment"). We will use the more mnemonic *wait()* and *release()* here. The *wait()* function simply waits until the semaphore, a Boolean value, is FALSE, holding the thread calling *wait()* in limbo. When the semaphore is finally FALSE, *wait()* sets it to TRUE and returns control to the calling thread. *release()* simply releases the resource by setting the semaphore to FALSE. This can be implemented in a very straightforward manner:

```
class semaphore {
private:
    int s;
public:
    semaphore() { s = 0; };
    int wait() { while (s); s = 1; return s; };
    void release() { s = 0; };
};
```

Of course, this naïve implementation has a number of problems. For example, many tasks simply cannot wait as is required by the balking rendezvous strategy. Only the calling task has enough contextual information to determine whether the inaccessibility of the resource is acceptable or constitutes a system fault. Balking can be implemented simply by returning a Boolean value from the wait method: 0 if not available and non-0 if the resource is available:

```
int wait() {
    if (!s) { // semaphore is available
        s=1;
        return s;} // lock it and return 1
    else
        return 0; // unavailable -- return 0
    };
```

Of course, other strategies are possible.

A difficulty arises when there are multiple tasks waiting for a resource—there is no control over who should get the resource. In some cases, FIFO (first-in, first out) is the best order; in others, the task priority should govern who gets the semaphore next. In the preceding code, the task that happens to check next, after the owner task releases the semaphore, becomes the owner. This can be resolved by including a queue of waiting tasks and ordering it appropriately, such as by first-come or by priority.

Many RTOSs supply mutex semaphore primitives. Those that do provide the *wait()* and *release()* operations to directly implement the standard waiting rendezvous. Some also support conditional mutex locking.[7] The conditional locking mutex allows the caller to lock the mutex if available, and to return immediately with a status code if not. This allows the other rendezvous policies to be implemented.

In general, to minimize priority inversion, synchronization primitives must use the same scheduling policy as the task scheduler. Many systems use priority-based preemption but handle tasks waiting for a resource in FIFO order (one of the difficulties with Ada-83 that was fixed in Ada-95) or with a fairness policy (for instance, random selection among waiting tasks). This clearly is at odds with an overall priority-based scheduling policy and can result in high levels of priority inversion.

11.4.2 Dekker's Algorithm

Another means to achieve synchronization, which does not assume atomicity among coordinating tasks, is Dekker's algorithm. This algorithm uses explicit signaling of the right of the other task to enter its critical section. The naïve solution of this has two problems. The first is that the explicit granting of permission to enter its critical section means that all tasks must progress at the same rate, following a set pattern of granting permission among the tasks. The second problem is that if a task currently granted permission to enter its critical section should become deadlocked or terminated (even if that task is not in its critical section), no other coordinating task can ever again enter its own

---

7. In POSIX, the function to conditionally lock a mutex is pthread_mutex_trylock().

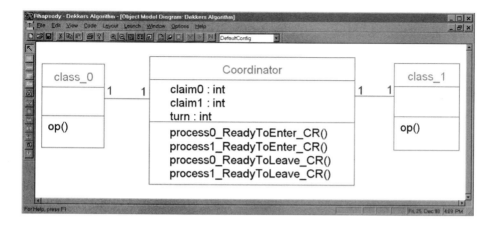

Figure 11-11: *Dekker's Algorithm Class Model*

critical section. This is required because the waiting task is waiting for the terminated task to explicitly grant permission.

Dekker's algorithm solves both difficulties with the addition of a *turn* attribute.

One difficulty with Dekker's algorithm, however, is the rather tight coupling among participating tasks. This can be resolved in an object model by extracting out the parts requiring coordination into a rendezvous class. The class diagram for this is shown in Figure 11-11. The relevant attributes and operations of the *Coordinator* class implementing Dekker's algorithm, are shown. The attributes *claim0* and *claim1* indicate the granting of permission to enter the critical section for *class_0* and *class_1*, respectively. The attribute *turn* is used only when a class wants to enter its critical section but does not have explicit permission.

Figure 11-12 shows how the classes coordinate to solve the mutual exclusion problem. This activity diagram shows operations from three classes: *class_0* (and its operation *op()*), *class_1* (and its own operation *op()*), and *Coordinator* (and its operations *process0_ReadyToEnter_CR()*, *process1_ReadyToEnter_CR()*, *process1_ReadyToLeave_CR()*, and *process1_ReadyToLeave_CR()*).

When *class_0::op()* wants to enter its own critical section, it sets *Coordinator::claim0* to *BUSY*. If *Coordinator::claim1* is *FREE*, then it may directly enter its critical section. Should *class_1*, running in a separate

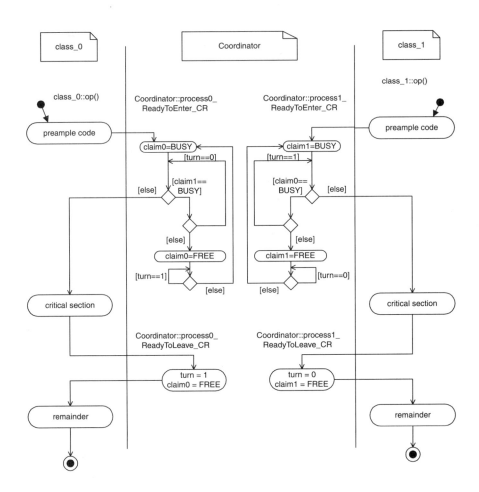

Figure 11-12: *Dekker's Algorithm*

thread, want to enter its critical section, it will be blocked by *Coordinator::claim0*, which has the value BUSY.

Things are more interesting when *class_0* finds that *class_1* currently has permission to enter its critical section (that is, *Coordinator::claim1* is BUSY). If *Coordinator::turn* is 0, then *class_0* will loop waiting for explicit permission.[8] If *Coordinator::turn* is FREE, then *class_1* is allowed

---

8. In a real system, you might not want to use a busy wait, but perhaps set a timer and periodically check for permission.

to proceed; *Coordinator::claim0* is set to FREE and loops until *Coordinator::turn* is 0. This gives *class_0* the right to try again. This algorithm solves the mutual-exclusion problem without hardware-assisted, atomic, set-and-test instructions. The *turn* attribute is considered only in the case of contention. In addition, deadlock is avoided. This algorithm can be easily extended to multiple tasks.

A proof of Dekker's algorithm is provided in [12]. Note that in Figure 11-12, the operations *class_0::op()* and *class_1::op()* terminate when done. They might also loop infinitely; in this case, the terminator pseudostate can be removed and the transition to it can be targeted back to the preamble activity state.

11.4.3 Spinlocks

A *spinlock* is a locking construct in which the calling thread loops iteratively, trying to lock a resource. Note that this construct makes sense only in a multiprocessing environment, because while the caller spins, he burns CPU cycles and does not allow the current resource owner to release the resource. In multiprocessing systems, spinlocks may improve throughput performance when resources are locked for a short period of time, but they can lead to excessive overhead if resources are locked for long periods. A variation on the spinlock is the *limited spinlock*. In this construct, the loop is limited to a maximum number of iterations before it gives up and becomes blocked. It is common to allow the limited spinlock to spin for about the time it takes to block on a mutex or perform a context switch. Both kinds of spinlocks can be implemented using conditional locking mutex semaphores.

11.4.4 Counting Semaphores

In the semaphore class above, the semaphore is binary-valued: TRUE or FALSE. This is sufficient because there is only a single resource that is protected. It is straightforward to extend this notion to a counting semaphore when a single semaphore is used to protect a finite pool of identical resources:

```
class counting_semaphore {
private:
    int s;
public:
```

```
counting_semaphore(int nResources) { s =
nResources; };
int wait( ) { s—; while (s<0);  return !s; };
void release() { s++; };
}
```

The last problem with this semaphore is more serious. The method *wait()* is not atomic, (i.e., a task switch can occur in the middle of the method call). Consider the example in Table 11-3.

In Step 1, Task 1 is running; it checks the semaphore S for availability and finds that it is available. In Step 2, Task 2 interrupts Task 1, and it also now checks S for availability and, likewise, finds it available. Task 2 then locks it (Step 4) and continues. In Step 5, Task 1 regains control and continues by claiming the semaphore for itself, even though it has been surreptitiously claimed by Task 2. By Step 6, both Task 1 and Task 2 think they each have exclusive access to the protected resource.

You might think that getting a task switch at the exact moment between falling through the *wait()* loop and setting the semaphore attribute *s* is so unlikely to happen that it isn't worth worrying about. However, the occurrence of this condition is not predictable. Improperly protecting shared resources from race conditions has been identified as the cause of several deaths from the use of the Therac-25, a radiation therapy machine, between 1985 and 1987. Despite the problems, the Therac-25 successfully treated thousands of patients, so the

Table 11-3: *Violation of Mutual Exclusion*

Step Number	Task 1	Semaphore (S) State	Task 2
1	Checks S	Free	
2	Ready to move on and claim it	Free	Interrupts Task 1
3		Free	Checks S
4		Locked	Claims it
5	Continues from interruption	Locked	Loses focus to Task 1
6	Claims S	Locked	

manufacturer was unwilling to believe the product had a fault.[9] Avoiding a single occurrence, however unlikely, is clearly worth the extra effort.

The problem can be avoided by making the *wait()* method atomic by disabling task switching before the test is done, reenabling it later. Note that if the entire wait loop is atomic, then the resource will never be released, because the task holding the semaphore can never execute to release it. Thus, the wait loop must be partitioned into atomic and nonatomic sections.

```
int wait () {
    int done = 0;
    while (!done) {
        disable();       // critical section
                         // disable interrupts and task
                         //   switches

        if (!s)  {
            s = 1;
            done = 1;
        } // end if
        enable();        // end critical section
                         // reenable interrupts and task
                         //   switches
    } // end while
} // end wait()
```

In most cases, an even better solution is to put the blocked task to *sleep* until the resource it needs in order to continue is available. Most real-time operating systems (RTOSs) offer such facilities. In this case, the RTOS probably also offers *event flags* to signal sleeping tasks that they may continue. These are low-cost means to wake a task that is waiting on a resource. The OS calls are usually called *pend()* (wait for event flag) and *post()* (send event flag).

11.4.5 Condition Variables

Condition variables are an appropriate method of synchronization when threads must wait for events to occur, such as when data becomes available to crunch, or when another thread has achieved a required pre-conditional state before moving on. The thread waits on

---

9. The Therac-25 story is discussed in [5].

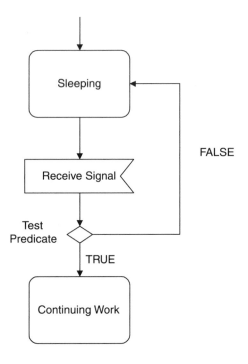

Figure 11-13: *Condition Variable Operation*

some condition in a sleeping state and is signaled when the predicate condition is changed. The behavior of the condition variable is shown in the activity diagram Figure 11-13. Note that the predicate condition variable is checked before continuing, even though the signal was received. This is to handle the condition of *spurious wakeup*, which is common to condition variable implementations.

If the RTOS does not provide condition variables, they can be constructed as instances of the Condition Variable Pattern, as shown in Figure 11-14. Note the explicit representation of callbacks (required to wake up the object waiting on the condition variable's predicate) and the policy.

Some RTOSs directly support condition variables. POSIX, for example, allows unconditional waiting on the condition (via the *pthread_cond_wait()* operation); as well as timed waiting (via *pthread_cond_timedwait()*). On the sender side, POSIX allows the signaling of threads waiting on a condition variable.

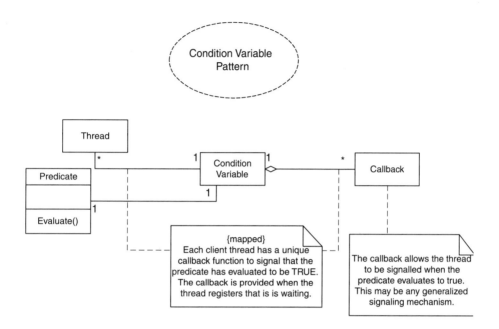

Figure 11-14: *Condition Variable Pattern*

Condition variables are often used in producer-consumer situations. In such cases, a consumer waits until data is available or work is ready to be performed. The producer threads generate the data or work, set the predicate to TRUE, and signal the consumer thread.

11.4.6 Barriers

A *barrier* is a condition variable in which the predicate on which the thread waits is a specific number of threads that are currently blocked on the condition variable. This allows the threads to meet at some synchronization point and continue only when all synchronizing threads are ready. For example, one can imagine a chemical plant in which two reagents must be ready to be mixed (precursor vats prefilled and reagents at the correct temperature), the mixing vat must be empty, and the output valve must be closed. This is shown in Figure 11-15. The details of the implementation of the join rendezvous are provided in the blow up.

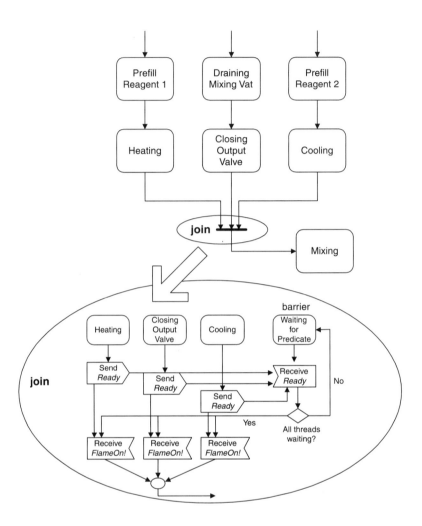

Figure 11-15: *Barrier for Thread Synchronization*

If barriers and condition variables are not provided by the underlying RTOS, they can be constructed. Figure 11-16 shows the pattern of object associations necessary to implement a barrier. Each thread that associates with the barrier object has a unique lock managed by the barrier object. As the threads register, they become locked. Once the pre-condition that the appropriate set of threads must register has been met, they are all released to continue. This is same as the Rendezvous Pattern from [1].

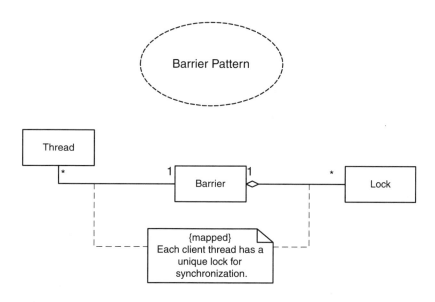

Figure 11-16: *Barrier Pattern*

11.4.7 Rendezvous Objects

The astute object modeler will notice that semaphores, condition variables, and barriers are really objects. They have data (values used within the predicate), state (TRUE or FALSE), and operations on its data (get, set, test, wait). They are specific cases of the more general notion of a *rendezvous object*. A rendezvous object is an object whose responsibility is to ensure the proper and reliable synchronization of multiple threads. When the RTOS does not provide the appropriate synchronization mechanism, a rendezvous object may be created.

11.5 Schedulability Analysis of Hard Real-Time Systems

Although several methods exist for predictable, real-time task scheduling, most published work for computing systems deals with rate monotonic analysis (RMA) and its various enhancements. The problems designers face with respect to schedulability are

- Predictability
  Time critical tasks have a hard deadline. Can you show that all task deadlines will always be met?

- Priority inversion
  Priority inversion occurs when a task of higher priority is prohibited from running by a task of lower priority. Whenever resources are shared among tasks, priority inversion is inevitable, but it needs to be at least upper-bounded.

- Deadlock
  Deadlock is related to priority inversion. It occurs when multiple tasks wait for resources to be released, but the release of resources requires tasks (which are blocked by the waiting tasks) to run. Because the waiting tasks cannot run until the blocked tasks run, and the blocked tasks cannot run until the waiting tasks release necessary resources, the system is kept from executing.

Rate monotonic analysis is not a single technique. It is a body of analytical methods that permits a set of tasks to be analyzed for schedulability. Individual techniques make different assumptions so that a wide range of scenarios may be analyzed. These techniques are organized in terms of their assumptions. The best reference for the techniques is the handbook by Klein, *et. al.* [4]. Anyone seriously interested in implementing these techniques should buy this excellent text.

11.5.1 Global Analysis

Global analysis, described earlier in this chapter, is the easiest method to apply. The technique assumes

- Tasks are infinitely preemptable.
  This means that whenever a high-priority task becomes ready to run, the lower-priority task immediately relinquishes control and the higher-priority task runs.

- A task's deadline is equal to its period.
  The period defines the frequency of task execution. When analyzing aperiodic tasks, the minimum inter-arrival interval may be substituted, although for many systems, this constraint is unreasonably restrictive.

- Priorities are based solely on period—the shorter the period, the higher the task priority.
- Tasks are independent and do not interact or share resources.

  Given these constraints, if

  $$\sum_{j=1}^{n} \frac{C_j}{T_j} \leq n(2^{\frac{1}{n}} - 1)$$

  where C_j is the execution time for task j
                  T_j is the period for task j
                  n is the number of tasks

then the set of tasks is guaranteed to meet all its deadlines.

For example, consider the simple class model shown in Figure 11-17. The three composite classes are all active (in the UML sense of being the roots of independent threads). The *data_acq_task* composite class is the root of one thread. It runs every 30 ms and requires 10 ms to execute (in the worst case). The *actuator_control_task* class is the root of another thread, and it runs every 20 ms and requires 8 ms to execute. Every so often, the *controller_task* runs (to adapt the closed-loop control values). It runs every 200 ms and requires only 5 ms to run. The basic execution information is shown in Figure 11-17, including the periods and worst-case execution times for each. The details of the sequence and the timing information for each task are also captured on a sequence diagram (see Figure 11-18 through Figure 11-20). Is this system schedulable—that is, can we guarantee that the system will always meet its deadlines?

The diagrams show the execution information required to apply the preceding equation. The intermediate results are shown in Table 11-4.

Table 11-4: *RMA Results for Simple Example*

Task	Execution Time (C_i)	Period (T_i)	C_i/T_i
Data acquisition	10 ms	30 ms	0.33333
Actuation	8	20	0.4
Master control	5	200	0.025
Computed utilization			0.758

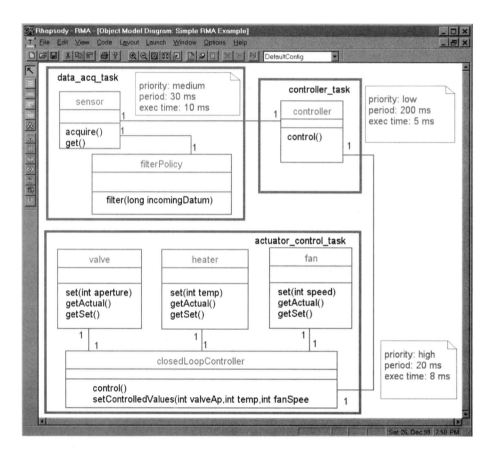

Figure 11-17: *Simple RMA Class Model*

The utilization bound for three tasks is 0.78 (taken from the right side of the simple utilization bound equation). Thus, because the computed utilization is less than the utilization bound for three tasks, the system is guaranteed to always meet its deadlines. Note that if the execution time for the actuation task was 10 ms rather than 8, the computed utilization would be 85.8 percent, well beyond the utilization bound of 78 percent. This does not necessarily mean that the tasks are not schedulable, merely that they cannot be guaranteed by this test to meet all their deadlines. A more detailed analysis may prove them to be schedulable.

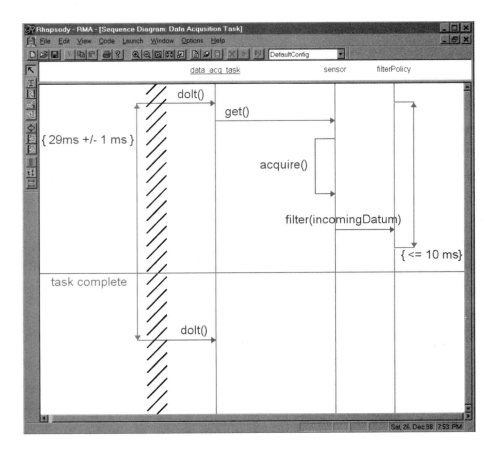

Figure 11-18: *Data Acquisition Task Sequence*

11.5.2 Global Method with Task Blocking

The constraints to this method are the same as with the global method, except that tasks may be *blocked* by other, lower-priority tasks. Generally, blocking occurs when:

- More than one task must share a protected resource
- A separate, lower-priority task cannot be interrupted during a critical section

In the latter case, tasks often have periods of time during which they cannot be interrupted. This can be true for the entire task duration,

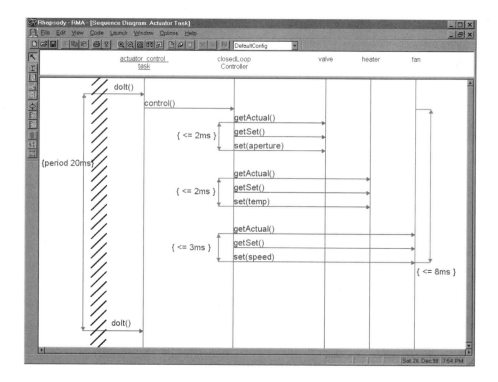

Figure 11-19: *Actuator Task Sequence*

as is often the case with interrupt handlers, or when the processing within a sequential section of a task is time-critical and delays due to higher-priority tasks cannot be tolerated. In implementation, this often means nothing more than turning interrupts off during the critical section.

To extend the global method to this broader context, it is necessary to determine the blocking term, B_j. This is the maximum amount of time Task j can be blocked from execution. To compute this, you must analyze all lower-priority tasks (it's not really blocking if a task is stopped from execution by a higher-priority task) to determine the length of their critical sections or their use of a resource shared with Task j. B_j is the largest of these.

Once the blocking terms for all tasks have been computed, the general formulation is

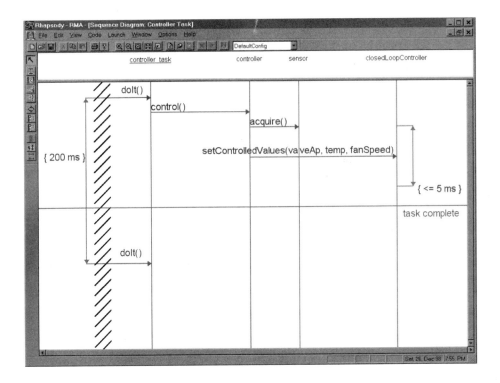

Figure 11-20: *Master Controller Sequence*

$$\sum_{j=1}^{n} \frac{C_j}{T_j} + \max\left(\frac{B_1}{T_1}, \cdots, \frac{B_n}{T_n} \right) \le n(2^{\frac{1}{n}} - 1)$$

Figure 11-21 shows an example in which blocking exists. *task_A* and *task_C* share a resource, which means that when *task_C* locks the resource, *task_A* must wait, even when it is ready to run. Note that in the absence of blocking, the tasks are easily schedulable, having a computed utilization of only 42.5 percent. In order to determine schedulability, we must compute the blocking.

task_C can block *task_A* for the time it can lock the resource—that is, 4 ms. However, because *task_B* can preempt *task_C* for 2 ms, the total amount of time that *task_A* can be blocked is 2+4=6 ms. Divide this blocking term by the period of *task_A*, and you get the value 6/20 = 0.3. Note that *task_B* cannot be blocked by *task_C*, because it does not need a resource that can be used by *task_C*. Also note that *task_C* can never be blocked in principle, because it is the lowest-priority task—by

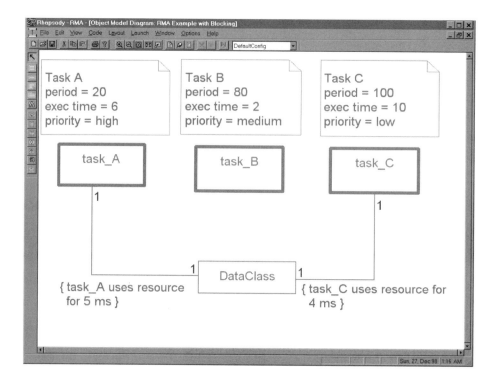

Figure 11-21: *RMA Example with Blocking*

definition, blocking can occur only when a higher-priority task is pre-vented from execution by a lower-priority task. The computational results are given in Table 11-5.

Table 11-5: *RMA Results for with Blocking*

Task	Execution Time (C_i)	Period (T_i)	C_i/T_i
task_A	6 ms	20 ms	0.3
task_B	2	80	0.025
task_C	10	100	0.10
Computed utilization without blocking			0.425
Blocking ($b_1/t_1 = (4+2)/20$)			0.3
Total computed utilization			0.725

11.5.3 Computing Blocking

Priority inversion is always limited to n-1 in a priority-based preemption scheme, where n is the number of running tasks. The analytical methods discussed so far do not deal directly with priority inversion. In more-complex systems than in the previous example, priority inversion bounding is required for the system to be schedulable in all cases. Imagine, for instance, the presence of 50 tasks between *task_A* and *task_C*, in terms of priority. *task_A* could be preempted by chained blocking of 51 tasks. Assuming that they require time to execute, it is extremely unlikely that *task_A* will meet its deadlines in this worst case. The problem could be avoided if we could find a way to limit the priority inversion to a single task—that is, so that one task could be blocked only by a single lower-priority task in the worst case.

There is a simple-minded approach to calculate the amount of time a lower-priority task (T_L) can block one of higher priority (T_H): Compute the maximum of T_L's critical sections and the longest use of all resources shared with T_H. The blocking term is the largest of these. This approach does not take into account secondary and tertiary blocking. Although there are no methods for eliminating it entirely, there are a number of methods for bounding the priority inversion.

The *highest locker protocol* uses dynamic task priorities. When the system is designed, all tasks that can use resources are known. It is therefore possible to identify the highest-priority task that uses each resource. This is called the *highest locker* (also called the *priority ceiling*). When an executing task uses a resource, it assumes the priority of the highest-priority task that can ever use that resource. In the preceding example, Task C's priority would be elevated to above that of Task A while it owns the resource, prohibiting Task B from preempting it. When Task C releases the resource, it is returned to its original priority. Because Task B is waiting, by the time Task C releases the resource, Task B would then preempt Task C. When Task A is ready to run, it will preempt Task B, if it is still running.

This technique requires that tasks do not voluntarily suspend themselves while they own a resource lock. Deadlock can occur if they do.

The *priority inheritance protocol* is implemented somewhat differently. A FIFO queue maintains a list of tasks waiting for the resource in question. The priority of the task currently using the resource is elevated to the priority of the highest-priority task in the FIFO for as long as it uses the resource. When it releases the resource, its priority is returned to its original value. This is typically implemented with a semaphore on the shared resource, to ensure mutual exclusion.

Highest locker and priority inheritance solve most deadlock problems, but a misbehaving task can still lead to deadlock by suspending itself when it owns a resource lock. Imagine two tasks, T_1 and T_2, that share resources X and Y. T_1 first locks X then Y, while T_2 first locks Y then X (see Figure 11-22). If T_1 locks X and then suspends itself, T_2 executes and locks Y. T_2 now wants X, but it is already locked by the suspended task T_1. Therefore, T_2 must suspend itself and wait until X is available. The system is now in classic deadlock. T_1 cannot run to completion and release its resources because it is blocked by T_2. T_2 cannot run because it is blocked by T_1. This is a possible scenario, but it requires ill-behaved tasks to happen. Nevertheless, permitting even ill-behaved tasks to deadlock themselves in a safety-critical application is not a good idea. Consequently, careful sequential locking of resources

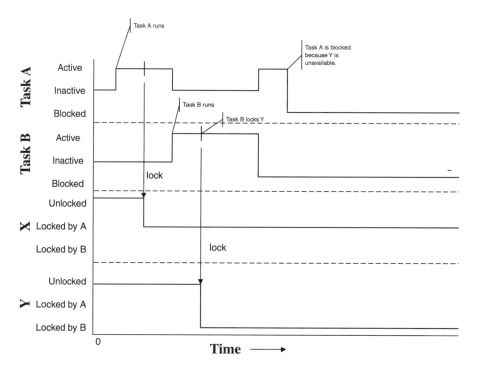

Figure 11-22: *Task Deadlock*

is recommended. Likewise, release of resources should be done in reverse order of their locking.

The *priority ceiling protocol* (PCP) circumvents even ill-behaved tasks from deadlocking. PCP is similar to the highest locker protocol in that the priority ceiling for each resource is precomputed. Each resource is controlled by a semaphore. Each semaphore has a priority ceiling that is equal to the highest priority of all tasks that can use the resource. As with the highest locker protocol, this can be determined during design. The system OS keeps track of the current value of the highest ceiling of *all* locked semaphores. This is the system priority ceiling. If a task is the holder of the semaphore corresponding to the system ceiling, then it is permitted to access another resource and lock its semaphore, as well. If the task is not the holder of the semaphore corresponding to the system ceiling but its priority is higher than the current system priority ceiling, it is permitted to lock semaphores of other resources. If it is not permitted to lock the semaphores, the OS blocks the task at the point at which the task requests the semaphore. If the task is blocked because it is stopped from using a resource, then the task owning the lock inherits the priority of the blocked task.

The disadvantage of this method is its complexity. Its advantage is that it can totally eliminate deadlock. In the example, when T_2 runs, it is not the task owning the lock of the current system ceiling (T_1 is). The priority ceilings of X and Y are both at least the maximum of the priority of T_1 and T_2. Thus, the priority of T_2 cannot be greater than T_1's currently elevated priority. Because T_2's priority is less than the current priority ceiling, it cannot access *any* locking semaphore, and the operating system will block T_2 the moment it tries. This may seem draconian, but it does mean that even ill-behaved tasks cannot cause deadlock. Eventually, when T_1 begins to run again, it will be able to access Y and so can run to completion, so even though T_1 is currently suspended, it is not deadlocked. Then T_2 will be able to run, as well.

11.5.4 Separate Task Utilization Bounds

The previous methods use a single utilization bound for the entire system. This is a rather gross analysis and its constraint is unnecessarily pessimistic. If the system does not pass these very restrictive constraints, further analysis may be done. This method computes individual worst-case task-response times and compares them with time available. The method assumes that the deadline for each task is less than or equal to its period.

Just as the world is composed of two kinds of people (those who categorize people into two groups and those who don't), this method iteratively categorizes tasks into two groups. For each task, the following steps must be employed:

1. First, find all tasks with a priority higher than or equal to the current task j. From this collection, H, subdivide the tasks further into H_1 and H_n. H_1 contains the tasks from H whose periods are greater than or equal to the deadline of the current task j. H_n consists of the tasks from H whose periods are less than j's deadline.

2. Once this division is made, compute the *effective utilization* of task j, where C_k is the execution time, B_k is the blocking time, and T_k is the period of task k.

$$f_j = \sum_{H_n} \frac{C_k}{T_k} + \frac{C_j + B_j + \sum_{H_1} C_k}{T_j}$$

3. Next, the utilization bound must be computed. Let n = the number of tasks in H_n + 1. and

$$\Delta_j = \frac{D_j}{T_j}$$

where D_j is the deadline for task j.

Clearly, if Δ_j is >= 1.0, then the task is not schedulable, because this method assumes that the deadline is no later than the period.

4. Compute the utilization bound U:

$$U = n((2\Delta_j)^{\frac{1}{n}} - 1) + 1 - \Delta_j, \ 0.5 < \Delta_j \le 1.0$$
$$= \Delta_j, \ 0 \le \Delta_j \le 0.5$$

5. Finally, if the computed effective utilization for task j is less than or equal to the utilization bound, then the task is schedulable. If, using this analysis, all tasks are schedulable, then the system is schedulable.

There are several more techniques available (interested readers are referred to the references, particularly Klein, *et al.*, 1993) that have a broader scope. There are methods that can apply to tasks with deadlines that extend past the task period, and others that can be applied to tasks that consist of actions that may have different priorities.

11.5.5 Aperiodic Tasks

Many tasks are fundamentally aperiodic, particularly those driven by user-generated events. The two main methods for dealing with aperiodic events are polling with periodic tasks and handling the events immediately. Polling tasks are frequently ineffective for high-priority, short-deadline aperiodic tasks, because the handling of the task is delayed until the next polling cycle. When analyzing polling tasks, the methods must take into account the worst-case response time, which is

$$R_j = Q_j + C_j$$

where R_j is the worst-case execute time, Q_j is the queuing time for the event, and C_j is the execute time for the task once it has begun. Polled tasks have the disadvantage that even when the system is idle, the event handling must wait until the next polling interval. In addition, polling tasks are executed even when the system is busy but the event has not occurred.

The other method for dealing with aperiodic tasks is to use a *sporadic server* task. When analyzing a sporadic server, the relevant time is the *minimum inter-arrival interval*. This is the smallest interval that separates two events of this type. For some events, classified as *bursty*, this is a realistic assumption. A bursty task is one generated by aperiodic events that may appear in clusters, even though there is an upper bound on the total number of events that may occur within any period. For nonbursty tasks, this assumption may be overly severe.

Sporadic servers permit analysis of aperiodic tasks. The research literature has shown that if the workload of a sporadic server is less than about 70 percent of the capacity of the server task, then the response time of the sporadic server is about six times faster than a periodic polling task and about ten times faster than handling the events as background activity. When the workload of the sporadic server approaches the server's budget, performance decays to that of a polling task.

The sporadic server is given a computational budget—that is, an amount of time it is permitted to execute. As long as this budget is not exhausted, a new event causes the server to preempt any lower-priority task that may be executing. As long as the server runs, it burns its budget. When the server's budget is exhausted, the aperiodic events serviced by the sporadic server are serviced only when the CPU is otherwise idle. Periodically, the server's budget is replenished. The priority of the sporadic server can be anywhere within the system priority scheme. For a full treatment, see [4].

11.6 Schedulability Analysis of Soft Real-Time Systems

Hard real-time means that absolutely all hard deadlines must be met for the system to be correct. "Softness," in this context, means that it is permissible to miss some deadlines or that the actions themselves do not have deadlines per se, as long as some other measure for timeliness must be met for the system to be schedulable.[10] The nebulous nature of soft real-time systems has resulted in their relative neglect in the real-time computing literature. However, with regard to schedulability analysis, as is often said, "Hard real-time is hard. Soft real-time is harder."

Determining schedulability for soft real-time systems is not easy. A natural example is the selection of the best line in a grocery store.[11] Even though, in this case, the criterion for "best" is clear (minimum time to [my] task completion), selecting the best line is difficult. It depends on a variety of variables, including the number of people in the line, the number of items each person has, how they are paying (credit or debit cards, cash, or check), how many coupons they have, and so on. This particular problem turns out to be so difficult that, in my own experience, random selection has, in fact, superior performance to planned computation.

In terms of maximizing the number of actions (purchase transactions), the solution is well-known—a single queue feeding n server resources (clerks). This is widely used in the operations management of banks for just that reason. One can only speculate about why this is not

---

10. It is usually, but not universally, true that the timeliness constraints of soft real-time actions are less severe than for hard real-time actions.
11. Therese Douglass, Air Traffic Software Architecture, Inc, private communication.

true in grocery stores. Perhaps it is to frustrate those of us that *can* do the math, or perhaps it is to provide the illusion to the customers of some control over their destiny. Stores try to minimize f_j (average frustration of customer j) by adding "10 items or less" lines.[12] However, this cannot *in principle* result in better overall schedulability than a single shared queue, even though it does shorten average handling of tasks with short execution times.

One common approach to schedulability analysis of soft real-time systems is to treat the system as though it had hard deadlines. Although it is true that if the system meets the criteria for hard real-time schedulability it also meets the requirements for soft schedulability, in fact in most circumstances, the assumptions are overly severe. This means that in order to ensure adequate performance, the system must be greatly overdesigned, resulting in increased recurring cost. The problem is exacerbated when one realizes that, in fact, most system performance requirements are actually soft.

A more optimal solution would allow one to:

- Define the criteria for timeliness relevant to the soft real-time system semantics

- Mathematically analyze a system, given known or estimated performance, to test whether these criteria can be predictably met

- Optimize a design to minimize recurring cost while ensuring that timeliness criteria are met

There is no general agreement on these issues, and no definitive answer is provided here. However, it is important to discuss and understand the issues.

11.6.1 Warm and Fuzzy: Timeliness in the Soft Context

One way to determine schedulability is to see to it that a certain percentage of deadlines are met. For example, one could set a threshold at 75 percent. The system is then determined to be schedulable if it will always meet 75 percent of its deadlines. Optimality scheduling is a matter of minimizing the number of missed deadlines. A problem with

---

12. Although I inevitably note to the clerk that it ought to be "10 items or *fewer*" nothing much seems to have changed.

this measure is that it ignores how late an action might be. A deadline missed by 1 percent counts as much as one missed by 10,000 percent.

On the other hand, we can see several ways in which this utility function can be generalized. The more obvious is that, in the hard deadline case, the utility function is a binary-valued step function. It is possible to envision that the utility of an action might assume multiple values or even vary smoothly with time. For example, consider the utility of a pacemaker stimulating a cardiac chamber. If the pace comes immediately following another or an intrinsic heart beat, the heart is refractory and will ignore the stimulation, regardless of its strength. Following that, the heart becomes extraordinarily sensitive to stimulation. Stimulation during this "supervulnerable period" can lead to fibrillation.[13] This is a bad thing, so its value is actually less than 0. Later, as it becomes the normal time for the heart to beat again, stimulating the heart becomes more valuable. Past the optimal heart rate, the utility decreases. Eventually, as myocardial tissue dies from hypoxia, the value of the pace reaches 0, where it remains. Such a function is shown in Figure 11-23. Whatever general formulation we come up with should be appropriate for the time semantics for both the binary-valued utility function and the multivalued continuous function shown in the figure.

Clearly, however, the concept of a deadline is very restrictive and doesn't seem to apply in any strict way to the pacemaker stimulation action. A hard deadline is a time at which the value of the utility function falls to zero. One can define (Boolean) lateness in a hard deadline context as:

Lateness = (Completion Time – Deadline > 0)

In soft real-time, it makes sense to think in terms of degrees of lateness (or earliness, for that matter). In such systems, a better definition is [8]:

Lateness = Completion Time – Deadline

which is then a linear function of time.

With such a measure, it is now possible to define another measure of overall timeliness—*mean lateness*—that is, the average lateness of a

---

13. Uncoordinated depolarization of myocardial tissue that prevents the pumping of blood.

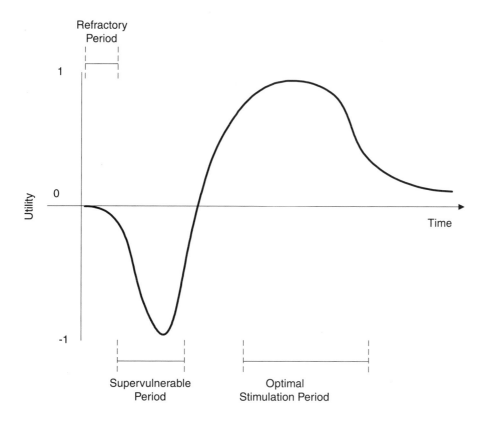

Figure 11-23: *Pacemaker Stimulation Action Utility Function*

repetitive action or of all actions. One might state that the soft real-time system is schedulable when the mean lateness is 0.5 seconds or perhaps 15 percent. This measure has the advantage that it incorporates the severity of lateness.

Compounding the issue is the relative importance of the action to the overall system functionality—an issue ignored in most real-time scheduling theory. In "classical" scheduling, a weight is applied to an action, allowing the completion of different actions to be compared with respect to their importance. This results in a scaling factor applied against the utility function so that some actions may have a utility function that ranges from –0.5 to +0.25 while another ranges from 0.0 to 1.0. Another optimization criterion is that the overall utility be as high as possible.

Another constraint in real-time scheduling is that an action is assumed to have no utility unless it completes. Partially completed actions may still have value. For example, it may be crucially important to get the control rods 75 percent of the way into the reactor core within a few seconds, but getting them the remaining 25 percent of the way may have decreasing relative value. Another example is iterative solutions that converge with increasing fidelity. Getting the rocket pointed at the correct rock in space quickly may be more important than aiming for a particular crevice if the computation takes much longer. In both these cases, considering an action to have value only upon completion may be an unwarranted oversimplification. This is the same as progressive utility, discussed earlier in the chapter.

It is also possible that a utility function may not be a function of a single variable (time). It may vary based on recent history. For example, it may be more important to complete an action earlier if the last action completed was very late. In such cases, the shape of the utility function might depend on the current mean lateness, average number of missed deadlines per unit time, or system state (such as *Parked, Taxiing on ground, Climbing in air, Falling like a rock*).

11.6.2 Soft Schedulability

Ideally, an optimal schedule is one in which all actions complete during their interval of maximum utility. This corresponds exactly to meeting all deadlines in the hard real-time situation. Barring that, a soft real-time system may be considered schedulable if the timeliness constraint measurement is acceptable. This generally means that the utility value of the actions satisfactorily compare with a fixed threshold value. As mentioned earlier, some timeliness criteria that may be used are

- All deadlines are met
- Minimized number of missed deadlines
- Minimized mean lateness
- Maximized weighted sum of utility

There are a number of barriers to analytical solutions of soft real-time schedulability, even when a simple criterion is used. The first is that the actions are performed in response to external events. The events have arrival patterns that may be as simple as a periodic arrival or may be totally unpredictable. Even if the arrival pattern is not periodic, it does not necessarily imply that the system eludes analysis. If the arrival pattern can be bounded or characterized in some way, it may be possible to determine its performance characteristics. For example, an aperiodic arrival pattern may be bounded by:

- Minimum inter-arrival time
- Burst length and a minimum inter-burst period
- Average arrival time, with an associated standard deviation and standard error

In large-scale systems, such as command and control (C^2) systems, these properties may not be knowable because of transmission delays, breakdowns and other failures, queuing delays, blocking, preemption, priority inversion, and so on. The only saving grace of such complex systems is that the timeliness constraints are generally less severe.

The other primary barrier to computable schedulability is that the execution time of the action may not be (and generally is not) fixed. Again, the standard solution is to assume the worst-case execution time. However, in some algorithms, the average or best-case execution is vastly superior to the worst case, and assuming worst case may be unduly restrictive. Further complicating the problem is that in some cases, the action need not complete to be of value. Statistical measures are often employed to solve these problems approximately—one can use worst case; best case; or some measure of central tendency, such as mean case.

As mentioned, predictability refers to the accuracy with which one can declare a priori the occurrence of the execution of an action. This is a very different concern from optimal use of resources, such as minimizing execution time. Many system designers trade off improved predictability for a less-optimal solution, particularly when the cost of failure is high. A periodic event is predictable. A periodic event with significant jitter is less so.

Because of the difficulties discussed so far, most soft real-time systems are difficult to analyze deterministically. Queuing theory can be applied to determine average throughput in some cases, provided the arrival patterns and action execution times can be well characterized. For the most part, there are no known closed-form solutions to soft (or hard, for that matter) real-time schedulability problems. For this reason, schedulability is frequently analyzed either ex post facto in a deployed system (where finding timeliness problems results in expensive redesign) or via simulation. Such simulations can exercise different scenarios of priority, arrival patterns, and so on to find an acceptable solution.

The most common scheduling policies for soft real-time computing systems use fixed-priority schemes. In a fixed-priority scheme, such as RMS, tasks (entities that perform actions) are assigned priorities at design-time. However, without a closed form solution, it is difficult to determine optimal (or even acceptable) priority assignments. For this reason, research has been focused in the last several years on the use of dynamic scheduling policies, such as earliest deadline, discussed earlier in the chapter.

11.7 Summary

Real-time systems are ones that contain computations whose correctness varies with time. The correction of a system action is given by its utility function—the value the completion of an action brings to the system's mission. Hard real-time systems are ones predominated by real-time actions whose utility functions are typically step functions. The point of time at which the discontinuity of the utility function occurs is called its deadline. Although the step function for virtually all known research and systems development is binary (that is, TRUE (valuable) and FALSE (either not valuable or actively bad)), it intuitively makes sense to scale the step function to account for the relative importance of different computational actions.

Priority is an implementation construct that takes into account importance or urgency, or some weighted combination of the two.

Soft real-time systems may be viewed as a more general form, with hard real-time constituting a specific case. Soft real-time systems contain actions whose correctness varies with time but may do so in any number of ways, including both smoothly varying and discontinuous utility functions. Because deadlines may be defined as the first discontinuity in the utility function after t=0, many soft real-time actions do not have deadlines because they may not have discontinuities.

The most common approach to scheduling is a simple FIFO (used in many distributed message-passing systems) or random (used in some communication systems, such as Ethernet). However, these approaches are problematic unless the system is significantly underloaded, because they will miss otherwise-schedulable deadlines. In most real-time systems in which schedulability is a concern, fixed priority scheduling is used to ensure those actions with higher priorities are executed first. In rate monotonic scheduling, for example, action priority depends on the period of the action.

In only a small percentage of real-time computing systems, priority can be fixed prior to system execution. Most often, action urgency and even importance varies during system execution. Dynamic scheduling algorithms can vary the priority of an action during system execution. Earliest deadline assigns priority on the basis of the closest deadline of actions ready to execute. Least laxity modifies earliest deadline to take into account the remaining computational effort required by the action. Maximum urgency first separates the actions into two sets—those with fixed deadlines (called the critical task set) and those scheduled by least laxity. All these algorithms are optimal in the sense that no other algorithm can do better, provided that all deadlines can be met. However, only RMS is stable. RMS is the only algorithm for which one can predict which actions will not complete in an overload situation.

Schedulability of an action means that it completes with an acceptably high utility value. For hard real-time actions, this means that the action completes prior to its deadline. Assuming "hardness" of deadlines allows you to make great simplifications, and it improves the tractability of formal off-line analysis of schedulability. However, only a tiny fraction of systems contain truly hard deadlines. Virtually all deadlines are soft to some extent, or the time value function may not actually contain deadlines at all. By pretending the deadline is hard, analysis is simplified. However, a large percentage of schedulable systems may fail these overly constraining tests.

11.8 Looking Ahead

Previously, we looked at the basic semantics of finite state machines (Chapter 2) and how to use them in system modeling (Chapter 7). We have not yet explored what constitutes "good" state machine design or how to reify state behavior. The next chapter identifies a number of commonly used patterns (ways to arrange states to solve common behavioral problems), as well as how to effectively test that a behavioral model is correct.

In the larger scale of things, a framework is a partially constructed application that the application specializes for its needs. Frameworks may be domain-specific and provide a significant savings of development time and effort. Chapter 13 discusses what constitutes a real-time framework, and what its advantages are, and explores an example of a real-time framework.

11.9 Exercises

1. Define the terms *periodic, aperiodic, period, inter-arrival time, deadline, execution time, jitter, predictability,* and *blocking*.

2. What are the two primary operations provided by a semaphore?

3. Identify four strategies for task execution following a failed request for resource access.

4. Using the data from Table 11-6, draw a timing diagram depicting system behavior.

Table 11-6: *Data for Timing Diagram*

Task Name	Arrival Pattern	Period/ Inter-arrival Interval	Jitter	Execution Time	Deadline	Priority
Task 1	Periodic	100 ms	2 ms	20 ms	100 ms	1
Task 2	Aperiodic	50 ms	n/a	5 ms	10 ms	2
Task 3	Periodic	250 ms	**10 ms**	40 ms	40 ms	3

5. From the additional information in Table 11-7, what is the maximum blocking term for the tasks?

6. Using RMA, determine whether the system is schedulable.

Table 11-7: *Data for Maximum Blocking Term*

Task Name	Resource A	Resource B
Task 1	8	
Task 2	2	10
Task 3		20

7. Consider the following specification:

The Acme Cruise Control user interface consists of four buttons (On/Off, Set Accelerator, Resume, and Coast). When the system is Off, the other buttons have no effect. When the system is On but a velocity has not been set, the system is *enabled,* but *paused.* When the system is *active* or *paused,* a momentary depression of the Set Accelerator button sets the velocity, making the system *active*; holding the button down more than 1.0 second acts identically to depressing the foot gas pedal, elevating the car's velocity. The Coast button temporarily *pauses* the system as long as it is held down. Once released, the system reverts to *active* velocity control. Any time the difference between the set velocity and the actual velocity exceeds 10 mph, the system *pauses* itself (is *enabled,* but not *active*). The system also *pauses* if the brake pedal is depressed. When the system is *paused,* reactivating the system by pressing the Resume button uses the previous set velocity. If the system is paused and the Set Accelerator button is pressed, then the system becomes *active,* with the current speed as the set velocity.

Create class and state models for the system. Draw up the external event list. Pick a strategy for identifying task threads, and create an initial set of tasks, complete with period and arrival pattern. Define the behavioral models for the Acme Cruise Control. Make initial estimates of deadlines and execution times. Make initial time budgets for the various method calls in the object model. Based on the task model, determine any opportunities for shared data, and estimate task blocking. Using RMA, determine if your system is schedulable.

9. Which of the following scheduling algorithms are optimal: rate monotonic, earliest deadline, least laxity? Which are stable?

10. What is priority inversion and under what circumstances does it arise? How can it be eliminated?

11. In what sense is the hard deadline a special case of a utility function? What is the difference between utility and progressive utility functions?

12. Name four criteria against which a soft real-time system may be optimized.

13. Write Dekker's algorithm for the case of n threads ($n>2$).

11.10 References

[1] Douglass, Bruce Powel. *Real-Time UML: Developing Efficient Objects for Embedded Systems,* Reading, Mass.: Addison-Wesley, 1998.

[2] Jensen, Douglas. "Real-Time Manifesto," *www.real-time.org*

[3] Lui, C. L. and J. W. Leyand. "Scheduling Algorithms for Multiprogramming in a Hard Real-Time Environment," *Journal of ACM,* January 1973; 20:40–61.

[4] Klein, Mark, et. al. *A Practitioner's Handbook for Real-Time Analysis,* Kluwer Academic Publishers, 1993.

[5] Leveson, Nancy. *Safeware,* Reading, Mass.: Addison-Wesley, 1995.

[6] Dijkstra, E. W. *Cooperating Sequential Processes,* Technology Report EWD-123, Eindhoven, Netherlands, 1965.

[7] Reisig, Wolfgang. *A Primer in Petri Net Design,* Berlin: Springer-Verlag, 1992.

[8] Pinedo, Michael. *Scheduling: Theory, Practice, and Systems,* Englewood Cliffs, N.J.: Prentice-Hall, 1995.

[9] Jensen, Douglas, C. Douglass Locke, and Hide Tokuda. *A Time-Driven Scheduling Model for Real-Time Operating Systems,* Proceedings of the Symposium on Real-Time Systems, IEEE, November 1985.

[10] Robinson, John, Thomas Davis, and Douglas Isaacson. *Fuzzy Reasoning-Based Sequencing of Arrival Aircraft in the Terminal Area,* New Orleans: AIAA Guidance, Navigation, and Control Conference, August 1997.

[11] Ben-Ari, M. *Principles of Concurrent Programming,* Englewood Cliffs, N.J.: Prentice Hall International, 1982.

Chapter 12

Dynamic Modeling

If life were easy, anyone could do it.
—Book of Douglass, Law 56

There are two primary problems in getting good dynamic execution models. The first is getting the models properly and completely captured. The second is testing and debugging those models to show they are correct.

Just as object patterns provide general object structural solutions to common problems, behavioral patterns provide general solutions to common problems of modeling object execution behavior. These patterns show idiomatic uses of statechart primitive constructs in ways that apply to a wide variety of problems. The patterns may then be instantiated and specialized for specific problems, leading to efficient and effective solutions to thorny dynamic puzzles.

Testing and debugging dynamic systems is much more effective when the models are examined at the same level of abstraction at which they were designed. This means that to efficiently test state machines, they must be tested using state machine primitive concepts and lower-level abstractions, which leads to the use of animated state machines in which graphical views depict states, actions, and transitions as the system executes.

12.1 Introduction

Earlier, in Chapter 1, we discussed some of the primitive semantics associated with state machines and statecharts. Later, in Chapter 7, we discussed the process of capturing dynamic behavior using statecharts during analysis. Those chapters did not provide guidance in good state machine design nor general organization of state machines to solve common problems. In the object space, those general solutions are abstracted into patterns of collaborations [1]. Similarly in the state space, many commonly used solutions can be abstracted into state patterns. In this chapter, we present a number of general state patterns that are useful in common design problems.

The other important issue in any kind of modeling is the correctness of the model. Specifically, in a development process, how does one effectively and efficiently execute the model and find and fix deficiencies?

When engineers began designing in high-level languages, debugging and testing those programs using assembly language proved difficult, because the problem was stated at a different level than that at which it was tested. The widespread introduction of source-code level debuggers greatly improved the quality and ease of testing and debugging. Now, as we use more-abstract models for representing systems, it is equally important that we test and debug those systems using the primitive concepts of the more-abstract modeling languages and that we do not test and debug using the lower-level abstraction set provided by source languages.

12.2 Terms and Concepts

In some respects, states collaborate to form an automaton that provides behavior for a class. This is analogous to the way objects collaborate to provide a mechanism. But while object mechanisms are structural things, state machines are dynamic things. The UML directly supports the notion of design patterns as sets of classes collaborating in ways that can be realized into a *mechanism*. The realization of a state pattern is a *state machine*. The UML itself does not directly support the notion of state patterns, but the UML metamodel does support the notion of a

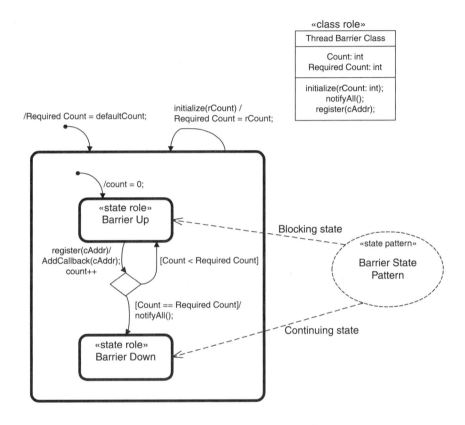

Figure 12-1: *Basic State Pattern Syntax*

state machine. To be more specific, we refer to the states within a pattern, but in actuality they are *state roles*. A state role is not a state per se—it is the role a state plays within the pattern.

Figure 12-1 shows the basic syntax for a state pattern. The dashed oval is a collaboration (pattern) icon. It is stereotyped to show that it is a «state pattern» kind of a collaboration. The rounded rectangles represent state roles. These are the roles the states will serve within the realized machine when the pattern is instantiated. The dashed arrows show the role within the pattern.

Note that the class is optionally shown in the pattern diagram. This is to facilitate understanding by listing the relevant class attributes and operations, which might be referenced within the state pattern. In addition, it may be appropriate to show states that are not part of the pattern

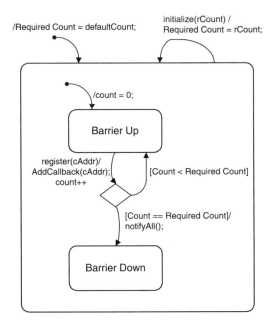

Figure 12-2: *Realized State Machine*

per se, but that serve to explain the pattern by providing context. To distinguish these illustrative states from essential pattern states, the pattern states are shown with heavy borders and the illustrative states are shown with thin borders.

As mentioned, the pattern is realized as a state machine. In this sense, the states in the realized machine are of the role stereotypes in the pattern, as shown in Figure 12-2. Usually, none of the stereotypes would be shown. They are provided here only to aid explanation.

The power of state patterns is that the expertise of state machine designers can be captured and reused in similar problems. In practice, there may be many ways to build a functionally equivalent state machine, all of which are equally valid and correct. However, individual solutions may optimize different properties. Some solutions may minimize complexity, others may provide maximum generality, extensibility, reusability, provability, or minimize code size or execution time. Evaluating tradeoffs and selecting a solution that is best for the application is clearly design work. In this spirit, the following state patterns are offered as solutions that may be good in a number of circumstances.

A pattern consists of three parts: a problem context, a solution, and a set of consequences ("features") of the solution. For example, the pattern in Figure 12-1 can be summarized as:

- Context
  A thread barrier is required when a set of threads must all reach a point at which they all wait to proceed before any of them is allowed to do so. A generalized mechanism should be able to easily accommodate any number of waiting threads.

- Solution
  The Thread Barrier State Pattern uses an orthogonal state pattern to count the threads as they register to indicate their readiness. When the specified number is reached, then the threads are signaled.

- Consequence
  State machines created using this pattern can handle any number of waiting threads, and this value can change by reinitializing the object. This is a low-cost implementation scheme for a thread barrier or rendezvous object when the order of thread registration is unimportant.

12.2.1 But Is It the *Right* State Machine?

State machines can be created through ad hoc methods or through the instantiation of state patterns. Developers still need a means to demonstrate that their state machines are complete (they describe the complete state space for the object), correct (the state machine has all the correct behavior), and robust (the state machine does the correct behavior in the face of novel conditions).

Complex state machines remain difficult to test in these ways. The traditional means for testing is

1. Model the finite state machine.
2. Decide on the code implementation strategies for each of the modeling construct metaclasses—states, events, transitions, actions, etc.
3. Write the code for each state machine by hand and compile the source code to produce an executable system.

4. Execute the source-code statements to ensure the state machine is "right." This is done by inserting "printf" style statements as actions in the state machine to track where it is, or by using a source code-level debugger to walk through the execution of the source code.

The fundamental problem with this approach, aside from the time and effort necessary before you can see if your state machine is correct, is that the testing is fundamentally at the wrong level of abstraction. Just as when you debug some C++ code that looks like this:

```
a += b % c;
```

you don't want to be looking at

```
0040102B    mov    eax,dword ptr [b]
0040102E    cwd
0040102F    idiv   eax,dword ptr [c]
00401032    mov    eax,dword ptr [a]
00401035    add    eax,edx
00401037    mov    dword ptr [a],eax
```

Even when you debug a relatively simple state machine, such as shown in Figure 12-3, you don't want to be looking at code like this:

```
switch(operating_active) {
   case shutting:
   { if(id == Timeout_id)
      { if(((Timeout*)event)->getTimeoutId() ==
         Reactor_Timeout_shutting_id)
            { myThread->unschedTm
               (Reactor_Timeout_shutting_id, this);
            pushNullConfig();
            operating_subState = idle;
            operating_active = idle;
            res = eventConsumed;
            }
      }
      break;
   };
   case idle:
   { if(id == Null_id)
      {
      //## transition 2
      if(heatReqs>0 && !IS_IN(faultS))
         {
```

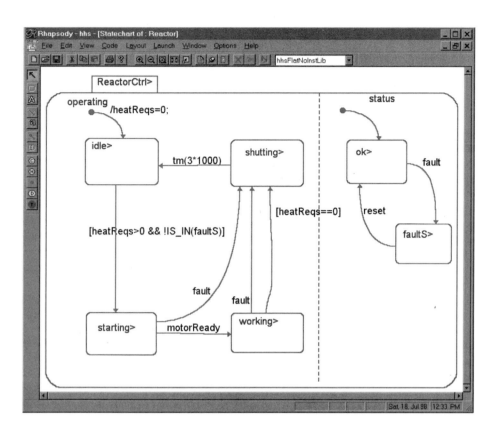

Figure 12-3: *Simple State Machine for Debugging*

```
            popNullConfig();
            operating_subState = starting;
            operating_active = starting;
            res = eventConsumed;
            }
        }
    break;
};
case working:
{
    switch(id) {
        case Null_id:
        {
        //## transition 5
        if(heatReqs==0)
```

```
{
   popNullConfig();
   operating_subState = shutting;
   operating_active = shutting;
   ROOT.reactorCtrl.operating.shutting.
   (Entry)
   { OMIterator<Room*> iter = get_itsRoom();
   while(*iter)
   {
      (*iter)->GEN(Fstopped);
      iter++;
   }
   }
   myThread->schedTm(3*1000,
      Reactor_Timeout_shutting_id, this,
      "ROOT.reactorCtrl.operating.shutting");
   res = eventConsumed;
}
         break;
};
case fault_Default_id:
{
   popNullConfig();
   operating_subState = shutting;
   operating_active = shutting;
   ROOT.reactorCtrl.operating.shutting.
   (Entry)
   { OMIterator<Room*> iter = get_itsRoom();
   while(*iter)
   {
      (*iter)->GEN(Fstopped);
      iter++;
   }
   }
   myThread->schedTm(3*1000,
      Reactor_Timeout_shutting_id, this,
      "ROOT.reactorCtrl.operating.shutting");
   res = eventConsumed;
   break;
   };
};
break;
};
case starting:
{
   switch(id) {
```

```
    case motorReady_Default_id:
    {
        pushNullConfig();
        operating_subState = working;
        operating_active = working;
        { OMIterator<Room*> iter =
          get_itsRoom();
        while(*iter)
        { (*iter)->GEN(Fstarted);
          iter++;
        }
        }
        res = eventConsumed;
        break;
        };
    case fault_Default_id:
    {
        operating_subState = shutting;
        operating_active = shutting;
        { OMIterator<Room*> iter =
          get_itsRoom();
        while(*iter)
        {
            (*iter)->GEN(Fstopped);
            iter++;
        }
        }
        myThread->schedTm(3*1000,
            Reactor_Timeout_shutting_id,
            this, "ROOT.reactorCtrl.operating.
            shutting");
        res = eventConsumed;
        break;
        };
        };
    break;
    };
    };
    return res;
};
```

It's not that the code is so difficult or onerous, but, just as in the earlier assembly language example, it is at *the wrong level of abstraction*. You'd rather be concerned with "Should the control rods be all the way in the reactor core?" rather than with how you are iterating over the associated objects to send them events.

The solution to the problem of the level of debugging abstraction is the notion of *executable objects* [2]. Objects that are sufficiently well-defined in their behavior (using sequence diagrams and statecharts) may be directly executable by a tool that understands the captured semantics. The UML provides sufficiently well-defined semantics for objects and state machines so that well-constructed UML models are executable.

This is important for several reasons. First, it means that automatic code generation tools can, in fact, be written for UML models.[1] It also means that, in principle, it is possible to build debugging and testing tools for the UML language rather than for the generated source code.

Objects may be executable in one of two ways. First, the object system may be simulated. This generally means that the objects execute on top of a virtual machine that interprets the UML statements and translates them at run-time into machine instructions. Simulation has a number of advantages. It is usually relatively easy to write a simulation interpreter (as opposed to a compiler), and the simulation can provide good debugging facilities easily. Simulation has some significant downsides, as well. It is usually much slower than executing native instructions because of the interpretation overhead. Also, simulations generally run in "simulation time," which means that they cannot handle real-time events, such as interrupts—such inputs must also be simulated rather than real. Another problem is that the simulation must generally run on the development machine rather than on the ultimate target, so the hardware peculiarities must also be (again) simulated. And probably most important, while the simulation can be tested, the real system must be tested again, resulting in at least two rounds of more-or-less identical testing. Many safety-critical application environments believe strongly in the adage: Test what you fly; fly what you test.

In such processes, simulation may not be an ideal solution.

The other approach to the execution of objects is to construct an object model compiler. Such a compiler reads one language (for example, the UML) and emits another, low-level language (for example, C++ or assembly code). The application of this approach to the execution of objects solves the primary pitfalls of simulation. It typically runs signif-

---

1. In fact, Rhapsody, from I-Logix, is the only UML-compliant, full code generation tool in existence at the time of this writing. A demo version is on the CD included with this book. See Appendix B for an overview of Rhapsody capabilities.

icantly faster than a simulation because there is no interpretation step to the model. It runs in real-time and can therefore handle interrupts and other "handle now" events. It can run on the development machine or on the ultimate target, and it is usually just a matter of retargeting the back end of the model compiler to the desired execution platform. Finally, the output of the compiler can be production-quality deployable code so that only a single set of tests must be performed.

Object model compilers do have their pitfalls, but they are less severe than those connected with simulations. Compilers are usually more work to write, for example. Also, it is more difficult (although not impossible) to debug compiled models than simulated ones. However, these problems are addressable, and a well-written compiler can provide a very capable debugging environment. One way to do this is via the same approach that source code compilers use—the insertion of instrumentation and symbolic information into the code stream to facilitate debugging. If this is done, the executable object model may be *animated*—that is, the execution flow of the model may be shown using graphical model constructs. State machines may be executed, and the user can see incoming events graphically activate transitions and current states become highlighted. Sequence diagrams can be drawn as messages are sent among relevant objects. The class attributes can be examined for their current values. All the things you would usually expect in a very high-powered debugging environment can be provided at the object model level.

The concept of executable object models is often met with some skepticism in the software engineering world. However, in my experience, anywhere from 60 percent to 90 percent of every application consists entirely of framework, or "housekeeping," code. For example, in order to implement a finite state machine, strategies for mapping modeling constructs to source code must be selected, whether automatically or manually. What is the code representation of an event, transition, action, state, conditional connector, or history connector? These selections are known as *representational invariants* (housekeeping code by any other name). If a sufficiently robust set of representational invariants is selected, they can be reused in a variety of applications. The other aspect of model compilation is the run-time environment. Most source code compilers link in one or more support libraries to provide services common to most applications. A model compiler is no different; it usually provides an execution environment, such as an operating system abstraction layer, container libraries, and a class framework[2] in which the application resides.

This is no different from what a source code language compiler does—provide a set of representation invariants (assembly code representations for source language constructs) and a set of services that may be invoked by the source language constructs. The technology is real and in use today.

12.3 Behavioral Patterns

A *pattern* is a parameterized collaboration of model constructs that achieve a higher-order purpose than the individual constructs. It is likely that many arrangements of constructs can meet the requirements of the collaboration, so a useful pattern optimizes one or more design criteria, such as complexity, reuse, extensibility, encapsulation, and so on. In general, patterns consist of three parts:

1. Problem context—the general problem the pattern addresses and important common contextual information
2. Solution—the parameterized solution provided by the pattern
3. Consequences—properties of the solution, both optimality and constraint properties

Virtually all work done in the object-oriented world with respect to patterns has been concerned with the collaboration of objects or collections of objects (packages or components). That is, they provide useful ways of structuring sets of objects to achieve some purpose with some degree of optimality. Object patterns are prototypical collaborations that experienced designers have found to be general solutions to commonly occurring problems. The patterns in this chapter are concerned with useful ways to structure *states* rather than objects. However, the same principles apply. The patterns provided here are collaborations of

---

2. A framework differs from a library in many respects. A library provides a set of services invoked by application objects. A framework provides a set of objects that invoke services of the application objects or are themselves subclassed to construct application objects. For more details on real-time frameworks, see Chapter 13.

states that are general enough to solve one or more common design problems and that optimize one or more criteria.

Many of these state patterns use orthogonal components to separate out independent aspects of the state machine. Although this does not appear to be widely understood, orthogonal components do not necessarily map to processor threads, so they are not necessarily concurrent at the operating system level. At an abstract modeling level, the distinction may not be important. However, at a design level, the overhead of orthogonal component implementation may be a concern. It is possible to have a single input event queue for each thread and have the thread manager dispatch the events to the relevant objects executing within the confines of that thread. It is also possible to implement orthogonal components within spawned threads. Thus, to avoid confusion, these partitions are called *orthogonal* (meaning "independent") rather than *concurrent*. That being said, the overhead for managing orthogonal components can be made very small, if desired. Also, in this section, the term *component* will refer to orthogonal state components rather than to UML components.

The following patterns certainly do not approach a complete set. The author is currently working on a forthcoming book on real-time design patterns. Readers who would like to submit structural (class, package, and component) or behavioral (state or activity) patterns for inclusion in the book are urged to send them to the author.[3] Table 12-1 provides a list of the state behavior patterns provided in this chapter.

12.3.1 Latch State Pattern

Problem
Many "work flow" style problems require a pre-condition state to have been passed through at some point in the past before an independent activity can progress. It is insufficient in these problems to require one component to be in a specific substate; rather, the more general condition is that the component has passed through the substate since the object's creation.

---

3. Email: *bpd@ilogix.com.* Patterns should include a three-part description, as they do here. The graphical image may be sent via Rhapsody project, JPEG, GIF, or PDF. Please send your personal information so that you may be credited with the pattern.

Table 12-1: *Table of State Behavior Patterns*

Section	State Pattern	Description
12.3.1	Latch	Remember that a pre-conditional state has been achieved for later synchronization
12.3.1	Persistent Latch	Provide a Latch Pattern that persists in a larger context by remembering the latch substate with the history connector
12.3.2	Polling	Periodically perform an action
12.3.3	Latched Data	Combine Polling and Latch Patterns to retain data even if the system isn't ready to process it yet
12.3.4	Device Mode	Model independent device modes of operation
12.3.5	Transaction	Model different quality-of-service transaction styles, such as for remote communications
12.3.6	Component Synchronization	General synchronization based on a set of ANDed pre-conditions
12.3.6	Waiting Rendezvous	Implement a waiting rendezvous with the Component Synchronization State Pattern
12.3.6	Timed Rendezvous	Implement a timed rendezvous with the Component Synchronization State Pattern
12.3.6	Balking Rendezvous	Implement a balking rendezvous with the Component Synchronization State Pattern
12.3.7	Thread Barrier	Implements a barrier for n components or threads
12.3.8	Event Hierarchy	Perform a general action on a class of events, as well as a specific action
12.3.8	Unexpected Event	A specialized subpattern of the Event Hierarchy Pattern used when it is a semantic error to ignore an unexpected event
12.3.9	Random State	Enter a new state using random selection
12.3.10	Null State	Use the results of a transition action in a guard by inserting a null state *(continued)*

Table 12-1: (*cont.*)

Section	State Pattern	Description
12.3.11	Watchdog	Execute a periodic liveness check to ensure the application is continuing properly by generating a stroke event for the watchdog orthogonal state component
12.3.11	Keyed Watchdog	A more elaborate watchdog, which checks for a proper sequence of events rather than a single stroke event
12.3.12	Retriggerable Counter	Decode pulse-modulated information with a retriggerable counter

Solution

Create a latch state orthogonal component that is initialized to "un-latched" with its default transition. When the appropriate pre-condition state is achieved, propagate an event to the latch component to go to the latched state. The coordinating component can use the latch sub-state in a guard to ensure the pre-condition has been satisfied.

Consequences

The Latch State Pattern is a simple behavioral pattern (see Figure 12-4). It is applicable in or out of the presence of concurrency. It is a light-weight means to synchronize independent behaviors when a latching condition is required. Other kinds of latches may be constructed. For example, an inhibitory latch (a latch that, when active, inhibits the progress of an independent activity) can be easily constructed by applying a NOT operator (for example, [!IN(Latched)]) within the guard condition.

The Latch State Pattern may be made persistent beyond the scope of the enclosing superstate by adding a history connector, as in Figure 12-5. The history connector (denoted with the circumscribed H) indicates that the orthogonal component must remember which substate it is in when the superstate is exited. The history initially points to the *Unlatched* state, indicating that when visiting this superstate for the very first time, *Unlatched* is the default.

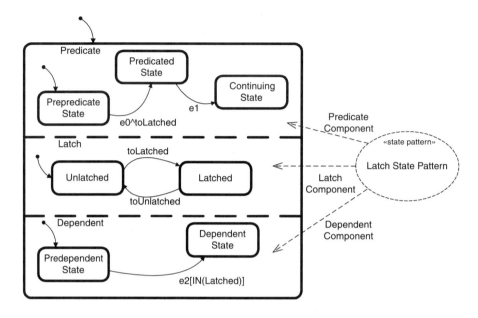

Figure 12-4: *Latch State Pattern*

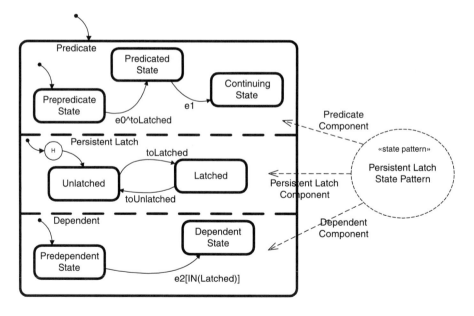

Figure 12-5: *Persistent Latch State Pattern*

12.3.2 Polling State Pattern

Problem

Many problems require active, periodic data acquisition. The object processing this data often has states associated with the problem semantics that are unrelated to the acquisition of the data.

Solution

The Polling State Pattern solves this problem by organizing the state machine for the object into two distinct orthogonal components. The first acquires the data periodically. The second component manages the object state.

Consequences

The Polling State Pattern provides a separation of two distinct behavioral concerns—the acquisition and the management of data (see Figure 12-6). This allows data handling to scale up to more-complex state behavior. One consequence of the pattern is that data that is acquired when the *Data Handler* component is in the *Crunching Data* substate is lost. To deal with situations that occur when data may potentially come in faster than it is handled, additional means must be employed, such as queuing the data or using the Latched Data Pattern.

12.3.3 Latched Data Pattern

Problem

Sometimes, we would like to use the Polling State Pattern but we do not want to lose data if a single datum is late. In this case, the construction of a single-element queue may be undesirable, even though it is more general.

Solution

The Latch and Polling State Patterns can be combined to solve this problem (see Figure 12-7). The Latched Data Pattern handles data immediately if the *Data Handler* component is in its *Idle* state. The handling is deferred if it is currently handling a datum, and the new datum is latched. If another datum comes in while the datum is latched, a detectable error occurs allowing for the intervention of error-recovery code.

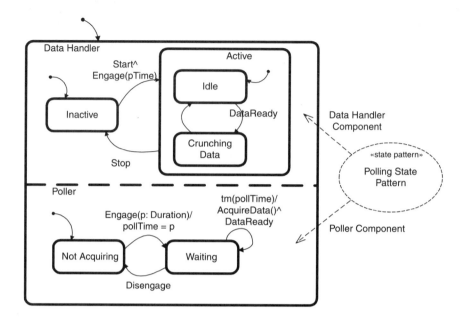

Figure 12-6: *Polling State Pattern*

Consequences

Notice that the *Data Loss Error* state is a dead end. In this pattern, a *Reset* event is required to restart the entire object to acquire and manipulate data. Other error-recovery means can be built in, as well. If more than a single datum may be late, associating the class with a queue object is probably most appropriate.

12.3.4 Device Mode State Pattern

Problem

Many systems are noticeably modal in their operation. For example, a device may be either Off or On; when it is On, it may be in *Demo, Boot Up, Operation,* or *Error* states. In any one of these high-level states, the system may transition to any other. Depicting this situation graphically as a flat state machine leads to a virtually unreadable state diagram. What you need is a simple way to represent overall machine state in a way that is clear and that scales up to different operational modes.

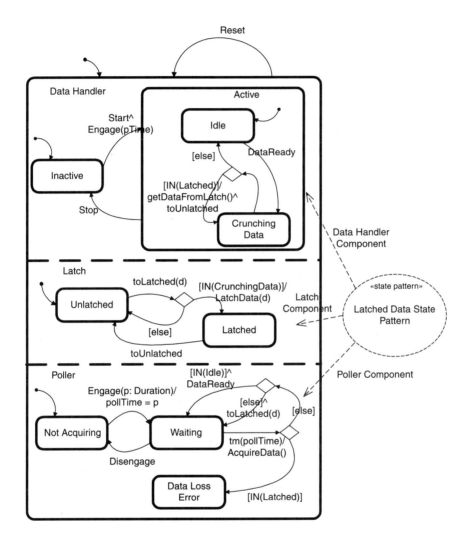

Figure 12-7: *Latched Data State Pattern*

Solution

This is such a common situation that it may be reified into a simple pattern, using nested states.

Consequences

The Device Mode State Pattern is a simple way to depict several independent modes that are all available (see Figure 12-8). The use of nesting

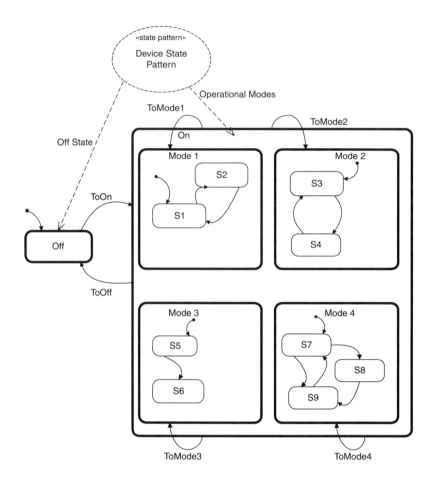

Figure 12-8: *Device Mode State Pattern*

avoids the "spaghetti" style of cross connecting all states. This state pattern is often applied to device controller objects that must track the state of the device has a whole.

12.3.5 Transaction State Pattern

Problem

Most messages or events are sent and forgotten—they need not persist. A *transaction* is a message or event that must persist for some period of time. This can occur, for example, during a reliable transmission service in which a message must be retransmitted if it is not received within a specified period of time.

Solution

The Transaction State Pattern is applied to transaction objects; the sent message or event is represented by an object. Each transaction object has its own state machine. This allows multiple transactions to be active simultaneously, each in its own state. Memory (that is, a count) is used to track the number of delivery attempts. When the number of delivery attempts reaches a set maximum, the sender of the message is notified of the failure. The transaction pattern in Figure 12-9 provides supports both sending and receiving transactions. This allows the construction of three service reliabilities: at most once (ATO), at least once (ALO), and exactly once (EO). The AMO service is a send-and-forget service (no transaction objects) similar to UDP. The ALO service tries to send reliably. If the receiver does not send a response within the appropriate time frame, then the transmission is repeated. It is called ALO because it is possible that the receiver will get more than one copy of the message rather than the original message, if the returning acknowledgement is lost. This makes this service appropriate for *set* and *get* style of messages, but not for increments or decrements. The last service reliability is EO. In this case, the receiver also maintains a transaction for each incoming message (for some set period of time). If multiple copies of the incoming message are received, the extras are quietly discarded.

Notice that the actual sending and receiving is done by other objects in the system. Specifically, the *Receiving* state responds to a *Msg Received* event. Objects (presumably in the communications subsystem) identify the message as matching the transaction in question (such as matching a unique message ID). The transition-to-self taken in the *Receiving* state has the semantic effect of resetting the timeout event *tm(Receive Time)*.

Consequences

This is a very common way to build communication services (such as TCP/IP transport) over potentially unreliable media. The pattern can be extrapolated should different reliability be required. Because the transaction object has an *Inactive* state, it need not be dynamically created and destroyed on message occurrence. This alleviates the problem associated with dynamic memory allocation in embedded systems.

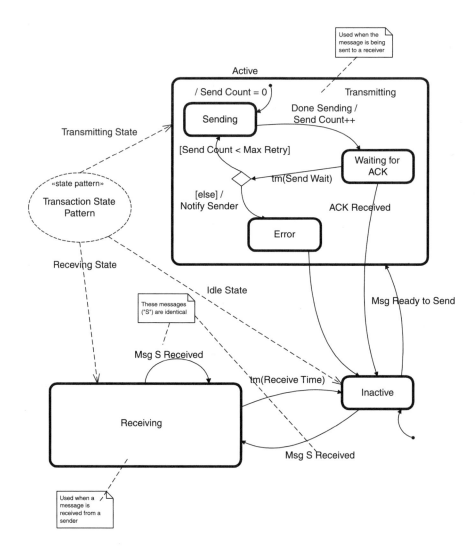

Figure 12-9: *Transaction State Pattern*

12.3.6 Component Synchronization State Pattern

Problem

Within statecharts, it is a simple modeling exercise to draw a superstate with multiple orthogonal components. An exiting event associated with that superstate (as opposed to one of its substates) terminates all orthogonal components nested within. Often, this event must be ignored if each component is not in an appropriate pre-conditional substate. For example, suppose a controller is shutting down several drainage valves prior to filling a vat. The *Filling Vat* state should not be entered until all the drainage valves are closed.

Solution
One solution is simply to use the pre-condition states of each of the participating components in a guard on the exiting event transition, such as:

```
e1[IN(Part1_Done) and IN(Part2_Done) and
IN(Part3_Done)]
```

The predicate guard may be arbitrarily elaborate. In some cases, an orthogonal component may use an associated latch (see the Latch State Pattern) to indicate that the pre-condition state was visited (and so is satisfied), even though it is not currently in that substate because of subsequent events.

Note, although three orthogonal components are shown in Figure 12-10, any number may be used.

Consequences
The use of guards as a means of ensuring predicate conditions are met greatly simplifies complex state machines that would otherwise require many latches. In most circumstances, the pre-conditional state should be a dead-end state within the context of its enclosing orthogonal component. When this is not true, it may be possible to nest substates within the pre-conditional state (so that the *IN( )* operator still returns TRUE). When this is not true, a latch may be required.

Also note that if the exiting event is anonymous (unnamed), then the transition is taken as soon as an event occurs that makes the entire predicate true.

Slight modifications to this pattern yield a variety of rendezvous subpatterns, as shown in Figure 12-11.

12.3.7 Barrier State Pattern

Problem
One of the common pre-conditional invariants for synchronization is that a number of threads all reach a shared synchronization point. When applied to threads, this synchronization mechanism is called a *barrier*.

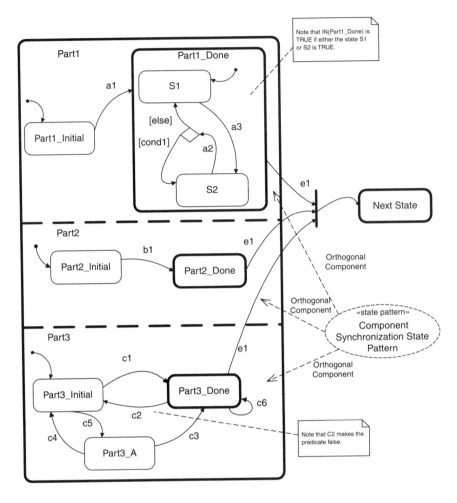

Figure 12-10: *Component Synchronization State Pattern*

Solution
Using a simple state machine, along with memory (that is, a count attribute), a barrier can be constructed (see Figure 12-12). As the threads register, they provide a means to be notified and the count is incremented. When it reaches the required count, the threads are released to continue, via notification.

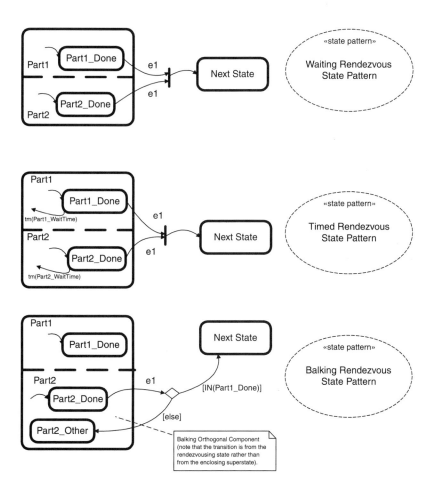

Figure 12-11: *Component Synchronization State Subpatterns*

Consequences

There is no enforced order of registration. In fact, other than the number of threads registering, this pattern provides no means to ensure that the proper threads have registered. In many cases, these are irrelevant to the application semantics. But if they are important, then a more elaborate state machine must be used. In addition, this pattern requires that some means must be provided to perform the notification of the released threads. In an RTOS, the threads may all wait upon a single

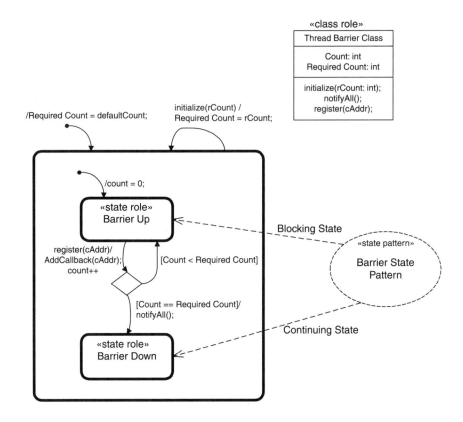

Figure 12-12: *Barrier State Pattern*

event, and this object can broadcast the event to all waiting threads. If this is a barrier to multiple orthogonal components within the same object, then they can all wait for the same release event to be propagated by the barrier. If the barrier is blocking multiple reactive objects within the same thread, then this object can iterate over the list of the objects, releasing them one at a time.

12.3.8 Event Hierarchy State Pattern

Problem
Some problems require transitions to be taken on several different events. The usual way to depict this is with one transition per relevant

event, leading to cluttered and hard-to-understand diagrams. This is usually done with nested states in which the superstate receives a set of events on which it must perform some action. Then it delegates the remainder of the behavior to a particular substate. One example would be an incoming message along a communication link, which may need to be preprocessed by the superstate. But various substates handle different kinds of messages.

Solution

One solution is to construct a taxonomy of event classes. The superstate then reacts to the event superclass and delegates to the proper substate based on the actual class of the event. Note in Figure 12-13 that the event *E* affects both orthogonal components. The processing component accepts it directly and performs its entry actions. The event-type-identification orthogonal component accepts the subtypes and, therefore, accepts the supertype, as well. If *e1* is a subclass of *E* and *E* occurs, then both components are affected immediately.

Consequences

This requires some run-time type identification (RTTI, in C++ speak) mechanism to identify the actual class of the event. If that doesn't exist conveniently in the target language, an orthogonal component can do this by responding to the actual event even while the other (superstate) component reacts to the superclass event. The event identification component can then store this information within a multistate latch or in an object enumeration attribute.

In the pattern shown in Figure 12-13, the type identification component sets an attribute and then generates a *done* event to signal the processing component that the event subclass is stored in the attribute and processing may continue.

Typically, unhandled events are quietly discarded. In some systems, however, the presence of an unexpected event indicates a serious failure, requiring immediate action. The *Event Processor* component in Figure 12-13 has an optional state in it called *Unexpected Event*. When present, this pattern is known as the *Unexpected Event Pattern*. If unexpected events can be quietly discarded, then the state-driven type identification mechanism used in Figure 12-13 can be greatly simplified by merely connecting the event trigger subtypes directly to their corresponding states, as shown in Figure 12-14.

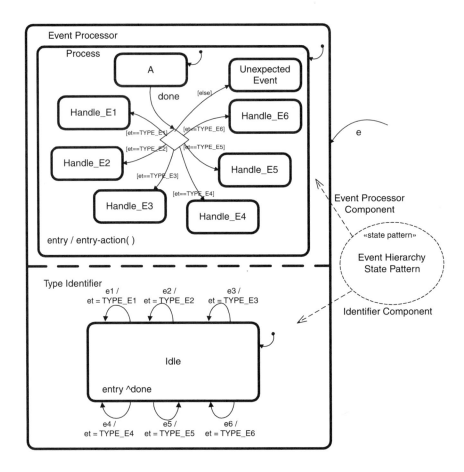

Figure 12-13: *Event Hierarchy State Pattern*

12.3.9 Random State Pattern

Problem
Because of an event, simulated systems often must change state randomly. But statecharts require precise definition of transition conditions.

Solution
Use a random number generator call within a guard to vary the target state.

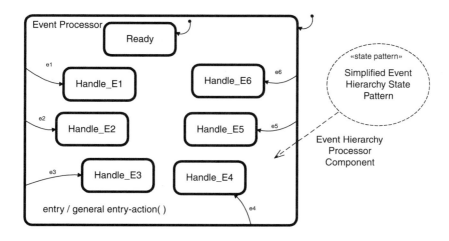

Figure 12-14: *Simplified Event Hierarchy Pattern*

Consequences

This pattern is of use when you don't want a deterministic state solution, so it is limited in its applicability to problems like simulation and genetic algorithms. Care must be taken so that only one of the concurrent guard predicates evaluates to TRUE. If this is not the case, the implementation is free to select from among the TRUE guarded transitions, and this will probably be a systematic, rather than random, selection.

If a random period of time is required for the transition from the *Waiting* state (see Figure 12-15), then the *e1* transition can be replaced with an event expression, such as

```
tm(100*rnd( ))
```

The timer must be triggered each time the *Waiting* state is entered. Thus, the timeout expression will be evaluated prior to executing the entry actions of the *Waiting* state.

12.3.10 Null State Pattern

Problem

The actions associated with a transition are executed only if the transition is taken, as determined by the occurrence of the proper event and

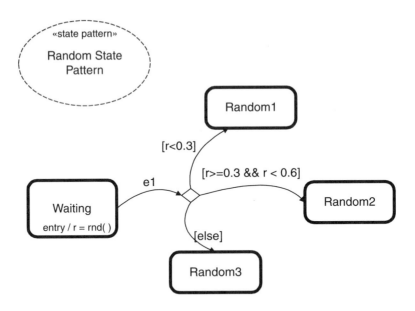

Figure 12-15: *Random State Pattern*

the guard evaluating to TRUE. That being the case, how can one use the results of an action within a guard on the transition? This happens when an event takes place that causes an action to occur (such as checking a message type or an external value), and based on that value, the state machine enters different states.

Solution
The solution is to insert a null or anonymous state between the initiating event and the guarding condition as shown in Figure 12-16.

Consequences
This is a simple pattern, but it adds an additional null state, leading to some clutter. However, it is the simplest approach when the action resulting in the value to be used cannot be invoked prior to the occurrence of a triggering event.

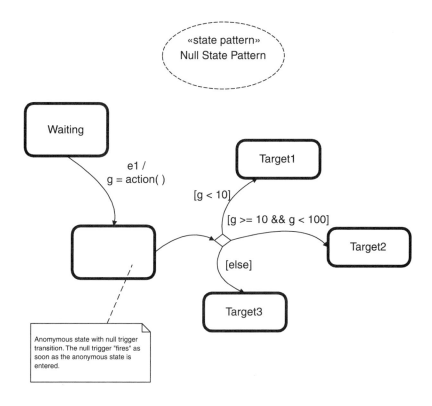

Figure 12-16: *Null State Pattern*

12.3.11 Watchdog State Pattern

Problem

In high-reliability and safety-critical applications, it may be necessary to continuously check the liveness of the application or object. If state transitions stop coming (indicative of missed events or a fault), the application must enter a fail-safe or error-recovery state.

Solution

A watchdog orthogonal state component may be constructed as shown in Figure 12-17. The *Watching* state is retriggered by the *Stroke* event (generated in this case, in the component above). Because the timeout is retriggered each time the *Watching* state is entered, the timeout occurs only if *WatchTime* has elapsed since that last *Stroke* event.

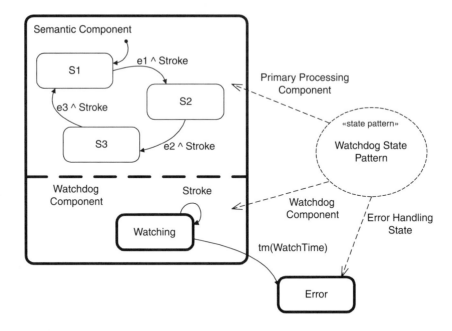

Figure 12-17: *Watchdog State Pattern*

Consequences

If implemented in a naïve fashion, this pattern suffers from a common mode failure. That is, if the CPU hangs or the processor crystal stops and the same processor is driving the semantic content and the watchdog, then it is impossible to enter the error state. For this reason, it is common to distribute the watchdog so that it has its own independent time source and executes on a different CPU. In this case, the *Waiting* state may be the only state of a watchdog object. Other objects signal events to the watchdog to indicate their liveness.

More-complex watchdogs, called keyed watchdogs, can be constructed by marching through a set of states in a particular sequence. This adds slightly more protection by ensuring that the repeated execution of a single block of code cannot be misinterpreted as liveness. The key can be a computed value passed with the event or different events. Both are shown in Figure 12-18.

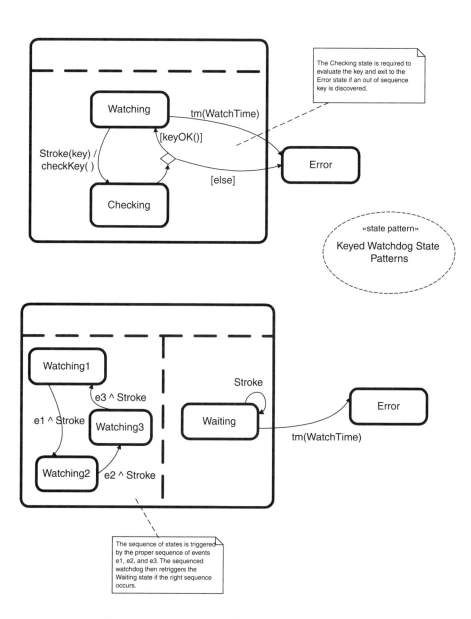

Figure 12-18: *Keyed Watchdog State Patterns*

12.3.12 Retriggerable Counter State Pattern

Problem

Many systems use pulse encoding for information transfer. Events occur in bursts of known length, followed by periods of quiet.

Solution

The solution is similar to the Watchdog State Pattern. As the countable events occur, they trigger a transition-to-self (see Figure 12-19). On each transition, a counter is incremented. Eventually, the countable events stop coming and the timeout occurs. The number of events occurring is then stored in the count attribute.

Consequences

Pulses must not come faster than the state transition mechanism, or they will be lost. The identification for the end of the pulse burst is a

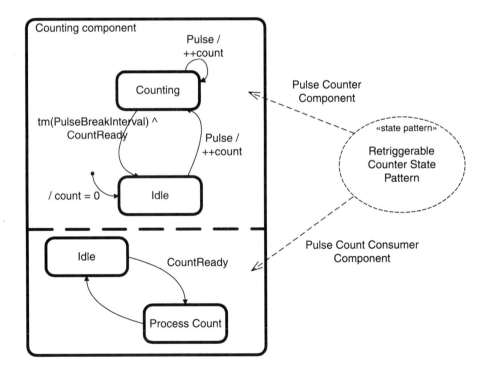

Figure 12-19: *Retriggerable Counter State Pattern*

quiet period of known duration. Processing of the last count may occur concurrently with the acquisition of a new datum from the counting component.

12.4 Model-Level Debugging and Testing

The reason why we, as developers, care about verifying models is because they are relatively unlikely to be correct. Oh, they're usually mostly correct, but that's just not good enough.[4] Most embedded and real-time systems have sets of requirements to meet, including quality-of-service (QoS) requirements, such as availability, reliability, and safety. Gone are the days when a developer could hold all the details of an application in his or her head. Most systems today are developed by teams of people (often teams of teams of people), and a single misbehaving line of code or model construct can have catastrophic consequences. In addition, the cost of fixing problems varies nonlinearly with the level of abstraction at which the problem was introduced. For this reason, defects introduced during the requirements analysis phase can cost 1,000 times more to fix in a deployed product than if they are caught during the requirements phase itself.

For this reason, many companies push to verify models as early as possible. This is the whole reason for the success of iterative lifecycle models[5]—they allow the early discovery of high-level defects, which are the highest risk and most expensive to repair. In keeping with this perspective, my key adage for developing high-reliability systems on time with as few defects as possible is: Execute early; execute often.

To practically implement this adage, it is important to build models that are *constructive*. By a constructive model, I mean:

- Model constructs (that is, metaclasses) have clear and unambiguous semantics.

- Metaclasses must be able to represent the structural and dynamic aspects of the system under development.

- Metaclasses can be mapped to source code in a repeatable fashion.

---

4. Not when I'm the one flying on the plane!
5. See Chapter 4 for one way to implement an iterative lifecycle development process.

- Metaclass → code translation can, and should, be done via machine translation.

By this definition, the following UML views are constructive:

- Object model diagrams, including class diagrams and object diagrams
- Statecharts
- Sequence diagrams
- Activity diagrams

Given the availability of a design automation tool that can compile object models into target source code, this approach has a number of advantages, the most important of which are

- Turnaround for an iterative prototype can be measured in terms of minutes or seconds rather than weeks or days.
- Code transcription errors are vastly reduced.
- Focus is more on doing the right thing (getting the analysis correct) than on the detailed issues of how best to do it (design and coding).

Naturally, in practice, we want control over how this translator works in order to optimize designs for speed, size (executable, heap, stack), and predictability, as well as to reuse existing designs and libraries.

As mentioned earlier, the best level of abstraction for verifying a model is the same level of abstraction used to capture the model semantics. To gain these advantages, we would like to employ the code-generation strategy discussed earlier to produce source code, but execute the model using the same graphical notation that captures and represents the model. Specifically, in terms of dynamic execution, we would like to see

- Object instances and their current attribute values
- Thread instances, along with their stacks and event queues
- Statechart animation for reactive classes
- Sequence diagrams drawn as messages are sent among objects of interest
- Operations being executed
- The ability to step through one operation at a time, as flow proceeds from object to object

- The ability to run to breakpoints based on such conditions as:
  a. Entry of a state
  b. Exit of a state
  c. Receipt of an event
  d. Execution of an operation

The view ideally provided by such a design automation tool would use class and object diagrams, state charts, and sequence diagrams as means to view, control, and navigate through the application as it executes.

A few design automation tools on the market today provide such capability. Object Designer, from ObjecTime, provides a simulation-style environment using the ROOM methodology [3], a proprietary object methodology. Project Technologies provides a tool based on the Shlaer-Mellor methodology [4,5]. Rhapsody, from I-Logix, is currently the only UML-compliant tool that provides these features. We will use that tool in our discussion here.

12.4.1 Animated Debugging

Figure 12-20 shows a typical debugging session. We can see several open debugging views. The browser shows the classes within the package and the currently instantiated objects. Viewing the object instance shows the current values of the object attributes. The statechart shows the state machine for one instance of class *T1* with the current state highlighted.[6] When the state machine accepts an event that causes a transition to a new state, the highlight changes to reflect the new state. Hierarchical states are highlighted at each level of nesting. The sequence diagram shows a mechanism of interest, consisting of several collaborating objects. As messages are sent from one object to another, the message is added to the sequence diagram, providing a "trace" of the collaboration.

The process for setting up a debugging session is as one would expect.

---

6. Rhapsody uses color coding to highlight the current state. But in these diagrams, we'll make the line weight heavy so that the current state is distinguishable in black and white.

1. Create the relevant portion of the model to be debugged.
2. Set the appropriate code generation options:
    *   Select the OS
    *   Select the compiler
    *   Enable animation instrumentation
3. Generate the code.
4. Compile and link the application.
5. Execute the application.

The first step is to construct the portion of the model that is to be debugged. This generally means adding a number of classes whose instances participate in the collaborations to be debugged, as well as adding some details of their behavior (operations, sequences, and states). Note that the entire model need not be present—only the classes and objects of interest. Statecharts and sequence diagrams are constructive views, so as actions and messages are added to them, matching operations are added to the class to support the behaviors. For early debugging, these operations may need to be only identified, not elaborated. At some point, operations like *EnableSensor* must contain code that you fill in, such as

```
int a = 0xff03;
outp a, ENABLE_CODE
```

But that can wait in most cases.

The remaining steps will be skipped here. Interested readers may turn to Appendix B or the on-line documentation on the CD.

12.4.2 Animated Testing

Debugging is a vital activity in the creation of any kind of executable systems, whether they are software, hardware, or a combination. Even more important for the development of highly reliable systems, however, is *testing*. Although debugging is an informal process of free-association examination of an executing system, testing is a more formal process in which the executable system is tested to ensure that it meets a set of specified criteria. The set of test cases for a particular test is called the *test suite*.

As mentioned in Chapter 4, most high-rel processes identify three purposes of tests: detailed tests of classes and their participation in mechanisms (unit test), testing of large collaborations of classes and mechanisms as they are integrated into components, subsystems, and systems (integration test), and testing of the entire system to ensure adherence to the behavioral specifications (validation test).

These categories of tests are different in many ways. One way they are different is in the design knowledge of the aspect under test that is utilized within the test itself. Unit tests fundamentally require detailed internal knowledge of the software or model structure. Such tests are commonly called *white-box,* because the details are visible. Validation tests do not test the design decisions themselves; rather, they test that the design, whatever it is, meets all the requirements of the system when viewed externally. Such tests generally hide all knowledge from the tester and so are known as *black-box* tests. Integration tests are in-between and require some, but usually not extensive, design knowledge.

In traditional environments, only the code is tested directly. Models are tested only indirectly, in the same way that testing at the assembly-language level also tests the source code. However, if we acknowledge that the code and the model ought to be completely isomorphic and that errors in modeling are vastly more expensive to repair than errors in code transcription, then we can only conclude that we would rather spend most of our testing effort testing the models rather than the code. The obvious questions arise: How do we best apply the animation modeling and debugging technology available? How do we effectively integrate this testing within the development process?

In Chapter 4, we introduced the *V* and iterative development models. The key to the success of this model (and its more-recent spiral and iterative derivatives) is that the earlier modeling activities provide the structure for the later testing. In early analysis, use cases and scenarios help to define the system requirements. Later in development, use cases can form the basis for the vertical prototypes, although other bases for vertical prototypes can be used, such as maximum-risk first. Use case scenarios define the required black-box behavior of the system and can therefore form the backbone of the detailed test suite for validation. Validation testing in the presence of an instrumented application becomes a matter of applying the same set of external messages and events to the application and dynamically constructing the sequence diagram as the system responds to those events. The resulting animated sequence diagram can then be compared, visually or automatically, to the original specification.

With such a toolset, this kind of validation testing can be applied on the host development environment, as well as directly on the target hardware. In the instance of Rhapsody, the target hardware can control the appropriate physical devices and read information from the actual sensors, and the execution of the system can still be shown on the development system.

One of the rules of testing that I employ is: Test first on the host, test last on the target.

The reasoning behind this adage (to which there are many exceptions, which will be noted) is

- You normally have better tools and quicker response on the host.
- The target hardware is often not available (or may itself be buggy).
- You have better control of the host environment.

When testing on the host environment, the problem arises of how to get the messages and events inserted into the application so that the system response can be examined. Because this is formalized testing, it is important that the tests be captured in such a way that the tests themselves are easy to create, review, modify, and repeat.

Tests that meet these criteria can be constructed in a variety of ways. One way is to use a scripting language that drives the insertion of events. In Rhapsody, for example, one can create a script like:

```
Go Idle
Break T2 stateEntered S3
T1->GEN(e1)
T1->GEN(e2)
Go
```

and save it as a text file. This script does the following:

Go Idle   Run until initial objects are created, the
                          stack is cleared, and no events are pending.

Break T2 stateEntered S3 Set a breakpoint in object T2 when it enters
                          its state S3.

T1->GEN(e1)	Generate (and enqueue) event e1 for object T1.
T1->GEN(e2)	Generate (and enqueue) event e2 for object T1.
Go	Free-run the application—that is, run until the application terminates or until a break point is reached.

A simple two-class system in the middle of these animation steps is shown in Figure 12-20. In this case, two classes, *T1* and *T2*, have an association. Both are reactive (that is, have state behavior). *T2* stays in state *S0* until it receives the event *f1* from object *T1*.[7]

Another way to test a system with these tools is to create actor classes that automatically insert events into the system. These actor classes can be arbitrarily complex, and it is frequently beneficial to construct them as finite state machines, especially because the modeling tool creates the executable behavior directly and automatically from its statecharts.

The same techniques can be applied to the other levels of testing. Unit testing is often ignored in many development environments, largely because of the work necessary to write and repeat the test suites on a per-class basis. However, by creating actors and making them friends,[8] they become repeatable test fixtures than can easily be excluded from the generated executable.[9]

12.4.3 Sample Debugging Session

The process of debugging is a free-form exploration of the execution of an application, with an eye toward finding defects. If a symptom of a

---

7. In this version of Rhapsody, propagated events are defined using the GEN(event-name) directive such as appears in the T1 statechart associated with the timeout transition from state A3. Standard UML syntax uses the "^event-name" operator.

8. In the C++ sense of: "You only show your friends your private parts."

9. One simple way to do this with Rhapsody is to put all actors in a special package, which is not built in the final system. Because the friend declaration in the application class can remain even without the testing classes' presence, building a deployable application is simply a matter of switching to the deployable configuration, a single action process. Other fully constructive tools should operate similarly.

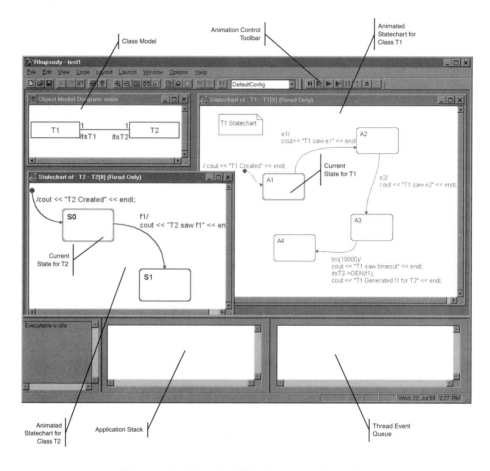

Figure 12-20: *Model Debugging Snapshot*

defect is found (for example, an attribute has an erroneous value or performs an erroneous action), there are usually several underlying defects that can create the symptom. Debugging consists of performing execution experiments to identify the actual underlying defect. The main rule of debugging is: Perform the experiment that eliminates the greatest number of defects from the list of possible causes for the identified symptom.

To illustrate the process, let us walk through a debugging session. This system is available in the Samples/PMx directory of the Rhapsody tool CD. The process is more intuitive if you actually execute the system while reading, but the diagrams should suffice for understanding the process.

The object model is shown in Figure 12-21. This depicts a simple cardiac pacemaker, dubbed the *Cardionada* (roughly meaning "heartless"). This particular model has many singletons. The purpose of the objects and classes is provided in Table 12-2.

Table 12-2: *Cardionada Class Responsibilities*

Object	Description/Responsibilities
Programmer	An actor (object external to the system) that allows the physician to configure and control the pacemaker.
Heart	An actor that provides cardiac electrical status to the pacemaker and receives electrical stimulation from the pacemaker.
Cardionada	The pacemaker device, which is composed of all the pacemaker component parts.
Communication_Coil_Driver	Object that both sends and receives bits (and bytes) via a telemetry coil. It pulses the coil 5 times to indicate a 1 bit and 15 times to indicate a 0 bit.
Reed_Switch	Magnetically activated switch that, when enabled, connects the telemetry coil to the Communication_Coil_Driver. This protects the pacemaker from inadvertent reprogramming.
Communication_Gnome	The object manages communications. It enqueues outgoing messages and queues incoming messages before identifying and dispatching them to relevant objects within the pacemaker. It does a small amount of interpretation of messages.
Chamber_Model	An abstract class that provides the basic behavior for pacing a cardiac chamber.
Atrial_Model	A version of Chamber_Model specialized for pacing the atrium.
Ventricular_Model	A version of Chamber_Model specialized for pacing the ventricle.
Battery	This object represents the battery. It can be queried by the external programmer for current voltage and estimated life expectancy.

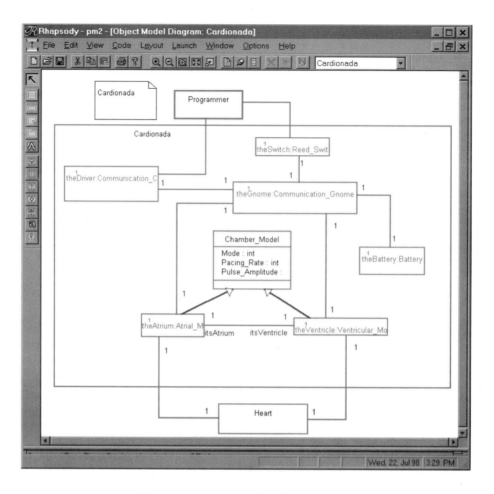

Figure 12-21: *Sample Object Model*

In this section, we'll focus exclusively on the pacing side of things. Figure 12-22 shows the statechart for this class. The Off state is used as a minimal-power storage mode. Once the physician implants the Cardionada pacemaker, he commands one or both chambers to the On state by sending the Cardionada a message that the *Communications_ Gnome* translates into propagated *CommandedOn* events. Then the physician can set the mode and pacing parameters, such as length of refractory period, pacing rate, pacing pulse width, and pacing pulse amplitude.

Pacing mode refers to the type of pacing delivered. In this example, several pacing modes are supported. Pacing modes are typically encoded using a three letter abbreviation. The first letter is the paced heart chamber; in this case *A* or *V*. This is the chamber that will receive the electrical stimulus when appropriate. The second letter is the sensed chamber, again *A* or *V*. This is the chamber watched for intrinsic heart activity. The third letter is the type of pacing—either *I* for "inhibited" or *T* for "triggered." Inhibited mode pacing works by sensing the specified chamber. If an intrinsic heartbeat does not occur in the selected chamber within a specified period of time, the pacemaker paces the chamber. Triggered mode is similar, except that a sensed heartbeat causes an immediate pace to ensure "capture" of the cardiac tissue.

The Cardionada supports the following pacing modes: AAI, VVI, AAT, VVT, and AVI. If the *Communications_Gnome* receives an AAI mode command, it sends the *ToIdle* event to the *Ventricular_Model* object and the *ToInhibited* event to the *Atrial_Model* object. Similarly, if the *Communications_Gnome* receives a VVT mode command, it sends a *ToIdle* event to the *Atrial_Model* object and a *ToTriggered* command to the *Ventricular_Model* object.

The astute object modeler may wonder why *Atrial_Model* and *Ventricular_Model* classes are subclasses of *Chamber_Model*, rather than instances of it. The reason they are not instances is that in AVI mode, the atrium must be paced and the ventricle must be sensed. It almost works to have the *Chamber_Model* fully define the AVI state and then instantiate both, but not quite. One must be in charge of pacing and the other in charge of sensing. Furthermore, these two objects must collaborate during the AVI pacing delivery. Thus, it is easier to model both of these as subclasses of *Chamber_Model* so that they inherit the general state behavior for the single-chamber pacing modes and specialize the one dual-chamber pacing mode into two different, but collaborating, subclasses.

The specialized AVI states are shown in Figure 12-23 and Figure 12-24. Because the rest of the state machine for each is provided by the superclass *Chamber_Model*, only the AVI state specializations are shown.

We can see in these figures that the *Atrial_Model* and *Ventricular_Model* objects collaborate by sending events back and forth to each

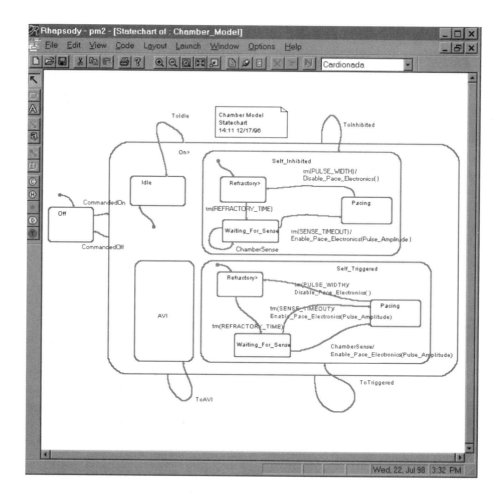

Figure 12-22: *Chamber Class Statechart*

other. It is this collaboration that we will briefly explore in our debugging example.

To build this model with Rhapsody, load the model into Rhapsody. Select the Code menu/Set Configuration option. That pops up a configuration menu. Click on Edit. In the Configuration dialog that appears, click on the Setting tab, and make sure that the following options are set:

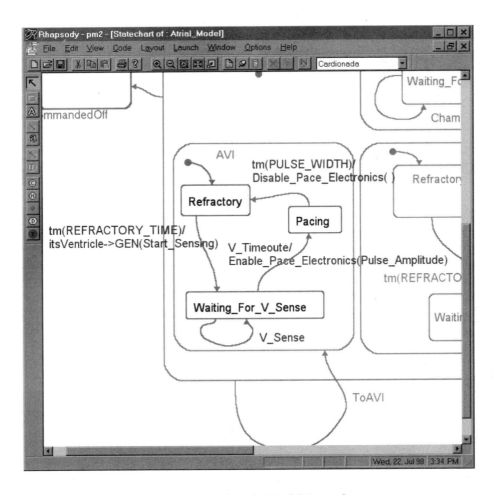

Figure 12-23: *Atrial_Model Statechart*

```
Type:                   Executable
Additional Sources:     bGlobals.cpp
Instrumentation:        Animation
Initial Instance:       Cardionada
```

In order to compile this, you must have the compiler that you indicated during the Rhapsody installation. Then accept the changes and close the dialog with OK. Now you can select

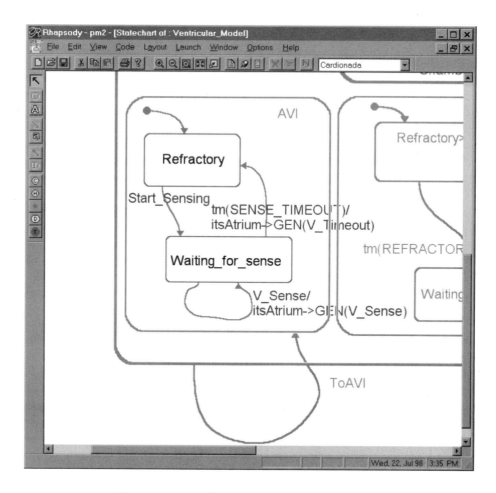

Figure 12-24: *Ventricular_Model Statechart*

```
Code/Generate
Code/Make
Code/Run
```

The executable is already compiled, so you needn't go through the steps unless you want to.

When you run the model, the animation control toolbar will appear. If you perform the following steps, you will get to the model condition shown in Figure 12-25.

```
Launch/Open Animated Sequence Diagram/Animated MSC2
Go Idle

[right click in sequence diagram on Atrial_Model
instance line and select Open Animated Statechart]
[right click in sequence diagram on Ventricular_Model
instance line and select Open Animated Statechart]

Cardionada->theAtrium->GEN(CommandedOn)
Cardionada->theVentricle->GEN(CommandedOn)
Cardionada->theAtrium->GEN(ToAVI)
Cardionada->theVentricle->GEN(ToAVI)
Go Idle
Go Idle
Go Idle
```

The first command uses the menu to open an animated sequence diagram. This diagram is predefined with the system border and the *Cardionada, Atrial_Model,* and *Ventricular_Model* objects already on it. These are the objects of interest to us in this debugging session. The Go Idle command is entered by clicking on the Go Idle button in the animation toolbar at the upper right of the screen (dark right-pointing triangle). This causes the executable to proceed until all events are consumed and the call stack is empty.

Once we've executed Go Idle, the system has created the initial instances of objects. In this case, the configuration specifies that a single instance of the *Cardionada* class is to be created upon startup. Because the *Cardionada* class is a composite, it also creates all its fixed-multiplicity components (the *Battery,* the *Reed_Switch,* the *Atrial_Model,* and so on). This is reflected in the construction messages drawn on the animated sequence diagram as the application executes.

Now that these objects are created, we can open their instance state charts. We do this by right-clicking on the instance lines in the sequence diagram and selecting "Open animated statechart." Both the *Atrial_Model* and the *Ventricular_Model* should be in their initial states of *Off*.

Now we'll enter some events to initialize the debugging session. The next four statements in the list are entered individually, using the "!" command from the animation toolbar. Type each one carefully. Each identifies the object, the GEN operator, and the event to generate for that object. If you look at the *Chamber_Model* statechart, you can see that the sequence of events cause both the *Atrial_Model* and *Ventricular_Model* objects to enter the *AVI* substate of the *On* state.

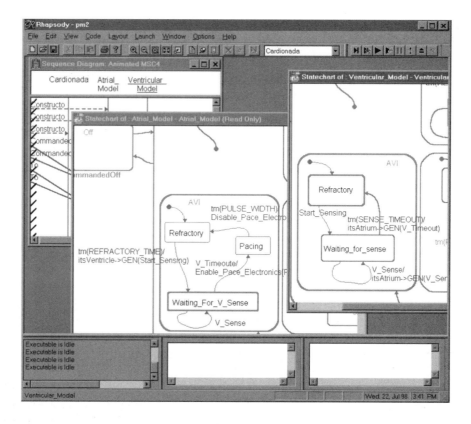

Figure 12-25: *Pacemaker Debugging View*

If you do several Go Idle steps, you see that the state machines for these objects get stuck; the *Ventricular_Model* object gets stuck in its *On.AVI.Refractory* state, and the *Atrial_Model* object gets stuck in the *On.AVI.Waiting_For_V_Sense* state (see Figure 12-25). Why is that?

In this case, we note a simple problem. The event specified on the *Atrial_Model* statechart is named *V_Timeoute*. This doesn't match the *V_Timeout* that is generated by the *Ventricular_Model* object.

To fix this, close the animation down by clicking on the Stop Animation button of the animation control toolbar. Open the state chart for the *Atrial_Model* and change the name of the event from *V_Timeoute* to *V_Timeout*. Regenerate the code, recompile, and rerun. You see that the application now cycles through the various states, just as you would expect (see Figure 12-26).

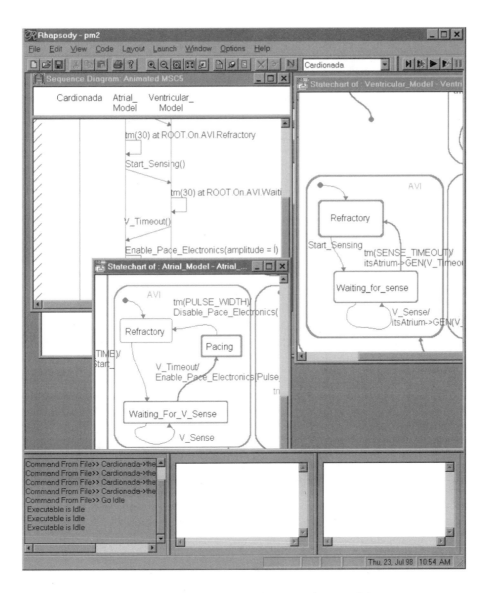

Figure 12-26: *Debugged Pacemaker Model*

12.5 Summary

This chapter dealt with a couple of important issues having to do with the effective modeling of dynamic systems. The first is the creation of reasonable state models that reflect the desired behavior. The second issue has to do with how dynamic models can be debugged and tested.

The approach taken for the first issue, the creation of good state models, is to identify a number of state patterns. A pattern is a generalized solution to a commonly occurring problem. Patterns are given in three different aspects: the problem context the pattern is trying to address, the solution provided by the pattern, and the consequences or implications of the pattern. A number of state patterns are provided in this chapter for your use. It is possible to specialize these patterns, merge them (such as was done with the Latch Data Pattern), or create entirely new patterns as they arise in your work.

The issue of testing and debugging complex dynamic systems is a difficult one. The biggest obstacle that I see in most development environments is that the applications are developed at one (more-abstract) level, but they are tested at another (less-abstract) level. This makes it difficult to identify conceptual defects, which have been shown to be the most expensive and difficult to repair. The suggested solution is to *debug at the same level as the system is designed*. Tools exist that can execute object models via both simulation and animation. These tools allow you to show that the models are correct, not by checking to see if the "jump on, no carry" assembly statement was correct, but at the "the control rods should be inserted into the reactor core" level.

12.6 Looking Ahead

The next chapter will look at the support environment for executable object systems. This support environment commonly takes the form of a framework, which is a set of interacting architectural patterns that provide the skeletal structure of a partially completed application. Frameworks can be specialized for their intended domain. Chapter 13 will focus on the features of frameworks that make sense in the context of a real-time embedded system.

12.7 Exercises

1. What is a pattern? What are the three important aspects of any pattern?

2. Why might it be a good idea to separate the timing aspects of an object that polls for information?

3. What is the difference between the Waiting, Timed, and Balking Rendezvous Patterns? What pattern are they specialized from?

4. What is another general way to create a pattern that randomly selects the next state?

5. In the chamber model statechart (see Figure 12-22), are any of the state patterns identified in this chapter used? If so, which one(s)?

6. Create a pattern based on the Thread Barrier Pattern that requires the three threads to register in a specific order.

7. What is the difference between testing and debugging?

8. What does the term *constructive model* mean?

9. What are the constructive object views of the UML?

10. What are some advantages of automatic code generation? What are some possible disadvantages?

12.8 References

[1] Gamma, Erich, Richard Helm, Ralph Johnson, and John Vlissides. *Design Patterns: Elements of Reusable Object-Oriented Software*, Reading, Mass.: Addison-Wesley, 1995.

[2] Harel, David and Evan Gery. *Executable Object Modeling with Statecharts*, IEEE Computer 1977; 30(7):31–42.

[3] Selic, Bran, Garth Gullekson, and Paul Ward. *Real-Time Object-Oriented Modeling*, New York: Wiley and Sons, 1994.

[4] Shlaer, Sally and Steven Mellor. *Object-Oriented Systems Analysis: Modeling the World in Data*, Englewood Cliffs, N.J.: Yourdon Press, 1988.

[5] Shlaer, Sally and Steven Mellor. *Object Lifecycles: Modeling the World in States*, Englewood Cliffs, N.J.: Yourdon Press, 1992.

Chapter 13

Real-Time Frameworks

The mind is the instrument of the heart.
—Book of Douglass, Law 185

Much of the infrastructure among applications is the same—the means for starting and ending tasks, task and resource scheduling, methods for implementing and executing state machines, and ways of implementing associations are not very application-specific. This is even more true among applications drawn from the same domain. Usually, anywhere from 60 percent to 90 percent of an application is common "housekeeping" code that can be reused if properly structured. The "traditional" way of building systems involves reconstructing the same implementation strategies over and over.

Another approach is to capture the common facilities required by all the applications of a domain in such a way that they can be reused as is, specialized as appropriate, or easily replaced if necessary. These facilities are generally a set of cooperating patterns that make up the backbone of the application. This infrastructure is called a framework.

> The use of appropriate frameworks can greatly facilitate the development of an application, because the common services need not be reimplemented. However, applications don't operate in a vacuum. The framework must provide an appropriate set of services for the application domain and must also work within the execution environment of the domain—including communication protocols, distribution algorithms, and operating systems. Domain-specific frameworks that meet these criteria result in applications that are robust and maintainable yet also support the rapid development lifecycles required in today's business world.

13.1 Introduction

There are several definitions for frameworks. The best definition that I've seen is: A framework is a partially completed application, pieces of which are customized by the user to complete the application [1].

Frameworks provide a number of significant, interrelated advantages for the quick development of robust applications:

- They provide a set of general ways to accomplish common programming tasks, which minimizes the complexity of the system, because there are fewer idioms to learn in order to understand the application structure and behavior.

- They provide service classes that perform many of the common housekeeping chores that make up most of all applications, which frees the developer to concentrate on domain-specific issues and problems.

- They provide a means to large-scale reuse for applications.

- They provide a common architectural infrastructure for your applications.

- They can greatly reduce the time-to-market for brand new applications.

- They can be specialized for domains so that they can capture domain-specific idioms and patterns.

One area in which frameworks have shown their value is in the development of Windows applications. Originally, Windows applications were hand-crafted C applications filled with complex and obscure Windows API calls to do everything imaginable. Windows applications were built totally from scratch each time. The development experience for Windows programming was that is was slow, painful, and error-prone—and the quality of the resulting Windows applications reflected it. Frameworks like the Microsoft Foundation Classes (MFC) and Borland's Object Windows Library (OWL) changed all that. Now, writing Windows applications with drop-down and pop-up menus, bitmaps, multiple document windows, and even database access, TCP/IP sockets, animation, and object linking and embedding (OLE) interfaces is almost as easy as writing DOS applications.

The tremendous decrease in perceived development effort is due to a single primary factor—frameworks. The use of frameworks also enabled a secondary technology, component-based development, to flourish by providing a common infrastructure in which to plug.

The same benefits are applicable in the world of real-time, embedded systems development. For the most part, real-time, embedded system development is now like Windows programming was a decade ago—slow, error-prone, and painful. However, through the development and use of frameworks that provide a common infrastructure, the development of real-time systems can be greatly improved. These improvements manifest themselves in higher quality and functionality and decreased development time.

13.2 Terms and Concepts

A modeling language, such as the UML, is defined in terms of a *metamodel*, which is a model of a model. In the UML, the metamodel itself is captured in terms of UML concepts. These concepts form metaclasses—that is, classes within the metamodel. The UML metamodel has metaclasses such as class, use case, signal, event, association, and so on. These metaclasses form the structural framework of the language and are used in the modeling of systems. Instances of these metaclasses are structural elements of an application model.

It is similar with frameworks. As mentioned earlier, frameworks are partially constructed applications. However, they also form a set of concepts in which an application model may be expressed. In this sense, a framework is a language for expressing a particular set of models. It is constructed using a more elemental language (such as the UML), so it is like having "scientific English" based on the more elemental language of "English." This doesn't mean that an application can't rise above the framework and add new application-specific concepts but, rather, that the framework provides a basis on which the application can be more easily constructed.

This perspective may be helpful because of the way frameworks are used in the course of application development. Frameworks are realized into executable applications by subclassing classes that may be thought of as the framework's *extension points* (which are analogous to use case extension points discussed in Chapter 5). This subclassing is obvious when doing source-level programming, but less obvious in design tools that generate code from UML models. In such tools, drawing a class *myClass* and associating it with a state machine may internally make the class create an instance of a framework metaclass "*reactiveClass*," which is a specialized form of the metaclass *class*. Making a class *active* (in the UML sense of being the root of a thread) may make it an instance of the metaclass "*activeClass*."

Of course, the framework is really nothing more than an extended or specialized metamodel of the underlying language of abstraction. Typically, some metaclasses and metarelations may be either omitted from (as unimportant to the domain of applications) or added to (as missing from the basic set of abstractions) the framework. For example, the framework may provide a number of ways to implement a state machine, set by user properties in the design tool. The framework metaclasses may optimize different aspects for enhanced run-time performance in various circumstances. Frameworks are typically optimized for certain types or domains of applications. They may be optimized for real-time systems (our interest), business applications, Internet applets, or simulation. By focusing on the needs of a particular domain, the concerns of that domain may be given special emphasis to enhance development, improve reuse, or optimize performance.

Frameworks may be oriented vertically or horizontally. Vertical frameworks are organized around a particular domain, such as financial systems or real-time systems. Vertical frameworks are typically more complete for that type of application because the knowledge of the domain allows them to have a richer metamodel. Horizontal frameworks know little, if anything, about the application domain. Instead, they provide a deployment infrastructure that allows them to operate in a common way (for example, a common user interface) or on a common platform. The Microsoft Foundation Classes, a commonly used framework for Windows programming, is an example of a horizontal framework.

One thing frameworks commonly provide that greatly assists the application developer is a library of useful *components*. You may remember from Chapter 1 that a component is a run-time thing that encapsulates and provides a cohesive set of services. For example, a framework may provide an abstraction of OS services so that applications may be written in an OS-independent (that is, portable) fashion. For example, the Windows metamodel provides a hardware abstraction layer for hardware control services, standard user interface services for a common look and feel, and abstract communication services, such as TCP/IP sockets, for networking. Components may also be purchased for specialized or enhanced services. Vertical frameworks may offer highly specialized components specific to the application domain of interest.

This view of frameworks is from the perspective of a modeler. An entirely different view of frameworks is from that of the framework implementer—namely, that a framework is a set of interacting and supporting design patterns. A design pattern, as we have already seen in several places in this book, is an abstraction of a collaboration that has been shown to be a general solution to a commonly occurring problem. The user's application creates instances of the collaborations.[1] This is typically accomplished in object-oriented frameworks by subclassing the classes in the collaboration and then instantiating them. It is common for a framework to provide one or more design patterns to meet a specific need, allowing the developer to fine tune the application's performance.

As discussed earlier, several kinds of patterns may be identified. *Architectural patterns* imply broad-scope, strategic decisions that have significant impact on the overall structure or performance of the system. *Mechanistic patterns* are abstractions of smaller collaborations, with primarily local effects—a relatively small set of interacting classes

---

1. We use the term *mechanism* for an instance of a collaboration.

that collaborate for a medium-scale purpose. Such collaborations often implement a single use case, for example. *Behavioral patterns* are a kind of *detailed design pattern,* because they implement patterns of state interactions that usually reside within a single class. Frameworks provide at least the first two kinds of patterns: architectural and mechanistic. They will provide the detail design patterns only when the domain is highly dependent on dynamic behavioral modeling.

13.3 Real-Time Frameworks

A *real-time framework* is a vertical framework optimized for real-time applications. Real-time frameworks usually provide all three kinds of patterns, as well as components optimized for predictability, speed, and size. The patterns presented in this section indicate the general flavor of patterns rather than a comprehensive list. The format of these patterns follows that of the behavioral patterns discussed in Chapter 12.

13.3.1 Architectural Support Patterns

One of the distinguishing characteristics of architectural patterns is that they represent strategic decisions that affect most or all of an application. Besides the fundamental organization of domains and layers, another key strategic decision for many real-time and embedded systems is the principles used for distribution across multiple processors and networks. A number of these patterns are provided elsewhere [2], but we will present a few of particular relevance here. Interested readers should check the references [2, 5, 6] at the end of this chapter.

13.3.1.1 Microkernel Architecture Pattern

Problem
Complex systems are often required not only to work properly (a difficult enough task), but also to be portable to multiple platforms and be easily adaptable to multiple sets of components. Unless care is taken, it is easy to propagate dependence on certain components or platform details throughout the system. This results in greatly increased maintenance costs and system fragility.

Solution

The Microkernel Architecture Pattern is a common way of building complex applications, because it allows a separation of concerns. These concerns may be separated in a couple of ways. One way is by level of abstraction. The more concrete layers of abstraction provide services to implement the more abstract layers above. The sending of a message from one object to another is a fairly abstract notion. The next lower level of abstraction may implement this by marshalling resources to construct a TCP/IP message for transmission to a remote object. A layer below that may concern itself with the actual byte and bit ordering of that message and the mechanics to send it along a bus. An even lower-level abstraction may use RTOS calls to invoke the remote communications services. An even lower level of abstraction deals with banging the bits out along a serial bus.

Consequences

The Microkernel Architecture Pattern in Figure 13-1 has no serious drawbacks. If a *closed architecture subpattern* is used (allowing a layer to call services of objects only in the layer immediately below it), the resulting system is more robust in the presence of modifications, but can be less efficient. An *open architecture subpattern* (allowing a layer to invoke services of any layer below, regardless of nesting depth) is more difficult to maintain, but can be more efficient. For this reason, open architectures are more common in real-time systems.

13.3.1.2 Six-Tier Microkernel Architectural Pattern

Problem

Optimal layer organization is not always obvious.

Solution

Another scheme for layering architectures is related but subtly different. Layers may be organized around *subject areas of interest*. Each subject area is termed a *domain* [3, 4]. Every domain contains a set of classes and objects related by subject matter.

Many architectures are actually mixtures of these two organizational principles. For example, the six-tier Microkernel Architectural Pattern in Figure 13-2 divides the system into domains and also into layers of abstraction. Table 13-1 provides the domain descriptions with

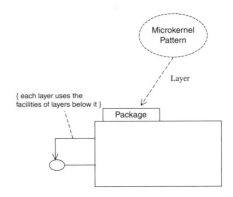

Figure 13-1: *Microkernel Architecture Pattern*

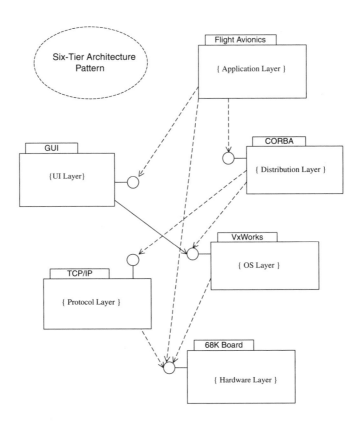

Figure 13-2: *Six-Tier Microkernel Architecture*

Table 13-1: *Domain Description for 6-Tier Architecture*

Domain	Description	Sample classes
Application	Concepts inherent in the specific problem domain reify into a set of related classes and objects	Flight Trajectory Speed Altitude
Distribution	Concepts related to the distribution of objects, data, and control flow in a distributed system	Distributed object Distributed message Naming service
User interface (UI)	Concepts related to the display of information and monitoring of user inputs	Window Scroll bar Bitmap Mouse click Button
Protocol	Concepts related to the reliable transmission and reception of messages across a communication medium	Protocol message Frame Message transaction CRC
OS	Concepts related to the management of task and resource scheduling control	Thread Mutex Barrier Heap Stack
Hardware	Concepts related to the direct control and monitoring of hardware devices	Register Interrupt Address Port

some sample classes to illustrate the partitioning of concerns within this architectural model.

Consequences

Domains are related to each other with one-way dependencies. More-abstract domains depend on more-concrete domains. These dependencies result in associations among the classes in the respective domains. For example, an application class, such as *flight,* may have an associated view in the UI domain and be distributed across multiple processors using the various object services in the distribution domain. On some of these nodes, the flight may be monitored using TCAS (running on the aircraft), GPS (running on multiple satellites and the aircraft), and active and passive radars. The application object may then combine this information based on sensor fusion techniques to a position and velocity vector with associated confidence factors for an air traffic controller.

Note that the domains are logically complete, because they contain all the relevant concepts and their interrelations within a certain subject matter. However, object collaborations almost always cross domain boundaries via associations and aggregations. However, generalization does *not* cross domain boundaries. There is no subclass of *Window,* for example, that belongs in any other domain. There are subclasses of *Window* that may be associated with objects in other domains, but the subclasses of *Window* must, in principle, remain within the UI domain.

13.3.2 Collaboration and Distribution Patterns

The patterns in this section are often provided in frameworks as solid and reliable solutions to common application domain problems.

13.3.2.1 Container-Iterator Pattern

Problem
Classes with nonunary multiplicities should resolve into a consistent implementation that handles the manipulation of 1-* associations. It is problematic and error-prone to populate the unary class with all the behavior necessary to manipulate an arbitrary number of client classes.

Solution
The use of containers is a standard approach to the storage and manipulation of multiple objects. A container class exists solely to manage the collections of objects. A 1-* multiplicity is resolved to a 1-1 association between the client and the container and a 1-* association from the container to the objects being contained. To be thread-reliable, iterators are used instead of internal, current-object pointers within the container. An iterator is a class (typically, a *friend* to the container class) that allows the unary class to select and manipulate objects held within the container. Figure 13-3 shows the container-iterator pattern.

Most often, the containers and iterators are parameterized classes, because the behavior of the container is identical, regardless of the class of objects contained. The unary class then has a pointer or reference to the container class and sends requests to the container by means of an iterator.

Consequences

The container pattern is widely used; in fact, it is so common that the Standard Template Library (STL), which consists mostly of containers and iterators, is part of the ANSI C++ standard. If containers provide a common interface, they can be interchanged, even at run-time, to optimize performance, if desired. There is generally a relatively small performance overhead exacted by the use of this pattern, but it is often offset by carefully crafting the set of containers and iterators.

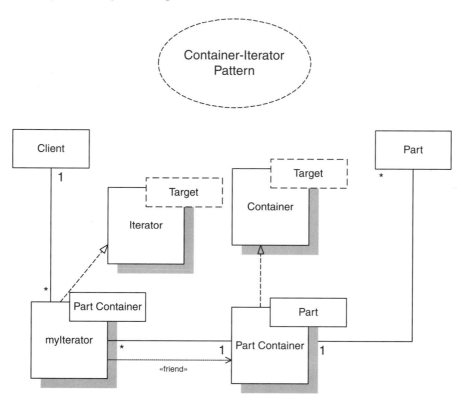

Figure 13-3: *Container-Iterator Pattern*

13.3.2.2 Observer Pattern

Problem

If a server associates to an arbitrary number of clients that depend on timely updates to server data, some means is necessary to get the data to the clients. It may be too inefficient to require each client to poll the server in order to get updated data, and it may increase the level of blocking and priority inversion in the system.

Solution

The Observer Pattern allows interested clients to subscribe to the server to receive automatic updates based on a changeable policy. Clients subscribe and detach, using related operations in the server class. The server class associates with one notification handle per registered client. The notification handle in Figure 13-4 is subclassed for episodic (that is, notification when the data changes), periodic notifications of the client, or both. Another solution is to associate the notification class with a policy class that manages the notification policy.

Consequences

The Observer Pattern is an efficient solution for systems in which the rate of change of data differs significantly from timeliness requirements for handling data changes. In addition, when there are many clients, it is inefficient to have each of them allocate timers for periodic updates, even if the period of the data is known.

13.3.2.3 Proxy Pattern

Problem

The Observer Pattern is inapplicable when the clients of the server are in different address spaces, either because they are in different threads or because they are running on different processors. This is because the normal notification scheme is through callback functions. Nevertheless, the Observer Pattern provides a number of advantages to such systems.

Solution

The Proxy Pattern in Figure 13-5 solves this problem by using local stand-ins for the server, called *proxies*. A proxy encapsulates the infor-

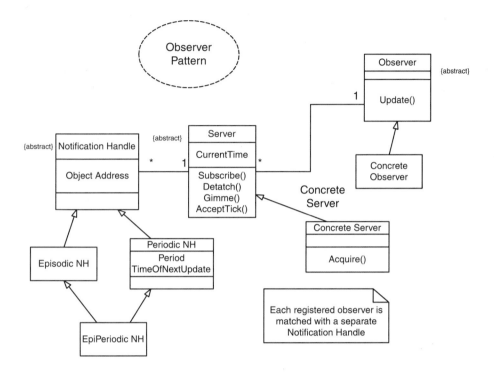

Figure 13-4: *Observer Pattern*

mation and operations necessary to get the data from the server. The proxy then, in turn, uses the Observer Pattern to provide data to clients within the proxy's address space.

Consequences

The Proxy Pattern is a conceptually simple extension to the Observer Pattern. It is frequently used in distributed, asymmetric processing systems in which the locations of the objects are known at design time. The use of this pattern optimizes bus traffic, because only the proxies are in direct communication with the remote server.

13.3.2.4 Broker Pattern

Problem

The Proxy Pattern is applied when the locations of objects are known at design time. However, in complex systems, the location of objects may

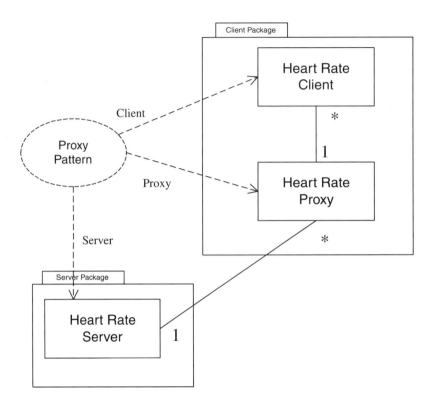

Figure 13-5: *Proxy Pattern*

not be known until the availability of computing resources can be assessed during run-time. The proxies then have no way of knowing the locations of the server objects.

Solution

The Broker Pattern in Figure 13-6 solves this problem by inserting an object broker that acts to connect object requests with object services. Server objects register with the broker, complete with enough information for the broker or other objects to request services. Later, when the proxies request an already registered server, the broker can return the current address of the object server to the proxy. If the object server must disconnect or migrate to a different location, the proxy discovers this when the request for service fails. At this point, the proxy can interrogate the broker for the new location of the server.

Consequences

This pattern works well for large distributed systems, particularly those that are multiprocessing-symmetric.[2] A variety of commercial object request brokers (ORBs) are available for the OMG CORBA (Common Object Request Broker Architecture) standard. While the definition of real-time CORBA is currently underway within the OMG, currently available ORBs tend to be nondeterministic in their behavior. Their performance and predictability is also determined by the underlying communications protocols. Most common are Ethernet and TCP/IP, both of which are not known for their predictability or performance under high load. Other protocols, such as bit-dominance, that do not require a potentially nondeterministic collision resolution policy, may be more appropriate.

13.3.3 Safety and Reliability Patterns

Safety concepts are discussed in Chapter 3. There are many safety-related patterns [2], but most are application-specific and unlikely to be

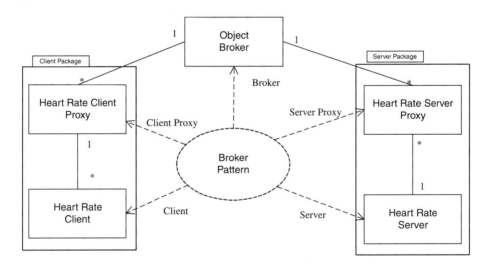

Figure 13-6: *Broker Pattern*

---

2. That is, the operating system performs dynamic load balancing by assigning processes to processors based on the processors' current computational loads.

provided by a general-purpose, real-time framework. Two such patterns are general enough to be provided by a vertical framework, however—the Watchdog and the Safety Executive Patterns.

13.3.3.1 Watchdog Pattern

Problem

In high-reliability and safety-critical applications, it may be necessary to continuously check the liveness of the application or object.

Solution

A watchdog is an object that observes the behavior of other objects and acts when they appear to misbehave. A watchdog is usually implemented as a passive receiver of strokes from the client objects. In the naïve version, the watchdog must be stroked within a specified period of time or it will timeout, causing some error-correcting action to occur. Watchdogs are often implemented with hardware support to handle the situation of a misbehaving task that locks up the software application. See Chapter 12 for details on a state behavioral watchdog pattern.

Consequences

The watchdog is a low-cost solution but does not provide very complete coverage. Specifically, a watchdog usually only checks the time base of the liveness checks (strokes). It may check both too fast and too slow. It may even check for simple sequence using keyed watchdog strokes (see Chapter 12). However, because it knows so little of the context, the normal action to be taken when the watchdog times out is draconian (e.g., system reset) and may not be appropriate in some set of circumstances.

13.3.3.2 Safety Executive Pattern

Problem

The watchdog is a very simplistic solution to the handling of exceptional and fault conditions that may occur within an application.

Solution

The Safety Executive Pattern uses a centralized coordinator for safety monitoring and control of system recovery from faults. It also goes by

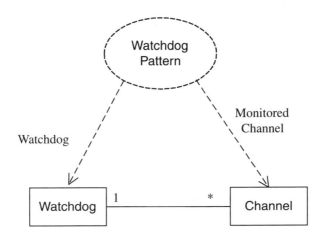

Figure 13-7: *Watchdog Pattern*

the name of the Safety Kernel Pattern. The safety executive tracks and coordinates all safety monitoring and ensures the execution of safety actions when appropriate. Typically it captures the following inputs:

- Watchdogs timeouts
- Software error assertions
- Continuous or periodic BITs
- Faults identified by monitors in the Monitor-Actuation Pattern

Consequences
For larger and more complex systems, a safety executive provides a consistent, centralized point for safety processing. This simplifies the application software which might otherwise be riddled with extra checks and resulting actions which obscure the primary application purpose. Because the safety control is centralized, it becomes a simpler process to verify and validate the safety measures.

13.3.4 Behavioral Patterns

The patterns in this section are *object patterns*, as opposed to the state behavioral patterns of Chapter 12 which arrangements of states within

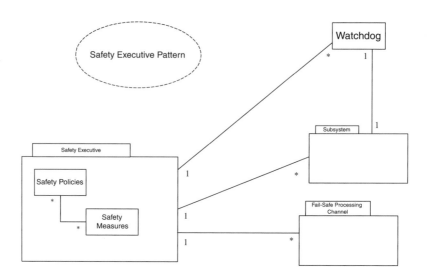

Figure 13-8: *Safety Executive Pattern*

a single object. They are different implementation solutions involving multiple objects.

13.3.4.1 State Pattern

Problem
Many objects spend most of their time in one or a small set of higher-level states, with relatively rapid transitions among child states. Constructing a large, flat state space can be inefficient. Also, many implementation strategies for state machines result in code bloat for reactive class hierarchies.

Solution
The State Pattern in Figure 13-9 constructs a set of modal or state objects, each corresponding to a high-level state of the *Context* object. Figure 13-9 shows the *Context* object as a composite, tightly aggregating the *Concrete* state component objects, each of which may have its own state machine for the child states. When a relevant transition occurs, the *Context* switches its focus to the proper *Concrete* state.

Consequences

High-level state transitions tend to be more heavyweight in some other implementation strategies. However, the internal transitions within the *Concrete* state classes can usually be made more efficient because the state space is smaller than if a single, large state space is considered. This pattern allows the user to set the optimization tradeoffs for the application.

If space is more critical than time, the *Concrete* state objects may be created when they are transitioned to, and deleted when exited. More commonly, however, they are all created when the *Context* is created and destroyed when the *Context* is destroyed.

The State Pattern is also more efficient when statecharts are inherited. If a nested-switch statement approach is used to implement a state machine, then a subclass may use exactly the same code—unless the subclass specializes the state machine. In that case, the entire flat, nested-switch construct must be reimplemented. However, if the State Pattern is used, then only the state that is modified must be reimplemented in the subclass. This results in a smaller application and fewer opportunities for introducing defects.

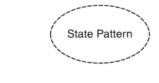

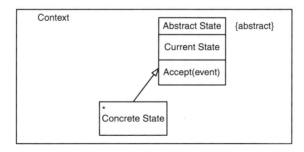

Figure 13-9: *State Pattern*

13.3.4.2 State Table Pattern

Problem

Many state implementation solutions require O(n) or worse time for transitions. In very large state spaces, this can lead to unacceptable performance.

Solution

The State Table Pattern provides a simple mechanism for managing state machines with an efficiency of O(c), where c is a constant. This makes it a preferred mechanism for very large state spaces, because the time to handle a transition is a constant (not including the time to execute actions associated with state entry or exit, or the transition itself). Another advantage is that this pattern maps directly to tabular state specifications, such as those used to develop many safety-critical systems.

The State Table Pattern in Figure 13-10 hinges upon the state table. This structure is typically implemented as an *s* x *t* array, where *s* is the number of states and *t* is the number of transitions. Each cell contains a

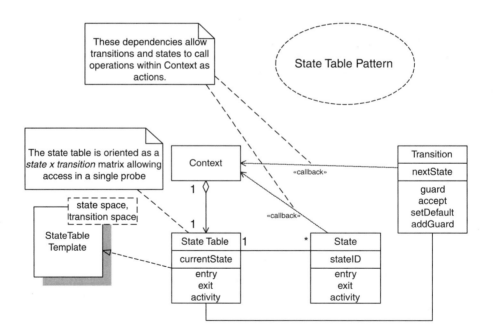

Figure 13-10: *State Table Pattern*

single pointer to a *Transition* object that "handles" the event with an *accept* operation. The operation returns the resulting state. Both events and states are represented as enumerated types. These enumerated types are used as indices into the table to optimize performance. Because this pattern is designed for fast execution, it has a relatively high initialization cost, but execution cost is low.

Consequences
The State Table Pattern provides O(c) performance, where c is a constant. That is, the time necessary to take a transition is independent of the number of transitions in the state machine. Although the state table is relatively expensive to construct, it is very efficient to execute. For more detail on the implementation of this pattern, see [2].

13.4 Framework Design Principles and Metrics

Building frameworks is just like building applications—only harder.[3] The reason why it's harder is primarily because you have to think about the universe of applications to be built with it, abstract an appropriate set of concepts and services, and design them in such a way that applications find them easy to use. A usable framework:

- Contains an appropriate set of services to be generally useful but not so many that a significant fraction is used by only a small set of applications
- Has a reasonable generalization hierarchy that is neither too broad nor too deep
- Has service components that are plug-replaceable by similar components
- Is portable to different platforms and provides a consistent set of services to various applications
- Uses consistent naming and parameter-passing syntax
- Meets the performance and resource constraints of the applications within its domain

---

3. A common rule for framework builders is to plan on building the framework at least twice. The first time allows you to make the primary mistakes. The second one, built from scratch, allows you to incorporate that knowledge and create a usable framework.

13.4.1 Set of Services

A key principle of frameworks is that they should be reusable in a variety of applications. Reusable means that the framework *does not require modification* in order to be reused. If you find that applications need to modify the framework, it is an indication that the framework itself is flawed. Reusable pieces of frameworks (typically, classes) are generally reused by *specialization* and *extension*. The latter two are realized by the application subclassing portions of the framework. Specializing a framework class means that the application subclasses a framework class and then alters behavior of polymorphic operations to be more semantically appropriate for the application. Extending a framework class is also done by subclassing, but in this case, operations and attributes are added to the class to meet the application's needs. Specialization and extension are commonly used together when building applications within the context of a framework.

To be included in a framework, the services must be of general need by the applications in the target domain, and the service must be sufficiently general to meet that need for most applications. For example, it would be inappropriate to build TCP/IP-specific communication features into the framework internals if a significant fraction of the applications use different communication protocols. It would be better to abstract the essential communication needs of the applications in such a way that they can be met by a replaceable protocol component (see the later section on replaceable components). As a general rule, if less than 20 percent of the applications in a domain cannot use a class, it is better to omit the class than to include it.

For example, many, if not most, embedded and real-time applications use finite state machines to model class behavior. A framework for this domain ought to include state machine execution semantics in such a way that the application can use them to execute the state machines of its application-specific classes.

Another example is the use of container libraries. All nontrivial applications must manage nonunary multiplicities on associations. The Container-Iterator Pattern provides the abstract pattern of this kind of collaboration. However, developers may want to use STL or Roguewave container libraries, so building an inherent dependency on the STL makes the framework less reusable.

Common sets of services for real-time frameworks may include

- Task creation and management
- Resource management and synchronization
- Object distribution
- Object containment
- Object persistence
- Intra-processor communication
- State machine execution and event generation
- Event and interrupt handling
- Debugging facilities

A framework may not provide services in all these areas. It all depends on its intended target domain.

13.4.2 Generalization Hierarchy Structure

In addition to providing a general set of structural and behavioral components, useful frameworks are *understandable*. This is important for two reasons. First, it greatly increases the chance that the framework is constructed properly. Second, it increases the likelihood that the user will use it properly. There are two generally opposing views on building hierarchies. The first is to provide a deeply nested hierarchy so that the framework contains many classes within the same taxonomy. This increases the likelihood that just the right base class for application specialization already exists. The other approach is to provide a shallower inheritance hierarchy in which each step in the specialization tree is more significant. Such a framework is smaller and easier to maintain, but it may require the application subclasses to reimplement more things in actual use. For example, the MFC Windows framework is fairly shallow, but individual classes within the hierarchies are relatively more complex. The OWL framework has a more complex hierarchy, but the classes within the hierarchy differ less importantly from their parents.

The generalization hierarchy is complicated when multiple inheritance is used. This is especially true if the two superclasses themselves share a common ancestor. In general, multiple inheritance can be used in frameworks, provided it is only used to mix totally independent hierarchies with no common ancestors, and when all lines of generalization are shallow.

13.4.3 Replaceable Components

Component libraries are an important facet of most applications in today's development environment. A component is a compiled object that provides a set of services. A component library includes a set of collaborating compiled objects that are reused at the object code level. As mentioned earlier in this chapter, frameworks enable the use of component libraries by providing abstract component interfaces. As long as a component implements the necessary abstract interface, it will successfully plug into the framework.

There are many examples of application domains that successfully incorporate reusable components into frameworks. The tremendous success of Visual Basic in the desktop applet market is due primarily to the extraordinarily broad set of components available from third parties to provide various kinds of GUI components, such as buttons, image frames, communication facilities (such as sockets), textual controls, graphical representations, and even complete spreadsheet engines. Components are also widely available for non-Windows applications. Communications protocols, such as SCSI, CAN, and TCP/IP, are often available as components. The same is true of container libraries, such as RogueWave components, Booch Components, and the STL.

A good framework does not lock the application into using only one component library. It is important for the application to be able to use a variety of similar components that are specialized for different needs. We've already seen how an application may need to use different communications protocols, depending on the target environment. Developers also want to be able to select the floating-point math library that meets their particular needs. The same is true for container libraries and other components.

13.4.4 Portability

There are two kinds of portability. The first kind is the ability to move the application, using the framework, to a different target execution environment. This generally consists of the underlying processor and support hardware and the operating system. The other kind of portability makes a supported environment available to a wide variety of applications. This is the concept of framework generality discussed earlier.

At the target end, a framework is portable if it is easy to move to a different platform. This usually means that the majority of the framework code is written so that it is independent of the underlying hardware characteristics. These characteristics include

- Primitive numeric word size (for example, sizeof (int))
- Endianism (big endian vs. small endian)
- Interrupt services
- Port and register I/O
- DMA services
- Display and control interfaces
- Memory space management

In most frameworks, this is accomplished by providing a hardware abstraction layer. In addition, the underlying RTOS must be abstracted away so that OS calls are made through an abstract OS interface. This need not be an expensive proposition, but it usually does entail some performance overhead.

13.4.5 Naming and Syntax Conventions

Good frameworks are easy to use. One of the ways to make them easy to use is to be consistent in naming conventions and parameter syntax. A simple example is the use of upper and lower case in naming. A common convention is to start with lower case but make the first letter of each word upper case, as in

```
mySeasonOfDiscontent
```

Another convention separates words with underscores, as in:

```
intelligent_sensor_interface_adaptor
```

Either convention is okay, but they should not be mixed; the developer will never be able to remember which convention is used with each set of services.

Another convention that should be followed has to do with the use of explicit checks for pre- and post-conditions. As a general rule, the user should not be required to remember and manually ensure that framework-provided service pre-conditions are met. For example, if *b()* is always called after *a()*, then perhaps a service *ab()* should be provided that internally calls *a()* and then *b()*. This enforces the protocol of the interaction between classes. Another way to enforce these pre-conditions is to use state machines. Exceptions are wonderful mechanisms to make sure that violations of pre-conditions result in a predictable and correct response.

13.4.6 Performance

A good framework allows applications to meet their performance requirements while providing for the application's functional needs. In the embedded and real-time domains, this does not mean that heavy-weight patterns should not be provided. It does mean that the application should not be forced to use heavyweight patterns to do lightweight things. For example, the Broker Pattern is a perfectly reasonable pattern when objects are distributed in a symmetric multitasking system. It is fine for a high-performance framework to provide such a pattern. However, it would not be appropriate to require all object interactions to use this pattern, as this would likely result in unacceptable performance if the objects were local or if their location was known at compile time. The user must be able to make generality/performance tradeoffs.

Some frameworks touted as real-time execute applications via a virtual machine rather than execute what is commonly called "bare-metal code." A virtual machine interprets an application in order to execute it. The application is generally compiled into a set of language tokens to ease the job of interpretation. This approach is attractive for a couple of reasons. First, an interpreter is easier to write than a full compiler, and it is easier to instrument for debugging purposes. The relative ease of creating an interpreter for the target environment makes porting the application to novel targets simpler. The Java language is implemented with a tokenizing compiler and a virtual machine, for example. However, a substantial performance penalty is typically paid for interpretation. This penalty means that the applications generally run five to twenty times slower than equivalent compiled applications.

In many systems, the absolute performance is not as important as the predictability of performance, especially as the system scales up in size. In this case, the application framework should provide O(c) or O(log n) performance patterns as much as possible. The State Table Pattern in the previous section is an example of such a pattern.

A good framework for real-time systems usually uses bare-metal code rather than a virtual machine, and provides a variety of user-selectable generality versus performance tradeoffs. This allows the developer to fine-tune the application to meet his or her needs. Heavy-weight patterns are fine, provided the application designer is not forced to use them. Finally, a good framework should provide a means to exclude parts of the framework that are not used in applications in the executable code image.

13.5 The Rhapsody Object Execution Framework (OXF)[4]

Rhapsody is a design automation tool that creates executable systems automatically from UML object models. It does this by generating code for the various constructive UML concepts and their specific user-defined properties that merge with a provided real-time framework. This section will introduce the user to this framework to illustrate how a commercially available framework is used in real systems.

13.5.1 Rhapsody Architecture

An overview of the Rhapsody structure is shown in Figure 13-11. The two large components are the Deployment Environment and the Development Environment. With Rhapsody, this can be the same (for example, in the same "space-time continuum" of a single machine) or different machines. It is common that early on, the generate-compile-execute sequence is done on the development machine, using Windows NT or 95/98. Later, as the application model matures, the actual hardware target provides the Deployment Environment, using an RTOS, such as pSOS or VxWorks. In either case, the Rhapsody execution session works the same.

---

4. OXF, along with other aspects of the Rhapsody tool, was designed by Eran Gery and Yachin Pnueli of I-Logix.

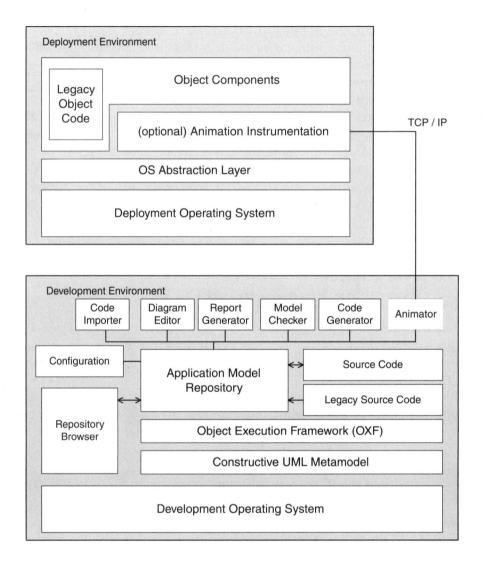

Figure 13-11: *Rhapsody Architecture*

The Development Environment consists of the components of the tool itself, represented by the boxes labeled "Diagram Editor," "Report Generator," "Model Checker," and so on. Underneath these is the Application Model Repository. This repository contains all the information about your application, whether or not it is shown in any diagram.[5] The various diagrams, the browser, and the report generator provide views of the model. The Model Checker performs completeness and correctness checks on the model. The Code Generator generates code from the model using the configuration settings from the Configuration component. The Development Environment Animator provides control of the (potentially remote) animation and is in charge of animating the other views (diagrams and browser) as the application executes in the deployment environment.

The model can link with legacy applications in several ways. First, legacy code can be imported into the model. This aspect of Rhapsody isn't complete at this time, so only certain model elements (classes and relations) import into the repository. Second, legacy source code may be "linked" in the sense that there are configuration options that allow legacy source code to be compiled and linked, along with the generated code. Finally, legacy compiled object code may be specified to link in during the link phase, without recompilation.

The Deployment Environment is shown in the upper part of Figure 13-11. As you can see, it contains three components provided by Rhapsody (Object Components, Animation Instrumentation, and the OS Abstraction Layer) and two components from elsewhere (precompiled legacy components and the RTOS itself). The Rhapsody-generated code provides the bulk of the Object Components. The OS Abstraction Layer is intentionally independent so that it is a simple matter to port the application to a different operating system. This layer is a very thin veneer that makes calls into the underlying OS with a minimum of overhead.

The Rhapsody design automation tool generates code that executes within its Object Execution Framework (OXF). The OXF consists of four primary parts:

1. Execution framework itself

2. Inter-object association patterns

3. Abstract operating system

4. Animation framework

---

5. Many beginner modelers are confused by this fact. The diagrams are merely views of the repository information. In fact, the generated code may be considered nothing other than yet another view of the model. The repository itself is where the model is captured.

13.5.2 Execution Framework

The purpose of the execution framework is to provide an infrastructure for the execution of a UML model. The appropriate elements from the UML metamodel are represented directly in the emitted source code stream. Classes within the application model are bound to these metaclasses by setting the appropriate properties, such as active, composite, reactive, and so on. Associations, aggregations, and compositions generate code that permits objects to call operations and to send events to other objects. The code associated with the various kinds of associations is discussed in the next section.

The execution framework, likewise, contains a metamodel. This metamodel captures the classes provided by the framework that will be subclassed by application classes. The execution framework is also configured by setting properties.[6] In code-based frameworks, such as MFC, use and subclassing of framework metaclasses is done explicitly by the user. In a graphically oriented modeling environment, subclassing is done implicitly by drawing classes and setting their properties. For example, in Rhapsody, if you set the *concurrency* property of a class to *active*, then the class automatically is a subclass of the frameworks *OMThread* metaclass. If you add a statechart to a class, it automatically is a subclass of *OMReactive*, which provides the machinery for the execution of state machines. The most important (from the user's standpoint) of these classes are found in Table 13-2.

The user is free to specify operations and attributes and thus use Rhapsody as a combination graphical and textual programming language, in much the same way that C++ is coded by hand. However, the full power of Rhapsody becomes more apparent when the user defines behavior using statecharts. The statechart execution model provided by Rhapsody supports both asynchronous and synchronous event triggers. Asynchronous state machines are handled by events. Each independent thread maintains its own event queue and parcels out the events to the appropriate objects executing within the thread. Events on state machines result in event acceptors in the target class. This is the default state behavior, because it is more general than synchronous state machine execution.

---

6. Rhapsody has in excess of 200 properties that may be set to control code generation, initial object instances, which framework classes are to be subclassed, how behavioral models are to be implemented, and so on.

Table 13-2: *Execution Framework Metaclasses*

Metaclass	Description
OMReactive	This metaclass provides the machinery to execute state machines, manage events, and related activities. Two implementations are available via property selection: State pattern and nested switch/case statements. Events are accepted by Rhapsody-generated event acceptor operations in the subclass. Event acceptors may be asynchronous (default) or synchronous (that is, "triggered operation"). This is settable by the operation type property (primitive, event, or triggered).
OMThread	Each thread has an event queue that holds events for objects executing within the thread. Several reactive objects share the same event queue.
OMEvent	Reactive classes communicate with each other by sending events of this type. This is the base class of all events in Rhapsody.
OMTimeout	Realizes timeouts in statecharts created using the *tm()* event trigger. When a state is entered, which has an exiting transition with a *tm()* event trigger, the framework requests an OS timer and catches the resulting event from the underlying OS via the abstract operating system.
OMTimerManager	Manages all pending timeouts.

Synchronous state machines are handled by specifying that the events are really triggered operations. This is done by setting the property of the event handler in the browser to "triggered operation." Rather than being queued, invoking a triggered operation completes the state transitions and associated actions before returning control. Nothing is queued in this case. Naturally, a single state machine should not mix normal events with triggered operations, to avoid potential race conditions.

13.5.3 Inter-Object Association Patterns

Rhapsody resolves all associations via pointers. When the multiplicity is 0 or 1, then a simple pointer is used to an object of the associated

Table 13-3: *Rhapsody Container Classes*

Association End Multiplicity	Ordered Property	Container Type	Implementation
0..1 or 1	Ignored	Scalar	Pointer
m..n, n, or *	False	Unordered	OMCollection
m..n, n, or *	True	Ordered	OMList
Qualified	Ignored	Qualified	OMMap
*where m and n are fixed scalars			

class. However, when the multiplicity is potentially greater than 1, a simple pointer won't suffice. In this case, Rhapsody automatically (and more-or-less invisibly) inserts a container class to handle the multiple object instances. By default, the *OMContainer* set that comes with Rhapsody is used, although STL is also directly supported. Other container libraries can be added via properties, if desired.

The properties of the association and the multiplicities are both used to determine the class of the container, as shown in Table 13-3.

To make the association thread-reliable, operations invoked across thread boundaries may be marked as *guarded* by setting that property of the operation. In this case, the operation will be protected by an operating system mutex to avoid mutual-exclusion problems.

13.5.3.1 Using Associations

If the association is implemented with a simple pointer, then the object may be referenced directly. The name of the role is used as the name of the pointer. For example, in Figure 13-12, the *Coyote* class can call operation *getInjuryList()* for its associated injuries with

```
hisinjuries->getInjuryList();
```

Directed associations are navigable in only one direction. For example, class *Coyote* can send a message to class *injuries,* but not vice versa. Bi-directional unary or optional associations are implemented using a pair of pointers, one in each class. *getRole* and *setRole* operations are provided to initialize and deinitialize the link, as desired.

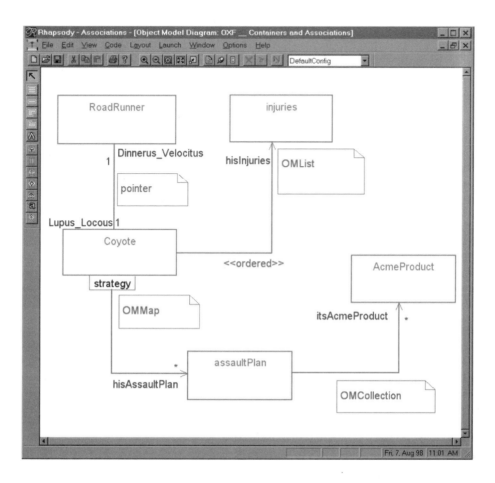

Figure 13-12: *Rhapsody Associations*

Nonunary multiplicities are a bit more complex, because Rhapsody uses the *OMContainer* classes to manage object collections. For example, because of the association from *assaultPlan* to *AcmeProduct* in Figure 13-12, Rhapsody inserts the following declaration

```
OMCollection<AcmeProduct*> itsAcmeProduct;
```

An iterator is provided to access the appropriate product. The four links can be initialized using this *OMCollection:*

```
itsAcmeProduct ->Add(new( "Acme RoadRunner Net",
   300.00 ))
```

```
itsAcmeProduct ->Add(new( "Acme RoadRunner Feed",
   47.00 ))
itsAcmeProduct ->Add(new( "Acme Superglue", 20.00 ))
itsAcmeProduct ->Add(new( "Acme Theromonuclear
   Device", 170000000.15 ))
```

Once initialized, the *OMIterator* can be used to access the products. To print the list of products and prices, you might use

```
OMIterator<product *> productLine(itsAcmeProduct);
productLine.reset();
while ( *productLine !=NULL) {
   (*productLine)->print();
++productLine;
};
```

Other relations work similarly. If the association is ordered (that is, its ordered property is set to TRUE), then an *OMList* is used instead. If the association has a qualifier, as does the association from *phoneBook* to customer, then an *OMMap* is used.

13.5.4 Using C++ Standard Template Library

Rhapsody also supports the STL directly. If you select the STL container library, the mapping rules in Table 13-4 are used.

13.5.5 Abstract Operating System

The point of abstracting the operating system away from the other parts of the framework is to enhance portability of the application to

Table 13-4: *STL Container Classes*

Association End Multiplicity	Ordered Property	Container Type	Implementation
0..1 or 1	Ignored	Scalar	Pointer
m..n, n, or *	False	Unordered	Vector
m..n, n, or *	True	Ordered	List
Qualified	Ignored	Qualified	Map
*where m and n are fixed scalars			

other operating systems. To move from VxWorks to pSOS, for example, is nothing more than a reimplementation of the lightweight operating system abstraction layer. The important classes in the abstract operating system are shown in Table 13-5.

Table 13-5: *Abstract OS Metaclasses*

Metaclass	Important Operations	Description
OMOSFactory		A singleton class (of name *theOSFactory*) that is an instance of the standard Factory design pattern [2]. Allows client classes to request object instances.
	`createOMOSMessageQueue`	Create a message queue.
	`createOMOSEventFlag`	Create an event flag.
	`createOMOSThread`	Create a thread.
	`createOMOSWrapperThread`	Create a wrapper thread.
	`createOMOSMutex`	Create a mutex.
	`createONOSTickTimer`	Create a tick timer.
	`createOMOSIdleTimer`	Create an idle timer.
OMOSThread		Concrete thread allocated by the OS Factory singleton.
	`suspend`	Suspend thread execution.
	`resume`	Resume thread execution.
	`start`	Begin thread execution.
	`getOSHandle`	Get the handle to the OS to call OS-specific operations.
	`setPriority`	Set the thread priority.
OMOSMutex		Concrete mutex allocated by the OS Factory singleton.
	`lock`	Lock the mutex.
	`free`	Free the mutex.
		(continued)

Table 13-5: (*continued*)

Metaclass	Important Operations	Description
OMOSMessage Queue		Concrete message queue used by the *OMOThread* class.
	put	Insert a message into the queue.
	pend	Wait for a message.
	isEmpty	Test if queue is empty.
	get	Get a message from the queue.
OMOSEventFlag		Concrete event flag class for signaling threads of the availability of events.
	signal	Signal an event.
	reset	Clear the event.
	wait	Wait for an event.

13.5.6 Animation Framework

The animation framework is the support Rhapsody generates in the emitted code stream for the animated design-level debugging of applications. Rhapsody does this through the insertion of instrumentation in-line in the code, which invisibly communicates back to the tool via a TCP/IP socket. This feature requires the underlying OS to provide TCP/IP communications and a socket interface.

The good side of using instrumentation to pass back execution status information to the Rhapsody tool is that Rhapsody can then graphically animate the model as the model executes. This requires no changes to the normal emitted code as defined by the UML model.

The downside of the instrumentation approach is that code that includes animation instrumentation is both larger and slower than otherwise. This makes animated code inappropriate for performance testing but perfectly valid for functional testing. The effects of instrumentation per se on the application are relatively small. However, to maintain the graphical animation synchronized with the execution, synchronization points are introduced in the instrumented application so that it can wait as the animated graphics hurry to capture the behavior. The requirement to maintain synchronicity between the host graphical animation and the target execution can result in a significant slowdown in overall execution speed.

To mitigate these problems, Rhapsody offers three levels of animation instrumentation (set from the Code/Configure menu option). The first of these is "none" and is meant to be shippable code. The second level is "tracing." This is a fairly lightweight option that results in a textual execution trace sent to the host's standard output. The third level, "graphical animation," requires the most resources (on the host side).

13.6 Sample Application Using the Rhapsody OXF Framework

Figure 13-13 shows a simple application with two classes related by a single directed association. One of the classes has a simple statechart. The code for the classes is shown below. Rhapsody generates two files per class as a default—a header (.h) file and an implementation (.cpp) file. It also generates two files for each package. In this example, there is one package ("default"). Rhapsody also generates two more files for the main execution state point, named after the configuration (in this case, "DefaultConfig").

```
class_0.h
/*****************************************************
    Rhapsody         :    2.0
    Login            :
    Configuration    :  DefaultConfig
    Model Element    :  Default::class_0
    Generated Date   :  Mon, 24, Aug 98
    File Path        :  DefaultConfig\class_0.h
*****************************************************/
//## package Default
//## class class_0

#ifndef class_0_H
#define class_0_H
```

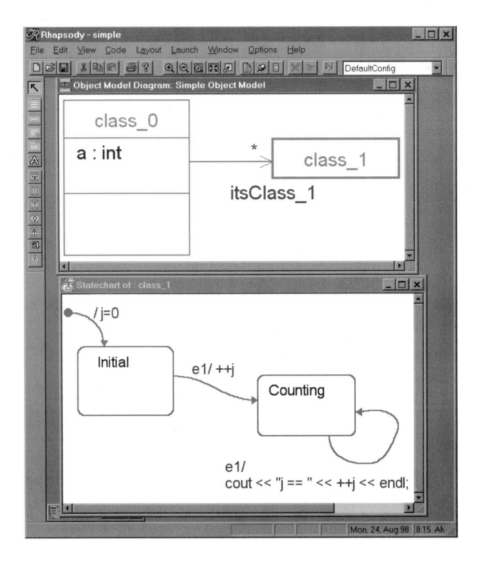

Figure 13-13: *Simple Rhapsody Application*

```
#include <oxf/oxf.h>
#include "Default.h"
//---------------------------------
// class_0.h
//---------------------------------
class class_1;
```

```
class class_0  {

////    User explicit entries     ////

protected :

   //## attribute a
   int a;

////    User implicit entries     ////

public :

   // Constructors and destructors:
   class_0();
   ~class_0();
   // Attribute accessors and mutators:
   int getA() const;
   void setA(int  p_a);
   OMIterator<class_1*> getItsClass_1() const;
   void addItsClass_1(class_1*  p_class_1);
   void removeItsClass_1(class_1*  p_class_1);
   void clearItsClass_1();

protected :

   OMCollection<class_1*> itsClass_1;

////    Framework entries     ////

protected :

   void cleanUpRelations();
};

#endif

/********************************************************
   File Path   : DefaultConfig\class_0.h
********************************************************/
```

You will note in the preceding code that Rhapsody automatically generates mutators and accessor operations for class attributes. In order to account for the nonunary, one-way association from *class_0* to *class_1,* an *OMCollection* container class from the OXF is inserted (as a protected member) along with an *OMIterator* to iterate the collection. Also, operations are added to add and remove *class_1* objects to and from the *OMCollection*.

class_0.cpp

```
/*********************************************************
   Rhapsody          :    2.0
   Login             :
   Configuration     :  DefaultConfig
   Model Element     :  Default::class_0
   Generated Date    :  Mon, 24, Aug 98
   File Path         :  DefaultConfig\class_0.cpp
*********************************************************/

//## package Default
//## class class_0

#include "class_0.h"
#include "class_1.h"

//-------------------------------
// class_0.cpp
//-------------------------------

class_0::class_0() {
};

class_0::~class_0() {
   cleanUpRelations();
};

   int class_0::getA() const {
   return a;

};
   void class_0::setA(int  p_a) {
   a = p_a;
};

OMIterator<class_1*> class_0::getItsClass_1() const {
   OMIterator<class_1*> iter(itsClass_1);iter.reset();
   return iter;
};

void class_0::addItsClass_1(class_1*  p_class_1) {
   itsClass_1.add(p_class_1);
};
```

```
void class_0::removeItsClass_1(class_1*  p_class_1) {
   itsClass_1.remove(p_class_1);
};

void class_0::clearItsClass_1() {
   itsClass_1.removeAll();
};

void class_0::cleanUpRelations() {
   {
       itsClass_1.removeAll();
   }
};

/*********************************************************
    File Path    : DefaultConfig\class_0.cpp
*********************************************************/
```

The preceding code fills in the implementation details of the class specification for *class_0*. The implementation is straightforward and should contain no surprises for the reader.

Class_1.h

```
/*********************************************************
    Rhapsody          :    2.0
    Login             :
    Configuration     : DefaultConfig
    Model Element     : Default::class_1
    Generated Date    : Mon, 24, Aug 98
    File Path         : DefaultConfig\class_1.h
*********************************************************/

//## package Default
//## class class_1

#ifndef class_1_H
#define class_1_H
#include <oxf/oxf.h>
#include "Default.h"

//-------------------------------
// class_1.h
//-------------------------------

class class_1 : public OMReactive {

////    User explicit entries      ////
```

```cpp
protected :

   //## attribute j
   int j;

////    User implicit entries    ////

public :

   // Constructors and destructors:
   class_1(OMThread*  p_thread = OMDefaultThread);
   ~class_1();
   // Attribute accessors and mutators:
   int getJ() const;
   void setJ(int  p_j);

////    Framework entries    ////
public :

   State* Initial;
   State* Counting;

   // rootState:
   void rootStateEntDef();
   // Initial:
   int InitialTakee1();
   // Counting:
   int CountingTakee1();
   virtual boolean startBehavior();

protected :
   void initStatechart();
   void cleanUpStatechart();

////    Events consumed    ////

public :
   // e1();
};

class class_1_ROOT : public ComponentState {

////    Framework entries    ////
public :

   class_1* concept;
```

```
    // Constructors and destructors:
    class_1_ROOT(class_1* c, State* p);
    // Attribute accessors and mutators:
    virtual void entDef();
};

class class_1_Initial : public LeafState {

////     Framework entries      ////

public :

    class_1* concept;

    // Constructors and destructors:
    class_1_Initial(class_1* c, State* p, State*
      cmp);
    // Attribute accessors and mutators:
    int takeEvent(short id);
};

class class_1_Counting : public LeafState {
////     Framework entries      ////

public :

    class_1* concept;

    // Constructors and destructors:
    class_1_Counting(class_1* c, State* p, State*
      cmp);
    // Attribute accessors and mutators:
    int takeEvent(short id);
};
#endif
/*******************************************************
    File Path   : DefaultConfig\class_1.h
*******************************************************/
```

Because *class_1* has a statemachine, Rhapsody generates it as a sub-class of the OXF class *OMReactive* (see preceding code). This enables it to handle the events. We used Rhapsody's default (that is, the state pattern), so a class is generated for each state.

Class_1.cpp

```
/***********************************************************
    Rhapsody          :    2.0
    Login             :
    Configuration     : DefaultConfig
    Model Element     : Default::class_1
    Generated Date    : Mon, 24, Aug 98
    File Path         : DefaultConfig\class_1.cpp
***********************************************************/

//## package Default
//## class class_1

#include "class_1.h"

//--------------------------------
// class_1.cpp
//--------------------------------

class_1::class_1(OMThread*  p_thread) {
   setThread(p_thread);
   initStatechart();
};

class_1::~class_1() {
   cleanUpStatechart();
};

int class_1::getJ() const {
   return j;
};
void class_1::setJ(int  p_j) {
   j = p_j;
};

void class_1::rootStateEntDef() {
   //#[ transition 0
   j=0;
   //#]
   Initial->entDef();
};

int class_1::InitialTakee1() {
   int res = eventNotConsumed;
   Initial->exit();
   //#[ transition 1
```

```
      ++j;
      //#]
      Counting->entDef();
      res = eventConsumed;
      return res;
   };

   int class_1::CountingTakee1() {
      int res = eventNotConsumed;
      Counting->exit();
      //#[ transition 2

      cout << "j == " << ++j << endl;
      //#]
      Counting->entDef();
      res = eventConsumed;
      return res;
   };

   void class_1::initStatechart() {
      delete rootState;
      rootState = new class_1_ROOT(this, NULL);
      Initial = new class_1_Initial(this, rootState,
         rootState);
      Counting = new class_1_Counting(this, rootState,
         rootState);
      rootState->subState = NULL;
      rootState->active = NULL;
   };

   void class_1::cleanUpStatechart() {
      delete rootState;
      rootState = NULL;
      delete Initial;
      Initial = NULL;
      delete Counting;
      Counting = NULL;
   };

   boolean class_1::startBehavior() {
      boolean done = FALSE;
      done = OMReactive::startBehavior();
      return done;
   };
   class_1_ROOT::class_1_ROOT(class_1*  c, State*  p) :
   ComponentState(p) {
```

```cpp
   concept = c;
};

void class_1_ROOT::entDef() {
   enter();
   concept->rootStateEntDef();
};

class_1_Initial::class_1_Initial(class_1*  c, State*
   p, State*  cmp) : LeafState(p, cmp) {
   concept = c;
};

int class_1_Initial::takeEvent(short  id) {
   int res = eventNotConsumed;
   if(id == e1_Default_id)
      {
          res = concept->InitialTakee1();
      }
   if(res == eventNotConsumed)
      {
          res = parent->takeEvent(id);
      }
   return res;
};
class_1_Counting::class_1_Counting(class_1*  c, State*
p, State*  cmp) : LeafState(p, cmp) {
   concept = c;
};

int class_1_Counting::takeEvent(short  id) {
   int res = eventNotConsumed;
   if(id == e1_Default_id)
      {
          res = concept->CountingTakee1();
      }
   if(res == eventNotConsumed)
      {
          res = parent->takeEvent(id);
      }
   return res;
};
/********************************************************
   File Path   : DefaultConfig\class_1.cpp
 ********************************************************/
```

The preceding code is a little more interesting, because it contains the implementation of *class_1* and its state machine. Note that the actions that appear on the statechart in Figure 13-13 show up in the generated code in operations *class_1::InitialTakee1()* and *class_1::CountingTakee1()*, operations that accept the event *e1*.

Default.h

```
/************************************************
    Rhapsody           :    2.0
    Login              :
    Configuration      : DefaultConfig
    Model Element      : Default
    Generated Date     : Mon, 24, Aug 98
    File Path          : DefaultConfig\Default.h
 ************************************************/
//## package Default

#ifndef Default_H
#define Default_H
#define e1_Default_id 1
#include <oxf/oxf.h>


//-------------------------------
// Default.h
//-------------------------------
class e1;
class class_1;
class class_0;
class e1 : public OMEvent {

////    Framework entries    ////

public :

   // Constructors and destructors:
   e1();
};
#endif


/************************************************
    File Path    : DefaultConfig\Default.h
 ************************************************/
```

The preceding code provides package-specific things, such as event classes, package types, and package instances. In this case, only the event *e1* is included.

Default.cpp

```
/*******************************************************
    Rhapsody          :    2.0
    Login             :
    Configuration     : DefaultConfig
    Model Element     : Default
    Generated Date    : Mon, 24, Aug 98
    File Path         : DefaultConfig\Default.cpp
*******************************************************/

//## package Default

#include "Default.h"
#include "class_1.h"
#include "class_0.h"


//--------------------------------
// Default.cpp
//--------------------------------

e1::e1() {
   lId = e1_Default_id;
};


/*******************************************************
    File Path   : DefaultConfig\Default.cpp
*******************************************************/
```

MainDefaultConfig.h

```
/*******************************************************
    Rhapsody          :    2.0
    Login             :
    Configuration     : DefaultConfig
    Model Element     : DefaultConfig
    Generated Date    : Mon, 24, Aug 98
    File Path         : DefaultConfig\MainDefaultConfig.h
*******************************************************/

#ifndef MainDefaultConfig_H
#define MainDefaultConfig_H
//--------------------------------
// MainDefaultConfig.h
```

```
//--------------------------------

#endif

/**************************************************
    File Path   : DefaultConfig\MainDefaultConfig.h
**************************************************/
```

The preceding two pieces of code are not particularly interesting in this case, but they provide placeholders for package-level implementation and for main initialization information, respectively.

MainDefaultConfig.cpp

```
/**************************************************
    Rhapsody          :    2.0
    Login             :
    Configuration     : DefaultConfig
    Model Element     : DefaultConfig
    Generated Date    : Mon, 24, Aug 98
    File Path         :
DefaultConfig\MainDefaultConfig.cpp
**************************************************/

#include "Default.h"
#include "MainDefaultConfig.h"
#include "class_0.h"
#include "class_1.h"

//--------------------------------
// MainDefaultConfig.cpp
//--------------------------------
int main(int  argc, char*  argv[]) {
   if(OXFInit(argc, argv, 6423))
      {
          class_0* p_class_0 = new class_0;
          class_1* p_class_1 = new class_1;
          p_class_1->startBehavior();
          OXFStart();
          delete p_class_0;
          delete p_class_1;
          return 0;
      }
   else
      return 1;
};
```

```
/*********************************************************
    File Path   : DefaultConfig\MainDefaultConfig.cpp
*********************************************************/
```

The last bit of code is the "main" for the generated application. The *OXFInit()* call initializes the framework. Prior to code generation, the configuration was set up to make initial instances of both *class_0* and *class_1;* their creation is placed following the initialization of the framework. Because *class_1* has a statechart, its state behavior is started next with a call to *startBehavior().* Finally, *OXFStart* is called to begin the application execution. When it returns, the application has terminated. At this point, the created classes are deleted and main exits.

One of the concerns I often hear about automatically generated code is that it is extremely opaque and unmodifiable. The code in our (admittedly) simple example shows that this need not be the case. The code looks very much like something a competent C++ programmer would write for the application. This continues to be true as the application scales up in size.

13.7 Summary

This chapter looked at frameworks in general, and real-time frameworks in particular. A framework is a partially written application with extension points where the user specializes and adds application-specific stuff. A framework consists of a set of interacting architectural and mechanistic patterns that provide a common set of ways of collaborating to meet application needs. Frameworks also typically include components that provide commonly needed services, such as communications and mathematical computations. Many frameworks provide pluggable components, allowing the user to replace the default components with ones specialized to more-closely meet application needs.

Horizontal frameworks are broadly applicable to many domains. They typically provide a large set of patterns and components to meet many application domains. Vertical frameworks provide few patterns, but compensate by specializing the patterns for optimal performance and applicability within a narrower set of domains.

Frameworks are often constructed as a set of layers (using the Microkernel Architecture Pattern). This allows the frameworks to be portable in two ways. By allowing the lower abstraction layers to be replaced, the framework may be easily ported to different target platforms. The lower abstraction layers contain the abstractions of the underlying operating system and hardware components. Frameworks also abstract away the application details at the higher levels of abstraction. This permits the same framework to be used in a variety of applications.

The Rhapsody OXF was examined as a particular example of a real-time framework. The OXF consists of four primary parts. The execution framework provides the infrastructure for managing threads, object creation and destruction, and the reactive object state machines. The second part, inter-object association patterns, manages the implementation of different kinds of associations (association, aggregation, and composition) through the insertion of container classes to manage nonunary multiplicities, and iterators to provide a thread-reliable means for accessing multiple objects. The third part, the abstract operating system, provides RTOS-independence for the application and the framework itself, allowing easy portability to different target platforms. The last part, the animation framework, enables the user to debug object models at the object and state level of abstraction, without having to "drill down" into source-level or assembly-level debuggers.

13.8 Exercises

1. Define and contrast the terms *mechanism, collaboration, pattern, framework,* and *application.*

2. What are the primary advantages of frameworks?

3. Name two kinds of frameworks.

4. Contrast the Observer, Proxy, and Broker Patterns.

5. What are the differences between the Rhapsody framework metaclasses *OMReactive* and *OMThread?*

6. What are the advantages (if any) of using an abstract operating system layer? What are the disadvantages (if any)?

7. Create a Rhapsody model that has two classes, both of which are "active." In one of the classes, attach a statechart that has both orthogonal regions and nested states. Generate the resulting code. Can you find any ways to improve the generated code?

13.9 References

[1] Rogers, Gregory. *Framework-Based Software Development in C++*, Upper Saddle River, N.J.: Prentice Hall, 1997.

[2] Douglass, Bruce Powel. *Real-Time UML: Developing Efficient Objects for Embedded Systems*, Reading, Mass.: Addison-Wesley, 1998.

[3] Shlaer, Sally, and Steven Mellor. *Object-Oriented Systems Analysis: Modeling the World in Data*, Englewood Cliffs, N.J.: Yourdon Press, 1988.

[4] Shlaer, Sally, and Steven Mellor. *Object Lifecycles: Modeling the World in States*, Englewood Cliffs, N.J.: Yourdon Press, 1992.

[5] Gamma, Erich, Richard Helm, Ralph Johnson, and John Vlissides. *Design Patterns: Elements of Reusable Object-Oriented Software*, Reading, Mass.: Addison-Wesley, 1995.

[6] Buschmann, Frank, Regine Meunier, Hans Rohnert, Peter Sommerlad, and Michael Stal. *A System of Patterns: Pattern-Oriented Software Architecture*, New York: John Wiley & Sons, 1996.

Appendix A

Summary of UML Notation

Class Diagram

Shows the existence of classes and
relationships in a logical view of a system

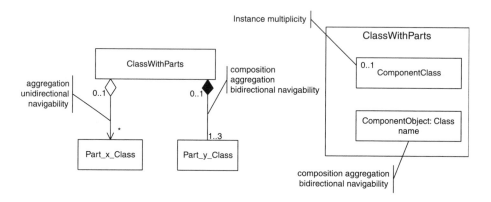

Aggregation and Composition

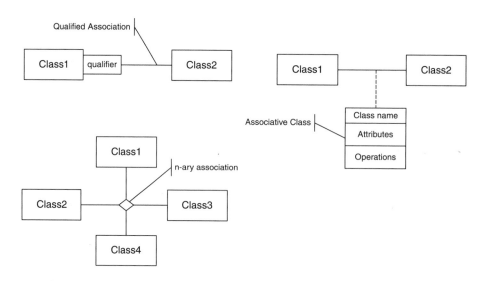

Advanced Associations

Class Diagram

Shows the existence of classes and
relationships in a logical view of a system

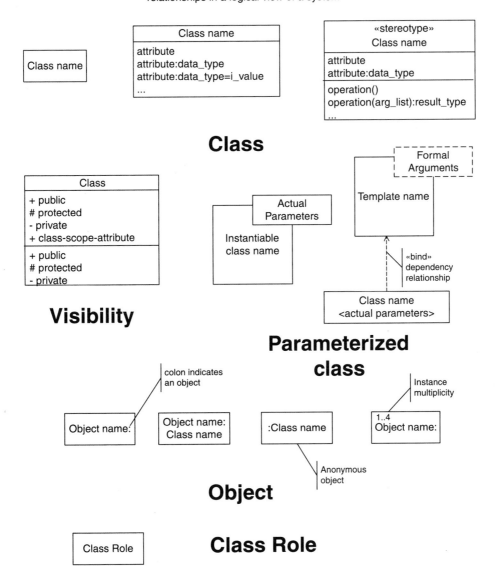

Class

Visibility

Parameterized class

Object

Class Role

Class Diagram

Shows the existence of classes and
relationships in a logical view of a system

Indicates speaking
perspective of
association name

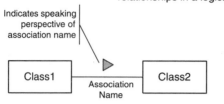

Role multiplicity

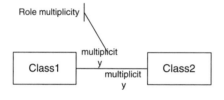

Multiplicity Symbol	Meaning
1	Exactly 1
0,1	Optionally 1
x..y	From x to y inclusive
a,b,c	Only specific values of a, b, and c
*	0 or more
1..*	1 or more

**Associations may be labelled using any
combination of names, role names, and
multiplicity**

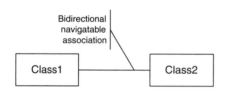

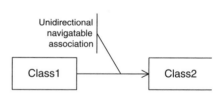

Association

Class Diagram

Shows the existence of classes and
relationships in a logical view of a system

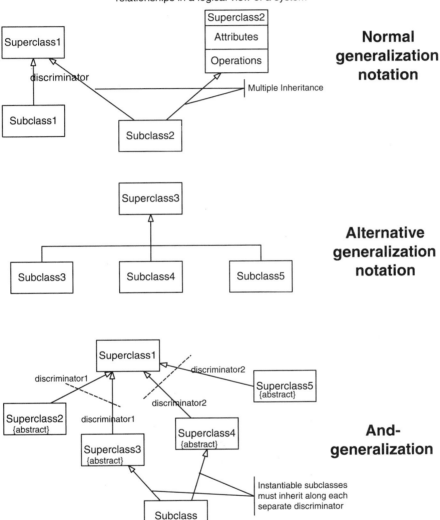

**Normal
generalization
notation**

**Alternative
generalization
notation**

**And-
generalization**

Generalization and Specialization

Class Diagram

Shows the existence of classes and
relationships in a logical view of a system.

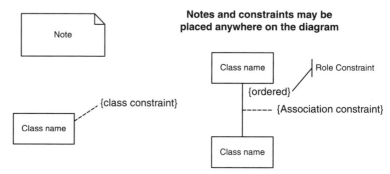

Notes and Constraints

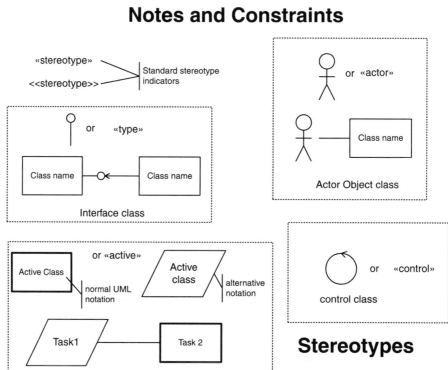

Stereotypes

Collaboration Diagram

Shows a sequenced set of messages illustrating a specific
example of object interaction.

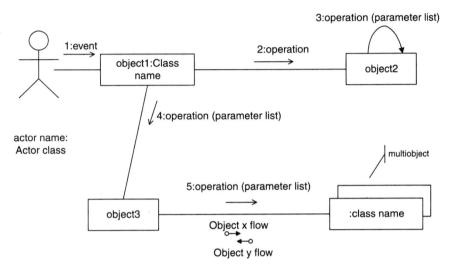

Object Collaboration

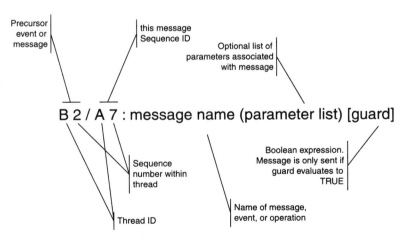

Message Syntax

Sequence Diagram

Shows a sequenced set of messages illustrating a specific example of object interaction.

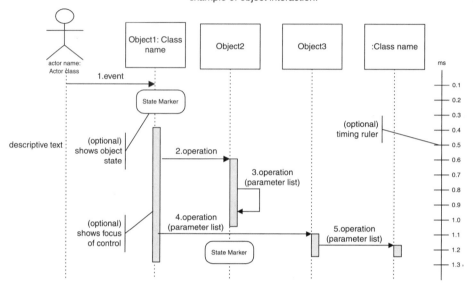

Sequence diagrams have two dimensions. The vertical dimension usually represents time, the horizontal represents different objects. (These may be reversed.)

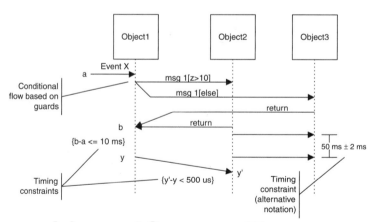

Advanced Sequence Diagrams

Use Cases

Use cases show primary areas of collaboration between the system and actors in its environment. Use cases are isomorphic with function points.

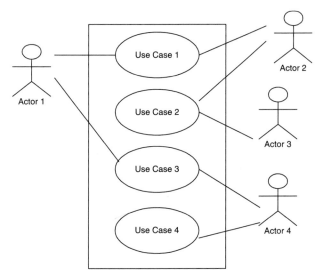

Use Case Diagram

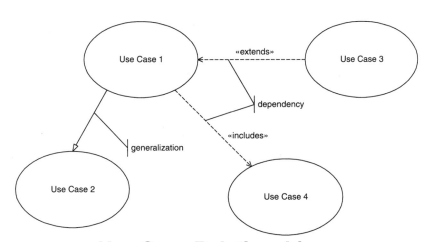

Use Case Relationships

Implementation Diagrams

Implementation diagrams show the run-time dependencies and packaging structure of the deployed system.

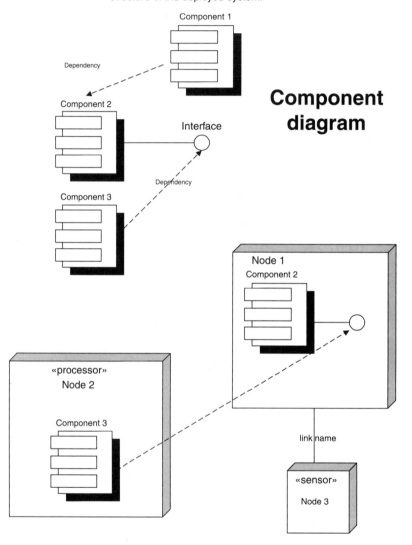

Deployment Diagram

Package diagram

Shows a grouping of model elements. Packages may also appear within class and object diagrams.

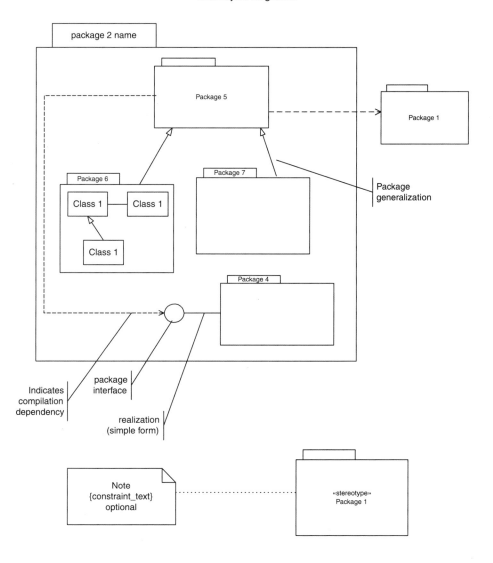

Statechart

Shows the sequences of states for a reactive class or interaction during its life in response to stimuli, together with its responses and actions.

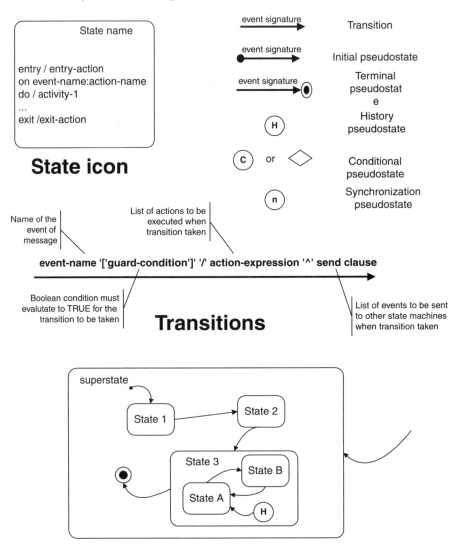

State icon

entry / entry-action
on event-name:action-name
do / activity-1
...
exit /exit-action

event signature → Transition

event signature → Initial pseudostate

event signature → Terminal pseudostate

H   History pseudostate

C or ◇   Conditional pseudostate

n   Synchronization pseudostate

Transitions

Name of the event of message

List of actions to be executed when transition taken

event-name '['guard-condition']' '/' action-expression '^' send clause

Boolean condition must evalutate to TRUE for the transition to be taken

List of events to be sent to other state machines when transition taken

Nested States

superstate
State 1 → State 2
State 3
State B
State A
H

Statechart

Shows the sequences of states for a reactive class or interaction during its life
in response to stimuli, together with its responses and actions.

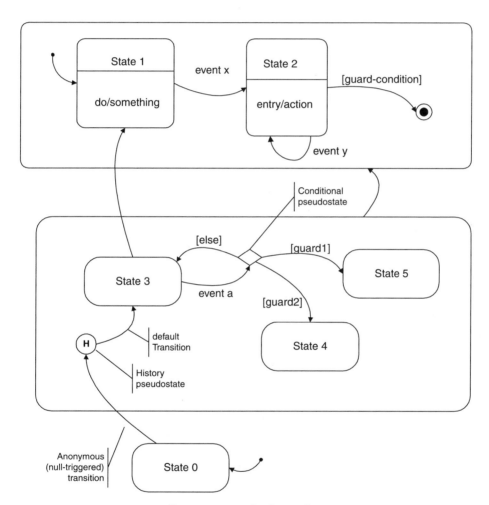

Sequential substates

Statechart

Shows the sequences of states for a reactive class or interaction during its life
in response to stimuli, together with its responses and actions.

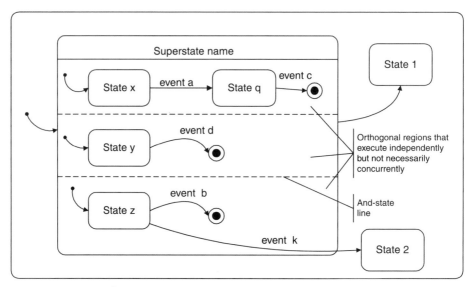

Orthogonal substates (and-states)

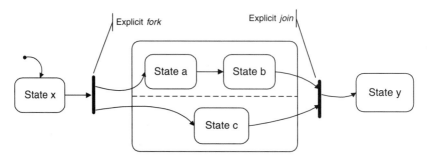

Complex state transitions

Activity Diagrams

Activity Diagrams are a specialized form of state diagrams in which most or all transitions are taken when the state activity is completed.

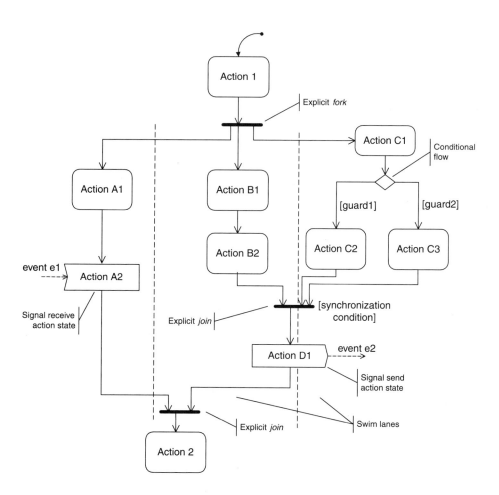

Timing Diagrams

Timing diagrams show the explicit change of state along a linear time axis
(Timing Diagrams are not in the UML standard)

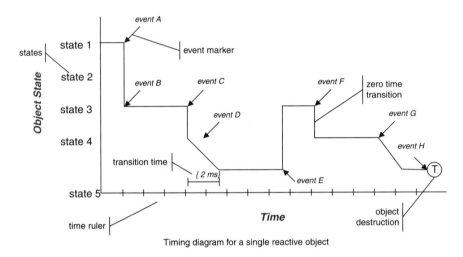

Timing diagram for a single reactive object

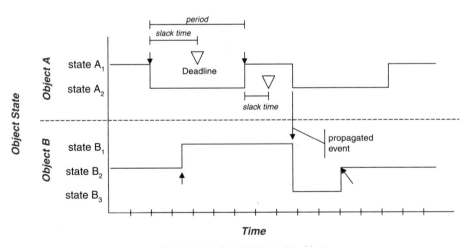

Timing diagram for multiple reactive objects

Timing Diagrams

Shading can be used to show execution state for «active» objects
(Timing Diagrams are not in the UML standard)

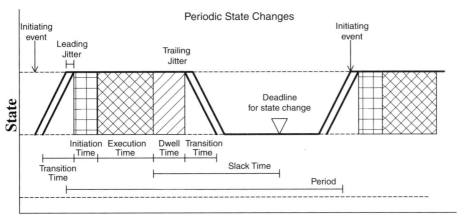

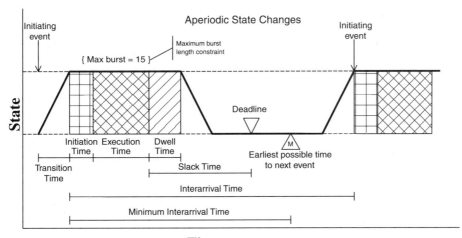

Appendix B

Rhapsody: A Fully Constructive UML Visual Programming Tool

This appendix provides a brief summary of Rhapsody, a visual, model-based programming environment for the analysis, design, and implementation of real-time and embedded systems. This tool is provided in demo mode on the CD-ROM that accompanies this book.

Rhapsody Overview

Rhapsody is a UML-compliant design automation tool used in the development of real-time and embedded systems. It maintains a central repository of all analysis and design information and offers several views of that repository.

- Analysis model view
- Object model view
- State model view
- Code model view
- Animation view

In addition to these graphical views, Rhapsody provides a repository browser that allows you to see, navigate, and modify the repository, and can generate reports containing the details held within the repository.

A typical project proceeds using the ROPES, or a similar, process. In such a process, work begins with the identification of use cases, actors, and scenarios. The project proceeds with the definition of classes, objects, and their relations. Some objects are reactive, so their state machines are defined using statecharts. Code is generated from these classes either automatically or manually. A built in code editor provides views of the generated code. Finally, the code can be executed, either on the development host platform or on a remote target platform. In either case, the model can be animated (shown graphically using UML diagrams) as it executes—statecharts can show the actual current state of the objects of interest; sequence diagrams can be drawn as messages are passed among the objects; the call stacks and event queues of the different threads can be shown; and the browser can display all the currently created objects and their current attribute values.

Rhapsody runs on Windows NT, Windows 95, and Windows 98. It targets multiple environments, including Windows NT, Windows 95, Windows 98, Windows CE, Arial, UNIX, pSOS, and VxWorks.

General Rhapsody Properties

Rhapsody provides a set of menus across the top of the main Rhapsody application window. Below that is a general-purpose toolbar for actions that are common to most or all Rhapsody views, such as cut/copy/paste, and the insertion of different kinds of notes in diagrams. Along the left side of the main Rhapsody window is a window-specific toolbar. It changes as different windows get focus. For example, the Class and Object Toolbar displays when the active window is an Object Model Diagram. This toolbar provides icons for dropping down classes and relations. If you select a sequence diagram, the Sequence Diagram Toolbar appears along the left edge, providing the ability to drop instance lines (objects on sequence diagrams), messages, partition lines, timing marks, and so on.

The Code Menu allows you to customize the project properties. These include optimizations for how the code will be generated, what kind of target you want to support (for example, VxWorks or pSOS), the compiler you want to use, where to find legacy code you want included or linked in, and so on. A complete set of properties is called a *configuration.* You may create as many configurations as you like. This permits, for example, the easy creation of an executable that runs under Windows with full animation, another that runs under VxWorks with tracing level of animation, and a noninstrumented version for the final deployed system—all of these configurations apply to the same object model. They can be selected easily from the pulldown menu on the Rhapsody toolbar along the top of the screen.

Because Rhapsody is a visual programming environment, it imposes some constraints that may not be present in standard CASE tools. For example, because fully executable code is generated from the object, state, and sequence diagrams, named model elements must be compilable (for example, no spaces or special characters in names). This facilitates moving up and down levels of abstraction during code execution and debugging as the names in the model map exactly to names in the code.

One of the key fundamental perspectives of Rhapsody is called "code-model bidirectional associativity." That means that each view (including the generated source code) reflects the *same underlying application model.* Although for the most part, the system is maintained from the higher level of abstractions first and code is then generated, it is also possible to update the method bodies separately and bring those changes back into the repository using a technique called "round-tripping." This means that the model and the code always remain in synch, which is crucial for real-time systems development. That is because it is sometimes easier and simpler to modify the code during a detailed debugging session, and you don't want to lose those changes the next time you generate code.

Analysis Model View

The analysis model view captures requirements using use cases and sequence diagrams as shown in Figure B-1.

Use case names can violate the fully constructive rule that all names must be legal identifiers. Use case names can, for example, contain spaces; class, state, event, and message names cannot.

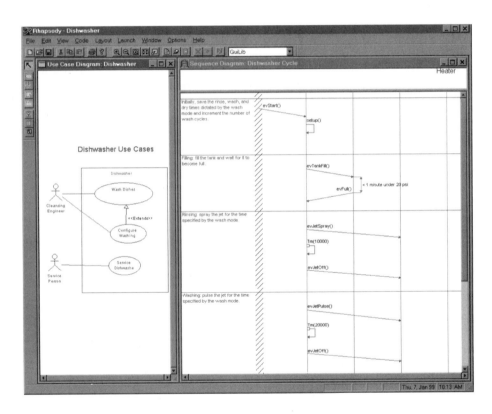

Figure B-1: *Rhapsody Analysis Model View*

Object Model View

The object model view captures the object structural analysis and design view (see Figure B-2). The various diagrams of the UML standard (class, object, and package) are all represented using a single diagram type that can contain all three element types. Optionally, attributes and operations can be shown. Either double clicking on the class or a right-click (to bring up a properties dialog) allows you to specify the properties of the class. These include the definition of the operations. These operations can be created and then populated with the lines of code you want them to contain. Later, should you modify the bodies of the generated code using an external code editor, these changes can be brought back into the model using a technique called

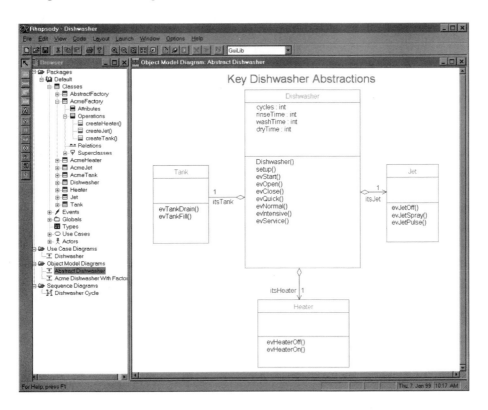

Figure B-2: *Rhapsody Object Model View*

"round-tripping." You may round-trip the code either by selecting the class and selecting Round-trip from the right-click menu, or the next time you generate code.

State Model View

Constructive statechart semantics and notation are provided (see Figure B-3). This means that the code that is generated from a statechart implements the state model. No additional coding (other than defining the code contents of any operation actions referenced in the statechart) is required. The generated code is complete and can accept and process the events used in the state machine.

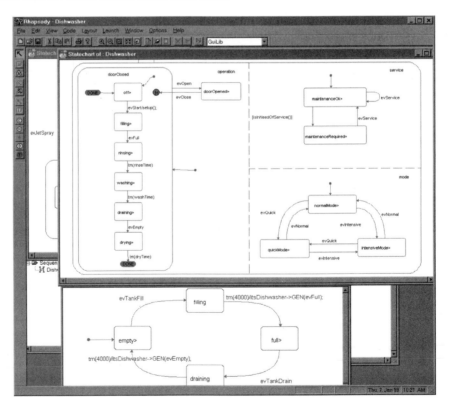

Figure B-3: *Rhapsody State Model View*

Code View

Rhapsody provides a number of editors for viewing and editing your code (see Figure B-4). The standard code editor in the browser is a simple editor for entering lines of code for the identified methods for your objects. In the browser, simply select the object and the operation, place the cursor in the method body text box, and type away. Click on the ellipsis button next to the text box to get a larger text window.

Alternatively, you can look at all the generated code by right-clicking on the class in the class diagram (or in the browser), and select Edit Code from the pop-up menu. This brings up the code that is actually sent to

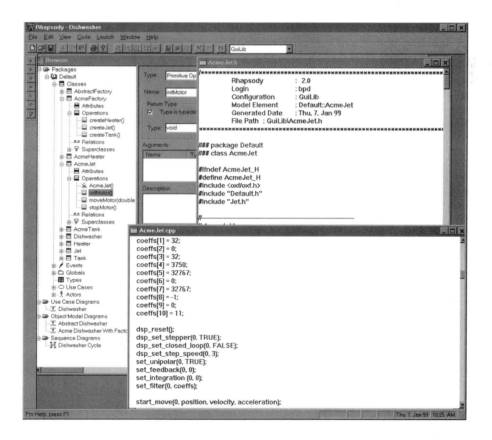

Figure B-4: *Rhapsody Code View*

the compiler during the compilation, which includes the method bodies you've defined and also the code that Rhapsody generates. Note: If you haven't generated code for a class, you may do so either from the right-click menu or from the main Rhapsody Code menu.

Animation View

Once an application is compiled with animation instrumentation (defined in the Configuration dialog box, available from the Code/Set Configuration menu), it may be run from the Code/Run menu. Rhapsody starts up your application. The default is a Windows console application. Then the animation control toolbar appears. This menu allows you to control the execution of your application. Options include

Go Step	Execute the next model step
Go	Free run your application
Go Idle	Run until the stack is empty and no events are pending
Go Event	Run until the next event is handled
Pause	Pause an application currently running
Command Prompt	Insert an event, set a break point, and so forth
Quit Animation	Stop running the application
Threads	Change the active thread view for call stack and event queue

From the Launch menu, you may open animated sequence diagrams or animated statecharts. These animated views show the execution of your application using standard UML model elements and highlighting (see Figure B-5). See Chapter 12 in the on-line Reference Manual for more information.

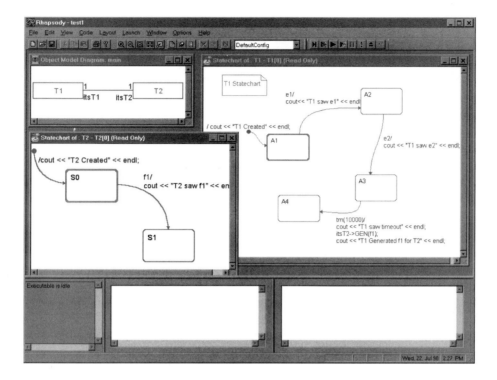

Figure B-5: *Rhapsody Animation View*

Installation

Navigate to the Rhapsody directory on the CD and run the SETUP.EXE file. You will be prompted for your compiler information. You must have one of the mentioned compilers installed on your system in order to compile and execute the object models provided on disk or one of your own models. You will be asked if you would like to have Adobe Acrobat installed, as well. Acrobat is required to view the on-line reference documentation.

The installation process installs Rhapsody in demo mode. This allows you to load and manipulate the models provided on disk and create and execute new ones, but not to save models. A number of models are provided in the Sample subdirectory. In addition, several design patterns are provided as Rhapsody projects in the Design Patterns subdirectory.

Both subdirectories are located in the directory in which Rhapsody is installed.

Note: The Rhapsody models on the CD-ROM should be copied to a read-write medium (such as your local hard disk) before opening them with Rhapsody.

Getting Help

The documentation for Rhapsody is provided online. Click on the Help menu to view the Rhapsody Reference Manual or other online documentation.

Using Rhapsody

Now that you've seen what Rhapsody can do, let's examine how to use it.

Create a Project

When you first run Rhapsody, you can create a project by selecting the File/New option. You will be prompted for a project name and location. The default will be under the Rhapsody directory.

For this example, let's create a project called TestProject in the default location.

Creating an Object Model

The initial window open is the browser. From here, you will want to start drawing diagrams. Diagrams can be created in any order. In this case, let's first create a use case diagram called Main Use Case Diagram.

Click on the Use Case Diagrams list item in the browser. Now type in *Main Use Case Diagram* in the Name text field at the right. When you press the Enter key, you will see that diagram added into the use case diagram list. Double click on it and the (currently blank) diagram will open.

To add modeling elements, click on the desired model element on the context-sensitive toolbar at the left of the screen. Then position the cursor at the point of insertion in the diagram and double click (dragging to a user-specified size also works). Each inserted model element is given a default name. You may change the name if desired. In this case, let's add a use case called Acquire Signal. Double click somewhere else, and another use case will be created. Name this one Format Signal. To resize the model element, select it to make the object handles appear, and drag one of them to get to the desired size. Actors and packages may be added in the same way. Create an actor called *User* and another called *Sensor.* Now add associations between the use cases and the actors by selecting the Create Association icon, then clicking on the source and then on the target modeling element.

To create an object model diagram, the process is virtually the same. In the Browser, click on the Object Model Diagram tree list and enter the name of the diagram in the Name field on the right. In this case, let's name it OMD 1. Hit Enter, and the diagram is created. Double click on the name of the diagram, and it is opened.

Notice that a different context-sensitive toolbar now appears on the left. The tool icons include classes (simple, three-compartment, and composite), packages, actors, and various relations. Feel free to experiment and draw a number of object diagrams.

Adding State Behavior

For reactive objects, statecharts must be drawn. Because the statechart maps to an individual class, the easiest way to create one is to select the class on an object model diagram, then select New Statechart from the right-click menu.

From here, statecharts may be drawn in the same way that object model and use case diagrams are drawn. Note that in this diagram, like the others, the tool does not like overlapping model elements. States are not permitted to partially overlap. States can be drawn within states (nested states) or outside states, but their borders are not allowed to intersect.

The context-sensitive toolbar includes states and two kinds of transitions. The usual kind is drawn from one state to another (which may be the same state). The other kind, the default connector, must originate by itself and terminate on a state. There is only one default connector within each level of context. To be well-formed, a default state must be defined for each state context—that is, for each level of nesting within a state and within each orthogonal region.

Executing the Model

Once you have an object model defined well enough to execute some portion of it, you must generate code. The Code/Set Configuration menu item allows you to specify how the code is to be generated. The Code/Generate menu item creates code from the object model. The Code/Make menu item runs the compiler on the generated code. The Code/Run menu item then executes it. If animation instrumentation has been specified, then Rhapsody will allow you to control it via the animation toolbar.

This just scratches the surface of Rhapsody's capabilities. Rhapsody contains some 200 customizable properties. You can link to third-party configuration management and requirements traceability tools, you can import models from Rational Rose, or you can import class directly from C++ code. You can link in legacy-compiled components or include legacy source code. You should feel free to peruse the online documentation and explore the tool's capabilities.

Contacting I-Logix

For more information about Rhapsody, or for consulting, mentoring, or training, you may contact I-Logix.

By phone:
888-8ILOGIX

By e-mail:
info@ilogix.com

On the Web:
www.ilogix.com

By smail:
I-Logix
3 Riverside Drive
Andover, MA 01810

Appendix C

TimeWiz: An Integrated Tool for Timing Analysis

This appendix provides a summary of TimeWiz, an integrated and comprehensive software tool for the modeling, analysis, simulation, and visualization of timing characteristics of single node or distributed, real-time, embedded systems (see Figure C-1). This tool is provided in demo mode on the CD-ROM that accompanies this book.

Traditionally, hardware engineers have used integrated tools to lay out the hardware, define timing characteristics, and perform timing analysis and simulation *prior* to prototype fabrication. Minor timing and logic issues are then ironed out during testing. Commercial production follows.

Software design often tends to ignore timing characteristics until the prototype or integration stage. This process may lead to significant architectural changes late in the process, in turn leading to significant cost overruns. Worst, timing glitches or surprises in the deployed system lead to loss of revenue, good will, property, and even life. TimeWiz

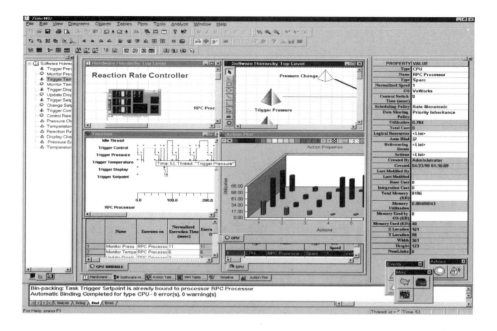

Figure C-1: *TimeWiz Analysis Windows*

allows the temporal (time-oriented) modeling, analysis, and simulation to be performed up-front to minimize late surprises in the design cycle and in deployment.

Predictability in Real-Time Systems

Real-time computing systems are critical components of an industrialized nation's technological infrastructure. Modern telecommunication systems, automated factories, defense systems, power plants, aircraft, airports, spacecraft, medical instrumentation, SCADA systems, people movers, railroad switching, and so forth cannot operate without them.

In real-time applications, the correctness of a computation depends not only upon its results but also upon the time at which its outputs are generated. Measures of merit in a real-time system include

- Predictability—Predictably fast response to urgent events.
- High degree of schedulability—Timing requirements of the system must be satisfied at high degrees of utilization.

- Stability under transient overload: When the system is overloaded by events and it is impossible to meet all deadlines, the deadlines of selected, critical tasks must still be guaranteed.

Rate-Monotonic Analysis

Rate-monotonic analysis (RMA) is a set of mathematical techniques that allows developers of real-time systems to meet application timing requirements by managing system concurrency and timing constraints at the level of tasking and message passing. In essence, the rate-monotonic scheduling theory guarantees that all tasks will meet their deadlines if the total system utilization of these tasks lies below a known bound, and if these tasks are scheduled using appropriate algorithms. This analytic, engineering basis makes real-time systems considerably easier to develop, modify, and maintain.

RMA began with the pioneering work of Liu and Layland [6] in which the rate-monotonic algorithm was introduced for scheduling independent periodic tasks. The RMS algorithm gives higher priorities to periodic tasks with higher rates. RMS is an optimal, static priority, scheduling algorithm for independent periodic tasks when task deadlines are at period boundaries. The optimality of RMS is in the sense that if any static priority scheduling algorithm can schedule a set of independent periodic tasks with end-of-period deadlines, then RMS can also schedule the task set. RMS theory has since been generalized to analyze the schedulability of aperiodic tasks with both soft deadlines and hard deadlines [11], inter-dependent tasks that must synchronize [7,8,9], tasks with deadlines shorter than the periods [5], tasks with arbitrary deadlines [4], and single tasks that have multiple code segments with different priority assignments [2]. An RMA-based technique allows a task set to meet its critical deadlines even under overload conditions as long as utilization of the critical tasks is below a schedulability bound [10]. An efficient, iterative, fixed-point technique has been developed to determine the schedulability of a set of periodic tasks using any fixed priority assignment [1,3].

RMA is described in Chapter 11 (and in more detail in [13]). In its simplest form, RMA states that

A set of n independent periodic tasks scheduled by the rate monotonic algorithm will always meet its deadlines, for all task phasings, if

$$\Sigma \left(\frac{C_i}{T_i}\right) \leq U(n) = n(2^{1/n}-1)$$

where,

> C_i = worst-case task execution time of task i
> T_i = period of task i
> $U(n)$ = utilization bound for n tasks.

The above equation applies to the simple case of independent periodic tasks. Techniques are also presented to represent, model, and analyze many more-complex, real-time situations, including shared resources, jitter requirements, aperiodic tasks, and so forth.

More often, the task execution time cannot be determined precisely, although the period needs to be specified as a parameter to the operating system. In these situations, worst-case schedulability and timing analysis may be performed using maximum estimated execution times. To arrive at average-case estimates, a) average estimates for execution times may be used and the process repeated, or b) a simulation, with execution times varying by known statistical distributions, or c) using actual data collected from a running system may be performed.

Technologies Used in TimeWiz

Two complementary approaches to timing analysis consist of worst-case timing analysis and average-case stochastic simulation.

Rate-monotonic analysis and its extensions have been built over several years to represent and analyze real-life scenarios with context switching, critical section, inter-process data sharing, communications, and synchronization. TimeWiz supports the basic theory and extensions. A number of data sharing policies (priority inheritance, priority ceiling) have also been developed to address problems with priority inversion and deadlocks. In addition to worst-case timing analysis based on RMA, TimeWiz has a built-in, process-oriented, simulation engine for stochastic modeling and for studying average-case behavior. Timing characteristics of the system can be studied within the scenario of discrete event simulation.

TimeWiz supplies processor and real-time operating system (RTOS) models. It also provides analysis and simulation models of networks using predictable transport protocols (for example, CanBus uses a priority-based scheme) and simulation models for other nondeterministic transport protocols (for example, the Ethernet exponential back-off scheme, keeping track of collisions). TimeWiz also provides an application programming interface (API) and a set of graphical tools to enable end-users' implementations of custom "plug-in" analysis and simulation models. The timing properties of these models are then automatically used by the TimeWiz framework when it performs analysis and simulation of distributed systems incorporating the custom models.

Using the above technologies, TimeWiz supports

- Graphical layouts of hardware and software architectures of single-node or distributed systems
- Timing parameter definition through object property sheets, tabular views
- Worst-case timing analysis (if possible)
- Timing simulation
- Visualization of timing behavior using Timelines, charts, reports
- Custom models of analysis and simulation

TimeWiz User Interface

The TimeWiz user interface is modeled after the Microsoft Visual C++ and Visual Basic environments. Office 97-style, dockable, customizable tool bars are designed to present a native, consistent Windows look and feel.

The default workspace consists of a tabbed hierarchy browser on the left for viewing the hardware and software hierarchies, and for interacting with the online help system. An object property inspector is docked on the right. The inspector displays the currently selected object. Objects may be selected via the diagrams, hierarchy navigators, or tables. Tabbed output windows at the bottom of the workspace keep your outputs organized. Various elements of the workspace can be rearranged or resized.

Multiple windows in the middle of the workspace provide user interaction. Hardware and software diagram views can be used to define the hierarchical structure of your entire architecture. Element connectivity information is retained and propagated across hierarchies. Element properties can be defined via the inspector. Using tabular views, you can view and change all properties of some types of elements.

Analysis and simulation is performed interactively or on demand. The results of analysis and simulation are displayed via the inspector or tabular views. Results can also be viewed graphically using Timeline, Chart, and Report views. Timeline view presents the exact execution sequence within your targets, representing your design choices. Chart view presents a means of comparing the parameters, such as utilization, execution time, and so forth. Report view integrates all the views into one integrated and coherent layout that can be viewed and printed.

The online user manual, accessed through the TimeWiz hierarchy navigator, provides more details on interaction and customization of the various views to further enhance your productivity.

Single Processor Model

TimeWiz single processor analysis can be used to provide answers to design decisions encountered in single processor, real-time system design:

- Assignment of periods and priorities for threads
- Setting the scheduling policy for the operating platform
- Design of shared resource accesses and their placements within the threads
- Setting the data access policies for shared resources
- Spare capacity available versus required
- Guaranteeing predictability of timing behavior
- Meeting deadlines under worst case
- Synchronization of multiple data streams (for example, audio, video, data)
- Performing average case studies with statistical data via simulation

TimeWiz's single processor analysis is built upon the SEI (Software Engineering Institute) model for real-time system analysis using the rate-monotonic analysis approach.

At a high level, the TimeWiz model of real-time systems is based upon the standard notions of *resources, events,* and *actions* as described in [13].

`TWZCPUMan.DOC` under the `Help` directory in your TimeWiz installation contains detailed information on the TimeWiz single processor model. The hardware is described in terms of *resources* and their properties. Software is described in terms of threads of executions and their interaction properties, captured via *events* and *actions*.

Resources can be physical or logical. Physical resources represent processing (or communication) media on which *actions* execute (or communicate). In addition, zero or more logical resources may be specified for consumption by an action. Logical resources represent shared data, locks, semaphores, and so forth, necessary for inter-task communication and synchronization. A *priority* can be associated with an action.

Actions by themselves need to be initiated by triggers. *Triggers,* or *trigger events,* signify periodic or aperiodic arrival of threads of execution. A trigger event and a chain of actions constitute a *thread of execution.*

Support for Distributed and Multiprocessor Systems

Tracers, or *tracer events,* are provided so that you can specify and study the behavior of events across system elements. Tracers act as a dye injected into the system. They are passive and do not influence the execution sequence of the components through which they flow. Their path through the system can be represented visually within TimeWiz. Worst-case analysis based upon mathematical techniques and simulation based on stochastic patterns can then be used to study the end-to-end system response to tracers.

The Temporal Model

The complete temporal, or timing, model of your distributed system consists of models of various elements (or *resources*) that contribute to latencies. Processors, real-time operating systems, networks, buses, and backplanes are examples of resources. TimeWiz provides detailed, standard plug-in models for processors, RTOSs, CanBus, and Ethernet. Other models can also be defined using the tools and the API provided with TimeWiz. These plug-in models can then be used to study end-to-end flows in your system.

Execution Target Support

Target profiling information is necessary for worst-case analysis and simulation. Commercial RTOSs, such as VxWorks and pSOS, have profiling tools that support the application of RMA technique. TimeWiz can interface with these tools to automate the model, building from execution traces of these RTOSs. WindView log files (*.WVR) and pSOS log files (*.EXP) can be directly imported into TimeWiz. Statistical models are constructed based upon the data contained within these files, and the TimeWiz temporal model is automatically built. For other RTOSs, an ASCII file interchange format is provided. By using it, a "filter" can be written. Documentation on this file format is in the Help subdirectory.

For Windows NT, CE, and RT-Mach targets, TimeTrace, from TimeSys Corp, provides detailed profiling information, consisting of context swaps and execution time monitoring. The files generated from TimeTrace can be imported directly into TimeWiz.

Installing TimeWiz

TimeWiz can be installed on any Windows platform. To install TimeWiz, use Windows Explorer to view the files located under the `TimeWiz` directory on the CD-ROM. Then, double-click on `setup.exe` and follow the on-screen instructions.

What Is Included in the CD-ROM

The distribution CD-ROM accompanying this book includes a demonstration version of TimeWiz and associated customization tools (the TimeWiz Catalog Designer and the TimeWiz Report Designer). The evaluation version also includes sample project files and tutorials. You can define your own projects, analyze, and simulate them. The evaluation version does *not* allow you to save the projects. Please contact TimeSys Corporation (888-432-TIME, *sales@timesys.com*) for further information on licensing options, modeling, analysis, and simulation support.

Further Information

TimeSys Corporation provides tools and solutions for real-time, embedded software development. These include design and analysis tools, profiling tools, and run-time services designed to facilitate the process of building predictable real-time systems. Seminars, courses, and consulting services are also provided. A concise but useful compilation of RMA techniques and TimeWiz standard notation, called *A Concise Handbook of Real-Time Systems*, can be obtained free from TimeSys Corporation (*www.timesys.com*, 1-412-681-6899 or 1-888-432-TIME).

Summary

The predictability of a real-time system should be considered from the early design stage and should not be an afterthought in the design and development process. Early consideration of timing issues results in robust designs and in significant cost savings in the product cycle. TimeWiz is a unique and powerful tool that lets one represent real-time system hardware and software, analyze and simulate its timing behavior, model processors and networks for end-to-end performance, plot and compare system parameters, and generate integrated system reports.

References

[1] Burns, A. "Scheduling Hard Real-Time Systems: A Review," *Software Engineering Journal*, May 1991: 116–128.

[2] Harbour, M.G., M.H. Klein, and J.P. Lehoczky. "Fixed Priority Scheduling of Periodic Tasks with Varying Execution Priority," *Proceedings of the IEEE Real-Time Systems Symposium*, December 1991.

[3] Joseph, M. and Pandya, "Finding Response Times in a Real-Time System," *The Computer Journal* (British Computing Society), 1986; 29(5): 390–395.

[4] Lehoczky, J.P., "Fixed Priority Scheduling of Periodic Task Sets with Arbitrary Deadlines," *IEEE Real-Time Systems Symposium*, December 1990.

[5] Leung, J., and J. Whitehead. "On the Complexity of Fixed-Priority Scheduling of Periodic, Real-Time Tasks," *Performance Evaluation* (2), 1982.

[6] Liu, C.L., and J.W. Layland. "Scheduling Algorithms for Multiprogramming in a Hard Real-Time Environment," *JACM,* 1973; 20(1): 46–61.

[7] Rajkumar, R., L. Sha, and J.P. Lehoczky. "Real-Time Synchronization Protocols for Multiprocessors," *Proceedings of the IEEE Real-Time Systems Symposium,* December 1988: 259–269.

[8] Rajkumar, R. *Synchronization in Real-Time Systems: A Priority Inheritance Approach,* Norwell, Mass.: Kluwer Academic Publishers, 1991.

[9] Sha, L., R. Rajkumar, and J.P. Lehoczky. "Priority Inheritance Protocols: An Approach to Real-Time Synchronization," *Proceedings of the IEEE Transactions on Computers,* September 1990.

[10] Sha, L., J.P. Lehoczky, and R. Rajkumar. "Solutions for Some Practical Problems in Prioritized Preemptive Scheduling," *Proceedings of the IEEE Real-Time Systems Symposium,* 1986.

[11] Sprunt, H.M.B., L. Sha, and J.P. Lehoczky. "Aperiodic Task Scheduling for Hard Real-Time Systems," *The Journal of Real-Time Systems,* 1989; 1:27–60.

[12] Sha, L., J.P. Lehoczky, and R. Rajkumar. "Solutions for Some Practical Problems in Prioritized Preemptive Scheduling," *Proceedings of the IEEE Real-Time Systems Symposium,* 1986.

[13] Klein, Mark, Thomas Ralya, Bill Pollak, Ray Obenza, and Michael Gonzalez Harbour, *A Practitioner's Handbook for Real-Time Analysis,* Norwell, Mass.: Kluwer Academic Publishers, 1993.

Index

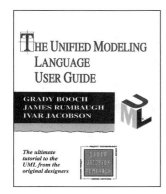

The Unified Modeling Language User Guide

Grady Booch, James Rumbaugh, and Ivar Jacobson
Addison-Wesley Object Technology Series

The Unified Modeling Language User Guide is a two-color introduction to the core eighty percent of the Unified Modeling Language, approaching it in a layered fashion and showing the application of the UML to modeling problems across a wide variety of application domains. This landmark book is suitable for developers unfamiliar with the UML or modeling in general, and will also be useful to experienced developers who wish to learn how to apply the UML to advanced problems.

0-201-57168-4 • Hardcover • 512 pages • ©1999

Objects, Components, and Frameworks with UML

The Catalysis Approach
Desmond Francis D'Souza and Alan Cameron Wills
Addison-Wesley Object Technology Series

Catalysis is a rapidly emerging UML-based method for component- and framework-based development with objects. The authors describe a unique UML-based approach to precise specification of component interfaces using a type model, enabling precise external description of behavior without constraining implementations. This approach provides application developers and system architects with well-defined and reusable techniques that help them build open distributed object systems from components and frameworks.

0-201-31012-0 • Paperback • 816 pages • ©1999

Real-Time UML

Developing Efficient Objects for Embedded Systems
Bruce Powel Douglass
Addison-Wesley Object Technology Series

The Unified Modeling Language is particularly suited to modeling real-time and embedded systems. *Real-Time UML* is the introduction that developers of real-time systems need to make the transition to object-oriented analysis and design with UML. The book covers the important features of the UML, and shows how to effectively use these features to model real-time systems. Special in-depth discussions of finite state machines, object identification strategies, and real-time design patterns to help beginning and experienced developers alike are also included.

0-201-32579-9 • Paperback • 400 pages • ©1998

Real-Time Programming
A Guide to 32-bit Embedded Development
Rick Grehan, Robert Moote, and Ingo Cyliax

This book teaches you how to write software for real-time embedded systems—software that meets unforgiving objectives under numerous constraints. The authors present the key topics that are relevant to all forms of real-time embedded development and offer complete coverage of the embedded development cycle, from design through implementation. A practical, hands-on approach is emphasized, allowing you to start building real-time embedded systems immediately using commercial, off-the-shelf hardware and software.

0-201-48540-0 • Paperback with CD-ROM • 720 pages • ©1999

The Unified Software Development Process
Ivar Jacobson, Grady Booch, and James Rumbaugh
Addison-Wesley Object Technology Series

The Unified Software Development Process goes beyond other object-oriented analysis and design methods by detailing a family of processes that incorporate the complete lifecycle of software development. This new book, representing the collaboration of Ivar Jacobson, Grady Booch, and James Rumbaugh, clearly describes the different higher-level constructs—notation as well as semantics—used in the models. Thus stereotypes such as use cases and actors, packages, classes, interfaces, active classes, processes and threads, nodes, and most relations are described intuitively in the context of a model.

0-201-57169-2 • Hardcover • 512 pages • ©1999

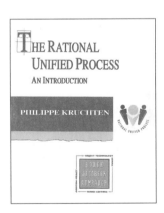

The Rational Unified Process
An Introduction
Philippe Kruchten
Addison-Wesley Object Technology Series

This concise book offers a quick introduction to the concepts, structure, content, and motivation of the Rational Unified Process. This revolutionary software development process provides a disciplined approach to assigning, managing, and completing tasks within a software development organization and is the first development process to exploit the full capabilities of the industry-standard Unified Modeling Language. *The Rational Unified Process* is unique in that it captures many of the proven best practices in modern software development and presents them in a form that can be tailored to a wide range of projects and organizations.

0-201-60459-0 • Paperback • 272 pages • ©1999

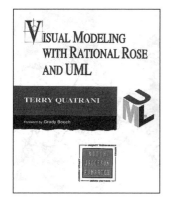

Visual Modeling with Rational Rose and UML

Terry Quatrani
Addison-Wesley Object Technology Series

Terry Quatrani, the Rose Evangelist for Rational Software Corporation, teaches you visual modeling and the UML, enabling you to apply an iterative and incremental process to analysis and design. With the practical direction offered in this book, you will be able to specify, visualize, document, and create software solutions. Highlights of this book include an examination of system behavior from a use case approach; a discussion of the concepts and notations used for finding objects and classes; an introduction to the notation needed to create and document a system's architecture; and a review of the iteration planning process.

0-201-31016-3 • Paperback • 240 pages • ©1998

Software Project Management

A Unified Framework
Walker Royce
Addison-Wesley Object Technology Series

This book presents a new management framework uniquely suited to the complexities of modern software development. Walker Royce's pragmatic perspective exposes the shortcomings of many well-accepted management priorities and equips software professionals with state-of-the-art knowledge derived from his twenty years of successful from-the-trenches management experience. In short, the book provides the software industry with field-proven benchmarks for making tactical decisions and strategic choices that will enhance an organization's probability of success.

0-201-30958-0 • Hardcover • 448 pages • ©1998

The Unified Modeling Language Reference Manual

James Rumbaugh, Ivar Jacobson, and Grady Booch
Addison-Wesley Object Technology Series

James Rumbaugh, Ivar Jacobson, and Grady Booch have created the definitive reference to the UML. This two-color book covers every aspect and detail of the UML and presents the modeling language in a useful reference format that serious software architects or programmers should have on their bookshelf. The book is organized by topic and designed for quick access. The authors also provide the necessary information to enable existing OMT, Booch, and OOSE notation users to make the transition to UML. The book provides an overview of the semantic foundation of the UML through a concise appendix.

0-201-30998-X • Hardcover with CD-ROM • 576 pages • ©1999

Applying Use Cases
A Practical Guide
Geri Schneider and Jason P. Winters
Addison-Wesley Object Technology Series

Applying Use Cases provides a practical and clear introduction to developing use cases, demonstrating their use via a continuing case study. Using the Unified Software Development Process as a framework and the Unified Modeling Language as a notation, the authors step the reader through applying use cases in the different phases of the process, focusing on where and how use cases are best applied. The book also offers insight into the common mistakes and pitfalls that can plague an object-oriented project.

0-201-30981-5 • Paperback • 208 pages • ©1998

Enterprise Computing with Objects
From Client/Server Environments to the Internet
Yen-Ping Shan and Ralph H. Earle
Addison-Wesley Object Technology Series

This book helps you place rapidly evolving technologies—such as the Internet, the World Wide Web, distributed computing, object technology, and client/server systems—in their appropriate contexts when preparing for the development, deployment, and maintenance of information systems. The authors distinguish what is essential from what is incidental, while imparting a clear understanding of how the underlying technologies fit together. The book examines essential topics, including data persistence, security, performance, scalability, and development tools.

0-201-32566-7 • Paperback • 448 pages • ©1998

The Object Constraint Language
Precise Modeling with UML
Jos Warmer and Anneke Kleppe
Addison-Wesley Object Technology Series

The Object Constraint Language is a new notational language, a subset of the Unified Modeling Language, that allows software developers to express a set of rules that govern very specific aspects of an object in object-oriented applications. With the OCL, developers are able to more easily express unique limitations and write the fine print that is often necessary in complex software designs. The authors' pragmatic approach and illustrative use of examples will help application developers to quickly get up to speed.

0-201-37940-6 • Paperback • 144 pages • ©1999

Addison-Wesley Computer and Engineering Publishing Group

How to Interact with Us

1. Visit our Web site

http://www.awl.com/cseng

When you think you've read enough, there's always more content for you at Addison-Wesley's web site. Our web site contains a directory of complete product information including:

- Chapters
- Exclusive author interviews
- Links to authors' pages
- Tables of contents
- Source code

You can also discover what tradeshows and conferences Addison-Wesley will be attending, read what others are saying about our titles, and find out where and when you can meet our authors and have them sign your book.

2. Subscribe to Our Email Mailing Lists

Subscribe to our electronic mailing lists and be the first to know when new books are publishing. Here's how it works: Sign up for our electronic mailing at **http://www.awl.com/cseng/mailinglists.html**. Just select the subject areas that interest you and you will receive notification via email when we publish a book in that area.

3. Contact Us via Email

cepubprof@awl.com

Ask general questions about our books.
Sign up for our electronic mailing lists.
Submit corrections for our web site.

bexpress@awl.com

Request an Addison-Wesley catalog.
Get answers to questions regarding your order or our products.

innovations@awl.com

Request a current Innovations Newsletter.

webmaster@awl.com

Send comments about our web site.

jcs@awl.com

Submit a book proposal.
Send errata for an Addison-Wesley book.

cepubpublicity@awl.com

Request a review copy for a member of the media interested in reviewing new Addison-Wesley titles.

We encourage you to patronize the many fine retailers who stock Addison-Wesley titles. Visit our online directory to find stores near you or visit our online store: **http://store.awl.com/** or call **800-824-7799**.

Addison Wesley Longman
Computer and Engineering Publishing Group
One Jacob Way, Reading, Massachusetts 01867 USA
TEL 781-944-3700 • FAX 781-942-3076

CD-ROM Warranty